Volume I

The Van de Walle Professional Mathematic

Teaching Student-Centered Mathematics

Developmentally Appropriate Instruction for Grades Pre-K–2

Second Edition

John A. Van de Walle
Late of Virginia Commonwealth University

LouAnn H. Lovin
James Madison University

Karen S. Karp
University of Louisville

Jennifer M. Bay-Williams
University of Louisville

PEARSON

Boston   Columbus   Indianapolis   New York   San Francisco   Upper Saddle River
Amsterdam   Cape Town   Dubai   London   Madrid   Milan   Munich   Paris   Montréal   Toronto
Delhi   Mexico City   São Paulo   Sydney   Hong Kong   Seoul   Singapore   Taipei   Tokyo

Vice President, Editor in Chief: Aurora Martínez Ramos
Executive Editor: Linda Bishop
Senior Development Editor: Christina Robb
Editorial Assistant: Laura White
Marketing Manager: Christine Gatchell
Production Editor: Karen Mason / Cynthia DeRocco
Editorial Production Service: Electronic Publishing Services Inc.
Manufacturing Buyer: Megan Cochran
Electronic Composition: Jouve
Interior Design: Electronic Publishing Services Inc.
Cover Designer: Laura Gardner

Image Credits: Chapter Opener Images: Left blocks, J. McPhail/Shutterstock; Middle tangrams, David Crehner/Fotolia; Right blocks, Sergey Galushko/Fotolia. Teaching Tip Icon: Koya79/ Fotolia. Standards for Mathematical Practice Icon: Xuejun Li/Fotolia

Cover Image: Paulrommer/Shutterstock

Credits and acknowledgments borrowed from other sources and reproduced, with permission, in this textbook appear on the appropriate page within text.

Library of Congress Cataloging-in-Publication Data

Van de Walle, John A.
    [Teaching student-centered mathematics. Grades K–3]
    Teaching student-centered mathematics. Developmentally appropriate instruction for grades pre-K–2.—2nd edition / John A. Van De Walle, Virginia Commonwealth University, LouAnn H. Lovin, James Madison University, Karen S. Karp, University of Louisville, Jenny M. Bay-Williams, University of Louisville.
        pages cm.—(The Van de Walle professional mathematics series; volume 1)
    Revision of: Teaching student-centered mathematics. Grades K–3 / John A. Van de Walle, LouAnn H. Lovin. c2006.
    Includes bibliographical references and index.
    ISBN-13: 978-0-13-282482-8
    ISBN-10: 0-13-282482-5
    1. Mathematics—Study and teaching (Primary) 2. Mathematics—Study and teaching (Early childhood) 3. Individualized instruction. I. Lovin, LouAnn H. II. Karp, Karen S. III. Bay-Williams, Jennifer M. IV. Title.
    QA13.V36 2014
    372.7—dc23   2012043394

10   9   8   7   6   5   4

ISBN 10: 0-13-282482-5
ISBN 13: 978-0-13-282482-8

The late **John A. Van de Walle** was a professor emeritus at Virginia Commonwealth University. He was a mathematics education consultant who regularly gave professional development workshops for K–8 teachers in the United States and Canada. He visited and taught in elementary school classrooms and worked with teachers to implement student-centered math lessons. He co-authored the Scott Foresman-Addison Wesley *Mathematics K–6* series and contributed to the Pearson School mathematics program, enVisionMATH. In addition, he wrote numerous chapters and articles for the National Council of Teachers of Mathematics (NCTM) books and journals and was very active in NCTM, including serving on the Board of Directors, as the chair of the Educational Materials Committee, and as a frequent speaker at national and regional meetings.

LouAnn H. Lovin is a professor of mathematics education at James Madison University (Virginia). She co-authored the first edition of the *Teaching Student-Centered Mathematics* Professional Development Series with John A. Van de Walle, as well as *Teaching Mathematics Meaningfully: Solutions for Reaching Struggling Learners* with special educators David Allsopp and Maggie Kyger. LouAnn taught mathematics to middle and high school students before transitioning to pre-K–grade 8. Over the last 15 years, she has worked in K–8 classrooms and engaged with teachers in professional development as they implement a student-centered approach to teaching mathematics. She has published articles in NCTM's *Teaching Children Mathematics* and *Mathematics Teaching in the Middle School* and has served on NCTM's Educational Materials Committee. LouAnn's research interest is investigating ways to develop teachers' mathematical knowledge needed to teach for understanding.

Karen S. Karp is a professor of mathematics education at the University of Louisville (Kentucky). Prior to entering the field of teacher education, she was an elementary school teacher in New York. Karen's research interest centers on teaching mathematics to diverse populations. She is also co-author of *Elementary and Middle School Mathematics: Teaching Developmentally, Growing Professionally: Readings from NCTM Publications for Grades K–8, Developing Essential Understanding of Addition and Subtraction for Teaching Mathematics in Pre-K–Grade 2*, and numerous book chapters and articles. She is a former member of the Board of Directors of NCTM and a former president of the Association of Mathematics Teacher Educators (AMTE). She continues to work in classrooms to support teachers of students with disabilities in their mathematics instruction.

Jennifer M. Bay-Williams is a professor of mathematics education at the University of Louisville (Kentucky). Jennifer has published many articles on teaching and learning in NCTM journals. She has also co-authored numerous books, including *Mathematics Coaching: Resources and Tools for Coaches and Leaders, K–12; Developing Essential Understanding of Addition and Subtraction for Teaching Mathematics in Pre-K–Grade 2; Math and Literature: Grades 6–8; Math and Nonfiction: Grades 6–8*; and *Navigating through Connections in Grades 6–8*. Jennifer taught elementary, middle, and high school in Missouri and in Peru, and continues to work in classrooms at all levels with students and with teachers. Jennifer served as member of Board of Directors for TODOS: Equity for All, as president of AMTE, and as editor for the 2012 NCTM Yearbook.

Brief Contents

Part I: Establishing a Student-Centered Environment

Part II: Teaching Student-Centered Mathematics

Contents

Part II: Teaching Student-Centered Mathematics

8 Developing Early Number Concepts and Number Sense   100

9 Developing Meanings for the Operations   126

15 Building Measurement Concepts 269

16 Developing Geometric Reasoning and Concepts 299

17 Helping Children Use Data   333

Preface

All children can learn mathematics with understanding! It is through the teacher's actions that every student, in his or her own way, can come to believe this important truth. We believe that teachers must create an environment in which children are trusted to solve problems and work together using their ideas to do so. Instruction involves posing tasks that will engage children in the mathematics they are expected to learn. Then, by allowing children to interact with and struggle with the mathematics using *their* ideas and *their* strategies—a student-centered approach—the mathematics they learn will be connected to other mathematics and to their world. Children will see the value of mathematics and feel empowered to use it. The title of this book, *Teaching Student-Centered Mathematics: Developmentally Appropriate Instruction for Grades Pre-K–2*, reflects this vision. This vision is so critical to the learning of mathematics that, in this second edition, we start with a new Part I that addresses how to build a student-centered environment in which children can become mathematically proficient.

What Are Our Goals for the Professional Math Series?

Creating a classroom in which children design their solution pathways, engage in productive struggle, and connect mathematical ideas is complex. Questions arise, such as, "How do I get children to wrestle with problems if they just want me to show them how? What kinds of tasks lend themselves to this type of engagement? Where can I learn the mathematics content I need in order to be able to teach in this way?" With these and other questions firmly in mind, we have three main objectives for the series:

1. Illustrate what it means to teach mathematics in a student-centered, problem-based manner.

2. Serve as a reference for all of the mathematics content suggested for grades pre-K–2, 3–5, and 6–8, as recommended in the *Common Core State Standards* and the *Curriculum Focal Points* (CCSSO, 2010; NCTM, 2006), as well as research-based strategies concerning how children learn this content.

3. Present a practical resource of robust, problem-based activities and tasks that can engage children in the mathematics that is important for them to learn.

These are also goals of *Elementary and Middle School Mathematics: Teaching Developmentally*, a comprehensive resource for teachers in grades K–8, which has been widely used in universities and in schools.

There is some overlap of both the text and activities between the comprehensive K–8 book and this Professional Series. However, we have adapted the Professional Series to be more useful for a practicing classroom teacher by focusing the content on specific grade bands and adding additional information on creating an effective classroom environment, engaging families, and aligning teaching to the new standards. We've also included more activities and lessons. We hope you will find that this is a valuable resource for teaching and learning mathematics!

Why Revise the Professional Math Series?

Since the writing of the first edition of this book began nearly a decade ago, many developments in mathematics education have occurred—from the publication of NCTM's *Curriculum Focal Points* (2006), to the development and implementation of the *Common Core State Standards* (CCSSO, 2010). Research has provided new information about how children learn particular mathematical ideas. We have also received great feedback from readers about what they *liked* about the first edition and what they *wished* would be in the second edition. It was time to incorporate these ideas into the book to ensure classroom teachers had access to strong support aligned with the latest developments in mathematics education.

What's New to the Second Edition of the Professional Math Series?

We made numerous significant changes to the Professional Series. They include:

- **A New Part I: Establishing a Student-Centered Environment.** The second edition is divided into *two* parts. Part I consists of seven chapters (all new) that address important ideas for creating a classroom environment in which all children can succeed. Part I focuses on what it means to teach mathematics *through* problem solving and how to differentiate instruction to meet the needs of *all* children. The final chapter in Part I expands the focus of mathematics education beyond the classroom, offering ideas for working with families, principals, and the community. These chapters focus on important "hot" topics that teachers and reviewers requested and that are important in making mathematics accessible to all learners. They are, by design, shorter in length than the content chapters in Part II, but are full of effective strategies and ideas. The intent is that these chapters can be used in professional development workshops, book study, or professional learning community (PLC) discussions. This new part replaces Chapter 1 in the first edition, which provided briefer attention to some of these topics. Part I includes:

  - A more in-depth definition of what we mean by *understanding*, using the eight mathematical practices identified in the *Common Core State Standards* (CCSSO, 2010), the five strands of mathematical proficiency from *Adding It Up* (NCTM, 2001), and NCTM's process standards (2000) (Chapter 1).

  - A discussion of what it means to teach mathematics *through* problem solving (as compared to teaching mathematics *for* problem solving). We include a discussion about criteria to use in the selection of problem-based tasks, and we present a set of recommendations for facilitating effective classroom discourse (Chapter 2).

  - Information on various formative assessment strategies including observations, diagnostic interviews, and tasks, as well as creating and using rubrics (Chapter 3).

  - Strategies to support the diverse range of learners in your classroom (Chapters 4–6).

  - Concrete ideas about how to communicate and engage with a variety of stakeholders to ensure children receive the support they need to be successful in mathematics (Chapter 7).

- **Connections to the** *Common Core State Standards.* A priority in preparing the second edition was to align the material to the *Common Core State Standards.* This has resulted in important changes:

  - Connections to the eight Standards for Mathematical Practice, critical components of the CCSSO recommendations, are highlighted in the text through marginal notes that focus readers' attention on examples in the nearby text of what these eight practices look like across content areas and grade levels.

  - Chapters have been reorganized and updated to reflect the CCSSO recommendations and present a more coherent progression of mathematical ideas and student learning. Explicit and specific attention is given to grade-level positioning of content throughout the discussion within each content chapter.

- **Increased Attention to Student Diversity.** A new emphasis on diversity can be seen with the addition of chapters on differentiating instruction (Chapter 4) as well as planning, teaching, and assessing culturally and linguistically diverse children (Chapter 5) and children with exceptionalities (Chapter 6). Additional strategies for supporting children with special needs and English language learners are included in Part II chapters, are highlighted in several activities in each chapter (noted with icons), and are incorporated into the revised expanded lessons at the end of each Part II chapter.

- **Coverage of Technology.** Since the first edition was published, technology has changed drastically. Now there is an increased availability of high-quality websites, applets, freeware, and so on. Throughout each chapter we identify effective, free technology that can help make content more visible, relevant, and interesting to children. To locate these examples, look for the Technology Notes in Part II.

- **Revised, Updated Expanded Lessons.** Every Part II chapter still has a lesson at the end, but they have all been revised. Lessons have been added or revised to explicitly focus on concepts central to mathematics in grades pre-K–2. All lessons now include (1) NCTM and CCSSO grade-level recommendations, (2) adaptation suggestions for English language learners and children with special needs, and (3) formative assessment suggestions for what to observe and what questions to ask children.

 What's New to Volume I?

The most obvious change in Volume I (*Developmentally Appropriate Instruction for Grades Pre-K–2*) might be the shift in grade band from K–3 to pre-K–2. Because we address grade 3 in Volume II (*Developmentally Appropriate Instruction for Grades 3–5*), we changed this book to span grades pre-K–2. This allowed us to explicitly focus on early childhood mathematical content and pedagogical issues. The recent recommendations from NCTM's *Curriculum Focal Points* and the *Common Core State Standards* informed our decisions about what to include in this volume. Major revisions to this book's contents focus on the following topics:

- **Early Number Concepts and Number Sense.** Number is such an important strand in pre-K–2 that we have expanded this chapter. Chapter 8 now includes a research-based learning trajectory that describes how young children develop an understanding of counting and numbers. There is more of an emphasis on building on children's natural tendency to use subitizing (i.e., quickly recognizing and naming small quantities without counting). We also introduce the arithmetic rack as a tool to help children develop benchmarks to 5 and 10.

- **Operations.** Chapter 9 offers an increased emphasis on problem structure that is also recommended in the *Common Core State Standards* and the National Research Council's publication *Mathematics Learning in Early Childhood: Paths toward Excellence and Equity.*

More attention is also paid to developing the meaning of the equal sign and helping children lay a foundation for multiplication.

- **Mastering the Basic Facts.** Chapter 10 has been completely restructured so that there are clearer connections to the number and operations chapters. The Make 10 strategy, which has been identified by research as most effective, has an increased emphasis. In this volume we focus on addition and subtraction facts and also have included a brief section on building a foundation for multiplication facts. In addition, we have included a new section with recommendations for supporting children as they develop reasoning strategies for and quick recall of basic facts.

- **Whole-Number Place-Value Concepts.** New to Chapter 11 is an increased emphasis on the role of counting in young children's development of base-ten ideas. You may also notice that money is no longer discussed in this chapter. Although money is often used to *reinforce* place value, for young children who are still developing an understanding of place value we recommend using groupable and proportional models, and therefore, we have moved money to the chapter on measurement.

- **Whole-Number Computation.** We have increased the number of activities in Chapter 12, and added many more example tasks, too. We have included a new section about issues related to teaching algorithms to culturally and linguistically diverse children as well as a new section that offers suggestions for creating a supportive classroom environment in which children can develop flexible computational skills.

- **Algebraic Reasoning.** Chapter 13 may be one of the most unrecognizable chapters from the first edition. It is now organized around three important areas of algebra identified in recent literature on developing algebraic reasoning. The chapter includes significantly more attention to content described in the *Common Core State Standards*, including generalization from arithmetic, meaningful use of the equal sign and variables, and understanding and using properties of our number system. Because of this increased attention to generalization from arithmetic, we moved this chapter so that it immediately follows the chapters on number and computation.

- **Early Fraction Concepts.** Chapter 14 has also changed considerably. Although recent standards recommend that instruction on fraction concepts begin in third grade, there are opportunities in pre-K–2 to build on children's everyday experiences to begin to develop informal knowledge and understanding about fractions (CCSSO, 2010; NCTM, 2006). Therefore, we have increased attention to the ideas of partitioning and iterating and children's initial halving strategies when reasoning about fraction tasks—effective ideas for developing children's fraction concepts that are recommended in the document *Developing Effective Fractions Instruction for Kindergarten through 8th Grade: A Practice Guide* (IES, 2010). New activities have also been created that target children's common misconceptions as they develop an understanding of fractions.

- **Measurement.** Chapter 15 now emphasizes length, time, and money for pre-K–2 as per the recommendations made in recent standards (CCSSO, 2010; NCTM, 2006). Increased attention is also given to the common misconceptions and difficulties children have with length.

- **Geometry.** Chapter 16 includes many more geometry activities that are appropriate for younger children. In the section describing the van Hiele levels, we have included a level proposed by researchers to exist prior to the first level in the van Hiele model. This additional level can help teachers make sense of younger children's geometric reasoning.

- **Data.** Chapter 17 also has undergone dramatic change. It now is organized around the process of doing statistics as described in the *Guidelines for Assessment and Instruction in Statistical Education (GAISE) Report* (American Statistical Association, 2005). Changes include new and revised sections on posing questions, data collection, data analysis, and interpreting results.

- **Probability.** Among other changes in Volume I, you may have noticed that we did not include a chapter about developing probability concepts. Given the recommendations made in recent standards that probability concepts should be delayed until middle school (CCSSO, 2010; NCTM, 2006), we have moved that content to Volume III (Grades 6–8) in the series.

What Special Features Appear in the Professional Series?

Throughout the Book

New! Teaching Tips.   Teaching Tips identify practical take-away ideas that can support the teaching and learning of specific chapter content being addressed. These might be an instructional suggestion, a particular point about language use, a common student misconception, or a suggestion about a resource.

Stop and Reflect.   Reflective thinking is the key to effective learning. This is true not only for your children but also for ourselves as we continue to learn more about effective mathematics teaching. Keep your eye out for these sections that ask you to solve a problem or reflect on some aspect of what you have read. These Stop and Reflect sections do not signal every important idea, but we have tried to place them where it seemed natural and helpful for you to slow down a bit and think. In addition, every chapter in Part I ends with a Stop and Reflect section. Use these for discussions in professional learning communities or for reflection on your own.

Blackline Master Icons.   Blackline Masters are used in some of the activities and Expanded Lessons. Look for the icon in the margin alerting you to the Blackline Masters. In Appendix C, you will find a thumbnail version of all Blackline Masters. A PDF version of each full-sized Blackline Master is available on the PDToolkit site.

Additional Features in Part II

Big Ideas.   Much of the research and literature espousing a developmental approach suggests that teachers plan their instruction around "big ideas" rather than isolated skills or concepts. At the beginning of each chapter, you will find a list of the key mathematical ideas associated with the chapter. These lists of learning targets can help you get a snapshot of the mathematics you are teaching.

Activities.   Numerous problem-based tasks are presented in activity boxes. Additional ideas are described directly in the text or in the illustrations. They are designed to engage your children in doing mathematics (as described in Chapter 2). Most of these activities are presented in the numbered activity boxes, and many have new adaptation and accommodation suggestions for English language learners and children with special needs. These are denoted with icons for easy reference. Following this Preface, you will find the Activities at a Glance table, which lists all the named and numbered activities with a short statement about the mathematical goal for each.

It is important that you see these activities as an integral part of the text that surrounds them. The activities are inserted as examples to support the development of the mathematics being discussed and how your children can be supported in learning that content. Therefore, we hope that you will not use any activity for instruction without carefully reading the full text in which it is embedded.

Formative Assessment Notes. Assessment should be an integral part of instruction. As you read, we want you to think about what to listen and look for (assess) in different areas of content development. Therefore you will find Formative Assessment Notes that describe ways to assess your children's developing knowledge and understanding. These Formative Assessment Notes can also help improve your understanding about how to help your children through targeted instruction.

New! *Technology Notes.* Integrated throughout the book are Technology Notes, which provide practical information about how technology can be used to help your children learn the content in that section. Descriptions include open-source software, interactive applets, and other Web-based resources—all of which are free.

New! *Standards for Mathematical Practice Notes.* Connections to the eight Standards of Mathematical Practice from the *Common Core State Standards* are highlighted in the margins. The location of the note indicates an example of the identified practice in the nearby text.

Expanded Lessons. The activities in the book are written in a brief format so as to provide many activities for the content without detracting from the flow of ideas. At the end of each Part II chapter, we selected one activity and expanded it into a complete lesson plan, following the *Before, During, After* structure described in Chapter 2. These Expanded Lessons provide a model for converting an activity description into a full lesson that can engage children in developing a strong understanding of the related concept. In this new edition, all lessons are now aligned with NCTM and CCSSO grade-level recommendations and include adaptation suggestions for English language learners and children with special needs.

New! **Common Core State Standards Appendixes.** The *Common Core State Standards* outline eight Standards for Mathematical Practice (Appendix A) that help children develop and demonstrate a deep understanding of and capacity to do mathematics. We initially describe these practices in Chapter 1 and highlight examples of the mathematical practices throughout the content chapters in Part II. We used the *Common Core State Standards* (CCSSO, 2010) as a guide to determine the content emphasis in each volume of the series. Appendix B provides a list of the critical content areas for each grade level discussed in this volume.

New! **PDToolkit.** The PDToolkit for *Teaching Student-Centered Mathematics: Developmentally Appropriate Instruction*, Second Edition (Volumes I, II, and III), together with the book, offers the tools you need to teach student-centered, problem-based mathematics.

The following resources are currently available:

- Video examples
- Virtual manipulatives
- Full-size, printable versions of the Blackline Masters from Volumes I, II, and III

In the future, we will continue to add additional resources.

To access the PDToolkit, go to http://pdtoolkit.pearson.com and enter the following code: PDTOOL-CLONK-LOSSY-SAVVY-HIGHS-LINES

Acknowledgments

We would like to begin by acknowledging *you:* the reader, the teacher, the leader, and the advocate for your children. The strong commitment of teachers and teacher leaders to always strive to improve how we teach mathematics is the reason this book was written in the first place. And, because of ongoing input and feedback, we endeavored to revise this edition to meet your changing needs. We have received input from so many teachers and reviewers, and all of it has informed the development of this substantially revised second edition!

In preparing the second edition, we benefited from the thoughtful input of the following educators who offered comments on the first edition or on the manuscript for the second: Alan Bates, Illinois State University; Rebecca L. Burghardt, College Station ISD; Sarah Lord, Madison Metropolitan School District; Allyson Moore, Elmira College; and Margaret Phillips, Tiger Creek Elementary. The reviewers' comments helped push our thinking on many important topics and many specific suggestions offered by these reviewers found their way into this book. We offer our sincere appreciation to these individuals for their suggestions and constructive feedback.

As we reviewed standards, research, and teaching articles; visited classrooms; and collected children's work samples, we were continually reminded of the amazing mathematics instruction going on in our profession. From the mathematics educators and mathematicians working on standards documents to the mathematics discussions occurring in pre-K–grade 8 classrooms that are then shared with others, we see great hope and vision in preparing all children to be mathematically proficient. It is for this broad commitment to mathematics education on the part of so many that we are so grateful, as well as the particular teachers with whom we have worked in recent years.

As authors, we also want to acknowledge the strong support of our editorial team throughout the process, from the first discussions about what a second edition might include, through the tedious editing at later stages in the development. Without their support, the final product would not be the quality resource we hope you find it to be. Specifically, we thank Kelly Villella-Canton for helping us envision our work, Linda Bishop for seeing this vision through, and both of them for their words of encouragement and wisdom. Working on three volumes of a book simultaneously is quite an undertaking! Christina Robb found a way to keep us organized and provided timely and much-needed feedback throughout our writing. We are grateful for Dana Weightman and the team at Pearson who patiently walked us through the permissions process. We also wish to thank Karla Walsh and the rest of the production and editing team at Electronic Publishing Services Inc.

Even with the support of so many, researching and writing takes time. Simple words cannot express the gratitude we have to our families for their support, patience, and contributions to the production of these books. Briefly we recognize them by name here: LouAnn thanks her husband, Ramsey, and her two sons, Nathan and Jacob. Karen thanks her husband, Bob Ronau, and her children and grandchildren, Matthew, Tammy, Josh, Misty, Matt, Christine, Jeff, Pamela, Jessica, Zane, Madeline, Jack, and Emma. Jennifer thanks her husband, Mitch, and her children, MacKenna and Nicolas.

The origin of this book began many years ago with the development of *Elementary and Middle School Mathematics: Teaching Developmentally* by John A. Van de Walle. What began as a methods book spread to the teaching community because it offered content support, activities, and up-to-date best practices for teaching mathematics. The series was developed as a way to focus on and expand the specific grade-level topics. John was adamant that all children can learn to reason and make sense of mathematics. We acknowledge his enduring vision, his commitment, and his significant contributions to the field of mathematics education. His ideas continue to inspire the work you see in this new edition.

The response to the first edition has been amazing. We hope the second edition will be received with as much interest and enthusiasm as the first and continue to be a valuable support to your mathematics teaching and your children's learning.

Activities at a Glance

This table lists the named and numbered activities in Part II of the book. In addition to providing an easy way to find an activity, the table provides the main mathematical goal or objective for each activity, stated as succinctly as possible. You should see the table only as a listing of the named activities, and not as an index of instructional ideas.

Rather than a book of activities, this is a book about teaching mathematics. Many practical and effective activities are used as examples. Every activity should be seen as an integral part of the text that surrounds it. Therefore, it is extremely important not to take any activity as a suggestion for instruction without reading carefully the full text in which it is embedded.

Activity		Mathematical Goal	Page Number
Chapter 11, Developing Whole-Number Place-Value Concepts			
11.1	Counting in Groups	Develop concept of groups of 10 as an efficient method of counting	182
11.2	Groups of Ten	Develop concept of groups of 10 as a method of counting	183
11.3	Estimating Groups of Tens and Ones	Use groups of 10 to count in a measurement context	184
11.4	Too Many Tens	Estimate and group quantities into hundreds, tens, and ones	185
11.5	Can You Make the Link?	Develop alternative groupings of 10 to represent a number	185
11.6	Three Other Ways	Develop alternative groupings of tens and hundreds to represent a number	186
11.7	Base-Ten Riddles	Develop alternative groupings of tens and hundreds to represent a number	187
11.8	Counting Rows of 10	Develop and connect three oral counting strategies	187
11.9	Counting with Base-Ten Models	Develop and connect three oral counting strategies	188
11.10	Tens, Ones, and Fingers	Develop and connect three oral counting strategies	188
11.11	Say It/Press It	Connect oral and symbolic names for numbers to physical representation	190
11.12	Digit Change	Apply place-value concepts to symbolic representations	191
11.13	Finding Neighbors on the Hundreds Chart	Explore patterns in numbers to 100	193
11.14	Models with the Hundreds Chart	Develop concepts of 1 more/less and 10 more/less for two-digit numbers	193
11.15	The Thousands Chart	Extend patterns for 1 to 100 to patterns to 1000	194
11.16	Who Am I?	Develop relative magnitude of numbers to 100	194
11.17	Who Could They Be?	Develop relative magnitude of numbers to 100	194
11.18	50 and Some More	Develop 50 as a part of numbers between 50 and 100	195
11.19	The Other Part of 100	Develop missing-part strategies with a whole of 100	196
11.20	Compatible Pairs	Explore combinations that make multiples of 10 or 100	196
11.21	Close, Far, and in Between	Explore relative differences between multidigit numbers	197
11.22	Calculator Challenge Counting	Develop mental addition strategies through skip counting	197
11.23	Numbers, Squares, Sticks, and Dots	Develop invented strategies for addition and subtraction	198
11.24	Hundreds Chart Addition	Practice adding two- or three-digit numbers	198
11.25	How Much Between?	Develop strategies to find the difference	199

Activity		Mathematical Goal	Page Number
Chapter 14, Exploring Early Fraction Concepts			
14.1	Fair and Unfair Shares	Develop an understanding of fractional parts	260
14.2	Finding Fair Shares	Develop an understanding of fractional parts	261
14.3	How Much Did She Share?	Develop an understanding of equal parts in fractions	262
14.4	More, Less, or Equal to One Whole	Develop an understanding of fractional parts	262
14.5	Cut Them Up Again!	Explore different ways to partition a quantity into equal parts	264
14.6	Keeping It Fair	Explore fraction equivalence	264
14.7	Who Is Winning?	Develop fraction concepts using a linear model	265
Chapter 15, Building Measurement Concepts			
15.1	About One Unit	Develop familiarity with standard units (any attribute)	274
15.2	Familiar References	Explore a variety of real-world benchmarks or references for standard units	275
15.3	Personal Benchmarks	Explore useful benchmarks using body lengths	275
15.4	Guess the Unit	Develop the concept of various units of measure	276
15.5	Estimation Quickie	Practice estimating measures of different attributes	279
15.6	Estimation Scavenger Hunt	Practice measurement estimation in real contexts	279
15.7	Longer, Shorter, Same	Explore the concept of length through direct comparisons	280
15.8	Length (or Unit) Hunt	Explore the concept of length through direct comparisons; develop familiarity with a standard unit	280
15.9	Will It Fit?	Explore the concept of length through indirect comparisons	281
15.10	Crooked Paths	Develop concept of length along paths that are not straight	281
15.11	How Long Is the Teacher?	Develop methods for measuring length	283
15.12	Estimate and Measure	Develop an understanding of length measurement	283
15.13	Changing Units	Explore the inverse relationship between unit size and measure	284
15.14	Make Your Own Ruler	Develop an understanding of rulers by making a ruler	285
15.15	One-Handed Clocks	Develop an understanding of the hour hand in reading a clock	288
15.16	Ready for the Bell	Practice reading a clock and develop an understanding of the relationship between an analog clock and a digital clock	288
15.17	Money Skip Counting	Practice skip counting in amounts related to coin values	290
15.18	Coin-Number Addition	Develop skill in counting money	290
15.19	How Much Is the Change?	Practice finding differences in amounts related to coin values	292
15.20	How Much Is the Change with Coins?	Develop skill in finding differences with money	292
15.21	Two-Piece Shapes	Develop an understanding of area; equivalent areas with different shapes	294

	Activity	Mathematical Goal	Page Number
17.3	Hidden Labels	Develop the concept of classification	340
17.4	Organizing Cards	Explore a bar diagram as a way to organize data	345
17.5	Storm Chaser	Use a bar diagram to display and analyze data	347
17.6	Story Bars	Use a bar diagram to display and analyze data	347
17.7	Stand By Me	Explore a line plot as a way to organize and analyze data	348

1

Teaching Mathematics for Understanding

An understanding can never be "covered" if it is to be understood.

Wiggins and McTighe (2005, p. 229)

Teachers generally agree that teaching for understanding is a good thing. But this statement begs the question: What is *understanding*? Understanding is being able to think and act flexibly with a topic or concept. It goes beyond knowing; it is more than a collection of information, facts, or data. It is more than being able to follow steps in a procedure. One hallmark of mathematical understanding is a student's ability to justify why a given mathematical claim or answer is true or why a mathematical rule makes sense (Council of Chief State School Officers, 2010). Although children might *know* their basic multiplication facts and be able to give you quick answers to questions about these facts, they might not *understand* multiplication. They might not be able to justify how they know an answer is correct or provide an example of when it would make sense to use this basic fact. These tasks go beyond simply knowing mathematical facts and procedures. Understanding must be a primary goal for all of the mathematics you teach.

Understanding and Doing Mathematics

Procedural proficiency—a main focus of mathematics instruction in the past—remains important today, but conceptual understanding is an equally important goal (National Council of Teachers of Mathematics, 2000; National Research Council, 2001; CCSSO, 2010). Numerous reports and standards emphasize the need to address skills and understanding in an integrated manner; among these are the *Common Core State Standards* (CCSSO, 2010), a state-led effort coordinated by the National Governors Association Center for Best Practices (NGA Center) and CCSSO that has been adopted by nearly every state and the District of Columbia. This effort has resulted in attention to *how* mathematics is taught, not just *what* is taught.

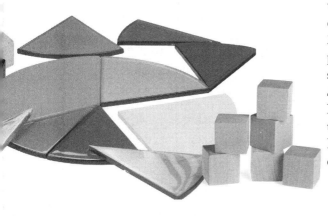

The National Council of Teachers of Mathematics (NCTM, 2000) identifies the process standards of problem solving, reasoning and proof, representation, communication, and connections as ways to think about how children should engage in learning the content as they develop both procedural fluency and conceptual understanding. Children engaged in the process of *problem solving* build mathematical knowledge and understanding by grappling with and solving genuine problems, as opposed to completing routine exercises. They use *reasoning and proof* to make sense of mathematical tasks and concepts and to develop, justify, and evaluate mathematical arguments and solutions. Children create and use *representations* (e.g., diagrams, graphs, symbols, and manipulatives) to reason through problems. They also engage in *communication* as they explain their ideas and reasoning verbally, in writing, and through representations. Children develop and use *connections* between mathematical ideas as they learn new mathematical concepts and procedures. They also build *connections* between mathematics and other disciplines by applying mathematics to real-world situations. By engaging in these processes, children *learn* mathematics by *doing* mathematics. Consequently, the process standards should not be taught separately from but in conjunction with mathematics as ways of learning mathematics.

Adding It Up (National Research Council, 2001), an influential research review on how children learn mathematics, identifies the following five strands of mathematical proficiency as indicators that someone understands (and can do) mathematics.

- **Conceptual understanding**: Comprehension of mathematical concepts, operations, and relations
- **Procedural fluency**: Skill in carrying out procedures flexibly, accurately, efficiently, and appropriately
- **Strategic competence**: Ability to formulate, represent, and solve mathematical problems
- **Adaptive reasoning**: Capacity for logical thought, reflection, explanation, and justification
- **Productive disposition**: Habitual inclination to see mathematics as sensible, useful, and worthwhile, coupled with a belief in diligence and one's own efficacy (Reprinted with permission from p. 116 of *Adding It Up: Helping Children Learn Mathematics*, 2001, by the National Academy of Sciences, Courtesy of the National Academies Press, Washington, D.C.)

This report maintains that the strands of mathematical proficiency are interwoven and interdependent—that is, the development of one strand aids the development of others (Figure 1.1).

Building on the NCTM process standards and the five strands of mathematical proficiency, the *Common Core State Standards* (CCSSO, 2010) outline the following eight Standards for Mathematical Practice (see Appendix A) as ways in which children can develop and demonstrate a deep understanding of and capacity to do mathematics. Keep in mind that you, as a teacher, have a responsibility to help children develop these practices. Here we provide a brief discussion about each mathematical practice.

Figure 1.1

Interrelated and intertwined strands of mathematical proficiency.

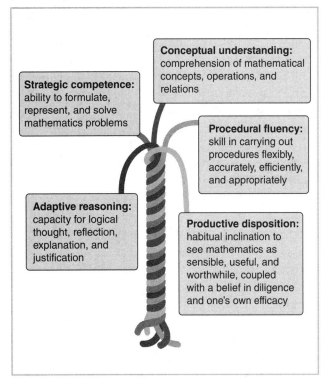

Source: Reprinted with permission from Kilpatrick, J., Swafford, J., & Findell, B. (Eds.), *Adding It Up: Helping Children Learn Mathematics.* Copyright 2001 by the National Academy of Sciences. Courtesy of the National Academies Press, Washington, D.C.

1. *Make sense of problems and persevere in solving them.* To make sense of problems, children need to learn how to analyze the given information, parameters, and relationships in a problem so that they can understand the situation and identify possible ways to solve it. Encourage younger students to use concrete materials or bar diagrams to investigate and solve the problem. Once children learn strategies for making sense of problems, encourage them to remain committed to solving them. As they learn to monitor and assess their progress and change course as needed, they will solve the problems they set out to solve!

2. *Reason abstractly and quantitatively.* This practice involves children reasoning with quantities and their relationships in problem situations. You can support children's development of this practice by helping them create representations that correspond to the meanings of the quantities and the units involved. When appropriate, children should also learn to represent and manipulate the situation symbolically. Encourage children to find connections between the abstract symbols and the representation that illustrates the quantities and their relationships. For example, when children use drawings to show that they made 5 bears from 3 red bears and 2 yellow bears, encourage them to connect their representation to the number sentence $5 = 3 + 2$. Ultimately, children should be able to move flexibly between the symbols and other representations.

3. *Construct viable arguments and critique the reasoning of others.* This practice emphasizes the importance of children using mathematical reasoning to justify their ideas and solutions, including being able to recognize and use counterexamples. Encourage children to examine each others' arguments to determine whether they make sense and to identify ways to clarify or improve the arguments. This practice emphasizes that mathematics is based on reasoning and should be examined in a community—not carried out in isolation. Tips for supporting children as they learn to justify their ideas can be found in Chapter 2.

4. *Model with mathematics.* This practice encourages children to use the mathematics they know to solve problems in everyday life. For younger students this could mean writing an addition or a subtraction equation to represent a given situation or using their number sense to determine whether there are enough plates for all the children in their class. Be sure to encourage children to determine whether their mathematical results make sense in the context of the given situation.

5. *Use appropriate tools strategically.* Children should become familiar with a variety of problem-solving tools that can be used to solve a problem and they should learn to choose which ones are most appropriate for a given situation. For example, second graders should experience using the following tools for computation: pencil and paper, manipulatives, calculator, hundreds chart, and a number line. Then in a situation when an estimate is needed for the sum of 23 and 52, some second graders might consider paper and pencil, manipulatives, and a calculator as tools that would slow down the process and would select a hundreds chart to quickly move from 50 down two rows (20 spaces) to get to 70.

6. *Attend to precision.* In communicating ideas to others, it is imperative that children learn to be explicit about their reasoning. For example, they need to be clear about the meanings of the operations and symbols they use, to indicate the units involved in a problem, and to clearly label the diagrams they provide in their explanations. As children share their ideas, make this expectation clear and ask clarifying questions that help make the details of their reasoning more apparent. Teachers can further encourage

Teaching Tip

Research suggests that children, in particular girls, may tend to continue to use the same tools because they feel comfortable with the tools and are afraid to take risks (Ambrose, 2002). Look for children who tend to use the same tool or strategy every time they work on tasks. Encourage all children to take risks and try new tools and strategies.

children's attention to precision by introducing, highlighting, and encouraging the use of accurate mathematical terminology in explanations and diagrams.

7. *Look for and make use of structure.* Children who look for and recognize a pattern or structure can experience a shift in their perspective or understanding. Therefore, set the expectation that children will look for patterns and structure and help them reflect on their significance. For example, look for opportunities to help children notice that the order in which they add two numbers does not change the sum—they can add $4 + 7$ or $7 + 4$ to get 11. Once they recognize this pattern with other examples, they will have a new understanding and the use of a powerful property of our number system, the commutative property of addition.

8. *Look for and express regularity in repeated reasoning.* Encourage children to step back and reflect on any regularity that occurs in an effort to help them develop a general idea or method or identify shortcuts. For example, as children begin adding numbers together, they will encounter situations in which zero is added to a number. Over time, help children reflect on the results of adding zero to any number. Eventually they should be able to express that when they add or subtract zero to any number, the number is unaffected.

Like the process standards, the Standards for Mathematical Practice should not be taught separately from the mathematics but should instead be incorporated as ways for children to learn and do mathematics. Children who learn to use these eight mathematical practices as they engage with mathematical concepts and skills have a greater chance of developing conceptual understanding. Note that learning these mathematical practices and, consequently, developing understanding takes time. So the common notion of simply and quickly "covering the material" is problematic. The opening quotation states it well: "An understanding can never be 'covered' if it is to be understood" (Wiggins & McTighe, 2005, p. 229). Understanding is an end goal—that is, it is developed over time by incorporating the process standards and mathematical practices and striving toward mathematical proficiency.

How Do Children Learn?

Let's look at a couple of research-based theories that can illustrate how children learn in general: constructivism and sociocultural theory. Although one theory focuses on the individual learner whereas the other emphasizes the social and cultural aspects of the classroom, these theories are not competing; they are actually compatible (Norton & D'Ambrosio, 2008).

Constructivism

At the heart of constructivism is the notion that learners are not blank slates but rather creators (constructors) of their own learning. All people, all of the time, construct or give meaning to things they think about or perceive. Whether you are listening passively to a lecture or actively engaging in synthesizing findings in a project, your brain is applying prior knowledge (existing schemas) to make sense of new information.

Constructing something in the physical world requires tools, materials, and effort. The tools you use to build understanding are your existing ideas and knowledge. Your materials might be things you see, hear, or touch, or they might be your own thoughts and ideas. The effort required to construct knowledge and understanding is reflective thought.

Through reflective thought people connect existing ideas to new information and in this way modify their existing schemas or background knowledge to incorporate new ideas. Making these connections can happen in either of two ways—*assimilation* or *accommodation*.

Assimilation occurs when a new concept "fits" with prior knowledge and the new information expands an existing mental network. Accommodation takes place when the new concept does not "fit" with the existing network, thus creating a cognitive conflict or state of confusion that causes what theorists call *disequilibrium*. As an example, consider what happens when children start learning about numbers and counting. They make sense of a number by counting a quantity of objects by ones. With larger numbers, such as two-digit numbers, they continue to use this approach to give meaning to the number (assimilation). Eventually, counting large amounts of objects becomes cumbersome and, at the same time, they are likely learning about grouping in tens. Over time they begin to view two-digit numbers differently—as groups of tens and ones—and they no longer have to count to give a number meaning (accommodation). It is through the struggle to resolve the disequilibrium that the brain modifies or replaces the existing schema so that the new concept fits and makes sense, resulting in a revision of thought and a deepening of the learner's understanding.

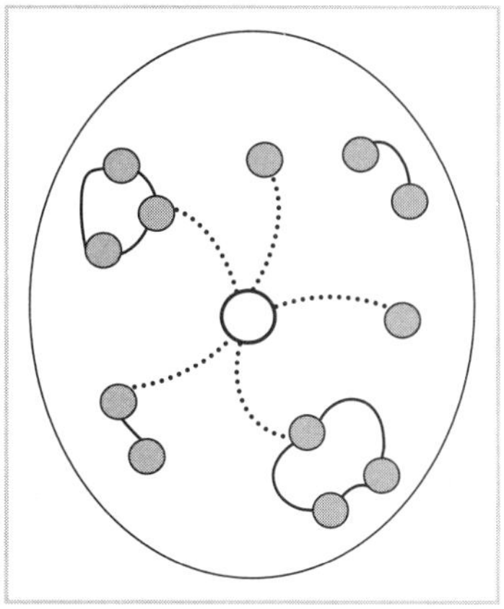

For an illustration of what it means to construct an idea, consider Figure 1.2. The gray and white dots represent ideas, and the lines joining the ideas represent the logical connections or relationships that develop between ideas. The white dot is an emerging idea, one that is being constructed. Whatever existing ideas (gray dots) are used in the construction are connected to the new idea (white dot) because those are the ideas that give meaning to the new idea. The more existing ideas that are used to give meaning to the new one, the more connections will be made.

Each child's unique collection of ideas is connected in different ways. Some ideas are well understood and well formed (i.e., connected), others less so as they emerge and build connections. Children's experiences help them develop connections and ideas about whatever they are learning.

Understanding exists along a continuum (Figure 1.3) from an instrumental understanding—knowing something by rote or without meaning (Skemp, 1978)—to a relational understanding—knowing what to do and why. Instrumental understanding, at the left end of the continuum, shows that ideas (e.g., concepts and procedures) are learned, but in isolation (or nearly so) to other ideas. Here you find ideas that have been memorized. Due to their isolation, poorly understood ideas are easily forgotten and are unlikely to be useful for constructing new ideas. At the right end of the continuum is relational understanding. Relational understanding means that each new concept or procedure (white dot) is not only learned, but is also connected to many existing ideas (gray dots), so there is a rich set of connections.

A primary goal of teaching for understanding is to help children develop a relational understanding of mathematical ideas. Because relational understanding develops over time and becomes more complex as a person makes more connections between ideas, teaching for this kind of understanding takes time and must be a goal of daily instruction.

Figure 1.2

How someone constructs a new idea.

Figure 1.3

Continuum of understanding.

◆ Sociocultural Theory

Like constructivism, sociocultural theory not only positions the learner as actively engaged in seeking meaning during the learning process, but it also suggests that the learner can be assisted by working with others who are "more knowledgeable." Sociocultural theory proposes that learners have their own zone of proximal development, which is a range of knowledge that may be out of reach for individuals to learn on their own but is accessible if learners have the support of peers or more knowledgeable others (Vygotsky, 1978). For example, when young children are learning to measure length, they do not necessarily recognize the significance of placing measurement units end to end. As children measure objects, they may leave gaps between units or overlap units. A more knowledgeable person (a peer or teacher) can draw their attention to this critical idea in measurement.

The best learning for any given child will occur when the conversation of the classroom is within his or her zone of proximal development. Targeting that zone helps teachers provide children with the right amount of challenge, while avoiding boredom on the one hand and anxiety on the other when the challenge is beyond the child's current capability. Consequently, classroom discussions based on children's own ideas and solutions to problems are absolutely "foundational to children's learning" (Wood & Turner-Vorbeck, 2001, p. 186).

Teaching for Understanding

◆ Teaching toward Relational Understanding

To explore the notion of understanding further, let's look into a learner-centered second-grade classroom. In learner-centered classrooms, teachers begin *where the children are*—with the *children's* ideas. Children are allowed to solve problems or to approach tasks in ways that make sense to them. They develop their understanding of mathematics because they are at the center of explaining, providing evidence or justification, finding or creating examples, generalizing, analyzing, making predictions, applying concepts, representing ideas in different ways, and articulating connections or relationships between the given topic and other ideas.

For example, in this second-grade classroom, the children have done numerous activities with the hundreds chart and an open number line. They have counted collections of objects and made many measurements of things in the room. In their counting and measuring, they often count groups of objects instead of counting by ones. Counting by tens has become a popular method for most but not all children. The class has taken big numbers apart in different ways to emphasize relationships between numbers and place value. In many of these activities, the children have used combinations of tens to make numbers. The children in the class have not been taught the typical procedures for addition or subtraction.

The teacher sets the following instructional objectives for the students:

1. Use number relationships (e.g., place-value ideas, such as 36 is 3 groups of 10 and 6 ones; 36 is 4 away from 40; etc.) to add two-digit numbers.

2. Apply flexible methods of addition.

As is often the case, this class begins with a story problem and the children set to work.

When Carla was at the zoo, she saw the monkeys eating bananas. She asked the zookeeper how many bananas the monkeys usually ate in one day. The zookeeper said that yesterday they ate 36 bananas but today they ate only 25 bananas. How many bananas did the monkeys eat in those two days?

Some children use counters and count by ones. Some use the hundreds chart or base-ten models and others use mental strategies or an open number line. All are expected to use words and numbers and, if they wish, drawings to show what they did and how they thought about the problem. After about 20 minutes, the teacher begins a discussion by having children share their ideas. As the children report, the teacher records their ideas on the board so everyone can see them. Sometimes the teacher asks questions to help clarify ideas but makes no evaluative comments. The teacher asks the children who are listening if they understand or have any questions to ask the presenters. The following solution strategies are common in classrooms where children are regularly asked to generate their own approaches.

Avery: I know that 25 and 25 is 50—like two quarters. And 35 is ten more so that is 60. And then one more is 61.

Teacher: What do you mean when you say "35 is ten more"?

Avery: Well, I used 25 of the 36 and 25 and ten more is 35.

Sasha: I did 30 and 20 is 50 and then 6 + 5 more. Five and five is ten and so 6 + 5 is 11. And then 50 and 11 is 61.

Juan: I counted on using the hundreds chart. I started at 36 and then I had to go 20 from there and so that was 46 and then 56. And then I went five more: 57, 58, 59, 60, 61.

Marie: I used an open number to help me. I started at 36 and went up 4 to 40. Then I went up a jump of 20 and then one more to get to 61. (Figure 1.4)

Teacher: Where is the "25" in your strategy?

Marie: It's above the jumps. 4 + 20 + 1 is the same as 25.

This vignette illustrates that when children are encouraged to solve a problem in their own way (using their own particular set of gray dots or ideas), they are able to make sense of their solution strategies and explain their reasoning. This is evidence of their development of mathematical proficiency.

During the discussion periods in classes such as this one, ideas continue to grow. The children may hear and immediately understand a clever strategy that they could have used but that did not occur to them. Others may begin to create new ideas to use that build from thinking about their classmates' strategies over multiple discussions. Some in the class may hear excellent ideas from their peers that do not make sense to them. These children are simply not ready or do not have the prerequisite concepts (gray dots) to understand these new ideas. On subsequent days there will be similar opportunities for all children to grow at their own pace based on their own understandings.

Figure 1.4

A child uses an open number line to solve 36 + 25 by starting at 36 and then adding 4, 20, and 1. The child wrote the numbers on the number line as the numbers move from 36 to 61.

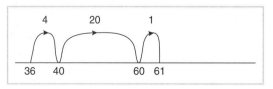

◆ Teaching toward Instrumental Understanding

In contrast to the lesson just described, in which children are developing concepts (understanding of place value) and procedures (ability to flexibly add) and seeing the relationship between these ideas, let's consider how a lesson with the same basic objective (addition using place-value concepts) might look if the focus is on instrumental understanding.

In this classroom, the teacher introduces only one way to solve multidigit addition problems—by modeling how to add numbers using base-ten materials. The teacher distributes base-ten blocks so that pairs of children have enough materials to solve any problem. The teacher reads to the class the same monkeys and bananas problem that was used earlier. The class quickly agrees that they need to add the two numbers in the problem. Using a projector to demonstrate, the teacher directs the children to make the two numbers on their place-value mats. Care is taken that the 25 is shown with the base-ten blocks beneath the base-ten blocks for 36. The children are directed to begin combining the pieces in the ones place. A series of questions guides them through each step in the standard algorithm.

1. How many ones are there all together?
2. What do we need to do with the 11 ones? (regroup, make a ten)
3. Where do we put the ten?
4. How many tens are there?
5. What is the answer?

Next, the children are given five similar problems to solve using the base-ten blocks. They work in pairs and record answers on their papers. The teacher circulates and helps anyone having difficulty by guiding them through the same steps indicated by the preceding questions.

In this lesson the teacher and children are using manipulatives to illustrate regrouping in addition problems. After engaging in several similar lessons, most children are likely to remember and possibly understand how to add with regrouping using the standard algorithm. Using manipulatives to illustrate why regrouping is needed does build a relational understanding, connecting place value to addition; however, because all children are instructed on one way to solve the problem, the lesson provides fewer opportunities to build connections between mathematical concepts. For example, students are not provided opportunities to use mental counting strategies, the hundreds chart, or the number line to add the numbers. Seeing that all of these methods work helps children build connections between mathematical ideas and across representations—fundamental characteristics of relational understanding. It is important to note that this lesson on the standard algorithm, in combination with other lessons that reinforce other approaches, *can* build a relational understanding, as it adds to children's repertoire of strategies. But if this lesson represents the sole approach to adding, then children are more likely to develop an instrumental understanding of mathematics.

◆ The Importance of Children's Ideas

Let's take a minute to compare these two classrooms. By examining them more closely, you can see several important differences. These differences affect what is learned and who learns. Let's consider the first difference: Who determines the procedure to use?

In the first classroom, the children look at the numbers in the problem, think about the relationships between the numbers, and then *choose* a computational strategy that fits these ideas. They have developed several different strategies to solve addition problems by exploring numbers and various representations, such as the open number line and the hundreds chart. Consequently, they are relating addition to various representations and employing number relationships in their addition strategies (taking numbers apart and putting them together differently). The children in the first classroom are being taught mathematics for understanding—*relational* understanding—and are developing the kinds of mathematical proficiency described earlier.

In the second classroom, the teacher provides one strategy for how to add—the standard algorithm. Although the standard algorithm is a valid strategy, the entire focus of the lesson is on the steps and procedures that the teacher has outlined. The teacher solicits no ideas from individual children about how to combine the numbers and instead is only able to find out who has and who has not been able to follow directions.

When children have more choice in determining which strategies to use, as in the first classroom, they can learn more content and make more connections. In addition, if teachers do not seek out and value children's ideas, children may come to believe that mathematics is a body of rules and procedures that are learned by waiting for the teacher to tell them what to do. This view of mathematics—and what is involved in learning it—is inconsistent with mathematics as a discipline and with the learning theories described previously. Therefore, it is a worthwhile goal to transform your classroom into a mathematical community of learners who interact with each other and with the teacher as they share ideas and results, compare and evaluate strategies, challenge results, determine the validity of answers, and negotiate ideas. The rich interaction in such a classroom increases opportunities for productive engagement and reflective thinking about relevant mathematical ideas, resulting in children developing a relational understanding of mathematics.

A second difference between the two classrooms is the learning goals. Both teachers might write "understand two-digit addition" as the objective for the day. However, what is captured in "understand" is very different in each setting. In the first classroom, the teacher's goals are for children to connect addition to what they already know and to see that two numbers can be combined in many different ways. In the second classroom, understanding is connected to being able to carry out the standard algorithm. The learning goals, and more specifically, how the teacher interprets the meaning behind the learning goals, affect what children learned.

These lessons also differ in terms of how accessible they are—and this, in turn, affects who learns the mathematics. The first lesson is differentiated in that it meets children where they are in their current understanding. When a task is presented as "solve this in your own way," it has multiple entry points, meaning it can be approached in a variety of ways. Consequently, children with different prior knowledge or learning strategies can figure out a way to solve the problem. This makes the task accessible to more learners. Then, as children observe strategies that are more efficient than their own, they develop new and better ways to solve the problem.

In the second classroom, everyone has to do the problem in the same way. Children do not have the opportunity to apply their own ideas or to see that there are numerous ways to solve the problem. This may deprive children who need to continue working on the development of basic ideas of tens and ones as well as children who could easily find one or more ways to do the problem if only they were asked to do so. The children in the second classroom are also likely to use the same method to add all numbers instead of looking for more efficient ways to add based on the relationships between numbers. For example, they are likely to add $29 + 29$ using the standard algorithm instead of thinking $30 + 30$ and then take away 2. Recall in the discussion of learning theory the importance of building on prior knowledge and learning from others. Student-generated strategies, multiple approaches, and discussion about the problem in the first classroom represent the kinds of strategies that enhance learning for a range of learners.

Children in both classrooms will eventually succeed at finding sums, but what they learn about addition—and about doing mathematics—is quite different. Understanding and doing mathematics involves generating strategies for solving problems, applying those approaches, seeing if they lead to solutions, and checking to see whether answers make sense. These activities were all present in the first classroom but not in the second. Consequently, children in the first classroom, in addition to successfully finding sums, will develop richer mathematical understanding, become more flexible thinkers and better problem solvers, remain more engaged in learning, and develop more positive attitudes toward learning mathematics.

Mathematics Classrooms That Promote Understanding

Three of the most common types of teaching are direct instruction, facilitative methods (also called a *constructivist approach*), and coaching (Wiggins & McTighe, 2005). With direct instruction, the teacher usually demonstrates or models, lectures, and asks questions that are convergent or closed-ended in nature. With facilitative methods, the teacher might use investigations and inquiry, cooperative learning, discussion, and questions that are more open-ended. In coaching, the teacher provides children with guided practice and feedback that highlight ways to improve their performances.

You might be wondering which type of teaching is most appropriate if the goal is to teach mathematics for understanding. Unfortunately, there is no definitive answer because there are times when it is appropriate to engage in each of these types of teaching, depending on your instructional goals, the learners, and the situation. Some people believe that all direct instruction is ineffective because it ignores the learner's ideas and removes the productive struggle or opportunity to learn. This is not necessarily true. A teacher who is striving to teach for understanding can share information via direct instruction as long as that information does not remove the need for children to reflect on and productively struggle with the situation at hand. In other words, regardless of instructional design, the teacher should not be doing the thinking, reasoning, and connection building—it must be the children who are engaged in these activities.

Regarding facilitative or constructivist methods, remember that constructivism is a theory of learning, not a theory of teaching. Constructivism helps explain how children learn—by developing and modifying ideas (schemas) and by making connections between these ideas. Children can learn as a result of different kinds of instruction. The instructional approach chosen should depend on the ideas and relationships children have already constructed. Sometimes children readily make connections by listening to a lecture (direct instruction). Sometimes they need time to investigate a situation so they can become aware of the different ideas at play and how those ideas relate to one another (facilitative). Sometimes they need to practice a skill and receive feedback on their performance to become more accurate (coaching). No matter which type of teaching is used, constructivism and sociocultural theories remind us as teachers to continually wonder whether our children have truly developed the given concept or skill, connecting it to what they already know. By shedding light on what and how our children understand, assessment can help us determine which teaching approach may be the most appropriate at a given time.

The essence of developing relational understanding is to keep the children's ideas at the forefront of classroom activities by emphasizing the process standards, mathematical proficiencies, and the Standards for Mathematical Practice. This requires that the teacher create a classroom culture in which children can learn from one another. Consider the following features of a mathematics classroom that promote understanding (Chapin, O'Conner, & Anderson, 2009; Hiebert, Carpenter, Fennema, Fuson, Wearne, Murray, Olivier, & Human,

1997; Hoffman, Breyfogle, & Dressler, 2009). In particular, notice who is doing the thinking, the talking, and the mathematics—the children.

- *Children's ideas are key.* Mathematical ideas expressed by children are important and have the potential to contribute to everyone's learning. Learning mathematics is about coming to understand the ideas of the mathematical community.

Listen carefully to children as they talk about what they are thinking and doing as they engage in a mathematical task. If they respond in an unexpected way, try to avoid imposing *your* ideas onto their ideas. Ask clarifying questions to try to make sense of the sense your children are making!

- *Opportunities for children to talk about mathematics are common.* Learning is enhanced when children are engaged with others who are working on the same ideas. Encouraging student-to-student dialogue can help children think of themselves as capable of making sense of mathematics. Children are also more likely to question each other's ideas than the teacher's ideas.

- *Multiple approaches are encouraged.* Children must recognize that there is often a variety of methods that will lead to a solution. Respect for the ideas shared by others is critical if real discussion is to take place.

- *Mistakes are good opportunities for learning.* Children must come to realize that errors provide opportunities for growth as they are uncovered and explained. Trust must be established with an understanding that it is okay to make mistakes. Without this trust, many ideas will never be shared.

- *Math makes sense.* Children must come to understand that mathematics makes sense. Teachers should resist always evaluating children's answers. In fact, when teachers routinely respond with "Yes, that's correct," or "No, that's wrong," children will stop trying to make sense of ideas in the classroom and discussion and learning will be curtailed.

To create a climate that encourages mathematics understanding, teachers must first provide explicit instruction on the ground rules for classroom discussions. Second, teachers may need to model the type of questioning and interaction that they expect from their children. Direct instruction would be appropriate in such a situation. The crucial point in teaching for understanding is to highlight and use children's ideas to promote mathematical proficiency.

Most people go into teaching because they want to help children learn. It is hard to think of allowing—much less planning for—the children in your classroom to struggle. Not showing them a solution when they are experiencing difficulty seems almost counterintuitive. If our goal is relational understanding, however, the struggle is part of the learning, and teaching becomes less about the teacher and more about what the children are doing and thinking.

Keep in mind that you too are a learner. Some ideas in this book may make more sense to you than others. Others may even create dissonance for you. Embrace this feeling of disequilibrium and unease as an opportunity to learn—to revise your perspectives on mathematics and on the teaching and learning of mathematics as you deepen your understanding so that you can help your children deepen theirs.

Stop and Reflect

Look back at the chapter and identify any ideas that make you uncomfortable or that challenge your current thinking about mathematics or about teaching and learning mathematics. Try to determine why these ideas challenge you or make you uncomfortable. Write these ideas down and revisit them later as you read and reflect further. ◼

2

Teaching Mathematics through Problem Solving

By inviting young children to solve problems in their own ways, we are initiating them into the community of mathematicians who engage in structuring and modeling their "lived worlds" mathematically.

Fosnot and Jacob (2007, p. 25)

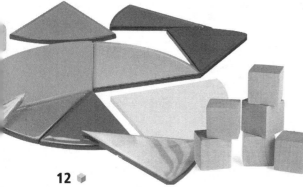

Teaching mathematics through problem solving is a method of teaching mathematics that helps children develop relational understanding. With this approach, problem solving is completely interwoven with learning. As children do mathematics—make sense of cognitively demanding tasks, provide evidence or justification for strategies and solutions, find examples and connections, and receive and provide feedback about ideas—they are simultaneously engaged in the activities of problem solving and learning. Teaching mathematics through problem solving requires you to think about the types of tasks you pose to children, how you facilitate discourse in your classroom, and how you support children's use of a variety of representations as tools for problem solving, reasoning, and communication.

Teaching through Problem Solving: An Upside-Down Approach

For many years and continuing today, mathematics has been taught using a teaching-*for*-problem-solving approach: The teacher presents the mathematics, the children practice the skill, and, finally, the children solve word problems that require using that skill. Unfortunately, this "do-as-I-show-you" approach to mathematics teaching has not been successful for many children in helping them to understand or remember mathematics concepts (e.g., Pesek & Kirshner, 2002; Philipp & Vincent, 2003).

Teaching mathematics *through* problem solving generally means that children solve problems to learn new mathematics, not just to apply mathematics after it has been learned. Children learn mathematics through real contexts, problems, situations, and models that allow them to build meaning for the concepts (Hiebert, Carpenter, Fennema, Fuson, Wearne, Murray, Olivier, & Human, 1997). So teaching *through* problem solving might be described as "upside down" from the traditional approach of teaching *for* problem solving because the problem is presented at the beginning of a lesson and skills and ideas emerge from working with the problem. An example of teaching through problem solving might have children explore the following situation before they are taught the basic facts related to five (e.g., 0 + 5; 1 + 4; 2 + 3, and so on).

Tatyana's mother is decorating a cake for Tatyana's fifth birthday but she only has green and blue candles. If she wants to use exactly 5 candles on the cake, how many green and blue candles could she use?

The teacher would explain to the class that there is more than one correct solution to this problem and that they are to find as many different solutions as they can. As children work on the problem, they may use green and blue counters, they may choose to draw the candles, or they may simply use numbers to capture their ideas.

Stop and Reflect

Find all the possible combinations of blue and green candles. How do you know you have found all the combinations? What is the significance of using two colors of candles? ■

Through this context and exploration, children could grapple with the commutative property of addition as they compare combinations such as 2 (green) + 3 (blue) and 3 (green) + 2 (blue). This problem also generates opportunities for children to investigate 0 as they consider whether they can have 5 green candles and 0 blue candles or vice versa.

Teaching *through* problem solving requires a paradigm shift, which means that teachers are doing more than just tweaking a few things about their teaching; they are changing their philosophy of how they think children learn best and how they can best help them learn. At first glance, it may seem that the teacher's role is less demanding because the children are doing the mathematics, but the teacher's role is actually more demanding in such classrooms. Here are some of the important teacher responsibilities:

- Select high-quality tasks that allow children to learn the content by figuring out their own strategies and solutions.

- Ask high-quality questions that allow children to verify and relate their strategies.

- Listen to children's responses and examine their work, determining in the moment how to extend and formalize their thinking through targeted feedback.

There is no doubt that teaching mathematics through problem solving can be challenging, but the results are worth the effort! It promises to be a better approach if our ultimate goal is deep (relational) understanding because teaching through problem solving accomplishes these goals:

- *Focuses children's attention on ideas and sense making.* When solving problems, children are necessarily reflecting on the concepts inherent in the problems. Emerging concepts are more likely to be integrated with existing ones, thereby improving understanding.

- *Emphasizes mathematical processes and practices.* Children who are solving problems will engage in all five of the processes of doing mathematics—problem solving, reasoning, communication, connections, and representation (NCTM, 2000), as well as the eight mathematical practices outlined in the *Common Core State Standards*, resulting in mathematics that is more accessible, more interesting, and more meaningful. Note that the first Standard for Mathematical Practice is "Make sense of problems and persevere in solving them" (CCSSO, 2010).

- *Develops children's confidence and identities.* Every time teachers pose a problem-based task and expect a solution, they implicitly say to children, "I believe you can do this." When children are engaged in problem solving and discourse in which the correctness of the solution lies in the justification of the process, they begin to see themselves as capable of doing mathematics and that mathematics makes sense.

- *Provides a context to help children build meaning for the concept.* Using a context facilitates mathematical understanding, especially when the context is grounded in an experience familiar to children and when the context uses purposeful constraints that potentially highlight the significant mathematical ideas (Fosnot & Dolk, 2001).

- *Allows entry and exit points for a wide range of children.* Good problem-based tasks have multiple paths to the solution, so each child can make sense of and solve the task by using his or her own ideas. Furthermore, children expand their ideas and grow in their understanding as they hear, critique, and reflect on the solution strategies of others.

- *Allows for extensions and elaborations.* Extensions and "what if" questions can motivate advanced learners or quick finishers, resulting in increased learning and enthusiasm for doing mathematics.

- *Engages children so that there are fewer discipline problems.* Many discipline issues in a classroom are the result of children becoming bored, not understanding the teacher directions, or simply finding little relevance in the task. Most children like to be challenged and enjoy being permitted to solve problems in ways that make sense to them, giving them less reason to act out or cause trouble.

- *Provides formative assessment data.* As children discuss ideas, draw diagrams, or use manipulatives, defend their solutions and evaluate those of others, and write reports or explanations, they provide the teacher with a steady stream of valuable information that can be used to inform subsequent instruction.

- *Is a lot of fun!* Children enjoy the creative process of problem solving and sharing how they figured something out. After seeing the surprising and inventive ways that children think and how engaged children become in mathematics, very few teachers stop using a teaching-*through*-problem-solving approach.

 Using Problems to Teach

When teachers teach mathematics *through* problem solving, children learn the desired content through problems (tasks or activities). A *problem* is defined here as any task or activity for which children have no prescribed or memorized rules or methods, and for which they do not have a perception that there is a specific "correct" solution method (Hiebert et al., 1997). In other words, the task or activity is a genuine problem.

◆ Features of a Problem

Problems that can serve as effective tasks or activities for children to solve have common features. Use the following points as a guide to assess whether a task or an activity has the potential to be a genuine problem.

- *The problem should engage children where they are in their current understanding.* Children should have the appropriate ideas to begin engaging with the problem and to solve the problem, and yet still find it challenging and interesting.

- *The problematic or engaging aspect of the problem must be a result of the mathematics that the children are to learn.* In solving the problem or doing the activity, children should be concerned primarily with making sense of and developing their understanding of the mathematics involved. Any context or external constraints used should not overshadow the mathematics to be learned.

- *The problem must require justifications and explanations for answers and methods.* In a high-quality problem, neither the process nor the answer is straightforward, so justification is central to the task. Children should understand that the responsibility for determining whether answers are correct and why they are correct rests on their mathematical reasoning, not on the teacher telling them that they are correct.

🔹 Examples of Problems

Problems can be used to develop both concepts and procedures, as well as the connection between concepts and procedures. In the following examples, the first two problems focus on concepts and the third problem focuses on a procedure.

CONCEPTS: Cardinality (how many), Decomposition of numbers

Four friends are playing in a playhouse at a park. The playhouse has two floors. Draw a picture to show how many friends might be on each floor. Can you find more than one way? How many ways do you think there are? Why?

CONCEPT: Equality

$$3 + 6 = 1 + \_\_\_$$

Find a number for the blank so that the equation is true. Is there more than one number that will make the equation true? Why or why not? Can you find more than one way to find a number for the blank so that the equation is true?

Note that a task in the form of a story problem does not automatically make the task a problem. A story problem can be "routine" if children read it and know right away that it is a subtraction problem and subtract to answer it. Conversely, an equation with no words, as in the second example above, is not necessarily routine and can actually be a rich problem to investigate.

PROCEDURE: Subtracting two-digit whole numbers

Solve this problem in two different ways: $32 - 17 = \_\_\_\_$
For each way, explain how you solved it.

The third example, although focused on a procedure, is a problem because children must figure out *how* they are going to approach the task (assuming they have not been taught the standard algorithm at this point). Children are also challenged to find more than one way to solve the problem. Implicit is the challenge to determine how the two solution strategies are different. The third example is important because it illustrates that virtually all mathematics—concepts and procedures—can be taught through problem solving.

🔹 Selecting Worthwhile Tasks

As noted earlier in the three features of a problem, a task must engage children where they currently are in their understanding and simultaneously must be problematic for the children. In selecting such a task, consider the level of cognitive demand, the potential of the task to have multiple entry and exit points, and the relevancy of the task to children.

Level of Cognitive Demand

Research supports the practice of engaging children in productive struggle to develop understanding (Bay-Williams, 2010; Hiebert & Grouws, 2007). Both words in the phrase "productive struggle" are important. Children must have the tools and prior knowledge to solve a problem and not be given a problem that is out of reach, because otherwise they will struggle without being productive; however, children should not be given tasks that are straightforward and trivial because they will not struggle with mathematical ideas and further develop their understanding. When children (even very young children) know that struggle is an expected part of the process of doing mathematics, they embrace the struggle and feel success when they reach a solution (Carter, 2008).

Figure 2.1 shows a useful framework for determining whether a task has the potential to challenge children (Smith & Stein, 1998). The framework distinguishes between tasks that require low levels and high levels of cognitive demand. Tasks that have low-level cognitive demand are routine and straightforward and do not engage children in productive struggle. Tasks with high-level cognitive demand not only engage children in productive struggle, but also challenge children to make connections between concepts and to other relevant knowledge. Although there are appropriate times to use low-level cognitive demand tasks, a heavy or sole emphasis on tasks of this type will not lead to relational understanding of mathematics. As an example of different levels of tasks, consider the degree of reasoning required when asking children to find the sum of three given numbers versus asking them to find three numbers whose sum is 35. The first task only requires children to add three numbers. The

Figure 2.1 Levels of cognitive demand.

Low-Level Cognitive Demand Tasks	High-Level Cognitive Demand Tasks
Memorization • Involve producing previously learned facts, rules, formulas, or definitions or memorizing • Are routine in that they involve exact reproduction of previously learned procedures • Have no connection to related concepts	**Procedures with Connections** • Focus children's attention on the use of procedures for the purpose of developing deeper levels of understanding of mathematical concepts and ideas • Suggest general procedures that have close connections to underlying conceptual ideas • Are usually represented in multiple ways (e.g., visuals, manipulatives, symbols, problem situations) • Require that children engage with the conceptual ideas that underlie the procedures in order to successfully complete the task
Procedures without Connections • Use procedures specifically called for • Are straightforward with little ambiguity about what needs to be done and how to do it • Have no connection to related concepts • Are focused on producing correct answers rather than developing mathematical understanding • Require no explanations or explanations that focus on the procedure only	***Doing* Mathematics** • Require complex and nonalgorithmic thinking (i.e., nonroutine—without a predictable, known approach) • Require children to explore and to understand the nature of mathematical concepts, processes, or relationships • Demand self-monitoring or self-regulation of children's own cognitive processes • Require children to access relevant knowledge in working through the task • Require children to analyze the task and actively examine task constraints • Require considerable cognitive effort

second task requires them to use number sense to generate three reasonable numbers that will result in a given sum. As a consequence of working on this second task, children have potential opportunities to think about and use number relationships while they work on their computational skills for adding.

Multiple Entry and Exit Points

A problem or task that has multiple entry points has varying degrees of challenge within it or it can be approached in a variety of ways. One of the advantages of a problem-based approach is that it can help accommodate the diversity of learners in every classroom because children are encouraged to use a strategy that makes sense to them instead of using a predetermined strategy that they may or may not be ready to use successfully. Some children may initially use less efficient approaches, such as guess and check or counting, but they will develop more advanced strategies through effective questioning by the teacher and by reflecting on other children's approaches. For example, for the task of finding three numbers whose sum is 35, one child may use a guess-and-check approach, listing three numbers and adding them to see if their sum is 35, whereas another child may use a more systematic approach, such as splitting 35 into 30 and 5 and then splitting 30 or 5 into two addends. Still other children may choose two numbers they estimate will sum to an amount less than 35 and then subtract that sum from 35 to find the third number.

Tasks should also have multiple exit points, or various ways that children can demonstrate an understanding of the learning goals. For example, children might draw a diagram, write an equation, use manipulatives, or act out a problem to demonstrate their understanding.

Consider the opportunities for multiple entry and exit points in the following tasks. Both tasks use an everyday classroom routine to provide children an opportunity to work on skills related to counting.

TASK 1:

(The teacher places snacks on a table.) Do we have enough snacks for everyone in the class?

TASK 2:

(The teacher gives each child a sheet of paper with a picture of the snack item copied in rows a certain number of times.) Do we have enough snacks for everyone in the class?

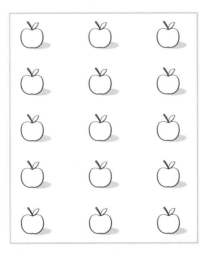

Source: Adapted with permission from *Young Mathematicians at Work: Constructing Number Sense, Addition, and Subtraction* by Catherine Twomey Fostnot and Maarten Dolk. Copyright © 2001 by Catherine Twomey Fosnot and Maarten Dolk. Published by Heinemann, Portsmouth, NH. All rights reserved.

Stop and Reflect

To what degree do these tasks offer opportunities for multiple entry and exit points? ■

If the snacks are readily available, as in the first task, the children will most likely pass them out to see if there are enough snacks and will miss any opportunity to think deeply about the situation. The second task offers more opportunity for children to engage with the task in a variety of ways, which also offers the teacher more information about each child's level of understanding. For example, how children organize their count of the pictured snacks is informative. Do they start at the top and count across the rows? Or do they haphazardly count and miss or double-count? Do they count by ones? Do they count from one or do they count on from a recognized amount? Once they know how many snacks are on the sheet, can they automatically state whether there are enough snacks for everyone? Or do they need to represent each child in the class, say, with a counter, and match a counter with a pictured snack? Clearly, the second task offers many more opportunities for all children to engage in the task in a variety of ways.

Teaching Tip

Before giving a selected task to your class, anticipate several possible responses to the task, including possible misconceptions, and think about how you might address these responses. Anticipating the responses gives you time to consider how you will respond to various approaches and it also helps you to quickly recognize different strategies and misconceptions when children are working on the task.

Relevant and Well-Designed Contexts

One of the most powerful aspects of teaching through problem solving is that the problem that begins the lesson can get children excited about learning mathematics. Compare the following two first-grade introductory tasks on counting in groups. Which one do you think would be more interesting to children?

Classroom A: "Today we are going to use straws to show the day of the month. We will bundle the straws into as many groups of ten as we can and then leave the leftovers loose."

Classroom B: "You all have been busy ordering seeds so we can plant a garden outside our classroom. One of the seed companies sends the seeds in multiple envelopes. In each envelope the seeds are taped in two groups of five onto a card. We are going to figure out how many envelopes we should expect to receive depending on how many seeds we order from this company." (Adapted with permission from *Young Mathematicians at Work: Constructing Number Sense, Addition, and Subtraction* by Catherine Twomey Fostnot and Maarten Dolk. Copyright © 2001 by Catherine Twomey Fosnot and Maarten Dolk. Published by Heinemann, Portsmouth, NH. All rights reserved.)

Familiar and interesting contexts increase children's engagement. Your goal as a teacher is to design problems that provide specific parameters, constraints, or structure that will support the development of the mathematical ideas you want children to learn. In the context used in Classroom B above, the situation involves seeds that are arranged in two groups of five. The teacher is aware that some of the children still need to count by ones, but the constraint that each card has two groups of five will require that they group their seeds into two groups of five, very likely after drawing and counting by ones. This constraint begins to incrementally move these children toward more efficient ways of counting. For those children who are already counting by fives, the two groups of five move them toward working with groups of ten. For children already working with groups of 10, they might not draw seeds at all and instead draw a rectangle to represent each envelope and label it with "10." By building in such constraints, parameters, or structure, teachers can support children in developing more sophisticated strategies that honor where the children currently are in their understanding (Fosnot & Dolk, 2001).

Orchestrating Classroom Discourse

Classroom discourse refers to the interactions among all the participants that occur throughout a lesson—in a whole-class setting, in small groups, between pairs of children, and with the teacher. The purpose of discourse is not for children to state their answers and get validation from the teacher, but to engage all learners and keep the cognitive demand high (Breyfogle & Williams, 2008/2009; Kilic, Cross, Ersoz, Mewborn, Swanagan, & Kim, 2010; Smith, Hughes, Engle, & Stein, 2009).

Classroom Discussions

The value of student talk throughout a mathematics lesson cannot be overemphasized. As children describe and evaluate solutions to tasks, share approaches, and make conjectures, learning will occur in ways that are otherwise unlikely to take place. As they listen to other children's ideas, they come to see the varied approaches in how problems can be solved and see mathematics as something that they can do. Questions such as those that ask children if they would do it differently next time, which strategy made sense to them (and why), and what caused problems for them (and how they overcame them) are critical in developing mathematically proficient children. Orchestrating discourse after children have worked on problems is particularly important because it is this type of discussion that helps children connect the problem to more general or formal mathematics and make connections to other ideas.

Implementing effective discourse in the classroom can be challenging. Finding ways to encourage children to share their ideas and to engage with others about their ideas is essential to productive discussions. Consider the following research-based recommendations that can be useful in a whole-class setting, in small groups, and in peer-to-peer discussions (Chapin, O'Connor, & Anderson, 2009; Rasmussen, Yackel, & King, 2003; Stephan & Whitenack, 2003; Wood, Williams, & McNeal, 2006; Yackel & Cobb, 1996).

- *Clarify children's ideas in a variety of ways.* You can restate children's ideas as questions in order to verify what they did as well as what they meant to confirm what you've heard or observed. You can also apply precise language and make significant ideas more apparent. Paying attention to children's ideas sends the message that their ideas are valued and, therefore, is a key step to encouraging participation of individual children. In addition, modeling how to ask clarifying questions demonstrates to children that it is okay to be unsure and that asking questions is appropriate. It is important to keep in mind that although you may understand a child's ideas and reasoning, there may be children in the class who do not. Therefore, look for opportunities to ask clarifying questions even if you do not need clarification. You can also ask children to restate someone else's ideas in their own words in order to ensure that ideas are stated in a variety of ways and to encourage children to listen to one another. This strategy of clarification is important for English language learners (ELLs) because it reinforces language and enhances comprehension.

- *Emphasize reasoning.* Ask follow-up questions whether the answer is right or wrong to place an emphasis on the reasoning process. Your role is to understand children's thinking (not to lead them to the correct answer and move on). Therefore, follow up with probes to learn more about their answer and their reasoning. Sometimes you will find that what you assumed they were thinking is not correct. Also, if you only follow up on wrong answers, children quickly figure this out and get nervous when you ask them to explain their thinking. In addition, move children to more conceptually based explanations when appropriate. For example, if a child says that he knows 5 + 3 is the same as 3 + 5, ask him (or another child) to explain why this makes sense. Also ask children what they think of the idea proposed by another child, or ask if they see a connection between two classmates' ideas or between a classmate's idea and a concept previously discussed.

• ***Encourage student–student dialogue.*** You want children to think of themselves as capable of making sense of mathematics so that they do not always rely on the teacher to verify the correctness of their ideas. Encouraging student-to-student dialogue can help build this sense of self. Children are also more likely to question one another's ideas than the teacher's ideas. When children have different solutions, ask them to discuss one another's solutions. Or ask someone to rephrase another child's ideas or to add something further to someone else's ideas. Provide opportunities that allow children to share their ideas in small groups or with a peer. This will ensure that all children are able to participate in sharing because not all children will be able to share during every whole-class discussion. Before a whole-class discussion, children can practice their explanations with a peer, which is one way to support ELLs and other children with special needs during mathematical discussions. See Chapters 5 and 6 for other ideas about how to support these particular groups of children with mathematical discussions. Figure 2.2 offers examples of teacher prompts that can support classroom discussions.

Be sure to explain to children that after they hear a question or a prompt they will have time to think so that silence in the classroom does not feel uncomfortable. For example, you can say, "This question is important. Let's take some time to think about it." There will be times when no one responds to your question or prompt. If the situation gets awkward, make sure children understand the question or prompt, then ask them to talk with a partner and try the discussion again.

$\mathcal{F}igure$ 2.2 Examples of teacher prompts for supporting classroom discussions.

Clarify Children's Ideas	"You used the hundreds chart and counted on?" "So, first you recorded your measurements in a table?" "What parts of your drawing relate to the numbers from the story problem?" "Who can share what Ricardo just said, but using your own words?"
Emphasize Reasoning	"Why does it make sense to start with that particular number?" "Explain how you know that your answer is correct." "Can you give an example?" "Do you see a connection between Julio's idea and Rhonda's idea?" "What if ...?" "Do you agree or disagree with Johanna? Why?"
Encourage Student–Student Dialogue	"Who has a question for Vivian?" "Turn to your partner and explain why you agree or disagree with Edwin." "Talk with Yerin about how your strategy relates to hers."

● How Much to Tell and Not to Tell

When teachers teach mathematics *through* problem solving, one of the most perplexing dilemmas is how much, if anything, to tell. On one hand, telling can diminish what is learned and lower the level of challenge in a lesson. On the other hand, telling too little can sometimes leave children floundering, or not productively struggling. Following are suggestions about three things that you need to tell children:

• *Introduce mathematical conventions.* Symbols, such as + and =, are conventions. Terminology is also a convention. As a rule of thumb, symbolism and terminology should be introduced *after* concepts have been developed and then specifically as a means of expressing or labeling ideas.

• *Discuss alternative methods.* If an important strategy does not emerge naturally from the children, then you should propose the strategy, being careful to identify it as "another" way, not the only or the preferred way.

• *Clarify children's methods and make connections.* Help children clarify or interpret their ideas and point out related concepts. A child may add 38 and 5 by noting that 38 and 2 more is 40 with 3 more making 43. This strategy can be related to the Make 10 strategy used to add 8 + 5. The selection of 40 as a temporary target in this child's strategy is an important place-value concept. Drawing everyone's attention to this connection can help other children see the connection while also building the confidence of the child who originally proposed the strategy (Hiebert et al., 1997).

▲ Representations: Tools for Problem Solving, Reasoning, and Communication

A representation can be thought of as a kind of tool, such as a diagram, graph, symbol, or manipulative, that expresses a mathematical idea or concept. Representations are not ends in themselves to be learned for the sake of learning, but are valuable tools in problem solving, reasoning, and communicating about mathematical ideas. Representations can help you think through a problem and better communicate your ideas to another person. How you represent the ideas in the problem will likely influence your solution process. In fact, the representations that children choose to use can provide valuable insight into their ways of interpreting and thinking about the mathematical ideas at hand.

Representations can be conventional or commonly used, such as a "+" to represent addition, or they can be created by children as they solve problems and investigate mathematical ideas. For example, a first grader, not having been introduced to the conventional notation for negative numbers, might create a representation by using the numeral with a slash through it (e.g., 3̶). The slash will remind him that he still needs to take that amount away. He created this representation as a way to record his ideas and share his thinking with others.

Models or representations, whether they are conventional or not, give learners something with which they can explore, reason, and communicate as they engage in problem-based tasks. The goal of using representations is that children be able to manipulate ideas, not manipulate symbols in a rote manner. By using personally meaningful representations to manipulate and communicate about mathematical ideas, children will make connections among mathematical ideas (relational understanding) and move toward mathematical proficiency.

◆ Tips for Using Representations in the Classroom

Because different representations can illuminate different aspects of a mathematical idea, multiple representations should be explored and encouraged. The more ways children are given to think about and test an emerging idea, the better they will correctly form and integrate it into a rich web of concepts and thereby develop a relational understanding. Figure 2.3 illustrates various representations for demonstrating an understanding of any topic. Children who have difficulty translating a concept from one representation to another also have difficulty solving problems and understanding computations (Clement, 2004; Lesh, Cramer, Doerr, Post, & Zawojewski, 2003; NCTM, 2000). Strengthening the ability to move between and among representations improves children's understanding and retention of ideas.

The following are rules of thumb for using representations in the classroom:

- Introduce new representations or tools by showing how they can represent *the ideas* for which they are intended. But keep in mind that, because the representations are not the concepts, some children may not "see" what you see.

- Allow children (in most instances) to select freely from available tools to use in solving problems.

- Encourage children to create their own representations. Look for opportunities to connect these student-created representations to more conventional representations.

- Encourage the use of a particular representation when you believe it would be helpful to a child having difficulty.

- Ask children to use representations, such as diagrams and manipulatives, when they explain their thinking.

Teaching Tip

Pay attention to children's choices of representations and use those representations as starting points for dialogues with them about their thinking. What they find important may be surprising and informative at the same time.

Figure 2.3

Mathematical understanding can be demonstrated through these different representations of mathematical ideas. Translations between each can help children develop new concepts and demonstrate a richer understanding.

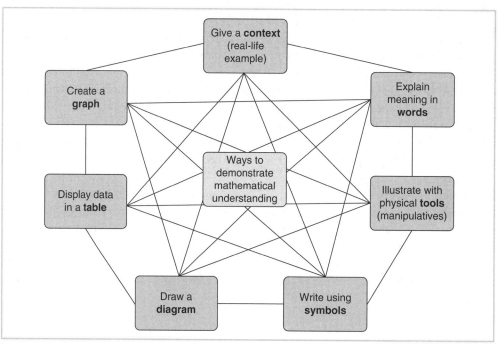

This will help you gather information about children's understanding of the idea and also their understanding of the representations that have been used in the classroom. It can also be helpful to other children in the classroom who may be struggling with the idea or the explanation being offered.

- In creating tasks and when facilitating classroom discussions, focus on making connections among the different representations used (and make sure each is understood). Helping children make these connections is very important to their learning.

⬢ Manipulatives

Let's turn to one kind of representation that is commonly used to support children's learning of mathematics: manipulatives or concrete objects. Used wisely, they can be a positive factor in children's learning, but just using manipulatives—particularly in a rote manner—does not ensure children will understand. It is important to consider how manipulatives can help, or fail to help, children construct mathematical knowledge.

First of all, manipulatives alone have no inherent meaning. A person has to impose meaning onto them. The manipulative is not the concept. Figure 2.4 shows three blocks commonly used to represent ones, tens, and hundreds. If a child is able to identify the rod as the "ten" piece and the large square block as the "hundred" piece, does this mean he has constructed the concepts of ten and hundred? No, all you know for sure is that he has learned the names typically assigned to the manipulatives. The mathematical concept of a ten is that a ten is the same as ten ones. This concept is the relationship between the rod and the small cube. This relationship called "ten" must be created by children in their own minds and imposed on the manipulative or the model used to represent the concept. For a child who does not yet understand the relationship, the model does not illustrate the concept for that individual. Through discussions that explicitly focus on the mathematical concepts over time, the connections between manipulatives and related concepts are developed.

Second, the most widespread misuse of manipulatives occurs when teachers tell children, "Do exactly as I do." There is a natural temptation to get out the materials and show children exactly *how to use them*. Children mimic the teacher's directions, and it may even look as if they understand, but they could be just following what they see. A rote procedure with a manipulative is still just that, a rote procedure.

A third and related misuse of manipulatives occurs when teachers always tell children which manipulative to use for a given problem. Children need opportunities to choose their own representations to use when reasoning through a problem (Mathematical Practice 5: Use appropriate tools strategically) and when communicating their ideas to others.

⬢ Visuals and Other Tools

There are other ways for children to represent and illustrate mathematical concepts. Drawings are one option and are important for a number of reasons. First, when children draw, you learn more about what they do or do not understand. For example, if

> **Teaching Tip**
>
> It is incorrect to say that a manipulative or object "illustrates" or shows a concept. Manipulatives can help children visualize the relationships and talk about them, but what they see are the manipulatives, not concepts.

Figure 2.4

Objects and names of objects are not the same as mathematical ideas and relationships between objects.

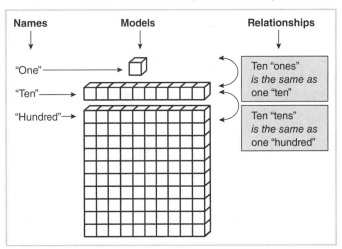

Figure 2.5

A kindergartner shows her thinking about ways to make 5.

How many ways can five people be on two stories of a house?

children are showing $\frac{1}{2}$ with their own drawings, you can observe whether they understand that each half must be the same size. Second, manipulatives can sometimes restrict how children can model a problem, whereas a drawing allows children to use any strategy they want. Plus, because children enter school with a limited ability to express their ideas in writing, a drawing may be the most appropriate way for them to express their ideas. Figure 2.5 shows an example of one kindergartner's solution for ways to make 5. Children should eventually be encouraged to connect their drawings to symbols, but they should not be forced to do so too soon. Some children will take longer than others to make this connection and that difference should be honored. Look for opportunities to use children's representations during classroom discussions to help them make sense of the more abstract mathematical symbols. Furthermore, as children use different representations to solve a problem, have them compare and contrast the various ways.

Representations generated and manipulated through technology can also support children as they reason about and communicate their mathematical ideas. In particular, virtual manipulatives often mirror the mental actions you want children to learn better than physical manipulatives do (Clements & Sarama, 2009). For example, with computerized base-ten blocks, children can break the blocks into ones using a hammer-like tool (decomposition) or they can glue or lasso ones together to form tens (composition) (see, for example, www.ejad.best.vwh.net/java/b10blocks/b10blocks.html). These actions can be done more quickly using a computer than using physical base-ten blocks, leaving more time for exploration. Plus, virtual manipulatives can help children link manipulatives to symbols. For example, at some websites a number representing the computerized base-ten blocks is displayed and changes as the base-ten blocks change, so children can see the results of the actions they take on the virtual manipulatives (e.g., go to http://nlvm.usu.edu/en/nav/category_g_2_t_1.html and select "Base Blocks," "Base Blocks Addition," or "Base Blocks Subtraction"). This dynamic link between these two representations helps children make sense of their activity as well as the numbers. An added bonus with technology is that sometimes the language displayed on the computer program can be changed for ELLs.

But don't forget about using real objects. Young children are better able to relate to a context when they work with real objects. Consider the example of the classroom in which children were ordering seeds to plant in their school garden. Part of the power of using contexts is to be able to use real objects for children to manipulate, organize, and count in ways that make sense to them.

A Three-Phase Lesson Format

A three-phase lesson format (*Before, During, After*) provides a structure for teaching mathematics through problem solving (see Table 2.1). *Before* refers to the time before the children start work on the problem. *During* refers to the time during which the children work on the problem, and *After* refers to the discussion that takes place after children work on the problem. The lesson may take one or more math sessions, but the three-phase structure can also be applied to shorter tasks, resulting in a 10- to 20-minute minilesson.

Table 2.1 Teaching Mathematics through Problem Solving Lends Itself to a Three-Phase Structure for Lessons

Lesson Phase		Teacher Actions in a Teaching Mathematics through Problem-Solving Lesson
Before	Activate prior knowledge.	Begin with a simple version of the task; connect to children's experiences; brainstorm approaches or solution strategies; estimate or predict if tasks involve a single computation or are aimed at the development of a computational procedure.
	Be sure the problem is understood.	Have children explain to you what the problem is asking. Go over vocabulary that may be troubling. Caution: This does not mean that you are explaining how to do the problem—just that children should understand what the problem is about.
	Establish clear expectations.	Tell children whether they will work individually, in pairs, or in small groups, or if they will have a choice. Tell them how they will share their solutions and reasoning.
During	Let go!	Although it is tempting to want to step in and "help," hold back and enjoy observing and learning from the children.
	Notice children's mathematical thinking.	Base your questions on the children's work and their responses to you. Use questions like "Tell me what you are doing"; "I see you have started to [add] these numbers. Can you tell me why you are [adding]?" [substitute any process/strategy]; "Can you tell me more about . . . ?"; "Why did you . . . ?"; "How does your diagram connect to the problem?"
	Provide appropriate support.	Look for ways to support children's thinking and avoid telling them how to solve the problem. Ensure that the children understand the problem (e.g., "What do you know about the problem?"); ask the children what they have already tried (e.g., "Where did you get stuck?"); suggest to the children that they use a different strategy (e.g., "Can you draw a diagram?"; "What if you used cubes to act out this problem?"; "Is this like another problem we have solved?"); create a parallel problem with simpler values (Jacobs & Ambrose, 2008).
	Provide worthwhile extensions.	Challenge early finishers in some manner that is related to the problem just solved. Possible questions to ask are "I see you found one way to do this. Are there any other solutions? Are any of the solutions different or more interesting than others?" Some good questions for extending thinking are "What if . . . ?" or "Would that same idea work for . . . ?"
After	Promote a community of learners.	You must teach children about your expectations for this time and how to interact respectfully with their peers. Role-play appropriate (and inappropriate) ways of responding to each other. The "Orchestrating Classroom Discourse" section provides strategies and recommendations for how to facilitate discussions that help create a community of learners.
	Listen actively without evaluation.	The goal here is noticing children's mathematical thinking and making that thinking visible to other children. Avoid judging the correctness of an answer so that children are more willing to share their ideas. Support children's thinking without evaluation by simply asking what others think about a child's response.
	Summarize main ideas and identify future problems.	Formalize the main ideas of the lesson, helping to highlight connections among strategies or different mathematical ideas. In addition, this is the time to reinforce appropriate terminology, definitions, and symbols. You may also want to lay the groundwork for future tasks and activities.

🔹 Before

In the *Before* phase of the lesson you are preparing children to work on the problem. As you plan for the *Before* part of the lesson, analyze the problem you will give to children in order to anticipate children's approaches and possible misinterpretations or misconceptions (Wallace, 2007). This can inform the questions you ask in the *Before* phase of the lesson to clarify children's understanding of the problem (i.e., knowing what it means rather than how they will solve it).

◈ During

In the *During* phase of the lesson children explore the problem (alone, with partners, or in small groups). This is one of two opportunities you will get in the lesson to find out what the children know, how they think, and how they are approaching the task you have given them (the other is in the discussion period of the *After* phase). You want to convey a genuine interest in what the children are doing and thinking. This is not the time to evaluate or to tell children how to solve the problem. When asking whether a result or method is correct, ask children, "How can you decide?" or "Why do you think that might be right?" or "How can we tell if that makes sense?" Use this time in the *During* phase to identify different representations and strategies children used, interesting solutions, and any misconceptions that arise that you will highlight and address during the *After* phase of the lesson.

◈ After

In the *After* phase of the lesson your children will work as a community of learners, discussing, justifying, and challenging various solutions to the problem that they have just worked on. It is critical to plan for and save ample time for this part of the lesson. Twenty minutes is not at all unreasonable for a good class discussion and sharing of ideas. It is not necessary to wait for every child to finish. Here is where much of the learning will occur as children reflect individually and collectively on the ideas they have explored. This is the time to reinforce precise terminology, definitions, or symbols. After children have shared their ideas, formalize the main ideas of the lesson, highlighting connections between strategies or different mathematical ideas.

What Do I Do When a Task Doesn't Work?

Sometimes children may not know what to do with a problem you pose, no matter how many hints and suggestions you offer. Do not give in to the temptation to "tell them." When you sense that a task is not moving forward, don't spend days just hoping that something wonderful may happen. You may need to regroup and offer children a simpler but related task that gets them prepared for the one that proved too difficult. If that does not work, set it aside for the moment. Ask yourself why it didn't work well. Did the children have the prior knowledge they needed? Was the task too advanced? Consider what might be a way to step back or step forward in the content in order to support and challenge the class. Nonetheless, trust that teaching mathematics *through* problem solving offers children the productive struggle that will allow them to develop understanding and become mathematically proficient.

Stop and Reflect

Describe in your own words what is meant by "teaching mathematics *through* problem solving." What do you foresee to be some opportunities and challenges to implementing problem-based mathematics tasks effectively in your classroom? ∎

3

Assessing for Learning

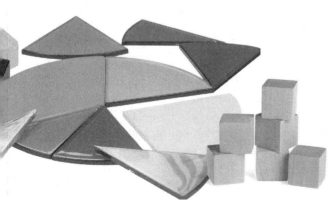

 Assessment That Supports Instruction

In a problem-based approach, teachers often ask, "How do I assess?" The assessment principle in *Principles and Standards for School Mathematics* (NCTM, 2000) stresses two main ideas: (1) Assessment should enhance children's learning, and (2) assessment is a valuable tool for making instructional decisions.

Assessment is not separate from instruction and in fact should include the critical mathematical practices (CCSSO, 2010) and processes (NCTM, 2000) that occur in the course of effective problem-based instructional approaches. The typical approach of an end-of-chapter test of skills may have value but rarely reveals the type of data that can fine-tune instruction so that it is tailored to improving the performance of individual children. In fact, Daro, Mosher, and Corcoran (2011) state that "the starting point is the mathematics and thinking the student brings to the lesson, not the deficit of mathematics they do not bring" (p. 48). Stiggins (2009) goes further to suggest that children should be informed partners in understanding their progress in learning and how to enhance their growth. They should begin to use their own assessment results to move forward as learners as they see that "success is always within reach" (p. 420). Using carefully selected assessment tasks allows you to integrate assessment into instruction and make it part of the learning process.

Assessments usually fall into one of two major categories: summative or formative. A summative assessment is a cumulative evaluation that may generate a single score, such as an end-of-unit test or a standardized test that is used in your state or school district. Although the scores are important for schools and teachers, used individually they often do not help shape teaching decisions on particular topics or identify misunderstandings that may hinder children's future growth.

A formative assessment is used to determine the point-in-time status of children's understanding, to preassess, or to attempt to identify children's naïve understandings or misconceptions so that the information is interpreted and used to provide feedback and make decisions about the next instructional steps (Wiliam, 2010). Wiliam (2010) goes on to note three key processes in formative assessment: "1) Establishing where the learners are in their learning, 2) establishing where they are going and 3) working out how to get there" (p. 45). As Wiliam (2010) states, "To be formative, assessment must include a recipe for future action" (slide 41).

For example, a formative assessment to see whether first graders can find a missing addend could be the following word problem: "If Lindy has 6 shells in her collection, how many more does she need to get 13?" The teacher observes one child taking out connecting cubes, counting out 6 and then adding more until she reaches 13. Then she goes back and takes out 6 and counts the remaining cubes, stating "seven." Another child places her hands on the table with fingers stretched out and, if observed carefully, shows signs that she is "counting on" from 6 by pressing 7 fingers down one at a time until she reaches 13. A different child just calls out 7 almost immediately. When asked how he arrived at that answer, he says that $6 + 6 = 12$, so $6 + 7 = 13$. The information gathered from observing these children reveals very different "paths" for next steps. This teacher is at the first step in Wiliam's three key processes, noting where children are in their learning. Moving into the second step, the teacher notes that one child should move to more challenging tasks while two children need to move closer to the standard of using addition and subtraction within 20 to solve a variety of word problems through more targeted instruction (CCSSO, 2010).

If summative assessment could be described as a digital snapshot, formative assessment is like streaming video. One is a picture of what a child knows captured in a single moment of time and the other is a moving picture demonstrating the child's active thinking and reasoning. In the following pages and throughout Part 2 of this book in the Formative Assessment Notes feature, various approaches are presented including Piaget's three broad categories of formative assessments: observations, interviews, and tasks (Piaget, 1976).

◆ Observations

All teachers learn useful bits of information about their children every day. When the three-phase lesson format (*Before*, *During*, and *After* phases described in Chapter 2) is followed, the flow of evidence about children's performance increases dramatically, especially in the *During* and *After* portions of lessons. If you have a systematic plan for gathering this information while observing and listening to children, at least two very valuable results occur. First, information that may have gone unnoticed is suddenly visible and important. Second, observation data gathered systematically can be combined with other data and used in planning lessons, providing feedback to children, conducting parent conferences, and determining grades.

Depending on the information you are trying to gather, several days to two weeks may be required to complete a single observation of how every child in a class is progressing on a standard. Shorter periods of observation will focus on a particular cluster of concepts or skills or on particular children. Over longer periods, you can note growth in mathematical processes or practices, such as the development of problem solving, representation, or reasoning. To use observation effectively, you should take seriously the following maxim: Only try to collect data on a reasonable number of children in a single class period.

Anecdotal Notes

One system for recording observations is to write short notes either during or immediately after a lesson in a brief narrative. One possibility is to have a card for each child taped to a clipboard (see Figure 3.1). Another option is to write anecdotal notes on an electronic tablet and store them in a spreadsheet. In either case, focus your observations on approximately five children a day. The children selected may be members of one or two cooperative groups or a group previously identified as needing additional support.

Checklists

To cut down on writing and to help focus your attention, a checklist duplicated for each child with several specific processes or content objectives can be devised (see Figure 3.2). As you build your checklist, include a place for comments. These comments should focus on big ideas and conceptual understanding rather than small skills. For example, you will probably find the comment "is beginning to see how addition facts can be related—such as using 6 + 6 to think about 6 + 16" more helpful than "knows the easy addition facts but not harder addition problems."

Another format involves listing all children in a class on a single page (see Figure 3.3). Across the top of the page are specific abilities or common misconceptions to look for (based on learning progressions or trajectories). Pluses and minuses, checks, or codes can be entered in the grid. A full-class checklist is more likely to be used for long-term objectives. Topics that might be appropriate for this format include mathematical practices and such skill areas as basic addition and subtraction fact fluency. Dating entries or noting specific observed performance is also helpful.

Figure 3.1

Preprinted cards for observation notes can be taped to a clipboard or folder for quick access.

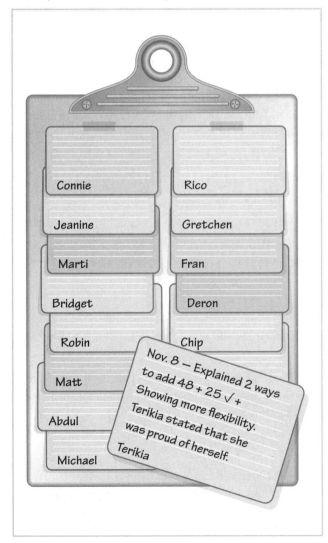

Connie
Jeanine
Marti
Bridget
Robin
Matt
Abdul
Michael

Rico
Gretchen
Fran
Deron
Chip

Nov. 8 — Explained 2 ways to add 48 + 25 ✓ + Showing more flexibility. Terikia stated that she was proud of herself.
Terikia

Figure 3.2

A focused checklist and rubric can be printed for each child.

NAME: *Sharon V.*

PLACE VALUE	NOT THERE YET	ON TARGET	ABOVE AND BEYOND	COMMENTS
Skip counts by tens		✓		
Skip counts by hundreds		✓		*Took out hundreds pieces while skip counting*
Understands 100 equals ten tens	✓			
Reads and writes numbers to 1000	✓			
Compares three-digit numbers		✓		*Showing greater reasonableness*
MATHEMATICAL PRACTICES				
Makes sense of problems and perseveres		✓		*Stated problem in own words*
Models with mathematics	✓			*Reluctant to use abstract models*
Uses appropriate tools		✓		

Figure 3.3

A full-class observation checklist can be used for long-term objectives or for several days to cover a short-term objective.

Topic: *Addition with sums to 20* **Names**	Not There Yet *Can't do mentally*	On Target *Has at least one strategy*	Above and Beyond *Uses different methods with different numbers*	Comments
Lalie		✓ 3-18-2013 3-21-2013		
Pete	✓ 3-20-2013	✓ 3-24-2013		*Difficulty with addends of 8 and 9*
Sid			✓ + 3-20-2013	*Flexible approaches used*
Lakeshia		✓		*Count up and over ten*
George		✓		
Pam	✓			*Beginning to look for ways to make ten*
Maria		✓ 3-24-2013		*Use a counting on strategy from the highest addend*

Questioning

Observations do not have to be silent. Probing into children's thinking through the use of questions can provide better data and more insights to inform instruction. As you circulate around the classroom, your use of questions is one of the most important ways to formatively assess and evaluate children's understanding in each lesson phase. Keep the following questions in mind (or on a clipboard, index card, or bookmark) as you move about the classroom to prompt and probe into children's thinking:

- What can you tell me about [today's topic]?
- How can you put the problem in your own words?
- Tell me how your picture fits with the story?
- Was there something in this problem that reminded you of another problem we've done?
- How did you decide what to do?
- How did you decide whether your answer was right?
- Did you try something that didn't work? How did you figure out that it was not going to work?

Getting the children used to responding to these questions (as well as getting accustomed to asking questions about their thinking and the thinking of others) will help prepare them for the more intensive questioning used in diagnostic interviews.

◆ Diagnostic Interviews

A diagnostic interview uses what we know about children's cognition to design an assessment (Huff & Goodman, 2007). The interview is usually a one-on-one investigation of a child's thinking about a particular concept or the processes that are being used to solve problems. The interview usually lasts from three to ten minutes. The challenge of diagnostic interviews is to remember that they are assessment opportunities and not teaching opportunities. It is hard to listen when children are making errors and not respond immediately. Instead, the interviews are used to listen and probe to discover strengths as well as gaps in children's understanding, which will lead to more targeted instruction.

Tasks should be aligned to recent work or your attempts to pinpoint underlying foundational gaps in understanding. Primary diagnostic interviews might include tasks such as counting a group of objects and writing down the number on paper, or asking children to solve a missing addend problem such as $4 + \square = 12$. As the child solves the task, the teacher is able to watch and listen.

Diagnostic interviews have the potential to provide information that you simply cannot get in any other way. Think of interviews as a formative assessment tool to be used for only a few selected children at a time—not for every child in the class. You can briefly interview a single child while the rest of the class is working on a task. Some teachers work with the child at an interactive whiteboard and record the whole conversation and written work.

The most obvious reason to consider conducting an interview is that you need more information concerning a particular child and how he or she is constructing concepts or using a procedure. In fact, these dialogues can be considered intense error analysis. Remediation will be more successful if you can pinpoint *why* a child is having difficulty before you try to fix the problem.

A second reason for conducting an interview is to gather information to plan your next instructional steps or to assess the effectiveness of your instruction. In an examination of hundreds of research studies, Hattie (2009) found the feedback that teachers received from children on what they knew and did not know was critical in improving children's performance. That is precisely what diagnostic interviews are designed to do!

For example, are you sure that your children have a good understanding of place value, or are they just doing the exercises according to rote procedures? Let's look at an actual classroom situation.

A teacher was working with a child who was displaying difficulty with calculating subtraction problems. To get the child to reveal where her thinking was in terms of what she understood and where some gaps might be, the teacher planned a diagnostic interview. Using an adaptation of a task (Philipp, Cabral, & Schappell, 2012), she showed the child a problem (see Figure 3.4) and asked the child to talk about her thinking as she answered. The child said, "Four from zero is four and five from eight is three, so my answer is 34." Although base-ten materials were on the table, they went untouched. The teacher resisted the temptation to immediately correct the child, as is necessary in these interviews, and instead probed further by asking the child if she could show the same problem using the base-ten materials. Showing fluency with the values of base-ten materials, the child took out the correct amounts and placed them on the table. She used the 54 that she took out as a reference and touched the other materials (in the group of 80) to show how many she would be taking away. This time she got 26 as the answer. The confusion was evident but when asked which answer was correct, she pointed back to her original calculation. She even redid the algorithm and repeated her mistaken "four from zero is four." The child quietly pondered and then pointed again to the answer of 34.

Figure 3.4

A child's work on a diagnostic interview task.

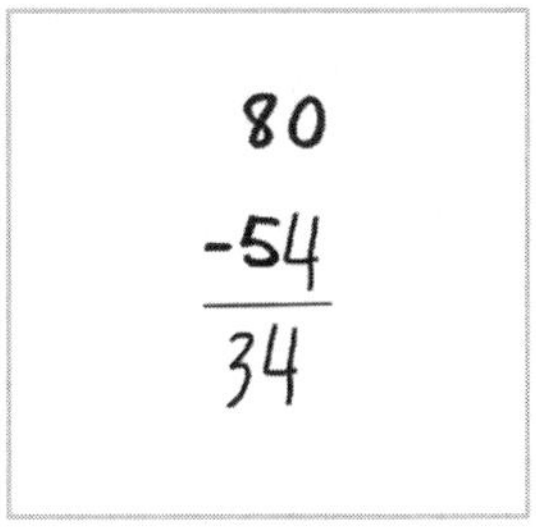

$$\begin{array}{r} 80 \\ -54 \\ \hline 34 \end{array}$$

Although this interview revealed that the child had a good grasp of the value of the base-ten materials, it also revealed that the child was not seeing the need to regroup and may not fully understand place-value concepts. The child also referred to the numbers in the tens column as "8" and "5" rather than 80 and 50. Notice that the teacher linked the assessment to the classroom instruction through the use of concrete materials. This connection provided a way for the child to think about the numbers rather than just the individual digits. Additionally, the cognitive dissonance caused by the difference in the two numerical outcomes, one responding to the procedure alone and the other with concrete materials, enabled the possibility for more connected ideas to emerge. Then planning for future instruction based on actual evidence could begin.

There is no one right way to plan or structure a diagnostic interview. In fact, flexibility is a key ingredient. You should, however, have an overall plan that includes an easier task and a more challenging task in case you have misjudged your starting point. Also, did you notice that the teacher in the vignette had instructional materials ready for the child to use? Be sure you have materials available that match those that the child has used during instruction and that will provide insights into what the child understands.

Begin by asking the child to complete the first task you've planned. When the opening task has been completed, ask the child to explain what was done. "How would you explain this to a kindergartner (or your younger sister)?" "What does this (point to something on the paper) stand for?" "Tell me why you did this that way." You may want to ask, "Can you show me what you are thinking with the materials?" If a child gets two different answers, as in the preceding scenario, ask "Why do you think you got two different answers? Which one do you think is correct? If you tried to do this problem again, which approach would you try first?" In each case it is important to explore if the child can connect actions using models to what he or she wrote or explained earlier.

Consider the following suggestions as you implement your diagnostic interview:

- *Avoid revealing whether the answer is right or wrong.* Often your facial expressions, tone of voice, or body language can give children clues that the answer they gave is correct or incorrect. Instead, use a response such as "Can you tell me more?" or "I think I know what you are thinking." If a child asks whether the answer is right, you can say "That's fine" or "I see what you are doing."

- *Avoid asking leading questions.* Comments such as "Are you sure about that?" or "Wait. Is that what you mean?" may indicate to children that they have made a mistake and cause them to reconsider their answer. This can hinder your ability to discover what they know and understand.

- *Wait silently for the child to give an answer.* Give ample time to allow the child to think and respond. Only then should you move to rephrase the question or probe for a better understanding of the child's thoughts. After the child gives a response (whether it is accurate or not), wait again! This second wait time is even more important because it encourages the child to elaborate on his or her initial thought and provide more information. Waiting can also provide you with more time to think about the direction you want the interview to take.

- *Remember that you should not interject clues or teach.* The temptation to do this is sometimes overwhelming. Watch and listen. Your goal is to use the interview not to teach but to find out where the child is in terms of conceptual understanding and procedural fluency.

- *Let children share their thinking freely without interruption.* Encourage children to use their own words and ways of recording. Interjecting questions or correcting language can be distracting to the flow of children's thinking and explanations.

- *Ask children to demonstrate their understanding in multiple ways.* For example, ask "Can you show me that with the materials? Can you draw a picture to help think about this problem? Can you write a word problem to go with that equation?" or "Can you explain what you just did?"

The benefits of the diagnostic interview become evident as you plan instruction that capitalizes on children's strengths while recognizing possible weaknesses and confusion. Also, unlike large-scale testing, you can always ask another question to find out more when children take an incorrect or unexpected path. These insights are invaluable in moving children to mathematical proficiency.

◆ Tasks

The category of tasks refers to written products and can include performance-based tasks, writing (e.g., journal entries, children's self-assessments), and tests. Good assessment tasks for either instructional or formative assessment purposes should permit every child in the class, regardless of mathematical ability, to demonstrate his or her knowledge, skill, or understanding.

Problem-Based Tasks

When problem-based tasks are used for assessment and evaluation, the intent is to find what children do know rather than only identifying what they do not know (e.g., he can't count and state how many he has—cardinality). The result is a broad description of the ideas and skills that children possess—for example, "Adam can identify triangles given a selection of three-sided figures, but he is challenged to select squares as rectangles when asked to find rectangles in a large group of four-sided figures."

Problem-based tasks have several critical components that make them good tasks for assessment, such as the following:

- Focus on a central mathematics concept or skill aligned to valued learning targets
- Stimulate the connection of content a child knows to new content
- Allow for multiple solution methods or approaches using a variety of tools
- Offer opportunities along the way for children to correct themselves
- Confront common misconceptions
- Encourage children to use reasoning and explain their thinking
- Create opportunities for observing children's use of mathematical processes and practices
- Generate data for instructional decision making as you "listen" to your children's thinking

Notice that the following examples of performance-based tasks are not elaborate, yet when followed by a discussion, each task could engage children for a large part of the lesson. What mathematical ideas and practices are required to successfully respond to each of these tasks? Will the task help you determine how well children understand these ideas?

SHARES (GRADES K–2)

Learning Targets: (1) Solve problems involving the operations. (2) Use manipulatives and words to describe a solution.

Leila has 6 gumdrops, Darlene has 2, and Melissa has 4. They want to share them equally. How will they do it? Draw a picture to help explain your answer.

At second grade, the numbers in the "Shares" task should be larger. What additional concepts would be involved if the task were about sharing cookies and the total number of cookies, 34, was given?

ONE UP, ONE DOWN (GRADES 1–2)

Learning Targets: (1) Work with addition equations. (2) Look for and make use of structure.

When you add 7 + 7, you get 14. When you make the first number 1 more and the second number 1 less, you get the same answer. Does this work any time the numbers are the same? Does it work when the addends are not the same?

PARTITIONING (GRADES K–1)

Learning Targets: (1) Decompose numbers in a problem situation. (2) Use reasoning and regularity of patterns to make sense of quantities and the relationships of quantities.

Six bowls of cereal are placed at two different tables. Draw a picture to show a way that six bowls might be placed at two tables. Can you find more than one way? How many ways do you think there are?

Translation Tasks

One important option is referred to as a *translation task*. Using the seven representations for concepts (see Figure 2.3), children are asked to use more than one representation (e.g., words, tools, and numbers) to demonstrate understanding of a single problem. As children move between these representations, there is a better chance they will form the concept correctly and integrate it into a rich web of ideas.

So what is a good way of structuring a translation task? Using an adaptation of a template for assessing concept mastery from Frayer, Fredrick, and Klauseier (1969) (Figure 3.5), children can be given a computational equation and be asked to

- Tell a story to match an equation.
- Illustrate the equation with materials or drawings.
- Draw a picture and write an equation to represent a story.

In particular, children's ability to communicate how they solved a problem is critical for responding to open-response questions on state assessments (Parker & Breyfogle, 2011).

Translation tasks can be used for whole-class lessons or for individual or small-group diagnosis. For example, second-grade children may be given an equation such as $36 + 49 = ?$ (see Figure 3.5). Their task could be to draw a model, say, of base-ten materials, in the "Manipulatives/Illustration" area (younger children could just show a manipulative), describe a real-world situation in which that addition is used in the "Real-World Story or Word Problem" area, and explain to another person in writing (or scripted or audio recorded by the teacher for younger children) how they solved the addition in the fourth area marked "Explanation."

Think about using translation tasks when you want to find out more about children's thinking. If children represent ideas in various forms and can explain why these representations are similar or different, you can use this valuable information to recognize misconceptions they may have and then identify the type of activity you can provide children to

Figure **3.5** Translation task template with example task.

Numbers/Equation	Real-World Story or Word Problem
$36 + 49 =$	
Manipulatives/Illustration	**Explanation**

advance their learning. Here are two other options for tasks that can be used with the translation template to assess children's understanding. Remember that a translation task may start off in any quadrant of the template and the children proceed to fill in the other three sections. Consider the following two "starters."

- Start with this word problem in the section labeled "Real-World Story or Word Problem":

Jack was at the pet store. A group of puppies came over and sat on Jack's lap. Two of the puppies jumped off. Now Jack has three puppies on his lap. How many puppies did Jack have on his lap in the beginning?

Then children create the equation that corresponds with the problem, make a matching drawing, and explain how they came to their answer in the last of the four sections.

- In the "Manipulatives/Illustration" section show two groups of coins in two circles. In one circle show an illustration of 2 quarters and 2 pennies (you can use a coin stamp) and in the other circle show 3 dimes, 1 nickel, and 3 pennies with the question, "How much money do you have?" Then children should write a corresponding equation to show the combining of both groups of coins, write a word problem, and in the last section explain to a friend how to approach this problem.

In some instances, the real value of a task is in what it can reveal about children's understanding, which will come primarily through discussion in the *After* phase of your lesson. It is important that you help children develop the habit of adding justifications to their answers and listening to and evaluating the explanations of others. Importantly, as illustrated here, do not always start with the same section—sometimes children can translate one way but not in reverse.

Writing for Early Learners

If you are working with pre-K–1 children, the writing prompts presented may sound too advanced; it may be difficult for prewriters and beginning writers to express ideas like those suggested. To begin the development of the writing-in-mathematics process in these early grades, use a language experience approach. After an activity, you can write the words "Giant Journal" and a topic or prompt on a large chart or interactive whiteboard. As children respond to the prompt verbally, the teacher writes down their thoughts, including the contributor's name and even drawings when appropriate, as in Figure 3.6.

All children can draw pictures of some sort to describe what they have done. Dots can represent counters or blocks. Shapes and figures can be cut out from duplicated sheets and pasted onto journal pages.

Rubrics and Their Uses

Appropriate assessment tasks yield an enormous amount of information that must be evaluated by examining more than a simple count of correct answers. A rubric is a scale based on predetermined criteria with two important functions: (1) It permits the children to see what is central to excellent performance, and (2) it provides the teacher with scoring guidelines that support analysis of children's work. In teaching through a problem-solving approach, you will often want to include criteria and performance indicators that measure whether children have accomplished the following:

- Solved the problem(s) accurately and effectively
- Explained strategies they used or justified their answer

Figure 3.6

A journal in kindergarten may be a class product on a flipchart.

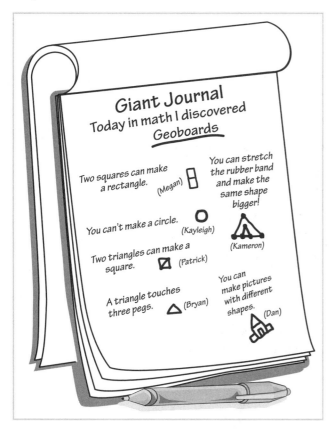

Teaching Tip

For very young children you many want to use three simple headings with visuals, such as "Yes, Got It!," "On Track," and "Need Help."

- Used logical reasoning
- Expressed a grasp of numerical relationships and structure
- Incorporated multiple representations and/or multiple strategies
- Demonstrated an ability to select and use tools and manipulatives
- Communicated using precise language and accurate units
- Identified general patterns of ideas that repeat, making connections from one big idea to another

Rubrics are usually built from the highest possible score. By describing what an outstanding performance would be on a given standard or learning target, you are then able to set the benchmarks for the other levels.

◆ Generic Rubrics

Generic rubrics identify general categories of performance instead of specific criteria for a particular task and, therefore, can fit multiple assignments. The generic rubric allows a teacher to score performances by first sorting them into two broad categories, as illustrated in the four-point rubric shown in Figure 3.7. The scale then allows you to separate each category into two additional levels. Note that a rating of 0 is given for no response or effort or for responses that are completely off task. The advantage of the four-point scale is that it is relatively easy to use when initially sorting performances into the two groupings "Got It" and "Not There Yet."

Another possibility is using a three- or four-point generic rubric on a reusable form, as in Figure 3.8, on page 38. Include space for content-specific indicators and a column to jot down names of children. A quick note or comment may be added to a name. This method is especially useful for planning purposes.

◆ Task-Specific Rubrics

Task-specific rubrics include specific statements, also known as *indicators*, that describe what performance looks like at each level of the rubric. In so doing, they establish criteria for acceptable performance. Initially, when you create a task-specific rubric, it may be difficult to predict what children's performances at different levels will or should look like. One important part of setting performance levels is predicting children's common misconceptions or the expected thinking or approaches to the same or similar problems.

Figure 3.7

With a four-point rubric, performances are first sorted into two categories. Then each performance is considered again and assigned to a point on the scale.

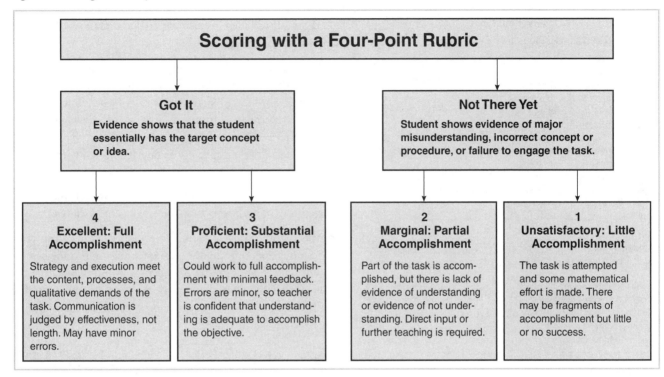

Scoring with a Four-Point Rubric

Got It
Evidence shows that the student essentially has the target concept or idea.

Not There Yet
Student shows evidence of major misunderstanding, incorrect concept or procedure, or failure to engage the task.

4
Excellent: Full Accomplishment

Strategy and execution meet the content, processes, and qualitative demands of the task. Communication is judged by effectiveness, not length. May have minor errors.

3
Proficient: Substantial Accomplishment

Could work to full accomplishment with minimal feedback. Errors are minor, so teacher is confident that understanding is adequate to accomplish the objective.

2
Marginal: Partial Accomplishment

Part of the task is accomplished, but there is lack of evidence of understanding or evidence of not understanding. Direct input or further teaching is required.

1
Unsatisfactory: Little Accomplishment

The task is attempted and some mathematical effort is made. There may be fragments of accomplishment but little or no success.

Stop and Reflect

Consider the preceding problem titled "Shares." Assume you are teaching first grade and wish to write performance indicators using a four-point rubric. What task-specific indicators would you use for level 3 and level 4 performances? Start with a level 3 performance, and then think about level 4. Try this before reading further. ■

Prior to teaching the lesson, write out indicators of "proficient" or "on target" performances. This excellent self-check will ensure that the task is likely to accomplish the purpose for which you selected it in the first place. Think about how children are likely to approach the activity. If you find yourself writing performance indicators in terms of the number of correct responses, you are most likely looking at drill or practice exercises and not performance-based tasks for which a rubric is appropriate.

Determining performance indicators is always a subjective process based on your professional judgment. Here is one possible set of indicators for the "Shares" task:

Level 3: Determines the correct answer or uses an approach that would yield a correct answer if not for minor errors. The picture drawn or the explanation does not fully explain the combining and sharing process.

Teaching Tip

When you return papers, review the indicators with the children, including examples of correct answers and successful responses. This will help children understand how they may have done better. Often it is useful to show work from classmates (anonymously) or from a prior class. Let children decide on the scores for these children. Children need to see models of what a level 4 performance looks like.

Figure 3.8

A rubric used over several days in a first-grade class during an activity on partitioning regions.

Observation Rubric		
Partition Regions into Equal Shares (3/17)		
Above and Beyond Clear understanding. Communicates concept in multiple representations. Shows evidence of using idea without prompting. *Can partition rectangles and circles into two, four, and eight equal shares. Explains that partitioning the same wholes into more shares makes smaller shares.*	Sally Latania Greg	 Zal
On Target Understands or is developing well. Uses designated models. *Can partition regions into equal shares and describes as "halves" and "fourths." May need prompt to compare halves and fourths.*	Lavant Julie George Maria	Tanisha Lee J.B. John H.
Not There Yet Some confusion or misunderstanding. Only models idea with help. *Needs help to do activity. No confidence.*	John S.	Mary

Level 4: Determines the total number of gumdrops and the amount of each equal share using words, pictures, and numbers to explain and justify the result and how it was obtained.

What about level 1 and level 2 performances? Here are suggestions for the same task:

Level 2: Uses only two numbers in addition instead of three and, therefore, fails to come up with the correct amount to share or adds correctly but does not carry out the division. The child shows some evidence of knowledge of addition but explanations and drawings are not properly aligned with the situation.

Level 1: Shows some effort but little or no understanding of addition or how to make equal shares.

Unexpected methods and solutions happen. Don't limit your children by expecting them to demonstrate their understanding only as you thought or hoped they would when there is evidence that they are accomplishing your objectives in different ways. Such occurrences can help you revise or refine your rubric for future use.

⬡ Self-Assessment with Rubrics

In the beginning of the year, post your rubric prominently and discuss it with the class. Many teachers use the same rubric for all subjects; others prefer to use a specialized rubric for mathematics. In your discussion, let children know that as they do activities and solve problems, you will sometimes look at their work and listen to their explanations and provide them with feedback in the form of a rubric rather than as a letter grade.

Make it a habit to discuss children's performance on tasks in terms of the rubric. You may also have children use the rubric to self-assess their work and give reasons for the rating. You can have class discussions about a completed task by talking about what might constitute "on target" and "above and beyond" performances. Also share student work from anonymous children as a way to highlight excellent responses as well as responses that need more detail or work shown. Use these work samples to get children to talk about what could make an answer stronger and better aligned with the rubric. This process of critiquing others' work is one of the Common Core Standards for Mathematical Practice and therefore is recognized as an essential element to becoming mathematically proficient.

A rubric is much more than a grade. It is a meaningful way to communicate feedback to children (and parents). It should let children know how well they are doing and encourage them to work harder by giving specific areas for improvement. When their performance is not progressing satisfactorily, children should understand that there are specific things they can work on. Your task is to target the follow-up instruction in response to their gaps and misunderstandings as well as their identified strengths.

You do not need to use rubrics with every task. Nor is it necessary to reserve rubrics for assessments that you want to grade. If you are using the four-point rubric just described, the language of the rubric can be used informally with your children. "Maggie, the rubric states that to get a 4 you need to solve the problem using two different methods and explain your thinking. Is that what you did?"

The rubric scale can also be used in recording observations of student performance. If you describe the task across the top of a class checklist and list the children's names down the left side, then it is useful to record a 1, 2, 3, or 4 next to each name. You may want to leave space for writing detailed comments for some children so that they can be grouped for follow-up instruction according to common misunderstandings.

Plan for Assessment

"An assessment system designed to help steer the instruction system must give good information about direction as well as distance to travel. A system that keeps telling us we are not there yet is like a kid in the back seat whining 'are we there yet?'" (Daro, Mosher, & Corcoran, 2011, p. 51). Instead we need a system in which teachers do the following (Wiliam, 2010):

- Establish where children are in their learning
- Identify the learning destination
- Carefully plan a route
- Begin the learning journey
- Make regular checks of progress along the way
- Make adjustments to the course as conditions dictate

Then assessments can more easily translate into tools that inform instruction and support children's growth.

Stop and Reflect

How can sharing samples of children's work (both strong and weak responses) support all children's ability to generate more in-depth responses? ■

Differentiating Instruction

[Differentiation] moves us away from seeing and teaching students as a unit toward reflecting on and responding to them as individuals.

Sousa and Tomlinson
(2011, p. 9)

All first graders do not learn the same thing in the same way and at the same rate. In fact, every classroom at every grade level contains a range of children with varying abilities and backgrounds. Perhaps the most important work of teachers today is to be able to plan (and teach) lessons that support and challenge *all* children to learn important mathematics.

Differentiation and Teaching Mathematics through Problem Solving

Teachers have for some time embraced the notion that children vary in reading ability, but the idea that children can and do vary in mathematical development may be new. Mathematics education research reveals a great deal of evidence demonstrating that children can vary in their understanding of specific mathematical ideas. Attending to these differences in children's mathematical development is key to differentiating mathematics instruction for your children.

Interestingly, the problem-based approach to teaching is the best way to teach mathematics while attending to the range of children in your classroom. In a traditional, highly directed lesson, it is often assumed that all children will understand and use the same approach and the same ideas as determined by the teacher. Children not ready to understand the ideas presented by the teacher must focus their attention on following rules or directions without developing a conceptual or relational understanding (Skemp, 1978). This, of course, leads to endless difficulties and can leave children with misunderstandings or in need of significant remediation. In contrast, in a problem-based classroom, children are expected to approach problems in a variety of ways that make sense to *them*, bringing to each problem the skills and ideas that they own. So, with a problem-based approach to teaching mathematics, differentiation is already built in to some degree.

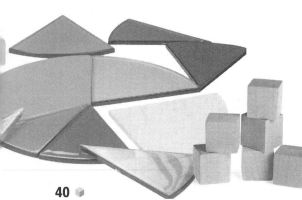

Figure 4.1 How many dogs are there? Nora's solution: 3 and 3 is 6.

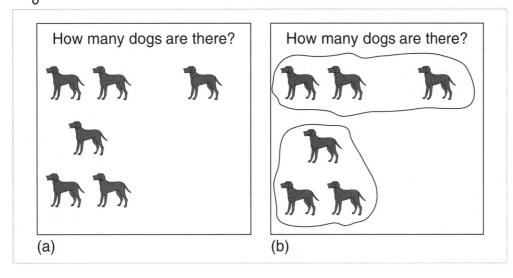

To illustrate, let's consider a first-grade classroom in which the teacher provided the children with a picture of six dogs as shown in Figure 4.1(a). She asked the children to determine how many dogs are in the picture and to be ready to explain how they know. Following are some of the children's explanations:

Carmen: I counted them and got 6. (Points to each dog and counts by ones.)

Sam: I counted them, too. But I counted by twos. (Puts two fingers over two dogs at a time and says, "Two, four, six.")

Edwin: I saw a pattern. I recognized the five, like on a die. I knew one more is six.

Nora: I also saw a pattern. But I saw a group of 3 and 3—that is 6. (See Figure 4.1(b).)

Some children are still counting by ones while others have begun skip counting or even recognizing the number of objects without counting. If the teacher had expected all children to count the dogs by ones, then many of the children may have been using less-efficient methods than they would have independently used. Also, the cognitive demand of the task would have been lowered! If the teacher had expected all the children to recognize the number of objects without counting, then some children may have been confused because they still need to count objects by ones to determine how many. Instead, the teacher allowed the children to use their own ideas to determine how many dogs are in the picture. This expectation and the recognition that different children will approach and solve the same problem in various ways honors children's varying mathematical development and sets the stage for differentiated mathematics instruction. In addition, by listening to how different children approach the task, the teacher has acquired important information that can be used to plan subsequent instruction that meets a variety of children's needs.

The Nuts and Bolts of Differentiating Instruction

Differentiation is an instructional approach that requires a shift from focusing on the "middle-of-the-road" child to attending to all children. As overwhelming as this may sound, differentiation does not require a teacher to create individualized lessons for each and every child in the classroom. Rather, it requires emphasizing three basic ideas (Sousa & Tomlinson, 2011):

- Planning lessons around meaningful content, grounded in authenticity
- Recognizing each child's readiness, interest, and approach to learning
- Connecting content and learners by modifying content, process, product, and the learning environment

Planning Meaningful Content, Grounded in Authenticity

Before you begin to think about differentiation, you first need to know where you want your students to "be" at the end of the learning experience. You must be explicitly aware of the content that children should know, understand, and be able to do after engaging in a given lesson or sequence of lessons. This awareness enables you to effectively guide children's learning by varying or differentiating instruction. If you do not have a clear idea about the specific learning outcomes, identifying how and when to differentiate can be difficult. In fact, Tomlinson (1999) claims that "If the 'stuff' [content] is ill conceived, the 'how' [differentiation] is doomed" (p. 16).

Note that the content must be authentic and grounded in important mathematics that emphasize the big ideas in ways that require children to develop relational understanding. Authentic content engages children in the heart of mathematics by requiring them to be problem solvers and creators of knowledge. Through this kind of engagement, children also develop a productive disposition toward mathematics and see it as sensible, useful, and worthwhile.

Recognizing Children as Learners

Knowing each child in the context of learning requires finding out who he or she is as an individual on traits such as readiness, interests, and learning profile. *Readiness* refers to a child's proficiency with the knowledge, understanding, and skills embedded in specific learning goals. *Interest* means a child's attraction to particular topics, ideas, and events. Using contexts that are interesting and familiar to children enhances their attention and motivation to engage and achieve (Sousa & Tomlinson, 2011). A *learning profile* identifies how a child approaches learning—how each child prefers to learn (e.g., in groups, alone); process and reason about information (e.g., by listening, observing, participating, or through talking; by thinking about details first and then the big picture or vice versa; by doing one task at a time or multitasking); and use or demonstrate what has been learned (e.g., writing, verbalizing, drawing). By using children's preferences for learning to structure the environment, tasks, and assessments, you are greatly facilitating the learning process.

Information about your children's traits can inform how you might modify different elements of the classroom (e.g., Sousa & Tomlinson, 2011; Tomlinson, 2003). You can gather information pertaining to children's readiness by using preassessments several days before a given unit so that you have time to analyze the evidence and assess each child's readiness for the unit. You can also use surveys, typically at the beginning and midpoint of the year, to gather information about children's interests and learning profiles. Interest surveys give children opportunities to share personal interests (e.g., what they like to do

Figure 4.2 Learning profile inventory.

When working on a task, I like to . . .	I like to work . . .	When working, I like the room to be . . .	When working, I like . . .	When learning about new ideas, I like to . . .	When sharing information, I like to . . .
☐ sit at my desk	☐ with a partner	☐ warm	☐ quiet	☐ hear about it	☐ talk
☐ sit somewhere other than my desk	☐ in a small group	☐ cool	☐ noise	☐ read about it	☐ show
☐ stand	☐ alone	☐ darker, lights off	☐ music	☐ see visuals about it	☐ write
☐ lie on the floor	☐ other	☐ bright	☐ other	☐ use materials to explore	☐ other
☐ other		☐ other		☐ talk about it	
				☐ other	

after school, on the weekends, and during the summer; what school subjects they find most interesting and why) and information about pets, siblings, and extracurricular activities. Increase your children's motivation and engagement by using their interests to provide contexts for the mathematics they are learning. Learning profile surveys or questionnaires also help children think about what helps them learn and what does not, such as preferring to work in pairs versus alone, being able to work with background noise, and needing to process ideas verbally (Figure 4.2). For younger children, use icons or images on the survey that they can circle to indicate their choice or conduct a quick informal interview using a checklist. Teacher observation can also provide valuable insights. By recording children's information on index cards, you can quickly refresh your memory by looking through the cards as you plan lessons. You can also sort the cards to help you create groups based on interests or learning profiles.

◆ Connecting Content and Learners

A critical component of differentiated lesson planning is determining how to modify four classroom elements to help the learner better connect with the content (Tomlinson, 2003). These four classroom elements are content, process, product, and the learning environment.

Content: What You Want Each Child to Learn

Generally, what is learned (the big ideas) should be relatively the same for all children. However, content can still be differentiated in terms of depth (level of complexity) and breadth (connecting across different topics) (Murray & Jorgensen, 2007; Small, 2009). Children's readiness typically informs the level of complexity or depth at which the content is initially presented for different groups of children. Interest and learning profiles tend to inform differentiation geared toward breadth.

An example of a depth adaptation for developing understanding and skill with organizing, representing, and interpreting data is a minilesson in which all children organize and represent data and answer questions based on the data. However, some children may have a smaller set of data to deal with, or they may be asked to answer given questions about the data, while others, who are ready for more sophisticated content, are asked to generate their own questions about the data. An example of a breadth adaptation for the same objective is to allow children a choice in terms of the kind of data with which to work. For example, based on their interests, children might choose to work with data pertaining to sports, books, science, or pets. By working with data from various contexts, children not only learn something about those contexts but also can begin to see the broader applications of organizing, representing, and interpreting data.

Process: How Children Engage in Thinking about Content

Although the big ideas of a learning experience remain relatively stable when differentiating, how children engage with and make sense of the content—the process—changes. Tomlinson (1999) described the process as children "taking different roads to the same destination" (p. 12). You can use different strategies or encourage children to take different "roads" to increase access to the essential information, ideas, and skills embedded in a lesson (Cassone, 2009; Tomlinson, 2003). For example, the use of manipulatives, games, and relevant and interesting contextual problems provides different ways for children to process their ideas while engaging with content.

The mathematical process standards (NCTM, 2000), which served as a basis for the Standards for Mathematical Practice in the *Common Core State Standards* (CCSSO, 2010), lend themselves well to differentiating how children engage with and make sense of content. In particular, the process standard of representation emphasizes the need to think about and use different ways to represent mathematical ideas, which can help children make connections between concepts and skills. With the process standard of communication, children can use verbal or written communication as they share their reasoning, depending on their strengths. In addition, the process standard of problem solving allows for differentiation because of the myriad of strategies that children can use—from drawing a diagram or using manipulatives to solving a simpler problem and looking for patterns.

Teaching Tip

> Be sure that the tasks you ask children to do are closely aligned with the learning objectives of the lesson.

Because of different levels of readiness, it is imperative that children be allowed to use a variety of strategies and representations that are grounded in their own ideas to solve problems. You can facilitate children's engagement in thinking about the content through a variety of methods. For example, teachers may

- Use visuals or graphic organizers to help children connect ideas and build a structure for the information in the lesson.

- Provide manipulatives to support children's development of a concept.

- Provide different manipulatives than those previously used with the same content.

- Use an appropriate context that helps children build meaning for the concept and that employs purposeful constraints that can highlight the significant mathematical ideas.

- Share examples and nonexamples to help children develop a better understanding of a concept.

- Gather a small group of children to develop foundational knowledge for a new concept.

- Provide text or supplementary material in a child's native language to aid understanding of materials written or delivered in English.

- Set up learning centers or a tiered lesson (a lesson that offers learners different pathways to reach a specific learning goal).

Product: How Children Demonstrate What They Know, Understand, and Are Able to Do after the Lesson Is Over

The term *product* can refer to what a child produces as a result of completing a single task or to a major assessment after an extended learning experience. The products related to a single task would be consistent with the ways children share their ideas in the *After* portion of a lesson, described in Chapter 2, which could include children explaining their ideas with manipulatives, through a drawing, in writing, or simply verbally. The products related to an extended experience can take the form of a project, portfolio, test, write-up of solutions to several problem-based inquiries, and so on. An important feature of any product is that it allows a variety of ways for children to demonstrate their understanding of essential content.

Learning Environment: The Logistics, Physical Configuration, and Tone of the Classroom

Consider how the physical learning environment might be adapted to meet children's needs. Do you have a child who prefers to work alone? Who prefers to work in a group? Who can or cannot work with background noise? Who prefers to work in a setting with brighter or dimmer lighting? Attending to these children's needs can affect the seating arrangement, specific grouping strategies, access to materials, and other aspects of the classroom environment. In addition to the physical learning space, establishing a classroom culture in which children's ideas and solutions are respected as they explain and justify them is an important aspect of a differentiated classroom. Refer to the recommendations provided in Chapter 2 pertaining to facilitating effective classroom discussions and establishing a supportive and respectful learning environment.

 # Examples of Differentiated Instruction

◆ Differentiated Tasks for Whole-Class Instruction

One challenge of differentiation is planning a task focused on a target mathematical concept or skill that can be used for whole-class instruction while meeting a variety of children's needs. Let's consider two different kinds of tasks that can meet this challenge: parallel tasks and open questions (Murray & Jorgensen, 2007; Small, 2009).

Parallel Tasks

Parallel tasks are two or three tasks that focus on the same big idea but offer different levels of difficulty. The tasks should be created so that all children can meaningfully participate in a follow-up discussion with the whole class. You can assign tasks to children based on their readiness, or children can choose which task to work on. If they choose a task that is too difficult, they can always move to another task. Consider how the following parallel tasks emphasize the big idea of subtraction, but at different levels of difficulty.

TASK 1:

There are 38 second graders on the playground; 22 of them come in for lunch. How many children are left on the playground?

TASK 2:

There are 108 second graders in our school; 29 of them leave on a field trip. How many second graders are left in the school?

Stop and Reflect

Which of the two tasks do you think would be more difficult, and why? ■

Both tasks provide opportunities for children to work with subtraction, but the numbers in the second task increase the level of difficulty regardless of the strategy a child uses. First, the numbers in the second task, 29 and 108, are further apart than the numbers in the first task, 22 and 38. In the second task, if children use a counting-up strategy to determine the difference, they will need to move across multiple decades while keeping track of the count. Plus, crossing over the 100 mark can also be difficult for children. Even if children use the typical procedure for multidigit subtraction, the second task requires regrouping whereas the first task does not.

You can facilitate a whole-class discussion by asking questions that are relevant to both tasks. For example, with respect to the previous two tasks, you could ask the following questions of the whole class:

- How did you determine how many children were left?

- Some of you indicated that you added to find your answer. Why does adding make sense?

- Suppose one more child left. How would that change your answer?

- Suppose there had been one more child to begin with. How would that change your answer?

Although children work on different tasks, because the tasks are focused on the same big idea, these questions allow them to extend their thinking as they hear others' strategies and ideas.

For many problems involving computation, you can simply insert multiple sets of numbers to vary the difficulty. In the following problem, children are permitted to select the first, second, or third number in each set of brackets. Giving a choice increases motivation and helps children become more self-directed learners (Bray, 2009; Gilbert & Musu, 2008).

LEARNING OBJECTIVE: Represent and solve problems involving addition. (Grade 1)

Mark had [9, 16, 43] stickers. Natalie gave him [5, 7, 15] more stickers. How many stickers does Mark have now?

The following parallel tasks for kindergarten focus on the big idea of cardinality or counting to tell the number of objects (see Figure 4.3).

TASK 1:

How many circles are there? (Circles are in a scattered configuration.)

TASK 2:

How many stars are there? (Stars are arranged in a rectangular array.)

With the first task, the teacher provides a task for children who are ready to find ways to organize their count. The parallel task still offers an opportunity for children to count but provides a built-in structure that can help children keep track of their count.

In thinking about how to create parallel tasks, once you have identified the big idea you wish to focus on, consider how children might differ in reasoning about that idea. The size of the numbers involved, the operations children can use, and the type of measurement with which children are most familiar are just a few differences to consider. Start with a task from your textbook and then modify it to make it suitable for a different developmental level. The original task and the modified task will serve as the parallel tasks offered simultaneously to your children. If you number the parallel tasks and allow children to choose the task they will work on, sometimes let the first task be the more difficult task. This randomness will ensure that children consider both options before they choose their task.

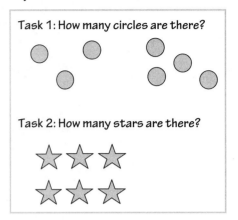

Figure 4.3

Parallel tasks for telling how many objects.

Open Questions

A question is open when it can be solved in a variety of ways or when it can have different answers. Following are two examples of open questions. Both questions can have different answers and can also be solved in a variety of ways.

- I measured an object in the classroom and found that it was 8 inches long. What could the object be?

- The sum of three numbers is 25. What could the three numbers be?

Stop and Reflect

How would you solve each of these tasks? Can you think of at least two different strategies or answers for each task? ■

Open questions have a high level of cognitive demand, as described in Chapter 2, because children must use more than recall or do more than merely follow steps in a procedure. As such, there are ample opportunities for them to approach the problems at their own level, which means open questions automatically accommodate for student readiness. Consequently, when given an open question, most children can find something appropriate to contribute, which helps to increase their confidence in doing mathematics and can inform you of their level of understanding.

A variety of strategies you can use to create open questions (Small, 2009; Sullivan & Lilburn, 2002) include the following:

- Give the answer and ask for the problem.

- Replace a number in a given problem with a blank or a question mark.

- Offer two situations or examples and ask for similarities and differences.

- Create a question in which children have to make choices.

The two preceding examples illustrate the first strategy of giving an answer and asking for the problem. The following are examples that show how to use the other strategies to convert standard questions to open questions.

Strategy	Standard Question	Open Question
Replace a number in a given problem with a blank or a question mark.	23 + 68 = _____	?3 + 6? = _____
Offer two situations or examples and ask for similarities and differences.	Draw a triangle.	How are these triangles the same and how are they different?
Create a question so that children have to make choices.	What number is 10 more than 25?	A number is 10 greater than another number. What could the numbers be?

Facilitating follow-up discussions is also important when you use open questions. While children work on an open question, walk around and observe the variety of strategies and answers children are finding. During this time, plan which children you will ask to share their ideas during the follow-up discussion to ensure that multiple strategies and answers are examined. During the discussion, look for opportunities to help children make connections between different ideas that are shared. For example, in the preceding task in which children are finding two numbers that are 10 apart from each other, suppose some children identified 45 and 55 as their two numbers. One child might explain that to find the two numbers she used the hundreds chart, started at 45, and then moved down a row to 55. Another child might say that he started at 45 and counted 10 more using his fingers. Ask the class how the strategy of counting on your fingers could be shown on the hundreds chart or how moving down one row on the hundreds chart is the same as counting 10 on your fingers. Asking questions that help children build connections can support those who need additional help and can also challenge children to extend their understanding.

◈ Learning Centers

Sometimes a mathematical concept or topic can be explored by having children work on different tasks at various classroom locations called *learning centers*. Children can work on concepts or topics in learning centers as an initial introduction, as a midway exploration, or as a follow-up task that provides practice or allows extension. Because you can decide which children will be assigned to which centers, you can differentiate the content at each center. For example, each center can use a different representation of the concept, require children to use a different approach to solve a problem, or vary in terms of the difficulty of the task (e.g., different centers can use different numbers that change the level of difficulty).

A good task for a learning center is one that can be repeated multiple times during one visit. This allows children to remain engaged until you are ready for them to transition to another center or activity. For example, at one center children might play a "game" in which they take turns covering part of a known number of counters while the other child names the amount in the covered part. Technology-enhanced tasks on the computer or interactive whiteboard that can be repeated can provide the focus of a center, but these tasks must be carefully selected. Among other aspects, you will want to choose technology-based tasks that require children to engage in reflective thought. For example, "Hiding Ladybug" in the National Council of Teachers of Mathematics online resources (www.nctm.org/standards /content.aspx?id=25009) offers children opportunities to plan and check a path for a ladybug to take so it can hide under a leaf. They can quickly check to see whether their plan works, make changes based on the results, and check the revised plan. As they engage in this interactive environment, they are enhancing their understanding of location and movement in space. Once they have successfully created a path, they can move the leaf and start the challenge again.

You may want children to work at centers in small groups or individually. Therefore, for a given topic, you might prepare four to eight different activities (you can also use the same activity at two different learning centers). However, be sure to keep the centers focused on the same topic or concept so that you can help children build connections across the centers. Using centers that focus on a variety of topics will more likely result in a disconnected learning experience for children.

To ensure greater student success at the centers, review with your whole class any instructions you have provided at each center on cards. For younger children or children who have difficulty reading, provide audio-recorded directions at each center. If necessary, model or teach again any necessary skills. After children have had time to work in several centers, follow up with individual or class discussions to ensure that children are learning the essential ideas and connections that the centers are meant to elicit.

◆ Tiered Lessons

In a tiered lesson, you set the same learning goals for all children, but different pathways are provided to reach those learning goals, thereby creating the various tiers. First, you need to decide which category you wish to tier: content, process, or product. If you are new to preparing tiered lessons, tier only one category until you become more comfortable with the process. Once you decide which category to tier, determine the challenge of each of the defined tiers based on student readiness levels, interests, and learning profiles (Kingore, 2006; Murray & Jorgensen, 2007; Tomlinson, 1999). Murray and Jorgensen (2007) suggest starting by creating three tiers to make the process more manageable: a regular tier or lesson, an extension tier that provides extra challenge, and a scaffolding tier that provides more background or support. Once you have this framework, you can design as many tiers as needed to meet your children's needs. All tiered experiences should have the following characteristics (Sousa & Tomlinson, 2011):

- Address the same learning goals

- Require children to use reasoning

- Be equally interesting to children

We have already considered some ways to tier the content by using parallel tasks and open questions. However, varying the degree of challenge is not just about the content. You can also tier lessons using any of the following four aspects (Kingore, 2006):

- **Degree of assistance.** If some children need additional support, you can partner children, provide examples, help them brainstorm ideas, or provide a cue sheet (Figure 4.4).

- **Structure of the task.** Some children, such as children with disabilities, benefit from highly structured tasks. However, gifted children often benefit from a more open-ended structure.

- **Complexity of the task.** Make tasks more concrete or more abstract and include more difficult problems or applications.

Figure 4.4 Problem-solving cue sheet.

Ways to help me think about the problem	5 + 7 =
	Counting chips
	Ten-frame
	Finger counting
	Drawing
	Other

- *Complexity of the process.* As you think about your learners, ask yourself these questions: How quickly should I pace this lesson? How many instructions should I give at one time? How many higher-level thinking questions are included as part of the task(s)?

Consider how the following original task is modified in the adapted task to change the level of challenge:

ORIGINAL TASK:

Elliot had 9 toy cars. Sasha came over to play and brought 8 cars. How many cars do Elliot and Sasha have together? Explain how you know.

The teacher has distributed cubes to children to model the problem and paper and pencil to illustrate and record how they solved the problem. He asks them to model the problem and be ready to explain their solution.

ADAPTED TASK:

Elliott had some toy cars. Sasha came over to play and brought her cars. How many cars do Elliott and Sasha have together? Explain how you know.

The teacher asks children what is happening in this problem, how they might solve the problem, and what tools might help them solve the problem. Then the teacher distributes task cards that tell how many cars Elliot and Sasha have. The teacher has varied the difficulty of the numbers, giving children who are struggling sums that are less than 10 and the more advanced children sums greater than 20.

Card 1 (easier)

Elliot has 5 cars and
Sasha has 3 cars.

Card 2 (middle)

Elliot has 9 cars and
Sasha has 8 cars.

Card 3 (advanced)

Elliot has 17 cars and
Sasha has 16 cars.

In each case, children must use words, pictures, models, or numbers to show how they figured out the solution. Various tools are provided (connecting cubes, counters, number line, and hundreds chart) for children's use.

Stop and Reflect

Which of the four aspects that change the challenge of tiered lessons was addressed in the adapted task? ◼

You would preassess your children to determine the best ways to use these task cards. One option is to give children only one card, based on their current academic readiness (e.g., easy cards to those who have not yet mastered addition of single-digit numbers). A second option is to give out cards 1 and 2 based on readiness, then use card 2 as an extension for those who successfully complete card 1, and card 3 as an extension for those who successfully complete card 2. In each of these cases, you will need to record at the end of the lesson which children were able to model and explain the various levels of the problems so that the next lesson can be planned appropriately. Notice that this tiered lesson addresses both the complexity of the task (difficulty of different cards) and the process (instructions are broken down by starting with the no-numbers scenario).

The following example illustrates how to tier a lesson based on *structure*. Notice that the different tasks vary in how open-ended the work is, yet all tasks focus on the same learning goal of analyzing and comparing two-dimensional shapes.

LEARNING OBJECTIVE: Analyze and compare two-dimensional shapes, in different sizes and orientations, using informal language to describe how they are the same and how they are different, or parts (e.g., number of sides and vertices/"corners"). (Grade K)

Children are given a collection of two-dimensional shapes (e.g., squares, a variety of triangles, nonsquare rectangles, hexagons). Some children may be given collections that have fewer shapes and fewer varieties of shapes in each category. The tasks are distributed to different groups based on their learning needs and prior knowledge of two-dimensional shapes.

- Group A: Explore the set of shapes. For each kind of shape, what do you notice about the shape? Make a list of the ideas that you think are true for each kind of shape. [open-ended]

- Group B: Explore the set of shapes. For each kind of shape, what do you notice about the number of sides and the number of corners (vertices)? [slightly structured]
- Group C: First, sort the shapes into like shapes. Count the number of sides and the number of corners (vertices) of each shape. Use the following table to record your findings. What do you notice about the number of sides and the number of corners (vertices) for each kind of shape? [most structured]

	Number of Sides	Number of Corners
Triangles		
Squares		
Rectangles		
Hexagons		

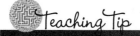

Teaching Tip

Make sure children understand the vocabulary used in tasks before they begin working independently. For instance, two of the tasks in the tiered lesson example use the words *sides* and *corners*. Before they start the tasks, have a group discussion with children who are assigned these tasks about the meaning of the terms.

The three tiers in this lesson reflect different degrees of difficulty in terms of task structure. However, all children are working on the same learning objective and they all must engage in reasoning about the shapes to complete their tasks.

In Chapter 6 you will read about response to intervention (RtI), a multitier student-support system that offers struggling children increasing levels of intervention. We want to distinguish between the tiers in RtI and tiered lessons used in differentiation. In RtI the tiers refer to the different degrees of intervention offered to children as needed—from the first tier, which occurs in a general education setting and involves the core instruction for all children based on high-quality mathematics curriculum and instructional practices, to the upper tier, which could involve one-on-one instruction with a special education teacher. Tiered lessons used in differentiation would be an avenue to offer high-quality core instruction for all children in the first tier or level of RtI.

● Flexible Grouping

Allowing children to collaborate on tasks supports and challenges their thinking and increases their opportunities to communicate about mathematics and build understanding. In addition, many children feel that working in groups improves their confidence, engagement, and understanding (Nebesniak & Heaton, 2010). Even children who prefer to work alone need to learn the life skill of collaboration and should be provided opportunities to work with others.

Determining how to place children in groups is an important decision. Avoid continually grouping by ability. This kind of grouping, although well-intentioned, perpetuates low levels of learning and actually increases the gap between more and less dependent children. Instead, consider using *flexible grouping*, in which the size and makeup of small groups vary in a purposeful and strategic manner (Murray & Jorgensen, 2007). When coupled with the use of differentiation strategies, flexible grouping gives all children the chance to work successfully in groups.

Flexible groups can vary based on children's readiness, interests, language proficiency, and learning profiles, as well as the nature of the tasks. For example, sometimes children can work with a partner because the nature of the task best suits two people working together. At other times, flexible groups might be created with four children because their assigned task has enough components or roles to warrant a larger team. Note that it can be effective to periodically place struggling learners with more capable children who are likely to be helpful. However, constantly pairing struggling learners with more capable children is not helpful for either group. The idea behind flexible grouping is that groups can and do easily change in response to all children's readiness, interests, and learning profiles and the nature of the task they will be doing.

Regardless of how you group your children, the first key to successful grouping is individual accountability. While the group is working together on a product, individuals must be able to explain the content, the process, and the product. Second, and equally important, is building a sense of shared responsibility within a group. At the start of the year, it is important to engage children in team-building activities and to set expectations that all group members will participate in the assigned group task(s) and that all group members will be responsible for ensuring that the entire group understands the concept.

Reinforcing individual accountability and shared responsibility may create a shift in your role as the teacher. When a member of a small group asks you a question, pose the question to the whole group to find out what the other members think. Children will soon learn that they must use teammates as their first resource and seek teacher help only when the whole group needs help. Also, when you are observing groups, rather than asking a child what she is doing, ask another child in the group to explain what the first child is doing. Having all children participate in the oral report to the whole class also builds individual accountability. Letting children know that you may call on any member to explain what the group did is a good way to ensure that all group members understand what they did. Additionally, having children individually write and record their strategies and solutions is important. Using these techniques will increase the effectiveness of grouping, which in turn will help children learn mathematical concepts more successfully.

Stop and Reflect

Why is teaching mathematics through problem solving (i.e., a problem-based approach) a good way to differentiate instruction and reach all children in a classroom? ■

5

Planning, Teaching, and Assessing Culturally and Linguistically Diverse Children

One of the aims of schools should be to produce citizens who treat one another with respect, who value the contributions of those with whom they interact irrespective of race, class, or gender, and who act with a sense of social justice.

Boaler (2006, p. 74)

Culturally and Linguistically Diverse Children

We are lucky to be in a country in which people from all over the world bring us rich diversity in cultural practices and languages. Children's native languages are an important part of their cultural heritage, and students also think, communicate, and learn in their native languages. Since 1980, the number of school-aged children who speak a language other than English at home has risen from 4.7 million to 11.2 million (National Center for Education Statistics, 2011).

Jo Boaler's quote captures the essence of the equity principle from *Principles and Standards for School Mathematics*: "Excellence in mathematics education requires equity—high expectations and strong support for all students" (National Council of Teachers of Mathematics, 2000, p. 12). Teaching for equity is much more than providing children with an equal opportunity to learn mathematics. Attention to language and culture, two interrelated and critical considerations, is important in planning, teaching, and assessing children from diverse backgrounds. Children who are given instructional tasks that are well supported and thought provoking—rather than low-level tasks with short-term gains—can reach higher levels of mathematics proficiency.

◈ Funds of Knowledge

Children from different countries, regions, or experiences, including those who speak different languages, are often viewed as challenges to a teacher or school. Rather, children's varied languages and backgrounds should be seen as a resource in teaching (Gutiérrez, 2009). Valuing a person's cultural background is more than a belief statement; it is a set of intentional actions that communicates to the child, "I want to know about you, I want you to see mathematics as part of your life, and I expect that you can do high-level mathematics." In getting to know these children, we access their funds of knowledge (the essential knowledge or information children use to survive and thrive) (Gonzáles, Moll, & Amanti, 2005). Instead of teaching English language learners (ELLs) from a deficit model (lack of knowledge and experience), we can connect their experiences from home and family to that of the mathematics classroom. The more we enhance learning for all children, regardless of their places of birth, the more enriched the opportunities for learning become.

◈ Mathematics as a Language

Mathematics is commonly referred to as a "universal language," but this is not entirely true. Conceptual knowledge (e.g., what division is) is universal. Procedures (e.g., how you add) and symbols are culturally determined and are not universal. Treating mathematics as universally the same can lead to inequities in the classroom. For example, the subtraction process varies from country to country in how it is notated and the language that is used to describe the process. Table 5.1 illustrates three ways to subtract, along with the countries that teach that process (Perkins & Flores, 2002; Secada, 1983). Commas and periods are sometimes used in reverse, for example, 1,400 meaning 1.400 as written in the United States. Numerals are sometimes written differently. For example, in many countries the numeral 1 is written more like a 7 with a sharper angle (*1*), and the 7 has a horizontal line through it to distinguish it from the one (*7*) (Secada, 1983). If these and other differences are not recognized, children from other cultures may not understand the symbols and processes being used in their class and, therefore, not be able to participate and learn.

How we do mathematics is also influenced by culture. For example, mental mathematics is highly valued in many countries, whereas in the United States recording every step is valued. Look again at the three strategies shared in Table 5.1, but imagine no "tick marks" recorded and no explanation provided. Could you follow what the first child did? Each represents different, yet equally efficient and effective, strategies for solving subtraction problems. The critical equity question, though, is not just whether you can follow an alternative approach, but how you will respond when you encounter children using such an approach.

- Will you require children to show their steps (disregarding the way they learned it)?
- Will you ask children to elaborate on how they did it?
- Will you have these children show other children their way of thinking?

The latter two responses communicate to children that you are interested in their way of knowing mathematics and that there are many ways in which different people and different cultures approach mathematics. Supporting invented strategies for algorithms is an important way to show that you value children as individuals and a good way to gain insights into useful and interesting culturally influenced strategies.

Table 5.1 Subtraction Algorithms from Around the World

Step in the Algorithm	Explanation or Think Aloud for the Step
Missing Addend Approach (used in France, Vietnam, Thailand, Laos, Mexico, Latin America, and other places)	
52 −17	(Done mentally) What number do I add to get from 7 to 12? 5. [Since 10 is added to the 2 (ones), 10 is also added to the lower number, so mentally the lower number is now 27.] What number do I add to get from 2 to 5? 3 (tens). The answer: 35.
5 2 −1¹7 ――― 5	[Because 10 is added to the 2 (ones), 10 is also added to the lower number, so mentally the lower number is now 27.]
5 2 −1¹7 ――― 3 5	What number do I add to get from 2 to 5? 3 (tens). The answer: 35.
Equal Addition Subtraction (used in Latin America and the United States, less common)	
52 −17	(Done mentally) I can't take 7 from 2, but I can add 3 to the 7 to get 0 (0 can be taken away from any number). If I add 3 to the bottom number, I must also add it to the top number.
⁵ 5 2̶ −1¹0 ――― 3 5	Note: This is notated for the reader but is often done mentally in actual practice. 2 from 5 is 3 (tens). The answer is 35.
Negative Numbers to Subtract (used in Eastern Europe, Russia, Latvia, Ukraine, and other places)	
52 −17	7 from 2 is −5.
52 −17 ――― −5	1 from 5 is 4.
5 12 −1 7 ――― 4 −5 3 5	40 minus 5 is 35.

Teaching Tip

Instead of requiring children to write all their steps, ask them to think aloud as they solve a problem or ask how they did it in their head.

◆ Culturally Responsive Instruction

Culture and language are interwoven and interrelated. Therefore, teaching strategies that support diverse learners often support both cultural diversity and language. For example, if you invite children to talk to a partner before sharing with the whole class, you not only provide ELLs with an additional speaking opportunity to support language, but you also distribute the sharing, listening, and teaching, so you are sharing power within the classroom community.

Culturally responsive mathematics instruction is not just for recent immigrants; it is for all children, including children from different ethnic groups, different socioeconomic levels, and so on. It includes consideration for content, relationships, cultural knowledge, flexibility in approaches, use of accessible learning contexts, a responsive learning community, and working in cross-cultural partnerships (Averill, Anderson, Easton, Te Maro, Smith, & Hynds, 2009). Differentiation, as described in Chapter 4, can be accomplished by adapting the content, process, product, and the classroom environment (Tomlinson, 2003). Following are four strategies for differentiating that address the specific needs of linguistically and culturally diverse children. These ideas are also presented in an at-a-glance format in Table 5.2.

Focus on Important Mathematics

Too often, our first attempt to help ELLs is to simplify the mathematics and/or remove the language from the lesson. Simplifying or removing language can take away opportunities to learn. Culturally responsive instruction stays focused on the big ideas of mathematics (i.e., based on standards such as the *Common Core State Standards*) and helps children engage in

Table 5.2 An At-a-Glance Focus on Culturally Relevant Mathematics Instruction

Aspect of Culturally Relevant Instruction	Reflection Questions to Guide Teaching and Assessing
Communicate high expectations.	Does the content include a balance of procedures and concepts? Are children expected to engage in problem solving and generate their own approaches to problems? Are connections made between mathematics topics?
Make content relevant.	In what ways is the content related to familiar aspects of children's lives? In what ways is prior knowledge elicited or reviewed so that all children can participate in the lesson? To what extent are children asked to make connections between school mathematics and mathematics in their own lives? How are children's interests (events, issues, literature, or pop culture) used to build interest and mathematical meaning?
Communicate the value of children's identities.	In what ways are children invited to include their own experiences within a lesson? Are story problems generated from children and teachers? Do stories reflect the real experiences of children? Are individual children's approaches presented and showcased so that children see their ideas as important to the teacher and their peers? Are alternative algorithms shared as a point of excitement and pride (as appropriate)? Are multiple modes to demonstrate knowledge (e.g., visuals, explanations, models) valued?
Model shared power.	Are children (rather than just the teacher) justifying the correctness of solutions? Are children invited to (expected to) engage in whole-class discussions in which children share ideas and respond to each other's ideas? In what ways are roles assigned so that all children feel that they contribute to and learn from other members of the class? Are children given a choice in how they solve a problem? In how they demonstrate knowledge of the concept?

and stay focused on those big ideas. For example, a critical area in grades 1 and 2 is addition, which includes moving between stories and equations. The stories can be carefully selected to use contexts that are familiar to ELLs and that lend themselves to using visuals (such as cars). Rather than having a new context for every story, the stories can focus on the same theme (and connect to the English that children are learning in their ESL instruction, if possible). This provides a context for the mathematics without adding unnecessary linguistic demands. The teacher can incorporate opportunities for children to share their approaches to adding and illustrate (with the visuals) how they thought about it. In this way, ELLs are able to learn the important content and engage in classroom discourse.

Make Content Relevant

There are really two components to making content relevant. One is to think about the mathematics: "Is the mathematics itself presented meaningfully and is it connected to other content?" The second is to contextualize the content so that it is grounded in familiarity.

Mathematical Connections.   Helping children see that mathematical ideas are inter-related will fill in or deepen their understanding of and connections to previously taught content. For example, consider the following first-grade problem:

Edwin has some trains. He gives 2 to Marta. Edwin now has 6 trains. How many did Edwin have before he gave some away?

You may recognize that this task connects addition and subtraction, and that the initial value (how many trains Edwin had before he gave any away) is the unknown amount. Although the mathematics is already presented in a conceptual and meaningful manner, it is important to connect addition and subtraction, as well as to connect the symbols to the situation. For example, one child might use a think-addition approach: "I know that he has 6 now and plus the 2 from Marta means he had 8." Another child might think: "I thought 'what minus 2 is 6 and I know that is 8." The symbols for each child's thinking are $6 + 2 = ?$ and $? - 2 = 6$, respectively. Having children connect the symbols back to their thinking and to the story helps build strong mathematical connections and understanding of addition and subtraction.

Context Connections.   Making content relevant is also about contexts. If the "trains" context is familiar, it can ground children's thinking so they can focus on reasoning about the mathematical relationships. Using problems that connect children to developmentally appropriate social or peer connections is one way to contextualize learning. Another is to make connections to historical or cultural contexts. Seeing mathematics from various cultures provides opportunities for children to "put faces" on mathematical contributions. For example, you can introduce the Mayan place-value system as a way to think about how we write numerals (grade K) and to think about our place-value (base-ten) system (grade 2). You can also have children create freedom quilts, which tell stories about the Underground Railroad (Neumann, 2005), or other geometric art patterns can be used to develop standards content such as partitioning circles or rectangles into halves and fourths (grade 1) or into halves, fourths, and thirds (grade 2).

Incorporate Children's Identities

Incorporating children's identities in the mathematics they do overlaps with the previous category, but it merits its own discussion. Children should see themselves in

Teachers can adapt the way children consider each other's ideas so that all members of the class feel comfortable participating in a discussion by asking specific prompts such as, "Which strategy would you use if the numbers were more difficult? Why? Talk to your partner and then we will share as a whole class."

mathematics and see that mathematics is a part of their culture. The classroom environment should incorporate children's cultural practices. For example, children from some countries may not feel comfortable challenging an approach used by other children in a classroom discussion.

Both researchers and teachers have found that telling stories about their own lives, or asking children to tell stories, makes the mathematics relevant to children and can raise student achievement (Turner, Celedón-Pattichis, Marshall, & Tennison, 2009). Table 5.3 provides ideas for making mathematics relevant to a child's home and community.

The following teacher's story illustrates one way to incorporate family history and culture by reading *The Hundred Penny Box* (Mathis, 1986). In Mathis's story, a 100-year-old woman remembers an important event in every year of her life as she turns over each of her 100 pennies. Each penny is more than a piece of money; it is a "memory trigger" for her life.

> Taking a cue from the book, I asked each child to collect one penny from each year they were alive starting from the year of their birth and not missing a year. Children were encouraged to bring in additional pennies their classmates might need. Then the children consulted with family members to create a penny time line of important events in their lives. Using information gathered at home, they started with the year they were born, listing their birthday and then recording first steps, accidents, vacations, pets, births of siblings, and so on.

Children in grades K–2 can prepare a time line of their key events too, determining when between 0 (i.e., the day they were born) and their current age a memorable event happened. The number line is an important model to use in counting, adding, and subtracting, and this context helps children better understand the number line, which is abstract and more challenging than using set models (e.g., counters). For example, you can ask children "How

Table 5.3 Where to Find Mathematics in Children's Homes and Communities

Where to Look	What You Might Ask Children to Record and Share (and Mathematics That Can Be Explored)
Grocery store or marketplace	Cost of an item of which they bought more than one (repeated addition or multiplication) Cost of an item that came with a quantity (e.g., dozen eggs) (division) Better buy of two different-sized items (division) Shapes of different containers (geometry) Different types/brands of foods they select, such as what kind of bread (data)
Photographs	A person they admire (data) A favorite scene (geometry, measurement) 2-D and 3-D shapes in their home or neighborhood (geometry) A flower (multiplication with number of petals, algebraic thinking)
Artifact (game or measuring device) from their culture or that is a favorite	A game that naturally involves mathematics Measuring devices (nonstandard and standard measures) for length and volume

many years between [these two events]?" and "How many years ago was [this event]?" These questions focus on subtraction as difference, rather than as take-away, an important and underemphasized subtraction situation.

Ensure Shared Power

When we think about creating a positive classroom environment, one in which all children feel as if they can participate and learn, we are addressing considerations related to power. The teacher plays a major role in establishing and distributing power, whether it is intentional or not. In many classrooms, the teacher has the power—telling children whether answers are right or wrong (rather than having children determine correctness through reasoning), demonstrating processes for how to solve problems (rather than giving choices for how children will engage in the problem), and determining who will solve which problems (rather than allowing flexibility and choice for children). The way that you assign groups, seat children, and call on children sends clear messages about who has power in the classroom.

Teaching Culturally and Linguistically Diverse Children

Creating effective learning opportunities for ELLs involves integrating the principles of bilingual education with those of standards-based mathematics instruction. When learning about mathematics, children may be learning content in English for which they do not know the words in their native language. For example, words such as *hexagons*, *cylinders*, and *prisms* may be entirely new terminology.

Teaching Tip

Any one of the categories in Table 5.4 could be the focus of a lesson study, discussion with colleagues, or the basis for individual reflection. The importance lies not in the specific suggestions but in the concept of having an eye on language development and mathematics content.

In addition, story problems are difficult for ELLs not only due to the language but also to the fact that sentences in story problems are often structured differently from sentences in conversational English (Janzen, 2008). Teachers of English to Speakers of Other Languages (TESOL), a professional organization focused on the needs of ELLs, argues that ELLs need to use both English and their native language to read, write, listen, and speak as they learn appropriate content—a position similarly addressed in NCTM standards documents and position statements. The strategies discussed in this section are the ones that appear most frequently in the literature as critical to increasing the academic achievement of ELLs in mathematics classrooms (e.g., Celedón-Pattichis & Ramirez, 2012; Echevarria, Vogt, & Short, 2008). Table 5.4 offers reflective questions related to instructional planning for and the teaching of English language learners.

◈ Focus on Academic Vocabulary

ELLs enter the mathematics classroom from homes in which English is not the primary language of communication. Although a person may develop conversational English language skills in a few years, it takes as many as seven years to learn "academic language," which is the language specific to a content area such as mathematics (Cummins, 1994). Academic language is harder to learn because it is not used in a child's everyday world. There are also unique features of the language of mathematics that make it difficult for many children, in particular those who are learning English. Teaching the academic language of mathematics evolves over time and requires thoughtful and reflective instructional planning.

Table 5.4 Reflective Questions for Planning and Teaching Mathematics Lessons for ELLs

Process	Mathematics Content Considerations	Language Considerations
Reflective Questions for Planning		
1. Determine the mathematics.	• What mathematical concepts (aligned to grade-level standards) am I teaching? • What child-friendly learning objectives will I post? • How does this mathematics concept connect to other concepts children have learned?	• What language objectives might I add (e.g., include reading, writing, speaking, and listening)? • What visuals or words will I use to communicate the content and language objectives?
2. Consider children's needs.	• How can I connect the content to be taught to content that children have learned? Or how will I fill in the gaps if children don't have prerequisite content needed for the lesson?	• What context or models might I select that are a good match to children's social/cultural backgrounds and previously learned vocabulary?
3. Select, design, or adapt a task.	• What task can I use that addresses the content identified in item 1 and the needs of my children identified in item 2? • How might I adapt a task so that it has multiple entry and exit points (i.e., is challenging and accessible to a range of children)?	• What context might I use that is meaningful to children's cultures and backgrounds? • What language pitfalls does the task have? Which of these will I eliminate and which of these need explicit attention? • Which words or phrases, even if familiar to children, take on new meaning in a mathematics context (e.g., homonyms, homophones, and words such as *mean, similar, find*)?
Reflective Questions for Teaching		
1. Introduce the task (the *Before* phase).	• How will I introduce the task in a way that elicits prior mathematics knowledge needed for the task? • Is a similar task needed to build background related to the content (or would such a preview take away from the purpose or challenge of the task)?	• How can I connect the task to children's experiences and to familiar contexts? • What key vocabulary do I want to introduce so that the words will be used throughout the lesson? (Post key vocabulary in a prominent location.) • What visuals and real objects can I use that bring meaning to the selected task? • How can I present the task in visual, written, and oral formats? • How will I be sure that children understand what they are to do in the *During* phase?
2. Work on the task (the *During* phase).	• What hints or assists might I give as children work to help them focus without taking away from their thinking? • What extensions or challenges will I offer for children who successfully solve the task? • What questions will I pose to push the mathematics identified in the learning goals?	• Have I grouped children for both academic and language support? • Have I encouraged children to draw pictures, make diagrams, and/or use manipulatives? • Have I used strategies to reduce the linguistic demands without hindering the problem solving (e.g., using a graphic organizer, sentence starters such as "I solved the problem by . . . ," recording tables, and concept maps)?

(*continued*)

Table 5.4 *(Continued)*

Process	Mathematics Content Considerations	Language Considerations
Reflective Questions for Planning		
3. Debrief and discuss the task and the mathematics (the *After* phase).	• How will children report their findings? • How will I format the discussion of the task? • What questions will I pose to push the mathematics identified in the learning goals?	• What ways can I maximize language use in nonthreatening ways (e.g., think-pair-share)? • How can I encourage and reinforce different formats (multiple exit points) for demonstrating understanding of the lesson content? • How might I provide advance notice, language support, or rehearsal to ELLs so that they will be comfortable speaking to their peers? • Am I using appropriate "wait time"?
Formative Assessment		
Throughout lesson and unit	• What questions will I ask during the lesson or what will I look for in the children's work as evidence of learning the objectives (*During* and *After* phases)? • What follow-up might I provide to children who are not demonstrating understanding of the mathematics?	• What words will I use in my questions to be sure the questions are understood? How might I use a translator to assist in assessing? • If a child is not succeeding, how might I diagnose whether the problem is with language, content, or both? • What accommodations can I provide to be sure I am accessing what the children know?

Honor Use of Native Language

Valuing children's native language is one of the ways you value their cultural heritage. In a mathematics classroom, children can communicate in their native language while continuing their English language development (Haas & Gort, 2009; Moschkovich, 2009; Setati, 2005). For example, a good strategy for children working individually or in small groups is having children think about and discuss the problem in their preferred language. If a child knows enough English, then the presentation in the *After* phase can be shared in English. If the child knows little or no English and does not have access to a peer who shares his or her native language, then a translator or a self-made mathematics-focused picture dictionary can be a strong support. Teachers can look up the essential terms in children's native languages to assist. Bilingual children will often code-switch, moving between two languages. Research indicates that this practice of code-switching supports mathematical reasoning because children select the language in which they can best express their ideas (Moschkovich, 2009).

Certain native languages can support learning mathematics words. Because English, Spanish, French, Portuguese, and Italian all have their roots in Latin, many mathematics words are similar across languages (Celedón-Pattichis, 2009; Gómez, 2010). For example, *aequus* (Latin), *equal* (English), and *igual* (Spanish) are cognates. See if you can figure out the English mathematics terms for the following Spanish words: *número, diferencia, hexágano, ángulo, triángulo, quadra,* and *cubo*. Children may not make this connection if you do not point it out, so it is important to explicitly teach children to look for cognates.

Use Content and Language Objectives

If children know the purpose of a lesson, they are better able to make sense of the details when they are challenged by some of the oral or written explanations. When language expectations are explicitly included, children will know that they will be responsible for reaching certain language goals alongside mathematical goals and will be more likely to attempt to learn those skills or words. Here are two examples of dual objectives:

1. Children will determine the defining attributes of a triangle (mathematics).
2. Children will describe in writing and orally characteristics that are true for any triangle (e.g., three angles) and which characteristics do not define a triangle (e.g., color, size) (language and mathematics).

Explicitly Teach Vocabulary

Intentional vocabulary instruction must be part of mathematics instruction for all children. This includes attention to terms within a lesson and additional opportunities to develop academic language. These additional opportunities can reinforce understanding as they help children learn the terminology. Examples include the following:

- Picture dictionaries, linking concepts and terms with drawings, or cut-out pictures
- Foldables of key words for a topic
- Games focused on vocabulary development (e.g., Pictionary or Concentration)
- Interactive word walls, including visuals and translations

In addition, many websites provide translations; children can create cards with terms and their translations and build personal mathematics dictionaries (Kersaint, Thompson, & Petkova, 2009).

Teaching Tip

Not all vocabulary should be "previewed," because the term (and its concept) can sometimes be better understood after some exploration.

All children benefit from an increased focus on language; however, too much emphasis on vocabulary can diminish the focus on mathematics. It is important that the language support be connected to the mathematics and the selected task or activity.

As you analyze a lesson, you must identify terms related to the mathematics and to the context that may need explicit attention. Consider the following kindergarten question:

MacKenna and Sydney pick red and yellow apples from the apple orchard. Sydney picks 5 apples to take home. How many of each kind of apple might she take?

In order for children to engage in this task, the contextual terms *pick*, *apples*, and *orchard* must be understood. The phrase *how many of each* must be understood, as it may not be clear that this means to have some apples of each color so that the total is five apples. In first and second grades, children could be asked to list all the combinations in a table.

Stop and Reflect

Table is among hundreds of words whose meanings in mathematics are different from everyday usage. Other such terms include *difference, foot, multiple, partition, side,* and *angle*. Can you name five others? ◼

◆ Lesson Considerations

Support for academic language use is a significant part of lesson considerations. In addition, facilitating discourse that provides access to ELLs is critical. This includes efforts to ensure

ELLs understand and have the background for engaging in the focus task(s) and the need to put structures in place for participation throughout the lesson.

Build Background

Similar to building on prior knowledge, building background also takes into consideration native language and culture, as well as content (Echevarria, Vogt, & Short, 2008). If possible, use appropriate visuals and context to help children understand the problem you want them to solve. This nonthreatening, engaging activity helps children make connections between what they have learned and what they need to learn.

Some aspects of English and mathematics are particularly challenging to ELLs (Whiteford, 2009/2010). For example, teen numbers sound a lot like their decade number—if you say *sixteen* and *sixty* out loud, you can hear how similar they are. Emphasizing the *n* sound helps ELLs hear the difference. For example, in a lesson on the teen numbers and place value, a teacher may have children partner and have one say the place-value words and the partner say the actual teen name (emphasizing the *n*):

Partner A: Ten and four
Partner B: Fourteen

And the teacher can help children see the connection between *ten* and *teen*.

Remember, too, that the U.S. measurement system may be unfamiliar to ELLs. When encountering content that may be unfamiliar or difficult for ELLs, devote additional time to build background so that children can engage in the mathematical tasks without also having to navigate language and background knowledge.

Use Comprehensible Input

Comprehensible input means that the message you are communicating is understandable to children. Modifications include simplifying sentence structures and limiting the use of nonessential or confusing vocabulary (Echevarria, Short, & Vogt, 2008). Note that these modifications do not lower expectations for the lesson. Sometimes teachers put many unnecessary words and phrases into questions, making them less clear to nonnative speakers. Compare the two sets of teachers' instructions:

NOT MODIFIED:

You have a worksheet in front of you that I just gave out. For every story problem, I want you to draw a picture and write an equation. You will be working with your partner, but each of you needs to record your answers on your own paper. If you get stuck on a problem, raise your hand.

MODIFIED:

Please look at your paper. (Holds paper and points to the first story, which now has a picture next to it). Let's read together. (Everyone reads.) What is this story about? (Waits) What words tell us what the story is about (points to story itself)? (Notes context-related words on board, as well as words that indicate the action in the problem, so they can be used for reference.) Talk to your partner about how to find the answer. (Points to mouth and then to a pair of children as she says this.) Write your answers. (Makes a writing motion over paper.)

Notice that four things have been done differently in the teacher talk: Sentences have been shortened, confusing words have been removed, attention is drawn to making meaning of the first example, and related gestures and motions have been added to the oral directives. Also notice the visuals that were added and the wait time the teacher gives. It is very important to provide extra time after posing a question or giving instructions to allow ELLs time to translate, make sense of the request, and then participate.

Another way to provide comprehensible input is to use a variety of tools to help children visualize and understand what is verbalized. In the preceding example, the teacher models the instructions and adds pictures to the stories. Real objects, manipulatives, and drawings that fit the context can be used to bring meaning to the problem and are important in helping the child think through and solve the problem. Effective tools include manipulatives, real objects, pictures, visuals, multimedia, demonstrations, and children's books (Echevarria, Vogt, & Short, 2008). Children should be expected to include various representations of their understandings, such as drawing and writing to explain what they have done. Doing so helps to develop children's understanding and language, and also gives the teacher a better idea of what they do and do not understand.

Engage Children in Discourse That Reflects Language Needs

Discourse, or the use of classroom discussion, is essential for the learning of all children, but is particularly important for ELLs who need to engage in productive language (writing and speaking) as well as receptive language (listening and reading). As noted in the *Application of Common Core State Standards for English Learners:*

> ELLs are capable of participating in mathematical discussions as they learn English. Mathematics instruction for ELL students should draw on multiple resources and modes available in classrooms—such as objects, drawings, inscriptions, and gestures—as well as home languages and mathematical experiences outside of school. Mathematical instruction should address mathematical discourse and academic language. (CCSSO, 2011, p. 2)

There are strategies you can use in classroom discourse that help ELLs understand and participate. As described in the preceding quote, the use of gestures and visuals is critical to learning English and mathematics. For example, revoicing is a research-based strategy that helps ELLs hear an idea more than once and hear it restated with the appropriate language applied to concepts. But, because ELLs cannot always explain their ideas fully, don't rush to call on someone else; instead, patiently press for details. Pressing for details is not done just so the teacher can decide whether the idea makes sense; it also allows other children to make sense of the idea (Maldonado, Turner, Dominguez, & Empson, 2009). Because practicing language is important for ELLs, offering opportunities for children to practice phrases or words through pair-share or choral response also is effective. Finally, children from other countries often solve or illustrate problems differently, so allowing time for them to explain or show their way can involve students in discourse while introducing a novel approach to other children.

Teaching Tip

Making the strategies of ELLs public and connecting these strategies to others is interesting and supports the learning of all children, while building the confidence of ELLs.

Plan Cooperative/Interdependent Groups to Support Language

The use of cooperative groups is a valuable way to differentiate instruction. For ELLs, groups provide the opportunity to use language, but only if the groups are carefully formed in a way that considers children's language skills. Placing an ELL with two English-speaking children may result in the ELL being left out. On the other hand, grouping all Spanish speakers together prevents these children from having the opportunity to hear and participate in mathematics in English. Consider placing a bilingual child in a group with a child with limited English, or place children that have the same first language together with native speakers so that they can help each other understand and participate (Garrison, 1997; Khisty, 1997).

◈ Implementing Strategies for ELLs

The strategies just described are subtle moves in teaching. As you read the following vignette, look for strategies that the teacher applies to provide support for ELLs while keeping expectations high.

> Ms. Cruz is teaching a second-grade lesson that involves the standard units for measuring length (in feet). The lesson begins with nonstandard units, and then moves to measuring in feet. Ms. Cruz has four English language learners in her class including a child from Korea, who knows very little English, and three children from Mexico, who speak English to varying degrees; all are recent arrivals in the United States. These children are not familiar with U.S. measurements and may or may not have had other experiences in measuring. Ms. Cruz knows she needs to build background to ensure they can participate in the lesson.
>
> The lesson begins by asking children to count how many thumbs to get from one side of their desk to the other. Ms. Cruz motions using the length of her thumb as a unit on a child's desk as she asks the question. She asks children to write their number of thumbs on a Post-it note and then stick the note on the board (using motions to illustrate instructions). After the answers are posted, she brings children up to the carpet. She states, "You measured your desk with your thumbs. What does measure mean?" After hearing responses and examples, she says, "Look at the answers when you measured. Can they all be right?" As children suggest that the thumb length might matter, she calls up pairs of children and has them compare their thumbs. She has the class state in full sentences whose is "longer" and "shorter" (e.g., Annie's thumb is longer than Eun's thumb). Ms. Cruz says that the big idea today is to figure out how we can measure so we all agree on how long something (like our desk) is.
>
> She then pulls out her book *How Big Is a Foot?* and begins to read, showing and pointing at pictures as she reads. When the bed turns out to be too small, she stops and asks, "What happened—any ideas?" She waits and then asks them to share with a partner before sharing with the group. One child explains that her foot is much smaller than Ms. Cruz's foot and gets up to show the difference.
>
> Ms. Cruz finishes the book and asks, "How is the king's problem with the bed like our thumb measures?" She then suggests that we all agree on one thumb length to use and to re-measure our desks to see if we agree on how many thumbs it is. She hands out thumb cut-outs and asks children to use this second grader's thumb to measure. She will see how they do in iterating the unit (not overlapping, end-to-end) and then bridge to measuring the carpet with a standard foot, being sure to talk about the meaning of the word *foot*.

Stop and Reflect

What specific strategies to support English language learners can you identify? ◼

There are a number of strategies in the vignette that provide support for ELLs: recognizing the potential language support for *measure* and later for *foot*, as well as lack of familiarity with measuring, which was supported by having an opportunity to measure prior to hearing the story (building background). Ms. Cruz has children saying in full sentences whose thumb is longer and shorter. She employs the think-pair-share technique, concrete models (the thumb cut-out), the story, and the children's own measures to build meaning and scaffold to measuring with a foot. Most importantly, Ms. Cruz did not diminish the challenge of the task with these strategies. If she had altered the task, for example, not expecting the ELLs to explain why their measures turned out differently or what they predicted would happen in the story, they would not be learning what they needed to learn. Conversely, if she had simply asked children to begin measuring in feet, she might have kept her expectations high but failed to provide the support that would enable her children to succeed.

◆ Assessment Considerations

Throughout the discussion of strategies for supporting ELLs are opportunities for assessment. Formative assessment, as described in Chapter 3, is embedded in instruction and informs instructional decisions. For example, the use of visuals and gestures is important in helping ELLs to

- Understand the instructions and mathematical ideas (comprehensible *input*)
- Participate in the lesson (small groups or discussion)
- Communicate their own understanding (formative assessment)

The use of native language is also important for assessment. Research shows that ELLs perform better when a test is given in their native language (Robinson, 2010). If a teacher wants to understand what a child knows about mathematics, then the child should be able to communicate that understanding in a way that is best for the child, even if the teacher may need a translation.

Several strategies can assist teachers in using formative assessments with ELLs, including tasks with multiple entry and exit points, diagnostic interviews, tasks that limit linguistic load, accommodations, and self-assessments.

Select Tasks with Multiple Entry and Exit Points

An aspect of teaching mathematics through problem solving that is important, particularly for ELLs, is to select tasks carefully. If a problem can be solved in multiple ways, an ELL is more likely to be able to design a strategy that makes sense and then illustrate that strategy. Inviting children to show and/or explain their strategies provides options for ELLs to use words and pictures to communicate their thinking.

Use Diagnostic Interviews

Chapter 3 provides a strong foundation on diagnostic interviews. Diagnostic interviews are critical for ELLs because of the insights they can provide related to language and mathematical understanding. When ELLs do not get a correct answer or cannot explain a response, teachers tend to think it is a lack of mathematical understanding rather than a language issue. This is particularly true with ELLs who have a pretty strong ability to communicate in everyday English (as opposed to academic English). Before drawing conclusions about what mathematics a child does and does not understand, it is important to observe whether it is content or language that is causing a problem. Consider the following task that could be part of a diagnostic interview focused on place value (grade 2):

If you have 2 dimes and 3 pennies, how many cents do you have?

Stop and Reflect

If a child missed this problem, what do you think might be the reason? ∎

There are numerous reasons children might have struggled with this problem, including a lack of understanding the mathematical concept of place value or the values of the coins. Or it could be due to vocabulary, such as not knowing what the word *cents* means. It also could be because of the sentence structure. Diagnostic interviews have found that the word *if*, and the implied "If…then" sentence structure common to mathematics but not in other reading, can prevent children from comprehending what the sentence is asking (a challenge for native English speakers as well) (Fernandez, Anhalt, & Civil, 2009). The fact that there are many possible reasons why a child might not be able to solve a task, some related to language and others to mathematics, is a strong argument for using diagnostic interviews. If we misdiagnose the reason for a child's struggles, our interventions will be misguided.

Diagnostic interviews also can be used prior to instruction in order to assess the mathematical and language needs of children. Hearing an English language learner's interpretation of a problem and seeing how the child approaches the problem provide valuable insights that you can incorporate into your planning and teaching. For example, a child might say "Forty-seven from one hundred eighty" rather than "One hundred eighty minus forty-seven," which indicates the way the child talks about subtraction in his or her home. Using and connecting both ways of talking about subtraction will strengthen everyone's understanding.

Limit Linguistic Load

If you are trying to assess understanding, look for language that can interfere with children's understanding the situation (e.g., unneeded elaboration in a story, difficult or unfamiliar vocabulary). Removing pronouns such as *they*, *this*, *that*, *his*, and *her* and using actual names can assist ELLs in understanding some problems. For example, a typical story problem follows:

Jacob has 9 comic books. For his birthday, his grandpa gives him some more for his collection. If he has 13 now, how many did he get for this birthday?

Rewritten, it might read:

Jacob has 9 comic books. <u>Jacob's</u> grandpa gave <u>Jacob</u> some more comic books. If he has 13 <u>comic books</u> now, how many <u>comic books</u> did <u>Jacob</u> get from his grandpa?

Notice that it is not only reducing unnecessary language (e.g., *birthday*), but also adding specific referents that make the meaning of the story more clear. Of course, this particular problem could be adapted further by using illustrations or actual comic books.

Another way to reduce the linguistic load is to pick a context and stay with it for an entire lesson or series of lessons. This allows children to focus their thinking on the mathematics without getting bogged down in the various contexts that might be on an assessment. For example, children need opportunities to interpret story problems in which different parts are missing (the starting part, the part being added, and the whole). In this example, the part being added is what was missing. A collection of stories can be created with different parts missing (and different values used). Using the comic book context but changing the problem type reduces the linguistic load while keeping the mathematical challenge high.

Provide Accommodations

In assessing, providing accommodations refers to strategies for making sure that the assessment itself is accessible to children. This might mean being able to hear the question (children often can understand spoken English better than written English), shortening the assessment, or extending the time (Kersaint, Thompson, & Petkova, 2009). In addition, you can provide sentence starters so that the child knows what type of response you want. For example, "My equation fits the story because. . . ."

Incorporate Self-Assessment

It may take time to help children learn what it means to self-assess, but creating a list of content from a unit and asking children to rate how well they know it can be one way to gather information on what children know. Similarly, after a lesson or problem, children can rate or describe how hard they thought the lesson or problem was (and why). This is valuable not only for you in the formative assessment process but also for children as they learn to self-monitor and look for ways to measure their own improvement.

Stop and Reflect

The goal of equity is to offer all children access to important mathematics. What might you have on the list of things to do (and things not to do) that provide culturally and linguistically diverse children with the opportunity to learn mathematics? ■

6

Planning, Teaching, and Assessing Children with Exceptionalities

Most low achievers in mathematics are probably "instructionally disabled," not cognitively or "learning disabled."

Baroody (2011, p. 31)

Talented [mathematics] students need teachers who can move beyond the traditional "teacher role" of a dispenser of information to that of a role model who is passionate about learning, able to translate that passion into action, aggressively curious, and comfortable with this change of role.

Greenes, Teuscher, and Regis (2010, p. 80)*

 **Instructional Principles for Diverse Learners**

The NCTM *Principles and Standards for School Mathematics* states, "All students, regardless of their personal characteristics, backgrounds, or physical challenges must have opportunities to study—and support to learn—mathematics" (NCTM, 2000, p. 12). Within the same document, and as noted previously in Chapter 5, the equity principle states, "Excellence in mathematics education requires equity—high expectations and strong support for all students" (NCTM, 2000, p. 12). We know that teaching for equity is much more than providing children with an equal opportunity to learn mathematics; instead, it attempts to attain equal outcomes for all children by being sensitive to individual differences.

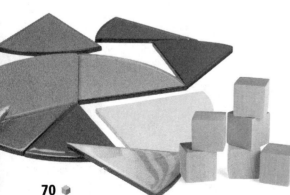

*Reprinted with permission from *Preparing Teachers for Mathematically Talented Middle School Students*, p. 80. Copyright 2010 by the National Council of Teachers of Mathematics. All rights reserved.

Many *achievement* gaps are actually *instructional* gaps or *expectation* gaps. It is not helpful when teachers establish low expectations for children, as when they say, "I just cannot put this class into groups to work; they are too unruly" or "My children with disabilities can't solve word problems—they don't have the reading skills." Operating under the belief that some children cannot "do mathematics" ensures that they don't have ample opportunities to prove otherwise. Instead, we suggest you consider Storeygard's (2010) mantra for teachers that proclaims "My kids can!"

As can be gleaned from the opening quotations, there is a spectrum of learners who need to be considered if we intend to have equity in our instruction. Figuring out how you will maintain equal outcomes (high expectations) while providing for individual differences (strong support) can be challenging. Equipping yourself with an ever-growing collection of instructional strategies for a variety of children is critical. A strategy that works for one child may be completely ineffective with another, even a child who has the same exceptionality. Addressing the needs of *all* means providing access and opportunity for

- Children who are identified as struggling or having a disability
- Children who are mathematically gifted
- Children who are unmotivated or need to build resilience

You may think, "I do not need to read the section on mathematically gifted children because they will be pulled out for math enrichment." Children who are mathematically talented need to be challenged in the daily core instruction, not just when they are participating in a program for gifted children.

The goal of equity is to offer all children access to important mathematics during their regular classroom instruction. Yet inequities exist, even if unintentionally. For example, if teachers do not build in opportunities for student-to-student interaction in a lesson, they may not be addressing the needs of girls, who are often social learners, or English language learners, who need opportunities to speak, listen, and write in small-group situations. It takes more than just wanting to be fair or equitable; it takes knowing the strategies that accommodate each type of learner and making every effort to incorporate those strategies into your teaching. "Equity does not mean that every student should receive identical instruction; instead, it demands that reasonable and appropriate accommodations be made as needed to promote access and attainment for all children" (NCTM, 2000, p. 12).

Across the wonderful and myriad diversities of your children, all of them learn mathematics in essentially the same way (Fuson, 2003). The authors of *Adding It Up* (National Research Council, 2001) conclude that all children are best served when you give attention to the following three principles:

1. Learning with understanding is based on connecting and organizing knowledge around big conceptual ideas.
2. Learning builds on what children already know.
3. Instruction in school should take advantage of children's informal knowledge of mathematics.

These principles, also reflected in the tenets of constructivist theory, apply to all learners and, therefore, are essential in making decisions about how you can adapt instruction to meet an individual learner's needs through accommodations and modifications. An accommodation is a response to the needs of the environment or the learner; it does not alter the task. For example, you might write down directions for a child instead of just presenting them orally. A modification changes the task, making it more accessible to the child. For example, if kindergartners are asked to try to use simple shapes to form larger shapes, you might show the outlines of the two smaller shapes for the children to find and place directly on the outline, then also give them the outline of the larger shape they will form. Subsequent shapes can be attempted without the modification. When modifications result in an easier or less demanding task, expectations are lowered. Modifications should be made in a way that leads back to the original task, providing scaffolding or support for learners who may need it. In the sections in this chapter, we share research-based strategies that reflect these principles while providing appropriate accommodations and modifications for the wide range of children in your classroom.

◆ Multitiered Systems of Support

In many areas, a systematic process for achieving higher levels of performance for all children often includes a multitiered system of support sometimes called *response to intervention* (RtI). This approach commonly emphasizes ways for struggling children to get immediate assistance and support rather than waiting for them to fail before they receive help. This same multitiered support system can also be used to identify children who are far exceeding standards and need additional challenges. Multitiered models are basically centered on three interwoven elements: high-quality curriculum, instructional support (interventions), and formative assessments that capture children's strengths and weaknesses. These systems of support were initially designed to determine whether low achievement is due to a lack of high-quality mathematics (i.e., "teacher-disabled children") (Baroody, 2011; Ysseldyke, 2002) or due to an actual learning disability. However, they can also help determine more intensive instructional options for children who need to catch up or who may need to have additional advanced mathematical challenges beyond what other children study.

Response to Intervention

RtI is a multitiered student support system that is frequently represented in a three-tier triangular format. As you move up the tiers, the number of children involved decreases, the teacher–child ratio decreases, and the level of intervention increases. As you might guess, there is a variety of RtI models in use as states and districts structure their unique approaches to meet local needs. Each tier in the triangle represents a level of intervention with corresponding monitoring of results and outcomes, as shown in Figure 6.1. The foundational and largest portion of the triangle (tier 1) represents the core instruction for all children based on a high-quality mathematics curriculum and instructional practices (i.e., manipulatives, conceptual emphasis, etc.), and progress-monitoring assessments. For example, if using a graphic organizer in tier 1 core instruction, the following high-quality practices would be expected in the three phases of the lesson—*Before*, *During*, and *After*:

- *Before.* States purpose, introduces new vocabulary, clarifies concepts from the prior knowledge in a visual organizer, and defines tasks of group members if groups are being used

Figure 6.1

Multitiered systems of support—using effective strategies to support all children.

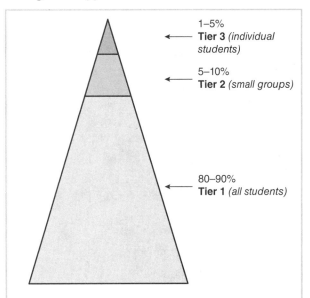

1–5%
Tier 3 *(individual students)*

5–10%
Tier 2 *(small groups)*

80–90%
Tier 1 *(all students)*

Common Features across Tiers

- **Research-Based Practices:** Prevention begins with practices based on students' best chances for success.
- **Data-Driven:** All decisions are based on clear objectives and formative data collection.
- **Instructional:** Prevention and intervention involve effective instruction, prompts, cues, practice, and environmental arrangements.
- **Context-Specific:** All strategies and measures are selected to fit individual schools, classrooms, or students.

Source: Based on Scott, T., & Lane, H. (2001). Multi-Tiered Interventions in Academic and Social Contexts. Unpublished manuscript, University of Florida, Gainesville.

- *During.* Displays directions in a chart, poster, or list; provides a set of guiding questions in a chart with blank spaces for responses
- *After.* Facilitates a discussion to highlight or make more explicit the significant concepts or skills and then presents a summary and list of important concepts as they relate to one another

Tier 2 represents children who did not reach the level of achievement expected during tier 1 instructional activities. Children in tier 2 should receive supplemental targeted instruction (interventions) outside the core mathematics lessons that uses more explicit strategies with systematic teaching of critical skills and concepts, more intensive and frequent instructional opportunities, and more supportive and precise prompts (Torgesen, 2002). The position statement of the National Council of Teachers of Mathematics on interventions (NCTM, 2011a) states, "Although we do not specifically state the precise interventions, we endorse the use of increasingly intensive and effective instructional interventions for children who struggle with mathematics." Interventions are "reserved for disorders that prove resistant to lower levels of prevention and require more heroic action to preclude serious complications" (Fuchs & Fuchs, 2001, p. 86).

Identifying and using these supplemental interventions is a flexible process that can be adapted or tailored based on how children respond. If further assessments, such as diagnostic interviews, reveal favorable progress, the children are weaned from the extra intervention sessions. However, if difficulties and struggles remain, the interventions can be adjusted in intensity, and in rare cases, children are referred to the next tier of support. Tier 3 is for children who need more intensive periods of instruction, sometimes with one-on-one attention, which may include comprehensive mathematics instruction or a referral for special education evaluation or special education services. Instructional strategies for the three tiers are outlined in Table 6.1.

Progress Monitoring

A key to the multitiered system of support is monitoring children's progress. One way to collect evidence of children's knowledge of concepts is through the use of diagnostic interviews, examples of which are described throughout the book in a feature called Formative Assessment Notes, marked with the following icon 📄. Another approach is to assess children's growth toward fluency in basic facts, an area that is a well-documented barrier for children with learning disabilities (Mazzocco, Devlin, & McKenney, 2008). Combining instruction with short daily assessments to monitor children's knowledge of number combinations that were already taught proved that the children with disabilities were better not only at remembering but also at generalizing to other facts (Woodward, 2006). The collection of information gathered from these assessments reveals whether children are making the progress expected or if more intensive instructional approaches need to be put into place.

▲ Planning, Teaching, and Assessing Children with Learning Disabilities

Because each child has specific learning needs, strategies that work for one child may not work for another. Yet there are some general ideas that can help as you plan instruction for children with learning disabilities. The following questions should guide your planning:

1. What organizational, behavioral, and cognitive skills are necessary for the children with disabilities to derive meaning from this activity?

2. Which children have known weaknesses in any of these skills or concepts?

3. How can I provide additional support in these areas of weakness so that children with learning disabilities can focus on the conceptual task in the activity? (Karp & Howell, 2004, p. 119).

Each phase of the lesson evokes specific planning considerations for children with disabilities. Some strategies apply throughout a lesson. The following discussion is not exhaustive, but it should provide you with specific suggestions for offering support to children throughout the lesson while you maintain the challenge.

Table 6.1 Interventions for Teaching Mathematics in a Multitiered System of Support

Tiers	Interventions

Tier 1	A highly qualified regular classroom teacher
	• Incorporates high-quality rigorous curriculum and has expectations for all children to be challenged
	• Builds in *Common Core State Standards* Mathematical Practices and NCTM Mathematical process standards
	• Commits to teaching the curriculum as defined
	• Supports children's use of multiple representations such as manipulatives, visual models, and symbols
	• Monitors progress to identify struggling children and children who excel at high levels
	• Uses flexible grouping of children
	• Fosters active involvement of children
	• Communicates high expectations
	• Uses graphic organizers in the *Before, During,* and *After* stages of the lesson
	  • *Before.* States purpose, introduces new vocabulary, clarifies concepts from the prior knowledge in a visual organizer, defines tasks of group members if using groups
	  • *During.* Lays out the directions in a chart, poster, or list; provides a set of guiding questions in a chart with blank spaces for responses
	  • *After.* Facilitates discussion of various student strategies and presents a summary and a list of important concepts as they relate to one another

Tier 2	A highly qualified regular classroom teacher with possible collaboration from a highly qualified special education teacher • Works with children (commonly in small groups) in supplemental sessions outside of the core instruction • Conducts individual diagnostic interviews to target strengths and weaknesses • Collaborates with special education, gifted, or English language learner (ELL) teachers • Creates lessons that emphasize the big ideas (focal points) or themes • Incorporates the CSA (concrete/semi-concrete/abstract) model • Shares thinking in a think-aloud to show children how to make problem-solving decisions • Incorporates explicit systematic strategy instruction (summarizes key points and reviews key vocabulary or concepts before the lesson) • Models specific behaviors and strategies, such as how to handle measuring materials • Uses mnemonics or steps written on cards or posters to help children follow problem-solving steps • Uses peer-assisted learning in which another child can provide help to a child in need • Supplies families with additional support materials to use at home • Encourages children's use of self-regulation and self-instructional strategies, such as revising notes, writing summaries, and identifying main ideas • Teaches test-taking strategies (e.g., allows children to use a highlighter on tests to emphasize important information) • Slices back (Fuchs & Fuchs, 2001) to material from a previous grade level to ramp back up
Tier 3	A highly qualified special education teacher • Works one-on-one with a child • Uses tailored instruction based on specific areas of weakness • Modifies instructional methods, motivates children, and further adapts curricula • Uses explicit contextualization of skills-based instruction

1. Structure the environment
   - *Centralize attention.* Move the child close to the board or teacher. Face the children when you speak to them and use gestures. Where possible remove competing stimuli.
   - *Avoid confusion.* Word directions carefully and ask the child to repeat them. Give one direction at a time. Use the same language for consistency. For example, talk about base-ten materials as ones, tens, and hundreds rather than interchanging those names with "flats," "rods," and other words about their shape rather than their value.
   - *Create smooth transitions.* Ensure that transitions between activities have clear directions and that there are limited chances to get "off task."

2. Identify and remove potential barriers
   - *Find ways to help children remember.* Recognize that memory is often not a strong suit for children with disabilities and develop mnemonics (memory aids) for familiar steps or write directions that can be referred to throughout the lesson. For example, **STAR** is a mnemonic for problem solving: **S**earch the word problem for important information; **T**ranslate the words into models, pictures, or symbols; **A**nswer the problem; **R**eview your solution for reasonableness (Gagnon & Maccini, 2001).

Note that searching the word problem for important information is different from identifying "key words," because the use of a "key word approach" is not effective.

   - *Provide vocabulary and concept support.* Give explicit attention to vocabulary and symbols throughout the lesson. Preview essential terms and related prior knowledge/concepts, create a "math wall" of words and symbols to provide visual cues, and connect symbols to their precise meanings.
   - *Use "friendly" numbers.* Instead of using $6.13, use $6.00 to emphasize conceptual understanding rather than mixing computation and conceptual goals. Incorporate this technique when computation and operation skills are *not* the lesson objective.
   - *Vary the task size.* Children with learning disabilities can become frustrated by the enormity of the task. One way to address this problem is to assign children with disabilities fewer problems to solve.
   - *Adjust the visual display.* Design assessments and tasks so that there is not too much on a single page. The density of words, illustrations, and numbers on a page can be overwhelming for children with disabilities. Find ways to put only one problem on a page, increase the font size, or reduce the visual display. Be sure the visual displays support the meaning of the problem (rather than just unrelated clip art).

3. Provide clarity
   - *Reiterate the timeframe.* Give children additional reminders about the time left for exploring materials, completing tasks, or finishing assessments. This helps children with time management.
   - *Ask children to share their thinking.* Use the think-aloud method or think-pair-share strategy.
   - *Emphasize connections.* Provide concrete representations, pictorial representations, and numerical representations. Have children connect them through carefully phrased questions. Also connect visuals, meanings, and words. For example, as you count a series of items, point out that you touch each item, say the number name in sequence, and write the last number said as the total amount.
   - *Adapt delivery modes.* Incorporate a variety of materials, images, examples, and models for visual learners. Some children may need to have the problem or assessment read to them or generated with voice creation software. Provide written instructions in addition to oral instructions.
   - *Emphasize the relevant points.* Some children with disabilities may inappropriately focus on the color of a cube instead of the quantity of cubes.

- *Use methods for organizing written work.* Provide tools and templates so that children can focus on the mathematics rather than on the creation of a table or chart. Also use graphic organizers, picture-based models, and paper with columns or grids.
- *Provide examples and nonexamples.* To define triangles, give examples of triangles as well as shapes that are not triangles. Help children focus on the characteristics that differentiate the examples from the nonexamples.

4. Consider alternative assessments
   - *Propose alternative products.* Provide options for how to demonstrate understanding (e.g., a verbal response that is written by someone else, voice recorded, or modeled with a manipulative). Use voice recognition software or word prediction software that can generate a whole menu of word choices when children type a few letters.
   - *Encourage self-monitoring and self-assessment.* Children with learning disabilities often are not good at self-reflection. Asking them to review an assignment or assessment to explain what was difficult and what they think they got right can help them be more independent and take greater responsibility for their learning.
   - *Consider feedback charts.* Help children monitor their growth by charting progress over time.

5. Emphasize practice and summary
   - *Help children bring ideas together.* Create study guides that summarize the key mathematics concepts and support students as they review key concepts. Older children can begin to develop class study guides to transition into creating their own study guides by identifying, summarizing, and coordinating the big ideas.
   - *Provide extra practice.* Use carefully selected problems (not a large number) and allow the use of familiar physical models.

Not all of these strategies will apply to every lesson and to every child with special needs, but as you are thinking about a particular lesson and certain children in your class, you will find that many of these will apply and will allow your children to engage in the task and accomplish the learning goals of the lesson.

◈ Implementing Interventions

NCTM (2007) has gathered a set of effective, research-based approaches for teaching children with difficulties in mathematics (such as children needing interventions in tier 2 or tier 3 of a support system such as RtI), highlighting the use of several key strategies that are also suggested by Gersten, Beckmann, Clarke, Foegen, Marsh, Star, and Witzel (2009). These strategies include systematic and explicit instruction, think-alouds, concrete and visual representations of problems, peer-assisted learning activities, and formative assessment data provided to children and teachers. These interventions, proven to be effective for children with disabilities, may represent principles quite different from those at tier 1. The strategies described here are interventions for use with the small subset of children for whom the initial core instruction was ineffective.

Explicit Strategy Instruction

Explicit instruction is often characterized by highly structured, teacher-led instruction on a specific strategy. When engaging in this explicit instruction, you do not merely model the strategy and have children practice it; instead you try to illuminate your decision making—a process that may be troublesome for these particular learners. In this instructional strategy, after you assess the children so that you know what to model, you use a tightly scripted sequence that goes from modeling to prompting children through the model to practice. Your instruction is highly organized in a step-by-step format and involves teacher-led explanations of concepts and strategies, including the critical connection building and meaning making that help learners relate new knowledge with concepts they know. Let's look at a classroom teacher who is using explicit instruction:

> As you enter Mr. Logan's classroom, you see a small group of children seated at a table listening to the teacher's detailed explanation and watching his demonstration of addition concepts. The children are using manipulatives, as prescribed by Mr. Logan, and moving through carefully selected tasks. He tells the children to take out three cubes and asks them then to take out five more cubes. He asks the children, "Now how many do you have?" Mr. Logan asks, "Is *add* a word you know?" Then, to make sure they don't overcount, he asks them to talk about their reasoning process with the question, "What are some things you need to keep in mind as you put the two groups together?" Mr. Logan writes their responses on the adjacent board along with $3 + 5 = 8$. Then he asks them to talk about how many more they have than when they started with the three cubes and records their responses. The children take turns answering these questions out loud. During the lesson, Mr. Logan frequently stops the group, interjects points of clarification, and directly highlights critical components of the task. For example, he asks, "Can you count from three by adding the five cubes on?" and "Would it be better to count on from the five? Why?" Vocabulary words, such as *combine* and *equals*, are written on the "math word wall" nearby and the definitions of these terms are reviewed and reinforced throughout the lesson. At the completion of the lesson, the children are given several similar examples of the kind of combinations discussed in the lesson as independent practice.

A number of aspects of explicit instruction can be seen in Mr. Logan's approach to teaching addition concepts. He employs a teacher-directed teaching format, carefully describes the use of manipulatives, and incorporates a model-prompt-practice sequence. This sequence starts with verbal instructions and careful demonstrations with concrete models, followed by prompting, questioning, and then independent practice. The children are deriving mathematical knowledge from the teacher's oral, written, and visual clues.

As children with disabilities solve problems, explicit strategy instruction can help guide them in carrying out tasks. First ask the children to read and restate the problem; draw a picture; develop a plan by linking this problem to previous problems; write the problem in a mathematical sentence; break the problem into smaller pieces; carry out operations; and check answers with a calculator, hundreds chart, or other appropriate tools. These self-instructive prompts, or self-questions, structure the entire learning process from beginning to end. Unlike during more inquiry-based instruction, the teacher models these steps and explains the components with terminology that is easily understood by children with disabilities—children who did not discover them independently through initial tier 1 or tier 2 activities. Yet, consistent with what we know about how all children learn, children are still developing an understanding of the meaning of addition and are engaged in problem solving (not just in skill development).

Concrete models can support explicit strategy instruction. For example, when you demonstrate the properties of two-dimensional shapes, you might say, "Watch me. Now make a rectangle with these four toothpicks that looks just like mine." In contrast, a teacher with a more inquiry-oriented approach might say, "Using toothpicks, how can you show me a rectangle?" Although initially more structured, the use of concrete models will provide access to more abstract concepts and can eventually lead to generalizations.

There are a number of possible advantages to using explicit strategy instruction for children with disabilities. This approach helps you make more explicit for these children the covert thinking strategies that others use in mathematical problem solving at a slower pace.

Although these students hear other children's thinking strategies in the *After* phase of each lesson, they frequently cannot keep up with the rapid pace of the sharing. Without extra time to reprocess the conversation, children with disabilities may not have access to these strategies. More explicit approaches are also less dependent on the children's ability to draw ideas from past experience or to operate in a self-directed manner.

Explicit strategy instruction can also have distinct disadvantages for children with disabilities. Some aspects of this approach rely on memorizing, which can be one of their weakest skills. Taking a known weakness and building a learning strategy around it is not productive. There is also the concern that highly teacher-controlled approaches promote long-term dependency on teacher assistance. This is of particular concern for children with disabilities because many are described as passive learners.

Children learn what they have the opportunity to practice. Children who are never given opportunities to engage in self-directed learning (based on the assumption that this is not an area of strength) will be deprived of the opportunity to develop skills in this area. In fact, the best explicit instruction is scaffolded, meaning it moves from a highly structured, single-strategy approach toward multiple models, including examples and nonexamples. It also includes immediate error correction followed by the fading of prompts to help children move to independence. Explicit instruction, to be effective, must include making mathematical relationships explicit (so that children, rather than only learning how to do that day's mathematics, make connections to other mathematical ideas). Because making connections is a major component in how children learn, it must be central to instructional strategies for children with disabilities.

Concrete, Semi-Concrete, Abstract (CSA)

The CSA (concrete, semi-concrete, abstract) intervention has been used in mathematics education in a variety of forms for years (Heddens, 1964; Witzel, 2005). Based on the reasoning theory of Bruner (1966), this model reflects a sequence that begins with an instructional focus on concrete representations (manipulative materials) and tools, then moves to semi-concrete representations (drawings or pictures) and abstraction (using only numerals or mentally solving problems) over time. Built into this approach is the return to visual models and concrete representations as children need them or as they begin to explore new concepts or extensions of concepts learned previously. As children share reasoning that shows they are beginning to understand the mathematical concept, there can be a shift to semi-concrete representations. This is not to say that CSA is a rigid approach that moves to abstraction only after the other phases. Instead, it is essential that there be parallel modeling of number symbols throughout this approach to explicitly relate concrete models and visual representations to their corresponding numerals and equations.

CSA also includes modeling the mental conversations that go on in your mind as you help children articulate their own thinking. Again, as you articulate your thought processes using an appropriate model for a child, your choice of a reasoning strategy and model should be based on evidence from the child's performance on targeted assessments. In the last component of CSA, children are capable of working with abstract aspects of the concepts without an emphasis on concrete or semi-concrete images.

Peer-Assisted Learning

Children with special needs also benefit from other children's modeling and support (Fuchs, Fuchs, Yazdian, & Powell, 2002). The basic notion is that children learn best when they are placed in the role of an apprentice working with a more skilled peer or "expert." Although the peer-assisted learning approach shares some of the characteristics of the explicit strategy instruction model, it is different because knowledge is presented on an "as-needed" basis as opposed to a predetermined sequence. The children can be paired with older children or peers who have a more sophisticated understanding of a concept. At other times, tutors and tutees can reverse roles during the tasks. Having children with disabilities "teach" others is an important part of the learning process, so giving children with special needs a chance to explain concepts to another child is valuable.

Think-Alouds

When you use a think-aloud as an instructional strategy, you demonstrate the steps to accomplish a task while verbalizing the thinking process and reasoning that accompany the steps. Remember, don't start where your thinking is—assess and start where the child's thinking is. The child follows this instruction by imitating your process of "talking through" a solution on a different but parallel task. This is similar to the model in which "expert" learners share strategies with "novice" learners.

Consider a problem in which first graders are given the task of determining which child is taller by lying on the floor. Rather than merely demonstrating, for example, how to use a ruler to measure the children, the think-aloud strategy would involve talking through the steps and identifying the reasons for each step while measuring each child with connecting cubes and comparing the difference between the children's heights. As you place a mark on the floor to indicate where the cubes start, you might state, "I used this line to mark off where Rebecca's foot ends. How should I use this line as I measure Rebecca? I know I have to add on cubes, but how do I know when to stop?" "How can I use both lines of cubes to figure out if Rebecca is taller than Emma?" All of this dialogue occurs prior to placing the ruler for a second measurement. Often teachers share alternatives about how else they could have carried out the task. When you use this metacognitive strategy, try to talk about and model possible approaches (and the reasons behind these approaches) in an effort to make your invisible thinking processes visible to the children.

Although you can choose any of these strategies as needed, your goal is always to work toward a high level of student responsibility for learning. Movement to higher levels of content understanding can be likened to the need to move to a higher level on a hill. For some, formal stair steps with support along the way are necessary (explicit strategy instruction); for others ramps with encouragement at the top of the hill will work (peer-assisted learning). Others can find a path up the hill on their own with some guidance from visual representations (CSA approach). All people can relate to the need to have different support during different times of their lives or under different circumstances, and it is no different for children with special needs (see Table 6.2). Yet these children must eventually learn to create a path to new learning on their own, as that is what will be required in the real world after formal education ends. Leaving children knowing only how to climb steps with support and face hills with constant assistance and encouragement from others will not help them attain their life goals.

◆ Adapting for Children with Moderate or Severe Disabilities

Children with moderate/severe disabilities often need extensive modifications and individualized supports to learn mathematics. This population of children may include those with severe autism, sensory disorders, limitations affecting movement, cerebral palsy, processing disorders such as intellectual disabilities, and combinations of multiple disabilities.

Originally, the curriculum for children with severe disabilities was called "functional," in that it often focused on life skills such as managing money, telling time, using a calculator, measuring, and matching numbers to complete such tasks as entering a telephone number or identifying a house number. Now directives and assessments have broadened the curriculum to address the content strands that were specifically delineated by grade level in the *Common Core State Standards* (CCSSO, 2010).

Table 6.2 Common Stumbling Blocks for Children with Disabilities

Stumbling Blocks	What Will I Notice?	What Should I Do?
Child has trouble forming mental representations of mathematical concepts	• Can't interpret a number line • Has difficulty identifying a triangle when the top of the triangle points down	• Use larger versions of the representation (e.g., number line) so that children can move to or interact with the model • Explicitly teach the representation—for example, exactly how to draw a triangle while identifying the critical properties
Child has difficulty accessing numerical meanings from symbols (issues with number sense)	• Has difficulty with basic facts; for example, doesn't recognize that 3 + 5 is the same as 5 + 3, or that 5 + 1 is the same as the next counting number after 5 • Does not understand the meaning of the equal sign • Can't interpret whether an answer is reasonable	• Explicitly teach multiple ways of representing a number showing the variations at exactly the same time • Use a number balance to support understanding of the equal sign • Use multiple representations for a single problem to show how it would be carried out in a variety of ways (base-ten blocks, illustrations, and numbers) rather than using multiple problems
Child is challenged to keep numbers and information in working memory	• Loses counts of objects • Gets confused when other children share multiple strategies during the *After* portion of the lesson • Forgets how to start the problem-solving process	• Use ten-frames or organizational mats to help the child organize counts • Explicitly model using counters or how to use skip counting to count • Record (in writing) the ideas of other children during discussions • Incorporate a chart that lists the main steps in problem solving as an independent guide or make bookmarks with questions the children can ask themselves as self-prompts
Child lacks organizational skills and the ability to self-regulate	• Misses steps in a process • Writes computations in a way that is random and hard to follow	• Use routines as often as possible or provide self-monitoring checklists to prompt steps along the way • Use graph paper to record problems or numbers • Create math word walls for reference
Child misapplies rules or overgeneralizes	• Applies rules such as "Always subtract the smaller from the larger" too literally, resulting in errors such as 25 − 9 = 24	• Always give examples as well as counterexamples to show how and when "rules" should be used and when they should not • Tie all rules into conceptual understanding; don't emphasize memorizing rote procedures or practices

At a beginning level, children work on identifying numbers by holding up fingers or selecting an amount on a picture. To develop number sense, counting up can be linked to counting daily tasks to be accomplished, and counting down can mark a period of cleanup after an activity or to complete self-care routines (brushing teeth). Children with moderate or severe disabilities should have opportunities to use measuring tools, compare graphs, explore place-value concepts (sometimes linked to money use), use the number line, and compare quantities. When possible, the content should be connected to life skills and features of jobs—shopping skills and activities in which food is prepared are both options for mathematical problem solving. At other times, you can link mathematical learning objectives to everyday events in a practical way. For example, when the operation of addition is studied, figuring how many forks are needed for two groups would be appropriate. Children can also undertake a small project such as making a placemat for lunch as a way to explore shapes and measurements.

Do not believe that all basic addition and subtraction facts must be mastered before children with moderate or severe disabilities can move forward in the curriculum; children can learn geometric or measuring concepts without having mastered all basic facts. Geometry for children with moderate or severe disabilities is more than merely identifying shapes; it is critical for being oriented in the real world through interpreting street signs in the local area. Children who learn to count bus stops and judge time can be helped to navigate their world successfully.

Table 6.3 offers ideas across the curriculum that are appropriate for teaching children with moderate to severe disabilities.

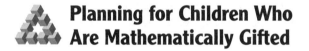

Planning for Children Who Are Mathematically Gifted

Children who are mathematically gifted include those who have a high level of ability or interest. Some may be gifted with an intuitive knowledge of mathematical concepts, whereas others have a passion for the subject even though they may have to work hard to learn it. Many children's giftedness becomes apparent to parents and teachers when they grasp and articulate mathematics concepts at an age earlier than expected. They are often found to make connections between topics of study easily and frequently are unable to explain how they quickly got an answer (Rotigel & Fello, 2005). Many teachers have a keen ability to spot talent when they note children who have strong number sense or visual/spatial sense (Gavin & Sheffield, 2010). Note that these teachers are not pointing to children who are fast and speedy with their basic addition and subtraction facts but to those who have the ability to reason and make sense of mathematics.

Do not wait for children to demonstrate their mathematical talent; instead develop it through a challenging set of tasks and inquiry-based instruction (VanTassel-Baska & Brown, 2007). Generally, as previously described in the RtI model, high-quality core instruction is able to respond to the varying needs of diverse learners, including the talented and gifted. Yet for some of your gifted children, the core instruction proves not to be enough of a challenge. The curriculum for these advanced learners should be adapted to consider level, complexity, breadth, depth, and pace (Assouline & Lupkowski-Shoplik, 2011; Renzulli, Gubbins, McMillen, Eckert, & Little, 2009; Saul, Assouline, & Sheffield, 2010).

There are four basic categories for adapting mathematics content for gifted mathematics children: *acceleration*, *enrichment* (depth), *sophistication* (complexity), and *novelty* (Gallagher & Gallagher, 1994; Ravenna, 2008). In each category, your children should apply rather than just acquire information. The emphasis on implementing and extending ideas must overshadow the mental collection of facts and concepts.

Table 6.3 Activities for Children with Moderate or Severe Disabilities

Content Area	Activity
Number and operations	• Count out a variety of items for general classroom activities. • Create a list of supplies that need to be ordered for the classroom or a particular event and calculate cost. • Calculate the number of calories in a given meal. • Compare the cost of two meals on menus from local restaurants.
Algebra	• Show a cumulating allowance on a chart to show growth over time. • Write an equation to show how much allowance the child will earn in a month.
Geometry	• Use spatial relationships to identify a path between two locations on a map. • Use tangrams to put shapes together or fill a space. This activity can develop important workplace skills such as packing boxes or organizing supplies on shelves.
Measurement	• Fill differently shaped items with water, sand, or rice to assess volume, ordering the containers from least to most. • Take body temperature and use an enlarged thermometer to show comparison to outside temperatures. • Calculate the amount of border needed to decorate the bottom edge of the bulletin board. • Identify the time for lunch.
Data analysis and probability	• Survey children on favorite games and use the top five as choices for the class. Make a bar graph to represent and compare the results. • Tally the number of children ordering school lunch. • Examine the outside temperatures for the past week and estimate the temperatures for the next two days.

Acceleration

Acceleration recognizes that your children may already understand the mathematics content that you plan to teach. Some teachers use "curriculum compacting" (Reis & Renzulli, 2005) to give a short overview of the content and assess the children's ability to respond to mathematics tasks that would demonstrate their proficiency. Another option is to reduce the amount of time these children spend on aspects of the topic or moving to more advanced content at the next grade level or beyond. Allowing children to increase the pace of their own learning can give them access to curriculum different from their grade level while demanding more independent study. However, moving children to higher mathematics (by moving them up a grade, for example) will not succeed in engaging them as learners if the instruction is still at a slow pace. Research reveals that when gifted children are accelerated through the curriculum, they become more likely to explore STEM (science, technology, engineering, and mathematics) fields (Sadler & Tai, 2007).

Enrichment

Enrichment activities go beyond the topic of study to content that is not specifically a part of your grade-level curriculum but is an extension of the original mathematical tasks. For example, while studying place value, mathematically gifted children can stretch their knowledge to study other bases, such as base five. This provides an extended view of how our base-ten numeration system fits within the broader system. Other times the format of enrichment can involve studying the same topic as the rest of the class while differing on the means and outcomes of the work. Examples include group investigations, solving real problems in the community, writing letters to outside audiences, and identifying applications of the mathematics learned.

Sophistication

Another strategy is to increase the sophistication of a topic by raising the level of complexity or pursuing greater depth of content possibly outside of the regular curriculum or by connecting mathematics to other subject areas. Frequently gifted children explore topics similar to those of their classmates but focus on higher-level thinking and more complex or abstract ideas. This can mean exploring a larger set of ideas in which a mathematics topic exists. For example, while studying a unit on place value, mathematically gifted children can deepen their knowledge to study other numeration systems such as Roman, Mayan, Egyptian, and Babylonian. This study provides a multicultural view of how our numeration system fits within the historical number systems (Mack, 2011).

Novelty

Novelty introduces completely different material from the regular curriculum and frequently occurs in after-school clubs, out-of-class projects, or collaborative school experiences. In collaborative experiences, children from a variety of grades and classes may volunteer for special mathematics projects with a classroom teacher, principal, or resource teacher taking the lead. The novelty category includes having children explore topics that are within their developmental grasp but outside the curriculum. For example, children may explore how to build structures with toothpicks and gumdrops or Styrofoam peanuts and then use the characteristics of the successful constructions to decide which designs are stable and which are not, sorting the structures using an "in or out" reasoning approach. They may also explore a large-scale investigation of the amount of food thrown away at lunchtime or the amount of water flushed in the school's bathroom. Another aspect of the novelty approach provides different options for children in culminating performances of their understanding, such as demonstrating their knowledge through inventions, experiments, simulations, dramatizations, visual displays, and oral presentations.

Strategies to Avoid

There are a number of ineffective approaches for gifted children that find their way into classrooms. Following are five common ones:

1. *Assigning more of the same work.* This is the least appropriate way to respond to mathematically gifted children and the most likely to result in children eventually hiding their abilities. This approach is described by Persis Herold as "all scales and no music" (quoted in Tobias, 1995, p. 168).

2. *Giving free time to early finishers.* Although children may find this rewarding, it does not maximize their intellectual growth and can lead to hurrying to finish a task.

3. *Assigning gifted children to help struggling learners.* Routinely assigning gifted children to teach other children who have not achieved what the gifted students have mastered does not stimulate their intellectual growth and can place them in a socially uncomfortable and undesirable situation. Consistently using this approach puts mathematically talented children in a constant position of tutoring rather than allowing them to create deeper and more complex levels of understanding.

4. *Providing gifted pull-out opportunities.* Unfortunately, generalized gifted programs are often unrelated to the regular mathematics curriculum (Assouline & Lupkowski-Shoplik,

2011). Although it can benefit students, add-on experiences are not enough. Gifted students need adaptations to the instruction in their mathematics classroom. Learners with a high level of ability can't get one-stop shopping in a gifted program that focuses on all academic subjects; they need individual attention to develop depth and more complex understanding of mathematics.

5. *Offering independent enrichment on the computer.* This practice often does not engage children with mathematics in a way that will enhance conceptual understanding and support their ability to justify their thinking to others. However, there are some excellent enrichment opportunities on the Internet that provide these kinds of experiences.

Sheffield (1999) writes that gifted children should be introduced to the "joys and frustrations of thinking deeply about a wide range of original, open-ended, or complex problems that encourage them to respond creatively in ways that are original, fluent, flexible and elegant" (p. 46). Accommodations, modifications, and interventions for mathematically gifted children must strive for this goal.

Stop and Reflect

How is equity in the classroom different from teaching all children equitably? ■

7

Collaborating with Families, Community, and Principals

With students, parents and teachers all on the same page and working together for shared goals, we can ensure that students make progress each year and graduate from school prepared to succeed in college and in a modern workforce.

CCSSO (2010)

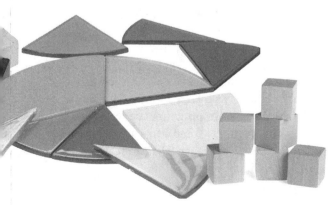

Parental and Community Support for Mathematics

Teaching mathematics developmentally, addressing the increased content demands articulated in the Common Core State Standards Initiative (CCSSO, 2010), and ensuring that children are mathematically proficient requires everyone's commitment. Numerous studies have found a positive relationship between the level of parental involvement and their child's achievement in school (e.g., Aspiazu, Bauer, & Spillett, 1998; Henderson et al., 2002).

We often hear educators make statements such as "You must have the principal's support" and "You need to get parents on board," and we nod our heads in agreement. But knowing what administrative and parental support looks like and recognizing how to get it are less clear. In this chapter, we discuss ideas for developing a collaborative community that understands and is able to support high-quality mathematics teaching and learning for every student.

Parents know the importance of mathematics for their child's future. They participate in their child's learning by supporting homework, volunteering at school, and meeting with teachers, even if they may recall unpleasant experiences or difficulties with school mathematics from their own schooling. Understanding that memories of mathematics classes are not always pleasant for parents and appreciating parental support will prepare us to suitably identify for parents the mathematics goals that children should be experiencing in the twenty-first century. Communication with parents is key to encouraging their support and involves using one-way, two-way, and three-way communication strategies (see Figure 7.1).

Figure 7.1 Ways to communicate with families.

One-Way Communication Strategies	Letters sharing the goals of a unit	Websites where resources and curriculum information are posted	Newsletters
Two-Way Communication Strategies	Log of student work (signed or commented on by parent)	PTA meetings, open house	One-on-one meetings, class or home visits
Three-Way (or More) Communication Strategies	Family math night	Conferences (with parent and child)	Log or journal of student learning with input from child, parent, and teacher

◆ Communicating Mathematics Goals

Every year, parents need opportunities to get information directly from the school leaders and teachers about their child's mathematics program, including the kind of instruction that might differ from what they experienced in their own schooling. For example, even if your school has been engaged in implementing a mathematics program for a decade that reflects the NCTM *Principles and Standards for School Mathematics* and now the *Common Core State Standards*, the program will still be new to the parents of your children. Changes to the mathematics curriculum—new textbooks, new technologies, new philosophies—are all perfect reasons for communicating with parents. This interaction is one of the most important components of successfully implementing a standards-based mathematics curriculum (Bay, Reys, & Reys, 1999). Without such opportunities, parents may draw their own conclusions about the effectiveness of the mathematics curriculum, develop frustrations and negative opinions about what is happening in their child's classroom or school, and communicate this apprehension to other parents. Table 7.1 highlights questions parents commonly ask about standards-based mathematics programs.

Providing a forum for parents around mathematics highlights the importance of the subject and gives parents confidence that your school is a great place for preparing their children for upper elementary school and beyond.

Be proactive! Don't wait for concerns or questions to percolate. Some early action strategies include engaging parents in family and community math nights, positive homework practices and parent coaching sessions, and sharing where to find mathematics-related resources for their children (e.g., websites and manipulatives). Let's discuss each.

◆ Family and Community Math Nights

There are many ways to conduct a family or community mathematics event, such as including a mathematics component in a back-to-school night, a PTA meeting, or hosting a showcase for a new mathematics program. Critical to this plan is to provide opportunities for parents to be learners of mathematics so they experience what it means to *do mathematics* (just like their children).

Teaching Tip

A back-to-school night is a great time to have parent–child teams experience working together on mathematics tasks.

Table 7.1 Categories of Parent Questions Related to Standards-Based Mathematics

Category	Types of Questions
Pedagogy	• Why isn't the teacher teaching? (And what is the point of reinventing the wheel?) • Are children doing their own work when they are in groups? Is my child having to do the work of children who don't understand the work? • Why is there so much reading and writing in math class? • Why is my child struggling more than before?
Content	• Is my child learning the basic skills? • Why is my child learning different ways (than I learned) for doing the operations? • Will my child be on track for Algebra I in eighth grade? Ninth grade? • Where are the math topics I am used to seeing and why are there topics I never learned? • Is my child learning mathematics or just doing activities?
Evidence	• Is there any evidence that this approach or curriculum is effective? • Will my child do better on state/national standardized tests with this new approach? • Will this prepare my child for middle school, high school, college, and beyond?
Understanding	• Why is mathematics teaching changing? • How can I help my child [with homework; to be successful]? • Where can I learn more about the *Common Core State Standards*?

Source: Adapted from Bay-Williams, J. M., & Meyer, M. R. (2003). What Parents Want to Know about Standards-Based Mathematics Curricula. *Principal Leadership, 3*(7), 54–60. Copyright 2003, National Association of Secondary School Principals. For more information on NASSP products and services to promote excellence in middle-level and high school leadership, visit www.nassp.org.

When choosing mathematical tasks to use with parents, be sure the tasks focus on content that really matters to them and relates to what they already know is a part of the elementary curriculum (e.g., addition and subtraction, including basic facts, as well as place value are good ideas in grades K–2). There are tasks throughout this text that are ideal for a math night. Figure 7.2 contrasts two examples of first-grade problems for learning about combinations (sums) that make 6—one that is a teaching-by-telling (traditional) experience (solve the problems as modeled by the teacher using counters) and one that is designed for a teaching-through-problem-solving experience (explore and find different combinations).

Stop and Reflect

What distinctions do you notice between the two tasks? What is valued as "doing mathematics" in both of the problems? ◾

The contrasting addition problems are perfect for discussing with parents what it means to do mathematics because they (1) address critical areas in the *Common Core State Standards* and focal points in the *Curriculum Focal Points*, (2) involve using manipulatives (color tiles or counters), (3) connect the mathematical ideas of partitioning and addition, and (4) (in the latter example) have multiple solution strategies.

Figure 7.2 Problems to explore at a parent or community night.

Problem Set 1: Find the answers to these equations. Use counters or draw pictures to show your work.

1 + 5 = _____   0 + 6 = _____

3 + 3 = _____   2 + 4 = _____

Problem Set 2: The parking lot has only blue and red cars. There are 6 cars parked. How many blue and how many red cars might be in the parking lot? Use counters to find as many ways as you can. Draw a picture and write an equation for each answer.

Extensions: Can you find all of the ways to have 6 red and blue cars in the parking lot? How many ways can you find to have a total of 5 cars? How many ways can you find to have a total of 7 cars? Do you see a pattern?

The potential each of these problems has to support and challenge children in making sense of mathematics should be made explicit during a discussion with parents. After giving parents time to do both tasks and discuss solution strategies (as you would with children), connect the learning experience to their questions and concerns. Ask participants to consider the learning opportunities in the two contrasting tasks. Ask questions such as the following:

- What skills are being developed in each problem?
- Which problem gives more opportunity to make connections between mathematics and the real world?
- Which task would your child be more motivated to solve? Why?

Help parents identify the depth of the mathematics in the teaching-through-problem-solving task. In grades K–2 children are building important foundations of number and operations through algebraic reasoning—looking for patterns, reasoning, and generalizing. Help parents see these aspects in the car combination problem. Share the CCSSO and or the NCTM standards (in parent-friendly language), and focus on the goal of having children becoming mathematically proficient as described in those standards. Ask "Where do you see these proficiencies being supported in the two tasks we did?"

Another good choice for family math nights is basic fact strategies, as addition and subtraction facts are a central part of the curriculum in grades 1–2, and developing *reasoning strategies* is essential to learning the facts well. (Parents may only know flash cards or other memorization activities.) See Chapter 10 for the three phases of fact mastery, as well as games and activities for developing reasoning strategies.

Teaching Tip

Provide copies of the appropriate *Common Core State Standards* Introduction and Overview pages (the first two pages for each grade) and allow parents time to think about each "Critical Area."

Address any or all of the questions in Table 7.1 that apply to your setting. One way to do this is to have parents write their questions on note cards and collect them so you can identify common questions and decide the order in which to discuss each question. The sections that follow provide possible responses to questions that parents (or community members) commonly ask.

Pedagogy

When parents ask questions that point to their belief that mathematics is best learned through direct instruction (just as they learned it), remind them of the experiences they had in *doing* mathematics with the car combination task. Point to the difference between *being shown* how to do something (e.g., "This is how you add; now practice this") and developing an understanding of something (e.g., "How many ways can you partition 6? How do you know if you have found all the ways?"). You can help parents identify the skills and concepts that are developed through these two experiences. Ask, "In what ways are children learning about addition? About subtraction? How do the different ways support eventual mastery of the basic facts?" Point out that skills are still important, and children benefit by generating their own procedures. Explicitly promote the fact that a developmental approach to learning mathematics provides the means for children to (1) use prior knowledge, (2) make connections, (3) use alternative strategies and reasoning, (4) apply mathematical ideas to new situations, and (5) develop positive dispositions about being able to do mathematics. Share example tasks such as these:

$$9 + 6 \qquad 6 + 28 \qquad 57 + 26$$

Ask parents to partition 6 to solve these problems mentally. Connect to the meaning of "procedural fluency" and the benefit in having children generate their own procedures, and connect those procedures to a strong understanding of number and operations.

Role of the Teacher

Similarly, address the role of the teacher as *organizer* (organizes a worthwhile mathematical task), *facilitator* (facilitates student interaction), and *questioner* (asks questions to help children make connections or to deepen their understanding). Remind parents that just because the teacher is not *telling* their child what to do does not mean that the teacher is not teaching. The teacher is orchestrating the class so that each child develops the ability to solve problems independently.

Cooperative Groups

Parents may also wonder about the frequency of their children working in cooperative groups because it may differ from their own mathematics learning experiences. Help parents see the role of others in their learning as they solved the problems and as they heard solutions from those who were working at other tables. Connect that experience to the value of cooperative learning. You can do this in a variety of ways:

1. *Include a feature in your parent newsletter*. Early in the year you can feature cooperative learning, addressing its importance across content areas. In mathematics this can include the following benefits: hearing different strategies, building meaning, designing solution strategies, and justifying approaches—all essential to building a strong understanding of mathematics and important life skills.

2. *Send home letters introducing mathematics units of study*. If you are about to teach a unit on adding and subtracting two-digit numbers, a letter can help parents know the important aspects of the content. This is a great time to mention that children will work in groups so that they can see different ways to add or subtract two numbers.

3. *Do a cooperative learning mathematics activity at a family math night or back-to-school event*. Use a task that involves assigning roles to different members of the group and that won't take long to solve. Have parents work with two to three others to solve the task.

4. *Invite parents to assist in a mathematics group assignment*. Seeing firsthand the dialogue and thinking that happens in cooperative groups can go a long way in illustrating how valuable cooperative groups can be!

Parents may worry that children working in groups are simply copying from others and not learning. Share strategies you use to build in individual accountability and shared responsibility. For example, teachers may ask each child to record explanations in his or her notebook. At other times, you may assign specific roles to each member of the group.

Teaching Tip

Being proactive about communicating the benefits of cooperative learning, as well as how you build in individual accountability and shared responsibility, will go a long way toward converting parent concerns into parent support.

Use of Technology

Parents may be avid users of technology yet still have concerns about their child using calculators and computers in grades pre-K–2, when they haven't yet mastered their basic facts for addition and subtraction. Even though research overwhelmingly finds that children using calculators achieve at least as much as those not using calculators, the calculator is widely blamed for children's lack of reasoning and sense making. Reassure parents that children *will* learn the basic facts and procedures and the calculator can support that learning. Consider sharing or doing any of the following activities:

1. Type in 5 + 5 = . Continue to push the = key (most calculators continue to add 5 every time you push =). What patterns do you notice as you count by fives?

2. Broken Key. Suppose the following keys do not work on your calculator: 5 and 8. Figure out another way to add or subtract these numbers using the calculator:

$$6 + 5 \qquad 15 - 6 \qquad 35 + 28$$

Teaching Tip

Families need to see specific ways to use the calculator to support learning of numbers and operations. Sharing or posting calculator activities is one way to help them understand the role calculators can play in young children's learning.

Debrief with parents about the ways in which the calculator can be used as a learning tool. Mastery of facts should *not* be a prerequisite to using a calculator. Instead, children and teachers should be making good decisions about whether a calculator supports or detracts from doing the problem at hand.

Practice and Problem Solving

Parents may also wonder why there are fewer skill/practice problems (and more story problems). Effective mathematics learning environments are rich in language. Real mathematics involves more "word" problems and far fewer "naked number" skill problems. Especially with young children, it is the context or story that provides the concrete experiences they need in order to reason about and understand the abstract numbers and symbols they are using. In contrast to when the parents went to school, computational skills are now less needed in the workplace because of available technology, but the importance of number sense, reasoning, and being able to solve real problems has increased. Because some children struggle with reading and/or writing, share with parents strategies you use to help children understand and solve story problems (see Figure 7.3).

Parents may worry when they see their child struggle with a single mathematics problem because they may believe that fast means successful. But faster isn't smarter! Cathy Seeley's book with this same title (Seeley, 2009) is a great read on this topic written for families, educators, and policy makers. Seeley offers 41 brief messages, many of which can address parent questions about mathematics (e.g., "A Math Message to Families: Helping Students Prepare for the Future," "Putting Calculators in Their Place: The Role of Calculators and Computation in the Classroom," and "Do It in Your Head: The Power of Mental Math"). Explain that engaging children in productive struggle is one of the two most effective ways teachers can help children develop conceptual understanding (the other being to make connections between mathematical ideas) (Bay-Williams, 2010; Hiebert & Grouws, 2007). Rather than presenting a series of simpler problems for children to practice, standards-based curriculum characteristically focuses on fewer tasks, each of which provides children with an opportunity for higher-level thinking, multiple-strategy solutions, and more time focused on mathematics learning.

Figure 7.3

Share with parents how you support reading and problem solving.

Reading Strategies for Math Problems

- Read math story problem aloud (whole class)
- Read a math story problem with a friend
- Say or write the question in the problem
- Draw a picture of the problem
- Act out the problem
- Use a graphic organizer (recording page with problem-solving prompts)
- Discuss math vocabulary
- Play math vocabulary games

Figure 7.4   Standard 1 from Standards for Mathematical Practice (CCSSO, 2010).

---

1. Make sense of problems and persevere in solving them.

Mathematically proficient students start by explaining to themselves the meaning of a problem and looking for entry points to its solution. They analyze givens, constraints, relationships, and goals. They make conjectures about the form and meaning of the solution and plan a solution pathway rather than simply jumping into a solution attempt. They consider analogous problems, and try special cases and simpler forms of the original problem in order to gain insight into its solution. They monitor and evaluate their progress and change course if necessary. Older students might, depending on the context of the problem, transform algebraic expressions or change the viewing window on their graphing calculator to get the information they need. Mathematically proficient students can explain correspondences between equations, verbal descriptions, tables, and graphs or draw diagrams of important features and relationships, graph data, and search for regularity or trends. Younger students might rely on using concrete objects or pictures to help conceptualize and solve a problem. Mathematically proficient students check their answers to problems using a different method, and they continually ask themselves, "Does this make sense?" They can understand the approaches of others to solving complex problems and identify correspondences between different approaches.

Share the first Standard for Mathematical Practice (see Figure 7.4) and ask the parents what they notice. Focus on the importance of *perseverance*. This is true in mathematics and in life. Reassure parents that some tasks take longer because of the nature of the task, not because their child lacks understanding. Mathematics is not nearly as much about speed and memorization as it is about being able to grapple with a novel problem, try various approaches from a variety of options, and finally reach an accurate answer.

Mathematics Content

A common concern of parents is that their children are not learning their basic facts and standard algorithms. You must address (at least) two points related to these issues. First, the skills that parents are looking for (e.g., U.S. standard algorithm for subtraction) are still there—they just look different because they are presented in a way based on understanding rather than memorization. Standard algorithms are still taught, but they are taught *along with* invented strategies that build on children's number sense and reasoning. Let parents experience that both invented and standard algorithms are important in being mathematically proficient by inviting them to solve the following problems.

$$69 + 47 = \underline{\hspace{1cm}} \qquad 309 - 288 = \underline{\hspace{1cm}}$$

$$487 + 345 = \underline{\hspace{1cm}} + 355$$

Ask for volunteers to share the ways that they thought about the problems. For the subtraction problem, for example, the following might be shared:

- 300 take away 288 is 12, then add the 9 back on to get 21.
- 288 up to 300 is 12 and up 9 more is 21.
- 309 to 300 is 9, then down to 290 is 10 more (19), and then to 288 is 2 more (21).

These invented strategies, over numerous problems, reinforce place-value concepts and the relationship between addition and subtraction. Noticing that these values are both near

300 helps the problem solver to select a strategy. This bird's-eye view of the problem is important in doing mathematics rather than always doing the same thing no matter what the numbers. This is very evident in the third example, which can be solved without computation if the relationship between the numbers is noticed first.

Second, what is "basic" in the twenty-first century is much more than computation. Many topics in the elementary curriculum were not a part of the curriculum a generation ago (e.g., connections of algebra to the operations). Looking together through the essential concepts in the *Common Core State Standards* or the NCTM *Curriculum Focal Points* helps parents see that the curriculum is not just an idea generated at their child's school but the national consensus on what students need to learn as well.

Student Achievement

At the heart of parents' interest in school mathematics is wanting their child to be successful, not only in the current classroom but also at the next level of school and later on in high-stakes assessments like the ACT or SAT for college entrance. If your state has implemented the *Common Core State Standards,* you can share that the standards are for K–12 and are designed to prepare students for college and future careers. The *Common Core State Standards* website (http://corestandards.org) has an increasing number of resources for parents to help them ensure their child is college and career ready.

Another approach to inform parents about student achievement is to share research on the *ineffectiveness* of the traditional U.S. approach to mathematics. The Trends in International Mathematics and Science Study (TIMSS), an international study conducted regularly and including many countries, continues to find that U.S. students achieve at an average level in fourth grade and then score lower in mathematics than international students from that point on. Discuss the implications of unpreparedness for students who want to seek higher-paying jobs on what is now an international playing field.

Parents may be more interested in how your specific school is doing in preparing children for the future. Share evidence from your school of mathematics success, including stories about an individual child (no name given) or the success of a particular classroom, like the following one received by a principal:

> I was worried at the start of the year because my son didn't have a lot of confidence in math and he was coming home with problems that he was supposed to figure out his own way to solve. I wondered why the teacher hadn't shown him how to add or subtract. But now I can really see his number sense—he has all kinds of ways he adds numbers and can do it in his head. And he is really good at solving and writing his own story problems! As an aside, I am also learning a lot—I didn't learn this way, but I am finding the homework problems are really interesting as we figure them out. I am just curious if this is something he will get to do again in second grade, or if this is just the way first-grade teachers introduce the ideas.

Such communications help parents see that there is a transition period and that in the end a standards-based approach helps engage children and build their understanding over time.

◈ Homework Practices and Parent Coaching

The way in which parents are involved in homework can make a difference in children's attitudes and learning, particularly at the elementary level (Cooper, 2007; Else-Quest, Hyde, & Hejmadi, 2008; Patall, Cooper, & Robinson, 2008). For example, children perform better when parents provide a quiet environment and establish rules about homework completion. Also, a parent's emotions are connected to the child's emotions, and positive emotions are connected to better performance (Else-Quest, Hyde, & Hejmadi, 2008). Therefore, parents who exhibit positive interest, humor, and pride in their child's homework support their child's mathematics learning.

You may have heard parents say, "I am not good at math" or "I don't like solving math problems." Parents may feel this way and, given the research just described, it is particularly important to redirect parents to portray mathematics in a positive light. For example, "Even though math can be hard, stick with it and you will figure it out." Teaching parents how to help their children has also been found to make a difference in supporting student achievement (Cooper, 2007).

How do you effectively encourage children and their families to support mathematics learning at home? Here we break down the many possible ways into four categories: parents' participation, homework support, resources for parents, and beyond-homework experiences.

Parents' Participation

If parents can witness firsthand your questioning and the many ways that problems can be solved, they will have a vision of how they can support learning at home. For example, they may notice that you encourage children to select their own strategy and explain how they know it works. They will also pick up on the language that you are using and will be able to reinforce that language at home. You can even provide a note-taking template that includes categories such as the following: What is the big idea of the lesson? What illustrations or tools are being used to help children understand? What are some questions the teacher is asking that I could also ask? What does the teacher do when a child is stuck?

Homework Support

Homework can be a positive experience for children, families, and the teacher. Take the following recommendations into consideration when thinking about the homework that you will assign to your children.

1. *Mimic the three-phase lesson model.* Complete a brief version of the *Before* phase of a lesson to be sure the children understand the homework task before they go home. At home, children complete the *During* phase. When they return with the work completed, apply the sharing techniques of the *After* phase of the homework. Children can even practice the *After* phase with their family if this is encouraged through communications to parents or guardians. Some form of written work must be required so that children are held responsible for the task and are prepared for the class discussion.

2. *Use a distributed-content approach.* Homework can address content that has been taught earlier in the year as practice, that day's content as reinforcement, or upcoming content as groundwork. Interestingly, research has found that distributed homework (homework that combines all three components) is more effective in supporting student learning (Cooper, 2007). The exception is children with learning disabilities, who perform better when homework focuses on reinforcement of skills and current class lessons.

3. *Promote an "ask-before-tell" approach with parents.* Parents may not know how best to support their child when he or she is stuck or has gotten a wrong answer. One important thing you can do is to ask parents to implement an "ask-before-tell" approach (Kliman, 1999). This means that before parents explain something they should ask their child to explain how he or she did it. The child may self-correct (a life skill) and, if not, at least the parents can use what they heard from their child to provide targeted assistance.

4. *Provide good questioning prompts for parents.* Providing guiding questions for parents or guardians supports a problem-based approach to instruction as they help their

Teaching Tip

Providing specific guidance to families makes a big difference in what they do (and do not do) to help their children learn mathematics and to be confident in doing mathematics.

Figure 7.5
Questions for families to help their children with homework.

> These guiding questions are designed to help your child think through their mathematics homework problems. When they get stuck, ask the following:
> * What do you need to figure out? What is the problem about?
> * What words are confusing? What words are familiar?
> * Did you solve problems like this one in class today?
> * What have you tried so far? What else can you try?
> * Can you make a drawing to help you think about the problem?
> * Does your answer make sense?
> * Is there more than one answer?
> * What words or pictures do you use in your class?

children. Figure 7.5 offers some guiding questions that can be included in the children's notebooks and shared with families. Translating questions for parents who are not native speakers of English is important. (Often, a child can help you with this task.)

Homework of this nature communicates to families the problem-based or sense-making nature of your classroom and might help them see the value in this approach. A final note: A little bit goes a long way—for example, about 10 minutes of homework a night is a good target for young children. If students are to spend time solving meaningful problems, then just a few engaging problems a night can accomplish more than a long set of practice problems.

Teaching Tip

Don't forget the value of your own website as the first site for parents to visit for support. Post your unit letters to families, newsletters, access to homework assignments, possible strategies for doing the homework, and even successful student solutions.

Resources for Families

Parents will be better able to help their child if they know where to find resources. The Internet can provide a wealth of information, but it can also be an overwhelming distraction. Help families locate good places to find mathematics support. First, check whether your textbook provides websites with online resources for homework including tutorials, video tutoring, videos, connections to careers and real-world applications, multilingual glossaries, audio podcasts, and more. Second, post websites that are good general resources. Here are some examples:

* *National Council of Teachers of Mathematics (NCTM)* (www.nctm.org/resources /families.aspx). This frequently updated site connects families with help on homework, current trends in mathematics, and resources.

* *Math Forum* (http://mathforum.org/parents.citizens.html). This site includes many features for teachers and families. Parents may want to read or participate in Math Discussion Groups, read about Key Issues for the Mathematics Community, or download some of the very interesting problems posted here.

* *National Library of Virtual Manipulatives* (http://nlvm.usu.edu/en/nav/vlibrary.html). This site has many applets and virtual tools for learning about many mathematics topics.

There are also great websites for specific content. For example, Thinking Blocks has excellent applets for exploring addition and subtraction.

Beyond Homework: Seeing Mathematics in the Home

In the same way that families support literacy by reading books with their children or pointing out letters of the alphabet when they encounter them, families can and should support numeracy. Since this has not been the practice in many homes, it means that you, as the teacher, have the responsibility to help parents see the connection between literacy and numeracy and everyday life. In her article, "Beyond Helping with Homework," Kliman (1999) offers some excellent suggestions, which include asking parents to share anecdotes, find mathematics in the books they read, do scavenger hunts, and create opportunities during household chores. Figure 7.6 provides a sample letter to send home that suggests these four ideas to parents.

Figure 7.6

Sample letter home to parents regarding ways to infuse mathematics into their interactions with their child.

Making Math Moments Matter (M⁴)

Dear Families:

As a second grader, your child is increasingly aware of what is going on in the world. In that world is a lot of math! In our class this year we are working on **place value**, as well as learning about **standard units of measurement, describing and analyzing shapes**, and **addition and subtraction of three-digit numbers**. It will really help your child to <u>understand</u> and <u>see the importance</u> of math if you find ways to talk about "math moments" (on any math topic, but especially these four critical areas). We call it Making Math Moments Matter (M⁴ for short). Here are some ways to have fun with M⁴ at home.

Share stories. Share a math moment at dinner (or in the car). When have you used math today (shopping, laundry, budgets, etc.)? Think of the many things you might have estimated—how long it will take to get to work, or to run a series of errands. Take turns sharing stories. We will share family math moments in class!

Connecting to reading. As they tell you about the book they are reading, ask quantity-type questions: How many shapes do you see in that picture? How many more pages do we have to finish the book? How long (in inches or centimeters) do you think that animal is?

Chores. Yes, chores! If it takes 45 minutes to do a load of laundry, how long will 3 loads take? If you walk the dog for 10 minutes twice each day, how many hours is the dog walked in 10 days? 100 days? If you earn $5 an hour walking dogs, what might you earn in a week?

Scavenger hunts. Riding in the car can be more interesting if there are things to look for. Consider challenging your child to look for numbers on signs and to say them correctly. Search for as many shapes as you can (e.g., a train car is a rectangular solid, a trash can is a cylinder, etc.).

Adults constantly use estimation and computation in doing everyday tasks. If you get parents to talk about these instances with their children, imagine how much it can help children learn about mathematics and its importance as a life skill.

◆ Involving All Families

Some families are at all school events and conferences, while others rarely participate. However, all families want their children to be successful in school. Parents who do not come to school events may have anxiety related to their own school experiences or they may feel complete confidence that the school and its teachers are doing well by their child and that they do not need to participate. In some cultures, questioning a teacher may be perceived as disrespectful. Rodríguez-Brown (2010), a researcher on Hispanic families, writes, "It is not that Latino parents do not want to support their children's learning . . . [They] believe that it is disrespectful to usurp the teacher's role" (p. 352).

Try to find ways to build a strong rapport with all families. Some strategies to consider include the following:

1. *Honor different strategies for doing mathematics.* While this is a recommendation in standards documents, it is particularly important for children from other countries, because they may have learned different ways to do the operations (Civil & Planas, 2010).

2. *Communicate with positive notes and phone calls.* Be sure to find a way to compliment each child's mathematical thinking (not just a good score on a quiz) at some point early in the school year.

3. *Host informal gatherings to discuss mathematics teaching and learning.* Having regular opportunities to meet with the parents allows for the development of rapport and trust. Consider hosting events in out-of-school facilities. Schools in high-poverty communities have found that having parent events at a community center or religious institution brings in families who are reluctant to come into a school.

4. *Incorporate homework that involves the family.* When a child brings in homework that tells about his or her family and you provide positive feedback or a personal comment, then you are establishing a two-way communication with the family via homework.

5. *Translate letters that are sent home.* If you are doing a class newsletter (for families) or a letter describing the next mathematics unit, make an effort to translate the letter to the native language of the families represented in your class. If you teach older children, consider having the first class session include a component in which children write to their families about what they are about to do. Ask them to write in their parents' first language and to include visuals to support their writing. Ask parents to respond (in their language of choice). This is a great practice for helping children know what they need to learn and communicates to families that they are an important part of that learning.

6. *Post homework on your webpage.* For parents who are not native speakers of English, posting problems on your site makes it easier for them to take advantage of online translations. Although these translations may not be perfectly accurate, they can aid in helping parents and children understand the language in the problems.

For more suggestions on ensuring that your mathematics tasks and homework are meeting the needs of culturally and linguistically diverse children, see Chapter 5 and read the NCTM research brief titled "Involving Latino and Latina Parents in Their Children's Mathematics Education" (Civil & Menéndez, 2010). For suggestions regarding children with special needs, see Chapter 6.

 ## Principal Engagement and Support

Teachers cite a supportive principal as one of the most essential components in successfully implementing a standards-based curriculum (Bay, Reys, & Reys, 1999). Therefore, a principal plays a pivotal role in establishing a shared vision for a problem-based mathematics program. Principals, who have many competing priorities, often cannot take time to attend the professional development workshops that are designed for teachers who will be teaching the mathematics program. And what they need to know is qualitatively different from what a classroom teacher needs to know.

Since the launch of the *Common Core State Standards*, school administrators, parents, and community members are more aware than ever about mathematics standards. If your state has not adopted the *Common Core State Standards*, there are still state-level standards that are the focus of mathematics goals and assessments. So, while it may seem that the need to communicate with administrators is something to simply check off your list, it *must* be a top priority.

Even though principals are hearing more about mathematics standards, higher standards, and the need to ensure that all children are successful, it does not mean they understand what standards-based mathematics curriculum *is* in terms of the content or the related CCSS Standards for Mathematical Practice or NCTM Process Standards. The principal is likely to get bombarded with broad or specific questions from parents: "Is New Math back? Why isn't the teacher teaching the procedure for adding and subtracting? What are the Standards for Mathematical Practice?" When principals are asked these questions, they need a convincing response that is both accurate and addresses the heart of the parents' concerns (that their child is going to get a good, sound, research-based mathematics experience).

Meyer and Arbaugh (2008) suggest professional development specifically for principals. While their focus is on the adoption of standards-based textbooks, the plan they outline applies to all principals who are seeking to be knowledgeable and effective advocates for implementing new standards or mathematics curricula. The following ideas are adapted from their suggested professional development to focus on one-on-one conversations.

1. *Contrast old and new curriculum.* As a first step, it is important to know what is new and different in the mathematics program. One way to start is to provide a set of materials that represents typical *Common Core State Standards*–aligned tasks alongside of what has been the previous curriculum. Point out the noticeable similarities and differences or the key features of the curriculum. (Note: It is important to focus on *both* similarities and differences—not *everything* is getting replaced and this is an important message.)

2. *Discuss how parents and children will respond.* Anticipate what will be noticed by parents (or their children). Which changes might be welcomed? Which changes might be worrisome? How will the welcome aspects be promoted and the worrisome aspects be explained?

3. *Experience the curriculum.* Invite the principal to visit your classroom or other classrooms where the Standards for Mathematical Practice or the NCTM Process Standards are being infused. Ask the principal to join a group of children and listen to their discussion of how they are solving a problem. Or organize a lesson in which the children actually present their solutions to the principal in the *After* phase. For example, in a kindergarten class, ask children to take pictures (or draw pictures) representing the two-dimensional shapes in the school. If possible, ask the principal to solve one of the problems children are doing and share his or her strategy with the class. This firsthand experience can provide the principal with a wonderful story to share with parents and insights that won't be gained from reviewing standards documents.

4. *Discuss emerging issues.* Plan a regular time to meet with the principal to discuss what he or she has heard from families about the mathematics program. Discuss what you might do to respond to questions (some of their anticipated issues may already have been described in the preceding section on parents' concerns). If there is a question about a problem-based approach, Chapter 2 should be a great read for a principal and contains talking points to share with others.

Finally, keep your principal apprised of successes and breakthroughs. These stories provide the principal with evidence to share when being pressed by parents or community members. Principals are very often your strongest advocate and are in the position to serve as buffers between school mathematics and the community.

▲ Communicating with Stakeholders

A final and critical point is to be careful in how we communicate with stakeholders (e.g., parents, district administrators, other teachers, community partners). Without knowing we are doing it, we sometimes say things that, although well-intentioned, increase concerns of stakeholders rather than help to ease stakeholder anxiety. Table 7.2 provides three such examples.

Stop and Reflect

Place your hand over the second and third columns in Table 7.2 and ask yourself how a parent might respond if they heard this statement. What might the parent misinterpret? How might my principal respond? Then read the responses in the table to see if they represent stakeholders like those in your setting. As a rule, it is a good idea to filter your statements through these questions. ■

Initially, the statements may not seem harmful, but they can set off alarms for the stakeholder. Consider these reactions, and then review the shifted language in the third column, which communicates a stronger (and less potentially disconcerting) message. Along these lines, it is very important to convey to parents an excitement for and pride in your mathematics program. Being tentative, reserved, vague, or silent on the mathematics program can

Table 7.2 Statements and Possible (Unintended) Interpretations of the Statements

Original Statement	What a Parent or Administrator Might Think	A Stronger, Carefully Composed Statement
"The [mathematics program] still addresses skills, but it also includes concepts."	"Why are they bringing skills up? They must be taking those away. My child/ U.S. kids have to know basics. How can I put a stop to this?"	"The skills in the [mathematics program] are expanding from what we once learned and now include . . ."
"It is important for children to learn from one another, so I will be more in the role of facilitator."	"The teacher is not teaching? My child does better when things are explained clearly. When I come see you teach, what am I looking for if you are just letting the kids learn on their own?"	"In our classroom, we learn from one another. I give carefully selected tasks for children to discuss and then we talk about them together so that everyone has a chance to learn the mathematics we are doing, and that approach gives me the chance to work one-on-one as needed."
"This year we are doing a whole new mathematics program that the state has adopted."	"My worst nightmare—an experiment of something new during the years my child is in elementary school. This will cause problems for the rest of his life."	"We are doing some new things in order to make sure your child is well prepared for . . . [or that our program is the best available]. You might have noticed that last year we [added writing as a component to our mathematics program]. This year, here are the big things we hope to accomplish. . . ."

only raise concerns in the community. Help parents and administrators to understand that the mathematics program children are experiencing aligns with best practices in education, represents what they need to know in today's world, and prepares them for mathematics at the next level as well as the mathematics they need for everyday life.

Stop and Reflect

What do you think the parents of your children would most value about teaching mathematics through problem solving? How will you use your response to this question to build strong family support and engagement? [Repeat the question for other stakeholders, such as your principal.] ■

Developing Early Number Concepts and Number Sense

Big IDEAS

1 Counting tells how many things are in a set. When counting a set of objects, the last word in the counting sequence names the quantity for that set.

2 Numbers are related to each other through a variety of number relationships. The number 7, for example, is three more than 4, two less than 9, composed of 3 and 4 as well as 2 and 5, is three away from 10, and can be quickly recognized in several patterned arrangements of dots. These ideas further extend to an understanding of 17, 57, and 370.

3 Number concepts are intimately tied to the world around us. Application of number relationships to the real world marks the beginning of making sense of the world in a mathematical manner.

4 Having number sense means that you can think about and use numbers and their relationships in many different ways.

To many adults number may seem like a simple idea. But number is actually a complex and multifaceted concept. A complete and rich understanding of number involves many different ideas, relationships, and skills. Although children may come to school with many ideas about number, it takes time and lots of experiences for them to develop a full understanding that will enhance all of the number-related concepts they will encounter in future years.

The emphasis that number and number sense receive in the National Council of Teachers of Mathematics' *Curriculum Focal Points* (NCTM, 2006) and the *Common Core State Standards* (CCSSO, 2010) speaks to their importance in the early childhood curriculum. This chapter looks at the development of number ideas for numbers up to about 20. These foundational ideas can all be extended to larger numbers, operations, basic facts, and computation—topics addressed in subsequent chapters.

Early Counting and Number

Families help children as young as 2 or 3 years of age count their fingers, toys, people at the table, and other small sets of objects, asking questions such as "Who has more?" or "Are there enough?" Considerable evidence indicates that when children have such experiences, they begin to develop understanding of the concepts of number and counting (Clements & Sarama, 2009). But even

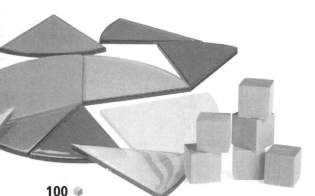

with these experiences, there is variability in how different children learn to count and develop number relationships. Much of this variability results from differences in opportunities to count and work with numbers and their relationships (National Research Council Committee, 2009).

◆ Early Counting

No matter what prior experiences children have had before coming to school, we need to strive to help all children develop the following four interrelated aspects of early numerical knowledge (Clements & Sarama, 2009):

1. *Number sequence.* The names and the ordered list of number words
2. *One-to-one correspondence.* Counting objects by saying number words in a one-to-one correspondence with the objects
3. *Cardinality.* Understanding that the last number word said when counting tells how many objects have been counted
4. *Subitizing.* Quickly recognizing and naming how many objects are in a small group without counting. Young children can recognize and name quantities of objects that are less than four without counting (Clements & Sarama, 2007).

Children must construct these ideas through a variety of experiences and activities. They cannot be forced. As children work on each of these aspects of early counting, their understanding about counting is continually refined. For example, children will learn *how* to count (matching counting words with objects) before they understand that the last count word indicates the *amount* of the set or the *cardinality* of the set. A teacher can at the same time use subitizing to emphasize the notion of cardinality and to help emphasize the notion that counting tells "how many."

Formative Assessment Note

To determine whether a young child understands cardinality, listen to how the child responds when you discuss counting tasks with him or her. After counting a set of objects you can ask, "How many are here?" If the child recounts the set, hesitates, or points to the last object counted, it's likely the child has not constructed the idea of cardinality of a set. Children with an understanding of cardinality are apt to emphasize the last count, will explain that there are nine "because I just counted them," and can use counting to find a matching set.

Although learning the number sequence may be considered a rote procedure, effort should be given to help children build the number sequence in a meaningful way, especially numbers in the teens. One recommendation is to connect English words with number words translated from other languages that are more explicit about the structure of the numbers. For example, map 11 to "ten and one," 12 to "ten and two," and so on. You can use a vertical number line to help children visualize how numbers change as they begin writing two-digit numbers (see Figure 8.1). A vertical number line is also more intuitive than a typical horizontal number line because it is consistent with the notion that as numbers become larger they go up the number line as opposed to moving to the right.

Although the forward number sequence is relatively familiar to most young children, mastering the backward number sequence or counting back can be difficult. Provide children frequent opportunities to practice both the forward and backward number sequences through short and engaging activities such as the following.

Standards for
Mathematical Practice

7 Look for and make use of structure

Teaching Tip

When learning the number sequence, some children do not realize that each number word represents a separate number, so they may touch two objects as they say two-syllable counting words such as "se-ven" or "thir-teen."

Figure 8.1

A vertical number line can help children visualize patterns in our written numbers.

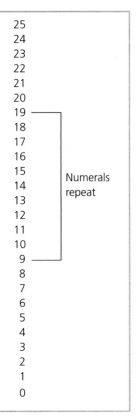

25
24
23
22
21
20
19 ┐
18
17
16
15
14   Numerals repeat
13
12
11
10
9 ┘
8
7
6
5
4
3
2
1
0

Activity 8.1 COUNTING UP AND BACK

Counting up to and back from a target number in a rhythmic fashion is an important counting exercise. For example, line up five children and five chairs in front of the class. As the whole class counts from 1 to 5, the children sit down one at a time. When the target number, 5, is reached, it is repeated; the child who sat on 5 now stands, and the count goes back to 1. As the count goes back, the children stand up one at a time, and so on, "1, 2, 3, 4, 5, 5, 4, 3, 2, 1, 1, 2, ..." Children find exercises such as this both fun and challenging. Any rhythmic movement (clapping, turning around, doing jumping jacks) can be used as the count goes up and back. You can modify the activity by varying the range of numbers. For example, use 15 to 20 if the class is working on the teen numbers and use something like 55 to 65 if the class is ready to move to larger numbers (both of these ranges fit with kindergarten expectations in CCSS). To modify this activity for English language learners, give each child who is in front of the class one card from a set of cards with the target numerals (e.g., 1 to 5, 15 to 20, or 55 to 65) and the corresponding number word. These cards will provide a visual to help children connect the written numeral and number word to the number being said.

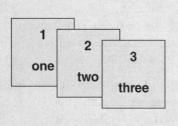

Another option involves having children stand in a circle and count around the circle to a target number. One child starts the count at number 1; the next child says the next number in the sequence, and so on, until a child says the target number. That child sits down and the next child starts the count again at number 1. The activity continues until one child is left standing. You can vary the activity by using shorter or longer sequences, by starting the count at a number other than 1, or by having the children count backward. Challenge children by asking them to predict who will sit down next or who will say a particular number.

Activity 8.2 LINE THEM UP!

To prepare for this activity, stretch a clothesline across a space in the classroom at a level where children can reach it. You can stretch it across a bulletin board or to the side of the room. Prepare a set of numeral cards that represents the sequence of numbers you want the children to work with, say, 1 through 15 for kindergarten. (You could also start at 0.) There should be one numeral on each card. Shuffle the cards so that they are in a random order and place the cards face down in a pile. Ask a child to take the top card from the pile and use a clothespin to place the card on the clothesline. Have a second child take the next card off the pile and place that card on the clothesline in what the child thinks is the appropriate position. As children place their numeral cards, ask questions such as "Is your number before or after . . ." and "Does your number go on the left or the right of . . .?" Continue placing the cards until all the cards are placed on the clothesline in a sequence. Once all the cards are placed, have the children read the sequence forward as well as backward. If any number is out of sequence, see if the children can determine how to correct the arrangement of cards. You can modify this activity by using shorter or longer sequences and by using number sequences that start at different numbers.

The last two activities are designed only to help children become fluent with the number words in both forward and reverse order and to begin counting with numbers other than 1.

To develop their understanding of counting, engage children in almost any game or activity in which they have to purposefully count objects and make comparisons between counts. The following is a simple suggestion.

Activity 8.3 FILL THE TOWERS

Create a game board with four "towers." Each tower is a column of twelve 1-inch squares with a star at the top. Children take turns rolling a die and collecting the indicated number of counters. They then place these counters on one of the towers. The object is to fill all of the towers with counters. As an option, require that the towers be filled exactly so that a roll of 5 cannot be used to fill four empty spaces. To modify this activity for a child with disabilities or for any child who is struggling with counting, use a die with only two or three dots on each side. Using a larger-sized die also makes it easier for the child to count the dots. You can increase the number choices on the die when you have evidence that the child is counting accurately. A good accommodation for gifted children is to have them use a die with larger numbers and a different game board to allow for the larger numbers.

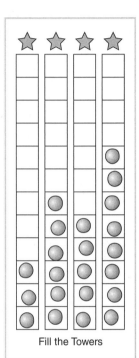

Fill the Towers

This game provides opportunities for you to talk with children about number and assess their thinking. Watch how the children count the dots on the die. Ask the children, "How do you know you have the right number of counters?" and "How many counters did you put in the tower? How many more do you need to fill the tower?"

Activity 8.4 HOW MANY ARE THERE?

Place wooden cubes numbered 1 to 10 in a box. In pairs, children pull out a cube and then collect that number of objects from a designated area in the classroom. The objects could be books, pencils, cubes, crayons, counting bears, and so on. They place their numbered cube and the collected objects in a container. Have pairs go around and check the other children's collections to make sure they have the correct number of objects. You can vary this activity by changing the range of possible numbers to either a smaller range (2–5) or a larger range (5–20) or by having each pair collect the same number of objects. Initially you may want children to collect the same kind of object, but eventually have them collect a mix of objects to reinforce the idea you can count different kinds of objects in a collection. For example, they can collect two crayons, one cube, and one pencil for the number 4.

Regular classroom activities, such as counting how many napkins or snacks are needed at snack time, how many materials are needed for an activity, how many children plan to eat the school lunch, or even simply taking attendance, are additional opportunities for children to engage in purposeful counting and to learn more about number and for teachers to listen to children's ideas. But make sure these activities involve more than the children simply following the teacher's count. Look for ways to make these situations into real problems. Chapter 2 includes an example of how to turn a routine snack time into an opportunity for children to learn more about number and counting (see section on multiple entry and exit points).

◆ Learning Trajectory for Counting

Research on children's counting schemes has identified a developmental progression of counting that varies in terms of mathematical sophistication (Steffe & Cobb, 1988; Wright, Stanger, Stafford, & Martland, 2006). To consider this framework, let's suppose a child is asked to determine "how many" items are in two sets of objects, say, one set of 6 objects and one set of 7 objects. Children will respond to this type of task in one of the following ways, depending on which type of counter they are:

- *Emergent counter.* The child is unable to count the collection of objects. The child may be unable to coordinate one number word with one object when counting or may not know the correct number sequence.

- *Perceptual counter.* The child can count the collection of objects only if the objects can be seen. A perceptual counter will count all objects by counting from the number 1.

- *Figurative counter.* The child can count the collection of objects even if the objects are blocked from view. The child is able to imagine or visualize the objects. A figurative counter will count all imagined objects by counting from the number 1.

- *Counting-on counter.* A counting-on counter is a child who can start counting from a given number other than 1 and who does not need to see the objects to count.

- *Non-count-by-ones counter.* A child who does not use counting by ones but partitions and combines the numbers involved is a non-count-by-ones counter. For example, the child may reason that 7 is 3 from 10, so partition the 6 into a 3 and 3. Combine 7 and 3 to get 10. Then combine 10 and 3 to get 13.

Teachers who are aware of this learning trajectory for counting are better able to design instructional tasks that are purposefully targeted at moving children from one level to the next. Let's consider two activities that are designed to help figurative counters move to counting on.

Figure 8.2

Counting on: "Hide four. Count, starting from the number of counters hidden."

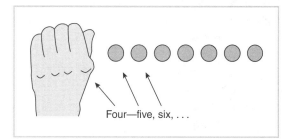

Four—five, six, . . .

Activity 8.5 COUNTING ON WITH COUNTERS

Give each child a collection of 10 or 12 small counters that the children line up left to right on their desks. Tell them to count four counters and push them under their left hands (see Figure 8.2). Then say, "Point to your hand. How many are there?" (Four.) "So let's count like this: f-o-u-r (pointing to their hand), five, six,. . . . " Repeat with other numbers of counters under the hand.

The following activity addresses the same concept in a more problem-based manner.

Activity 8.6 REAL COUNTING ON

This game for two children requires a deck of cards (numbers 1 to 7), a die, a paper cup, and counters. The first player turns over the top number card and places the indicated number of counters in the cup. The card is placed next to the cup as a reminder of how many are inside. The second player rolls the die and places that many counters next to the cup. (See Figure 8.3.) Together they decide how many counters in all. A record sheet with columns for "In the Cup," "On the Side," and "In All" will support children's organization. Increase the highest number in the card deck when children have mastered the smaller numbers. For children with disabilities, keep the number of counters in the cup constant (say, 3) and have them count on from that number until they are fluent with that number.

Observe how children determine the total amounts in the preceding activity. Children who are not yet counting on may want to empty the counters from the cup or will count up from 1 without emptying out the counters. Be sure to permit these strategies. As children continue to play, they will eventually use counting on as that strategy becomes meaningful and useful.

◆ Initial Number Relationships: More, Less, and Same

The concepts of "more," "less," and "same" are basic relationships contributing to children's overall understanding of number. Almost any child entering kindergarten can choose the set that is *more* if presented with two sets that are quite obviously different in number. Classroom activities should help children build on and refine this basic notion.

Though the concept of less is logically related to the concept of more (selecting the set with more is the same as *not* selecting the set with less), the word *less* proves to be more difficult for children than the word *more*. A possible explanation is that children have many opportunities to use the word *more* but have limited exposure to the word *less*. To help children with the concept of less, frequently pair it with *more* and make a conscious effort to ask "Which is less?" questions as well as "Which is more?" questions. For example, suppose that your class has correctly selected the set that has more from the two sets that are given. Immediately follow with the question "Which is less?" In this way, the concept is connected with the better-known idea and the term *less* becomes familiar.

For all three concepts (more/greater than, less/less than, and same/equal to), children should construct sets using counters as well as make comparisons or choices between two given sets. The following activities should be conducted in a spirit of inquiry with requests for explanations: "Can you show me how you know this group has less?"

Figure 8.3

How many in all? How do children count to tell the total? Dump the counters? Count up from 1 without dumping the counters? Count on?

▶ *Activity 8.7* **MAKE SETS OF MORE/LESS/SAME**

At a workstation, provide about eight cards with pictures of sets of 4 to 12 objects (or use large dot cards); a set of small counters; word cards labeled More, Less, and Same; and paper plates or low boxes to support children with disabilities by defining the work space. Next to each picture card have children make three collections of counters: a set that is more than the amount in the picture, one that is less, and one that is the same. They then place the appropriate word cards (More, Less, Same) on the sets (see Figure 8.4). Have children with disabilities begin by creating a collection that matches the picture. Once they are consistently successful with creating a set that matches, move to creating sets with more and then to sets with less.

Figure 8.4

Making sets that are more, less, and the same.

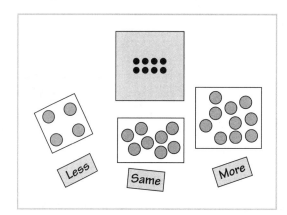

Initially when young children begin comparing sets, they may be easily confused by perceptual cues such as the length of the row of counters or the spacing of counters in one set

Figure 8.5
Dot cards can be made using Blackline Masters.

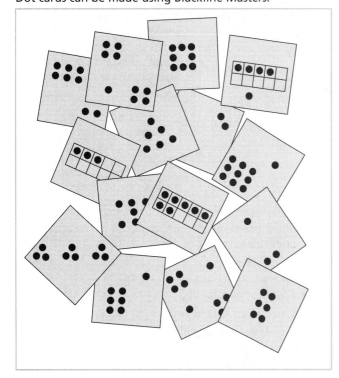

versus another set. So you may need to encourage some children to use matching or counting to compare sets. You can suggest in Activity 8.7 that they stack counters on top of the images to match the sets. As they create a set with counters, they have the opportunity to reflect on the sets and adjust them as they work. The next activity is done without counters. Although it addresses the same basic ideas, it provides a different problem situation.

Activity 8.8 FIND THE SAME AMOUNT

Give children a collection of cards with pictures of sets on them. Dot cards are one possibility (see Figure 8.5; see also Blackline Masters 3–8). Have the children pick up any card in the collection and then find another card with the same amount to form a pair. Continue to find other pairs. Some children with disabilities may need a set of counters with a blank ten-frame to help them "make" a pair instead of finding a pair.

Activity 8.8 can be altered to have children find dot cards that are "less" or "more."

Formative Assessment Note

Observe children as they do this task. Children whose number ideas are completely tied to counting and nothing more will select cards at random and count each dot. Others will begin by selecting a card that appears to have about the same number of dots. This shows a significantly higher level of understanding. Also observe how the dots are counted. Are the counts made accurately? Is each counted only once? A significant milestone for children occurs when they begin recognizing small patterned sets without counting (subitizing).

You can also have children play Okta's Rescue (http://illuminations.nctm.org/ActivityDetail.aspx?ID=219), which is an interactive activity that requires children to gather a given number of animals either by counting by ones or by grouping the animals. The activity is timed to provide that additional push to move children beyond counting by ones.

Helping children relate numerals to number words and to quantities is important. Consider using a computerized version of the game Concentration that offers options to limit the numbers between 1 and 6 or between 1 and 10 (http://illuminations.nctm.org/ActivityDetail.aspx?ID=73). Children can play individually or with another player. You can also reduce the level of difficulty by selecting the option to have all the numerals, numbers, and quantities visible so that the child can focus on moving back and forth between the representations without having the added difficulty of remembering the locations of specific cards.

Developing Number Sense by Building Number Relationships

Number sense is not a set of skills that children can develop in a short period of time. It is something that grows and develops over time. Howden (1989) described *number sense* as a "good intuition about numbers and their relationships. It develops gradually as a result of exploring numbers, visualizing them in a variety of contexts, and relating them in ways that are not limited by traditional algorithms" (p. 11).

In the remainder of this chapter we look at the kinds of relationships and connections children should be making about smaller numbers up to about 20. But "good intuition about numbers" does not end with these smaller whole numbers. Children continue to develop number sense as they begin to use numbers in operations, build an understanding of place value, devise flexible methods of computing, and make estimates involving large numbers. Flexible, intuitive reasoning with numbers—number sense—should continue to be developed throughout the school years as fractions, decimals, and percentages are added to children's repertoire of number ideas.

Relationships between Numbers 1 through 10

Once children have acquired a concept of cardinality and can meaningfully use their counting skills, little more can be gained from the kinds of counting activities described so far. But too often teachers move directly from the beginning ideas of counting to addition and subtraction, leaving children with a very limited collection of ideas about number to bring to these new topics. The result is often that children continue to count by ones to solve simple story problems and have difficulty mastering basic facts. Emphasizing number relationships is key to helping children fully develop number sense. Figure 8.6 illustrates the four different types of relationships that children can and should develop with numbers:

- *Spatial relationships.* Children can learn to recognize sets of objects in patterned arrangements and tell how many without counting. For most numbers, there are several common patterns. Patterns can also be made from two or more easier patterns of smaller numbers.

- *One and two more, one and two less.* The two-more-than and two-less-than relationships involve more than just the ability to count on two more or count back by two. Children should know that 7, for example, is 1 more than 6 and also 2 less than 9.

- *Anchors or "benchmarks" of 5 and 10.* Since the number 10 plays such a large role in our numeration system and because two fives make up 10, it is very useful to develop relationships for the numbers 1 to 10 to the important anchors of 5 and 10.

Figure 8.6

Four relationships to be developed involving small numbers.

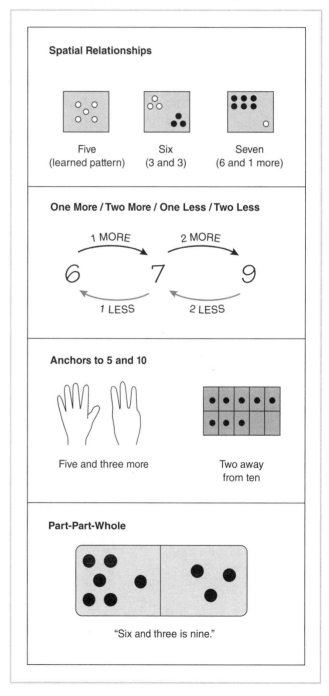

- *Part–part–whole relationships.* To conceptualize a number as being made up of two or more parts is the most important relationship that can be developed about numbers. For example, 7 can be thought of as a set of 3 and a set of 4 or a set of 2 and a set of 5.

The principal tool that young children will use as they construct these relationships is the one number tool they possess: counting. Initially, then, you will notice a lot of counting, and you may wonder if you are making progress. Have patience! Counting will become less and less necessary as children construct new relationships and begin to use more powerful ideas.

Figure 8.7

A collection of dot patterns for "dot plates."

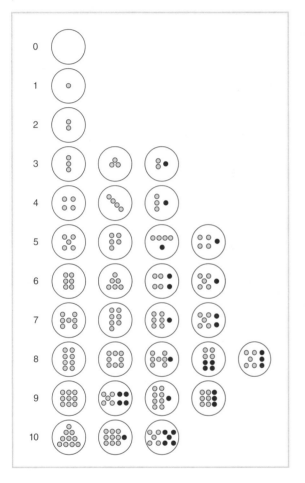

Spatial Patterns: Patterned Set Recognition

Many children learn to recognize the dot arrangements on standard dice due to the many games they have played that use dice. Similar instant recognition can be developed for other patterns as well. This instant and intuitive recognition of quantities up to four or five, that ability to "just see it," is called subitizing and is one of the four interrelated aspects of early numerical knowledge described earlier in the chapter. While some children seem to automatically use subitizing, others need more support to do so. There are also times when a child is able to instantly recognize even larger amounts without counting. In these cases, the child sees and uses small groups within the larger amount to quickly determine how many. For example, a child can mentally break apart dots in a pattern of eight by seeing four in one row and mentally doubling it to get a total of eight. The activities suggested here encourage reflective thinking about the patterns so that the relationships will be constructed to support the development and use of subitizing. This can aid in counting on (from a known patterned set) or learning combinations of numbers (seeing a pattern of two known smaller patterns).

A good set of materials to use in pattern recognition activities is a set of dot plates. These can be made using small paper plates and the peel-off dots commonly available in office supply stores. A reasonable collection of patterns is shown in Figure 8.7. Note that some patterns are combinations of two smaller patterns or a pattern with one or two additional dots. These should be made in two colors. Keep the patterns compact. If the dots are spread out, the patterns are hard to see.

Activity 8.9 LEARNING PATTERNS

To introduce the patterns, provide each child with about 10 counters and a piece of cardstock or paper plate as a mat. Hold up a dot plate for about 5 seconds and say, "Make the pattern you saw on the plate using the counters on the mat. How many dots did you see? What did the pattern look like?" Spend some time discussing the configuration of the pattern and the number of dots. Then show the plate so they can self-check. Do this with a few new patterns each day. One way to modify this activity for a child with disabilities is to show a small selection of plates and, instead of the child creating a given pattern with counters, have the child find the plate that matches a given pattern.

The next activity displays images quickly so that children do not have time to count the dots one by one. Consequently, they are challenged to find another way to determine how many. Dot plates that have three to five dots are useful in helping children work on subitizing. Dot plates that have more than five dots are useful in helping children work on advanced subitizing or decomposition where they quickly see and use small groups within the larger amount to quickly determine how many.

> **Teaching Tip**
>
> Use quick images to encourage children to move beyond counting by ones.

Activity 8.10 DOT PLATE FLASH

Hold up a dot plate for only 1 to 3 seconds and say, "How many dots do you see? What did the pattern look like?" Include easy patterns first and then add more dots as children's confidence builds. Initially you may need to show a plate a second time so that children can get a second look. Children like to see how quickly they can recognize and say how many dots. Children can also flash dot plates to each other as a workstation activity.

The instant recognition activities with the plates are exciting and can be done in 5 minutes at any time of day or between lessons. There is value in using them at any primary grade level and at any time of year.

In addition to dot plates, a good set of materials is a set of dot-pattern dominoes. Make a set of dominoes out of cardstock and put a dot pattern on each end. The size of the dominoes can be about 2 inches by 4 inches. The same patterns can appear on lots of dominoes with different pairs of patterns making up each one. Let the children play dominoes in the regular way, matching up the ends. As a speed activity, spread out all of the dominoes and see how fast the children play all of the dominoes or play until no more can be played. Regular dominoes could also be used, but there are not as many patterns.

Speedy Pictures (www.fi.uu.nl/toepassingen/00204/toepassing_rekenweb.xml?style=rekenweb&language =en&use=game) is an interactive website where children can work on identifying amounts using quick images. They can select from a variety of images such as dice, arithmetic racks (a rack with one or two rows of 10 beads in two colors), egg cartons, and finger patterns. You can set a timer that ranges from about 10 seconds to 40 seconds.

One and Two More, One and Two Less

When children count, they have no reason to reflect on the way one number is related to another. The goal is only to match number words with objects until they reach the end of the count. To learn that 6 and 8 are related by the twin relationships of "two more than" and "two less than" requires reflection on these ideas within tasks that permit counting. Counting on (or back) one or two counts is a useful tool in constructing these ideas.

The following activities are named for one of the more-than/less-than relationships, but each activity can be done for any of these relationships.

> ### Activity 8.11 ONE-LESS-THAN DOMINOES
>
> Use the dot-pattern dominoes or a standard set to play "one-less-than" dominoes. Play in the usual way, but instead of matching ends, a new domino can be added if it has an end that is one less than the end on the board. A similar game can be played for two less, one more, or two more.

> ### Activity 8.12 MAKE A TWO-MORE-THAN SET
>
> Provide children with about six dot cards. For each card, their task is to display a set of counters that is two more than the set shown on the card. Similarly, spread out eight to ten dot cards and, for each card, find a card that is two less than it. (Omit the 1 and 2 cards for two less than, and so on.)

In activities in which children find a set or make a set, they can select the appropriate numeral card (a small card with a number written on it) that identifies the quantity in the set. They can also be encouraged to take turns reading a number sentence to their partner. If, for example, a set has been made that is two more than a set of four, the child can read this by saying the number sentence "Two more than four is six."

Anchoring Numbers to 5 and 10

Here again, we want to help children relate a given number to other numbers, specifically 5 and 10. These relationships are especially useful in thinking about various combinations of numbers.

> ### Stop and Reflect
>
> Consider the role that 5 and 10 play in helping to think about tasks such as these: $8 + 7$, $8 - 2$, $8 - 3$, $8 - 4$, $13 - 8$. ∎

Figure 8.8
Ten-frames.

The knowledge of 8 as "5 and 3 more" and as "2 away from 10" can play a role in how a child thinks about these examples. Later, similar relationships can be used in the development of mental computation skills on larger numbers such as $68 + 7$.

The most common models to help children anchor numbers to 5 and 10 are five-frames and ten-frames. The ten-frame is a 2×5 array in which counters or dots are placed to illustrate numbers (see Figure 8.8). Ten-frames can be simply drawn on a full sheet of cardstock (or use Blackline Master 1). Nothing fancy is required, and each child can have one. The ten-frame has been incorporated into a variety of activities in this book and is now a popular representation found in standard textbooks for children.

For children in pre-kindergarten or kindergarten who have not yet explored a ten-frame, it is a good idea to begin with a five-frame. This row of five sections can also be drawn on a sheet of cardstock (or use Blackline Master 2). Provide children with about 10 counters that will fit in the five-frame sections and conduct the following activity.

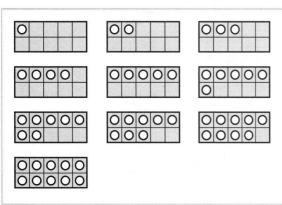

Activity 8.13 FIVE-FRAME TELL-ABOUT

Explain that only one counter is permitted in each section of the five-frame. No other counters are allowed on the five-frame mat. Have the children show 3 on their five-frame. "What can you tell us about 3 from looking at your mat?" After hearing from several children, try other numbers from 0 to 5. Children initially may place their counters on the five-frame in any manner. What they observe will differ a great deal from child to child. For example, with four counters, a child with two on each end may say, "It has a space in the middle" or "It's two and two." There are no wrong answers. Focus attention on how many more counters are needed to make 5 or how far away from 5 a number is. Next try numbers between 5 and 10. The rule of one counter per section still holds. As shown in Figure 8.9, numbers greater than 5 are shown with a full five-frame and additional counters on the mat but not in the frame. In discussion, focus attention on these larger numbers as 5 and some more: "Eight is five and three more."

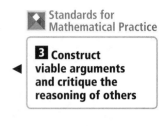

Standards for
Mathematical Practice

3 Construct
viable arguments
and critique the
reasoning of others

◀

Figure 8.9

A five-frame focuses on the 5 anchor. Counters are placed one to a section, and children tell how they see their number in the frame.

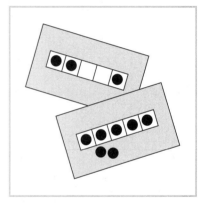

Notice that the five-frame really focuses on the relationship to 5 as an anchor for numbers but does not anchor numbers to 10. After five-frames have been used for a week or so, introduce ten-frames. You may want to play a ten-frame version of a "Five-Frame Tell-About" but soon introduce the following rule for showing numbers on the ten-frame: Fill the top row first, starting on the left, the same way you read. When the top row is full, counters can be placed in the bottom row, also from the left. This rule will help children see the significance of a full row in the ten-frame—in particular, if the row is full, they do not need to count because it will always be 5. This observation needs to come from the children, not the teacher. So look for opportunities to draw children's attention to this characteristic of the ten-frame. Filling the ten-frame in this fashion also provides a visualization of numbers as 5 and some more, as can be seen in Figure 8.8. Make sure to spend time asking questions such as "What are you looking at in the ten-frame to help you find how many?" and "How does knowing you have a full row help you determine how many?"

For a while, many children will count every counter on their ten-frame. When making a new number, some children will remove all the counters from the ten-frame and begin from a blank frame. Others will soon learn to adjust numbers by adding on or taking off only what is required, often capitalizing on a row of five without counting. Do not pressure children to use one approach or another. With continued practice, all children will grow. How they are using the ten-frame provides insight into children's current number concept development.

You can find virtual five- and ten-frames at http://illuminations.nctm.org/Activity Detail.aspx?ID=74 and http://illuminations.nctm.org/activitydetail.aspx?id=75, respectively. These versions can be used not only with the whole class or small groups but also with individual children because these activities feature a computerized voice that asks the children questions. These versions allow children to build target numbers and include an option that asks children to determine how many counters are displayed as well as how many empty spaces are in a given frame.

Activity 8.14 NUMBER MEDLEY

First, have all children show the same number on their ten-frame. Then call out random numbers between 0 and 10. After each number, the children change their ten-frames to show the new number. Children can also do this activity independently by using a prepared list of about 15 random numbers. One child plays "teacher" while the rest use the ten-frames.

"Number Medley" is much more of a problem-solving situation than it first appears. How do you decide how to change your ten-frame to make the new number? Some children will clear off the entire frame and start over with each new number. Others will have learned what each number looks like. To add another dimension, have the children tell, *before changing their ten-frames,* how many more counters need to be added ("plus") or removed ("minus"). They then call out plus or minus whatever amount is appropriate. If, for example, the frames showed six, and the teacher called out "Four," the children would respond "Minus two!" and then change their ten-frames accordingly. A discussion of how they know what to do is valuable.

Ten-frame flash cards are an important variation of ten-frames. Make cards from cardstock about the size of a small index card with a ten-frame on each and dots drawn in the frames. A set of 20 cards consists of a 0 card, a 10 card, and two each of the numbers 1 to 9. The cards allow for simple practice activities to reinforce the 5 and 10 anchors (see Blackline Masters 17 and 18).

◆ *Activity 8.15* TEN-FRAME FLASH CARDS

Flash ten-frame cards to the class or group and see how quickly the children can tell how many dots are shown. This fast-paced activity takes only a few minutes, can be done at any time, and is a lot of fun.

Important variations of "Ten-Frame Flash Cards" include

- Saying the number of empty spaces on the card instead of the number of dots
- Saying one more than the number of dots (or two more and also less than)
- Saying the "ten fact"—for example, "Six and four make ten"

Ten-frame tasks are surprisingly challenging for children. Children must reflect on the two rows of five, the spaces remaining, and how a particular number is more or less than 5 and how far away from 10. The earlier discussions about how children can describe how they see numbers on the five-frames or ten-frames are examples of brief discussions that can take place in the *After* portion of the lesson, in which children learn from one another.

Another model for benchmarks of 5 and 10 is an arithmetic rack. An arithmetic rack can have one row of 10 beads or two rows of 10 beads. Each row has 5 beads of one color and 5 beads of another color (see Figure 8.10). Arithmetic racks are available commercially or you can make an arithmetic rack with cardstock, pipe cleaners, and small plastic beads. You can also find an electronic version of an arithmetic rack at http://maine.edc.org/file.php/1 /AssessmentResources/ArithmeticRack132_L.html, where you can set the rack as a single row of 10 or as a double row of 10, depending on the readiness of your children.

The different colors and embedded five structure of the arithmetic rack help children build mental images of numbers. Children can be asked to name the number displayed on an arithmetic rack—and if flashed quickly as with the ten-frame, children can be asked how they know how many beads are displayed. They can also be asked to show a particular number using the arithmetic rack. The class can then share the different ways that the same number was displayed.

Standards for Mathematical Practice

7 Look for and make use of structure ▶

Figure 8.10

An arithmetic rack provides a visual model of the benchmarks of 5 and 10.

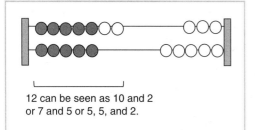

12 can be seen as 10 and 2 or 7 and 5 or 5, 5, and 2.

Part–Part–Whole Relationships

Stop and Reflect

Before reading on, get some counters or coins. Count out a set of eight counters in front of you as if you were a kindergartner. ■

Any child who has learned how to count meaningfully can count out eight objects as you just did. What is significant about the experience is what it did not cause you to think about. Nothing in counting a set of eight objects will cause a child to focus on the fact that it could be made of two parts. For example, separate the counters you just set out into two piles and reflect on the combination. It might be 2 and 6 or 7 and 1 or 4 and 4. Make a change in your two piles of counters and say the new combination to yourself. Focusing on a quantity in terms of its parts has important implications for developing number sense. The ability to think about a number in terms of parts is a major milestone in the development of number sense. Of the four number relationships we have discussed, part–whole ideas are easily the most important.

Most part–part–whole activities focus on a single number for the entire activity. Kindergarteners can usually begin these activities working on the number 4 or 5. As concepts develop, the children can extend their work to numbers 6 to 12. It is not unusual to find children in the second grade who have not developed firm part–part–whole constructs for the numbers 7 through 12, even though by that time they should be adding up to 100.

The following activity and its variations may be considered the "basic" part–part–whole activity.

Figure 8.11
Assorted materials for building parts of 6.

Activity 8.16 BUILD IT IN PARTS

Provide children with one type of material, such as connecting cubes or squares of colored paper. The task is to see how many different combinations for a particular number they can make using two parts. (If you wish, you can allow for more than two parts.) Each different combination can be displayed on a small mat, such as a quarter-sheet of cardstock. Here are just a few ideas, each of which is illustrated in Figure 8.11.

- Use two-color counters such as lima beans spray-painted on one side (also available in plastic).
- Make bars of connecting cubes. Make each bar with two colors. Keep the colors together.
- Make combinations using two dot strips—strips of cardstock about 1 inch wide with stick-on dots. (Make lots of strips with one to four dots and fewer strips with five to ten dots.)
- Make combinations of "two-column strips." These are cut from cardstock ruled in 1-inch squares. All pieces except the single squares are cut from two columns of the cardstock.
- Color rows of squares on 1-inch grid paper.
- Use arithmetic racks that have 10 beads in two rows.

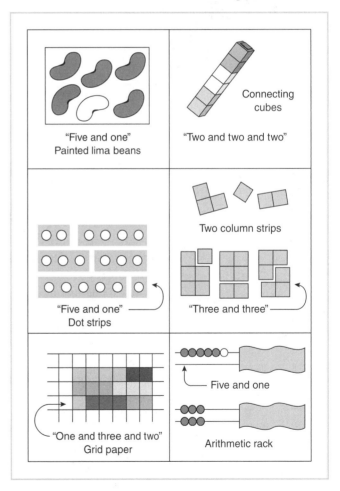

"Five and one"
Painted lima beans

Connecting cubes
"Two and two and two"

"Five and one"
Dot strips

Two column strips

"Three and three"

"One and three and two"
Grid paper

Five and one

Arithmetic rack

Standards for Mathematical Practice

◀ **4 Model with mathematics**

As you observe children working on the "Build It in Parts" activity, ask them to "read" or write a number sentence to go with each of their representations. Reading or writing the combinations serves as a means of encouraging reflective thought focused on the part–whole relationship. Writing can be in the form of drawings, numbers

Figure **8.12** Representations for 6.

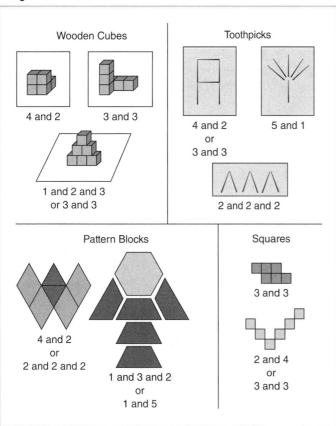

written in blanks (_____ and _____), or addition equations if these have been introduced (3 + 5 = 8). There is a clear connection between part–part–whole concepts and addition and subtraction ideas.

In the "Build It in Parts" activity, the children are focusing on the combinations. To add some interest, vary the activity by adding a design component. Rather than creating a two-part illustration for a number, children create an interesting design with an assigned number of elements. For each design, they are then challenged to see and read the design in two parts. Here are some ideas.

- Make arrangements of wooden cubes.
- Make designs with pattern blocks. It is a good idea to use only one or two shapes at a time.
- Make designs with flat toothpicks. These can be dipped in white glue and placed on small squares of cardstock to create a permanent record.
- Make designs with touching squares or triangles. Cut a large supply of small squares or triangles out of cardstock. These can also be pasted down.

It is both fun and useful to challenge children to see their designs in different ways, producing different number combinations. In Figure 8.12, notice how children look at the designs to get the combinations listed under each.

You can also use ten-frames to help children build and visualize numbers in parts. When most of your children know that there are 5 in a full row, allow them to fill in the ten-frame without filling the top row first. For example, you could show 7 as 4 and 3 or 6 and 1, using different colored counters to emphasize the different parts (see Figure 8.13). Again, take time to draw children's attention to the empty spaces in the ten-frame to build parts of 10. Virtual five- and ten-frames available at http://maine.edc.org/file.php/1/AssessmentResources/5Frame10Frame32_L.html allow you to display counters in two colors so that you can highlight two parts of the target number.

A special and important variation of part–part–whole activities is referred to as missing-part activities. In a missing-part activity, children are given the whole amount and they use their already-developed knowledge of the parts of that whole to try to tell what the covered or hidden part is. If they do not know or are unsure, they simply uncover the unknown part and say the full combination as they would normally. Missing-part activities can be challenging for children not only because the missing part increases the difficulty level but also because they encourage children to continue to reflect on the combinations for a number. They also serve as the forerunner to subtraction concepts. With a whole of 8 but with only 3 showing, the child can later learn to write "8 − 3 = 5."

Missing-part activities require some way for a part of the whole to be hidden or unknown. Usually this is done with two children working together or in a teacher-directed manner with the class. The next four activities illustrate variations of this important idea of a missing part.

Figure **8.13**

Using ten-frames to show part–part–whole relationships.

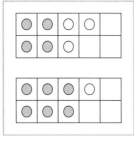

Activity 8.17 COVERED PARTS

A set of counters equal to the target amount is counted out, and the rest are put aside. One child places the counters under a margarine tub or piece of cardstock. The child then pulls some out into view. (This amount could be none, all, or any amount in between.) For example, if 6 is the whole and 4 are showing, the other child says, "Four and *two* is six." If there is hesitation or if the hidden part is unknown, the hidden part is immediately shown (see Figure 8.14).

Activity 8.18 MISSING-PART CARDS

For each number from 4 to 10, make missing-part cards using strips of cardstock measuring 3 × 9 inches. Each card has a numeral for the whole and two dot sets with one set covered by a flap. For the number 8, you need nine cards with the visible part ranging from 0 to 8 dots. Children use the cards as in "Covered Parts," saying, "Four and two is six" for a card showing four dots and hiding two (see Figure 8.14).

Activity 8.19 I WISH I HAD

Hold out a bar of connecting cubes, a dot strip, a two-column strip, or a dot plate showing 6 or less and say, "I wish I had six." The children respond with the part that is needed to make 6. Counting on can be used to check. The game can focus on a single number (a good starting point for children with disabilities), or the "I wish I had" number can change each time (see Figure 8.14). Consider adding a familiar context, such as "I wish I had six books to read."(See the Expanded Lesson based on "I Wish I Had" at the end of this chapter.)

𝓕𝒾𝑔𝓊𝓇𝑒 8.14
Missing-part activities.

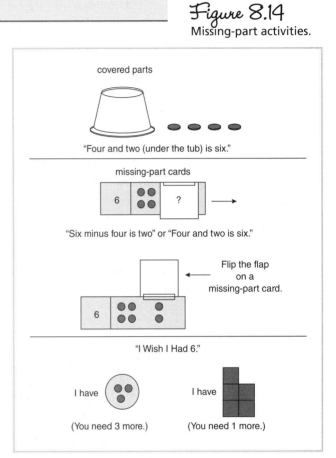

You can also use a virtual format for any of the preceding activities by using the part–part–whole model found at http://maine.edc.org/file.php/1/AssessmentResources/Add Models_PPW-NumLine32_L.html. Counters are dragged into the boxes that represent the parts. The whole and either part can be hidden from view as well as the corresponding numerals.

Activity 8.20 NUMBER SANDWICHES

Select a number between 5 and 12 and partner children to find combinations of two dot cards totaling that number (see Blackline Masters 3–8). Children make a "sandwich" with the two cards by placing them back-to-back with the dot sides out. When they have found at least 10 pairs, the next challenge is for the partner to name the number on the other side. The cards are turned over to confirm. The same sandwiches can then be used again to name the other hidden part.

Constructing Number Relationships through Story Problems

Children often construct number relationships as they work to solve story problems prior to their mastery of basic facts. Consider the following problem:

Standards for Mathematical Practice

1 Make sense of problems and persevere in solving them

Molly has 2 more toy cars than Jack has. Jack has 5 cars. How many cars does Molly have?

In solving this problem, children might

- Use counters for each set.
- Use counters for Molly's cars starting with 5 and adding 2 more.
- Count on from 5.

Each of these possibilities can contribute to the development of the two-more-than relationship between 5 and 7. Problems that involve 5 and 10 as one of the numbers are useful for developing those numbers as reference points. Use problems, such as the following, that involve separation of a number into two parts to promote missing-part thinking:

Doug has a pocketful of pennies and nickels. He has 9 coins in all. He has 3 pennies. How many nickels does Doug have?

Research has demonstrated that when kindergarten and first-grade children are regularly asked to solve word problems, not only do they develop a collection of number relationships, but they also learn addition and subtraction facts based on these relationships. The key is to allow them to figure out ways to solve the problems. Simply telling them to solve the problems in a particular way robs them of the opportunities to build number relationships. This approach is further discussed in the next chapter.

Formative Assessment Note

The four types of number relationships (spatial representations, one and two more or less than, 5 and 10 anchors, and part–whole relationships) provide an excellent reference for assessing where your children are relative to number concepts. If you have station activities for these relationships, careful observations alone will tell a lot about children's number concepts. For a more careful assessment, each relationship can be assessed separately in a one-on-one interview, taking only a few minutes.

With a set of dot plates and a set of ten-frame cards you can quickly check which dot patterns children recognize without counting and whether they recognize quantities on ten-frames. To check their grasp of relationships involving one and two more or less than, simply write a few numbers on a sheet of paper. Point to a number and have the child tell you the number that is *"two less than* this number," varying the specific request with different numbers. It is not necessary to check every possibility.

For part–whole relationships, use a missing-part assessment similar to Activity 8.17 ("Covered Parts") on p. 115. Begin with a number you believe the child has "mastered," such as 5. Have the child count out that many counters into your open hand. Close your hand around the counters and confirm that child knows how many are hidden there. Then remove some and show them in the palm of your other hand. (See Figure 8.15.) Ask the child, "How many are hidden?" Repeat with different amounts removed, although it is only necessary to check three or four missing parts for each number. If the child responds quickly and correctly and is clearly not counting in any way, call that a "mastered number." If a number is mastered, repeat the entire process with the next higher number. Continue until the child begins to stumble. In early kindergarten you will find a range of mastered numbers from 4 to 7 or 8. By the end of kindergarten, children should have mastered numbers up to 10 (CCSSO, 2010).

Figure 8.15

A missing-part number assessment. Eight in all. "How many are hidden?"

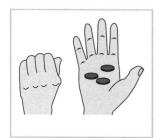

◆ Relationships for Numbers 10 to 20

Even though pre-kindergartners to second graders experience daily numbers up to 20 and beyond, it should not be assumed that they will automatically extend the set of relationships they have developed with smaller numbers to numbers beyond 10. And yet these numbers play a big part in many simple counting activities, in basic facts, and in much of what we do with mental computation. Relationships with these numbers are just as important as relationships involving the numbers through 10. In fact, an emerging approach to number instruction is to expose children to numbers beyond 10 and even beyond 20 as soon as possible—even before formal place-value instruction (Fosnot & Dolk, 2001; Wright, Stranger, Stafford, & Martland, 2006). Although children may count by ones to count sets beyond 10, the experiences of counting and grouping help children build important initial place-value knowledge. The emphasis should be on helping children learn the number words and numerals beyond 10 rather than the traditional notions of place value (e.g., names of places). That will come in time as children develop strategies to add and subtract two-digit numbers.

> *Teaching Tip*
>
> Children do not have to have formal place-value instruction before working with numbers beyond 10.

A Pre–Place-Value Relationship with 10

Stop and Reflect

Say to yourself, "One ten." Now think about that from the perspective of a child just learning to count to 20! What could one ten possibly mean when ten tells me how many fingers I have and is the number that comes after nine? How can it be one? ∎

Wright and his colleagues (2006) outlined a progression of three levels in children's understanding of ten:

1. *An initial concept of ten.* The child understands ten as ten ones and does not see ten as a unit. When children at this level work on a task involving tens, they will count by ones.

2. *An intermediate concept of ten.* The child understands ten as a unit composed of ten ones but relies on materials or representations to help complete tasks involving tens.

3. *A facile concept of ten.* The child can solve tasks involving tens and ones without using materials or representations. At this level children can mentally think about two-digit numbers as groups of tens and ones.

In order to help children begin to think about counting in ways that can move their understanding of "ten" forward, consider providing lots of purposeful opportunities for them to count and group objects. For example, Fosnot and Dolk (2001) describe a K–1 teacher who used the context of making necklaces using five beads of one color, then five beads of another color, and then repeating these groups of five. Children could count by ones if they needed to, but the teacher built in the constraint of creating necklaces with a five structure to encourage the children to begin to count by fives. Eventually she introduced the idea of selling the necklaces as a school fundraiser and suggested charging a penny per bead. Since the beads are in groups of five, the children begin to work with nickels and dimes, further encouraging the children to begin to see five and ten as units.

Building from the idea mentioned earlier, mapping the teens number names to a ten and one structure is an important idea (i.e., matching thirteen to "ten and three"). The activity that follows provides a way to help children visualize and reinforce the meaning of multidigit numbers.

Standards for Mathematical Practice

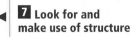
◀ **7** Look for and make use of structure

Figure 8.16

Building numbers with a set of cards.

Activity 8.21 BUILD THE NUMBER

From cardstock create a set of cards so that the tens card is twice as long as the ones card and the hundreds card is three times as long as the ones card (see Figure 8.16). To start, children use the cards to create two-digit numbers. Write a two-digit number, say, 26, where children can see it. Children are to find the two cards that can be used to make 26 (a 20 and a 6). Select children to demonstrate to the class how to make the given number. Point out that you can still see the 20 hiding under the overlay of the 6. Repeat the activity with different two-digit numbers. When children are ready, you can extend the activity to three-digit numbers. You can also have children model the numbers with materials, such as base-ten materials or ten-frames.

Given that their understanding of "ten" is likely to be at an initial concept level, the idea of a single ten can be strange for a kindergarten or early first-grade child to grasp. The difficulty of discussing "one ten and six ones" (what's a one?) does not mean that a set of ten should not figure prominently in the discussion of the teen numbers. The following activity illustrates this idea.

Activity 8.22 TEN AND SOME MORE

Using a simple two-part mat, have children count out ten counters onto one side. Next have them put five counters on the other side. Together count all of the counters by ones. Chorus the combination: "Ten and five is fifteen." Turn the mat around: "Five and ten is fifteen." Repeat with other numbers in a random order but without changing the ten side of the mat.

Activity 8.22 is designed to teach new number names and, thus, requires a certain amount of directed teaching. Following this activity, explore numbers to 20 in a more open-ended manner. Provide each child with two ten-frames drawn one under the other on a cardstock mat, or use Blackline Master 14. In random order, have children show numbers to 20 on their mats. There is no preferred way to do this as long as the number of counters is correct.

BLM

Formative Assessment Note

It is interesting to discuss how the counters can be placed on the mat so that it is easy to see how many are there. Have children share their ideas. Not every child will use a full set of 10, but as this idea becomes more popular, the notion that 10 and some more is a teen amount will soon be developed. Do not forget to include numbers less than 10 as well. As you listen to your children, you may want to begin challenging them to find ways to show larger amounts, such as 26 counters or even more.

Extending More and Less Relationships

Standards for
Mathematical Practice

8 Look for and express regularity in repeated reasoning ▶

The relationships of one more than, two more than, one less than, and two less than are important for all numbers. However, these ideas are built on or connected to the same concepts for numbers less than 10. The fact that 17 is one less than 18 is connected to the idea that 7 is one less than 8. Children may need help in making this connection.

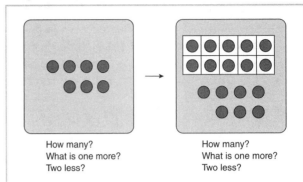

Figure 8.17 Extending relationships to the teens.

How many?	How many?
What is one more?	What is one more?
Two less?	Two less?

Activity 8.23 MORE AND LESS

EXTENDED

On a projector, show seven counters, and ask what is two more, or one less, and so on. Now add a filled ten-frame to the display (or 10 in any pattern) and repeat the questions. Pair up questions by covering and uncovering the ten-frame as illustrated in Figure 8.17.

Numbers to 100: Early Introductions

According to the *Common Core State Standards* (CCSSO, 2010), kindergartners are expected to be able to count to 100 by the end of the school year. Therefore, early exposure to numbers to 100 is important even in kindergarten. Although it is extremely unlikely that children in kindergarten or first grade will have a facile understanding of tens and ones or place value, they can learn much about the sequence of numbers to 100, if not beyond. Most important at this early level is for children to become familiar with the counting patterns to 100.

The hundreds chart (Figure 8.18) is an essential tool for every K–2 classroom. An extremely useful version of the chart is made of transparent pockets into which each of the 100 numeral cards can be inserted. You can hide a number by inserting a blank card in front of a number in the pocket. You can insert colored pieces of paper in the slots to highlight various number patterns. And you can remove some or all of the number cards and have children replace them in their correct slots.

A hundreds chart displayed using a projection device is almost as flexible as the pocket chart version. Numbers can be hidden by placing opaque counters on them. Patterns can be marked with a pen or with transparent counters. A blank 10×10 grid serves as an empty hundreds chart on which you can write numbers. These charts can be made from Blackline Masters 9–10 and are also available commercially. Computerized versions are also available online. A particular version found at www.nctm.org/standards/content.aspx?id=25013 uses a calculator and hundreds chart together so that children can visually see the patterns generated by the calculator.

There are many useful hundreds-chart activities for the K–2 level. If nothing else, children should orally count to 100 as you or a child points to each number on the chart. Whenever collections of things are counted, a good idea is to pause long enough to find the number on the chart. This can help put numbers for large quantities in perspective. Point out, for example, that 87 is a big number that is close to 100. The number 35 is also big but is closer to 20 than 100 and is far away from 87. Consider the following activities.

Figure 8.18
A hundreds chart.

1	2	3	4	5	6	7	8	9	10
11	12	13	14	15	16	17	18	19	20
21	22	23	24	25	26	27	28	29	30
31	32	33	34	35	36	37	38	39	40
41	42	43	44	45	46	47	48	49	50
51	52	53	54	55	56	57	58	59	60
61	62	63	64	65	66	67	68	69	70
71	72	73	74	75	76	77	78	79	80
81	82	83	84	85	86	87	88	89	90
91	92	93	94	95	96	97	98	99	100

BLM

◢ *Activity* 8.24 **PATTERNS ON A HUNDREDS CHART**

Have children work in pairs to find patterns on the hundreds chart. Solicit ideas orally from the class. Have children explain patterns found by others to be sure that all understand the ideas that are being suggested.

There are many different patterns on the hundreds chart. In a discussion, different children will describe the same pattern in several ways. Accept all ideas. Here are some of the patterns they may point out:

- The numbers in a column all end with the same number, which is the same as the number at the top.
- In a row, one number "counts" (the ones digit goes 1, 2, 3, . . . , 9, 0); the "second" number (ones digit) goes up by ones, but the first number (tens digit) stays the same.
- In a column, the first number (tens digit) "counts" or goes up by ones.
- You can count by tens going down the right-hand column.
- If you count by fives, you get two columns: the 5 column and the last column.

For children, these patterns are not at all obvious or trivial. For example, one child may notice the pattern in the column under the 4—every number ends in a 4. Two minutes later another child will "discover" the parallel pattern in the column headed by 7. That there is a pattern like this in every column may not be completely obvious.

Although not essential, skip-count patterns can also be explored at an early level. Skip counts by twos, fives, and tens are the easiest and the most important. Help children see the column patterns that these counts make.

◢ *Activity* 8.25 **MISSING NUMBERS**

Provide children with a hundreds chart on which some of the number cards have been removed. (You can use a classroom pocket chart.) The children's task is to replace the missing numbers in the chart. Beginning versions of this activity have only a random selection of individual numbers removed. Later, remove sequences of several numbers from three or four different rows. Finally, remove all but one or two rows or columns. Eventually, challenge children to replace all of the numbers in a blank chart.

The "Missing Numbers" activity can also be done with the full class. Use cardstock tabs to cover numbers on the chart. Have children write the missing numbers as you point to them. You may think that the adjacent numbers are too much of a clue, but the clue is itself a help in learning the number sequence.

📄 *Formative Assessment Note*

Replacing the number cards or tiles from a blank chart is a good learning center activity for two children to work on together. By listening to how children go about finding the correct locations for numbers, you can learn a lot about how well they have constructed an understanding of the 1-to-100 sequence.

Number Sense and the Real World

Here we examine ways to broaden early knowledge of numbers. Relationships of numbers to real-world quantities and measures and the use of numbers in simple estimations can help children develop flexible, intuitive ideas about numbers.

Calendar Activities

There are significant issues with calendar activities being considered the kind of mathematics instruction that will support young learners in reaching mathematical literacy.

Although the calendar may be helpful in developing a sense of time, the National Research Council Committee (2009) has stated that "using the calendar does not emphasize foundational mathematics" (p. 241) and has pointed out that the calendar does not support the development of key mathematical relationships related to 10 because the calendar is based on groups of seven. The committee concludes, "Doing the calendar is not a substitute for teaching foundational mathematics" (p. 241). Therefore, doing calendar mathematics should be thought of as an "add on" and should not take time away from developing essential pre-K–2 mathematics concepts.

Estimation and Measurement

One of the best ways for children to think of real quantities is to associate numbers with measures of things. In the early grades, measures of length, weight, and time are good places to begin. Just measuring and recording results will not be very effective, however, because there is no reason for children to be interested in or to think about the result. To help children think or reflect a bit on the numbers and what they mean, ask them to first write down or tell you an estimate. To produce an estimate is, however, a very difficult task for young children. They do not understand the concept of "estimate" or "about." For example, suppose that you cut out of cardstock an ample supply of very large footprints all the same size, say, about 18 inches long each. You would ask the class, "About how many footprints will it take to measure across the rug in our reading corner?" The key word here is *about*, and it is one that you will need to spend a lot of time helping children understand. To this end, the request for an estimate can be made in ways that help develop the concept of *about*. For example, rather than asking children for a specific number, begin by asking whether the amount will be more or less than a target number.

The following estimation questions can be used with most early estimation activities:

- *More or less than* _____ ? Will it be more or less than 10 footprints? Will the apple weigh more or less than 20 blocks? Are there more or less than 15 connecting cubes in this long bar?

- *Closer to* _____ *or to* _____ ? Will it be closer to 5 footprints or closer to 20 footprints? Will the apple weigh closer to 10 blocks or closer to 30 blocks? Is this bar closer to 10 cubes or closer to 50 cubes?

- *About* _____ ? Use one of these numbers: 5, 10, 15, 20, 25, 30, 35, 40, ... About how many footprints wide is the hallway? About how many blocks will the apple weigh? About how many cubes are in this bar?

Asking for estimates using these formats helps children learn what you mean by *about*. Every child can make an estimate without having to pull a number out of the air.

To help with numbers and measures, estimate several things in succession using the same unit. For example, suppose that you are estimating and measuring "around things" using a string. The string is wrapped around the object and then measured in some unit such as popsicle sticks. After measuring the distance around Demetria's head, estimate the distance around the wastebasket or around the globe or around George's wrist. Each successive measure helps children with the new estimates. See Chapter 15 for a complete discussion of measurement.

Activity 8.26 ADD A UNIT TO YOUR NUMBER

Write a number on the board. Now suggest some units to go with it, and ask the children what they can think of that fits. For example, suppose the number is 9. "What do you think of when I say 9 dollars? 9 hours? 9 cars? 9 kids? 9 meters? 9 o'clock? 9 hand spans? 9 gallons?" Spend some time in discussion of each. Let children suggest units as well. Be prepared to explore some of the ideas either immediately or as projects or tasks to share with parents at home.

Activity 8.27 IS IT REASONABLE?

Select a number and a unit—for example, 15 feet. Could the teacher be 15 feet tall? Could your living room be 15 feet wide? Can a man jump 15 feet high? Could three children stretch their arms 15 feet? Pick any number, large or small, and a unit with which children are familiar. Then make up a series of these questions.

◆ Standards for
Mathematical Practice

**3 Construct
viable arguments
and critique the
reasoning of others**

▶

Once children are familiar with Activity 8.27, have them select the number and the unit or things (e.g., 10 kids, 20 bananas), and see what kinds of questions children create. When a difference of opinion develops, capitalize on the opportunity to explore and find out. Resist the temptation to supply your adult-level knowledge. Say instead, "Well, how can we find out whether it is reasonable? Who has an idea about what we could do?"

◆ Graphs

Graphing activities are another good way to connect children's worlds with numbers. Chapter 17 discusses ways to make graphs with children in grades K–2. Graphs can be quickly made from almost any data that can be gathered with children: favorite ice cream, color, sports team, type of pet; number of sisters and brothers; kids who ride different buses; types of shoes; number of pets; and so on. Graphs can be connected to content in other subjects. A unit on sea life might lead to a graph of favorite sea animals.

Once a simple bar graph is made, it is very important to take a few minutes to ask as many number questions as are appropriate for the graph. In the early stages of number development (grades pre-K–1), the use of graphs for number relationships and for connecting numbers to real quantities in the children's environment is a more important reason for building graphs than the graphs themselves. The graphs focus attention on counts of realistic things. Equally important, bar graphs clearly exhibit comparisons between and among numbers that are rarely made when only one number or quantity is considered at a time. See Figure 8.19 for an example of a graph and questions that can be asked. At first, children will have trouble with the questions involving differences, but repeated exposure to these ideas in a bar graph format will improve their understanding. These comparison concepts add considerably to children's understanding of number.

Figure 8.19 Relationships and number sense in a bar graph.

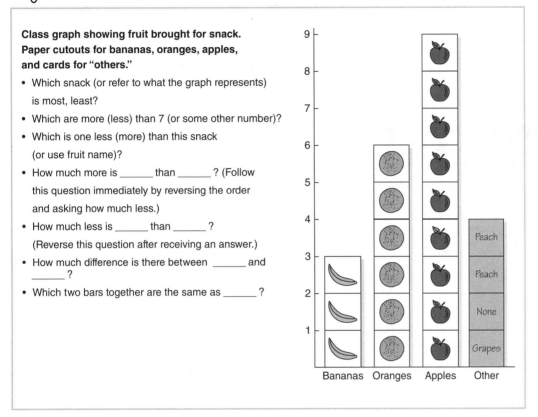

Class graph showing fruit brought for snack. Paper cutouts for bananas, oranges, apples, and cards for "others."

• Which snack (or refer to what the graph represents) is most, least?

• Which are more (less) than 7 (or some other number)?

• Which is one less (more) than this snack (or use fruit name)?

• How much more is _____ than _____? (Follow this question immediately by reversing the order and asking how much less.)

• How much less is _____ than _____? (Reverse this question after receiving an answer.)

• How much difference is there between _____ and _____?

• Which two bars together are the same as _____?

Expanded Lesson

I Wish I Had

Content and Task Decisions

Grade Level: K–1

Mathematics Goals

- To develop part–whole relationships by focusing on the missing part

Grade Level Guide

NCTM Curriculum Focal Points	Common Core State Standards
Children in **kindergarten** use written numerals to represent quantities and to solve quantitative problems in the joining and separating of sets. In **grade 1,** children use strategies for adding and subtracting whole numbers. They use part–whole models to support their problem-solving strategies.	Under the domain of Operations and Algebraic Thinking, children in **kindergarten** understand addition as putting together and adding to: "Represent and solve problems involving addition and subtraction." Moving to **grade 1,** children use addition within 20 to solve a variety of problem situations including adding to, putting together, and comparing.

Consider Your Children's Needs

Children can count meaningfully and, at least for the numbers in this lesson, have spent considerable time exploring decomposing and composing a number. For example, they have decomposed 7 into two parts, naming the parts as 2 and 5 or 6 and 1. Though not necessary, it would be good for children to have already worked with decomposing and composing the number that you select to use in this lesson using the two-column cards.

For English Language Learners

- Practice saying the numbers together in the *Before* phase.
- If a context is added (e.g., balloons), be sure it is familiar to all children.
- If children do not know the English words for each number, try to pair children to do the activity in their native language. Other possibilities are for them to show the answer by holding up the appropriate number of fingers. Or, if they are readers, provide a translation list of the numbers.

For Children with Disabilities

- Instead of the two-column cards, use connecting cubes.
- Use a part–part–whole mat such as the one in Chapter 9. Let children place the "I wish I had" number in the area representing the whole. Then use the other number as a part to help structure their thinking about the relationship.

Materials

Each child will need:

- A set of two-column cards in a plastic storage bag. These are best if copied onto cardstock and cut out for the children.

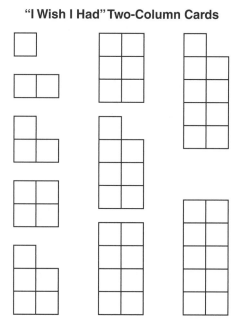

"I Wish I Had" Two-Column Cards

Two-column cards

Teacher will need:

- Either a projection device or a large demonstration set of two-column cards (see Blackline Master 34)

  BLM

- *Note:* Several alternative materials can be used, such as connecting cubes, dot plates, or ten-frames.

Lesson

Before

Present the focus task to the class:

- This lesson will be described for the number 7, but it can be done for any number from 6 to 10.

- Have children place a 7 card in front of them and return all cards greater than 7 to the bag.

- Show the class a two-column card for any number less than 7 and say, "I wish I had 7." The children's task is to find the two-column card from their set that goes with your card to make 7. For example, if you hold up (or place on the floor) a 2 card, they would have to find the 5 card.

- When children have found the card that makes 7 when combined with your card, they should hold it up *silently.* Call on a child to say the 7 combination: "Five and two makes seven."

- Add context to make it more interesting. Then student responses would include the context: "Five balloons and two more balloons makes seven balloons for my party!"

Provide clear expectations:

- This lesson can be done with a small group of children or the full class sitting in a circle on the floor. All children must be able to see the teacher materials clearly.

During

Ongoing:

- Occasionally stop and ask children how they decided on the card so that you can get insights into their thought processes.

- Do not forget to include 0 (indicate "no card" by miming the placing of a card) and also 7.

- For both right and wrong responses, ask whether other children agree. Another idea is to ask "How can we tell if that is correct?" Be sure to do this for both right and wrong responses.

- Pay attention to the methods that children use to find the required card. Do they count squares? Can they easily tell how many squares are on your card? Are they counting on from your card? Are they using card shapes instead of number of squares? You may want to have them put the 7 card away; however, some children may need to have it visible.

- Listen to how confident children are as they say their combinations.

- If 7 seems to present little challenge for all in the group, make a big deal out of changing the game to "I wish I had 8." Alternately, if 7 seems difficult, simply switch to 5 or 6.

After

Bring the class together to share and discuss the task:

- "Suppose that I show the 3 card. Tell me how you decide which card should go with it to make 7." Get responses from several children. Repeat the question with another card.

- "Is there any number that is easy for you? Why?"

- "Does the shape of the card help you? How?"

Assessment

Observe

- Children's success with this task depends somewhat on their familiarity with the two-column cards, though it depends more on their experiences with part–part–whole activities for the number 7 (or whatever number you have selected).

- There are many ways that children may use to find the correct card. They may first count the squares on your card and then select a card and count on. They may seem to know which card is needed but still have to count to find it. Others may use a purely spatial approach, comparing the shape of your card to the 7 card that is in front of them and locating the missing piece.

- Children for whom the game is easy and who do not need to count or rely on the spatial characteristics of the cards can be said to "know 7," at least in terms of parts and wholes.

- It is not a goal to be able to recognize numbers in this set without counting, but some children will quickly be able to recognize each of the cards without counting (subitize). This provides another way to think about numbers.

Ask

- "Suppose I show the 4 card. Tell me how you decide which card should go with it to make 7."

- "How did you find the missing part?"

Developing Meanings
for the Operations

Big IDEAS

1 Addition can be thought of as physically or conceptually placing two or more quantities together.

2 Subtraction can be thought of as taking an amount away from a given quantity, comparing two quantities, or finding a missing part given the whole and the other part.

3 Multiplication in grades pre-K–2 involves counting groups of equal size and determining how many are in all.

4 Division in grades pre-K–2 can be thought of as sharing equal amounts among a given number of groups or as repeatedly measuring out the same amount from a given total.

5 The operations are related to each other. Addition names the whole in terms of the parts, and subtraction names a missing part. Multiplication can be thought of as repeated addition. Division names a missing factor in terms of the known factor and the product. Division can also be thought of as repeated subtraction.

6 Models can be used to solve contextual problems for all operations and to figure out what operation is involved in a problem. Models also can be used to give meaning to number sentences.

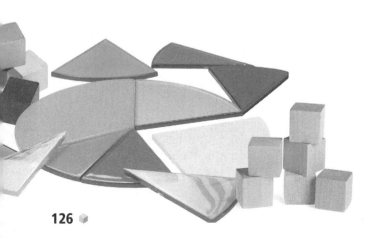

This chapter is about helping children connect different meanings, interpretations, and relationships to the four operations of addition, subtraction, multiplication, and division so that they can accurately and fluently apply these operations in real-world settings. As they make these connections, children develop what might be termed *operation sense*, a highly integrated understanding of the four operations and the many different but related meanings these operations take on in real contexts. As children develop their operation sense through problem solving and concept development, they can and should simultaneously develop more sophisticated ideas about number as well as different ways of thinking about basic fact combinations.

Teaching Operations through Contextual Problems

Contextual problems are the primary teaching tool that you can use to help children construct a rich understanding of the operations. What might a good lesson that is built around contextual problems look like? The answer comes more easily if you think about children not just solving the problems but also using words, pictures, and numbers to explain how they went about solving the problem and why they think they are correct. Children should solve problems using whatever techniques they wish including whatever physical materials they feel they need to help them, or they can simply draw pictures. What is important is that they explain what they did and why it makes sense within the context of the situation. If they are recording their ideas on paper, whatever they put on their paper, whether a written explanation or a drawing they used to help them solve the problem, it should explain what they did well enough to allow someone else to understand it. With the emphasis on children explaining their ideas and reasoning, lessons should focus on two or three problems and the related discussion.

Standards for Mathematical Practice

3 Construct viable arguments and critique the reasoning of others

Addition and Subtraction

From an adult's perspective the ideas of addition and subtraction seem quite simple. For example, think about how you would solve the following problem.

Aidan had 7 beads. After she bought some more beads, she had 15 beads. How many beads did Aidan buy?

Most adults and older students solve the problem by subtracting $15 - 7$. But young children do not initially view this as a subtraction situation because $15 - 7$ is the "opposite" operation or action implied in the problem. Instead they will mimic the implied action in the problem and solve it by adding on or counting up from 7 until they reach 15. Their approach may seem less efficient than simply subtracting, but it makes sense to young children because it mirrors the situation in the problem. Eventually, after much experience making sense of story problems, working with different combinations of numbers, and examining the results of using addition and subtraction in these situations (possibly at their teacher's request), they will begin to generalize that they get the same result by subtracting and will join older students and adults in using subtraction for these kinds of problems. This example illustrates how children's initial conceptions are different from those of adults—even with something we consider so basic as addition and subtraction.

Standards for Mathematical Practice

1 Make sense of problems and persevere in solving them

Children's conceptions are the best foundation on which to build future learning. Therefore, the perspective on addition and subtraction taken in this chapter is based on what has been learned from numerous research studies (Gutstein & Romberg, 1995; Carpenter, Fennema, Franke, Levi, & Empson, 1999; NRC, 2009; Verschaffel, Greer, & De Corte, 2007; Clements & Sarama, 2009). Through this research, we are aware that children can solve contextual or story problems with appropriate numbers by reasoning through the relationships in the problems. We also know that different problems have different structures that can affect the difficulty level of the problem. When teachers are familiar with these structures, they are better able to plan and differentiate instruction.

Addition and Subtraction Problem Structures

Addition and subtraction situations have been studied extensively and categorized in multiple ways (Gutstein & Romberg, 1995; Carpenter, Fennema, Franke, Levi, & Empson, 1999;

Standards for
Mathematical Practice

**7 Look for and make
use of structure**

Verschaffel, Greer, & De Corte, 2007; Clements & Sarama, 2009; NRC, 2009; CCSSO, 2010). Table 9.1 illustrates one categorization scheme that identifies four types of problems based on the relationships involved. The problem types include join (add to) problems, separate (take from) problems, part–part–whole (collection) problems, and comparison problems.

Table 9.1 Addition and Subtraction Problem Types Using the Number Family 4, 8, 12

Problem Type and Structure	Result Unknown	Change Unknown	Start Unknown
Physical Action Involved			
Join (Add To) Change → Start → Result	Sandra had 8 pennies. George gave her 4 more. How many pennies does Sandra have altogether?	Sandra had 8 pennies. George gave her some more. Now Sandra has 12 pennies. How many did George give her?	Sandra had some pennies. George gave her 4 more. Now Sandra has 12 pennies. How many pennies did Sandra have to begin with?
Separate (Take From) Change ← Start → Result	Sandra had 12 pennies. She gave 4 pennies to George. How many pennies does Sandra have now?	Sandra had 12 pennies. She gave some to George. Now she has 8 pennies. How many did she give to George?	Sandra had some pennies. She gave 4 to George. Now Sandra has 8 pennies left. How many pennies did Sandra have to begin with?

	Whole Unknown	**One Part Unknown**	**Both Parts Unknown**
No Physical Action Involved			
Part–Part–Whole (Collection) Whole / Part | Part	George has 4 pennies and 8 nickels. How many coins does he have?	George has 12 coins. Eight of his coins are pennies, and the rest are nickels. How many nickels does George have? George has 12 coins. Four of his coins are nickels, and the rest are pennies. How many pennies does George have?	George has 12 coins. Some are pennies and some are nickels. How many of each could he have?

	Difference Unknown	**Bigger Unknown**	**Smaller Unknown**
Comparison Bigger amount / Smaller ←→ Difference	George has 12 pennies and Sandra has 8 pennies. How many more pennies does George have than Sandra? (Alternative: How many fewer pennies does Sandra have than George?)	Sandra has 8 pennies. George has 4 more pennies than Sandra. How many pennies does George have? (Alternative: Sandra has 4 fewer pennies than George.)	George has 12 pennies. George has 4 more pennies than Sandra. How many pennies does Sandra have? (Alternative: Sandra has 4 fewer pennies than George.)

Join/Add To Problems. *Join* problems describe situations in which quantities are physically being brought together. These problems are also known as *add to* problems because the action or change occurring in the problem is a result of adding or joining quantities.

Separate/Take From Problems. *Separate* problems are commonly known as *take away* or *take from* problems in which part of a quantity is physically being removed or taken away. Notice that in the separate problems, the start amount is the whole or the largest amount, whereas in the join problems, the result is the whole.

Part–Part–Whole Problems. *Part–part–whole* problems, also known as *put together* and *take apart* problems in the *Common Core State Standards* (CCSSO, 2010), involve two parts that are conceptually or mentally combined into one collection or whole. These problems are different from joining problems in that there is no action of physically joining the two quantities. These kinds of problems often conceptually combine different kinds of objects, such as 5 red balls and 6 blue balls or 3 cars and 4 trucks, into one collection. The third situation in this problem type, in which the whole or total is known and the two parts are unknown, creates opportunities to think about all the possible decompositions of the whole.

Comparison Problems. Comparison problems involve comparing two quantities. The third quantity in these problems does not actually exist but is the difference between the two amounts. Like part–part–whole problems, comparison situations do not typically involve a physical action.

Structure versus Operation. Each type of problem involves a number "family," such as 4, 8, 12, that can be related through addition or subtraction. Note that the problems are described in terms of their structure and not as addition or subtraction problems. A different problem results within each problem type depending on which of the three quantities in the structure is unknown.

In most curricula, the overwhelming emphasis is on the easier join and separate problems with the result unknown. These become the de facto definitions of addition and subtraction: Addition is "put together" and subtraction is "take away." But these are not the only situations in which we use addition and subtraction, as you can see from Table 9.1. When children develop these limited put-together and take-away definitions for addition and subtraction, they often have difficulty later when addition or subtraction is called for but the structure of the problem is something other than put together or take away. It is important that children experience all the problem types to ensure they are developing a broader understanding of addition and subtraction. You can find more examples of these problem types in the *Common Core State Standards* (see Table 1 in the CCSSI Math Standards Glossary; CCSSO, 2010, p. 88).

Stop and Reflect

Go back through the problems in Table 9.1 and match the numbers in each problem with the components of the problem structure. For example, which numbers in the Join Problems match to Start, Change, and Result? Then for each problem, first use a set of counters to model (and solve) the problem as you think children in the primary grades might do. Second, write either an addition or subtraction equation that you think best represents the problem as you modeled it with counters. ∎

In writing an equation for each of the problems in Table 9.1, you may have written some equations where the unknown quantity is not isolated on one side of the equal sign. For example, a likely equation for the join problem with start unknown is $\square + 4 = 12$. This is referred to as the semantic equation for the problem since the numbers are listed in the order that follows the sequence in the problem. When the semantic form does not isolate the unknown, an equivalent equation can be written for the same problem. In this case, the equation $12 - 4 = \square$ is referred to as the computational form of the equation; it isolates the unknown and is typically how most adults think about the problem. This may be an efficient way to solve the problem, but children typically begin to think about and model the situation based on the sequence played out in the problem, which is modeled more appropriately by the semantic equation. When the two forms are not the same, you should help children eventually come to see the equivalence of these equations. However, initially they should be allowed to use the semantic form of the equation if this equation better represents their way of reasoning through the problem.

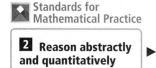

◆ Standards for Mathematical Practice

4 Model with mathematics

◆ Standards for Mathematical Practice

2 Reason abstractly and quantitatively

Children's Strategies for Solving Addition and Subtraction Problems

Research in mathematics education describes three levels through which children progress as they solve addition and subtraction situations (Carpenter, Fennema, Franke, Levi, & Empson, 1999; Clements & Sarama, 2007; NRC, 2009). The levels are direct modeling, counting strategies, and derived facts. Over time, after having multiple experiences with different addition and subtraction situations, children eventually become fluent with individual sums and differences and these become known facts to the children.

Let's consider how children might solve the following word problem depending on the level at which they are functioning.

Jacob has 5 cards. His brother gives him 8 more cards. How many cards does Jacob have now?

Children who use direct modeling to find a solution model every number and action the situation describes using actual objects, fingers, or drawings. So a child who is working at the direct modeling level would count out 5 blocks, then count out 8 more blocks, and then count them all to find 13—this is called a "count all" strategy. A child who is using counting strategies does not need to model every number in the situation. So this child might start at 8 and count up 5, holding up one finger for each number word from 9 up to 13—this is called a "counting on" strategy. A child functioning at the derived facts level often looks for ways to decompose the numbers in a given situation to make an easier problem. This child may reason that because 8 is 2 away from 10, he can decompose 5 into 2 and 3, add the 2 to the 8 to get 10, and then add 3 more to get 13—this is called an "up over 10" strategy. A child who is using derived facts may reason so quickly that it appears that the fact is a known fact. In this case, the distinction between derived and known facts is arbitrary.

◆ Problem Difficulty

Structure

The various types of problems are not at all equal in difficulty for children. Problems in which a physical action is taking place, as in join and separate problems, are easier because children can model or act out the situation. However, even within these types of problems, some problems are more difficult than others. Consider each of the following three problems.

Maggie had 7 bracelets. She bought 8 more bracelets. How many bracelets does Maggie now have?

Maggie had 7 bracelets. She bought some more bracelets. She now has 15 bracelets. How many did Maggie buy?

Maggie had some bracelets. She bought 8 more bracelets. She now has 15 bracelets. How many bracelets did Maggie start with?

Stop and Reflect

Use a set of counters to model (and solve) these problems as you think children in the primary grades might do. Rank order the problems in terms of which ones you think would be more difficult for children. Why do you think one problem might be more difficult than the others? ■

Unknown start problems are more difficult than unknown change problems and unknown change problems are more difficult than unknown result problems. Unknown start problems are among the most difficult probably because children modeling the problems directly do not know how many counters to put down to begin with. For these problems, children initially use a trial-and-error approach (Carpenter, Fennema, Franke, Levi, & Empson, 1999) to determine the unknown start amount. The easiest of the three problems is the first one, in which the start and change are known because to find the unknown result the known quantities are simply combined, an action that is implied in the problem. The result unknown problems tend to be the most commonly used in classrooms. Make sure to provide your children a wide range of experiences by also posing join and separate problems with more difficult structures.

Teaching Tip

Many children have difficulty with problems in which the start is unknown because they try to model the problem in chronological order and they cannot make the set that represents the beginning of the problem. Write a question mark on an index card and have children use the card to represent the unknown amount.

Part-part-whole problems can be difficult for children for two reasons. First, there is no action to model because the situation describes a conceptual bringing together of quantities, which is difficult to directly model. Second, it is a challenge for children to grasp that a quantity can represent two things at once. For example, if the problem describes 3 cars and 4 trucks in a parking lot and asks how many vehicles are in the lot, children have to understand that the cars and trucks are also part of the larger category of vehicles.

The challenge of comparison problems comes from the fact that two quantities are being described using language that can be complex for children. Fewer, less than, more, bigger, and greater than are the terms typically used to describe the relationships in comparison problems. Children often have more experiences with the relationships of more and bigger than, so you need to ensure they have opportunities to think about relationships described using fewer and less than. Note that when the bigger amount is unknown, stating the problem using the term *more* is easier for children because the relationships between the quantities and the operation more readily correspond to each other. In the

Teaching Tip

If children struggle to make sense of the relationship between the quantities in a comparison problem, suggest they cover up the number that comes before the word more/fewer (e.g., George has ■ more pennies than Sandra; Sandra has ■ fewer pennies than George). This strategy helps them determine which quantity is bigger or smaller.

smaller unknown situation, stating the problem using the term *fewer* is easier for children for the same reason. Similar to the part–part–whole problems, the lack of a physical action in these situations makes it difficult for children to model or act out these kinds of problems.

Choosing Numbers for Problems

You can vary the difficulty of the problem by the numbers you choose to use. If a child is struggling with a problem, use smaller numbers to see if it is the size of the numbers causing the difficulty. You can also increase the challenge by increasing the size of the numbers if a child needs the added challenge. In general, the numbers in the problems should be in accord with the children's number development. According to the *Common Core State Standards* (CCSSO, 2010), by the end of their respective school years, kindergartners should be able to count as many as 20 objects to answer "how many?"; first graders should be able to add and subtract up to 20 and demonstrate fluency up to 10; and second graders should be able to add and subtract fluently up to 20. Kindergartners are also expected to decompose numbers between 11 and 19 into tens and ones; first graders are learning about decomposing two-digit numbers up to 100; and second graders are learning about decomposing three-digit numbers up to 1000. Clearly, children in grades K–2 are learning about multidigit numbers and are beginning to understand how our base-ten system works. Rather than wait until children have developed techniques for computing numbers, you can use word problems as a problem-based opportunity for them to learn about number and computation at the same time. For example, a problem involving the combination of 30 and 42 has the potential to help first and second graders focus on sets of 10. As they begin to think of 42 as 40 and 2, it is not at all unreasonable to think that they will add 30 and 40 and then add 2 more. The structure of a word problem can strongly influence the type of strategy a child invents to solve a multidigit problem. This is especially true for children who have not been taught the standard algorithms for addition and subtraction. For example, consider the following problem.

A school of 28 fish was swimming together in the ocean. Another school of fish decided to join them, making a larger school of fish. The new larger school had 64 fish. How many fish were in the second school of fish that joined the first group of fish?

Because the preceding problem has a join action, this increases the probability that children will use a counting-on or an add-on approach to solve the problem. Using an open number line to support a more efficient strategy than simply counting on by ones, a child might reason as follows: Add 2 to 28 to get to 30, add 30 more to get to 60, add 4 more to get to 64. Then add 2 + 30 + 4 (what was added to 28 to get 64). Another child might add on 40 to 28 making 68 and then take off the 4 extra—4 from 40 is 36. You can learn more about student-invented strategies for computation in Chapter 12.

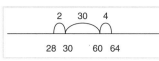

Wording of Problems

Problems that are worded so that the actions and quantities follow in a chronological or natural story order are generally easier than those in which the problem order is inverted. For example, in the following pair of problems, notice how the second problem matches a natural order of events:

Mike's grandpa gave him some money for his birthday. Mike already had 6 dollars. Now Mike has 9 dollars. How much did Mike's grandpa give him?

Mike had 6 dollars. His grandpa gave him some money for his birthday. Now he has 9 dollars. How much did Mike's grandpa give him?

Join problems in which the change is unknown can be thought of in terms of "how much more is needed" or in terms of "how much was added." Some children find actions that happened in the past more difficult to grasp—as in "how much was added?" These children would find the first of the following two problems easier:

Joyce has 3 eggs in her basket. How many more eggs does she need to find to have 8 eggs?

Joyce has 3 eggs in her basket. She found some more eggs for her basket in the chicken coop. Now she has 8 eggs. How many more eggs did Joyce find in the chicken coop?

When you think that issues with wording are the cause of difficulty, pose problems with *similar structure* but with wording in which the actions and quantities follow a chronological or natural story order. If it is the wording that is causing the difficulty, have children gain confidence with the easier wording, but eventually they need to be challenged to make sense of the more difficult wording. Here are some strategies to help support children when they are challenged with more difficult wording:

- When children do not seem to know what to do with a problem, ask them first to talk about what is happening in the problem. (See the suggestions in the later section, "Encourage Problem Analysis.")

- Have children use counters to act out the problem. Have them say out loud what each set of counters stands for and explain with the counters what is happening in the problem. This can help children with similar analyses when you are not there to make these suggestions.

- Have children draw out pictures that represent each of the quantities in the problem. Then have them try to articulate the relationships between these quantities.

If you have English language learners (ELLs) in your classroom, you may be tempted to avoid using story problems because of the concern that language might present a challenge for them. However, contextual problems are good for ELLs because they connect to life experiences. Some strategies to support comprehension of story problems include structuring the sentences to use present and past tenses, using a noun-verb word order, replacing terms such as *his/her* and *it* with a name, and removing unnecessary vocabulary words. Also ensure that ELLs understand the meaning of any contextual terms (e.g., *chicken coop, model boat, savings account*) as well as any mathematical terms (e.g., *how many, fewer, feet*) used in story problems.

◆ Introducing Symbolism

Very young children initially have no need for the symbols +, −, and =. However, these symbolic conventions are important. When you feel your children are ready to use these symbols, introduce them in the discussion portion of a lesson where children have solved story problems. Say, "You had the number 12 in your problem and the number 8 was one of the parts of 12. You found out that the part you did not know was 4. Here is a way we can write that: $12 - 8 = 4$." The minus sign should be read as "minus" or "subtract" but not as "take away" because not all subtraction situations are take away situations. The plus sign

◀ **Standards for Mathematical Practice**

4 Model with mathematics

is easier since it is typically a substitute for "and." Alternatively, for the same problem, you could introduce the equation as $8 + 4 = 12$, especially if a child has described a counting-up strategy to find 4.

Some care should be taken with the equal sign. The equal sign means "is the same as." However, many children come to think of it as a symbol that tells you that the "answer is coming up" or "it is time to do a computation." It is interpreted in much the same way as the = key on a calculator. That is, it is the key you press to get the answer. Find opportunities to write equations like $12 = 8 + 4$ to counter this misinterpretation of the equal sign. So, for example, if a child has described how she broke or decomposed 8 into 3 and 5, you could record that idea as $8 = 3 + 5$. The next activity helps to emphasize the meaning of the equal sign.

Teaching Tip

Use the phrase "is the same as" in place of or in conjunction with "equals" as you read equations with children.

Activity 9.1 **TRUE OR FALSE**

Create a list of number sentences to introduce children to the idea of determining whether a number sentence is correct. For example, show children the following number sentences and ask whether each is true or false and how they know: $3 + 4 = 7$; $7 + 8 = 15$; $10 - 4 = 5$; and $8 - 5 = 3$. Once they are familiar with true/false number sentences, introduce number sentences that will encourage them to examine their understanding of the equal sign. The following are some examples: $7 = 3 + 4$; $3 + 6 = 6 + 3$; $2 + 6 = 4 + 4$; $3 = 10 - 7$; and $5 = 5$. You can also pose problems such as $3 + 4 = \square + 5$ in which the task is for children to make a true number sentence. Encourage children to explain their thinking.

Standards for Mathematical Practice

5 Use appropriate tools strategically

Using Model-Based Problems for Addition and Subtraction

▶ Many children will use models such as counters, diagrams, or number lines to solve story problems. The model is a thinking tool to help them both understand what is happening in the problem and a means of keeping track of the numbers and solving the problem. Problems can also be posed using models when there is no context involved.

Addition

When the parts of a set are known, addition is used to name the whole in terms of the parts. This simple definition of addition serves both action situations (join and separate) and static or no-action situations.

Each part–part–whole model shown in Figure 9.1 is a model for $5 + 3 = 8$. Some of these are the result of a definite add to or joining action, and some are not. Notice that in every example, both of the parts are distinct, even after the parts are joined. For children to see a relationship between the two parts and the whole, the image of the 5 and 3 must be kept as two separate sets. For example, if counters are used, the two parts should be kept in separate piles or in separate sections of a mat or should be two distinct colors. This helps children reflect on the action after it has taken place. "These red chips are the ones I started with. Then I added these five blue ones, and now I have eight altogether."

Figure 9.1 Part–part–whole models for 5 + 3 = 8 and 8 − 3 = 5.

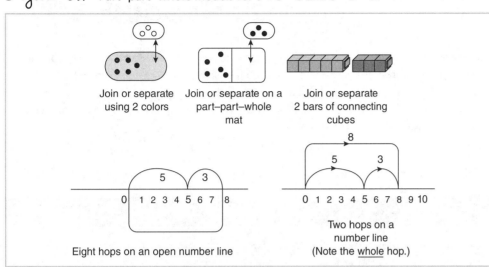

Join or separate using 2 colors

Join or separate on a part–part–whole mat

Join or separate 2 bars of connecting cubes

Eight hops on an open number line

Two hops on a number line (Note the whole hop.)

Activity 9.2   BUILD IT IN PARTS EQUATIONS

Recall Activity 8.16, called "Build It in Parts," and its variations in which children made designs or built sets to represent different combinations for a particular number. In this activity, children are challenged to find different combinations for the same number. When children are ready to deal with written symbolism, simply show them how to write an addition number sentence (equation) for each design. Initially with "Build It in Parts" children said a combination, such as "Four and five is nine." Now they have a new symbolic way to represent and record what they say.

Figure 9.1 includes two different versions of a number line model. A number line model can present some conceptual difficulties for younger children. A number line measures distances from zero the same way a ruler does and children mistakenly might focus on the hash marks or numerals on a number line instead of the spaces (units of length) when using a number line to count. Figure 9.2 shows a sequence of four number line models that can be used to introduce children to the more commonly used number line model and then the open number line model. The first of the number lines in Figure 9.2 accentuates the spaces (or the units) between the numerals by using thin rectangular strips in alternating colors. Eventually introduce the hash marks and over time move to the more commonly seen number line. The fourth model in Figure 9.2, the open number line, has been found to be an effective way for children to keep track of and communicate their reasoning (Fosnot & Dolk, 2001). But before using open number lines, children need to know what the units and numbers on a number line represent. So the open number line model should be introduced only after children demonstrate the understanding that they are counting spaces as opposed to numbers or hash marks. To model the part–part–whole concept of 5 + 3 on any version of the number line, start by drawing an arc from 0 to 5 and saying, "This much is five." The arcs or hops are used to explicitly illustrate the notion of length. This technique is demonstrated in the first and fourth models in Figure 9.2. It is extremely important that you do not point to the hash mark for 5 and say, "This is five."

Figure 9.2

Sequence of number lines.

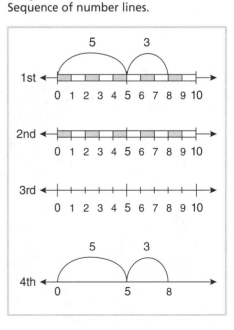

You can find an interactive number line at www.eduplace.com/kids/mw that emphasizes the unit by using animals (a frog, a rabbit, or a kangaroo) to hop along the number line. Once at the site, select the grade level (K, 1, or 2), e-Manipulatives, and then Number Line. Each hop is marked with an arc and a length and you can change the length of the hops from one to ten. You can also change the direction of the hop so that the animal hops forward (addition) or backward (subtraction).

The next activity provides an opportunity for children to make sense of a number line.

Activity 9.3 UP AND DOWN THE NUMBER LINE

Create a large number line on the floor of your classroom by using colored tape. (Masking tape comes in a variety of colors and will not leave adhesive on your floor.) Make sure to start with zero and include arrows at each end of the line. Alternatively you could display a number line in the front of your room. Use a stuffed animal, like a frog or rabbit, for hopping along the number line, or ask a child to walk on the number line if using the floor model. Pose a variety of problem situations and talk about the movement required for each situation. To begin with, your problem situations should mirror the idea of moving a distance to emphasize the spaces (units of length) between the numbers on the number line. For example, use a scenario of a baby rabbit making 5 hops away from its mother and then making 3 hops back. The children's task is to determine how many hops away the baby is from its mother. This activity can help children create a mental image for thinking about the meaning of addition and subtraction.

Subtraction

In a part–part–whole model, when the whole and one of the parts are known, subtraction can be used to name the other part. If you start with a whole set of 8 and remove a set of 3, the two sets that you know are the sets of 8 and 3. The expression 8 − 3, read "eight minus three," names the five remaining. Notice that the models in Figure 9.1 are models for subtraction as well as addition (except for the action). Helping children see that they are using the same models or pictures aids in connecting the two operations.

Activity 9.4 MISSING-PART SUBTRACTION

Use a context or story about something that is hiding to introduce this activity. For example, the books *Five Little Monkeys Play Hide-and-Seek* (Christelow, 2004) and *What's Hiding in There?* (Drescher, 2008) offer scenarios that can be used as contexts. Explain to the children that they will model whatever is hiding using a fixed number of tiles placed on a mat. One child separates the tiles into two parts while another hides his or her eyes. The first child covers one of the two parts with a sheet of paper or a large index card, revealing only the other part (see Figure 9.3). The second child says the subtraction sentence. For example, "Nine minus four [the visible part] is five [the covered part]." The covered part can be revealed for the child to self-check. Have children record both the subtraction equation and the addition equation. ELLs may need sentence prompts such as "_____ minus _____ is _____."

◆ Standards for Mathematical Practice

2 Reason abstractly and quantitatively ▶

Figure 9.3

Models for 9 − 4 as a missing-part problem.

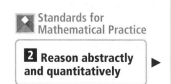

No action

Start with 9 in all.
Remove some.
How many covered?

Start with a bar of 9.
Break some off.
How many hidden?

The other part of the bar is hidden.

Subtraction as Think-Addition

Note that in Activity 9.4, the situation ends with two parts clearly distinct, even when there is a remove action. The removed part remains in the activity or on the mat as a model for an addition equation to be written after writing the subtraction equation. A discussion of how these two equations can be written for the same model is an important opportunity to connect addition and subtraction. This is significantly better than the traditional worksheet activity of "fact families" in which children are given a family of numbers, such as 3, 5, and 8, and are told to write two addition equations and two subtraction equations. Very quickly this becomes a matter of putting the numbers in the various slots without much meaning.

Subtraction as "think-addition" is extremely significant for mastering subtraction facts. Because the tiles for the remaining or unknown part are left hidden under the cover, when children do these activities they are encouraged to think about the hidden part: "What goes with the part I see to make the whole?" For example, if the total or whole number of tiles is nine, and six can be seen, the child is likely to think in terms of "6 and what makes 9?" or "What goes with 6 to make 9?" The mental activity is "think-addition" instead of a "count what's left" approach. Later, when working on subtraction facts, a subtraction fact such as $9 - 6 = \square$ should trigger the same thought pattern: "6 and what makes 9?"

Formative Assessment Note

The techniques that children use to solve problems provide you with important information concerning their number development, strategies that they may be using to answer basic facts, and methods that they are using for multidigit computation. Therefore, it is essential that you look at more than the answers children get. These methods can give you clues as to what numbers to use in problems for the next day. The information can also be used to give special number or computation development work to children who need it. Key papers can be saved in folders and used in conferences to show parents how their child is working and progressing.

For example, a child who counts out counters for each of two addends and then counts all of the counters might be encouraged to count on by posing a problem involving adding 14 + 3, a large number and a small one. If you have been working on the meaning of the teens or other ideas about tens, you should pose problems that offer opportunities for children to use these ideas. For example, pose problems for 14 − 10 or 10 + 10 + 10 + 6. Then you can observe children's use of the ideas you have been working on.

Similarly, you can pose problems involving number concepts or computations that you have not yet explored with your children. How they approach the problems will give you clues as to where that portion of your number program can best begin.

The point is to use story problems to assess more than problem solving. Number and computation skills are often much more clearly visible in children's work with story problems than on exercises devoid of a context.

Comparison Models

Comparison situations involve two distinct sets or quantities and the difference between them. Several ways of modeling the difference relationship are shown in Figure 9.4. The same kind of model can be used whether the difference or one of the two quantities is unknown.

Figure 9.4

Models for the difference between 8 and 5.

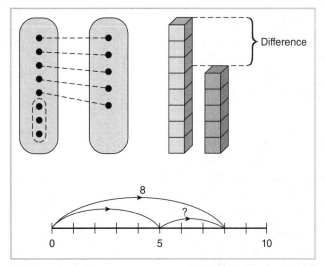

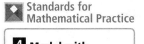

4 Model with mathematics

Note that it is not immediately clear how you would associate either the addition or subtraction operations with a comparison situation. From an adult vantage point, you can see that if you match part of the larger amount with the smaller amount, the large set is now a part–part–whole model that can be used to solve the problem. In fact, children may model compare problems in just this manner. But that is a very difficult idea to show children if they do not construct the idea themselves.

Have children make two amounts, perhaps with two bars of connecting cubes. They can match the cubes in the two bars until all the cubes are used from the shorter bar. The unmatched cubes in the longer bar represent the difference. Discuss the difference between the two bars to generate the third number. For example, if the children make a bar of 10 and a bar of 6, the difference is 4. "What equations can we make with these three numbers?" Have children make up story problems that involve two amounts of 10 and 6 that they are comparing. Discuss which equations go with the problems that are created.

◆ The Commutative Property and the Zero Property

The commutative property (sometimes known as the order property) for addition says that it makes no difference in which order two numbers are added. Most children find little difficulty with this idea after they have had many opportunities to verify for themselves that the order in an addition problem does not matter. Since it is quite useful in problem solving, mastering basic facts, and mental mathematics, there is value in spending some time helping children construct the relationship. Having children state the name of the property is not important, but the idea behind the property is important for them to understand.

To help children focus on the order property, pair problems that have the same addends but in different orders. Using a different context for each problem can help children focus on the significant similarities that go beyond context. For example:

Tania is on page 8 in her book. Tomorrow she hopes to read 6 more pages. What page will she be on if she reads that many pages?

The recycling bin in the cafeteria had 6 bottles in it. During lunch 8 more bottles were put in the bin. How many bottles were in the bin after lunch?

Ask if anyone notices how these problems are alike. If done as a pair, some children will see that having solved one they have essentially solved the other. You will likely need to pose multiple problem pairs across time before children become convinced that the order does not matter.

The following activity helps with the same idea.

◆ Activity 9.5   MORE THAN TWO ADDENDS

Give children six sums to find involving three or four addends. Prepare these on one page divided into six sections so that there is space to write beneath each sum. Within each, include at least one pair with a sum of 10 or perhaps a double: $4 + 7 + 6$, $5 + 9 + 9$, or $3 + 4 + 3 + 7$. Children should discuss and show how they added the numbers. Allow children to find the sums without any other directions.

Figure 9.5 illustrates how children might show what they did. As they share their solutions, almost certainly there will be children who added in different orders but got the same result. From this discussion you can help them conclude that you can add numbers in any order. But continue to find opportunities to highlight this idea because some children will need additional time to be convinced that the order does not matter. You are also using the associative property, but it is the commutative property that is more important here. This is also an excellent number sense activity because many children will find combinations of 10 in these sums or will use doubles (easy facts for many children). Learning to adjust strategies to fit the numbers is the beginning of the road to computational fluency. Note that some children will attempt to overgeneralize the commutative property to subtraction. Use contextual situations or story problems to help children confront this misconception.

Using story problems with zero or with zero in the three-addend sums (e.g., $4 + 0 + 2$) is also a good method of helping children understand zero in addition or subtraction. Occasionally children think that $6 + 0$ must be more than 6 or that $12 - 0$ must be 11 since "addition makes numbers bigger" or "subtraction makes numbers smaller." Instead of making meaningless rules, create opportunities for discussing adding and subtracting zero using contextual situations.

Standards for
Mathematical Practice

◀ **8 Look for and express regularity in repeated reasoning**

Figure 9.5
Children show how they added.

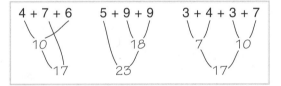

▲ Laying the Foundation for Multiplication and Division

The *Common Core State Standards* recommends that second graders should work with equal groups of objects to build a foundation for the formal study of multiplication (CCSSO, 2010). In fact, kindergarten through second-grade children can be quite successful at solving multiplication and division contextual problems, even division involving remainders, prior to being taught computational methods for multiplication and division or even before they have learned the terms or symbols used in multiplication and division (Carpenter, Fennema, Franke, Levi, & Empson, 1999; Schifter, Bastable, & Russell, 1999; Roberts, 2003). Young children engage in situations such as counting equal groups (multiplication) and fairly sharing or measuring out (division) in their daily lives outside of school. Capitalizing on these kinds of informal experiences with multiplication and division situations can help lay a good foundation for more formal study of these operations in later grades. Multiplication and division problems also provide children with opportunities to work with the idea of groups, which helps with the development of place value and grouping in tens.

◆ Multiplication and Division Problem Structures

Although there are meanings for multiplication other than equal groups or repeated addition, we will focus on this particular meaning because it relates well to the addition work in which children in grades pre-K–2 have been involved and is typically how multiplication and division are introduced. Equal group problems involve three quantities: the number of groups, the size of each group, and the total. These quantities are illustrated in the following problem:

Jill has 4 bags of crayons. There are 3 crayons in each bag. All together she has 12 crayons.

In a given problem, any of these three quantities can be unknown. When the total is unknown, the problem is a multiplication situation. When either the number of groups or the size of the groups is unknown, the problem is a division situation. But note that these latter two situations are not alike. Problems in which the size of the groups is unknown are called fair-sharing or partition problems. The whole is shared or distributed among a known number of groups to determine the size of each. If the number of groups is unknown but the size of the equal groups is known, the problems are called measurement or repeated subtraction problems. The whole is "measured off" in groups of the given size.

There is also a subtle difference between problems that might be termed equal-group problems (e.g., If 3 children have 4 apples each, how many apples are there?) and those that might be termed rate problems (e.g., If there are 4 apples per child, how many apples would 3 children have?). Rate problems may be more difficult for children because they involve a rate rather than a number of countable objects. However, because they can be thought of in much the same way as the equal-group problems, you should consider posing such problems.

Standards for Mathematical Practice

7 Look for and make use of structure

Examples of the problem types for multiplication and division are shown in Table 9.2. Problems matching these structures can be modeled with sets of counters, number lines, or arrays. (The term multiplicative is used here to describe all problems that involve multiplication and division structure.) You can find more examples of these problem types in the *Common Core State Standards* (see Table 2 in the CCSSI Math Standards Glossary; CCSSO, 2010, p. 89).

In multiplicative problems, one number or factor counts how many groups or parts of equal size are involved. The other factor tells the size of each group or part. The third number in each of these two structures is the whole or product and is the total of all of the parts. The parts and wholes terminology is useful in making the connection to addition.

Table 9.2 Multiplication and Division Problem Types

Problem Type	Multiplication (Whole Unknown)	Partition Division (Size of Groups Unknown)	Measurement Division (Number of Groups Unknown)
Equal groups	Mark has 4 bags of apples. There are 6 apples in each bag. How many apples does Mark have altogether?	Mark has 24 apples. He wants to share them equally among his 4 friends. How many apples will each friend receive?	Mark has 24 apples. He put them into bags containing 6 apples each. How many bags did Mark use?
Rate	If apples cost 7 cents each, how much did Jill have to pay for 5 apples?	Jill paid 35 cents for 5 apples. What was the cost of 1 apple?	Jill bought apples at 7 cents apiece. The total cost of her apples was 35 cents. How many apples did Jill buy?

Children's Strategies for Solving Multiplication and Division Problems

As with addition and subtraction situations, children progress through different levels of strategies as they solve multiplication and division situations. Initially they solve these kinds of problems by directly modeling the relationships and action described in the problems. In time children move from directly modeling to using counting strategies and then to using derived facts.

Let's consider how children who are using different levels of strategies might solve the following multiplication problem:

There are 3 golf balls in a tube. How many balls are in 6 tubes?

A child who is directly modeling would make 6 groups with 3 counters in each group and would count all the counters to find the answer. A child who has moved to the next level might hold up a finger one at a time as she counts by three 6 times: 3, 6, 9, 12, 15, 18. Another child who is not as proficient at skip counting by threes may start skip counting and then revert to counting by ones: 3, 6, 9, 12, . . . 13, 14, 15, . . . 16, 17, 18. This child is still using a counting strategy. When a child is using derived facts, he uses known facts to find unknown facts. For this problem, a child might reason that 3×5 is 15 and 3 more is 18.

For partition division, let's look at the following problem:

Arielle has 12 lollipops. She wants to share them equally among 4 of her friends. How many will each friend get?

When direct modeling, a child will count out 12 counters and then separate them into 4 groups, probably placing one counter in each of the 4 groups until all 12 counters are distributed. He would then count the counters in one of the groups to find the answer. For a child who is using a counting strategy to solve a partition division problem, the child will typically use trial and error to determine how many might be in each group because she is trying to mimic the action in the problem. So the child might first skip-count by twos, keeping track of the number of twos on her fingers: 2, 4, 6, 8. Because 4 twos is not enough, she tries another number, say, 3: 3, 6, 9, 12. When she reaches 12 with 4 fingers raised, she realizes each friend would get 3 lollipops.

For measurement division, consider this problem:

> **Standards for Mathematical Practice**
>
> **1** **Make sense of problems and persevere in solving them**

Parker has 24 cupcakes. He wants to store the cupcakes 6 to a box. How many boxes will he need?

A child who is directly modeling will count out 24 counters and then repeatedly measure out groups of 6 counters until no more groups of 6 are possible. He will then count the number of groups to find the answer. For a child who is using a counting strategy, he will count by sixes, keeping track of each count, say, by extending a finger: 6, 12, 18, 24. Looking at 4 extended fingers, he knows Parker will need 4 boxes. If a child is using derived facts, he may think 5×6 is 30, but one less 6 would be 24—so, 4 boxes.

Symbolism for Multiplication

When children solve simple multiplication story problems before learning about multiplication symbolism, they will most likely write repeated addition equations to represent what they did. In fact, the *Common Core State Standards* recommends that second graders begin

▶

to write equations to express the total as a sum of equal addends (CCSSO, 2010). If you feel your children are ready, introduce the multiplication sign and explain what the two factors mean. You can also write one sentence that expresses both concepts at once, for example, $9 + 9 + 9 + 9 = 4 \times 9$.

In the United States, the usual convention is that 4×8 refers to four sets of eight, not eight sets of four. (In other countries such as Japan and Korea, the convention is that 4×8 refers to eight sets of four.) The more important idea at this level is the informal explorations with multiplication and division situations and not the introduction of symbolism.

◢ Choosing Numbers for Problems

Choose numbers that are within your children's grasp when creating multiplication and division problems. In the early grades, it is a mistake to only pose problems without remainders. Rather, it is useful to include story problems with remainders and explore the different ways that children handle these in context. For children who are beginning to talk about fractions, include partition problems in which items can be subdivided into fractional parts (brownies, pies, cups of milk, etc.). For example,

Griffin has 11 brownies and he wants to share them with 4 people. How many brownies will each person get?

Figure 9.6

Remainders expressed as fractions.

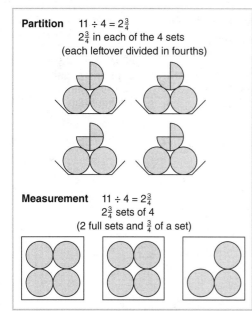

Partition $11 \div 4 = 2\frac{3}{4}$
$2\frac{3}{4}$ in each of the 4 sets
(each leftover divided in fourths)

Measurement $11 \div 4 = 2\frac{3}{4}$
$2\frac{3}{4}$ sets of 4
(2 full sets and $\frac{3}{4}$ of a set)

Some children will handle partition problems like this one by fairly sharing, as can be seen in the first part of Figure 9.6.

It is a bit more difficult to conceptualize a measurement problem with a fractional remainder. Consider the following problems:

Tania was filling crates with special oranges. Each crate holds 4 oranges. If Tania has 11 oranges, how many crates will she need?

Toby has 11 cups of milk in a pitcher. If he pours all 11 cups into jars that hold 4 cups each, how many jars will Toby fill?

The first problem can be modeled as 2 full crates and $\frac{3}{4}$ of another crate (see the second part of Figure 9.6). This requires thinking of each crate as a whole and assumes that the child will think about a partial crate as part of the answer. In the milk problem, there may be a greater chance of thinking about a jar being $\frac{3}{4}$ full. If you want to introduce these fractional ideas and no one in the class suggests them, offer them yourself. You can say, "If someone said that Toby filled two and three-fourths jars with milk, would that make sense? Do you think that could be a correct answer?" There is no need to be afraid of these ideas even if they do not appear in your curriculum.

More often than not, division situations in real life do not result in a simple whole number. In the absence of a context, a remainder can be dealt with in only two ways: It can either remain a quantity left over or be partitioned into fractions. In Figure 9.6, the problem $11 \div 4$ is modeled to show fractions.

In real contexts, remainders sometimes have three additional effects on answers:

1. The remainder is discarded, leaving a smaller whole-number answer.

2. The remainder can "force" the answer to the next highest whole number.

3. The answer is rounded to the nearest whole number for an approximate result.

The following problems illustrate all five possibilities.

- *Left over.* You have 10 pieces of candy to share fairly with 3 children. How many pieces of candy will each child receive? *Answer:* 3 pieces of candy and 1 left over.
- *Partitioned as a fraction.* You have 9 brownies and you want to fairly share with 4 children. How many brownies will each child receive? *Answer:* 2 and $\frac{1}{4}$ brownies.
- *Discarded.* A rope is 15 feet long. How many 7-foot jump ropes can be made? *Answer:* 2 jump ropes.
- *Forced to next whole number.* If 4 children can ride in each car, how many cars are needed to take to 23 children to the museum? *Answer:* 6 cars.
- *Rounded, approximate result.* If 6 children are planning to share a bag of 50 pieces of bubble gum, about how many pieces will each child get? *Answer:* About 8 pieces for each child.

Using Model-Based Problems for Multiplication and Division

Standards for Mathematical Practice

5 Use appropriate tools strategically

In the beginning, children will be able to use the same models—sets and number lines—for all four operations. A model not generally used for addition but extremely important and widely used for multiplication and division is the array. An array is any arrangement of objects in rows and columns, such as a rectangle of square tiles or blocks. A variety of models is shown in Figure 9.7.

The *Common Core State Standards* recommend that second graders experience using the array model with no more than five rows and five columns to lay the foundation for

Figure 9.7 Models for equal-group multiplication.

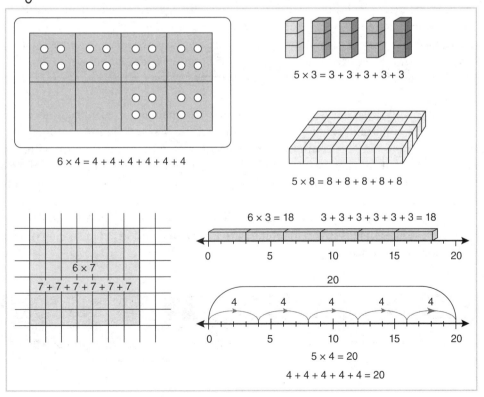

multiplication (CCSSO, 2010). However, even younger children can use the array model to begin to help them organize quantities and skip-count. Because you want to move children beyond counting by ones and encourage children's use of rows and columns as units, you need to use small quantities to play off their ability to subitize (quickly recognize the amount without counting).

Figure 9.8

Using arrays to help children construct efficient multiplication strategies. Which array subtly suggests skip counting?

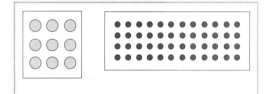

The following activity uses contexts and the idea of using small numbers of rows and columns to help children make sense of the array model as well as move beyond counting by ones.

◀ *Activity 9.6* **QUICK! HOW MANY ARE THERE?**

To use contexts to introduce the array model, find places where you live that organize objects into arrays, such as a bakery or a grocery store. Take pictures of a tray of doughnuts or muffins or a box of oranges or apples. You can also find pictures online for this purpose. (Check out the website for the Harry & David stores as one possibility.) Show these pictures to your children and set up the task by telling them that the baker, grocer, or person making an online order needs their help to determine how many items are on the tray or in the box. Allow children to use a strategy that makes sense to them, which initially may be counting by ones. Look for children who are using skip counting and make sure to have them share their strategy so that this idea is introduced to other children. You can repeat this activity several times with different contexts and different pictures.

Keep in mind that even if you use arrays that are arranged in quantities more likely to be subitized, some children may not be ready to move beyond counting by ones. Allow them to count by ones but continue to provide them opportunities to work with these kinds of arrays and to hear how other children are paying attention to and using small amounts to efficiently skip-count. Given time, these children will also begin to use more efficient strategies.

Using contexts also helps to encourage children to explore division situations. Snack time provides lots of opportunities for children to explore the notion of fair sharing or partition division as the next activity illustrates.

◀ *Activity 9.7* **SNACK TIME SHARING**

Read *Snack Attack* (Ruschak & Carter, 1990) as a lead-in to this activity. In groups, children work with a bag of snacks, such as crackers or cookies, to determine how many each child in the group will get. Because the children will be handling the snacks, you can either use pictures of the snacks that have been cut out or have additional snacks on hand for children to eat after the activity. To differentiate, you can prepare baggies of different amounts of the snack and place children in different size groups. For example, you can give a bag of 12 cookies to a group of 3 children; a bag of 10 cookies to 3 children; a bag of 16 cookies to 4 children; or a bag of 15 cookies to 4 children. The scenarios depend on your children and whether they are ready for the challenge of dealing with leftovers. Circulate as children are engaged in this sharing activity, asking children to explain their reasoning. You can capture their ideas on chart paper to help them share their ideas later in a discussion. Look for ways that children dealt with leftovers as well as whether children distributed the snacks in amounts other than by ones.

Roberts (2003) described a teacher who used *Snack Attack* and a similar sharing activity with her kindergartners. The article describes the various strategies children used to fairly share their snack and how the teacher supported the children as they shared their strategies during discussion time. You can refer to the article for more ideas. *One Hundred Hungry Ants* (Pinczes, 1999) and *Remainder of One* (Pinczes, 2002) are two additional children's books that provide engaging contexts for children to explore multiplication and division.

As with addition problems, children who are investigating multiplication and division situations can benefit from a few activities with models and no context. The purpose of such activities is to focus on the meaning of the operation and the associated symbolism, if children are ready for symbolism. Activity 9.8 has a good problem-solving spirit. The language you use depends on what you have used with your children in the past.

Activity 9.8 DIVIDE AND CONQUER!

Provide children with an ample supply of counters and a way to place them into small groups. Small paper cups work well. Have children count out a number of counters to be the whole or total set (e.g., start with 18). They then record this number. Next specify either the number of equal sets to be made or the size of the sets to be made: "Separate your counters into four equal-sized sets," or "Make as many sets of four as possible." Next, if ready for symbolism, have the children write the corresponding repeated addition or multiplication equation for what their materials show. You can also challenge children to write a corresponding story problem.

Be sure to include both types of exercises: number of equal sets and size of sets. Discuss with the class how these two situations are different yet how each is related to multiplication and can be written as repeated addition and multiplication equations. Do Activity 9.8 several times. Start with whole quantities that are multiples of the divisor (no remainders) but soon include situations with remainders.

Vary the activity by changing the model used. Have children build arrays using square tiles or have them draw arrays on centimeter grid paper. Present the exercises by specifying how many squares are to be in the array. You can then specify the number of rows that should be made (partition) or the length of each row (measurement). How could children model fractional answers using drawings of arrays on grid paper?

Figure 9.9

Two ways an array can be used to illustrate the commutative (order) property for multiplication.

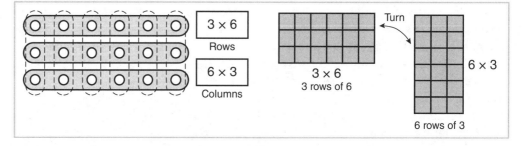

Formative Assessment Note

A good way to check on children's understanding of the operations is to provide several story problems with different operations. It is not necessary to have children do all the problems in one day. Have them work on two or three problems a day over the course of a week. If your objective is to find out about their understanding of the operations, you can do this by not having them actually do the computations. Rather, have them indicate what operation they would use and with what numbers. To avoid guessing, you can have children draw a picture to explain why they chose the operation that they did. Alternatively, you can have the children come up with story problems to go with given equations.

◆ Readiness for Multiplication Properties

As with addition and subtraction, there are some multiplicative properties that are useful and, although they will be highlighted in third grade and beyond, are still worthy of attention in the earlier grades. The emphasis should be on the ideas and not on the terminology or definitions.

The Commutative Property of Multiplication

It is not intuitively obvious that 3×8 is the same as 8×3 or that, in general, the order of the numbers makes no difference. A picture of 3 sets of 8 objects cannot immediately be seen as 8 piles of 3 objects. Eight hops of 3 land at 24, but it is not clear that 3 hops of 8 will land at the same point.

The array, by contrast, is quite powerful in illustrating the order property, as shown in Figure 9.9. Children can draw or build arrays and use them to demonstrate why each array represents two different multiplications with the same product.

The Role of Zero and One in Multiplication

Zero and, to a lesser extent, one as factors can cause difficulty for children. Have children make up story problems to reason about situations such as 0×5 or 3×0. Note that on a number line, 5 hops of 0 land at 0 (5×0). What would 0 hops of 5 be? Another fun activity is to try to model 6×0 or 0×8 with an array. (Try it!) Arrays for factors of one are also worth investigating. Avoid telling children rules. Instead, challenge children to articulate general statements about the role of zero and one in multiplication based on their experiences thinking about different contexts.

More Thoughts about Children Solving Story Problems

Solving word problems of all sorts on a regular basis should be a significant part of your number and computation curriculum. But your goals for children should go beyond being able to solve story problems. At the pre-K–2 level, there are many interrelated objectives that you should have in mind when you pose story problems:

- *Understanding the various meanings of the four operations.* It is primarily through story problems that children will gain a full understanding of which operation to use in any given situation.

- *Development of number skills and concepts.* As children solve problems, they are forced to deal with the numbers involved. Initially, they will use inefficient counting techniques. Later these techniques will give rise to more efficient skills and eventually will provide the foundations for mastery of basic facts.

- *Computational fluency.* Related to their number skills are the many different methods that children will develop for computing. Place-value ideas will be enhanced and utilized as children find new and better ways to break numbers apart and combine them. The structure of the problem can significantly influence the way children compute.

This broad array of goals suggests that there is much more to story problems than simply having children get answers. We want them to develop number skills and computational techniques as well as to have a rich understanding of the operations. To attend to these goals requires that we think carefully about the problems we pose. What operation structures do children need to work on? What numbers will challenge children but not overwhelm them? In other words, think of story problems as a means to an end rather than an end in themselves.

◆ Caution: Avoid Key Words!

It is often suggested that children should be taught to find "key words" in story problems. For example, "altogether" and "in all" mean you should add and "left" and "fewer" indicate you should subtract. To some extent, teachers have been reinforced to use key words by the overly simple and formulaic story problems often found in textbooks. When problems are written in this way, it may appear that the key word strategy is effective.

In contrast with this belief, researchers and mathematics educators have long cautioned against the strategy of key words. Here are four arguments against the key word approach.

1. The key word strategy sends a terribly wrong message about doing mathematics. The most important approach to solving any contextual problem is to analyze its structure—to make sense of it. The key word approach encourages children to ignore the meaning and structure of the problem and look for an easy way out. Mathematics is about reasoning and making sense of situations. A sense-making strategy will *always* work.

2. Key words can be misleading. Often the key word or phrase in a problem suggests an operation that is incorrect. For example:

> ◆ Standards for Mathematical Practice
>
> ◀ **1 Make sense of problems and persevere in solving them**

Maxine gave 28 stickers she no longer wanted to Zandra. Now Maxine has 73 stickers *left*. How many stickers did Maxine have to begin with?

If you look through the story problems in this chapter, you will find other examples of misleading key words.

3. Many problems have no key words. Especially when you get away from the overly simple problems found in primary textbooks, you will find that a large percentage of problems have no key words. A child who has been taught to rely on key words is left with no strategy. In both the addition and the multiplication problems in this chapter, you will find numerous examples of problems with no key words.

4. Key words cannot be used to solve multistep problems, which begin in grade 3 in the *Common Core State Standards* (2010). Using key words for simpler problems does not require children to learn to read for meaning. When faced with multistep or more complex problems in later grades, they will struggle if they have not learned to read word problems for meaning.

◆ Encourage Problem Analysis

Many children in kindergarten and first grade will do better at solving problems than will children in the upper grades. Once children have learned computational techniques, they often think that is what solving story problems means—grab the numbers and compute. These are the children who ignore problem context and often use extraneous numbers in their computations. In contrast, kindergarten and first-grade children have little or no means of computing. They pay attention to the problem, often use counters or other models, and figure out the solution based on the meaning in the story. Regardless of what grade you are teaching, it is important to always have children think through the problem before they get started. For example, let's consider the following problem:

Luke is saving up to buy a new model boat that costs $33. Each week his dad agrees to put $6 in a savings account if Luke does chores around the house. How many weeks will Luke have to work before he has enough money to buy the model boat?

Here are some questions that you might have the class discuss or answer on paper. Similar questions can be used for most any problem:

- *What is happening in this problem?* Luke is working to save money to buy a boat.
- *What will the answer tell us?* The answer will tell us how many weeks Luke will have to work in order to have enough money.
- *Do you think it will be a big number or a small number?* Well, each week he gets $6. If he works 10 weeks, he would have $60. He only needs $33. So it must be less than 10.
- *About how many weeks do you think he will have to work?* [Although some children may be able to compute the answer mentally, others may not even be able to make a good guess.]

With these questions, children are asked to focus on the problem and the meaning of the answer. The analysis of the problem leads to an idea of the size of the answer or a rough estimate of the answer. Knowing about how big the answer might be—even knowing if it will be more or less than one of the numbers in the problem—is a big first step in solving the problem. It is also useful information in judging the answer when the problem is solved.

◆ **Standards for Mathematical Practice**

3 Construct viable arguments and critique the reasoning of others

◆ Require Explanations

▶ In the early years, solving story problems provides an excellent place to begin children's habit of providing explanations. This is especially true before children have developed methods of computation. For children in grades pre-K–2, explanations can range from verbal statements to drawings to written words. You may find that children who know their basic facts or have learned traditional methods of computing will write little more than the computations they used. It is important to make clear that you want explanations, nearly always using words and numbers and often using drawings as well.

The solutions shown in Figure 9.10 are from children aged 4 to 7. Laura, a beginning second grader, used separate equations to represent the amounts. Emma, who was just beginning first grade, chose to use a weekly calendar format to help her think about the problem. She explained that the calendar helped her keep track of the amounts. She had

Figure 9.10

Three pre-K–2 children solve a complex problem using different types of drawings and explanations for their work.

I went to visit Mrs. Sato's farm last week.
- On Monday, I found 1 egg.
- On Tuesday, I found 2 eggs.
- On Wednesday, I found 3 eggs.
- On Thursday, I found 4 eggs.
- On Friday, I found 5 eggs.

How many eggs did I find last week?

Laura

$1+2=3 \quad 3+3=6 \quad 6+4=10$
$10+5=15$

Emma

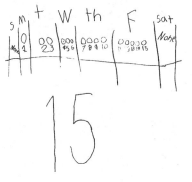

initially drawn only circles for each day, counted the circles, and wrote the large numeral 15 on her paper. When asked how she got 15, she labeled each circle as she counted by ones to reach 15. Abby, a pre-kindergarten child, drew her picture on her own after hearing the story problem read twice. Notice how Abby used spacing to help organize her ideas. When asked how many eggs were found, she said she counted and got 15. She wrote the numeral 15 with help.

As children continue to attempt to show their reasoning, they will improve both from practice and from seeing the methods used by others. For the examples in Figure 9.10, the children are showing how they solved the problem. To extend their explanations, you might ask questions such as, "Why do you think your answer is correct?" or "Why did you decide that addition (or whatever operation was used) was the right thing to do in this problem?"

📄 *Formative Assessment Note*

If a child is having difficulty solving word problems, first find out what is causing the difficulty. If you cannot tell from the child's written efforts or from observation, a short interview session is highly recommended to gain insight into the child's difficulties. Do not use the interview as a time to intervene or teach! Prepare some problems written out on paper, one problem to a page. To avoid issues of reading, read the problem together. Provide manipulatives but encourage the child to use whatever he or she wishes to solve the problem. Explain that you want to hear what the child is thinking so that you will know how to help him or her. Do not make the session too long. Consider the aspects identified in the earlier sections "Problem Difficulty" and "Children's Strategies" as you try to identify the difficulty. Is it the structure of the problem, the numbers in the problem, or the wording of the problem that is causing the difficulty? Is the child trying to use a strategy that is more sophisticated than he or she is ready for, such as using derived facts when the child is still at the direct modeling stage? If you cannot identify the difficulty with one or two problems, use additional problems on another day. Use any information gleaned to prepare problems or other tasks for a later interview or lesson.

Expanded Lesson

Divide and Conquer!

Content and Task Decisions

Grade Level: 2

Mathematics Goals

- To develop the measurement (repeated subtraction) concept of division. (Note that division is considered a multiplicative operation.)
- To connect the measurement concept of division to multiplication and addition.

Grade Level Guide

NCTM Curriculum Focal Points	Common Core State Standards
A connection to the Number and Operations focal point identified at second grade states that in preparing children for grade 3, they should "solve problems involving multiplicative situations, developing initial understanding of multiplication as repeated addition" (NCTM, 2006, p. 14).	As part of the Standards for second-graders, they are expected to "Work with equal groups of objects to gain foundations for multiplication" (CCSSO, 2010, p. 18).

Consider Your Children's Needs

Children have explored multiplicative concepts, which include division, using word problems and contexts such as in Activity 9.7. So the lesson can further develop early ideas and help connect the ideas to contextual situations.

For English Language Learners

- Rather than have ELLs write a story, they can illustrate the story.
- Stories about a lot of different topics can be overwhelming for children learning English. Instead, you can ask them to write stories about something specific (e.g., apples).
- Be sure that children know the terms *sets* and *groups* as well as *remainder*.

For Children with Disabilities

- Have children match a story problem with an equation if they are not able to write their own.

Materials

Each child will need:

- 35 counters
- Small paper cups or portion cups that will hold at least 6 counters (alternatively, children can stack counters in piles)

Lesson

Before

Begin with a simpler version of the task:

- Draw or display 9 counters (dots) on the board and ask children to put out 9 counters on their workspace. Ask, "How many sets of 4 can we make if we have 9? How many will be left over?" Some children may be able to answer this question mentally. Others may need to work with manipulatives to find the answer, so make sure to give everyone enough time to think about the question. After receiving several answers, have a child come to the board and demonstrate how to verify the answer of two sets of 4 and 1 left. (*Note:* Depending on your children, you may want to precede the first step using a number such as 8 or 12 so that there are no remainders. Do not wait too long before remainders are addressed.)
- Say, "Think of a situation in which someone might have 9 things and wants to find out how many sets of 4 can be made."
- Make up a story problem about your situation. Have several children share their story problems.
- Ask, "What equation could we write for what we have on the board?" Accept children's ideas. Correct ideas include:
  - $4 + 4 + 1 = 9$
  - $2 \times 4 + 1 = 9$ ($4 \times 2 + 1$ technically represents 4 sets of 2 and 1 more.)
  - $9 \div 4 = 2$ with 1 left over (No child may come up with this symbolism, which is fine. Do not introduce unless you feel your children are ready for this particular symbolism.)

Present the focus task to the class:

- Distribute small paper cups or portion cups and counters to children. Pose the following two problems:
  1. Use 17 counters to see how many sets of 4 you can make.
  2. Use 26 counters to find out how many sets of 6 you can make.
- Ask children for ideas of how they might use the cups to help them solve the problems.

Provide clear expectations:

- Write the directions on the board:
  1. Find how many sets of 4 you can make using 17 counters.
  2. Write a story problem to go with the situation.
  3. Write two equations: one addition and one multiplication. (Note that you can omit this step if your children are not ready for symbolism.)
  4. Repeat steps 1, 2, and 3 using 26 counters to make sets of 6.

During

Initially:

- Observe that each child understands the task and is in the process of attempting to solve the first situation.
- If you find that some children, particularly those with disabilities, are struggling, you may need to get them started by supporting them in the placement of 4 counters in the first cup. Then they should be able to use that model to continue.

Ongoing:

- Ask children to explain and show (on their workspace) why their story problems and equations go with what they did with the counters.
- Do not correct incorrect equations or story problems. You only want to be sure children are attempting to connect the activity with the stories and symbolism.
- Challenge early finishers to see if they can do the same thing for 37 things in sets of 5. However, they will have to figure it out without using counters.

After

Bring the class together to share and discuss the task:

- Ask children to show how they know how many sets of 4 can be made with 17 counters. A picture may be drawn on the board or counters can be used with a projection device.
- Have several children share their story problems. Children should explain how the story situation matches the action of finding how many sets of 4 are in 17. For example: "There were 17 apples in the basket. If each apple tart requires 4 apples, how many tarts can be made?"
- Have several children share their equations. Ask those who have different equations to share theirs as well.
- Have children explain how their equations match what was done with the counters. If children disagree, have them respectfully explain their reasoning. Because children are still learning how to use symbolism with multiplication, you should correct any misunderstandings about the multiplication and repeated addition equations and what they mean.
- If time permits, repeat with the 26 ÷ 6 situation.

Assessment

Observe

- Story problems should indicate the action of measuring equal sets of 4 rather than dividing the quantity into 4 sets in a process of sharing or partitioning. If children make this error, simply have them discuss whether or not the story fits well with the action. Do not indicate that the story is incorrect.
- It is also possible that children will create addition stories with 17 being the sum and 4 being one of the addends. Here, ask children to look back at what the number 4 refers to in the task.

Ask

- How does your story problem connect to subtraction?

10

Helping Children
Master the Basic Facts

Big IDEAS

1   Number relationships provide the foundation for strategies that help children to remember basic facts or figure out unknown facts from those already known. For example, knowing how numbers are related to 5 and 10 helps children master facts such as 3 + 5 (think of a ten-frame) and 8 + 6 (since 8 is 2 away from 10, take 2 from 6 to make 10 + 4 = 14).

2   Finding the total number of objects arranged in equal-sized groups helps children to build a foundation for multiplication. This situation can be represented using repeated addition.

3   Mastery of the basic facts is a developmental process. Children move through stages starting with counting, then moving to more efficient reasoning strategies and eventually to quick recall. Instruction must help children move through these phases without rushing them to memorization.

4   Children who are not developing fluency with the basic facts may need to revisit foundational ideas, such as number relationships. Simply continuing to drill will not address the cause of their difficulty and can negatively affect their confidence and attitude toward and success in mathematics.

Basic facts for addition refers to combinations in which both addends are less than 10. Subtraction facts correspond to the addition facts. Thus, $15 - 8 = 7$ is a subtraction fact because both the corresponding addition parts are less than 10.

Mastery of a basic fact means that a child can give a quick response (in about 3 seconds) without resorting to nonefficient means, such as counting. According to the *Common Core State Standards* (CCSSO, 2010), by the end of second grade, children should have mastered their basic addition and subtraction facts. It is critical that children know their basic facts well, but mastery does not just start in second grade. If you teach in grades pre-K–1, this chapter is also for you because you have a very important role in helping children to be ready to master their basic addition and subtraction facts by the end of second grade.

Aspects of number sense that are critical to children developing fluency with basic facts begin in pre-kindergarten and continue throughout the primary grades. The *Common Core State Standards* (CCSSO, 2010) indicate that kindergartners should represent and solve addition and subtraction situations (putting together and adding to; taking apart and taking from) within 10 using any method that makes sense to them, such as using objects, their fingers, drawings, or mental images. First graders extend addition and subtraction to a wider variety of situations and to within 20, still using any method that makes sense to them.

This chapter explains strategies for helping children learn their facts, including instructional approaches to use and instructional approaches to avoid. It may surprise you to hear that flash cards and timed tests are not the answer. Focusing on number sense is key to teaching basic facts effectively.

Approaches to Fact Mastery

Three somewhat different approaches to helping children master their basic facts can be identified. One is memorization of each fact in isolation. A second approach suggests that we teach children a collection of strategies and thought patterns for various categories of basic facts. A third approach also emphasizes the use of strategies to learn facts; however, the strategies are generated, or reinvented, by the children. Each of these approaches is briefly described in the following sections.

◆ Memorization

Some textbooks and teachers move from presenting concepts of addition and subtraction straight to memorization of facts, feeling that developing strategies is not essential to learning facts (Baroody, Bajwa, & Eiland, 2009). This "passive storage view" (the idea that children can just store the facts when they are practiced extensively) means that children have 100 separate addition facts for the various combinations of 0 through 9 that must be memorized and practiced frequently. They may even have to memorize subtraction separately, bringing the total to over 200! There is strong evidence that this method simply does not work. Too many fourth and fifth graders have not mastered addition and subtraction facts and continue to count on their fingers. You may be tempted to say that you learned your facts in this manner, as did many other children. However, studies as long ago as 1935 found that despite of the amount of isolated drill that they experienced, children independently develop a variety of different thought processes or strategies for basic facts (Brownell & Chazal, 1935). You may even be aware that you found your own strategies for facts that were difficult to remember. Unfortunately, drill does not encourage or support the refinement of these strategies. Baroody (2006, p. 27) notes that this approach to basic fact instruction works against the development of the five strands of mathematical proficiency, pointing out the following limitations:

- *Inefficiency.* There are too many facts to memorize in a rote fashion.
- *Inappropriate applications*. Children misapply the facts and don't check their work.
- *Inflexibility.* Children don't learn flexible strategies for finding sums and, therefore, continue to count by ones. (Reprinted with permission from *Why Children Have Difficulties Mastering the Basic Number Combinations and How to Help Them*, copyright 2006, by the National Council of Teachers of Mathematics. All rights reserved.)

When taught basic facts via rote memorization, many children with learning disabilities continue to use counting strategies because they do not independently develop thought processes or other strategies that move beyond counting (e.g., Mazzocco, Devlin, & McKenney,

2008). However, they can be very successful in learning their basic facts when the emphasis is on using strategies. In addition, drill can cause unnecessary anxiety and undermine children's interest and confidence in mathematics. Connecting to what children know and building on that knowledge allows all children to learn the basic facts and to learn them for life.

Explicit Strategy Instruction

This approach to basic fact instruction involves explicitly teaching efficient strategies that are applicable to a collection of facts. Children practice these strategies as they are shown to them. There is strong evidence to indicate that such methods can be effective (e.g., Baroody, 1985; Bley & Thornton, 1995; Fuson, 1984, 1992). Many of the ideas developed and tested by these researchers are discussed in this chapter.

The intent of this approach is to *support* children's thinking rather than to give them something new to remember. Sometimes textbooks and teachers emphasize memorization of the strategy and which facts work with that strategy. This emphasis on memorization does not work for the same reasons that memorizing isolated facts does not work. A recent study found that children whose teachers emphasized memorization of basic fact strategies had lower number-sense proficiency (Henry & Brown, 2008). The key is to help children see the possibilities and then let them *choose* strategies that help them determine the answer without counting.

Guided Invention

With this approach, basic fact instruction and mastery are intricately tied to children's collection of number relationships (Gravemeijer & van Galen, 2003). Some children may think of 6 + 7 as "double 6 is 12 and one more is 13." Others in the same class may recognize that 7 is 3 away from 10, so they take 3 from 6 to add to 7 to make 10, and then add the remaining 3 to get 13. Still other children may take 5 from each addend to make 10 and then add the remaining 1 and 2 to get 13. The crucial point is that children are using number combinations and relationships that make sense to them.

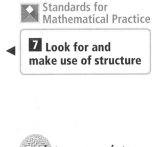

Standards for Mathematical Practice

◀ **7 Look for and make use of structure**

Gravemeijer and van Galen (2003) called this approach *guided invention* because not all children will independently develop many of the strategies that are efficient without some guidance. That is, we cannot put all of our efforts on number relationships and the meanings of operations and hope that fact mastery will magically happen. Instead you need to purposefully design tasks and problems that will promote the invention of effective strategies by children. And then you need to ensure that these strategies are shared and clearly articulated in the classroom.

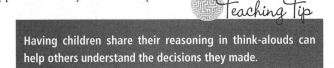

Teaching Tip

Having children share their reasoning in think-alouds can help others understand the decisions they made.

Developmental Nature of Basic Fact Mastery

For a long time it was believed that children learned their basic facts through drill and memorization. However, now psychologists and mathematics educators believe that developing quick and accurate recall with basic facts is a developmental process that depends on the development of reasoning strategies (Baroody, 2003; Fuson, 1992; Henry & Brown, 2008; Verschaffel, Greer, & De Corte, 2007). Baroody, Bajwa, and Eiland (2009, p. 70) identify three phases in the process of learning basic facts:

1. *Counting strategies.* Using objects (e.g., blocks, fingers, marks) or verbal counting to determine answers. (Example: For 4 + 7, the child starts with 7 and verbally counts on 8, 9, 10, 11.)

Figure 10.1
The developmental process for basic fact mastery for addition and subtraction.

	Addition	**Subtraction**
Counting	Direct modeling (counting objects and fingers) • Counting all • Counting on from first • Counting on from larger	Counting objects • Separating from • Separating to • Adding on
	Counting abstractly • Counting all • Counting on from first • Counting on from larger	Counting fingers • Counting down • Counting up
		Counting abstractly • Counting down • Counting up
Reasoning	Properties • $a + 0 = a$ • $a + 1 =$ next whole number • Commutative property	Properties • $a - 0 = a$ • $a - 1 =$ previous whole number
	Known-fact derivations (e.g., $5 + 6 = 5 + 5 + 1$; $7 + 6 = 7 + 7 - 1$)	Inverse/complement of known addition facts (e.g., $12 - 5$ is known because $5 + 7 = 12$)
	Redistributed derived facts (e.g., $7 + 5 = 7 + (3 + 2) = (7 + 3) + 2 = 10 + 2 = 12$)	Redistributed derived facts (e.g., $12 - 5 = (7 + 5) - 5 = 7 + (5 - 5) = 7$)
Retrieval	Retrieval from long-term memory	Retrieval from long-term memory

Source: Reprinted with permission from First-Grade Basic Facts: An Investigation into Teaching and Learning of an Accelerated, High-Demand Memorization Standard. *Journal for Research in Mathematics Education,* copyright 2008, by the National Council of Teachers of Mathematics. All rights reserved.

2. *Reasoning strategies.* Using known facts and relations to logically determine the answer for an unknown combination. (Example: For $4 + 7$, the child knows that $3 + 7$ is 10, so $4 + 7$ is one more or 11.)

3. *Mastery.* Producing answers quickly and accurately. (Example: For $4 + 7$, the child quickly responds, "11; I just know it.") (Reprinted with permission from *Why Children Have Difficulties Mastering the Basic Number Combinations and How to Help Them,* copyright 2006, by the National Council of Teachers of Mathematics. All rights reserved.)

Figure 10.1 outlines the developmental methods children use to solve basic addition and subtraction problems. You will see some ideas, such as the different counting strategies, which were discussed in Chapters 8 and 9. In this chapter, we will focus on reasoning strategies and how to teach children to use reasoning to master the basic facts (phases 2 and 3).

Formative Assessment Note

How will you know when your children are ready to work on reasoning strategies? Based on the research, they are ready to apply reasoning strategies when they can use counting-on strategies (start with the larger number and count up) and are able to decompose numbers (e.g., 6 as $5 + 1$). Pose one-digit addition problems to children in a one-on-one setting to see whether they demonstrate these skills. If they lack one skill, provide additional experiences to develop it. Once they have all the needed skills, begin working on reasoning strategies.

Reasoning Strategies

The purpose of developing reasoning strategies is to help children move from counting to more efficient ways of recalling facts quickly and accurately. In order for you to support your children in using effective strategies, you need to have a command of as many successful strategies as possible. With this knowledge you will be able to recognize effective strategies as your children develop them and then help others make sense of their peers' ideas.

◆ Supporting Strategy Development

We discuss two effective approaches that you can use to help children move from counting to strategies to recall. One approach is to have children solve story problems using strategies that make sense to them. The second approach is to explicitly teach reasoning strategies. You will find a combination of these two approaches will serve your children well.

Use Story Problems

A story problem provides a context that can help children make sense of the situation and provides opportunities for children to apply a variety of strategies for doing computations. Suppose that you want your class to consider the Make 10 strategy. The idea is to use story problems that increase the likelihood that children will develop that target strategy. You might pose the following question:

◄ **Standards for Mathematical Practice**

1 Make sense of problems and persevere in solving them

Rachel sold 9 boxes of Girl Scout cookies on Friday and 6 boxes on Saturday. How many boxes did she sell?

Stop and Reflect

How does this problem increase the likelihood that children will develop the Make 10 strategy? ■

Suppose that Sammie explains that because 9 is 1 away from 10, she took 1 from 6 to make 9 into 10 and then added the remaining 5 to get to 15. Make explicit the expectation that children are to attend to their classmates' ideas. You can ask another child to explain what Sammie just shared. You can also explore with the class what other facts might work with Sammie's strategy.

◄ **Standards for Mathematical Practice**

3 Construct viable arguments and critique the reasoning of others

Continue to develop and use story problems that are readily solved using the Make 10 strategy to give children more opportunities to make the strategy their own.

Posing a story problem such as the preceding one each day, followed by a brief discussion of the strategies that children used, can improve children's accuracy and efficiency with basic facts (Rathmell, Leutzinger, & Gabriele, 2000). Research has found that when a strong emphasis is placed on children solving problems, they not only become better problem solvers but they also master more basic facts than children in a drill program (National Research Council, 2001).

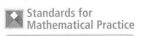 Teaching Tip

 Children with disabilities may find it difficult to keep all of their peers' ideas in working memory, so display the ideas on a board or on chart paper as an effective support.

Some teachers hesitate to use story problems with ELLs or children with disabilities because of the additional language or reading required, but because language supports understanding, using story problems is important for all children. It is crucial, however, that the contexts you use are relevant and understood by all the children.

Explicitly Teach Reasoning Strategies

A second approach is to directly model a reasoning strategy. This approach can help children expand their own collection of strategies that will help them move away from counting. Do not, however, expect to introduce a strategy and have children understand and use the strategy with just one exposure. Just as when using story problems, children need lots of opportunities to make the strategy their own. Many children will simply not be ready to use an idea the first few days, and then suddenly something will click and they will meaningfully use the strategy.

Teaching Tip

Write new strategies on the board or make a poster of strategies that children develop. Give strategies names that make sense so that children can use the names to describe what they did (e.g., Make 10, Doubles).

As an example, you can design a lesson to help children examine a specific collection of facts for which a particular type of strategy is appropriate. Discuss as a class how these facts are alike in some way, or you might suggest an approach and see if children are able to use it with similar facts.

Remember to keep the focus on reasoning and continue to discuss strategies invented in your class and plan lessons that encourage the use of strategies. You can encourage children to use particular strategies, but do not require them to do so—this is the opposite of what you are trying to accomplish as it takes the reasoning right out of strategy development. Instead emphasize making good choices and justifying those choices.

◆ Reasoning Strategies for Addition Facts

The reasoning strategies children can and will develop are directly related to one or more number relationships that were discussed in Chapter 8. In that chapter, numerous activities were suggested to help children develop these relationships. Now the teaching task is to help children connect these number relationships to the basic facts.

+	0	1	2	3	4	5	6	7	8	9
0		1	2							
1	1	2	3	4	5	6	7	8	9	10
2	2	3	4	5	6	7	8	9	10	11
3		4	5							
4		5	6							
5		6	7							
6		7	8							
7		8	9							
8		9	10							
9		10	11							

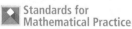

Standards for Mathematical Practice

3 Construct viable arguments and critique the reasoning of others ▶

One More Than and Two More Than

Each of the 36 facts highlighted in the accompanying chart has at least one addend of 1 or 2. These facts are a direct application of the one-more-than and two-more-than relationships described in Chapter 8. Research suggests that children need to be able to count on before they are able to successfully use this strategy (Baroody et al., 2009).

Story problems in which one of the addends is a 1 or a 2 are easy to create. For example: *Six children were waiting in line for ice cream. Two more children got in line. How many children are waiting in line?* Ask different children to explain how they got 8 as the answer. Some will count on from 6. Some may still need to count 6 and 2 and then count all. Others will say they knew that 2 more than 6 is 8. To help children move from counting to reasoning strategies, draw their attention to the connection between counting on two and adding two.

Activity 10.1 **HOW MANY FEET IN THE BED?**

Read *How Many Feet in the Bed*? by Diane Johnston Hamm. On the second time through the book, when a new person gets in the bed, ask children how many *more* feet are in the bed. Have children record the equation (e.g., 4 + 2) and tell how many feet in all.

As family members get out of the bed, two less can be explored. If children continue to count all, let them use a number line or ten-frame. Find opportunities to make the connection between counting on two and adding two using a number line or ten-frame. For ELLs, clarify the meaning of *foot* (it is used here as a body part, not as a unit of measure) and be sure to they know what the phrases "two more" and "two less" mean. You can further support ELLs and children with disabilities by acting out the story with children in the classroom.

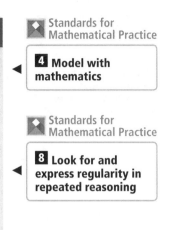

Standards for Mathematical Practice

4 Model with mathematics

Standards for Mathematical Practice

8 Look for and express regularity in repeated reasoning

The different responses will provide you with a lot of information about children's number sense. As children are ready to use the two-more-than idea without counting all, they can begin to practice with activities such as the following.

Figure 10.2

One more and two more activities.

Activity 10.2 **ONE MORE THAN AND TWO MORE THAN WITH DICE AND SPINNERS**

Make a die labeled +1, +2, +1, +2, "one more," and "two more." Label another die with the values 3, 4, 5, 6, 7, and 8, or whatever values children need to practice. After each roll of the dice, children should say the complete fact: "Four and two is six." Alternatively, use a spinner with "1 more" on one half and "2 more" on the other half in place of the first die (see Figure 10.2). For children with disabilities, you may want to start with a die that just has +1 and "one more" and then move to a +2 and "two more" die on another day. This approach will help these children focus on and practice one approach.

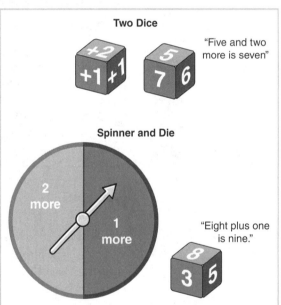

Activity 10.2 can be modified for almost all of the strategies in the chapter.

Adding Zero

Nineteen facts shown in the accompanying chart have zero as one of the addends. Though such problems are generally easy, some children overgeneralize the idea that answers to addition problems are bigger than the addends. Word problems involving zero and subsequent discussions will be especially helpful in avoiding this overgeneralization. In the discussion, use drawings that show two parts with one part empty.

The following activity provides children opportunities to generalize from a set of problems, which reinforces reasoning.

+	0	1	2	3	4	5	6	7	8	9
0	0	1	2	3	4	5	6	7	8	9
1	1									
2	2									
3	3									
4	4									
5	5									
6	6									
7	7									
8	8									
9	9									

Activity 10.3 WHAT'S ALIKE? ZERO FACTS

Write about 10 zero facts on the board, some with the zero first and some with the zero second. Discuss how the equations are alike. Ask children to create their own stories and then use counters and a part–part–whole mat to model the situations.

Using 5 as an Anchor

Using an anchor (5 or 10) is a reasoning strategy that builds on children's knowledge of number relationships and so is a great way to reinforce number sense while learning the basic facts. Using 5 as an anchor means looking for fives in the numbers in the problem. For example, in $7 + 6$, a child may think of 7 as $5 + 2$ and 6 as $5 + 1$. The child would add $5 + 5$ and then the extra 2 from the 7 and the extra 1 from 6, adding up to 13.

The five- and ten-frames and the arithmetic rack discussed in Chapter 8 can help children visualize numbers as 5 and some more. The following activity extends the use of these visual models to support children's reasoning strategies for addition.

Activity 10.4 FLASH

Project two ten-frames on the board. Without letting children see, place counters on each ten-frame so that the top row is full (five counters) and the extras are in the bottom row of each ten-frame. Uncover the two ten-frames for about 3 to 5 seconds and then recover. First, ask children to share how many counters they saw and accept all answers. Then ask children to explain how they saw it. Again quickly uncover and then cover the ten-frames and ask if anyone wants to change their answer. Finally, uncover the ten-frames and have children explain how they saw the counters. Alternatively, you can use two ten-frame cards from Blackline Master 18 or two arithmetic racks.

Make 10

Perhaps the most important strategy for children to know is the Make 10 strategy, or the combinations that make 10. The ten-frame and the arithmetic rack are useful tools for creating visual images of the number relationships. The next activity is a good way to introduce the Make 10 strategy. Story problems using two numbers that make 10 or that ask how many are needed to make 10 can provide children additional opportunities to develop the Make 10 strategy.

Activity 10.5 MAKE 10 ON THE TEN-FRAME

Place counters on a ten-frame and ask, "How many more to make 10?" (See Figure 10.3.) This activity can be repeated using different starting numbers. Eventually, show an empty ten-frame and say a number less than 10. Children start with that number and complete the "10 fact." If you say, "four," they say, "four plus six is ten." This activity can be completed in small groups or individually. Children who are still in phase 1 of learning the facts (using counting strategies) may need to model the numbers using their own ten-frame.

Figure 10.3
Make 10 on ten-frames.

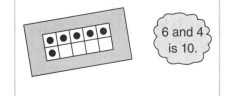

6 and 4 is 10.

Knowing number combinations that make 10 also builds a foundation for working on addition with larger numbers. For example, when adding 28 + 7, a child can use the Make 10 strategy by adding 2 to 28 to get to 30 and then adding 5 more. This strategy can even be extended to make 100.

Up Over 10

This strategy is also known as Make 10 Extended. Many facts have sums greater than 10, and all those facts can be solved using the Up Over 10 strategy, making this a very useful strategy. With this strategy, children use their known facts that equal 10 and then add the rest of the number onto 10. For example, to solve 6 + 8, children may recognize that 8 is 2 from 10; so they take 2 from the 6 and add the 2 to 8 to make 10 and then add on the remaining 4 to get 14. This process is called Break Apart to Make Ten, or BAMT (Sarama & Clements, 2009), and aligns with children's previous experiences with ten-frames and arithmetic racks. If you are trying to encourage children to come up with this strategy on their own, pose problems that have at least one addend of 8 or 9.

Notice that many of the basic addition facts can be solved using the Up Over 10 strategy (about a third). Moreover, this strategy can be later applied to adding up over other benchmark numbers such as 20 and 50. Therefore, you should spend a significant amount of time and attention to helping children develop this strategy.

Activity 10.6 MOVE IT, MOVE IT

Give children a mat with two ten-frames. Flash cards are placed next to the ten-frames, or a fact can be given orally. Children should cover each frame with counters to represent the problem. For example, for the problem 9 + 6, children would cover nine places on one frame and six on another. Then children are to decide on a way to move the counters so that they can find the total without counting. Ask children to explain what they did and connect their ideas to the new equation.

For example, 9 + 6 may become 10 + 5 by moving one counter to the first ten-frame.

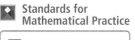

Standards for Mathematical Practice

◀ **4** Model with mathematics

Activity 10.7 FRAMES AND FACTS

Make little ten-frame cards (Blackline Master 18) and display an 8 (or 9) card on a projector. Place other cards beneath it one at a time and ask children to respond with the total. Have children say what they are doing. For 8 + 4, they might say, "Take 2 from the 4 and put it with 8 to make 10. Then 10 and 2 left over is 12." Move to more difficult cards, like 7 + 6. Have children record each equation as shown in Figure 10.4. Find opportunities to highlight that filling in the little ten-frame starting with the larger number is a faster approach. Show and talk about how it is more challenging to start with the smaller number as a counterexample. The activity can also be done independently with the little ten-frame cards.

BLM

Figure 10.4 Frames and facts activity.

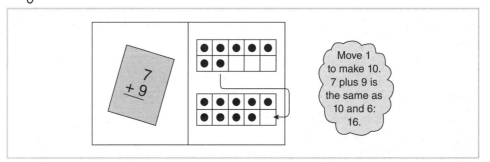

Note that children may have many other ways of using 10 to add with 8 or 9. For example, with the fact $9 + 5$, some will add $10 + 5$ and then subtract 1. This is a perfectly good strategy that uses 10.

+	0	1	2	3	4	5	6	7	8	9
0	0									
1		2								
2			4							
3				6						
4					8					
5						10				
6							12			
7								14		
8									16	
9										18

Doubles

There are ten doubles facts from $0 + 0$ to $9 + 9$, as shown in the chart here. These facts can be anchors for other facts.

Many children find doubles easier to grasp than other facts. However, all children, and especially children with disabilities, can benefit from using and creating picture cards for each of the doubles as shown in Figure 10.5. Story problems can focus on pairs of like addends:

Alex and Zack each found 7 seashells at the beach. How many did they find together?

Activity 10.8 CALCULATOR DOUBLES

For this activity, children work in pairs with a calculator. The children enter the "double maker" ($2 \times$ __) into the calculator. Then one child says a double—for example, "Seven plus seven." The other child should press 7 on the calculator, say what the double is, and then press = to see the correct double (14) on the display. The children then switch roles. For ELLs who are just learning English, invite them to say the double in their native language or in both their native language and English. (Note that the calculator is also a good way to practice +1 and +2 facts.)

Figure 10.5 Double facts.

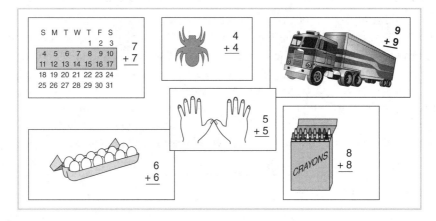

 **10.6** Near-double facts.

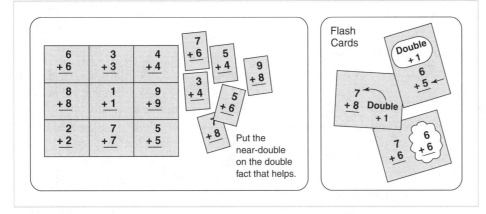

Near-Doubles

Near-doubles are also called the "doubles-plus-one" or "double-minus-one" facts and include all combinations in which one addend is one more or one less than the other. This strategy uses a known fact to derive an unknown fact. Double the smaller number and add 1 or double the larger number and subtract 1. Be sure children solidly know the doubles before you focus on this strategy.

To introduce the strategy to the class, write several near-doubles facts on the board. Place the smaller addend first for some of the problems and second for others. Have children solve problems independently and then discuss their strategies. Some may double the smaller number and add one and others may double the larger and subtract. If no one uses a near-double strategy (they may use the Up Over 10 strategy), write the corresponding doubles for some of the facts and ask how these facts could help. This strategy is more difficult for students to recognize and, therefore, may not be a strategy that all children find useful. In that case, do not force it.

◀◣ *Activity* 10.9 **ON THE DOUBLE!**

Create a display (on a board or on paper) that illustrates the doubles and prepare cards with near-doubles (e.g., 4 + 5) (see Figure 10.6). Ask children to take a near-doubles card and to find the doubles fact on the display that could help them solve the fact on the card and place the card on that spot. Ask children if there are other doubles that could help as well.

🔷 Reasoning Strategies for Subtraction Facts

Subtraction facts prove to be more difficult than addition. This is especially true when children have been taught subtraction through a "count-count-count" approach; for $13 - 5$, *count* 13, *count* off 5, *count* what's left. Remember that counting is the first phase in reaching basic fact mastery. You need to move children beyond counting strategies to ensure they master their basic facts. Figure 10.1 lists the ways children might subtract as they move from counting to reasoning to mastery. Children need opportunities to learn and use reasoning strategies; otherwise they continue to rely on counting strategies for subtraction, which can be slow and too often result in inaccurate answers. Spending sufficient time on the following reasoning strategies can help children move to phase 2 and eventually on to mastery (phase 3). You can also help children build stronger connections between addition and subtraction by posing more join and separate story problems with start and change unknowns as well as more part–part–whole and comparison story problems (see Chapter 9).

Subtraction as Think-Addition

Figure 10.7

Using a think-addition model for subtraction facts.

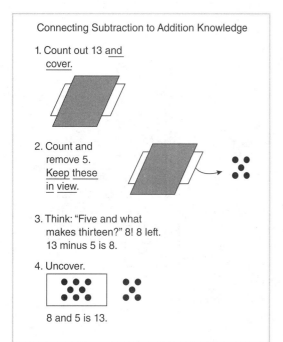

Connecting Subtraction to Addition Knowledge

1. Count out 13 <u>and</u> <u>cover.</u>

2. Count and remove 5. <u>Keep these in view.</u>

3. Think: "Five and what makes thirteen?" 8! 8 left. 13 minus 5 is 8.

4. Uncover.

8 and 5 is 13.

In Figure 10.7, subtraction is modeled in such a way that children are encouraged to think, "What goes with this part to make the total?" When done in this *think-addition* manner, children use known addition facts to produce the unknown quantity or part. If this important relationship between parts and wholes—between addition and subtraction—can be made, subtraction facts will be much easier. As with addition facts, it is helpful to begin with facts whose totals (minuends) are 10 or less (e.g., $8 - 3$, $9 - 7$) before working on facts that have a total higher than 10 (e.g., $13 - 4$).

The value of think-addition cannot be overstated. However, if children are to effectively use the think-addition strategy, they first must master the basic addition facts. Evidence suggests that children learn very few, if any, subtraction facts without first mastering the corresponding addition facts. So, for example, mastery of $3 + 5$ is prerequisite knowledge for learning the facts $8 - 3$ and $8 - 5$.

Story problems that promote think-addition are those that sound like addition but have a missing addend: *join, start unknown; join, change unknown;* and *part–part–whole, part unknown* (see Chapter 9). Consider this problem:

Janice had 5 fish in her aquarium. Grandma gave her some more fish. Then she had 12 fish. How many fish did Grandma give Janice?

Notice that the action is *join* and, thus, suggests addition. There is a high probability that children will think, "Five and how many more make 12?" In the discussion in which you use problems such as this, your task is to connect this thought process with the subtraction fact, $12 - 5$. Children may use the Up Over 10 strategy to solve this problem, just as they did with the addition facts. For example, they may think, "It takes 5 to get to 10 and 2 more to get to 12, so that's 7."

Stop and Reflect

Before reading further, look at these three subtraction facts and reflect on the thought processes you use to get the answers. Even if you "just know them" think about what a likely process might be. ■

$$\begin{array}{ccc} 14 & 13 & 15 \\ \underline{-9} & \underline{-7} & \underline{-6} \end{array}$$

Down Over 10

You may have used a think-addition strategy for any of the problems in the previous Stop and Reflect. Or you may have started with the 14 and counted down to 10 (4) and then down 1 more to 9 for a total difference of 5. This reasoning strategy is called Down Over 10. If you did not use this strategy, try it with one of the examples.

This strategy is based on a derived fact strategy because children use what they know (14 minus 10 is 4) to figure out a related fact ($14 - 9$). This strategy helps children move to mastery while supporting their number sense.

One way to develop the Down Over 10 strategy is to give children five or six pairs of facts in which the difference for the first fact is 10 and the second fact is 8 or 9 (e.g., $16 - 6$ and $16 - 7$ or $14 - 4$ and $14 - 6$). Have children solve each pair of problems and discuss their strategies. If children do not naturally see the relationship, ask them to think about how the first fact can help them solve the second. Reinforce the Down Over 10 strategy by posing story problems such as the following:

Bekah had 15 bracelets. She gave 6 to a friend. How many does Bekah have left?

Take from 10

This strategy capitalizes on children's knowledge of the combinations that make 10 and it works for all subtraction problems in which the starting value (minuend) is more than 10. For example, consider the problem $16 - 8$. Children would take the minuend (16) apart into $10 + 6$, and then subtract $10 - 8$ (because they know this fact). They would then add the 2 back to the 6 to get 8. Try this strategy on these examples:

$$15 - 8 = \qquad 17 - 9 = \qquad 14 - 8 =$$

This is a great reasoning strategy, although it may seem uncomfortable at first. It may be helpful to use story problems to make it easier to keep track of the quantities. For example, for $14 - 8$, you might use a story problem such as "Andy had 14 toy animals. He gave 8 to a friend. How many does Andy have left?" To reason through the strategy, children can either use manipulatives or imagine taking the 14 toy animals and splitting them into a group of 10 and a group of 4. Then they have to take 8 from the group of 10 to get 2. Then they add the 2 to the 4 to see they have 6 left.

❖ Reinforcing Reasoning Strategies

It is important to note that while the strategies explained so far may appear as if they are best used for particular basic facts, the reality is there is no one "best" strategy for any fact. For example, $7 + 8$ could be solved using Up Over 10 or near-doubles. The more you emphasize choice, the more children will be able to find strategies that work for them, which will lead to fact fluency.

Stop and Reflect

Most addition facts lend themselves to a variety of different reasoning strategies. What are three strategies children could use to get the answer to $8 + 6$? ■

The following activity is good for helping children realize that if they just don't know a fact, they can rely on reasoning.

Activity 10.10   **IF YOU DIDN'T KNOW**

Pose the following task to the class: If you did not know the answer to $8 + 5$ (or any fact that you want students to think about), how could you figure it out without counting? Encourage children to come up with more than one way (hopefully using the strategies suggested earlier). To support children's communication skills, especially ELLs and children with disabilities, use a think-pair-share approach in which children discuss their ideas with a partner before they share them with the class.

Formative Assessment Note

Using diagnostic interviews with children learning their basic facts is critical. Many children will be stuck on counting strategies (phase 1) and can be so adept at counting that you may be unaware that they are counting. Quick counting is not a substitute for fact mastery. Use a short diagnostic interview that includes a variety of facts that lend themselves to different strategies. After the child records or states the answer, ask the child to explain how his or her thinking led to the answer.

◆ Building a Foundation for Multiplication Facts

According to the CCSSO (2010), children in second grade should start to work with equal groups of objects arranged in rectangular arrays (up to 5 rows and up to 5 columns) to lay a foundation for multiplication. Although it will be appropriate for second graders to use skip counting at this stage, emphasizing reasoning strategies is just as important for moving toward mastery of multiplication facts (Baroody, 2006; Wallace & Gurganus, 2005).

You can begin to draw children's attention to the commutative property of multiplication. As discussed in Chapter 9, this property can be best visualized by using arrays as opposed to equal groups of objects. For example, a 2×8 array can be described as 2 rows of 8. When rotated 90 degrees, it is an 8×2 array and described as 8 rows of 2. In both cases, the total is 16. It will take time for children to understand this significant idea but understanding it will reduce by half the number of multiplication basic facts to be memorized.

Teaching Tip

As with addition and subtraction facts, start with story problems as you develop reasoning strategies for multiplication facts.

Standards for Mathematical Practice

7 Look for and make use of structure ▶

For a virtual site that connects arrays to multiplication facts, go to http:// nlvm.usu.edu/en/nav /category_g_2_t_1.html and click on "Rectangle Multiplication."

Doubles

+	0	1	2	3	4	5	6	7	8	9
0			0							
1			2							
2	0	2	4	6	8	10	12	14	16	18
3			6							
4			8							
5			10							
6			12							
7			14							
8			16							
9			18							

Facts that have 2 as a factor are equivalent to addition doubles and should already be known by children by the time you begin introducing them to multiplication. So the goal is to help children realize that 2×7 is the same as double 7, as is 7×2. Start with story problems in which 2 is the number of groups. Later, use problems in which 2 is the size of each group.

Our field trip is in 2 weeks. How many days will we need to wait? [two groups of 7]

A kindergarten class was making clay animals. If there were 7 rabbits made, how many rabbit ears were there? [seven groups of 2]

Fives

Facts with 5 as the first or second factor can be related to skip counting by fives. Practice counting by fives to at least 45. Connect counting by fives with arrays that have rows of 5 dots (see Figure 10.8a). Point out that such an array with six rows is a model for 6×5, eight

 Fives facts.

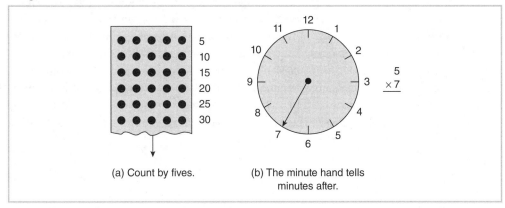

(a) Count by fives.

(b) The minute hand tells minutes after.

rows is 8 × 5, and so on. As illustrated in the following activity, you can also connect fives facts to telling time on a clock to the nearest five minutes, an expectation for second graders in the *Common Core State Standards*.

Activity 10.11 CLOCK FACTS

Focus on the minute hand of the clock. When it points to a number, how many minutes after the hour is it? Point to numbers 1 to 9 on a large clock face in random order. Children respond with the minutes after. (See Figure 10.8b.) Connect this idea to the multiplication facts with 5. In this way, the fives facts become the "clock facts."

+	0	1	2	3	4	5	6	7	8	9
0						0				
1						5				
2						10				
3						15				
4						20				
5	0	5	10	15	20	25	30	35	40	45
6						30				
7						35				
8						40				
9						45				

Zeros and Ones

Thirty-six facts have at least one factor that is either 0 or 1. These facts, though apparently easy on a procedural level, tend to get confused with "rules" that some children learned for addition. The fact 6 + 0 is 6, but 6 × 0 is 0; and n + 1 fact is the next counting number, but n × 1 is n. Using story problems to develop the concepts underlying these facts is the best approach. To reinforce the concepts, ask children to put words to the equations. For example, for 6 × 0, they could say something such as six rows of chairs with no people in each. For 0 × 6, they could say something such as we have zero spiders with six legs each. Avoid rules that aren't conceptually based, such as "Any number multiplied by zero is zero."

+	0	1	2	3	4	5	6	7	8	9
0	0	0	0	0	0	0	0	0	0	0
1	0	1	2	3	4	5	6	7	8	9
2	0	2								
3	0	3								
4	0	4								
5	0	5								
6	0	6								
7	0	7								
8	0	8								
9	0	9								

Mastering Basic Facts

Children must master the basic facts (develop quick recall) because those who continue to struggle with basic facts often fail to understand higher mathematics concepts. Their cognitive energy is spent doing computation when it should be spent focusing on the more sophisticated concepts being developed (Forbringer & Fahsl, 2010).

As stated in the *Common Core State Standards*, the expectation is that by the end of second grade children will know from memory their basic facts for addition and subtraction. This achievement is a result of repeated experiences with reasoning strategies over time and not because of time spent memorizing. Children can know something from memory through immersion in the reasoning strategies, game playing, and life experiences, without *ever* having to memorize a fact from a flash card. Drill without moving children from counting strategies (phase 1) to reasoning strategies (phase 2) to mastery (phase 3) has repeatedly been found to be ineffective. The distinction between mastering basic facts via rote memorization and mastering basic facts via an emphasis on reasoning strategies is the most significant message in this chapter.

◆ Effective Drill

The fact that drill—repetitive non-problem-based activity—can strengthen memory and retrieval capabilities (Ashcraft & Christy, 1995) is important to consider once children are effectively using reasoning strategies that they understand but that they have not yet memorized. For drill to be effective, pacing and focus are crucial. Too often children become frustrated and overwhelmed because drill includes too many facts too quickly. Children will progress at different rates—gifted children tend to be good at memorizing whereas children with intellectual disabilities have difficulty memorizing (Forbringer & Fahsl, 2010).

When working on moving children to phase 3 (know from memory), use groups of related facts. By organizing the work around related facts, if a child needs any further discussion and illustrations, the focus will be beneficial. For example, if given a stack of ×1 facts, some children will quickly learn these facts by noting the generalization described earlier. However, some children—in particular, children with disabilities—may need more discussion and illustration to support their learning.

There are several websites and software programs that provide children opportunities to drill basic facts. These programs can be a great support for children who are near mastery or who are maintaining mastery because they can be fun. Try to use websites or programs for which you can target groups of related facts, rather than ones that drill on all the facts at one time. Fun 4 the Brain (www.fun4thebrain.com) and Math Fact Café (www.mathfactcafé.com) are two such websites.

◆ Use Games to Support Basic Fact Mastery

Games are another option that can keep children engaged while supporting the mastery of basic facts. Use games and activities in which children can choose from the strategies discussed in this chapter to help them become more fluent at choosing strategies and eventually to become more fluent with the basic facts. You can also focus on clusters of related facts with games. Games increase children's involvement, encourage student-to-student interaction, and improve communication—all of which are related to improved academic achievement (Forbringer & Fahsl, 2010; Kami & Anderson, 2003; Lewis, 2005). When all the facts are learned, continued reinforcement through occasional games and activities is important.

Activity 10.12 SALUTE!

Place children in groups of three and give each group a deck of cards (omit face cards and use aces as ones). Two children draw a card without looking at it and place it on their forehead facing outward so the others can see it. The child with no cards tells the sum of the two cards. The first of the other two to correctly say the number on their forehead "wins" the round. For ELLs, children with disabilities, or reluctant learners, speed can increase anxiety and inhibit participation. You can remove speed of response by having each child write down the card they think they have (within 5 seconds) and they get a point if they are correct. This activity can be differentiated by including only certain cards (e.g., addition facts using only the numbers 1 through 5).

Activity 10.13 MISSING-NUMBER CARDS

Show children families of numbers with the sum circled, as in Figure 10.9a. Ask why they think the numbers go together and why one number is circled. When this number family idea is understood, draw a different card and cover one of the numbers with your thumb, asking, "What is missing?" Ask children how they figured it out. After you have modeled this process, children can do this with partners. Alternatively, you can create cards with one number replaced by a question mark, as in Figure 10.9b. When children understand this activity, you can introduce missing-number cards such as those in Figure 10.9c. Ask children to name the missing number and explain their thinking.

Figure 10.9 Introducing missing-number cards.

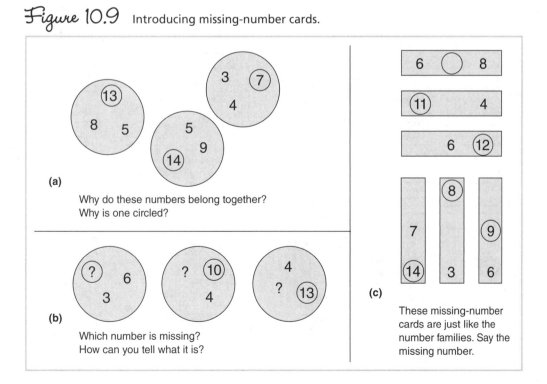

(a) Why do these numbers belong together?
Why is one circled?

(b) Which number is missing?
How can you tell what it is?

(c) These missing-number cards are just like the number families. Say the missing number.

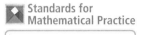

Standards for
Mathematical Practice

**4 Model with
mathematics** ▶

As a follow-up to Activity 10.13, children can complete "cards" on missing-number handouts (Blackline Master 11). You can create differentiated worksheets for children using clusters of facts that each child is ready to work on. For example, in one column of 13 "cards," you can put Make 10 facts, in another column you can put near-doubles facts, and in the third column you can put combinations from two families. Put combinations with different numbers missing, some addends and some sums. Also make sure to put blanks in different positions. An example is shown in Figure 10.10. Have children write an equation for each missing-number card.

This is an important step because many children are able to give the missing part in a family but do not connect this knowledge with subtraction.

Formative Assessment Note

As children are engaged in games and activities, interview them to determine if they are using counting strategies, reasoning strategies, or quick recall. Ask them to tell you what strategy they just used. If you observe counting, ask the child to try a particular reasoning strategy. If children are counting, more experiences to develop number relationships, such as activities with ten-frames, are needed.

Figure 10.10

Missing-number handouts. The blank version can be used to fill in any sets of facts you wish to emphasize (see Blackline Master 11). (Note that the columns are not labeled on student pages.)

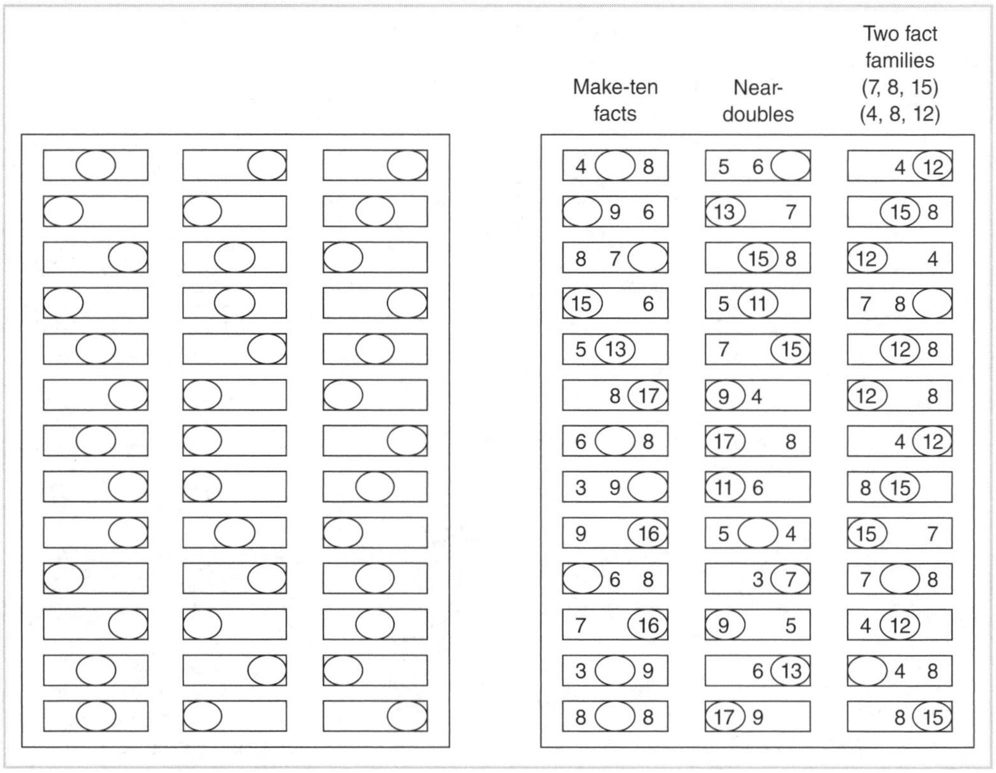

Dos and Don'ts for Teaching Basic Facts

This is such an important life skill for all learners that it is important that you use what research suggests are the most effective practices. The following list of recommendations can support the development of quick recall.

1. *Ask children to self-monitor.* Having a sense of what you know, what you don't know, and what you need to learn is important. Have children identify which basic facts are difficult for them and which reasoning strategies they want to work on to help them with those facts.

2. *Focus on self-improvement.* If you are working to improve a child's quickness at recalling facts, then the only person he should be compared with is himself. For example, children can keep track of how long it took them to go through their "fact stack" and then two days later, work through the same stack and check to see whether they were quicker or more accurate than the last time. Celebrate successes.

3. *Drill in short time segments.* Long periods (10 minutes or more) for drill are not effective. Use the first 5 to 10 minutes of the day, or extra time before lunch, to provide continued support on fact development and retention without using mathematics instructional time better devoted to other topics. Other quick ideas include projecting numerous examples of double ten-frames, doing a story problem and taking 5 minutes to share strategies, and having children pair up and go through each of their individualized sets of flash cards in 2 minutes.

4. *Work on facts over time.* Plan to work on facts over months and months, emphasizing reasoning strategies, then memorization, and then continued review and monitoring.

5. *Involve families.* Share your plan for how you will work on learning facts over the year and will first emphasize reasoning strategies. Ask family members to help children by using reasoning strategies when they don't know a fact.

6. *Make drill enjoyable.* Use games and activities designed to reinforce facts without competition and without inducing anxiety.

7. *Use technology.* Technology offers children immediate feedback and reinforcement, helping them to self-monitor.

The following list describes strategies that may have been designed with good intentions but hinder children's recall of basic facts.

1. *Don't use lengthy timed tests.* Children can get distracted by the pressure and abandon their reasoning strategies during timed tests. They can also develop anxiety as a result of timed tests, which works against learning mathematics. Instead have children self-monitor the time it takes them to go through a small set of facts and then work to improve their speed.

Formative Assessment Note

If there is any purpose for a timed test of basic facts, it may be for diagnostic purposes to determine which number combinations are mastered and which remain to be learned. Follow up with the child to identify possible misconceptions or misapplication of strategies as well as which facts are mastered and which need more practice.

2. *Don't use public comparisons of mastery.* Avoid using public comparisons, such as a bulletin board display that shows which children have mastered which basic facts. Similarly, avoid public competition with flash cards. It is great to celebrate children's successes, but avoiding public comparisons between children can go a long way in preventing children's anxiety as they learn mathematics.

3. *Don't proceed through the facts in order from 0 to 9.* Instead work on collections of facts based on strategies and conceptual understanding to emphasize connections and sense making.

4. *Don't work on all the facts all at once.* Select a strategy (starting with the easier ones) and then work on memorization of that set of facts (e.g., doubles). Be sure children really know these facts before moving on; otherwise, they may become confused and your goal for them to master all the facts will backfire. Because some children will learn some facts more quickly than other children, you will need to differentiate.

5. *Don't move to quick-recall activities too soon.* Quick recall or mastery can be attained only after children have a robust collection of reasoning strategies to apply as needed.

6. *Don't use facts as a barrier to good mathematics.* Mathematics is not solely about computation. Mathematics is about reasoning, using patterns, and making sense of things. Children who have mastered their basic facts do not necessarily reason better than those who, for whatever reason, have not yet mastered their facts. There is no reason that a child who has not yet mastered all basic facts should be excluded from any mathematical experiences.

7. *Don't use fact mastery as a prerequisite for calculator use.* Insisting that children master the basic facts before allowing them to use a calculator denies them important learning opportunities. For example, if the learning objective for a lesson is for children to explore even and odd numbers, then they might be building different array representations of numbers, recording different parts of the representations while they look for patterns. A child who has not yet developed fluency could get too bogged down in computation without a calculator. With a calculator, the same child can participate and hopefully attain the learning goals of the lesson.

Missing-Number Cards

Content and Task Decisions

Grade Level: 1–2

Mathematics Goals

- Practice part–part–whole thinking in developing connections between addition and subtraction
- Use think-addition as a strategy for solving subtraction facts

Grade Level Guide

NCTM *Curriculum Focal Points*	Common *Core State Standards*
Basic fact strategies begin in grade 1 and are mastered in grade 2 in the Number and Operations and Algebra strands. In grades 1 and 2, focal points target basic fact strategies: "Developing understandings of addition and subtraction and strategies for basic addition facts and related subtraction facts" (National Council of Teachers of Mathematics, 2006, p. 13) and "Developing quick recall of addition facts and related subtraction facts and fluency with multi-digit addition and subtraction" (p. 14).	Adding and subtracting within 20 are addressed in grades 1 and 2. In grade 1, children develop strategies (such as relating addition to subtraction) and add fluently to 10. "By end of grade 2, know from memory all sums of two one-digit numbers" (CCSSO, 2010, p. 19).

Consider Your Children's Needs

Children who are still very weak with addition facts will not benefit very much from this activity. The ultimate goal is to use think-addition when the whole and part are known and then later connect this thinking to subtraction.

For English Language Learners

- Children from other countries are often very good at mental mathematics. ELLs may have no trouble finding the missing number but may struggle to explain

how they thought about it. Encourage such children to illustrate their solution on a hundreds chart or with double ten-frames.

- The phrase "fact families" or "families of values" may sound odd to ELLs because they probably know a different meaning of the word *family*. Use the everyday meaning to connect to the grouping of the numbers in the missing-number sets.

For Children with Disabilities

- If children are struggling, you may want to use a part–part–whole mat along with counters to model the arrangements of the fact families.

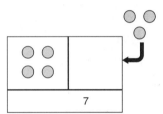

Materials

Each child will need:

- Missing-part recording sheet (Blackline Master 11). The combinations on the worksheet should address the specific facts children need to master.

Teacher will need:

- Missing-number flash cards. (The specific combinations on the cards are dependent on the facts that children still need to master. They should include roughly an equal number of missing-part and missing-whole numbers. See Figures 10.9 and 10.10 in the text.)

Lesson

Before

Present the focus task to the class:

- Draw several three-unit number families on the board. For example, you might show 4, 8, and 12; 6, 9, and 15; or 6, 7, and 13. In each number family, the whole is always circled. Have children tell why the numbers go together and how they are related.

- Next draw some number families with one number in the family missing. If the whole is missing, put an empty circle where it would be. If a part and a whole are given, circle the whole. For example, for 9, 4, and an empty circle, the missing number is the whole, 13. For 5 and a circled 12, the missing number is 7, the part that goes with 5 to make 12. Ask children to tell which number you have left out and why. They need to understand the convention of the circled number being the whole and the other two numbers being the parts.

- Introduce the missing-number flash cards. Show at least five cards with two numbers and a space for a third (either in a circle or not) and have children tell which number is missing on the card.

- Pass out the missing-part recording sheets prepared with number families on which children can practice. Their task is to fill in the missing number on each "card" of the recording sheet.

Provide clear expectations:

- This activity may be presented in small groups to address specific weaknesses.

During

Ongoing:

- Watch to see how fluently children are able to fill in the cards on the recording sheets. If you see hesitation or finger counting, stop and ask children to try to think of an addition fact (or related fact) that can help them figure out the missing number. Children can also use double ten-frames to help think about the problem.

- Ask children what strategies they are using to find the missing number.

- Note which types of problems are difficult for children.

After

Bring the class together to share and discuss the task:

- Select specific cards on the recording sheet and ask children to describe how they decided on the answer.

- Discuss strategies children used on the missing-part examples. Listen carefully for reasoning that approximates the following: "I saw a 5 and a 14 in a circle so I had to figure out what goes with 5 to make 14. Since 5 and 9 make 14, I put down 9."

Assessment
Observe

- The format of this practice activity encourages a think-addition approach. Do you see this with your children?

- For children who struggle with missing parts, it is important to see how fluent they are with the corresponding missing-whole cards. You can similarly check their mastery of addition facts.

- Prepare a page of addition and subtraction facts that correspond to the facts on the missing-part recording sheets. Children who complete the missing-part recording sheets fluently should also know the corresponding addition and subtraction facts.

- Children who revert to counting, especially counting backward (a take-away approach), but who can do the missing-part sheets have not yet made a connection between missing parts and subtraction. This calls for explicit work on connecting subtraction to missing-part thinking. Ask questions to help build this connection.

Ask

- How did you find the missing number?

- How is this missing-number card related to addition and subtraction?

Developing Whole-Number Place-Value Concepts

Big IDEAS

1   Sets of ten (and tens of tens) can be perceived as single entities or units. For example, "three sets of ten and two singles" is using base-ten language to describe 32 single objects.

2   The positions of digits in numbers determine what they represent—which size group they count. This is the major organizing principle of place-value numeration and is central to developing number sense.

3   There are patterns to the way that numbers are formed. For example, each decade has a symbolic pattern reflective of the 0-to-9 sequence (e.g., 20, 21, 22, . . . 29).

4   The groupings of ones, tens, and hundreds can be taken apart in different but equivalent ways. For example, beyond the typical way to decompose 256 into 2 hundreds, 5 tens, and 6 ones, it can be represented as 1 hundred, 14 tens, and 16 ones as well as 25 tens and 6 ones. Decomposing and composing multidigit numbers in flexible ways is a necessary foundation for computational estimation and exact computation.

5   Children progress through three levels of understanding the concept of "ten" starting with understanding ten not as a unit but only as ten ones. They then move to seeing ten as a unit but rely on physical or mental reconstructions of models to help them work with units of ten. Finally, they are able to easily work with units of ten without the need of physical or mental reconstructions of base-ten models.

6   Children's ability to label the tens place and the ones place or to count by tens does not guarantee that they understand that one ten is the same as ten ones.

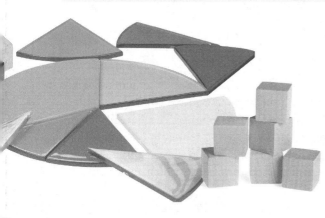

A complete understanding of place value, including extensions to decimal numeration, develops over the elementary and middle grades. However, the most critical period in this development occurs in grades pre-K to 2. In kindergarten and first grade, children count and are exposed to patterns in the numbers to 100. Most importantly, they begin to think about groups of ten objects as a unit. The *Common Core State Standards* (CCSSO, 2010) recommend that kindergartners work with numbers between 11 and 19 by putting them together (composing) and taking them apart (decomposing) into tens and ones using materials and drawings. By second grade, these initial ideas are extended to three-digit numbers.

As a significant part of this development, children should engage in composing and decomposing numbers in a wide variety of ways as they solve addition and subtraction problems with two- and three-digit numbers. In other words, there is no need to separate place-value instruction from computation instruction. Children's efforts with the invention of their own computation strategies will both enhance their understanding of place value and provide a firm foundation for flexible methods of computation.

Children's Pre–Place-Value Understandings

Children know a lot about numbers with two digits (10 to 99) as early as kindergarten. After all, most kindergartners can and should learn to count to 100 and count out sets of items with as many as 20 or 30 objects (CCSSO, 2010). They count children in the room, turn to specific page numbers in their books, and so on. However, to begin with, their understanding is quite different from yours. It is based on a count-by-ones approach to quantity and so the number 18 to them means 18 ones. They are not yet able to separate the quantity into place-value groups. For example, even after counting 18 teddy bears, a young child might tell you that the 1 in the number stands for 1 teddy bear and the 8 stands for 8 teddy bears.

Researchers have identified three levels of understanding about the concept of "ten" through which children progress (Wright, Martland, Stafford, & Stanger, 2008).

- *Level 1:* Initial Concept of Ten. Children understand ten not as a unit but only as ten ones. When solving addition or subtraction problems involving tens, they count only by ones.

- *Level 2:* Intermediate Concept of Ten. Children see ten as a unit that consists of ten ones, but they must rely on physical or mental reconstructions of models to help them work with units of ten.

- *Level 3:* Facile Concept of Ten. Children are able to easily work with units of ten without the use of physical or mental reconstructions of base-ten models.

Formative Assessment Note

Ask first- or second-grade children to count out 35 tiles. Watch closely to note whether they count out the tiles one at a time and put them into a pile without any type of grouping or if they group them into tens. Have the children write the number that tells how many tiles they just counted. Some may write "53" instead of "35," a simple reversal. You will likely find that early on children count the tiles one by one and are not yet thinking of ten as a unit (level 1 or initial concept of ten).

The children just described know that there are 35 tiles "because I counted them." Writing the number and saying the number are usually done correctly, but their understanding of 35 derives from and is connected to the count-by-ones approach. Children do not easily or quickly develop a meaningful use of groups of ten to represent quantities.

Even if children can tell you that in the numeral 35 the 3 "is in the tens place" or that there are "5 ones," they might just know the name of the positions without understanding that the "tens place" represents how many groups of ten. Similarly, if children use base-ten blocks, they may name a rod of ten as a "ten" and a small cube as a "one" but may not be able to tell how many ones are required to make a ten.

Children may know that 35 is "a lot" and that it's more than 27 (because you count past 27 to get to 35). They think of the "35" that they write as a single numeral. In this stage, they do not know that the 3 represents three groups of ten things and the 5 represents five single things (Fuson, 2006). Fuson and her colleagues refer to children's pre–place-value understanding of number as "unitary." That is, there are no groupings of ten, even though a two-digit number is associated with the quantity. They rely on unitary counts to understand quantities.

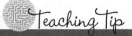
Teaching Tip

It is easy for children to attach words to both materials and groups without realizing what the materials or symbols represent.

Foundational Ideas in Place Value

Place-value understanding requires an integration of new and sometimes difficult-to-construct concepts of grouping by tens (the base-ten concept) with procedural knowledge of how groups are recorded in our place-value system and how numbers are written and spoken.

Teaching Tip

Children must understand the word *grouping*, especially English language learners (ELLs) who may become confused because the root word *group* is frequently used to instruct children to work together.

Integration of Base-Ten Groupings with Counting by Ones

Recognizing that children can count out a set of 35 by ones, you want to help them see that making groupings of tens and leftovers is a way of counting that same quantity. Each of the sets in Figure 11.1 has 35 tiles. You want children to construct the idea that all of these are the same and that the sameness is evident by virtue of the groupings of tens.

There is a subtle yet profound difference between children at this stage: Some know that set B in Figure 11.1 is 35 because they understand the idea that three groups of 10 and 5 more is the same amount as 35 counted by ones; others simply say, "It's 35," because they have been told that when things are grouped this way, it's called 35. The children who understand place value will see no need to count set B by ones. They understand the "thirty-fiveness" of sets A and B to be the same. The children in the pre–base-ten stage may not be sure how many they will get if they count the tiles in set B by ones or if the groups were "ungrouped" how many there would then be.

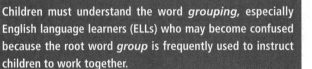
Standards for Mathematical Practice

◄ **7 Look for and make use of structure**

Stop and Reflect

What are some defining characteristics of "pre–place-value" children and children who understand place value? ∎

Recognition of the equivalence of sets B and C is another step in children's conceptual development. Groupings with fewer than the maximum number of tens are referred to as *equivalent groupings* or *equivalent representations*. Understanding the equivalence of sets B and C indicates that grouping by tens is not just a rule that is followed but also that any grouping by tens, including all or some of the singles, can help tell how many. Many computational techniques (e.g., regrouping in addition and subtraction) are based on equivalent representations of numbers.

Figure 11.1

Three equivalent groupings of 35 objects. Set A is 35 because "I counted them (by ones)." Set B has 3 tens and 5 more. Set C is the same as B, but now some groups of 10 are broken into singles.

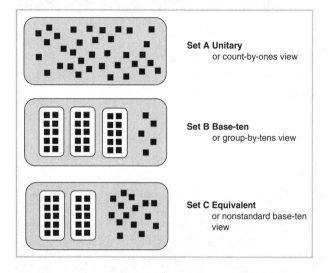

Set A Unitary
or count-by-ones view

Set B Base-ten
or group-by-tens view

Set C Equivalent
or nonstandard base-ten view

The Role of Counting in Constructing Base-Ten Ideas

Counting plays a key role in constructing base-ten ideas about quantity and in connecting these concepts to symbols and oral names for numbers.

Children can count sets such as those in Figure 11.1 using three distinct approaches. Each approach helps children think about the quantities in a different way.

1. *Counting by ones.* Children usually begin with this method. Initially, a count-by-ones approach is the primary way they can name a quantity or "tell how many." All three of the sets in Figure 11.1 can be counted by ones. Before base-ten ideas develop, counting by ones is the only approach by which children can be convinced that all three sets are the same amount.

2. *Counting by groups and singles.* In set B in Figure 11.1, counting by groups and singles would go like this: "One, two, three groups of 10, and one, two, three, four, five singles." Consider how novel this method would be for a child who had never thought about counting a group of objects as a single item. Also notice how this approach to counting does not tell directly how many items there are. This counting must be coordinated with counting by ones before it can be a means of telling "how many."

3. *Counting by tens and ones.* This is the way adults would probably count set B and perhaps set C: "Ten, twenty, thirty, thirty-one, thirty-two, thirty-three, thirty-four, thirty-five." Although this count ends by saying the number of objects, it is not as explicit as the second method in counting the number of groups.

Regardless of the specific activity that you may be doing with children, your foremost objective should be helping them integrate the grouping-by-tens concept with what they know about number from counting by ones. If they first counted by ones, the question might be, "What will happen if we count these by groups and singles (or by tens and ones)?" If a set has been grouped into tens and singles and counted accordingly, "How can we be really certain that there are 35 things here?" or "How many do you think we will get if we count by ones?" You cannot *tell* children that these counts will all be the same and hope that will make sense to them. It is a relationship they must construct.

◈ Integration of Groupings with Words

The way we say a number such as "thirty-five" must also be connected with the grouping-by-tens concept. The counting methods provide a way to help children make this connection. Counting by tens and ones results in saying the number of groups and singles separately: "three tens and five." Saying the number of tens and singles separately in this fashion can be called base-ten language. Children can associate base-ten language with standard language: "three tens and five—thirty-five."

There are several variations of base-ten language for 35: "3 tens and 5," "3 tens and 5 ones," "3 groups of 10 and 5 ones;" "3 tens and 5 singles," and so on. Each may be used interchangeably with the standard name "thirty-five." If you have ELLs, it is best to select one variation (e.g., 3 tens and 5 ones) and consistently connect it to the standard language.

Figure 11.2

Groupings by 10 are matched with numerals, which are recorded in labeled places and eventually written in standard form.

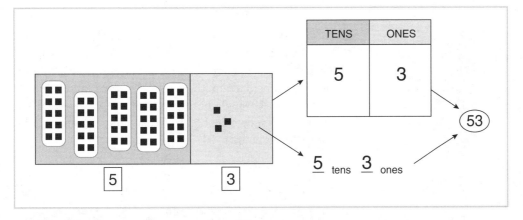

Other languages often use base-ten terminology, so this can be a good cultural connection for children (e.g., 17 in Spanish is *diecisiete*, literally meaning "10 and 7").

◆ Integration of Groupings with Place-Value Notation

The symbolic scheme that we use for writing numbers (ones on the right, tens to the left of ones, and so on) must be coordinated with the grouping scheme. Activities can be designed so that children physically associate groupings of tens and ones with the correct recording of the individual digits, as Figure 11.2 indicates.

Language again plays a key role in making these connections. The explicit count by groups and singles matches the individual digits as the number is written in the usual left-to-right manner. A similar coordination is necessary for hundreds and other place values.

Figure 11.3 summarizes the ideas of integrated place-value understanding that have been discussed so far. Note that in addition to counting by ones, children should have experiences counting in two other ways: by groups and singles and by tens and ones. All three methods of counting are coordinated as the principal method of integrating the base-ten concepts, the written names, and the oral names.

🔺 Base-Ten Models for Place Value

Physical models for base-ten concepts can play a key role in helping children develop the idea of "a ten" as both a single entity and as a set of 10 units. Remember, though, that the physical models do not "show" the concept to the children. The children must mentally construct the "ten makes one" relationship and impose it on the model.

When first teaching place value, the base-ten model for ones, tens, and hundreds should be proportional. That is, a model for ten is physically ten times larger than the model for a one, and a model for one hundred is ten times larger than the ten

Figure 11.3

Relational understanding of place value integrates three components: base-ten concepts, oral names for numbers, and written names for numbers.

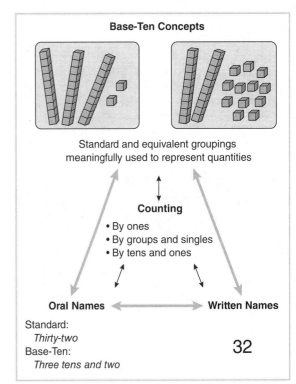

Figure 11.4

Groupable and pregrouped base-ten models.

(a) Groupable base-ten models

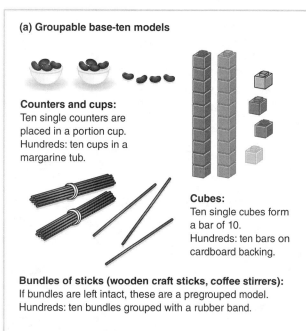

Counters and cups:
Ten single counters are placed in a portion cup. Hundreds: ten cups in a margarine tub.

Cubes:
Ten single cubes form a bar of 10. Hundreds: ten bars on cardboard backing.

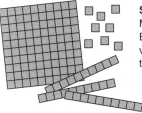

Bundles of sticks (wooden craft sticks, coffee stirrers):
If bundles are left intact, these are a pregrouped model. Hundreds: ten bundles grouped with a rubber band.

(b) Pregrouped base-ten models

Strips and squares:
Make from cardstock. See Blackline Master 13. Plastic versions are available through catalogs.

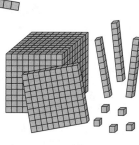

Base-ten blocks:
Wooden or plastic units, longs, flats, and blocks. Expensive, durable, easily handled, the only model with 1000.

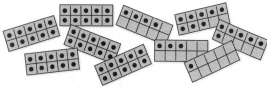

Little ten-frame cards:
Good for illustrating how far to the next multiple of ten. Ones are not loose but are organized in a ten-frame. No model for 100. Inexpensive and easy to make. See Blackline Masters 17 and 18.

Standards for Mathematical Practice

7 Look for and make use of structure ▶

---

model. Base-ten models can be categorized as groupable and pregrouped.

Groupable Models

Models that most clearly reflect the relationships of ones, tens, and hundreds are those for which the ten can actually be made or grouped from the single pieces. When children put 10 beans in a cup, the cup of 10 beans literally is the same as the 10 single beans. Examples of these groupable models are shown in Figure 11.4a. These could also be called "put-together–take-apart" models.

Teaching Tip

As children begin to make groupings of ten, start introducing the language of "tens" by matching the objects being used, such as "cups of ten and ones" or "bundles of ten and singles." Then move to a general phrase, such as "groups of ten and ones."

Of the groupable models, beans or counters in cups are inexpensive and easy for children to use. Plastic linking cubes also provide a good transition to pregrouped tens rods as they form a similar shape. Bundles of wooden Popsicle sticks or coffee stirrers can be grouped with rubber bands, but small hands may have trouble using rubber bands.

As children become more and more familiar with these models, collections of tens can be made in advance by the children and kept as ready-made tens (e.g., Popsicle sticks can be left bundled, linking cubes can be left connected). This is a good transition into the pregrouped models described next.

Pregrouped or Trading Models

Models that are pregrouped are commonly shown in textbooks and are often used in instructional activities. Pregrouped models, such as those in Figure 11.4b, cannot be taken apart or put together. When 10 single pieces are accumulated, they must be exchanged or traded for a ten, and likewise, tens must be traded for hundreds. With pregrouped models you need to make extra efforts to make sure that children understand that a ten piece really is the same as 10 ones. Here children combine multiplicative understanding (each piece is ten times the value of the place to the right) with a positional system (each place has a value)—something hard to do prior to learning multiplication! The chief advantage of these physical models is their ease of use and the efficient way they model large numbers.

The little ten-frames (see Blackline Masters 17–18) are less common but are very ef-fective. If children have been using ten-frames to think about numbers to 20 as discussed in Chapters 8 and 10, the value of the filled ten-frame may be more meaningful than the ten rods and squares of base-ten materials. Although the ones are fixed on the cards, this model has the distinct advantage of always showing the distance to the next decade. For example, when 47 is shown with 4 ten cards and a seven card, a child can see that three more ones will make five full cards, or 50.

A significant disadvantage of the pregrouped physical models is the potential for children to use them without reflecting on the ten-to-one relationships or without really understand-ing what they are doing—this is especially true if children have not had adequate experience working with groupable models.

For example, if children are told to trade 10 ones for a ten, it is quite possible for them to make this exchange without attending to the "ten-ness" of the piece they call a ten. Similarly, children can learn to "make the number 42" by simply selecting 4 tens and 2 ones pieces without understanding that if the pieces all came apart there would be 42 ones pieces that could be counted by ones.

Standards for
Mathematical Practice

◄ **5** **Use appropriate tools strategically**

technology note

Electronic versions of pregrouped base-ten manipulatives (such as the Base Blocks applet at http://nlvm .usu.edu/en/nav/frames_asid_152_g_3_t_2.html) are computer representations of the three-dimensional base-ten blocks. With simple mouse clicks, children (including those with disabilities) can place ones, tens, hundreds, or thousands on the screen. To break a piece into 10 smaller pieces, simply move the piece to the right one column. Lasso 10 pieces and they are automatically grouped into a larger base-ten piece. As pieces are moved onto the place value mat, a corresponding numeral that shows the current quantity is displayed. You can also adjust the columns to display two, three, or four place values.

Compared to real base-ten blocks, these virtual materials are free, can be easily grouped and ungrouped, can be shown to the full class on a projection device, and are available in "endless" supply—even the thousands blocks. Even with all these advantages, the computer models, like the physical models, are only a representation for children who understand the relationships involved.

◆ Nonproportional Models

Nonproportional models (e.g., money, an abacus) can be used by children who understand that 10 units make "a ten." These are models, such as money, in which the ten is not physi-cally ten times larger than the one. Many children can grasp place-value relationships using pennies, dimes, and dollars to represent the ones, tens, and hundreds on their place-value mat. Using coin representations, they can display amounts and exchange 10 dimes for a dol-lar and represent and carry out a variety of calculations. However, like a bead frame that has the same-sized beads on wires in different columns (i.e., an abacus) or chips that are assigned different place values by color, nonproportional representations are not used to introduce place-value concepts. They are used once children have a conceptual understanding of the numeration system and need additional reinforcement.

🔺 Developing Base-Ten Concepts

Now that you have a sense of the important place-value concepts, we turn to activities that can assist children in developing these concepts. This section focuses on base-ten concepts or grouping by tens (see the top of Figure 11.3). Connecting this important idea with the oral and written names for numbers (the rest of Figure 11.3) is discussed separately. However, in the classroom, the oral and written names for numbers can and should be developed in concert with conceptual ideas.

◆ Grouping Activities

Reflect for a moment on how strange it must sound to say "seven ones." Certainly, children have never said they were "seven ones" years old. The use of the word *ten* as a singular group name is even more mysterious. Consider the phrase "Ten ones makes one ten." The first ten carries the usual meaning of 10 things, the amount that is 1 more than 9 things. But the other ten is a singular noun, a thing. How can something the child has known for years as the name for a lot of things suddenly become one thing? And if you think this is confusing for native speakers, imagine the potential difficulty for ELLs.

Because children come to their development of base-ten concepts with a count-by-ones idea of number, you must begin there. You cannot arbitrarily impose grouping by ten on children. Children need to experiment with showing amounts in groups of like size and eventually come to an agreement that ten is a very useful size to use. The following activity could be done in first grade and is designed as an example of a first effort at developing grouping concepts.

Standards for Mathematical Practice

1 Make sense of problems and persevere in solving them

Activity 11.1 COUNTING IN GROUPS

Find a collection of things that children might be interested in counting—perhaps the number of shoes in the classroom, a tub of cubes, a long chain of plastic links, or the number of crayons in the classroom crayon box. The quantity should be countable, somewhere between 25 and 100. Pose the question, "How could we count our shoes in some way that would be easier than counting by ones?"

Whatever suggestions you get, try to implement them. After trying several methods, you can have a discussion of what worked well and what did not. If no one suggests counting by tens, you might casually suggest that as an idea to try.

One teacher challenged her children to find a good way to count all the linking cubes being held by the class after each child had been given a cube for each of their pockets. The first suggestion was to count by sevens. That was tried but did not work very well because none of the children could count by sevens. In search of a more efficient way, the next suggestion was to count by twos. This did not seem to be much better than counting by ones. Finally, they settled on counting by tens and realized that this was a pretty good method.

This and similar activities provide you with the opportunity to suggest that materials be arranged into groups of tens before the "fast" way of counting is begun. Remember that children may count "ten, twenty, thirty, thirty-one, thirty-two" but not fully realize the "thirty-two-ness" of the quantity. To connect the count-by-tens method with their understood method of counting by ones, the children need to count both ways and discuss why they get the same result.

The idea in the next activity is for children to make groupings of ten and record or say the amounts. Number words are used so that children will not mechanically match tens and ones with individual digits. It is important that children confront the actual quantity in a manner meaningful to them.

Activity 11.2 GROUPS OF TEN

Prepare bags of different types of objects such as toothpicks, buttons, beans, plastic chips, linking cubes, Popsicle sticks, or other items. Children should have a recording sheet similar to the top example in Figure 11.5. The bags can be placed at stations around the room or given to pairs of children. Children empty the bags and count the contents. The amount is recorded as a number word. Then the objects are grouped in as many tens as possible. The groupings are recorded on the form. After returning the objects to the bags, bags are traded or children move to another station. Note that children with disabilities may initially need to use a ten-frame to support their counting. Then the use of the ten-frame should eventually fade.

Variations of the "Groups of Ten" activity are suggested by the other recording sheets in Figure 11.5. On the "Get This Many" sheet, children count the dots and then count out the corresponding number of objects. Provide small cups to put the groups of ten in. Notice that the activity requires children to first count the set in a way they understand (e.g., count

Figure 11.5 Activities involving number words and making groups of ten.

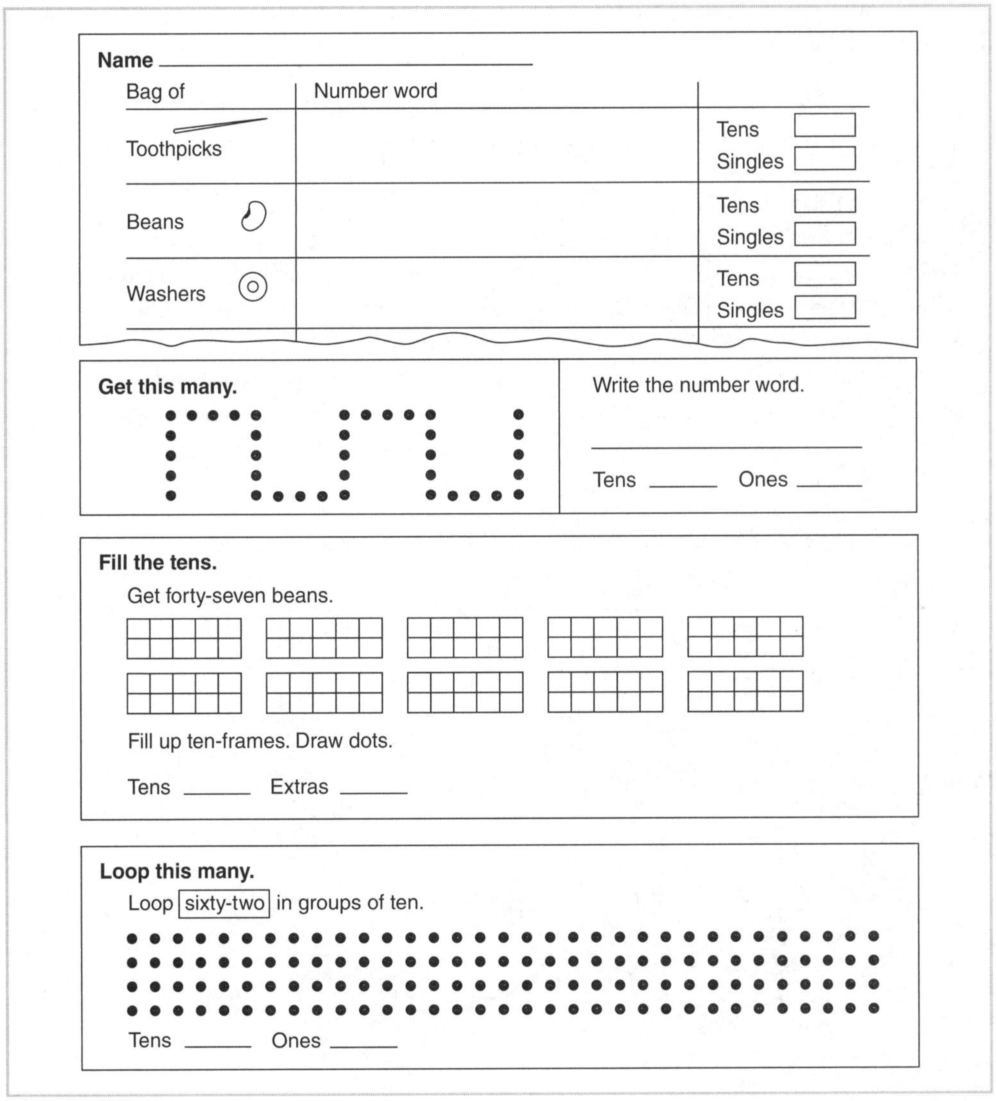

by ones), record the amount in words, and then make the groupings. The "Fill the Tens" and "Loop This Many" sheets begin with a verbal name (number word), and children must count the indicated amount and then make groups.

The following activity is another variant of the grouping activities but includes an estimation component that adds interest, makes the activity more problem based, and contributes to number sense. Listening to children's estimates is a useful assessment opportunity that tells you a lot about children's concepts of numbers.

Activity 11.3 ESTIMATING GROUPS OF TENS AND ONES

Show children a length that they are going to measure—for example, the length of a child lying down or the distance around a sheet of newspaper. At one end of the length, line up 10 units (e.g., 10 linking cubes, toothpicks, rods, or blocks). On a recording sheet (see Figure 11.6), children write down an estimate of how many groups of 10 and ones they think will fit into the length. Next they find the actual measure, placing units along the full length. These are counted by ones and also grouped in tens. Both results are recorded. Estimating the groups of ten requires children to pay attention to the ten as a group or unit.

Children can work in pairs to measure several lengths around the room. A similar estimation approach could be added to "Groups of Ten" (Activity 11.2), where children first estimate the quantity in the bags.

Formative Assessment Note

As you watch children doing these activities, you can learn a lot about their base-ten concept development. For example, how do children count out the objects? Do they make groupings of ten? Do they count to 10 and then start again at 1? Children who do that are already using the base-ten structure. But what you will more likely see early on is children counting a full set without stopping at tens and without any effort to group the materials in piles. You can also ask a child in a diagnostic interview to count a jar of small beans. Ask the child, "If you were to place each group of 10 beans in a small cup, how many cups would you need?" If a child has no idea or makes random guesses, what would you know about the child's knowledge of place value?

Figure 11.6 Recording sheet for estimating groups of tens and ones.

NAME Jessica

OBJECT	ESTIMATE	ACTUAL
desk	5 TENS 6 SINGLES	3 TENS 2 SINGLES Thirty-two Number Word
______	____ TENS ____ SINGLES	____ TENS ____ SINGLES ______ Number Word

◆ Grouping Tens to Make 100

In second grade, numbers up to 1000 become important (CCSSO, 2010). Here the issue is not one of connecting a count-by-ones approach to a group of 100 but rather seeing how a group of 100 can be understood as a group of 10 tens as well as 100 single ones. In textbooks this is often illustrated on one page showing how 10 rods of ten can be put together to make one hundred. This quick demonstration may be lost on many children.

As a means of introducing hundreds as groups of 10 tens and also 100 singles, consider the following estimation activity.

Activity 11.4 TOO MANY TENS

Show children any quantity with 150 to 1000 items. For example, you might use a jar of lima beans, a clear bag full of plastic necklace beads, a long chain of connecting links or paper clips, or a box of Styrofoam packing peanuts. Suppose you are using the bag of plastic beads. First, have children make and record estimates of how many beads are in the bag. Discuss with children how they determined their estimates. Then give portions of the beads to pairs or triads of children to put into cups of 10 beads. Collect leftover beads and put these into groups of ten as well. Now ask, "How can we use these groups of ten to tell how many beads we have? Can we make new groups from the groups of ten? What is 10 groups of ten called?" If using cups of beads, be prepared with some larger containers or baggies into which 10 cups can be placed. When all groups are made, count the hundreds, the tens, and the ones separately. Record the totals on the board as "4 hundreds + 7 tens + 8 ones."

In this activity, it is important to use a groupable model so that children can see how the 10 groups of ten are the same as 100 individual items. This connection is often too implicit in the display of a hundreds flat or a paper hundreds square in the pregrouped base-ten models.

◆ Equivalent Representations

An important variation of the grouping activities is aimed at the equivalent representations of numbers. After children have just completed the "Groups of Ten" activity (Activity 11.2) with a bag of objects, pose the following task.

What is another way you can show 42 besides 4 groups of ten and 2 singles? Let's see how many ways you can find.

Interestingly, most children will go next to 42 singles. The following activities focus on creating other equivalent representations.

Activity 11.5 CAN YOU MAKE THE LINK?

Show a collection of materials that is only partly grouped in sets of ten. For example, you may have 5 chains of 10 links and 17 additional links. Be sure the children understand that each chain is a group of 10 links. Have children count the number of chains, and also count the singles, in any way they wish to count. Ask, "How many in all?" Record all responses and discuss how they got their answers. Next change the groupings (make a

◆ Standards for
Mathematical Practice

8 Look for and
express regularity in
repeated reasoning ▶

ten from the singles or break apart one of the tens) and repeat the questions and discussion. Do not change the total number from one time to the next. Once children begin to understand that the total does not change, ask in what other ways the items could be grouped if using tens and singles.

If you teach second grade, equivalent representations for hundreds as groups of tens can help children with the concept of a hundred as 10 tens. The next activity is similar to "Can You Make the Link?" but is done using pregrouped materials and includes hundreds.

◢ *Activity* 11.6 **THREE OTHER WAYS**

Children work in groups or pairs. First, they show 463 on their desks with base-ten materials in the standard representation. Next, they find and record at least three other ways of representing this quantity.

A variation of "Three Other Ways" is to challenge children to find a way to show an amount with a specific number of pieces. For example, ask children to show 463 with 31 pieces. (There is more than one way to do this.)

After children have had sufficient experiences with pregrouped materials, a semiabstract "dot-stick-square" notation can be used for recording ones, tens, and hundreds (see Figure 11.7). Use the drawings as a means of telling the children which type of pieces to use to solve problems and also as a way for children to record results.

The next activity begins to incorporate oral language with equivalent representation ideas.

Figure 11.7 Equivalent representation exercises using square-stick-dot pictures.

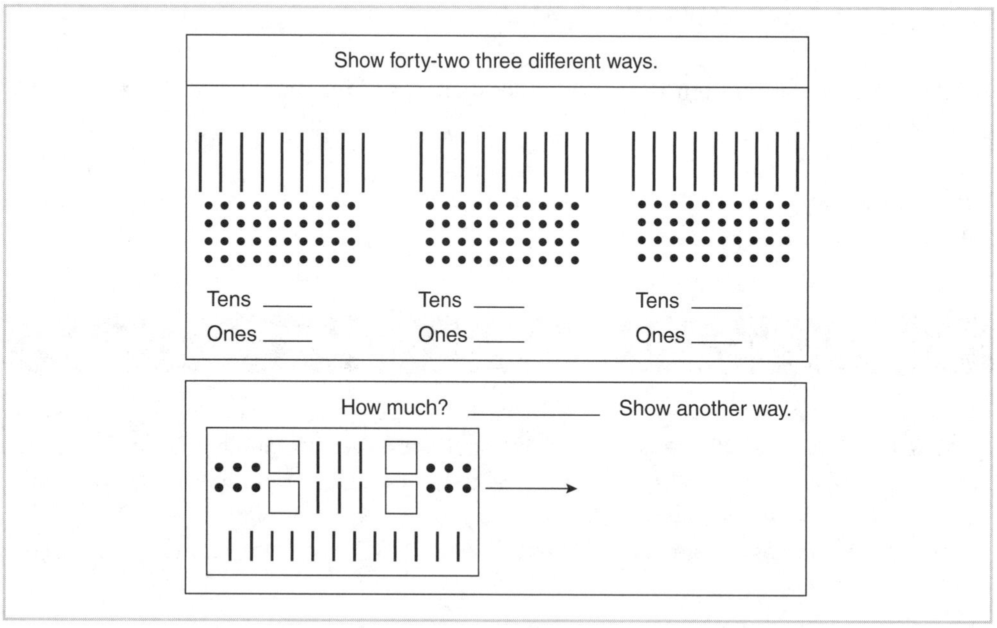

◆ *Activity* 11.7 **BASE-TEN RIDDLES**

Base-ten riddles can be presented orally or in written form. In either case, children should use base-ten materials to help solve the riddles. The examples here illustrate a variety of different levels of difficulty. After children solve the following riddles, have them write new ones.

• I have 23 ones and 4 tens. Who am I?
• I have 4 hundreds, 12 tens, and 6 ones. Who am I?
• I have 30 ones and 3 hundreds. Who am I?
• I am 45. I have 25 ones. How many tens do I have?
• I am 341. I have 22 tens. How many hundreds do I have?
• I have 13 tens, 2 hundreds, and 21 ones. Who am I?
• If you put 3 more tens with me, I would be 115. Who am I?
• I have 17 ones. I am between 40 and 50. Who am I? How many tens do I have?

Oral and Written Names for Numbers

In this section, we focus on helping children connect oral and written names for numbers (see bottom of Figure 11.3) with their emerging base-ten concepts of using groups of ten or one hundred as efficient methods of counting. Note that the ways we say and write numbers are conventions, not concepts. Children must learn these by being told rather than through problem-based activities.

Teaching Tip

It is important to note that the patterns in our English number words are probably not the same as those in ELLs' native language, especially for the numbers 11 to 19.

◆ Two-Digit Number Names

In kindergarten and first grade, children need to connect the base-ten concepts with the oral number names they have used many times. They know the words but may have not thought of them in terms of tens and ones. In fact, early on they may want to write twenty-one as 201.

Almost always use base-ten models while teaching oral names. Initially, rather than use standard number words, use the more explicit base-ten language (e.g., "4 tens and 7 ones" instead of "forty-seven"). Base-ten language is rarely misunderstood. When it seems appropriate, begin to pair base-ten language with standard language. Emphasize the teens as exceptions. Acknowledge that they are formed "backward" and do not fit the patterns. The next activity helps introduce oral names for numbers.

◆ *Activity* 11.8 **COUNTING ROWS OF 10**

Use a 10 × 10 array of dots on the projector. Cover up all but two rows, as shown in Figure 11.8a. "How many tens? (2.) Two tens is called twenty." Have the class repeat. Show another row. "Three tens is called thirty. Four tens is forty. Five tens could have been fivety but is just fifty. How many tens does sixty have?" The names *sixty, seventy, eighty,* and *ninety* all fit the pattern. Slide the cover up and down the array, asking how many tens and the name for that many. ELLs may not hear the difference between *fifty* and *fifteen, sixty* and *sixteen,* and so on, so explicitly compare these words and clearly enunciate and even overemphasize the word endings.

Use the same 10 × 10 array to work on names for tens and ones. Show, for example, four full lines, "forty." Next expose one dot in the fifth row. "Four tens and one. Forty-one." Add more dots one at a time. "Four tens and two. Forty-two." "Four tens and three. Forty-three." This is shown in Figure 11.8b. When that pattern is established, repeat with other decades from 20 through 90.

Figure 11.8

10×10 dot arrays are used to model sets of 10 and singles (Blackline Master 12).

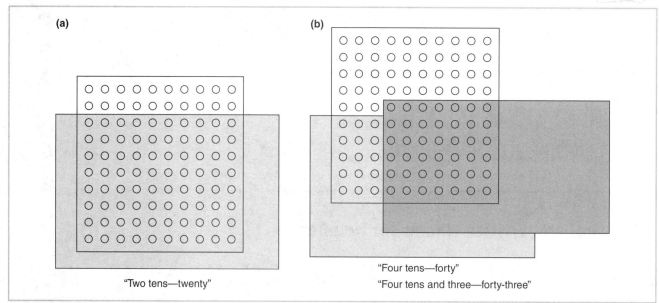

(a)

"Two tens—twenty"

(b)

"Four tens—forty"
"Four tens and three—forty-three"

Repeat this basic approach with other base-ten models. The next activity shows how this might be done.

Activity 11.9 COUNTING WITH BASE-TEN MODELS

Show some tens pieces on the projector or just place them on the carpet in a mixed arrangement. Ask how many tens. Add a ten or remove a ten and repeat the question. Next add some ones. Always have children give the base-ten name and the standard name.

Continue to make changes in the materials displayed by adding or removing one or two tens and by adding and removing ones. Avoid the standard left-to-right order for tens and ones so the emphasis is on the names of the materials, not the order they are in.

Reverse the activity by having children use base-ten blocks at their desks. For example, say, "Make 63." The children make the number with the models and then give the base-ten name (6 tens and 3 ones) and standard name (63).

Teaching Tip

Post examples of base-ten names and the corresponding standard names on the math word wall. This is particularly helpful for ELLs and children with disabilities and will be helpful for other children as well.

Note that Activities 11.8 and 11.9 will be enhanced by having children explain their thinking. If you don't require children to reflect on their responses, they soon learn how to give the response you want, matching number words to models without actually thinking about the total quantities. The next activity has the same objective as Activities 11.8 and 11.9.

Standards for Mathematical Practice

2 Reason abstractly and quantitatively ▶

Activity 11.10 TENS, ONES, AND FINGERS

Ask your class, "Can you show 6 fingers (or any amount less than 10)?" Then ask, "How can you show 37 fingers?" Some children will figure out that at least four children are required.

Line up four children, and have three hold up 10 fingers while the fourth child holds up 7 fingers. Have the class count the fingers by tens and ones. Ask other children to show different numbers. Emphasize the number of sets of 10 fingers and the single fingers (base-ten language) and pair this with standard language.

In the last three activities, it is important occasionally to count an entire representation by ones. Remember that counting by ones is the young child's principal linkage with the concept of quantity. For example, suppose you have just had children use linking cubes to make 36. Try asking, "Do you think there really are 36 blocks there?" Many children may not be convinced, so the count by ones is very significant.

◆ Three-Digit Number Names

The approach to three-digit number names is essentially the same as for two-digit names. Show mixed arrangements of base-ten materials. Have children write the base-ten name and the standard name. Vary the arrangement from one example to the next by changing only one type of piece. That is, add or remove only ones or only tens or only hundreds. It is important for children with disabilities to see counterexamples, so purposefully point out that some (anonymous!) children wrote 200803 for two hundred eighty-three, and ask them whether that is correct. These discussions allow children to explore their misunderstandings and to more explicitly focus on the place-value system.

Similarly, have children at their desks model numbers that you give to them orally using the standard names. By the time that children are ready for three-digit numbers, the two-digit number names, including the difficulties with the teens, have usually been mastered. The major difficulty is with numbers involving no tens, such as 702. As noted earlier, the use of base-ten language is quite helpful here. The difficulty with zero tens (or more generally the internal zero) is more pronounced when writing numerals. At first children do not see the importance of zero in place value and do not understand that zero helps to distinguish between such numbers as 703, 73, and 730 (Dougherty, Flores, Louis, & Sophian, 2010). Try posing tasks similar to the following to emphasize the importance of zero in place value.

Standards for Mathematical Practice

◀ **4 Model with mathematics**

Use the standard names to say the following numbers: 203, 23, and 230. As you say a number, have children write the number and then model the number with base-ten materials. Then repeat the numbers orally using base-ten language and have children check their models and written numerals.

Children frequently incorrectly write 2003 for two hundred three. The emphasis on the meaning in the oral base-ten language will be a significant help. ELLs may need additional time to think about how to say and write numerals because they are translating all the terms within the number.

◆ Written Symbols

Place-value mats are simple mats divided into two or three sections to hold ones and tens or ones, tens, and hundreds pieces as shown in Figure 11.9. You can suggest to children that the mats are a good way to organize their materials when working with base-ten blocks. Explain that the standard way to use a place-value mat is with the space for the ones on the right and tens and hundreds places to the left.

Although not commonly seen in textbooks, it is strongly recommended that two ten-frames (see Blackline Master 15) be drawn in the ones place as shown. That way, the amount of ones on the ten-frames is always clearly evident, eliminating the need for repeatedly counting

BLM

Figure 11.9

Place-value mats with two ten-frames in the ones place to organize the counters and promote the concept of groups of ten.

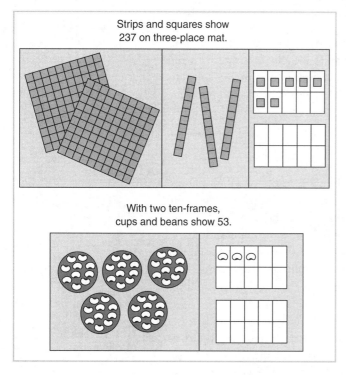

Strips and squares show 237 on three-place mat.

With two ten-frames, cups and beans show 53.

Figure 11.10

Building numbers with a set of cards.

the ones. The ten-frame also makes it very clear how many additional counters would be needed to make the next set of ten. If children are modeling two numbers at the same time, one ten-frame can be used for each number.

Be aware of how easy it is for a child to show a number on a mat using base-ten blocks and learn to write the number without any understanding of what the number represents. First- and second-grade textbooks often show a picture of base-ten materials and have children record numbers in this manner:

_7_ tens and _3_ ones is _7_ _3_ in all.

It is all too easy to copy down the number of rods and single blocks and rewrite these digits in a single number 73 and not confront what these symbols stand for. Consider the following approach to address this issue.

As children use their place-value mats, they can be shown how the left-to-right order of the pieces is also the way that numbers are written. To show how the numbers are "built," have a set of 27 cards—one for each of the hundreds (100–900), one for each of the tens (10–90), and ones cards for 1 through 9 (see Figure 11.10). Notice that the cards are made so that the tens card is twice as long as the ones card and the hundreds card is three times as long as the ones card.

As children place the materials for a number (e.g., 457) on the place-value mat, have them also place the matching cards (e.g., 400, 50, and 7) below the materials. Then starting with the hundreds card, layer the others on top, right aligned. This approach will show how the number is built while allowing children to see the individual components of the number. This is especially helpful when there are zero tens. The place-value mat and the matching cards illustrate the important link between the base-ten models and the written form of the numbers.

The next two activities are designed to help children make connections between models, oral names (base ten and standard), and written forms. The activities can be done with two- or three-digit numbers depending on children's needs.

Activity 11.11 SAY IT/PRESS IT

Display some ones and tens (and hundreds) in a mixed arrangement. (Use a projector or simply draw on the board using the square-stick-dot method.) Children say the amount shown in base-ten language ("four hundreds, one ten, and five ones") and then in standard language ("four hundred fifteen"); next they enter it on their calculators. Have someone share his or her display and defend it. Make a change in the materials and repeat. You can also do this activity as "Show It/Press It" and start by saying the standard name for a number (with either two or three digits). At their desks, children use base-ten materials to show that number and press it on their calculators (or write it). Again, pay special attention to numbers in the teens and the case of zero tens. ELLs may need additional time to think of the words that go with the numbers, especially as the numbers get larger.

These activities are especially good for numbers that pose problems for children, such as the teens and three-digit numbers with zero tens. If you show or say 7 hundreds and 4 ones, the class says, "seven hundreds, zero tens, and four ones—seven hundred (slight pause) four." The pause and the base-ten language suggest the correct three-digit number to press, write, and model.

The next activity is a wonderful challenge for children in early stages of place-value development. It can also be used as an assessment to see whether children really understand the value of digits in two- and three-digit numbers.

Activity 11.12 DIGIT CHANGE

Have children enter a specific two- or three-digit number on the calculator. The task is to change one of the digits in the number without simply entering the new number. For example, change 48 to 78. Change 315 to 305 or to 295. Changes can be made by adding or subtracting an appropriate amount. Children should write or discuss explanations for their solutions. Children with disabilities may need the visual support of having cards that say "add ten" or "add one" first to explore how the number changes. They may also need to use base-ten materials to be able to conceptualize the number before moving to more abstract work using only the calculator.

Formative Assessment Note

Children are often able to disguise their lack of understanding of place value by following directions, using the tens and ones pieces in prescribed ways, and using the language of place value.

The diagnostic tasks presented here are designed to help you look more closely at children's understanding of the integration of the three components of place value. Designed to be used in diagnostic interviews rather than whole-class activities, these tasks have been used by several researchers and are adapted primarily from Kami (1985), Labinowicz (1985), and Ross (1986).

The first interview task is referred to as the Digit Correspondence Task. Take out 36 blocks. Ask the child to count the blocks, and then have the child write the number that tells how many there are. Circle the 6 in 36 and ask, "Does this part of your 36 have anything to do with how many blocks there are?" Then circle the 3 and repeat the question. As with all diagnostic interviews, do not give clues. Based on responses to the task, Ross (1989, 2002) has identified five distinct levels of understanding of place value:

1. *Single numeral.* The child writes 36 but views it as a single numeral. The individual digits 3 and 6 have no meaning by themselves.
2. *Position names.* The child correctly identifies the tens and ones positions but still makes no connections between the individual digits and the blocks.
3. *Face value.* The child matches 6 blocks with the 6 and 3 blocks with the 3.
4. *Transition to place value.* The 6 is matched with 6 blocks and the 3 with the remaining 30 blocks but not as 3 groups of 10.
5. *Full understanding.* The 3 is correlated with 3 groups of 10 blocks and the 6 with 6 single blocks.

For the second interview, write the number 342. Have the child read the number. Then have the child write the number that is 1 more. Next, ask for the number that is 10 more. You may wish to explore further with models. One less and 10 less can be checked the same way. Watch to see whether the child is counting on or counting back or if the child immediately knows that 10 more is 352. This interview can also be done with a two-digit number.

A third interview can also be revealing. Ask the child to write the number that represents 5 tens, 2 ones, and 3 hundreds. Note that the task does not give the places in order. What do you think will be the common misunderstanding? If the child does not write 352, then ask the child to show you the number with base-ten materials. What information can you obtain from the results of this interview?

Figure 11.11

A hundreds chart (Blackline Master 10).

1	2	3	4	5	6	7	8	9	10
11	12	13	14	15	16	17	18	19	20
21	22	23	24	25	26	27	28	29	30
31	32	33	34	35	36	37	38	39	40
41	42	43	44	45	46	47	48	49	50
51	52	53	54	55	56	57	58	59	60
61	62	63	64	65	66	67	68	69	70
71	72	73	74	75	76	77	78	79	80
81	82	83	84	85	86	87	88	89	90
91	92	93	94	95	96	97	98	99	100

BLM

Patterns and Relationships with Multidigit Numbers

Now we move beyond a snapshot view of individual numbers to look at patterns in our number system and how numbers are related. In particular we are interested in helping children develop an understanding of the relationships of numbers to special numbers called benchmark numbers. These ideas begin to provide a basis for computation.

◆ The Hundreds Chart

The hundreds chart (Figure 11.11) is such an important tool in the development of place-value concepts that it deserves special attention. K–2 classrooms should have a hundreds chart displayed prominently.

As mentioned in Chapter 8, a pocket-chart version of a hundreds chart is very useful. You can hide a number in the chart by inserting a blank card in front of the number in the pocket. You can also insert colored pieces of paper in the slots to highlight various number patterns such as skip-counting patterns. You can also remove some or all the number cards and have children return them to their correct positions. A blank 10 × 10 grid (see Blackline Master 9) serves as an empty hundreds chart on which you can write numbers.

In kindergarten and first grade, children can count and recognize two-digit numbers with the hundreds chart. In first and second grades, children can use the hundreds chart to develop base-ten understanding, noticing that jumps up or down are jumps of ten, while jumps to the right or left are jumps of one.

There are lots of patterns on the hundreds chart. In a discussion, different children will describe the same pattern in several ways. Accept all ideas. In addition to the patterns described in Chapter 8, you might have children explore various skip-count patterns.

You can use online versions of a hundreds chart, one of which (called Hundred Square) can be found at www.crickweb.co.uk/ks2numeracy-tools.html. This online tool allows you to hide numbers behind opaque screens as well as highlight particular numbers or patterns using transparent colored screens. You can also change where the hundreds chart begins (e.g., 0 or 1) and change the increments between numbers to explore skip-counting patterns.

Have children skip-count together by twos, threes, or fours. Then have children record a specific skip-count pattern on their own copy of the hundreds chart by coloring in each number they count. Discuss the patterns on the chart as well as the patterns in the numbers.

Once you've discussed some of the patterns on the chart, try Activity 8.25, "Missing Numbers" (p. 120).

Replacing the number cards from a blank chart is a good station activity for two children to try. By listening to how children determine the correct places for numbers, you can assess how well they have constructed an understanding of the 1-to-100 sequence.

Activity 11.13 FINDING NEIGHBORS ON THE HUNDREDS CHART

Begin with a blank or nearly blank hundreds chart. Circle a particular missing number. Children are to fill in the designated number and its "neighbors"—the numbers to the left, to the right, above, and below. This can be done with the full class on a projector or with blank hundreds chart worksheets. Especially for children with disabilities, it is important to use a "think-aloud" to describe what key features of the numbers you think about as you determine the missing number and its neighbors. After children become comfortable naming the neighbors of a number, ask what they notice about the neighboring numbers. The numbers to the left and right are one more and one less than the given number. Those above and below are ten less and ten more, respectively. What about those numbers on the diagonal? By discussing these relationships on the chart, children begin to see how the sequence of numbers is related to the numerical relationships.

Notice that children will first use the hundreds chart to learn about the patterns in the sequence of numbers. Many children, especially at the kindergarten or first-grade level, will not understand the corresponding numeric relationships such as those discussed in the last activity. In the following activity, number relationships on the chart are made more explicit by including the use of base-ten materials.

Activity 11.14 MODELS WITH THE HUNDREDS CHART

Use any base-ten model for two-digit numbers with which the children are familiar. The little ten-frame cards are recommended (see Blackline Masters 17–18). Give children one or more numbers to first make with the models and then find on the chart. Use groups of two or three numbers either in the same row or the same column. Ask children, "How are the numbers in the row (or column) alike? How are they different?"

Indicate a number on the chart. Ask children, "What would you have to change to make it into each of its neighbors (the numbers to the left, to the right, above, and below)?"

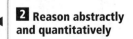

◀ **2 Reason abstractly and quantitatively**

It is also helpful for children to have a chart that extends to 200, even in the first grade. Perhaps a more powerful idea is to extend the hundreds chart to 1000.

◆ *Activity* **11.15** THE THOUSANDS CHART

Provide children with several sheets of the blank hundreds charts (see Blackline Master 9). Assign groups of three or four children the task of creating a 1-to-1000 chart. The chart is made by taping 10 blank hundreds charts together in a long strip. Children should decide how they are going to divide up the task of filling in the chart with different children working on different parts of the chart.

The thousands chart should be discussed as a class to examine how numbers change as you count from one hundred to the next, what the patterns are, and so on. In fact, the earlier hundreds chart activities can all be extended to a thousands chart.

◆ Relationships with Benchmark Numbers

One of the most valuable features of both the hundreds chart and the little ten-frame cards is how clearly they illustrate the distance to the next multiple of 10 (e.g., the end of the row on the chart or the blank spaces on the ten-frame card). Multiples of 10, 100, and occasionally other special numbers, such as multiples of 25, are referred to as benchmark numbers. Children might learn to use this term as they work with informal methods of computation. For example, when finding the difference between 74 and 112, a child might say, "First I added 6 onto 74 to get to a benchmark number. Then I added 2 tens onto 80 to get to 100 because that's another benchmark number." No matter the terminology used, understanding how numbers relate to these special numbers is an important step in children's development of number sense and place-value understanding.

In addition to the hundreds chart, the number line is an excellent way to explore these relationships. The next two activities are suggestions for using number lines.

◆ *Activity* **11.16** WHO AM I?

Sketch a line (or use a piece of cash register tape) and label 0 and 100 at opposite ends. Mark a point with a "?" that corresponds to your secret number. (Estimate the position the best you can.) Children use estimation to try to identify your secret number. For each estimate, place and label a mark on the line. Continue marking each estimate until your secret number is discovered. Have children explain how they are making their estimates. Highlight any use of benchmark numbers in their estimations. As a variation, the endpoints can be other than 0 and 100. For example, try 0 and 1000, 200 and 300, or 500 and 800.

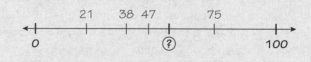

◆ *Activity* **11.17** WHO COULD THEY BE?

Label two points on a number line (not necessarily the ends) with benchmark numbers. Show children different points labeled with letters; ask what numbers these points might be and why the children think that. In the example shown here, B and C are less than 100 but probably more than 60. E could be about 180.

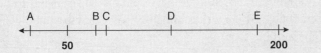

You can also ask where 75 might be or where 400 is. About how far apart are A and D? Why do you think D is more than 100? For ELLs and children with disabilities, say as well as write the numbers on a note card, or ask children to both write and say the numbers.

🔷 Connecting Place Value to Addition and Subtraction

As you can see, there is much more to learning about place value than having children state how many ones, tens, or hundreds are in a number. Children need ample time and opportunity to fully understand place value because it is a complex concept—so complex that it took humans centuries to develop. One relatively recent shift has been to blend instruction on numeration and place value. The NCTM *Principles and Standards for School Mathematics* suggest, "It is not necessary to wait for students to fully develop place-value understandings before giving them opportunities to solve problems with two- and three-digit numbers. When such problems arise in interesting contexts, students can often invent ways to solve them that incorporate and deepen their understanding of place value, especially when students have the opportunities to discuss and explain their invented strategies and approaches" (National Council of Teachers of Mathematics, 2000, p. 82*). Researchers also suggest that problems involving addition and subtraction are a good context for learning place-value concepts (Wright et al., 2008). We know that children who only understand computation as a digit-oriented exercise and not with full understanding of the numbers involved make many errors and have little judgment of the reasonableness of their answers. Chapter 12 focuses on helping children build flexible computational strategies using place-value knowledge. Here, in this section, we lay the groundwork for developing both conceptual and procedural knowledge as we connect place value to addition and subtraction.

Stop and Reflect

As you consider the activities in this section, you will find that although you are adding and subtracting multidigit numbers, the activities are structured so that you will not be regrouping or trading. If you find yourself using a standard procedure, do the activity again. Focus on decomposing and composing numbers rather than regrouping. ∎

The key purpose of the following activities is to provide opportunities for children to apply their emerging understanding of place value to computation.

◢ *Activity 11.18* 50 AND SOME MORE

Say or write a number between 50 and 100. Children respond with "50 and _____." For 63, the response is "50 and 13." Any benchmark number can be used instead of 50. For example, you could use any number that ends in 50 (e.g., 450). You could also use numbers such as 70 or 230.

*Reprinted with permission from *Principles and Standards for School Mathematics,* copyright 2000, by the National Council of Teachers of Mathematics. All rights reserved.

Benchmark numbers are often used in computational strategies to make the computations easier to do. The next activity is aimed at what may be one of the most important benchmark numbers, 100.

Activity 11.19 THE OTHER PART OF 100

Two children work together with a set of little ten-frame cards. One child makes a two-digit number. Then both children work mentally to determine what goes with the ten-frame amount to make 100. They write their solutions on paper and then check by making the other part with the cards to see if the total is 100. Children take turns making the original number. Figure 11.12 shows three different thought processes that children might use.

Figure 11.12

Using little ten-frames to help think about the "other part of 100."

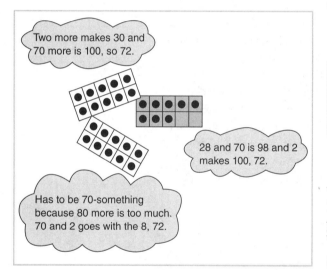

If children are adept at finding parts of 100, you can change the whole from 100 to another number. At first try other multiples of 10, such as 70 or 80. Then extend the whole to any number less than 100.

Stop and Reflect

Suppose that the whole is 83. Sketch four little ten-frame cards showing 36. Looking at your "cards," what goes with 36 to make 83? How did you think about it? ■

What you might have done in finding the other part of 83 was subtract 36 from 83. Or you might have added up from 36. Either way, notice that you did not regroup. Most likely you did it in your head, possibly using benchmark numbers. With more practice you (and children as early as the second grade) can do this without the aid of the cards.

Compatible numbers for addition and subtraction are numbers that go together easily to make benchmark numbers. Numbers that make tens or hundreds are the most common examples. Compatible sums also include numbers that end in 5, 25, 50, or 75, because these numbers are easy to work with as well. The teaching task is to get children accustomed to looking for combinations that work together and then looking for these combinations in computational situations.

Figure 11.13 Compatible pair searches.

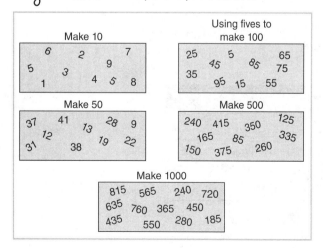

Activity 11.20 COMPATIBLE PAIRS

Searching for compatible pairs can be done as an activity with the full class. Project one at a time the five suggested compatible pair searches shown in Figure 11.13. The possible searches are at different difficulty levels. Children name or connect the compatible pairs as they see them.

The next activity has children apply some of the same ideas about benchmark numbers that we have been exploring.

Activity 11.21   CLOSE, FAR, AND IN BETWEEN

Put any three numbers on the board. Use two-digit numbers if those are more appropriate for the children.

With these three numbers as referents, ask questions such as the following, encouraging discussion of all responses:

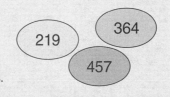

- Which two numbers are closest? How do you know?
- Which number is closest to 300? To 250?
- Name a number between 457 and 364.
- Name a multiple of 25 between 219 and 364.
- Name a number that is more than all of these numbers.
- About how far apart are 219 and 500? 219 and 5000?
- If these are "big numbers," what are some small numbers? Numbers that are about the same? Numbers that make these seem small?

For ELLs, modify this activity by using prompts that are similar to each other. Changing the prompts each time increases the linguistic demand for these children. ELLs and children with disabilities will also benefit from using a visual, such as a number line, and from writing the numbers rather than just hearing them or saying them.

The following activity takes the next step to making addition more explicit.

Activity 11.22   CALCULATOR CHALLENGE COUNTING

Children press any number on the calculator (e.g., 17), then ⊞ 10. They say the sum before they press ⊟. Then they continue to add 10 mentally, challenging themselves to say the number before they press ⊟. Challenge them to see how far they can go without making a mistake.

You can adjust the difficulty level by adjusting the numbers. You may want to begin with a starting number that is less than 10 (e.g., 6) for children with disabilities or start with a larger number, such as 98 or 327, for children who need a challenge. The constant addend (⊞ 10 in the preceding example) can also be changed to any number with one, two, or three digits. Some children will even find jumps of 5 to be challenging if the starting number is not a multiple of 5. Skip counting by 20 or 25 will be easier than counting by 7 or 12 and will help develop important patterns and relationships.

You can also go in reverse. That is, enter a number such as 53 in the calculator and press ⊟ 6. As before, children say the result before pressing ⊟. Each successive press will subtract 6 or whatever constant was entered.

Children can work together in pairs quite profitably on this activity. The activity can be used repeatedly and varied according to the skill level to challenge children while they improve their mental skills with numbers.

This next activity combines base-ten representations with symbolism.

Figure 11.14
Flexible counting on or addition using both models and numerals.

Figure 11.15
Take away or take from subtraction using both models and numerals.

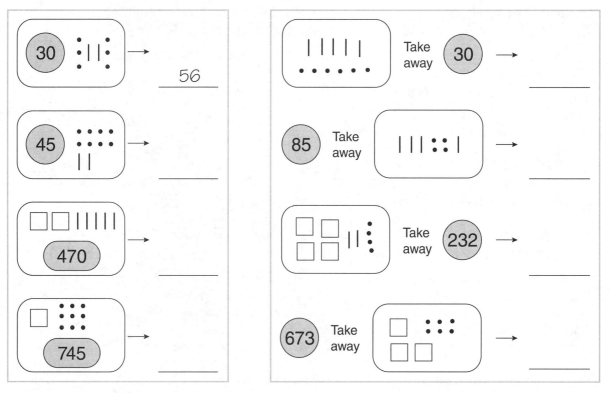

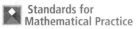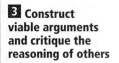

Activity 11.23 NUMBERS, SQUARES, STICKS, AND DOTS

As illustrated in Figure 11.14, prepare a worksheet or display that includes a numeral and some base-ten pieces. Use small squares (hundreds), sticks (tens), and dots (ones) for base-ten pieces to keep drawings simple. Children then mentally compute the totals.

Figure 11.15 is a take-away version of the same activity. As shown, the amount removed can be represented either by a numeral or the squares and sticks. You may want to start with the removed amount represented by the numeral first before using the square-stick-dot representation for the removed amount.

If this activity is done as a whole class, discuss each task before going on to the next. If you use a worksheet format, include only a few examples and have children write how they solved them. But it is still important to have a discussion with the class.

The next activity extends the use of the hundreds chart by using it for addition.

Standards for Mathematical Practice

3 Construct viable arguments and critique the reasoning of others

Activity 11.24 HUNDREDS CHART ADDITION

Display a hundreds chart (or thousands chart) for all children to see or, alternatively, give children their own individual charts (see Blackline Master 10). Children use the hundreds chart to add two numbers (e.g., 38 and 24). There are many ways that children can use the hundreds chart to add two numbers so class discussions are a must. Have children work on one sum at a time and then have a discussion to compare the different methods children used.

The hundreds chart can be thought of as a stacked number line—one that accentuates the distance from any number to the next multiple of 10. A jump down a row is the same as adding 10, and a jump up a row is 10 less. To begin, pose problems with relatively small second numbers such as the following:

$$17 + 14 \qquad 23 + 12 \qquad 35 + 13 \qquad 78 + 15$$

Many children will initially count on by ones from the first number, which is an indication that they may not understand how to count by tens from any starting value (an important place-value concept). A child who is using ten as a unit might explain for the problem $17 + 14$ that she started at 17 on the hundreds chart and added 10 by jumping down a row to 27, and then added 3 more by counting over 30, and then one more to 31. Alternatively, a child might add $17 + 14$ by adding $10 + 10$ by starting at 10 and jumping down a row to 20, then moving over 7 spaces to 27, and then counting 4 more spaces to 31.

The following activity is similar to "Hundreds Chart Addition" but explores the idea of adding up as a method of subtraction.

◀ *Activity 11.25* **HOW MUCH BETWEEN?**

Children must have access to a hundreds chart for this activity. Give them two numbers. Their task is to determine how much from one number to the other.

In "How Much Between?" the choice of the two numbers has an impact on the strategies children will use. The easiest pairs are ones in the same column on the hundreds chart (e.g., 26 and 76), which is a good place to begin. When the larger number is in a different column from the smaller number (e.g., 24 and 76), children can add on tens to get to the target number's row and then add or subtract ones. There are also other possible approaches. Consider the numbers 26 and 72, where the column of 72 is to left of the column that 26 is in. A child might count by tens from 26 to get to 66 (the row before 72) and then count by ones to get to 72. Or a child might count by tens from 26 to get to 76 and then count back by ones to get to 72.

You may be so accustomed to thinking about addition and subtraction computation as involving "regrouping"—the trading of 10 ones for a ten or vice versa—that you tend to believe that regrouping is an integral part of computation. In fact, as you will see in Chapter 12, virtually all invented strategies for computation as well as mental strategies involve no regrouping at all. Rather, what happens in most cases might be called "bridging a ten." The row structure of the hundreds chart is especially useful in developing this understanding of bridging across ten. Children should have ample opportunities to develop their ideas in activities like the ones in this section. Many children are likely still developing their ideas about numbers and distances between them. These ideas are as much about place-value understanding as about addition and subtraction.

📝 *Formative Assessment Note*

Children who exhibit difficulty with any of these activities may also be challenged with invented computation strategies. Conduct a diagnostic interview with children to determine how they are reasoning in activities, such as Activity 11.23, "Numbers, Squares, Sticks, and Dots." That activity requires that children have sufficient understanding of base-ten concepts to use them in meaningful counts. If children are counting by ones, then more practice with activities like "Numbers, Squares, Sticks, and Dots" may be ineffective. Rather, consider additional counting activities in which children have opportunities to see the value of grouping by ten. Using the little ten-frames may help.

Connections to Real-World Ideas

As children study place-value concepts, encourage them to see numbers in the world about them. Children in the first grade should be thinking about numbers up to 100 and second graders should be thinking about numbers up to 1000 (CCSSO, 2010). Where are numbers like this? Look around your school: the number of children in a particular grade, the number of children who ride to school on school buses, the number of minutes devoted to mathematics each day, or the number of days since school has started. And then there are measurements and numbers at home, on a field trip, in the news, and so on.

You do not need a prescribed activity to bring real numbers into the classroom. So, what do you do with these numbers? Turn them into interesting graphs, write stories using them, and make up problems.

As children become more skilled, their interest in numbers can expand beyond the school and classroom. All sorts of things can and should be measured to create graphs, draw inferences, and make comparisons. For example, consider posing the following problem to your class.

How many cartons of chocolate and plain milk are served in the cafeteria each month?

Collecting data for such problems and grouping them into tens and hundreds will help reinforce the value of grouping to count and compare quantities.

The particular way you bring numbers and the real world together in your class is up to you. But do not underestimate the value of connecting the real world to the classroom.

Estimating Groups of Tens and Ones

Content and Task Decisions

Grade Level: 1–2

Mathematics Goals

- To connect a count-by-ones understanding to a count based on the number of groups of 10 and leftovers for quantities to 100

- To measure lengths using nonstandard measures

Grade Level Guide

NCTM *Curriculum Focal Points*	*Common Core State Standards*
In grade 1, children measure by "laying multiple copies of a unit end to end and then counting the units by using groups of tens and ones." This "supports children's understanding of number lines and number relationships" (NCTM, 2006, p. 13). In second grade one of the main Focal Points is "Developing an understanding of the base-ten numeration system and place-value concepts" (NCTM, 2006, p. 14).	In first grade, as part of the Measurement and Data domain, children should measure the length of an object by laying multiple lengths of a unit end to end without gaps or overlaps. Also in first grade, children begin to understand place value by thinking of two-digit numbers as groups of tens and ones.

Consider Your Children's Needs

Children have not yet developed a full understanding of two-digit numbers in terms of tens and ones. They are able to count a collection of objects to 100. They have talked about numbers in terms of groups of tens and have discussed number patterns on the hundreds chart.

For English Language Learners

- You may want to write the words for the objects on the recording sheet and place name tags next to the objects so that the children know which object they are measuring.

- Model an example prior to doing the lesson to clarify the directions.

For Children with Disabilities

- Make sure your selection of a unit is one that children with disabilities are familiar with from other experiences. Avoid introducing a material for the first time as you are also introducing estimation with this unit.

- As the two children actually measure the length in the *Before* component of the lesson, ask them to share aloud how they are deciding where to put the connecting cubes or other unit.

Materials

Each child will need:

- "How Long?" recording sheet (Blackline Master 45)

Each measurement station will need:

- Object that can be measured by placing measurement units end-to-end along the full length (vertical distances can be measured with connecting cubes)

- Corresponding measurement "kit" consisting of more than enough individual nonstandard units to measure the length and 10 connected units (a bar of 10 connecting cubes, a chain of 10 paper clips, or a row of 10 toothpicks point to point sandwiched between two pieces of transparent tape)

For Unit	*Use Lengths*
Connecting cubes	2 to 5 feet (60 cm to 180 cm)
Small paper clips	2 to 9 feet (60 cm to 270 cm)
Large paper clips	3 to 12 feet (90 cm to 4 m)
Toothpicks	5 to 12 feet (1.8 m to 4 m)

Teacher will need:

- The recording sheet for projection

- A kit of nonstandard units that can be used in the *Before* portion of the lesson

Lesson

Before

Begin with a simpler version of the task:

- Show the children a length that is somewhere between 25 and 45 connecting-cube units long. For example, you might use the edge of a teacher's desk, a length of ribbon or rope, or a poster.

- Explain that you want to make an estimate of how long the item is in terms of connecting cubes. Accept estimates and record them where the children can see. Expect the children's guesses to be quite varied. Then suggest that it might be helpful to estimate in terms of groups of 10 units and leftovers. Show the children a bar of 10 connecting cubes.

- Hold the 10 units at one end of the length to be measured and accept children's new estimates. Write the first child's estimate on the projected recording sheet. Explain that an *estimate* is what you think it might be by looking at the 10 units; it is not just a wild guess.

- Pass out the recording sheets and have the children record their own estimates in the first box. Ask several children what their estimates are.

- Have two children use individual units (e.g., connecting cubes) to measure the length. It is important that they line the units end to end along the entire length so that when they have finished they will have as many actual units as required for the measure. Have two children put the units into groups of 10. Count the groups of 10, and count any leftovers separately. Record this in blanks labeled "Actual" on the projected recording sheet and have the children do likewise on their papers.

- Finally, ask the children how many units there are. Have the class count the entire group by ones as you set them aside or point to each. Write the number word and the number (e.g., *thirty-four 34*) on the projected recording sheet and the unit (e.g., 34 connecting cubes or 34 toothpicks). Have children write this on their recording sheets.

Present the focus task:

- At three stations, children are to see if they can make reasonable estimates of lengths in terms of groups of 10 and leftovers.

- They then check their estimates by actually measuring, making and counting groups of 10 and leftovers, and finally counting all the units.

- Explain that there are measuring kits and a length for each station. For each length, children are to:

  - Hold the 10 units at one end of the length and estimate the measure of the length in terms of 10 and leftovers. Each child should record his or her estimate on the recording sheet.

  - They are then to measure the lengths using individual units—laying them end to end with no gaps or overlaps.

  - When they have placed units along the full length, they should make sets of 10, then count and record the number of groups of 10 and leftovers.

- Finally, they should count all of the units and record this as a number word and as a number. Refer to your example.

Provide clear expectations:

- Have the children work in groups of two to four. Tell them that they will work together to measure each object, but each child should make his or her own estimate. Over the course of the three stations, each child should have the opportunity to measure an object using individual units and to measure using groups of 10 and leftovers.

During

Initially:

- Observe that the children understand the task and are in the process of making a reasonable estimate before measuring each object.

- Be sure that the children are making and recording estimates by comparing the length to the provided group of 10. They are not to change their estimates.

Ongoing:

- Check that the children are lining individual units along the edge of the object without gaps or overlaps when measuring.

- Pay attention to how the children count the total number of units. Some may already know that 4 tens and 6 leftovers is 46. However, many will count by ones. Challenge the children who just count groups: "Are you sure you will get 46 if you count them all by ones?"

After

Bring the class together to share and discuss the task:

- Discuss what it means to estimate—it is not the same as a guess. Ask, "How did using a group of 10 units help you make an estimate? How does counting the groups of tens and leftovers help tell you how many units you had?" This last question is the key to this lesson. Avoid telling children how to relate the groups and leftovers to the actual number.

Assessment

Observe

- Look for children who do not make connections between the groups and leftovers and the actual counts. These children have not yet developed base-ten concepts.

- Those who confidently state the total when they have the number of groups and leftovers have indicated at least a beginning understanding of base-ten concepts.

Ask

- How did using a group of 10 units help you make an estimate?

- How does counting the groups of tens and leftovers help tell you how many units you had?

Building Strategies for Whole-Number Computation

Big IDEAS

1 Flexible methods of addition and subtraction involve taking apart (decomposing) and combining (composing) numbers in a wide variety of ways. Most of the decomposition of numbers is based on place value or "compatible" numbers—number pairs that work easily together, such as 25 and 75.

2 Invented strategies are flexible methods of computing that vary with the numbers and the situation involved. Strategies can be invented by a child, a peer, or the class as a whole; they may even be suggested by the teacher.

3 Flexible methods for computation require a strong understanding of the operations and properties of the operations, especially the commutative (turn-around) property and the associative property. How addition and subtraction are related as inverse operations is also important.

4 The standard algorithms are clever strategies for computing that are based on performing the operation on one place value at a time with transitions to an adjacent position (trading or regrouping). Standard algorithms tend to cause children to think in terms of digits rather than the composite number that the digits make up.

5 Multidigit numbers can be built up or taken apart in a variety of ways. These parts can be used to create estimates in calculations rather than using the exact numbers involved. For example, 17 can be thought of as 15 and 2 or 3 less than 20.

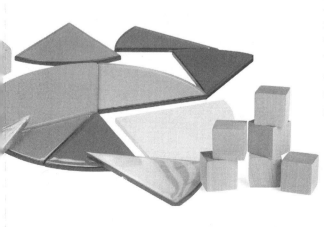

Much of the public sees computational skill as the hallmark of what it means to know mathematics at the elementary school level. Although this is far from the truth, the issue of computational skills with whole numbers is, in fact, a very important part of the elementary curriculum. Expectations for competency in today's workforce as well as in daily life mean that changes are warranted in how computation is approached.

Toward Computational Fluency

The days of children memorizing computational algorithms are fading fast. Rather than constant reliance on a single method of adding or subtracting, methods can and should change flexibly as the numbers and the context change. In the spirit of the *Common Core State Standards* (CCSSO, 2010) and the *Principles and Standards for School Mathematics* (National Council of Teachers of Mathematics, 2000), the issue is no longer a matter of "knows how to subtract three-digit numbers"; rather it is the development over time of an assortment of flexible skills that will best serve children in the real world. *Adding It Up* (National Research Council, 2001) describes it this way:

> More than just a means to produce answers, computation is increasingly seen as a window on the deep structure of the number system. Fortunately, research is demonstrating that both skilled performance and conceptual understanding are generated by the same kinds of activities. (p. 182)

According to the *Common Core State Standards*, children in grades K–2 should solve addition and subtraction problems with numbers appropriate for their grade level (within 10 for kindergartners; within 100 for first graders; and within 1000 for second graders). First graders are expected to add two-digit numbers to one-digit numbers or to a multiple of 10. Second graders are expected to add two-digit and three-digit numbers. The solution methods range from using concrete models or drawings to strategies based on place value, meanings of operations, and number sense. To support the development of flexible addition and subtraction strategies, the *Common Core State Standards* also expect children to be able to compose and decompose numbers (numbers less than 20 for kindergartners; numbers less than 100 for first graders; and numbers less than 1000 for second graders).

Addition and subtraction strategies that build on decomposing and composing numbers in flexible ways contribute to children's overall number sense. In most everyday instances, these alternative strategies for computing are easier and faster than the standard algorithms (procedures for computing) and can often be done mentally.

Consider the following problem.

Mary has 114 spaces in her photo album. So far she has 89 photos in the album. How many more photos can she put in before the album is full?

Stop and Reflect

Try solving the photo album problem using some method other than the one you were taught in school. Can you solve it mentally? Can you solve it in more than one way? Work on this before reading further. ∎

Here are just four of many methods that have been used by children in the primary grades to solve the computation in the photo album problem:

- 89 + 11 is 100. 11 + 14 is 25.
- 90 + 10 is 100 and 14 more is 24 plus 1 (because we should have started at 89, not 90) is 25.

Figure 12.1

A general instructional sequence for three types of computational strategies.

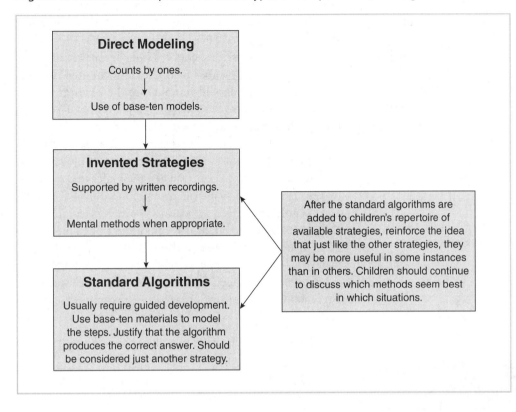

- Take away 14 to get to 100, then take away 10 more to get to 90, and then 1 more to get to 89, or take away 25 in all.
- 89, 99, 109 (that's 20). 110, 111, 112, 113, 114 (keeping track on fingers) is 25.

Strategies such as these can be done mentally, are generally faster than the standard algorithms, and make sense to the person using them. Every day, children and adults resort to often error-prone, standard algorithms when other, more meaningful methods would be faster and less susceptible to error. Flexibility with a variety of computational strategies is an important tool for successful daily living. It is time to broaden our perspective of what it means to compute.

Figure 12.1 lists a general instructional sequence for three types of computing. The direct modeling methods can, with guidance, develop into an assortment of more flexible and useful student-invented strategies, many of which can be carried out mentally. The standard algorithms remain in the mainstream curricula; however, an emphasis on a variety of strategies is critical to developing number sense as well as procedural proficiency. The standard algorithms should be seen simply as another strategy that can be added to children's repertoire of available strategies.

◆ Direct Modeling

The developmental step that usually precedes invented strategies is called *direct modeling*: The use of manipulatives, drawings, or fingers along with counting to directly represent the meaning of an operation or story problem. Figure 12.2 shows an example of direct modeling in which a child has modeled the numbers in the problem using counters and then counted by ones to find the answer.

Figure 12.2

A possible direct modeling solution for a story problem.

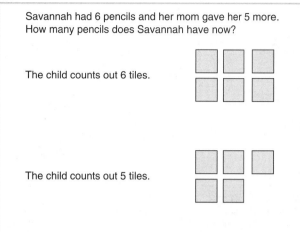

Savannah had 6 pencils and her mom gave her 5 more. How many pencils does Savannah have now?

The child counts out 6 tiles.

The child counts out 5 tiles.

Then the child counts all tiles to get the answer 11.

Teaching Tip

Accepting direct modeling as a necessary developmental phase allows children who are not ready for more efficient methods a way to explore the same problems as classmates who have progressed beyond this stage.

Children who consistently count by ones most likely have not developed base-ten grouping concepts. That does not mean that they should not solve problems involving two-digit numbers. As you work with children who are still struggling to see 10 as a unit, suggest that they group counters by tens as they count, either by making bars of 10 from connecting cubes or organizing counters in cups of 10. Some children will initially use the base-ten rod of 10 as a counting device to keep track of counts of 10, even though they are counting each segment of the rod by ones.

When children have constructed the idea of 10 as a unit, they begin to use this idea in the direct modeling of problems. They will soon transfer their ideas to methods that do not rely on materials or counting. But it is important to note that direct modeling is a necessary phase for children to work through. It is important not to push children to prematurely abandon concrete approaches using materials—including their fingers!

Children may need encouragement to move away from direct modeling. Here are some ideas to promote the fading of direct modeling:

- Record children's verbal explanations on the board in ways that they and others can model.

- Ask children who have just solved a problem with models to see if they can do it mentally.

- Ask children to make a written numeric record of what they did when they solved the problem with models. Explain that they are then going to try to use the same written method on a new problem.

◈ Invented Strategies

We refer to any strategy, other than the standard algorithm, that does not involve the use of physical materials or counting by ones as an *invented strategy* (Carpenter, Franke, Jacobs, Fennema, & Empson, 1998). In the expectations for first and second graders, the *Common Core State Standards* (CCSSO, 2010) describe these as "strategies based on place value, properties of operations, and/or the relationship between addition and subtraction" (pp. 16, 19). More specifically, children are expected to "develop, discuss, and use efficient, accurate, and generalizable methods to compute sums and differences of whole numbers in base-ten notation, using their understanding of place value and the properties of operations" (p. 17). At times, invented strategies become mental methods after ideas have been explored, used, and understood. For example, after some experience, children may be able to do 75 + 19 mentally (75 + 20 is 95, less 1 is 94). For 648 + 257, children may need to write down intermediate steps to aid in memory as they work through the problem. (Try that one yourself.) In the classroom, written support is often encouraged as strategies develop. Written records of thinking are more easily shared and help children focus on the ideas. Distinctions among written, partially written, and mental computation are not important, especially in the development period.

A number of research studies have focused attention on how children handle computational situations when they have been given options for multiple strategies (see, for example,

Keiser, 2010; Rittle-Johnson, Star, & Durkin, 2010; Verschaffel, Greer, & De Corte, 2007). "There is mounting evidence that children both in and out of school can construct methods for adding and subtracting multi-digit numbers without explicit instruction" (Carpenter et al., 1998, p. 4). But not all children invent their own strategies. So strategies invented by class members are shared, explored, and tried out by others. However, children should not be permitted to use any strategy without understanding it.

Contrasts between Invented Strategies and Standard Algorithms

Consider the following significant differences between student-invented strategies and the standard algorithms.

- *Invented strategies are number oriented rather than digit oriented.* Using the standard algorithm for 45 + 32, children never think of 40 and 30 but rather 4 + 3. Kamii, long a crusader against standard algorithms, claims that they "unteach" place value (Kamii & Dominick, 1998). On the other hand, an invented strategy for 618 − 254 might begin with 600 − 200 is 400. Another approach might begin with 254. Adding 46 is 300 and then 300 more to 600. In either case, the computation begins with complete three-digit numbers.

- *Invented strategies tend to be left-handed rather than right-handed.* Invented strategies often begin with the largest parts of numbers, those represented by the leftmost digits. For 86 + 17, an invented strategy might begin with 80 + 10 or 86 + 10, providing some sense of the size of the eventual answer in just one step. The standard approach begins with 6 + 7 is 13. By beginning on the right with a digit orientation, standard methods typically hide the result until the end. Long division is an exception.

- *Invented strategies represent a range of flexible options rather than "one right way."* Invented strategies tend to change with the numbers involved in order to make the computation easier. Try each of these mentally: 465 + 230 and 526 + 98. Did you use the same method? The standard algorithm suggests using the same approach on all problems. The standard algorithm for 7000 − 25 typically leads to student errors, yet a mental strategy is relatively simple.

Benefits of Invented Strategies

The development and use of invented strategies generate procedural proficiency. The positive benefits are difficult to ignore.

- *Children make fewer errors.* Research indicates that when children use their own computational strategies they tend to make fewer errors because they understand their own methods (Gravemeijer & van Galen, 2003). Even if well explained and illustrated with base-ten blocks, many children do not understand the underlying concepts of standard algorithms. Not only do these children make more errors, but the errors are often systematic and difficult to remediate as well. Errors with invented strategies are less frequent and rarely systematic.

- *Less reteaching is required.* Often teachers are concerned when children's early efforts with invented strategies are slow and time consuming. But the extended time for these early stages results in a meaningful and well-integrated network of ideas that is robust and long lasting. The increase in development time results in a significant decrease in reteaching and remediation.

- *Children develop number sense.* Children's development and use of number-oriented, flexible algorithms help them cultivate a rich understanding of the number system, especially place-value concepts.

- *Invented strategies are the basis for mental computation and estimation.* When invented strategies are the norm for computation, there is no need to talk about mental computation as if it were a separate skill. As children become more and more proficient with these flexible methods, they find they are able to use them mentally without having to write down even intermediate steps.

- *Flexible methods are often faster than the standard algorithms.* Consider 300 − 98. A simple invented strategy might use 300 − 100 = 200. Adding 2 back (because we subtracted 2 too many), we get 202. This is easily done mentally, or even with some recording, in much less time than the steps to the standard algorithm. Those who become adept with invented strategies will consistently perform addition and subtraction computations more quickly than those using a standard algorithm.

- *Strategy invention is itself an important process of "doing mathematics."* Children who invent a computational strategy or who adopt a meaningful strategy developed by a classmate are involved in the process of sense making. This development of procedures is a process that is often hidden from children. By engaging in this aspect of mathematics, a significantly different and valuable view of "doing mathematics" is revealed to learners.

- *Children who use invented strategies perform similarly or outperform their counterparts who are taught only standard algorithms.* Children in other countries such as the Netherlands are not taught to use standard algorithms, and they perform significantly better than U.S. children on international measures of proficiency (Fleischman, Hopstock, Pelczar, & Shelley, 2010).

Mental Computation

A mental computation strategy is simply any invented strategy that is done without recording steps. What may be a mental strategy for one child may require written steps by another child. Initially, children may not be ready to do computations mentally, as they may still be at the direct modeling stage or need to notate parts of the problem as they think it through. As children become more adept, they can and should be challenged to do appropriate computations mentally. You may be quite amazed at the ability of children (and at your own ability) to do mental mathematics.

Try this example using mental mathematics:

$$342 + 153 + 481$$

Stop and Reflect

For the preceding addition task, try this method: Begin by adding the hundreds, saying the totals as you go—3 hundred, 4 hundred, 8 hundred. Then add on to this the tens in successive manner and finally the ones. Give it a try. ■

◆ Standard Algorithms

More than a century of tradition combined with pressures from families who were taught only the standard algorithm may result in thinking that there is only one best approach and one "right" algorithm. Arguments for a single algorithm generally revolve around efficiency and the need for methods that work with all numbers. For addition and subtraction, however, well-understood and practiced invented strategies are sometimes more efficient and often more accurate.

Although teaching only the standard algorithm does not allow children to explore other useful approaches, including it among the strategies children learn is important. The main focus in teaching the standard algorithm is not learning a memorized series of steps but making sense of it as a process.

Standard Algorithms Must Be Understood

Children often pick up the standard algorithm from older siblings and family members. Children who already know the standard algorithm may resist the development of more flexible strategies. What do you do then?

First and foremost, apply the same rule to standard algorithms as to all strategies: *If you use it, you must understand why it works and be able to explain it.* In an atmosphere that says, "Let's figure out why this works," children can profit from making sense of standard algorithms just as they can with invented strategies. But the responsibility for the explanations should be theirs, not yours!

Delay Standard Algorithms

Children are not likely to invent the standard algorithms because methods that begin with the smaller numbers are not as intuitive. Therefore, you will need to introduce and explain each algorithm and help children understand how and why they work. No matter how carefully you introduce these algorithms as simply another alternative, children may sense that "this is the real way" or the "one right way" to compute.

Before teaching standard algorithms, spend a significant amount of time with invented strategies—months, not weeks. Do not feel that you must rush to the standard algorithms. Delay! The understanding that children gain from working with invented strategies will make it much easier for you to teach the standard algorithms. If you think you are wasting precious time by delaying, think of how many years teacher teach the same standard algorithms over and over to children who are still unable to use them without making errors or who still do not understand them.

Continue to Value All Methods

The standard algorithm (once it is understood) is one more strategy children can put in their "toolbox of methods." Reinforce the idea that just like the other strategies, it may be more useful in some instances than others.

Pose problems in which invented strategies are much more useful, such as $504 - 498$ or $61 + 19$. Discuss which method seems best. Point out that for a problem such as $568 + 347$, the standard algorithm has advantages.

◄ Standards for Mathematical Practice

1 Make sense of problems and persevere in solving them

Cultural Differences in Algorithms

Chapter 5 discusses issues that you need to be aware of when planning, teaching, and assessing culturally and linguistically diverse children. Here we specifically revisit issues related to algorithms. As noted in Chapter 5, there are many international differences in notation, conventions, and algorithms. Knowing more about the diverse algorithms English language learners (ELLs) bring to the classroom and their ways of recording symbols for "doing mathematics" will assist you in supporting these children and responding to their families. It is important to realize that an algorithm we call "standard" may not be customary in other countries. Encouraging a variety of algorithms is important in valuing the experiences of all children.

For example, one popular subtraction algorithm used in many Latin and European countries, and briefly described in Chapter 5, is known as "equal addition" or "add tens to both" and is based on the knowledge that adding (or subtracting) the same amount to both the minuend and the subtrahend will not change the difference (answer). Therefore, if the expression to solve is $15 - 5$, there is no change to the answer (or the difference) if you add 10 to the minuend and subtrahend and solve $25 - 15$. There is still a difference of 10. Consider the problem $62 - 27$. Using the algorithm you may think of as "standard," you will likely regroup by crossing out the 6 tens, adding the 10 with a small "1" to the 2 in the ones column (making

Figure 12.3

The "equal addition" algorithm.

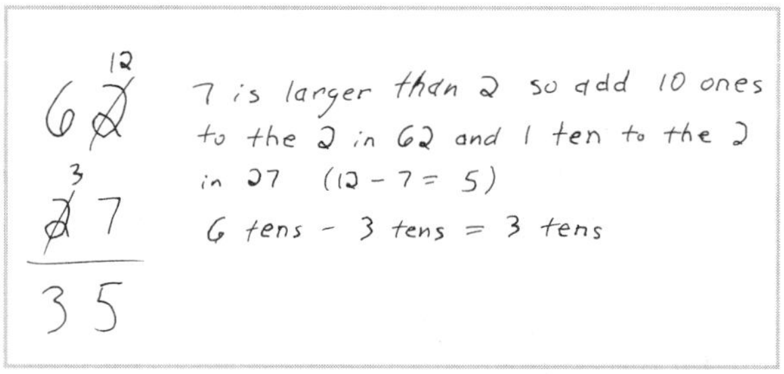

12 ones), and then subtract 7 from the 12, and so forth. In the "equal addition" approach (see Figure 12.3), you add 10 to the ones place (2) in 62 to get 12 ones. You would then counteract the addition of 10 to the minuend by adding 10 to the 27 (subtrahend), making 37. Now you subtract the 37. This may sound confusing to you, but try it. Especially when there are zeros in the minuend (e.g., 302 − 178), you may find this an easier approach than our "standard" algorithm. More importantly, your possible confusion can give you a sense of how your children (and their families) may react to a completely different procedure from the one they know and find successful.

Invented Strategies for Addition and Subtraction

Children should be able to use strategies for addition and subtraction that they understand and can use efficiently. Your goal might be that each of your children has at least one or two methods that are reasonably efficient, mathematically correct, and useful with lots of different numbers. Expect different children to settle on different strategies that play to their strengths.

Children do not spontaneously invent wonderful computational methods while the teacher sits back and watches. In various experimental programs, children tended to develop or gravitate toward different strategies, suggesting that teachers and the programs do have an effect on the methods children develop (Verschaffel et al., 2007). The following two sections discuss general pedagogical methods for creating an environment that will help children develop invented strategies while the subsequent sections describe a variety of invented strategies that children often use.

Creating a Supportive Environment

Children who are attempting to investigate new ideas in mathematics need a safe and nurturing classroom environment in which they can take risks, tests conjectures, and try new approaches. The characteristics of such a classroom have already been discussed in Chapters 1 and 2. Here are some factors to keep in mind:

Standards for Mathematical Practice

3 Construct viable arguments and critique the reasoning of others

- Avoid immediately identifying the right answer when a child states it. Give other children a chance to consider whether they think it is correct.
- Expect and encourage student-to-student interactions, questions, and discussions.
- Promote curiosity and openness to new ideas and trying new things.
- Talk about both right and wrong ideas in nonevaluative or nonthreatening ways.
- Move less sophisticated ideas to more sophisticated thinking through coaxing, coaching, and strategic questioning.
- Use familiar contexts and story problems to build background and connect to children's experiences.

Models to Support Invented Strategies

There are three common types of invented-strategy models that children come up with to solve addition and subtraction situations: split strategy (which can also be thought of as decomposition), jump strategy (similar to counting on or counting back), and shortcut strategy

Figure 12.4

Two methods of recording children's thought processes on the board so that the class can follow the strategy.

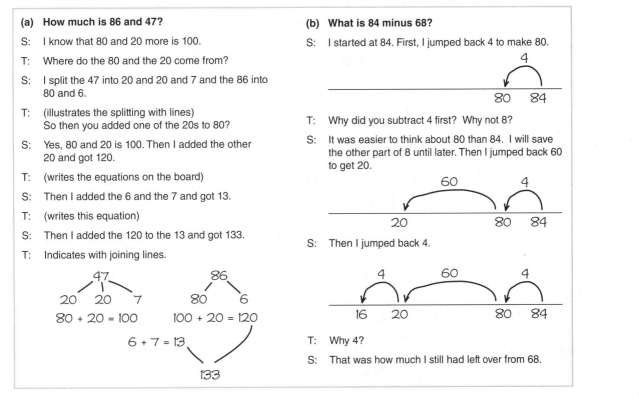

(a) How much is 86 and 47?

S: I know that 80 and 20 more is 100.

T: Where do the 80 and the 20 come from?

S: I split the 47 into 20 and 20 and 7 and the 86 into 80 and 6.

T: (illustrates the splitting with lines)
So then you added one of the 20s to 80?

S: Yes, 80 and 20 is 100. Then I added the other 20 and got 120.

T: (writes the equations on the board)

S: Then I added the 6 and the 7 and got 13.

T: (writes this equation)

S: Then I added the 120 to the 13 and got 133.

T: Indicates with joining lines.

(b) What is 84 minus 68?

S: I started at 84. First, I jumped back 4 to make 80.

T: Why did you subtract 4 first? Why not 8?

S: It was easier to think about 80 than 84. I will save the other part of 8 until later. Then I jumped back 60 to get 20.

S: Then I jumped back 4.

T: Why 4?

S: That was how much I still had left over from 68.

(sometimes known as *compensation*) (Torbeyns, De Smedt, Ghesquiere, & Verschaffel, 2009). The notion of "splitting" a number into parts is a useful strategy for all operations. Both the word *split* and the use of a visual diagram have been found to help children develop strategies (Verschaffel et al., 2007). When recording children's ideas, try using arrows or lines to explicitly indicate how two computations are joined together, as shown in Figure 12.4a.

The *empty number line* shown in Figure 12.4b uses a sequential *jump strategy* developed in the Netherlands. This model has been found to be much more flexible than the usual number line because it works with any numbers and eliminates the confusion with hash marks and the spaces between them and children are less prone to making computational errors when using it (Gravemeijer & van Galen, 2003; Klein, Beishuizen, & Treffers, 2002; Verschaffel et al., 2007). You can introduce the empty number line (also called an *open number line*) by using it to model a child's thinking for the class. With time and practice, children find the empty number line to be an effective tool to support and explain their reasoning.

◆ **Standards for Mathematical Practice**

◄ **5 Use appropriate tools strategically**

You will find an interactive number line at www.ictgames.com/numberlineJumpMaker/index.html where children can practice using a jump strategy to find the distance between two numbers. You can change where the number line starts (−100 to 200) as well as the number of spaces on the number line (26 spaces versus 66 spaces).

The *shortcut strategy* involves the flexible adjustment of numbers. For example, just as children used 10 as an anchor in learning their basic facts, they can move numbers such as 38 or 69 to the nearest 10 and then take the 2 or 1 off to compensate later. In this case, $40 + 70$ equals 110, and then take off the three extras to get 107. As another example, $51 - 37$ can be thought of as $51 + 6$ to get 57 and $57 - 37 = 20$; then subtract 6 (because you added 6 to make the problem easier) to get 14. So $51 - 37 = 14$.

As these examples suggest, the numbers involved in a computation will tend to influence how children approach a problem. You also learned in Chapter 9 that the type of story problems used can also influence strategies children use. Therefore, it is important to think carefully about the type of story problem you pose as well as the numbers you use in problems.

◆ Adding and Subtracting Single Digits

When adding or subtracting small amounts or finding the difference between two reasonably close numbers, many children will use counting to solve the problem. One goal should be to extend children's knowledge of basic facts and the ten-structure of the number system so that counting is not required. When the calculation crosses a ten (e.g., $58 + 6$), using the decade number (60) and thinking $58 + 2 + 4$, for example, extends children's use of the Up Over 10 strategy (e.g., add on to get up to 10 and then add the rest). Similarly, for subtraction, children can extend the Down Over 10 strategy. For instance, for $53 - 7$, take off 3 to get to 50, then 4 more is 46.

The next activity helps children think explicitly about making this extension.

Teaching Tip

Using the empty number line model to support and make explicit children's initial reasoning with jumps can help children develop mental models that will allow them to solve problems in their head.

◆ Activity 12.1   CROSSING A DECADE

Quickly review the Up Over 10 and Down Over 10 strategies from basic facts using ten-frames. Then pose an addition or subtraction story problem that crosses a decade number and involves a change or difference of less than 10. The following problems are examples.

- Tommy was on page 47 of his book. Then he read 6 more pages. What page did he end up on?
- How far is it from 68 to 75?
- Meghan had 42 cents. She bought a small toy for 8 cents. How much money does she have left?

Two children can work together to determine how to quickly find the total.

Listen for children who are counting on or counting back by ones without paying attention to the ten. For these children, suggest that they use either a hundreds chart or the little ten-frames, shown in Figure 12.5, to support their thinking. Also find out how they solve fact combinations such as $8 + 6$ and $13 - 5$. The use of tens for these facts is essentially the same as for the higher decade problems. Have children who are using the ten to solve these problems share their strategy. For $47 + 6$ you should expect something like *I added 3 from the 6 to the 47 to get to 50. Then I added the remaining 3 to get to 53.*

Adding and Subtracting Tens and Hundreds

As you move children from single-digit to two-digit numbers, adding and subtracting tens and hundreds is an important transition. Sums and differences involving multiples of 10 or 100 are easily computed mentally. Write a problem such as the following on the board:

300 + 500 + 20

Challenge children to solve it mentally. Ask them to share how they did it. Listen for the use of place-value words: "3 *hundred* and 5 *hundred* is 8 *hundred, and 20 is 820.*" Early problems should not require any regrouping. For example, start with problems such as 420 + 300 and then move to more difficult problems that require re-grouping such as 70 + 80. Using base-ten models can help children think in terms of units of tens and hundreds.

Adding Two-Digit Numbers

Problems involving the sum of 2 two-digit numbers will usually produce a wide variety of strategies. Some of these strategies will involve starting with one or the other number and working from that point, either by adding on to get to the next ten or by adding tens to get from one number to the other.

Figure 12.5

Little ten-frame cards can help children extend the Up Over 10 idea to larger numbers (see Blackline Masters 17–18).

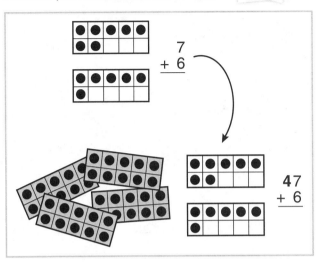

Formative Assessment Note

Periodically you will want to focus on a child to determine which strategies he is and is not using. Pose a problem such as 46 + 35. See if the child begins by splitting the numbers. That is, for 46 + 35, he may add on 4 to get from 46 to 50 and then add the remaining 31. Or he may add 30 to 46 to get to 76, then add 4 more to get to 80, and then add the remaining 1.

Children will often use a counting-by-tens-and-ones technique. That is, instead of "46 + 30 is 76," they may use an open number line and count up "46, 56, 66, 76." These jumps can be written down as they are said to help children keep track. In each case, be mindful of how flexibly children use ten as a unit or how they use the shortcut strategy. If children are not using the ten as a unit, they may need more work on place-value activities.

◄ **Standards for Mathematical Practice**

2 Reason abstractly and quantitatively

Figure 12.6 illustrates four different strategies for the following story problem, which involves addition of 2 two-digit numbers. The recording methods in Figure 12.6 are suggestions.

Two Scout troops went on a field trip. There were 46 Girl Scouts and 38 Boy Scouts. How many Scouts went on the trip?

The shortcut and compensation strategies that focus on making ten are useful when one of the numbers ends in 8 or 9. To promote these strategies, present problems with addends like 39 or 58. Note that it is only necessary to adjust one of the two numbers.

Figure 12.6 Four different invented strategies for addition with two-digit numbers.

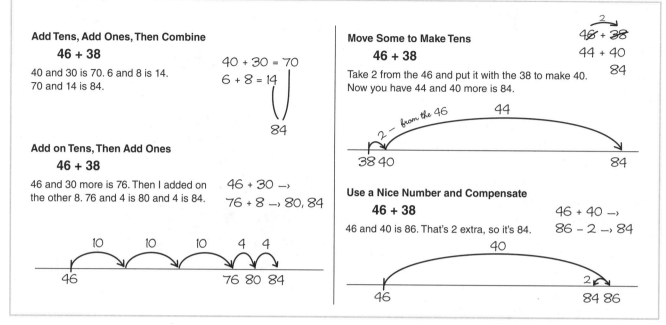

Stop and Reflect

Try adding 367 + 155 in as many different ways as you can. How many of your ways are like those in Figure 12.6? ∎

The next activity provides children opportunities to add multidigit numbers outside a story problem context.

Activity 12.2 SUM THEM UP!

Children work in pairs for this activity. Without communicating to each other, each child writes down a two-digit number. (You can also use three-digit numbers depending on the children.) The children work together to find out the sum of the two numbers. Once a sum is determined, they should use little ten-frame cards to represent the two numbers they started with and use those to check their sum. Children with disabilities may initially need to use the little ten-frames to help them determine the sum.

This activity could also be completed by displaying two numbers on a projector and having children work in pairs at their desks. Follow up by having children share their strategies for finding the sum.

The following activity encourages children to think about different ways to adjust numbers as they solve problems.

Activity 12.3 JUST ADJUST IT

Suppose you want to help children think about adjusting numbers by using 10 as an anchor. Create a series of problems using numbers that will increase the likelihood that children will gravitate toward this idea, but do not require children to use this idea and do not be disappointed if they do not use this idea. The point is to try to help children become more aware of different ways to adjust numbers. Following is one possible series of problems:

$$50 + 30 \qquad 48 + 30 \qquad 50 + 32 \qquad 51 + 28 \qquad 20 + 60 \qquad 18 + 58$$

Project one problem at a time and give children time to solve it before you ask first for answers and then for explanations. Record children's strategies so that you can refer back to them when appropriate. If no child suggests the idea of using $50 + 30$ or $20 + 60$ to help solve the subsequent related problems, you may want to challenge them to determine how they could use that problem to help them solve the others.

Note that there are multiple ways to add the numbers from the preceding activity and there are multiple ways to use 10 as an anchor to solve the series of problems. For example, for $51 + 28$, a child may change 51 to 50 and 28 to 30, add $50 + 30$ to get 80, and then adjust for the 30 and 50—subtract 2 to adjust for adding 30 (instead of 28) and add 1 for adding 50 (instead of 51)—to get 79. Other children may think that 51 is really close to 50 and they move 1 to the 28 and add $50 + 29$ to get 79. Still other children may add the tens ($50 + 20$) and then the ones ($1 + 8$) to get 79. This last strategy did not use $50 + 30$, which is fine. Again, your goal is to help children develop strategies that are efficient and that make sense to them. Listening to how some of their classmates used $50 + 30$ can help others be more aware of different ways to adjust numbers.

◆ Subtracting by Counting Up

This is an amazingly powerful way to subtract. Children working on the *think-addition* strategy for their basic facts can also be solving problems with larger numbers. The concept is the same. For example, for $45 - 19$, the idea is to think, "How much do I add to 19 to get to 45?" Notice that this strategy is not as efficient for $45 - 6$. Using *join with change unknown* problems or *missing-part* problems (discussed in Chapter 9) will encourage the counting-up strategy. Here is an example of each.

Sam had 46 baseball cards. He went to a card show and got some more cards for his collection. Now he has 73 cards. How many cards did Sam buy at the card show?

Juanita counted all of her crayons. Some were broken and some were not. She counted 73 crayons in all. 46 crayons were not broken. How many were broken?

Figure 12.7 shows invented strategies for these story problems. As you can see, using tens is also an important part of these strategies. Simply asking for the difference between two numbers may also prompt these strategies.

> **Standards for Mathematical Practice**
>
> **1** Make sense of problems and persevere in solving them

Figure **12.7** Three different invented strategies for subtraction by counting up.

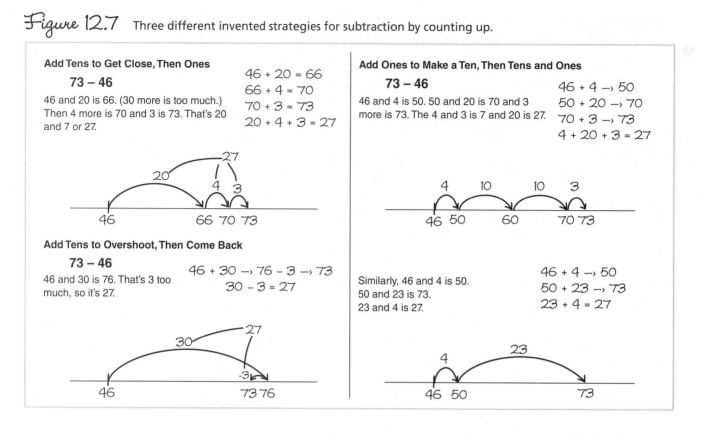

Take-Away Subtraction

Using take-away subtraction is considerably more difficult to do mentally. However, take-away strategies are common, probably because many textbooks emphasize take-away as the meaning of subtraction. Four different strategies are shown in Figure 12.8 for the following story problem.

There were 73 children on the playground. The 46 second-grade students came in first. How many children were still outside?

The two methods that begin by taking tens from tens are reflective of what most children do with base-ten pieces. The other two methods leave one of the numbers intact and subtract from it. When the subtracted number is a multiple of 10 or close to a multiple of 10, take-away subtraction can be an easy method to do mentally. Try 83 − 29 in your head by first taking away 30 and adding 1 back. Some children will become confused when they hear a classmate describe this strategy for 83 − 29. In particular, they do not understand why you add 1 back. They think because you added 1 to 29 to make it 30, then you should subtract 1 from the answer. Use a story problem with the numbers and let them act it out so that they can see that when they take away 30, they took 1 too many away and that is why they need to add 1 back.

Remember the "equal addition" algorithm that was described in the section on standard algorithms? There are some children who use this strategy as an invented strategy with take-away subtraction. For example, for 32 − 17, children might think that 32 is 2 away from 30, so if they subtract 2 from 32 to get 30, they need to subtract 2 from 17 to get 15. Now the problem is 30 − 15 or 15.

Figure 12.8 Four different invented strategies for take-away subtraction.

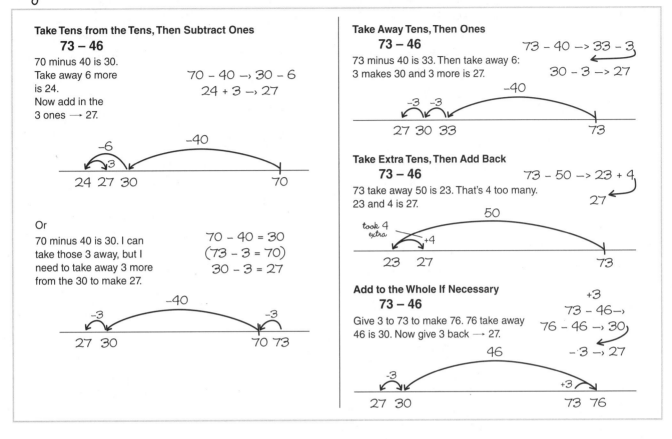

Stop and Reflect

Try computing 82 − 57. Use both take-away and counting-up methods. Can you use all of the strategies in Figures 12.7 and 12.8 without looking? ■

For many subtraction problems, especially those with three digits, an adding-on approach is significantly easier than a take-away approach. Try not to force the issue with children who do not use an add-on strategy. However, you may want to revisit some simple missing-part activities that are more likely to encourage that type of thinking.

Activity 12.4   **HOW FAR TO MY NUMBER?**

Children work in pairs for this activity. Without communicating to each other, one child writes down a number less than 50 while the other child writes down a number greater than 50. You may choose to limit the size of the second number (e.g., less than 100; less than 500) depending on the children. The children work together to find out how much more must be added to the smaller number to get to the larger number. Once an answer is determined, they should use little ten-frame cards to represent the smaller number and the amount they found to see whether the total matches the larger number. Children with disabilities may initially need to use the little ten-frames to help support their work in finding out how much more to add on.

"How Far to My Number?" can also be done by displaying two numbers on a projector and having children work in pairs at their desks. Another idea to help children think about using an adding-on approach is to show a number such as 28 with little ten-frame cards and ask, "What goes with 28 to make 53?" You can do the same with three-digit numbers with or without the use of models. As always, it is important to have children share their strategies during a discussion.

● Extensions and Challenges

Each of the examples in the preceding sections involved sums less than 100 and all involved *bridging* or *crossing a ten*; that is, if done with a standard algorithm, they require regrouping or trading. Bridging, the size of the numbers, and the potential for doing problems mentally are all issues to consider.

Bridging

For most of the strategies, it is easier to add or subtract when bridging is not required. Try each strategy with $34 + 52$ or $68 - 24$ to see how it works. Easier problems instill confidence. They also permit you to challenge children with a "harder one." There is also the issue of bridging 100 or 1000. Try $58 + 67$ with different strategies. Bridging across hundreds is also an issue for subtraction. Problems such as $128 - 50$ or $128 - 45$ are more difficult than ones that do not cross a hundred.

Larger Numbers

The *Common Core State Standards* recommend that second graders add and subtract three-digit numbers using a variety of strategies. Try seeing how *you* would do these without using the standard algorithms: $487 + 235$ and $623 - 247$. For subtraction, a counting-up strategy is usually the easiest. Occasionally, children will use other strategies with larger numbers. For example, "chunking off" multiples of 50 or 25 is often a useful method. For $462 + 257$, pull out 450 and 250 to make 700. That leaves 12 and 7 more, making 719.

Standard Algorithms for Addition and Subtraction

As noted earlier, children are not likely to invent the standard algorithms because they are less intuitive, so your instruction when teaching these algorithms will be more directed. Given that, it is critical that you teach the algorithms in a conceptual manner, helping children understand the tens and ones as they work.

The standard algorithms require an understanding of *regrouping*, exchanging 10 in one place-value position for 1 in the position to the left—or the reverse, exchanging 1 for 10 in the position to the right. The corresponding terms *borrowing* and *carrying* are obsolete and conceptually misleading. The word *regroup* may have little meaning for young children. A preferable term to use initially is *trade*. Ten ones are *traded* for a ten. A hundred is *traded* for 10 tens. Notice that none of the invented strategies involves regrouping.

Be sure to emphasize to children that the standard algorithm is just one possible algorithm that is a good choice in some situations, just as invented strategies are good choices in some situations.

Teaching Tip

Even after you have taught the standard algorithms, it is important to continue to encourage and promote the use of invented strategies. Children must learn to choose the method that best fits the numbers in the problem.

● Standard Algorithm for Addition

As with any procedure (algorithm), you need to begin with the concrete. Explicit connections must be made between the concept (regrouping) and the procedure.

Begin with Models Only

In the beginning, simply focus on regrouping with base-ten materials without recording the numerical process. Provide children with place-value mats (see Blackline Master 15) and base-ten models.

Have children use base-ten materials to make one number at the top of the mat and a second beneath it as shown in Figure 12.9. If children are still developing base-ten concepts, a groupable model such as counting chips in cups is helpful.

Point out this one rule: *Begin in the ones column*. Then let children solve the problem on their own. Allow plenty of time and then have children explain what they did and why. Let children display their work on a projector or on the board to help with their explanations.

One or two problems in a lesson with lots of discussion are much more productive than a lot of problems based on rules children don't understand.

Develop the Written Record

Reproduce pages with simple place-value charts similar to those in Figure 12.10 (p. 220). The charts will help children record numerals in columns as they do each step of the procedure with the base-ten models.

The first few times you do this, guide each step carefully through questioning, as shown in Figure 12.11 (p. 220). A similar approach would be used for three-digit problems.

Have children work in pairs. One child is responsible for the models and the other records the steps. They can reverse roles with each problem.

Figure 12.12 (p. 221) shows a variation of the traditional recording scheme that is quite reasonable, at least for up to three digits. It avoids the "carried ones" and focuses attention on the value of the digits. If children were permitted to start adding on the left as they are inclined to do, this would just be a vertical recording scheme for the invented strategy "add tens, add ones, then combine" (see Figure 12.6 on p. 214). This slight adaptation can be particularly effective for children with disabilities.

Standard Algorithm for Subtraction

The general approach to developing the subtraction algorithm is the same as for addition. When the procedure is completely understood with models, a do-and-write approach connects it with a written form.

Begin with Models Only

Start by having children model only the top number in a subtraction problem on the top half of their place-value mats. For the amount to be subtracted, have children write each digit on a small piece of paper and place these pieces near the bottom of their mats in the respective columns, as in Figure 12.13 (p. 221). To avoid errors, suggest making all trades first. That way, the full amount on the paper slip can be taken off at once. Also explain to children that they are to begin working with the ones column first, as they did with addition.

Standards for Mathematical Practice

4 Model with mathematics

Figure 12.9

Working from right to left with the standard addition algorithm.

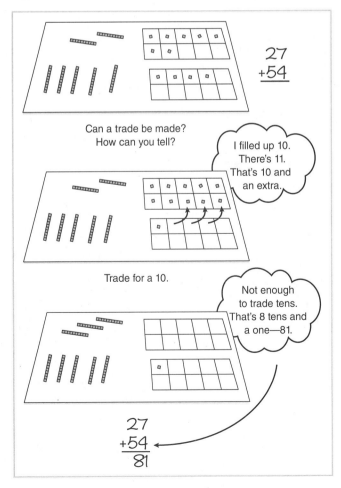

Figure 12.10

Blank recording charts are helpful for children to record their work.

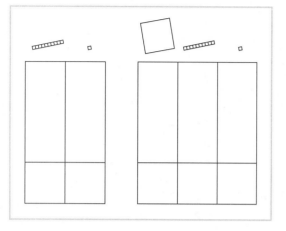

Anticipate Difficulties with Zeros

Exercises in which zeros are involved anywhere in the problem tend to cause special difficulties. Give extra attention to these cases while still using models.

The common errors that emerge when "regrouping across zero" are best addressed at the modeling stage. For example, in 403 − 138, children must make a double trade, trading a hundreds piece for 10 tens and then a tens piece for 10 ones. Use the following activity before giving children any hints about how they might deal with regrouping across a zero.

Activity 12.5 TRICKY TRADING

Pose a problem to the class that requires regrouping across zero. The problem should be one that will be easy for children to check using an invented strategy, such as 103 − 78. Children work in pairs using base-ten models and place-value mats. Once they have identified an answer, they should check their answer using an invented strategy.

Figure 12.11 Help children record on paper each step they do on their place-value mats.

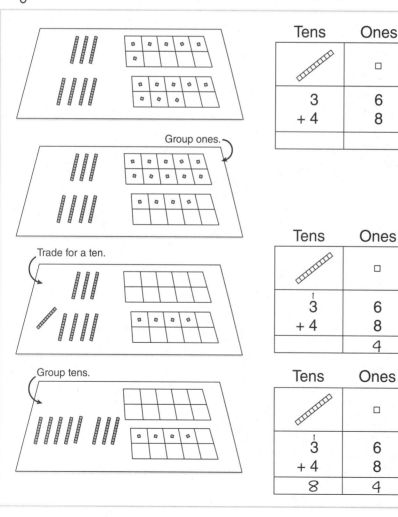

How much is in the ones column? (14)

Will you need to make a trade? (yes)

How many tens will you make? (1)
How many ones will be left? (4)

Good! Make the trade now.

Let's stop now and record exactly what we have done. You had 14 ones, and you made 1 ten and 4. Write a "1" in the tens column to show the ten you put there and a "4" in the answer space of the ones column for the 4 ones left.

Look at the tens column on your mat. You have 1 ten on top, 3 from the 36, and 4 more from the 48. See how your paper shows the same thing?

Now add all the tens together. Write how many tens that is in the answer space for the tens column.

If they did not get the same answer using base-ten models and their invented strategy, encourage them to try to determine why. Follow up with a discussion that starts with children sharing their ideas.

There are several versions of base-ten blocks online. One example called "Base Blocks Addition" is found at the National Library of Virtual Manipulatives (http://nlvm.usu.edu/en/nav/grade_g_1.html). You can create any problem up to four digits or you can let the applet generate problems. When you want to regroup, simply drag a rectangle around the pieces you wish to join.

Figure 12.12

An alternative recording scheme for addition. Notice that this can be used from left to right as well as from right to left.

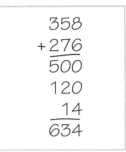

$$
\begin{array}{r}
358 \\
+\,276 \\
\hline
500 \\
120 \\
14 \\
\hline
634
\end{array}
$$

Develop the Written Record

The process of recording each step as it is done is the same as was suggested for addition. You can also use the same recording sheets (see Figure 12.10).

When children can explain the use of the symbols involved in the recording process, move them away from the use of the physical materials and on to a completely symbolic level. Again, be attentive to problems with zeros.

If children are permitted to follow their natural instincts and begin with the big pieces (from the left instead of the right), recording schemes similar to that shown in Figure 12.14 are possible. The trades are made from the pieces remaining *after* the subtraction in the column to the left has been done. In this case, a "regroup across zero" situation will still occur in problems like 462 − 168. Try it.

Figure 12.13 Two-digit subtraction with the standard algorithm and models.

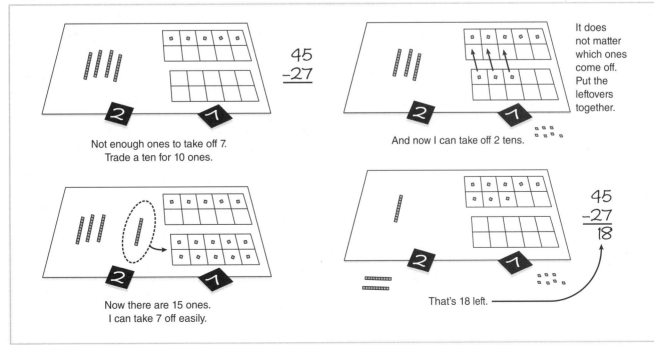

Figure 12.14

A left-hand recording scheme for subtraction. Other methods can also be devised.

$$
\begin{array}{r}
{}^{13}7{}^{14}\cancel{3}\cancel{4} \\
-\ 275 \\
\hline
\cancel{5}00 \\
4\cancel{6}0 \\
59 \\
\hline
459
\end{array}
$$

Once children understand the standard algorithms for addition and subtraction of multidigit numbers, it is important to provide them opportunities to determine which strategy from a variety of strategies might be more useful, given the specific numbers involved. The following activity provides this experience.

technology note

"Base Blocks Subtraction" is an applet found at the National Library of Virtual Manipulatives (http://nlvm .usu.edu/en/nav/grade_g_1.html). You can create any problem up to four digits or you can let the applet generate problems. The applet uses blue blocks to represent the top number and red blocks to represent the bottom number (the number being subtracted). When the blue blocks are dragged onto the red blocks, they disappear. Although you can begin in any column, if you start in the ones column and trade when necessary, the applet reinforces the standard algorithm by displaying a corresponding written record.

◢ *Activity* 12.6 **PICK YOUR PROCESS**

Project a list of strategies related to how children might solve addition (or subtraction) problems. This could include whatever names you have used to label the invented strategies as well as the standard algorithm. Tell children you are going to project a problem for them to see, but they are NOT to solve it—they are simply to tell which of the various methods they would choose to solve the problem and be ready to explain why. After they have made their choice, have children raise their hand as you say each method to indicate that is the method they have selected. Then tell them they are going to solve the given problem using their selected method and, once they are finished, they are to raise their thumb and hold it to their chest to indicate they are finished. Have children share solutions for each different method. Then ask which method seemed to work best for this situation. Make sure to use a variety of problems whose numbers lend themselves to different strategies.

Helping children develop flexible methods of adding and subtracting strengthens their understanding of place value, number relationships, and operations. Comparing methods used, including the standard algorithm, supports children in better understanding these methods, which results in their making fewer computational errors. This assortment of computational methods will serve children well in the real world.

Expanded Lesson

Exploring Subtraction Strategies

Content and Task Decisions

Grade Level: 2

Mathematics Goals

- To use invented strategies for subtracting two-digit numbers
- To use efficient strategies for subtracting two-digit numbers (beyond counting on by ones)

Grade Level Guide

NCTM *Curriculum Focal Points*	*Common Core State Standards*
At grade 2 children are expected to develop quick recall of addition and subtraction facts as well as fluency with two-digit addition and subtraction of whole numbers. There is an expectation that they will be able to estimate and calculate answers mentally.	Children in grade 2 use their understanding of place value to subtract. They should "fluently add and subtract within 100 using strategies based on place value, properties of operations, and/ or the relationship between addition and subtraction" (CCSSO, 2010, p. 19).

Consider Your Children's Needs

Children should have experience using a variety of invented strategies for adding two-digit numbers. Children should have had experience subtracting with smaller values and may have had experience subtracting two-digit from two-digit numbers. The assumption is that children have not been taught the standard algorithms for addition and subtraction. Consider using manipulatives or drawings as a tool to support children's thinking.

For English Language Learners

- Reading comprehension is central to this task. If ELLs have limited English, you can modify this lesson by using the same subject in all the stories. If proficiency is stronger, ensure that the contexts are understood in the *Before* phase.

For Children with Disabilities

- Cut the recording sheet into three pieces to reduce the visual display or put one problem on a page.
- If children are struggling explicitly, suggest the use of a particular strategy (such as the empty number line) but do not suggest how to do the problem.

Materials

Each child will need:

- "Looking at Collections" recording sheet (Blackline Master 46)
- Manipulatives (for counting)

Lesson

Before

Present the task to the class:

- Read the first problem together with the children. Ask children questions to make sure they understand the situation (not how to solve it). For example, ask "What do we know?" or "Can you put the problem in your own words?"
- Record what children know on the board.
- Ask children to brainstorm ideas about how they might solve the problem. Call on several children and elicit their thoughts. For example, if a child says, "I would start with 35 and count up to 72," ask how he or she will count or what model he or she might use to do the problem. It is not sufficient to say, "I would subtract."
- Summarize by encouraging children to use one of the ideas they heard or one of their own ideas. Also encourage them to use manipulatives or models (e.g., hundreds chart, empty number line).

Provide clear expectations:

- Explain to children that they will be working individually (or you may choose to have them work in pairs).
- Explain that they are to show how they solved each problem. They can show how with words, drawings, or equations.

- They should provide enough information on their paper so that, if they shared it with other second-grade children, other children would understand what they did.

- Tell children to continue on to the second and third problems after they finish the first one.

During

Initially:

- Observe that children have access to the materials needed to solve the problem.

- Observe that each child understands the question and is in the process of attempting to solve the first situation.

Ongoing:

- Observe children's work—notice the methods they are using and the models they are using to solve the problem. See the "Assessment" section of this lesson for details. Keep these in mind for selecting who will share in the *After* phase of the lesson.

- As children work, ask them to tell you what the problem is asking and how they are thinking about solving it. See the "Assessment" section at the end of the lesson for details.

- If a child is stuck, try to make a suggestion that builds on the child's ideas. For example, if the child says, "I want to take 35 from 72, but I don't know how to start," you might ask the child if the hundreds chart might help. Or you might suggest that the child try one of the ideas that was mentioned in the *Before* phase of the lesson. After making a suggestion, walk away and check back later.

- If you notice an error, rather than correct it, ask children to explain how they solved the problem (children often catch their mistakes while explaining and showing).

After

Bring the class together to share and discuss the task:

- Ask children to explain how they solved the problem. Record their ideas on the board, sketching any visuals that they describe, or show their work on a document camera.

- Be careful to write the equations both horizontally and vertically so that children recognize that these are equivalent representations.

- One good visual representation is to use an empty number line. You can use the number line when a child suggests a strategy that involves skip counting by tens (e.g., "I started with 35, added 10 and 10 and 10 to get to 65, then counted by five to 70, and then by ones to 72, and got 37."). Your number line on the board may look like this:

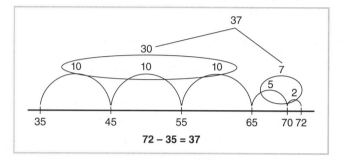

- If there are different answers, allow the children with different answers to explain their thinking, and the class as a whole can determine if the answer makes sense. The responsibility for deciding what is correct falls to the class, not you.

- Repeat the process for the second and third problems.

Assessment

Observe

- Use a checklist to identify children using strategies that involve counting by ones. You may need to meet with these children in a small group to encourage them to use skip counting or landmark numbers as a faster, more efficient strategy.

- Look to see whether children are using different strategies across the problems or using the same strategy.

Ask

- What strategy are you using?

- Can you show me (with manipulatives or a hundreds chart) how you found the answer?

- Can you use skip counting or benchmark numbers to find the answer more quickly?

13

Promoting Algebraic Reasoning

BigIDEAS

1 Algebra for pre-K–2 children is more than recognizing and extending repeating and growing patterns. It should emphasize generalization.

2 Algebra is a useful tool for generalizing arithmetic and representing patterns and regularities in our world.

3 Symbolism, especially that involving equality and variables, must be understood conceptually. For example, children need to understand that the equal sign is used to express the relationship of equality and is not an indication to do a computation.

4 The structures in our number system can and should be generalized. For example, the generalization that $a + b = b + a$ tells us that $38 + 72 = 72 + 38$ without computing the sums on each side of the equal sign.

Algebraic reasoning for grades pre-K–2 involves forming generalizations from experiences with number and computation, formalizing these ideas using meaningful representations and symbols, and exploring the concepts of pattern and functions. The core idea of algebraic reasoning or algebraic thinking is looking for and finding relationships and building a structure with those relationships. This type of reasoning prepares children to think mathematically across all areas of mathematics and is essential for making mathematics useful in daily life.

Teaching Tip

Your success in helping children see relationships and think algebraically is driven by your questions. Record the questions suggested throughout this chapter on note cards and keep them handy for lesson planning and classroom discussions.

In *Young Mathematicians at Work: Constructing Algebra*, Fosnot and Jacob (2010) write, "It is human to seek and build relations. The mind cannot process the multitude of stimuli in our surroundings and make meaning of them without developing a network of relations" (p. 12).*

According to the *Curriculum Focal Points* (National Council of Teachers of Mathematics, 2006), algebraic

---

*Reprinted with permission from *Young Mathematicians at Work: Constructing Algebra*, copyright 2010, by the National Council of Teachers of Mathematics. All rights reserved.

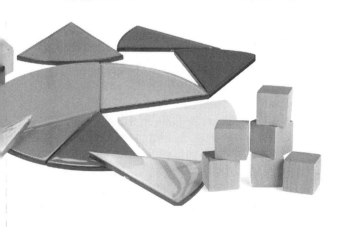

225

thinking should be connected to the focal points at every grade level with the primary topics being the use of patterns leading to generalizations (especially with operations), the study of change, and a rudimentary concept of function. In the *Common Core State Standards* (CCSSO, 2010), the close connection between arithmetic and algebra is evident by an identified domain called "Operations and Algebraic Thinking." This chapter on promoting algebraic reasoning follows the number and operation chapters so that you can see the close relationship between number concepts, operations, and algebraic reasoning.

Strands of Algebraic Reasoning

Three strands of algebraic reasoning are commonly identified (Carraher & Schliemann, 2007; Kaput, 2008). Notice that the central notions of generalizations and symbolism are embedded in all three strands.

1. Study of structures in the number system, including those arising in arithmetic (algebra as generalized arithmetic).
2. Study of patterns, relations, and functions.
3. Process of mathematical modeling, including the meaningful use of symbols.

Although algebra can be thought of as composed of different components and is often considered a separate area of the curriculum, algebra can and should be approached as an integral part of all areas of mathematics. The three strands of algebra that we have identified form a foundation for the existing mathematics curriculum in grades pre-K–2. Let's see how.

Generalization from Arithmetic

To generalize a concept, one uses specific examples to identify commonalities that can be used to describe any example of the concept. The process of generating generalizations from number and arithmetic begins as early as pre-kindergarten and continues as children learn about all aspects of number and computation, including basic facts and meanings of the operations.

⬢ Generalization with Operations

When young children explore addition families, they learn how to decompose, compose, and recompose numbers. Consider the following problem that provides children a chance to think about ways to decompose the number 9:

Nine frogs are sitting on two lily pads, one small lily pad and one big lily pad. Show the different ways that the nine frogs could sit on the two lily pads.

This problem can also provide children with the occasion to notice generalizable characteristics, such as increasing the number on the big lily pad by one means reducing the number on the small lily pad by one. To facilitate this opportunity, children can be challenged to find all the ways the frogs can be on the two lily pads. The significant algebraic question is how to decide when all the solutions have been found. To begin with, children will just reply they cannot think of any more ways. By asking questions to focus children's attention on the relationship between adjacent solutions (e.g., 2 + 7 and 3 + 6) (asking questions, not

Teaching Tip

In these kinds of problems, children often do not consider the combinations with zero. If this happens, simply ask, "Could one of the lily pads be empty?"

telling!), children will eventually begin to strategically use each number from 0 to 9 for one lily pad and the corresponding number for the other lily pad.

Continue to work toward generalization by looking at other quantities of frogs (e.g., how many ways for 5 frogs? for 6 frogs?), asking children what patterns they notice across these cases. When a child explains that for each number 0 to 9 there is one solution, he or she is no longer partitioning 9 into parts to find solutions but is making a generalization about how to determine the number of solutions without having to list them. For example, the child might explain, "There is always one more way than the number of frogs."

This reasoning can be applied to other numbers and in other contexts, which is an important step in generalization. The children's book *The Sleepover* (Fosnot, 2007) describes a context of eight children rearranging themselves on a pair of bunk beds that would offer another opportunity for children to grapple with the idea of finding all the possible combinations for a number. (Fosnot's book *The Sleepover* can be found at www.heinemann.com /products/E01084.aspx.)

The following activity purposefully focuses children's attention on the adjacent facts in an effort to help them generalize and reason more strategically.

◀ *Activity* 13.1 **ONE UP AND ONE DOWN WITH ADDITION**

Have children select a number, such as 7, and add it to itself. The task is to find out what happens to the sum if you add 1 to one of the sevens and subtract 1 from the other seven (e.g., 8 + 6). Ask children, "Does this work with other numbers? Does it only work if you start with a number plus itself? Can you explain why it works? What else can you find out?"

Activity 13.1, "One Up and One Down with Addition," poses a significant task for first and second graders. Some children may wonder if it works for "really big numbers." Suggest they test their ideas with a calculator. It is also useful to explore the idea of two up and two down, and so on. Of course, the results are the same as long as the same amount is added and subtracted from each number. The result of this exploration can be useful when learning basic facts (6 + 8 is the same as 7 + 7 or double 7). Children may want to know if the one-up/one-down idea works for subtraction. (It does not.) But there is an important pattern to discover: If both numbers change in the same direction, up or down, the result is the same. (This is called "equal additions" and is described in Chapters 5 and 12.) Recognizing this allows us to change 12 − 8 to 10 − 6, or 83 − 48 to 85 − 50, changing potentially difficult problems to easier ones.

Generalizing can be extended to symbols, even with first and second graders. For example, in the frogs and lily pad problem, the teacher might respond to the child who states that there will always be one more solution than the number of frogs by asking, "How about if there were *n* frogs?" Children will typically respond using their own words with something like, "It would just be one more than that." Challenge them to determine how they might write this if *n* indicates the number of frogs. Children will struggle with this question but it extends the opportunity for them to think about the generalization and how they might communicate about it.

Contexts like the frogs on lily pads can provide opportunities to address commutativity. For example, some children might consider pairs of solutions such as 2 + 7 and 7 + 2 as different solutions because of the contextual situation; that is, 2 + 7 could represent 2 frogs on the small lily pad and 7 frogs on the big lily pad and then 7 + 2 would represent 7 frogs on the small lily pad and 2 frogs on the big lily pad. Others may argue that they are the "same," meaning that although 2 + 7 and 7 + 2 are modeling different situations, they still result in 9 frogs on lily pads. It is important to allow children to work through this idea

Standards for Mathematical Practice

8 **Look for and express regularity in repeated reasoning**

Standards for Mathematical Practice

2 **Reasoning abstractly and quantitatively**

**Standards for
Mathematical Practice**

8 **Look for and
express regularity in
repeated reasoning**

of commutativity so look for multiple places to revisit the idea. Consider the suggestion in the next paragraph.

Slight shifts in how arithmetic problems are presented can open up opportunities for ▶ generalizations (Blanton, 2008). For example, instead of a series of unrelated addition problems, consider the following list:

$$4 + 7 \qquad 7 + 4 \qquad 23 + 15 \qquad 15 + 23$$

Once children have solved these problems, you can focus their attention on the addends, asking questions such as, "What do you notice?" "Will this always be true?" and "How could we write that using symbols?" In their own words, children will explain that the numbers can be added in any order. Even if children show some understanding of commutativity of single-digit addends, it is important to help them recognize the *generalizability* of the property with larger numbers.

◆ Generalizations in the Hundreds Chart

The hundreds chart is a rich representation for exploring number relationships. Activities in Chapters 8 and 11 had children exploring the hundreds chart and looking for patterns (see Activities 8.24–8.25 and 11.13–11.14). To connect arithmetic to algebra, you can ask children, "What did we add to get from 72 to 82? From 5 to 15? From 34 to 44?" When children stop counting and note the generalized idea that they are adding 10 and moving ▶ down exactly one row, they are deepening their understanding of number concepts and how adding 10 changes numbers.

**Standards for
Mathematical Practice**

7 **Look for and make
use of structure**

Moves on the hundreds chart can be represented with arrows (for example, → means right one column or plus 1, and ↑ means up one row or less 10). Consider asking children to complete these problems:

$$14 \rightarrow \rightarrow \leftarrow \leftarrow \qquad 63 \uparrow \uparrow \downarrow \downarrow \qquad 45 \rightarrow \uparrow \leftarrow \downarrow$$

What do you anticipate children will do? Children may count up or back using a count-by-ones approach. Others may know to jump 10 (up or down) and will do all four moves. Still others may recognize that a downward arrow "undoes" an upward arrow—an indication that these children are moving toward generalizations (Blanton, 2008). In other words, they recognize that +10 and −10 results in zero change.

✑ Formative Assessment Note

As children work on tasks like the one just described, observe, using a checklist, which children solve tasks by counting by ones, by jumping, or by noticing the "doing" and "undoing." What you observe can help you identify which children's approaches to highlight during the subsequent discussion. For example, you can start the discussion by having children who used a count-by-ones approach or a jumping strategy to share and then have children who have generalized the situation share how they think about it.

The next activity continues to have children explore patterns involving place value and addition.

◢ *Activity* 13.2 DIAGONAL SUMS

BLM

Provide children with a hard copy of a hundreds chart (see Blackline Master 10) or you can have them use an interactive virtual hundreds chart (see, for example, www.crickweb .co.uk/ks2numeracy-tools.html). Have children select any four numbers in the hundreds chart that form a square. They are to add the two numbers on each diagonal as in the example shown here.

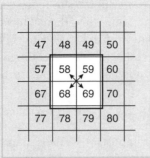

Children should explore other diagonal sums on the chart. Expand their search to diagonals of any rectangle. For example, the numbers 15, 19, 75, and 79 form four corners of a rectangle. The sums 15 + 79 and 19 + 75 are equal. Challenge children to figure out why this happens. (See Figure 13.1.)

Stop and Reflect

Before reading further, stop and explore why the diagonal sums described in the previous activities are the same. Decomposing the numbers may help. ■

Here are some additional tasks you might explore on a hundreds chart.

- When skip counting, which numbers make diagonal patterns? Which numbers make column patterns? Can you describe a rule for explaining when a number will have a diagonal or column pattern?

- If you move down two and over one on the hundreds chart, what is the relationship between the original number and the new number?

- Can you find two skip-count patterns with one color marker "on top of" the other (i.e., all of the shaded values for one pattern are part of the shaded values for the other)? How are these two skip-count numbers related? Is this true for any pair of numbers that have this relationship?

These examples extend number concepts to algebraic reasoning. Asking questions such as "When will this be true?" and "Why does this work?" requires children to generalize and thereby strengthen their understanding of the number concepts they are learning.

Figure 13.1

Diagonals on a hundreds chart. For any four numbers forming a rectangular arrangement on the hundreds chart, the sum of the corner numbers on one diagonal equals the sum of the corner numbers on the other diagonal.

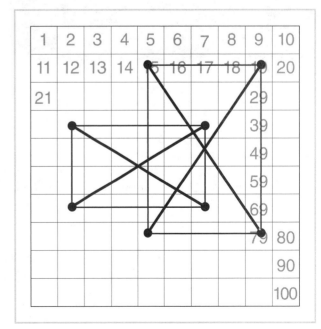

Meaningful Use of Symbols

The equal sign and variables are powerful tools in representing mathematical ideas and the primary grades are not too early to begin using them. However, many misconceptions often develop in these early years that unfortunately stay with children into later years. In this section, we emphasize how pre-K–2 teachers can help children develop a strong understanding of the equal sign and variables through meaningful instruction.

The Meaning of the Equal Sign

The equal sign is one of the most important symbols in mathematics, especially in elementary arithmetic and in early algebra. We teach children to write equations using the equal sign as early as kindergarten, and they continue to experience equations in every subsequent grade. Unfortunately, research dating from 1975 to the present indicates that students have a very poor understanding of the equal sign (RAND Mathematics Study Panel, 2003). In addition, the equal sign is rarely represented in U.S. textbooks in ways that facilitate children's understanding of the equivalence relationship—an understanding that is critical to understanding algebra (McNeil et al., 2006).

Stop and Reflect

In the following equation, what number do you think belongs in the box?

$$8 + 4 = \square + 5$$

How do you think children in the early grades or in middle school typically answer this question? ∎

Teaching Tip

Do not connect multiple expressions using equal signs unless they are equal. For example, when adding 6 and 6 and then adding 3 more to that sum, do not write that as $6 + 6 = 12 + 3 = 15$. Doing this incorrectly reinforces the idea that the equal sign means "and the answer is" rather than indicating equivalence.

In one study (Falkner, Levi, & Carpenter, 1999), no more than 10 percent of children in grades 1 to 6 put the correct number (7) in the box. None of the sixth graders (out of 145) put a 7 in the box. The common responses were 12 and 17. (How did children get these answers?)

Most, if not all, equations that children encounter in elementary school are similar to $5 + 7 = \underline{\quad}$ or $4 \times 3 = \underline{\quad}$. As a consequence, children come to see = as signifying "and the answer is" rather than as a symbol that indicates equivalence (Carpenter, Franke, & Levi, 2003; McNeil & Alibali, 2005; Molina & Ambrose, 2006). Subtle shifts in how you approach teaching computation can alleviate this significant misconception. For example, a simple change such as writing basic facts as $7 = 2 + 5$ can cause children to stop and question why this is the same as $2 + 5 = 7$. Also, rather than always asking children to solve a problem like $19 + 23$, ask them to find an equivalent expression and use both to write an equation (Blanton, 2008). For $19 + 23$, children might write $19 + 23 = 20 + 22$. Activity 13.3 (adapted from Fosnot & Jacobs, 2010) works on this idea using the basic facts and emphasizes the Up Over 10 strategy.

Activity 13.3 TEN AND THEN SOME

For this activity, each pair of children will need eight note cards labeled with the equations $10 + 1$ to $10 + 8$. They lay those cards out on their desks face up.

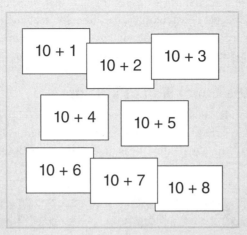

They will also need a deck of playing cards with all the face cards, aces, and tens removed. Each child draws one playing card from the deck. Together the partners decide which note card is equivalent to the sum of their playing cards. They place the playing cards behind the identified note card. If the sum of the playing cards is less than 10, they slide the cards back in the deck in random places. Have children write the two expressions as an equation (e.g., $5 + 8 = 10 + 3$) to reinforce the idea that these quantities are equal. Children can also play this game independently.

To begin with, children struggle to understand how amounts that look different can actually be equivalent. In other words, they wonder why the numbers do not have to be identical. Consequently, children will initially need to add the numbers on each side to verify for themselves that they are the same quantity. As they come to understand compensation (e.g., how part of one number can be moved to another number), they begin to understand how equivalent quantities do not have to be identical. Once you know children can use compensation, challenge them to find the equivalent expression without computing first.

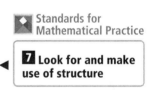

◄ Standards for Mathematical Practice

7 Look for and make use of structure

The next activity continues to challenge children to find different ways to express equivalent amounts.

▰ *Activity* 13.4 **DIFFERENT BUT THE SAME**

Challenge children to find different ways to express a particular number, say, 6. Give a few examples, such as $3 + 3$ or $12 - 6$. Encourage children to use both addition and subtraction in the same expression. Ask questions such as, "How many ways can you make 6 using at least one number greater than 10?" Have children write equations using their expressions (e.g., $12 - 6 = 0 + 6$; $15 - 9 = 2 + 4$). In your discussion, emphasize that each expression is a way of representing the same quantity. Adding a context (e.g., trading cards) can support children's reasoning.

Why is it so important that children in grades pre-K–2 correctly understand the equal sign? First, it is important for children to understand and symbolize relationships in our number system and the equal sign is a principal method of representing these relationships. For example, $8 + 5 = 8 + 2 + 3$ shows a basic fact strategy. When ideas that are initially and informally developed through arithmetic are generalized and expressed symbolically, children have access to powerful relationships for working with other numbers in a generalized manner. A second reason, although removed from the pre-K–2 classroom, is that when older students have a poor understanding of the equal sign, they typically have difficulty working with algebraic expressions (Knuth, Stephens, McNeil, & Alibali, 2006). Helping pre-K–2 children develop a solid understanding of the equal sign can in turn help them avoid such difficulties in later grades.

Conceptualizing the Equal Sign as a Balance

You can help children understand the idea of equivalence through concrete methods. The next two activities use kinesthetic approaches, tactile objects, and visualizations to reinforce the "balancing" notion of the equal sign (ideas based on Mann, 2004).

Activity 13.5 SEESAW COMPARISONS

Ask children to raise their arms to look like a seesaw. Explain that you have softballs, all weighing the same, and tennis balls, all weighing the same. The softballs are heavier than the tennis balls. (Have some softballs and tennis balls in case children, especially ELLs, are not familiar with these items.) Tell children to imagine that you have placed a softball in each of their left hands. Ask them what would happen to their seesaw (children should bend to the left side). Tell children to imagine that you place another softball in their right hands (children should level off). Next with the softballs still there, ask them to imagine a tennis ball added to the left. Finally, say you are adding another tennis ball in the left hand again. Then ask them to imagine a tennis ball moving over to the right hand. This is a particularly important activity for children with disabilities who may be challenged with the abstract idea of balancing values of expressions.

After acting out the seesaw several times, you can ask children to create and share their observations. For example, one child may share, "If you have a balanced seesaw and add something to one side, it will tilt to that side." Another child may explain, "If you take away the same object from both sides of the seesaw, the seesaw won't change."

Activity 13.6 WHAT DO YOU KNOW ABOUT THE SHAPES?

Prepare a balance scale with objects on both sides. Here is an example:

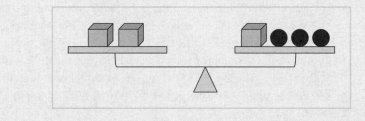

Tell children that the cubes weigh the same and the balls weigh the same. Then ask the children to think about what they know about the shapes. Have children share with a partner what they think they know. If children do not focus on the weights, ask a more directed question such as, "What do you know about how the weights of the balls and the cubes compare?" Have children explain their thinking.

Standards for
Mathematical Practice

2 Reason abstractly
and quantitatively ▶

Figure 13.2 shows a series of other examples for the pan balance. Two or more balances for a single problem provide different information about the shapes or variables. Problems of this type can be adjusted in difficulty for children in grades K–2. When no numbers are involved, as in the top three examples in Figure 13.2, children can find combinations of numbers for the shapes that make the pans balance. The different shapes represent different variables and so would have different values. There are often different paths to finding a solution.

To create your own pan balance problems, start by giving values to two or three shapes. Place shapes in groups and add the values. Be sure your problems can be solved!

Stop and Reflect

How would you solve the last problem in Figure 13.2? Can you solve it in two ways? ■

Figure 13.2   Examples of problems using pan balances.

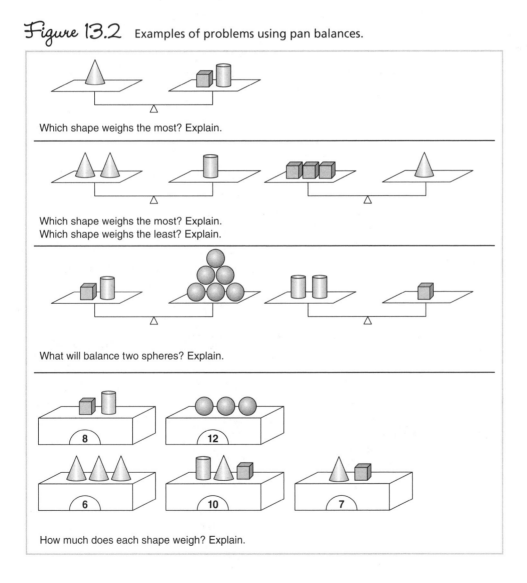

Which shape weighs the most? Explain.

Which shape weighs the most? Explain.
Which shape weighs the least? Explain.

What will balance two spheres? Explain.

How much does each shape weigh? Explain.

Figure 13.3

Using expressions and variables in equations and inequalities. The two-pan balance helps develop the meaning of =, <, and >.

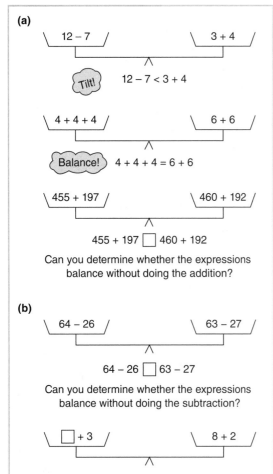

(a)

12 − 7 | 3 + 4

(Tilt!) 12 − 7 < 3 + 4

4 + 4 + 4 | 6 + 6

(Balance!) 4 + 4 + 4 = 6 + 6

455 + 197 | 460 + 192

455 + 197 ☐ 460 + 192

Can you determine whether the expressions balance without doing the addition?

(b)

64 − 26 | 63 − 27

64 − 26 ☐ 63 − 27

Can you determine whether the expressions balance without doing the subtraction?

☐ + 3 | 8 + 2

Can you determine how to make the expressions balance without doing the addition?

You can find more "Pan Balance" explorations at http://illuminations.nctm .org/ActivityDetail.aspx?id=33. Use the directions under "Explorations" so that you can help your children strategically explore the tasks found at this site.

technology note

After children have experiences with tasks involving shapes, they can explore numbers and then variables using pan balances.

Activity 13.7 TILT OR BALANCE

On the board, draw or project a simple two-pan balance. In each pan, write a numeric expression and ask which pan will go down or whether the two will balance (see Figure 13.3a). Challenge children to write their own expressions for each side of the scale to make it balance. Include examples such as the third and fourth balances for which children can analyze the relationships on both sides (as opposed to doing the computation) to determine whether the pan tilts or balances. For children with disabilities, rather than have them write their own expressions, initially have them identify from a small collection of cards with expressions the ones that will make the scale balance.

True/False and Open Sentences

Carpenter, Franke, and Levi (2003) suggest that a good starting point for helping children make sense of the equal sign is to explore equations as either true or false. Clarifying the meaning of the equal sign is just one of the outcomes of this type of exploration, as seen in the next activity.

Activity 13.8 TRUE OR FALSE EQUATIONS

Introduce true/false sentences or equations with simple examples to explain what you mean by a true equation and a false equation (e.g., $2 + 3 = 5$ is a true equation; $4 + 3 = 2$ is a false equation). Then put several simple equations on the board, some true and some false. Here are some examples:

$$5 + 2 = 7 \qquad 4 + 1 = 6$$
$$8 = 10 - 1 \qquad 7 = 12 - 5$$

To begin with, keep the computations simple. The children's task is to decide which of the equations are true and which are false. For each response, they must explain their reasoning.

After this initial exploration, have children explore equations that are in a less familiar form:

$$3 + 7 = 7 + 3 \qquad 10 - 3 = 11 - 4 \qquad 9 + 6 = 0 + 14$$

$$8 = 8 \qquad\qquad 15 + 7 + 3 = 16 + 10$$

Listen to the types of reasons children use to justify their answers and plan additional equations accordingly. ELLs and children with disabilities will benefit from first explaining (or showing) their reasoning to a partner as a low-risk speaking opportunity and then sharing with the whole group.

Children will typically agree about equations when there is an expression on one side and a single number on the other, although initially equations such as $7 = 12 - 5$ may generate discussion. For equations with no operation (e.g., $8 = 8$), the discussion may be lively. Children often believe there must be an operation on one side and an "answer" on the other. Reinforce that the equal sign means "is the same amount as" by using that language as you read the symbol.

After children have experiences with true/false sentences, introduce open sentences—that is, equations with a box or letter to be replaced by a number. To develop an understanding of open sentences, encourage children to look at the number sentence as a whole and describe in words what the equation represents.

◆ *Activity* 13.9 OPEN SENTENCES

Write several open sentences on the board. These can be similar to the true/false sentences that you have been exploring. Here are some examples:

$$5 + 2 = \square \qquad 4 + \square = 6 \qquad 4 + 5 = \square - 1$$

$$6 - n = 7 - 4 \qquad n + 5 = 5 + 8 \qquad 15 + 27 = n + 28$$

Ask children to decide what number can replace the box (or letter) to make the sentence true. They should be ready to explain their reasoning.

Relational Thinking

Once children understand that the equal sign means that the quantities on both sides are the same amount, they can use relational thinking to solve problems. Relational thinking occurs when a child observes and uses number relationships between the two sides of the equal sign instead of actually computing the amounts. Relational thinking of this sort is the first step toward generalizing relationships found in arithmetic to relationships used when variables are involved.

Standards for
Mathematical Practice

◄ **2** **Reason abstractly and quantitatively**

To illustrate this kind of thinking, consider the two explanations for placing an 8 in the box for $7 + \square = 6 + 9$.

Explanation 1: Since $6 + 9$ is 15, I need to figure out 7 plus what equals 15. It is 8, so the box is 8.

Explanation 2: Seven is one more than the 6 on the other side. That means that the box should be one less than 9, so it must be 8.

The first child computed the sum on one side of the equation and then used the sum to determine the missing part on the other side. The second child used a relationship between the expressions on either side of the equal sign. This child did not need to compute the values on each side.

Stop and Reflect

How are the two children's responses for $7 + \square = 6 + 9$ different? How would each of these children solve the following open sentence? ■

$$534 + 175 = 174 + \square$$

Teaching Tip

Having children share their reasoning promotes relational thinking and can help other children to improve analyzing relationships in a problem.

The first child would likely do the computation and may have difficulty finding the correct addend. The second child would use relational thinking to reason that 174 is one less than 175, so the number in the box must be one more than 534.

Formative Assessment Note

As children work on these types of tasks, listen to individual children for whether they are using relational thinking. If they are not, ask them, "Can you find the answer without actually doing any computation?" This questioning helps nudge children toward relational thinking and helps you decide the next instructional steps.

To facilitate relational thinking and the meaning of the equal sign, continue to have children explore increasingly complex true/false and open sentences that are designed to elicit relational thinking rather than computation. Although not a guarantee, posing problems with larger numbers that make computation difficult (not impossible) can prompt children to try a relationship approach. Here are some examples to consider.

TRUE/FALSE:

$674 - 369 = 664 - 379$ $37 + 54 = 38 + 53$ $376 - 329 = 76 - 29$

OPEN SENTENCES:

$73 + 56 = 71 + \square$ $126 - 37 = \square - 40$ $68 + 58 = 57 + 69 + n$

Stop and Reflect

One of the previous true/false sentences is false. Can you explain why using relational thinking? ■

The following activity will help to solidify children's understanding of the equal sign.

◀ Activity 13.10 TRUE OR FALSE CHALLENGES

After children have had ample time to discuss true/false and open sentences, ask them to make up their own true/false sentences that they can use to challenge their classmates. Each child should write a collection of three or four sentences with at least one true and at least one false sentence. Encourage them to include one "tricky" one. Their equations can be either traded with a partner or shared with the whole class. Repeat for open sentences.

When children write their own true/false sentences, they often are intrigued with the idea of using large numbers and lots of numbers in their sentences, especially if you have challenged them to include "tricky" sentences. Support their efforts, as these kinds of problems tend to help move children toward relational thinking.

◆ The Meaning of Variables

Expressions or equations with variables are a means for expressing patterns and generalizations. Variables can be used as unique known values or as quantities that vary. Unfortunately, children often think of variables as placeholders for specific numbers, not representations for multiple or even infinite values. Children need experiences that build meaning for both.

Variables Used as Known Values

The $\square$ used in some of the examples of open sentences is a precursor of a variable used in this way. You can also use letters instead of a box to stand for the missing number, which was also seen in some of the examples. To avoid children thinking of the box as the answer space, ask them what number the box could be to make the sentence true. You can also use this language when you use letters instead of boxes. Initially children should rely on relational reasoning when finding the value of the variable that makes the sentence true.

Consider the following open sentence:

$$\square + \square + 7 = \square + 17$$

This equation could have also been written as $n + n + 7 = n + 17$. When the same symbol or letter is used in multiple places in an expression or equation, the convention is that it stands for the same number every place it occurs. In this example, the $\square$ or n must be 10.

Recall from Chapter 9 that there are different types of story problems, and that in each type, what is missing from the problem can be the initial value, the change, or the answer. This is a major emphasis in the *Common Core State Standards* in grades 1 and 2. Too often our story problems have the result unknown. But children need many experiences with other parts missing, as in the following example:

Rebekah had 5 apples in her basket. She picked some more after lunch. Then she had 13. How many apples did she pick after lunch?

Children may recognize this as a difference and realize the answer is 8. The equation that fits this story is $5 + \_\_\_ = 13$. Note the change is unknown. Therefore, this is a missing-part situation. This notion of missing addend is a precursor for children's work with variables

▶ Standards for Mathematical Practice

6 Attend to precision

and algebraic expressions and equations. You can begin to use variables instead of leaving a blank space: $5 + a = 13$.

When writing equations for story problems, different equations may occur. For example, consider this story problem:

If Gabbie has 12 cards and Karl has 5 cards, write an equation for how many more cards Gabbie has than Karl.

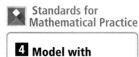
Standards for
Mathematical Practice

4 Model with
mathematics ▶

Notice the instructions did not ask children to solve the problem but rather to write an equation. Some children might write $12 - 5 = \square$ while others may write $5 + \square = 12$. The latter equation can be interpreted as "Karl's 5 cards plus some more cards are the same as Gabbie's 12 cards." Facilitate a discussion with children to help them understand that both equations show the same relationships and either is correct. Although either is correct, it is important that children can write and justify *both* equations, connecting the equations to the story.

Within a context, children can even explore three variables, each one standing for an unknown value as in the following activity (based on Maida, 2004).

Activity 13.11 TOYS, TOYS, TOYS

Children can figure out the cost of three toys, given the following three facts:

Ask children to look at each fact and make observations that can help them figure out the cost of each toy. For example, they may notice that the soccer ball costs $1 more than the teddy bear. Help children write this observation as the other statements. Continue until these discoveries lead to finding the cost of each toy. Encourage children to use manipulatives to represent and explore the problem.

Stop and Reflect

Work on the problem in Activity 13.11 before reading further. Using the observation that the soccer ball cost $1 more than the bear, that means that the third fact can be thought of as a bear + $1 + bear = $5. So, how much is a teddy bear? ■

Variables as Quantities That Vary

The shift from the variable representing a specific quantity to a variable representing multiple possibilities can be difficult for children. Using contexts (again, story problems!) is significant in helping children develop this second meaning of variables. As Blanton (2008) suggests, use slight alterations to a number task:

NUMBER TASK:
Sandra has 8 pennies. George has 4 more pennies than Sandra. How many pennies does George have?

ALGEBRA TASK:
Sandra has some pennies. George has 4 more pennies than Sandra. How many pennies does George have?

Notice in the new version there is no way to do a computation because you are not given specific values. Children can list possible ways in a table (see Figure 13.4) and eventually represent the answer as *George = Sandra + 4*.

Another place to use variables as quantities that vary is when children make conjectures about the number system (e.g., when you add zero to any number, you get that number back). These statements are true for all numbers. At first children will use their own language to describe the situation, but you can introduce the use of variables to help refine their ideas. For example, for the commutative property of addition, children might explain, "It does not matter which order you add the numbers. You get the same amount." After children have discussed this idea multiple times and created several examples, suggest writing this idea as $a + b = b + a$.

Figure 13.4

Possible ways variables can vary in quantity.

Number of Pennies for Sandra	Number of Pennies for George
2	6
3	7
4	8
10	14
23	27

Making Structure in the Number System Explicit

Chapter 9 discusses several properties for addition and subtraction and begins to lay the foundation for some properties for multiplication—all of which are important for children as they learn basic facts and computational strategies. For example, understanding the commutative property for addition substantially reduces the number of facts to be mastered. This and other properties are likely to be used informally as children develop relational thinking and learn about computation.

A next step is to have children examine these properties and to begin to express them in general terms without reference to specific numbers—first in their own language and then using symbols. For example, after examining several examples of adding zero, a child might observe, "When you add zero to any number, you get that number back." Articulating this property (and any other properties of our number system) in a general way, in either words or symbols (e.g., $a + 0 = a$), noting that it is true for all numbers, makes the structure of our number system explicit. When these structures are made explicit and are understood, they not only add to children's tools for computation, but they also enrich their understanding of the number system, providing a base for even higher levels of reasoning (Carpenter, Franke, & Levi, 2003).

⬥ Making and Justifying Conjectures about Properties

Properties of the number system can be built into children's explorations with true/false and open number sentences. For example, children will eventually agree that the true/false sentence $4 + 7 = 7 + 4$ is true. The pivotal question, however, asks, "Is it true for any numbers?" Some children will agree that although it seems to be true all of the time, maybe there are two numbers that haven't been tried yet for which it does not work.

Consider the following discussion that occurs after children have had several opportunities to discuss true/false sentences such as $4 + 7 = 7 + 4$. The following discussion focuses on investigating the commutative property of addition, not on whether the equation is true or false.

Teacher: [*Pointing at $5 + 3 = 3 + 5$ on the board*] Is it true or false?

Carmen: True, because $5 + 3$ is 8 and $3 + 5$ is 8.

Andy: There is a 5 on both sides and a 3 on both sides and nothing else.

Teacher: [*Writing $6 + 9 = 9 + 6$ on the board*] True or false?

Children:	True. Same reasons!
Teacher:	[*Writing 25 + 48 = 48 + 25 on the board*] True or false?
Children:	True!
Teacher:	Who can describe what is going on with these examples?
Rene:	If you have the same numbers on each side, you get the same thing.
Teacher:	Does it matter what numbers I use?
Children:	No.
Teacher:	[*Writing a + 7 = 7 + a on the board*] What is *a*?
Michael:	It can be any number because it's on both sides.
Teacher:	[*Writing a + b = b + a on the board*] What are *a* and *b*?
Children:	Any number!

Notice how the teacher is developing the aspects of the commutative property in a conceptual manner—focusing on exemplars to guide children to generalize rather than asking them to memorize the properties as their first experience, which can be a meaningless, rote activity.

You can follow specific examples, such as those used in the preceding dialogue, by asking children to try to state the idea in words without using specific numbers. If the generalization is not clear or entirely correct, have children discuss and modify the wording until all agree with and understand the wording. Write this verbal statement of the property on the board.

Making a conjecture and attempting to justify or prove that conjecture is true is a significant form of algebraic reasoning and is at the heart of what it means to do mathematics (Ball & Bass, 2003; Carpenter, Franke, & Levi, 2003; Schifter, 1999; Schifter, Monk, Russell, & Bastable, 2007). Therefore, when children make conjectures in class, rather than respond with an answer, ask, "Do you think that is always true? How can we find out?" Children need

**Standards for
Mathematical Practice**

**3 Construct
viable arguments
and critique the
reasoning of others**

**Standards for
Mathematical Practice**

**7 Look for and
make use of structure**

Table 13.1 Properties of the Operations for Pre-K–2

Name of Property	Symbolic Representation	How Children Might Describe the Pattern or Structure
Commutative	$a + b = b + a$	"When you add two numbers in any order, you'll get the same answer."
Associative	$(a + b) + c = a + (b + c)$	"When you add three numbers, you can add the first two and then add the third or add the last two numbers and then add the first number. Either way, you will get the same answer."
Additive Identity	$a + 0 = 0 + a = a$	"When you add zero to any number, you get the same number you started with."
	$a - 0 = a$	"When you subtract zero from any number, you get the number you started with."
Additive Inverse	$a - a = 0*$	"When you subtract a number from itself, you get zero."
Inverse Relationship of Addition and Subtraction	If $a + b = c$ then $c - b = a$ and $c - a = b$	"When you have a subtraction problem you can 'think addition' by using the inverse."

*The additive inverse property is usually written as $a + (-a) = 0$, but the symbolic representation $a - a = 0$ will make more sense to elementary children.

to reason through ideas based on their own thinking rather than simply relying on the word of others.

The most common form of justification for young children is the use of examples. Some children will be satisfied to try one or two examples. Others will try several but will not vary those examples in terms of size or other characteristics, such as using even and odd numbers. Still others will try very large numbers as substitutes for "any" number. Encourage children to use a wide variety of examples. After trying their examples, they may respond, "See? It works for any number you try." Proof by example will hopefully lead to someone asking, "How do we know there aren't some numbers that it doesn't work for?"

Children may reason with physical materials or illustrations to show the reasoning behind the conjecture (see Figure 13.5). What moves this beyond "proof by example" is an explanation such as "It would work this way no matter what the numbers are."

Figure 13.5

Using manipulatives to generalize the commutative property.

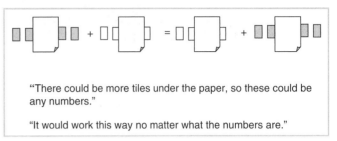

"There could be more tiles under the paper, so these could be any numbers."

"It would work this way no matter what the numbers are."

♦ Odd and Even Relationships

The categorization of numbers as odd or even is an important structure in our number system. All too often children are simply told that the even numbers are those that end in 0, 2, 4, 6, or 8 and odd numbers are those that end in 1, 3, 5, 7, or 9. Although this is true, it is only an attribute of even and odd numbers rather than a definition that explains what *even* or *not even* (i.e., *odd*) really means. The next two activities help children develop conceptual ideas of even and odd numbers without forcing definitions. In fact, after these activities children should be able to describe in their own words what we mean by odd and even numbers.

◀ *Activity* 13.12 **FAIR SHARES FOR TWO**

Tell a story about two twin sisters (or brothers). The twins always shared whatever they had equally. If they found some pretty seashells, they would count them out and share them so that each had the same number of shells. When Mom gave them cookies for lunch, they would be sure that each got the same number of cookies. Sometimes they were not able to share things fairly because there would be something left over. This happened once when Dad gave them five marbles. (Discuss why they could not share five marbles equally.) Whenever there was a leftover, the twins put the extra item in a special box of "leftovers" that they decided to keep for their baby brother.

After discussing the way that the twins shared things, ask children to find out what numbers of things they could share fairly and what numbers would have a leftover when they shared them. Assign three or four numbers from 6 to 40 to pairs of children. Their task is to decide which of their numbers could be shared fairly and which would have a leftover. Provide linking cubes to help them in their investigation. Collect the information and make lists of numbers that can be shared and those that will have a leftover. Examine the lists as a class and ask for observations. Select numbers not in the list and ask if children can tell which list they belong in and why they think so.

The critical portion of the last activity is the discussion. Notice how the children used the linking cubes in their investigation. Some children counted out the number of cubes and then distributed the cubes one by one to each twin. They either kept track of the fair

Figure 13.6

Sharing cubes fairly with two people.

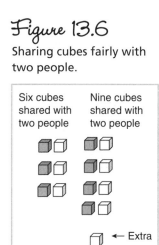

sharing (e.g., one for this twin, one for that twin; two for this twin, two for that twin, and so on) or they had to count at the end to determine if each twin received the same amount. Others may have organized their cubes by pairing them together to make sure that each twin received the same amount (see Figure 13.6). Have children share how they used their linking cubes and ask which ways (or to identify a way to) help them quickly see that the twins received the same amount. Based on this activity, *an even number is an amount that can be shared fairly or split into two equal parts with no leftovers. An odd number is one that is not even or cannot be split into two equal parts.* Challenge the children to use their own words to describe the numbers. The number endings of 0, 2, 4, 6, and 8 are only an interesting and useful pattern or observation and should not be used as the definition of an even number.

The next activity focuses on the same concept of even and odd but this time children start with visual representations of even and odd numbers.

Activity 13.13 BUMPS OR NO BUMPS

Create sets of "two-column cards" on card stock (see Figure 13.7) for groups of three to four children (see Blackline Master 34). In their groups, children are to see how many things they can find to tell about the pieces. (For example: There is a piece for each number 1 to 10. Some are like rectangles. Some have a square sticking out.) For those who might need a start, suggest that they put the pieces in order from one square to ten. After having some time to explore and share ideas they have noticed, have children sort their pieces into two sets. It is very likely that some group will sort the pieces as shown in Figure 13.7. (If no one sorts the pieces this way, do so on a projector and ask what rule you are using to sort them.) Use children's language to describe the pieces representing the odd numbers. For example, someone may describe the seven piece as having a "bump."

Next, assign the groups of children three or four numbers between 11 and 50 and have them decide whether two-column cards for these numbers would have bumps or no bumps (or whatever language children used). Have linking cubes available for their investigation. Have them use words and pictures to explain their conclusions.

Figure 13.7

Two-column pieces are separated into pieces with "bumps" and "no bumps." Note that these are also odd and even numbers. Why?

Stop and Reflect

Think for a moment how you might prove that the sum of two odd numbers is always even. How might the two-column pieces used in the activity "Bumps or No Bumps" be useful? ◼

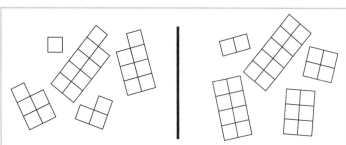

Once children have described in their own words a general way to describe these numbers, introduce the terminology *odd* and *even* numbers. As in "Fair Shares for Two," children will eventually see that numbers with "bumps" end in 1, 3, 5, 7, or 9 and even numbers end in 0, 2, 4, 6, or 8.

As an extension exploration to "Bumps or No Bumps," ask children what kind of piece they will get when two pieces in the set are added together to create a new two-column piece.

Patterns and Functions

Patterns are found in all areas of mathematics. Learning to look for, describe, and extend patterns are important processes in thinking algebraically. Two of the eight mathematical practices (CCSSO, 2010) actually begin with the phrase "look for," implying that children who are mathematically proficient pay attention to patterns as they do mathematics.

In grades pre-K–2 repeating and then growing patterns have often been a strong focus, but they are not explicitly mentioned in the *Common Core State Standards*. This does not mean that patterns are not useful. In fact, patterns provide opportunities for children to look for structure and express regularity in situations. The point is that the goal is not to have children do patterns just to do patterns. Rather children should be engaged in looking for, describing, and extending patterns to help them develop the skills to look for structure and express regularity in all mathematical situations.

When possible, patterning activities should involve some form of physical materials. Many kindergarten and first-grade textbooks have pages where children are given a pattern such as a string of colored beads. The task may be to color the last bead or two in the string. There are two differences between this and the same activity done with actual materials. First, by coloring on the page, the activity takes on an aura of right versus wrong. If a mistake is made, correction on the page is difficult and can cause feelings of inadequacy. Physical materials, on the other hand, allow a trial-and-error approach to be used. Second, pattern activities on worksheets prevent children from extending patterns beyond the few spaces provided by the page. By using materials such as colored blocks, buttons, and connecting cubes to create and extend their patterns, children gain more experience thinking about patterns because the patterns can be extended well beyond a few elements. Plus, when patterns are built with materials, children are able to test the extension of a pattern and make changes without fear of being wrong.

Standards for Mathematical Practice

7 Look for and make use of structure

8 Look for and express regularity in reasoning

Repeating Patterns

The concept of a repeating pattern and how a pattern is extended or continued can be introduced to the full class in several ways. One possibility is to draw simple shape patterns on the board and extend them in a class discussion. Oral patterns can be recited. For example, "do, mi, mi, do, mi, mi, . . ." is a simple singing pattern. Body movements such as moving the arm up, down, and sideways can be used to make patterns: up, side, side, down, up, side, side, down.

technology note

There are several websites that offer children opportunities to explore repeating patterns. For example, PBS Kids offers an interactive site for young children (www.pbs.org/teachers/connect/resources/7661/preview). NCTM's Illuminations Activity called "Patch Tool" (http://illuminations.nctm.org/ActivityDetail.aspx?ID=27) allows children to flip and rotate shapes to create various patterns, which informally introduces them to geometric transformations. The National Library of Virtual Manipulatives also has several applets that support the exploration of repeated (and growing) patterns, including Attribute Trains, Color Patterns, and Pattern Blocks (http://nlvm.usu.edu/en/nav/grade_g_1.html).

An important concept in working with repeating patterns is for children to identify the core of the pattern (Warren & Cooper, 2008). The core of a repeating pattern is the shortest string of elements that repeats. Notice in Figure 13.8 that the core is always fully repeated and never only partially shown.

Children can explore patterns with all sorts of materials, as shown in the following activity.

Figure 13.8

Examples of repeating patterns using manipulatives.

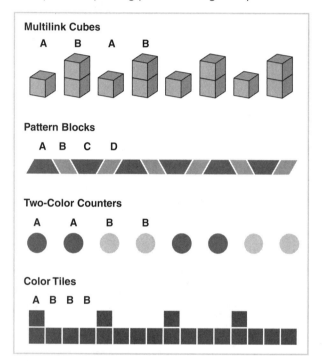

Activity 13.14 REPEAT THAT PATTERN

Children can work independently or in groups of two or three to extend patterns made from simple materials: buttons, colored blocks, connecting cubes, toothpicks, geometric shapes—items you can gather easily. For each set of materials, draw or build two or three complete repetitions so the core is obvious. The children's task is to extend it. Figure 13.8 illustrates one possible pattern for a variety of manipulatives. Children can build their own patterns and then trade with a partner and work on identifying the core and extending their partner's pattern. In the follow-up discussion, children should be able to identify the patterns as AB, ABC, ABBA, or whatever core is represented. For children with disabilities, you may need to ask them to say the name of the color or shape as they look at the manipulatives to help support identifying the pattern.

Alternatively, you can create several pattern strips using various materials that have been glued onto strips of card stock in a repeating pattern (see Figure 13.9) and place the pattern strips and corresponding sets of materials at a center. Children identify the core of the pattern on the pattern strips and then use the sets of materials to extend the pattern. They can take digital pictures to record their finished product.

The following activity helps children work on identifying the core of a pattern.

Activity 13.15 CAN YOU MATCH IT?

Using the board or a projector, show six or seven patterns with different materials or pictures. Half of the class closes their eyes while the other half uses the A, B, C method to read a pattern that you point to. After hearing the pattern, the children who had their eyes closed examine the patterns and try to decide which pattern was read. If two of the patterns in the list have the same structure, the discussion can be very interesting.

Standards for
Mathematical Practice

7 Look for and
make use of structure

A significant step forward mathematically is to see that two patterns constructed with different materials are actually the same pattern. For example, the third pattern in Figure 13.8 and the third pattern in Figure 13.9 can both be "read" A-A-B-B-A-A-B-B, and the pattern above those in both figures is A-B-C-D-A-B-C-D. Translating two or more essentially alike patterns to a common format helps children to move beyond the materials making up the pattern to see the fundamental mathematical structure involved. Using some form of symbolism (in this case, the alphabet) to represent the structure of a pattern helps children generalize the pattern.

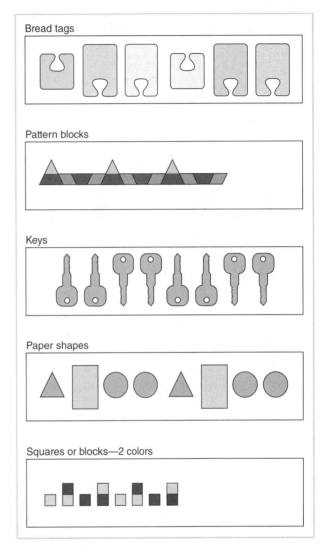

Figure 13.9

Examples of pattern cards on card stock. Each pattern completely repeats its core at least twice.

Bread tags

Pattern blocks

Keys

Paper shapes

Squares or blocks—2 colors

Activity 13.16 SAME PATTERN, DIFFERENT STUFF

Give each child a pattern strip like those shown in Figure 13.9 and a set of materials that is different from that on the pattern strip. Have children make a pattern with the set of materials that has the same structure as the pattern on the strip. You can also mix up the pattern strips and have children find strips that have the same pattern structure. To test if two patterns are the same, children can translate each of the strips into a third set of materials or they can write down the A, B, C pattern for each.

Though geometric patterns and motions like clapping are good ways to introduce patterns, it is important that children see patterns in the world around them. The seasons, days of the week, and months of the year are just a beginning. Challenge children to identify AB patterns in their daily activities—for example, "set the table before eating, clear the table after eating."

Children's books can also be a great resource for patterns. For example, a very long repeating pattern can be found in *If You Give a Mouse a Cookie* (Numeroff, 1985), in which each event eventually leads back to giving a mouse a cookie, implying that the sequence should be repeated.

◆ Growing Patterns

Beginning in the primary grades, children can begin to explore patterns that involve a progression from step to step. In technical terms, these are called *sequences;* we will simply call them *growing patterns*. Figure 13.10 shows different examples of growing patterns. With growing patterns, children identify the core, as with repeating patterns, but they also look for a generalization or a relationship that will tell them how the pattern is changing—and ultimately, in later grades, what the pattern will be at any point along the way (e.g., the *n*th term). Figure 13.10d is a growing pattern in which design 1 requires 4 cubes, design 2 requires 8 cubes, and so on—so we can say that the number of cubes needed is a function of the design (which happens to be the function: number of cubes = 4 × design number).

For children in grades K–2, the first thing to do with growing patterns is to have children build the pattern (replicate what they see) and extend the pattern (build the next one in the sequence). Geometric patterns made with physical materials (e.g., tiles, counters, cubes) make good exemplars because the pattern is easier to see (than with numbers) and because children can manipulate the objects. Some growing patterns get quite large quickly and can require more materials than you may have. One solution to this dilemma is to have children make a step with materials and then draw it on grid paper. In this way, they will only need enough materials to make one step at a time.

The following activity will introduce growing patterns to your children.

Figure 13.10

Geometric growing patterns using manipulatives.

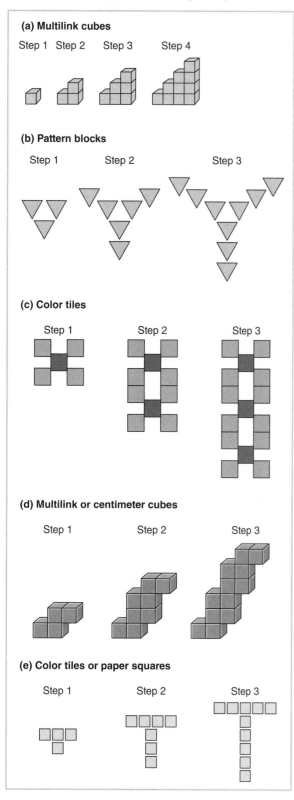

(a) Multilink cubes

Step 1   Step 2   Step 3   Step 4

(b) Pattern blocks

Step 1   Step 2   Step 3

(c) Color tiles

Step 1   Step 2   Step 3

(d) Multilink or centimeter cubes

Step 1   Step 2   Step 3

(e) Color tiles or paper squares

Step 1   Step 2   Step 3

Activity 13.17 **EXTEND AND EXPLAIN**

Show children the first three or four steps of a pattern. Provide them with appropriate materials and grid paper, have them extend the patterns recording each step, and explain why their extension indeed follows the pattern.

When discussing a pattern, children should try to determine how each step in the pattern differs from the preceding step.

Teaching Tip

Two important questions help children analyze growing patterns in order to determine the general relationship: What is staying the same? What is changing?

If each new step can be built by adding on to or changing the previous step, the discussion should include how this can be done.

Stop and Reflect

Before reading further, what is the relationship between the steps in the each of the patterns shown in Figure 13.10? What changes from the first step to the second step? From the second step to the third step? ■

Each stair step in Figure 13.10a can be made by adding a column of blocks to the preceding stair steps. The pattern in Figure 13.10e involves adding three tiles to each new figure, two to the vertical part and one to the horizontal part of the figure. Circling the part that is the same in adjacent terms may help identify what is changing.

The children's book *Two of Everything* (Hong, 1993) describes a magic pot in which anything that falls into it is doubled. This scenario is a growing pattern. McNamara (2010) describes using this book with second graders who determined a rule for explaining how much would come out of the magic pot (output) when told how much went in (input).

The next activity builds on a similar idea by creating a function machine.

Figure 13.11

A function machine is used to play "Guess My Rule." Children suggest input numbers and the machine operator records the output value.

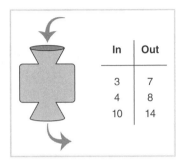

In	Out
3	7
4	8
10	14

Activity 13.18 GUESS MY RULE

Draw a simple in–out "machine" on the board, as shown in Figure 13.11. The "operator" of the machine knows the secret rule that is stored in the machine that changes whatever is put into it. For example, the secret rule might be "double the input number and add 1." Children try to guess the rule by putting numbers into the machine and observing what comes out. A list of in–out pairs is kept on the board. Children who think they have guessed the rule raise their hands. As more numbers are put into the machine, those children who think they know the rule tell what comes out. Continue until most have guessed the rule.

"Guess My Rule" can be played with the whole class, or children can play in small groups, perhaps as a station activity. Provide a collection of rules on cards. Include at least three examples so that the function machine operator is sure to understand the rule.

The guesses can be kept in a chart on paper that all players can see. Eventually children can make up their own rules to try to stump their classmates.

◆ Number Patterns

Our number system is also full of wonderful patterns. Numbers not only offer children an opportunity to explore patterns but also to learn to expect, see, and use patterns in all of mathematics.

The simplest form of a number pattern is a string of numbers that follows some rule for determining how the string continues. Consider the following activity, which includes some repeating patterns and some growing patterns as well as some other kinds of relationships.

Skip counts by 2, 5, and 10, already a part of most K–2 curricula, can be an excellent source of patterns and can help children reason about number relationships (e.g., comparing skip counting by twos and by threes leads to revealing that both counts include 6, 12, 18, . . .).

> ### Teaching Tip
> With a large empty box, you can have a volunteer inside a function machine generating the output. This can become a fun daily routine, switching who is the function machine operator.

Activity 13.19 WHAT'S NEXT AND WHY?

Show children five or six numbers from a number pattern. The task is to extend the pattern for several more numbers and to explain the rule for generating the pattern. The difficulty of the task depends on the number pattern and how familiar the children are with searching for patterns. Here are some recommended patterns to try.

1, 2, 1, 2, 1, 2, . . .	a simple alternating scheme
1, 2, 2, 3, 3, 3, . . .	each digit repeats according to its value
2, 4, 6, 8, 10, . . .	even numbers—skip counting by 2
1, 2, 4, 8, 16, . . .	double the previous number
2, 5, 11, 23, . . .	double the previous number and add 1
1, 2, 4, 7, 11, 16, . . .	successively increase the skip count
2, 2, 4, 6, 10, 16, . . .	add the preceding two numbers

Most of the preceding examples also have variations you can try. Challenge children to make up their own number pattern rules.

The calculator can skip-count by any amount beginning anywhere. For example, to count by threes, enter 0 [+] 3 [=]. (The 0 isn't necessary but is a good idea with young children.) Successive presses of the [=] key will count on from 3 by threes. To skip count by threes from a different number, say, 16, simply press 16 [+] 3 and continue pressing the [=] key. What is happening is that the calculator "remembers" the last operation, in this case "[+]3," and adds that to whatever is currently in the window whenever the [=] key is pressed. The [=] will continue to have this effect until an operation key is pressed.

◀ *Activity* 13.20 **CALCULATOR SKIP COUNTING**

If you have not done so previously, teach children how to make their calculators count by twos. When the children are able to do this without pressing a new operation key— which is what they have a tendency to do—show them how to change the beginning number. For example, press 5 [+] 2 [=], [=], [=], ... They can return to beginning the count at 5 (or any other number) by pressing 5 and continuing to press [=].

Now challenge children working in pairs to say the next number before they press the [=] key. Have them hold their finger over the [=] button and say the next skip count, press the [=] to confirm or correct, and then continue, always trying to say the next count before pressing the key.

As children skip count on the calculator, discuss the patterns that they see. For example, when counting by twos starting with 0, they see numbers ending in 0, 2, 4, 6, and 8, and then that pattern repeats. Note that this same sequence appears if you begin with any even number, such as 34 (although the sequence begins with 4 instead of 0). If counting by twos beginning with 1, the numbers are odd: 1, 3, 5, 7, and 9.

When children have become comfortable skip counting by small numbers, suggest that they try a "big" number. Suggest they count by 20 or 50. These large numbers will seem very difficult to children, who will then be surprised to recognize familiar patterns in the tens and hundreds places. Continue as appropriate with challenges to count by 25 or by 30 or 40. Other good skip-count numbers are 9, 11, 12, 15, or 21.

Focusing on patterns in skip counting will support children's use of invented strategies for multiplication. In fact, the key to exploring patterns in the elementary curriculum is not to identify patterns for patterns' sake but to strengthen children's understanding of number relationships and properties. The more often you can ask children, "Did you notice a pattern?" the more they are considering and making sense of the mathematics they are doing.

Standards for
Mathematical Practice

1 Make sense
of problems and
persevere in
solving them

Expanded Lesson

One Up and One Down

Content and Task Decisions

Grade Level: K–1

Mathematics Goals

- To discover and explore number patterns within the context of addition
- To understand how complementary changes in two addends leave the sum unchanged

Grade Level Guide

NCTM *Curriculum Focal Points*	Common *Core State Standards*
In a focal point connection under "Algebra" at both kindergarten and grade 1, children work with number patterns to explore relationships that will eventually result in the creation of generalizable rules.	In the domain of Operations and Algebraic Thinking, kindergartners add by using a variety of ways to represent the problems. In first grade, children add using the relationship between addition and subtraction and are expected to understand the meaning of the equal sign.

Consider the Children's Needs

Children need not know their addition combinations to engage in this lesson. However, they should have been exposed to the plus and equal signs and understand how an addition equation is a representation of two parts of a whole.

For English Language Learners

- Be sure that the children know the words "up" and "down," which can be acted out by asking children to stand up and sit down (emphasizing the words *up* and *down*).
- As needed, provide translations for the numbers.

For Children with Disabilities

- Use a mathematics balance (a plastic "number line" on a fulcrum). This can be used to dramatically model the movement of one hanging weight and the effect it has on the balance of the equation. If you do not have such a balance, use a two-sided mat with an equal sign in the middle to have the children demonstrate making equations that show that what is on the left side of the mat is the same as (or equal to) what is on the right side of the mat.

Materials

Each child will need:

- Counters
- Calculators (optional)

Lesson

Before

Present the focus task to the class:

- Explain this problem: "The other day, a friend of mine was thinking about adding 7 + 7." Write 7 + 7 on the board. "She wondered what would happen if she made the first 7 one more and the second 7 one less." With the children's help, write this new sum, 8 + 6, on the board. Have the children complete each equation.
- Ask, "Why do you think the answers are the same?" Have the children offer their ideas. Ask, "Do you think this same plan will work if we started with 5 + 5 or 8 + 8?" Discuss this briefly.
- To differentiate the task, some children could use counters to try to figure out why 7 + 7 and 8 + 6 have the same answers. Then try another sum, such as 5 + 5, and see if it works for that sum also.
- For more advanced children, the task is to use counters and try to figure out why 7 + 7 and 8 + 6 have the same answers. Will it work for any double (e.g., 5 + 5, 6 + 6, 8 + 8, and so on)? What if the two numbers you begin with are not the same?
- The children should use pictures, numbers, and words to show their thinking. If others pick up the papers, they should be able to understand the children's ideas.

Provide clear expectations:

- You may want to have children work in pairs. Work could be shown on large chart paper to be shared with the class.

During

Initially:

- Observe that children have access to the materials they need to solve the problem. Observe that each child understands the question and is in the process of attempting to solve the first situation.

Ongoing:

- Some children may use their counters and complete each sum independently without relating one to the other. Ask these children to show you 7 + 7 with counters. Be sure that there are two separate piles of 7 and not a single pile of 14. Ask, "How could you change these piles to show 8 + 6?" Observe how the children make the changes so that later you can invite the children to show their different ways.

- Encourage children to get their ideas on paper for the 7 + 7 case before they explore further.

- How much you push children to explore further depends on the abilities and maturity of the children. In the lower grades, you might remind them to try another double such as 5 + 5 and see if the same thing works there. Older children can be challenged with more open-ended explorations, such as "Does it always work? Do you have to start with a double? What if you change the numbers by 2 or some other number? What about really big numbers like 87 + 87?" (For large numbers, children should be encouraged to use calculators, even if they cannot compute the sums by hand.)

- For those children who may find this exploration rather easy, challenge them to see how this might work for subtraction.

After

Bring the class together to share and discuss the task:

- Select children to share their ideas. Perhaps call first on children who have struggled and need to be en-couraged. Although it is good for children to see the more sophisticated ideas, it is important to also focus on emerging ideas as well. For each child who shares, encourage the children to ask questions or to offer additional ideas.

- Some children may have difficulty articulating their ideas. Suggest that they use counters on the overhead or magnetic counters on the board so that they can show the class their thinking.

- Ask the children how this idea could help them if they forgot how much 5 + 7 was. (5 + 7 will be the same as 6 + 6. Similarly, 6 + 8 is double 7, and so on.)

Assessment

Observe

- Especially for very young learners, be aware of children who do not have a clear connection between a model for addition—especially a part-part-whole model—and the symbolic equation that represents this. Many children learn only to use counters to get answers but do not see the counters as a way to show what the equation means.

- Children who shove counters together and begin counting at once to solve an addition equation are the most likely to have difficulty with this activity.

- A few children will see this activity as rather simple. These children have a good understanding of what addition means.

Ask

- How does changing one number (or pile of counters) up one and the other pile down one affect the sum? Why is that?

- Did you see a number pattern with your problems?

- What do you think would happen if we change the numbers by adding two to each?

14

Exploring Early Fraction Concepts

Big IDEAS

1 Fractions are numbers. They indicate a quantity and can be compared with other quantities.

2 Partitioning and iterating are two ways children can reason about fractions. Partitioning can be thought of as cutting or splitting an amount equally. Iterating can be thought of as physically or mentally making copies of a piece (unit fraction) and counting those pieces.

3 Fractional parts are equal shares or equal-sized portions of a whole or unit. A unit can be one object or a collection of objects.

4 Fractional parts have special names that tell how many parts of that size are needed to make the whole. For example, thirds require three parts to make a whole.

5 The more fractional parts used to make a whole, the smaller the parts. For example, thirds are smaller than halves.

Fractions have always presented a considerable challenge for students, even into the middle grades. NAEP results have consistently shown that students have a weak understanding of fraction concepts (Sowder & Wearne, 2006; Wearne & Kouba, 2000). You can help children in the primary grades begin to construct a foundation for fraction concepts that will prepare them for the more complex concepts and skills that come later in the elementary and middle school curricula.

The *Curriculum Focal Points* (National Council of Teachers of Mathematics, 2006) and the *Common Core State Standards* (CCSSO, 2010) recommend that formal instruction on fraction concepts begin in third grade. However, that does not mean that you cannot build on children's everyday experiences to begin to develop informal knowledge and understanding about fractions before third grade. In fact, the *Common Core State Standards* include partitioning geometric shapes into equal shares at both the first and second grade levels. In first grade, children are introduced to fractions through the partitioning of circles and rectangles into two and four equal-sized shares (Standard 1.G.A.3). First graders are also expected to know the vocabulary *halves, fourths,* and *quarters* and to tell time to the nearest half hour. Second graders extend this work to partitioning circles and rectangles into *thirds* or three equal-sized shares (Standard 2.G.A.3).

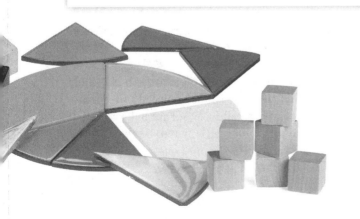

 **Meanings of Fractions for Pre-K–2 Children**

To help children develop a comprehensive understanding of fractions, a report completed by the Institute of Education Sciences (IES) (Siegler et al., 2010) recommends that children have experiences involving the different meanings of fractions. The different meanings include part–whole, division, measurement, ratio, and operator. For grades pre-K–2, we emphasize part–whole, division, and measurement.

◆ Part–Whole

One of the most commonly used meanings of fractions is the part–whole relationship. In early childhood classrooms, part–whole fractions are typically represented by shading part of a whole that has been partitioned into equal parts ($\frac{3}{4}$ of a rug). Part–whole situations can also be described as part of a group of children ($\frac{1}{3}$ of the class brought their lunch) or as part of a length (we walked $1\frac{1}{2}$ miles). The first example (shading part of a whole to indicate area) and the third example (walked $1\frac{1}{2}$ miles) use continuous quantities, that is, quantities that are measured and that can be cut into as many equal parts as we wish. The second example ($\frac{1}{3}$ of the class) uses discrete quantities, that is, quantities that represent objects that cannot be divided further (e.g., a person, a chair, a car).

Although the part–whole meaning of fractions is important, too often instruction based only on the part–whole relationship leaves children with little sense that fractions are numbers. Also fractional amounts arise naturally from partitioning amounts in everyday life. For these reasons, initial instruction should focus on the next meaning of fractions: equal sharing.

◆ Equal Sharing

Standards for Mathematical Practice

2 **Reason abstractly and quantitatively** ▶

Equal sharing is an idea that young children understand intuitively because of their experiences sharing things with brothers, sisters, friends, and so on. Consider the idea of four children fairly sharing two sticks of clay so they can make clay animals. Fractions emerge naturally from this scenario. Because of the meaningful connections that can be made, early fraction instruction should build from young children's experiences of sharing and partitioning (Empson & Levi, 2011; Lamon, 2012; Siegler et al., 2010).

Equal sharing situations can use continuous or discrete quantities. The example with two sticks of clay is an example of a continuous quantity because theoretically we could cut the stick into as many equal pieces as we want. For equal sharing situations that use discrete quantities, it is best with young children to use story problems that have whole-number solutions with no remainders. (These story problems with discrete quantities are the same as the partition problems discussed in Chapter 9.) Consider these story problems:

- There are 12 chairs and 4 tables in a classroom. If we want the same number of chairs around each table, how many chairs will be placed around a table?
- There are 14 chairs and 4 tables in a classroom. If we want the same number of chairs around each table, how many chairs will be placed around a table?

The solution for both problems (how many chairs will be placed around a table) is a whole number (3). But in the second problem there are 2 chairs that cannot be placed and, because chairs are discrete objects, they cannot be split or cut into smaller parts that can be shared. If your goal is to have children think about fractional parts, you want them to be able to share fairly all the objects in the situation. So it is important to use continuous quantities when there are remainders so those can be cut into as many equal parts as needed.

◈ Measurement

Although the *Common Core State Standards* recommend limiting linear measurement in grades K–2 to whole units (e.g., inches, feet, centimeters, meters), fractions often emerge naturally in many measurement situations. Linear measurement involves identifying a unit of length and then using that unit to determine the length of an object. For example, using the unit of an inch, a child could use multiple copies of an inch to determine that a pencil is 5 inches long. Similarly for fractions, a child can use a fraction strip that represents the unit fraction $\frac{1}{3}$ to count or measure to show that it takes four units to reach $\frac{4}{3}$.

Measurement also includes time. The most obvious place to relate fractions and time is when telling time to the half hour and quarter hour. This would involve identifying the unit of time as an hour. Making the hour unit explicit is key. Emphasize how the minute hand sweeps a full turn around an analog clock face to measure an hour. Halfway measures half that time or half of an hour. Half of that measures a quarter of the time by splitting the hour into four equal quantities of time. When second graders progress to telling time in smaller increments of 5-minute intervals, the connection between time and fractions becomes less obvious.

Measurement situations by their very nature consist of measuring a quantity that we could cut into as many equal-sized pieces as we need and so involve continuous quantities.

Fractions Are Numbers, Too!

One of the most significant ideas for children to develop about fractions is the sense that fractions are numbers—quantities that have values. You may have never heard the terms *partitioning* (splitting equally) and *iterating* (counting a repeated amount) but, as you will see, they connect to whole-number concepts you will recognize. Researchers have acknowledged for some time the importance of these two actions to meaningfully working with fractions (e.g., Olive, 2002; Pothier & Sawada, 1990). These actions, in particular, emphasize the numerical nature of fractions. When children explain how they thought about fractional situations, listen for these ideas.

◈ Partitioning

Partitioning can be thought of as splitting or cutting a quantity equally. Young children are engaged in the act of partitioning from an early age when they split a group of 6 into 3 and 3. Connecting this informal knowledge to *fair* sharing and then to more formal fraction concepts is key to providing effective initial fraction instruction in grades pre-K–2. You can do this by posing story problems that involve equal sharing. In fact, using story problems is the primary method for facilitating children's fraction learning at the pre-K–2 level. Consider the following example that uses a continuous quantity (candy bars) that can be cut into as many equal-sized pieces as we wish.

Six children want to share 5 candy bars fairly. How much will each child get?

When children answer questions such as "how much will each child get?" the idea that fractions are numbers will be reinforced.

Iterating

In whole-number learning, counting precedes learning to add and subtract. This is also true of fractions. Children should come to think of counting fractional parts in much the same way they might count apples or any other objects. Counting fractional parts to see how multiple parts compare to the whole helps children to understand the relationship between the parts of the whole. Children should be able to answer the question, "How many fourths are in one whole?" just as they know how many ones are in ten. This counting a repeated amount (e.g., unit fraction) is called *iterating*. Understanding that $\frac{3}{4}$ can be thought of as a count of three parts called *fourths* is an important idea for children to develop (Post, Wachsmuth, Lesh, & Behr, 1985; Siebert & Gaskin, 2006; Tzur, 1999).

 Models for Fractions

Substantial evidence suggests that the effective use of physical models in fraction tasks is important (Cramer & Henry, 2002; Empson & Levi, 2011; Siebert & Gaskin, 2006). Unfortunately, when textbooks use physical models, they tend to use only area models, in particular fraction circles, with little attention to length or set models (Hodges, Cady, & Collins, 2008). Using a variety of physical models that represent both continuous and discrete quantities is critical for children to make sense of fractions as they explore fractions in a variety of situations.

◆ Area Models

Circular fraction pieces are by far the most commonly used area model. One of the advantages of the circular model is that it emphasizes the part–whole concept of fractions and, in particular, the relative size of a part to the whole (Cramer, Wyberg, and Leavitt, 2008). What is being compared is the area of the part to the area of the whole. Because we can cut area into as many equal-sized pieces as we want and because area is measured, it falls into the category of a continuous quantity. Note that when drawing circles, children (and adults) can find it difficult to partition the circle into reasonably equal-sized parts. There are many other area models including pattern blocks, geoboards, color tiles, and fraction bars. Regions, such as rectangles, can also be drawn on blank or grid paper. The other physical models in Figure 14.1 demonstrate how different shapes can represent the whole.

◆ Length Models

With length models, lengths or linear measurements are compared instead of areas. In this model, a unit of length is compared to the whole length. We can cut a length into as many equal-sized pieces (units) as we want; therefore, length models represent continuous quantities. Length models appropriate for pre-K–2 include fraction strips, paper strips (e.g., adding-machine tape), Cuisenaire rods, and line segments (see Figure 14.2). All of these models provide flexibility because any length can represent the whole.

Researchers have identified number line models as useful in fraction instruction because they emphasize the idea that a fraction represents a quantity (Siegler et al., 2010). Locating fractions on a number line also highlights their relationship to other numbers, including other fractions. The number line has been shown as extremely effective with young children when working with whole numbers (e.g., Booth & Siegler, 2008; Fosnot & Dolk, 2001; Siegler & Ramani, 2009). Using this model with whole numbers can help prepare

Figure 14.1 Area models for fractions.

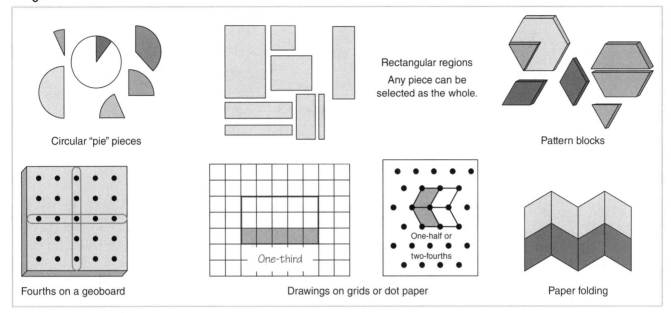

Circular "pie" pieces

Rectangular regions
Any piece can be selected as the whole.

Pattern blocks

Fourths on a geoboard

One-third

Drawings on grids or dot paper

One-half or two-fourths

Paper folding

these children to be ready to use this model with fractions in later grades. Using a modified version, line segments, for fraction instruction in grades pre-K–2 is ideal.

◆ Set Models

The whole in a set model is understood to be a set of objects, and subsets of the whole make up fractional parts. For example, 3 red counters are one-fourth of a set of 12 counters. The set of 12, in this example, represents the whole or 1. The idea of referring to a collection of counters as a single entity can make set models difficult for young children. To help children see the set of objects as a whole, put a loop of yarn around the set. Another challenge with set models is that children may focus on the size of the subset rather than the number of equal-sized subsets in the whole. For example, if 12 counters make a whole, then a subset of 4 counters is *one-third*, not one-fourth, because 3 equal-sized subsets make the whole. Discrete objects, like two-color counters, are frequently used for set models. They can easily be flipped to change their color to model various fractional parts of a whole set (see Figure 14.3).

Figure 14.2 Length or measurement models for fractions.

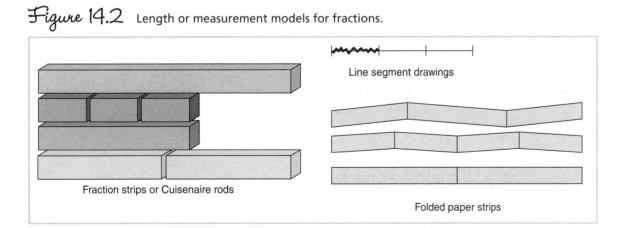

Line segment drawings

Fraction strips or Cuisenaire rods

Folded paper strips

Figure 14.3 Set models for fractions.

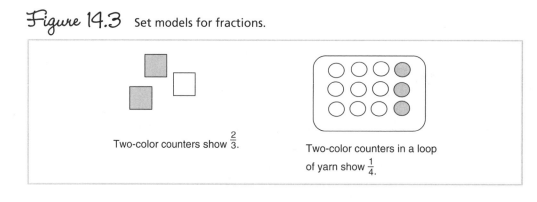

Two-color counters show $\frac{2}{3}$.

Two-color counters in a loop of yarn show $\frac{1}{4}$.

Introducing Fraction Language

Fraction symbolism represents a fairly complex convention that can be misleading to children. That is why it is important in grades pre-K–2 to use fraction words and postpone introducing fraction symbolism (e.g., Empson & Levi, 2011). Let children first focus on making sense of fractions without the complication of also trying to make sense of the symbolism.

Children will need to learn fraction vocabulary, such as *halves*, *thirds*, *fourths*, and *quarters*. A good time to introduce the vocabulary of fractional parts is *during* the discussions of children's solutions to story problems and not before. When a brownie or other whole has been partitioned into equal shares, simply say, "We call these *fourths*. The whole is cut into four equal-sized parts—fourths."

Children need to be aware of two aspects of fractional parts: (1) the number of parts and (2) the equality of the parts (in size, not necessarily in shape). Emphasize that the number of equal parts or fair shares that make up a whole determines the name of the fractional parts or shares. Children will likely be familiar with halves but should quickly learn to describe thirds and fourths.

Formative Assessment Note

Some children think that all fractional parts are called halves. Once a child has completed a partitioning story problem, ask the child to tell you how much each person gets. The word the child uses to describe the fractional amount will tell you if the child is overgeneralizing the word *half*.

Note that in the *Common Core State Standard for Mathematics*, halves and fourths are developed in first grade prior to thirds in second grade. This is done because successive halving of parts is a natural process for young children. Once children have been successful dealing with and explaining halves and fourths, pose sharing tasks that involve eighths. They will likely rely on their halving strategy to find a solution. Likewise, once children have demonstrated an understanding of thirds, pose sharing tasks that involve sixths.

In addition to helping children use the words *halves*, *thirds*, *fourths*, and *quarters*, be sure to make regular comparisons of fractional parts to the whole. Make it a point to use the term *whole*, *one whole*, or simply *one* so that children have a language that they can use regardless of the model involved.

Standards for
Mathematical Practice

**6 Attend to
precision**

Equal Sharing Tasks

Given children's experiences with fairly sharing items among family and friends, sharing tasks are a good place to begin the development of fractions. The sharing tasks allow children to develop concepts of fractions from an activity that makes sense to them, rather than having the structure imposed on them. In this approach children do not begin with traditional part–whole tasks of identifying halves, thirds, fourths, and so on. These fractional parts and children's understanding of part–whole fractions emerge as a result of their fair sharing in meaningful contexts.

Sharing tasks are generally posed in the form of a story problem involving a given number of objects that are to be shared equally among a given number of people. The problems and variations that follow are adapted from Empson (2002).

◆ Standards for
Mathematical Practice

1 Make sense of problems and persevere in solving them

Four children are sharing 10 brownies so that each one will get the same amount. How much will each child get?

Stop and Reflect

Before reading further, use a drawing with rectangles to represent the brownies and act out this problem as if you were a child. Based on your drawing, how much will each child get? ∎

For 10 brownies and 4 sharers, many children will deal out 2 brownies to each child and then halve each of the remaining brownies (see Figure 14.4).

These kinds of story problems include the following features:

- The objects in the story are easy to draw and partition (e.g., apples, bagels, cookies, brownies, quesadillas, pancakes, sticks of gum, sandwiches, pizzas, crackers, cake, candy bars, sticks of modeling clay, pretzel sticks, and so on).

- The story problem does not contain fractions. The fractions emerge as a result of the relationship between the number of objects to be shared and the number of people sharing. This allows children to make connections between their whole-number knowledge and their developing fraction knowledge.

◆ Standards for
Mathematical Practice

2 Reason abstractly and quantitatively

- Children can solve these kinds of problems without formal instruction and without knowing anything about fraction symbols. They can represent how much one person gets by shading in one share or showing one share with manipulatives.

You can differentiate these tasks by changing the numbers involved. Consider these variations in numbers:

- 5 brownies shared with 2 children
- 2 brownies shared with 4 children
- 5 brownies shared with 4 children
- 4 brownies shared with 8 children
- 3 brownies shared with 4 children

Figure 14.4 Ten brownies shared with four children. Each child gets $2\frac{1}{2}$ brownies.

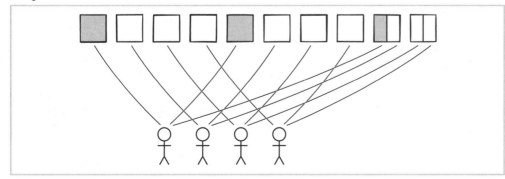

Stop and Reflect

Try drawing pictures for each of the preceding sharing tasks listed. Which do you think is most difficult? Which of these represents essentially the same degree of difficulty? What other tasks involving two, four, or eight sharers would you consider as similar, easier, or more difficult than these tasks? ■

When the numbers allow for some items to be distributed whole (five shared with two), some children will first share whole items and then cut up the leftovers. Others will slice every piece in half and then distribute the halves. When there are more sharers than items, some partitioning must happen at the beginning of the solution process. When children who are still using a halving strategy try to share five things among four children, they will eventually get down to two halves to give to four children. For some, the solution is to cut each half in half; that is, "each child gets a whole (or two halves) and a half of a half."

Stop and Reflect

Try solving the following variations using drawings. Can you solve them in different ways? ■

* 4 pizzas shared with 6 children
* 4 pizzas shared with 3 children
* 5 pizzas shared with 3 children

Figure 14.5 Three different sharing processes.

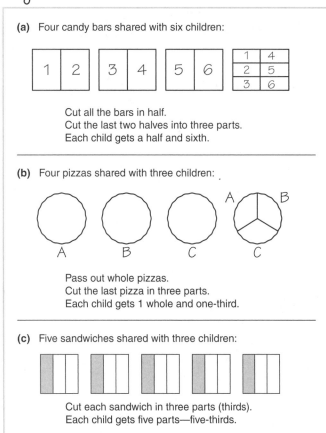

(a) Four candy bars shared with six children:

Cut all the bars in half.
Cut the last two halves into three parts.
Each child gets a half and sixth.

(b) Four pizzas shared with three children:

Pass out whole pizzas.
Cut the last pizza in three parts.
Each child gets 1 whole and one-third.

(c) Five sandwiches shared with three children:

Cut each sandwich in three parts (thirds).
Each child gets five parts—five-thirds.

Partitioning into 3 and 6 equal parts is challenging for children because they naturally want to use a halving strategy that does not work in these cases. Figure 14.5 shows some different sharing solutions that might be observed.

Considerable research has been done with children from first through eighth grades to determine how they go about the process of forming fair shares and how the tasks posed to children influence their responses (e.g., Empson & Levi, 2011; Lamon, 2012; Mack, 2001; Pothier & Sawada, 1990; Siegler et al., 2010). Researchers recommend following a progression of sharing tasks that builds on children's understanding of whole-number quantities and informal partitioning strategies (e.g., Empson & Levi, 2011; Siegler et al., 2010). Table 14.1 captures the following progression and provides examples of corresponding story problems.

1. *Begin with equal sharing problems whose solutions are whole numbers.* To begin with, it is easier for young children to share fairly a number of discrete objects (e.g., 14 apples with 7 people) than for them to share fairly one object (e.g., 1 pancake with 4 children). So begin with equal sharing situations in which the quantities to be shared

Table 14.1 Progression for Teaching with Equal Shares Story Problems.

Progression	Example Problems
1. Problems whose solutions are whole numbers.	Three children want to fairly share 15 grapes. How many grapes will each child get?
2. Problems with 2, 4, or 8 sharers and whose solutions are mixed numbers (greater than 1).	Two children want to share 5 quesadillas so that everyone gets the same amount. How much will each child get?
3. Problems with 2, 4, or 8 sharers and whose solutions are less than 1.	Four children want to share 3 cookies so that everyone gets the same amount. How much will each child get?
4. Problems with 3 sharers and whose solutions are mixed numbers (greater than 1).	Three children want to share 10 sticks of clay to make clay animals. If everyone gets the same amount, how much does each child get?
5. Problems with 3 sharers and whose solutions are less than 1.	Three children want to equally share 2 pizzas. How much does each child get?

are discrete objects. (Again, these situations are the same as the partition or fair sharing problems discussed in Chapter 9.) In the *Before* and the *After* portions of the lessons, emphasize that all of the objects must be shared and shared equally. This is an important idea to stress because once the scenarios require partitioning quantities into smaller pieces, some children will either not share all of the objects or not share them equally.

2. *Use equal sharing problems with 2, 4, or 8 sharers and whose solutions are mixed numbers.* Because children's initial strategies for sharing single objects involve halving, begin with 2, 4, and then 8 sharers. Using problems that have solutions that are larger than 1 enable children to relate their understanding of whole numbers to fractions and they actually find them easier to solve than problems whose solutions are less than 1.

3. *Use equal sharing problems with 2, 4, or 8 sharers and whose solutions are less than 1.* Again, problems with 2, 4, or 8 sharers capitalize on children's halving strategies. Problems with solutions less than 1 tend to be more difficult for young children.

4. *Next, use equal sharing problems with 3 sharers and whose solutions are mixed numbers.* For 3 sharers, children have to anticipate how to slice or cut the objects. Many children will attempt to use a repeated halving strategy or trial and error. Moving to 3 (and then 6 sharers) will force children to confront their tendencies to use halving strategies.

5. *Use equal sharing problems with 3 sharers and whose solutions are less than 1.* Again, children have to anticipate how to partition the objects.

As discussed in other chapters, when using story problems to help children construct mathematical ideas, having children share their solutions and explain their reasoning to each other is key. Make sure to look for significant ideas in children's work while they are solving the story problems that you can then highlight in the discussion (*After*) portion of the lesson.

Standards for
Mathematical Practice

3 Construct
viable arguments
and critique the
reasoning of others

technology note

"Kids and Cookies" (http://mathlanding.org/content/kids-and-cookies) is an interactive website where children can work on partitioning strategies in the context of fairly sharing cookies with friends. You can change the number of friends (up to 6), the shape of the cookie (round or rectangular), the number of cookies to share (up to 12), and the number of equal pieces you can cut a cookie into (halves, thirds, quarters, fifths, and sixths). If children want to change a partition, they can drag the cookie back to the cutting board or click a button to put one or all cookies back. The applet is also available in Spanish.

Formative Assessment Note

Young children can have difficulty drawing equal parts because they will not initially anticipate how to slice the object into equal parts (Empson & Levi, 2011; Siegler et al., 2010). Observe children as they draw pictures and begin to partition the objects. Note if they automatically begin halving for every scenario, even those for which halving will not work (e.g., 5 children equally sharing 3 bananas). This could be an indication that they are not anticipating how to partition objects. Especially when partitioning into equal groups of 3 and 6, children have to pay attention to the relationship between the number of objects and the number of sharers.

Teaching Tip

For children who have difficulty drawing equal parts, give them wooden coffee stirrers or thick uncooked spaghetti noodles to show the partitioning. This allows children to easily move the partitions as needed.

Initially some children do not partition amounts into equal-sized groups and, in particular, some children do not distinguish between the number of objects shared and the quantity shared—in other words, they may find an equal number of pieces without considering the size of the pieces. The next activity targets this difficulty.

Activity 14.1 FAIR AND UNFAIR SHARES

Standards for Mathematical Practice

▶ **3 Construct viable arguments and critique the reasoning of others**

As in Figure 14.6, show examples and nonexamples of fair shares. (Note that examples and nonexamples are very important to use with children with disabilities.) Have children identify the amounts that are equally partitioned and those that are not. For each response, have children explain their reasoning.

The activity should be done with a variety of models, including length and set models. The *Common Core State Standards* set as an expectation for second graders that they will recognize that "equal-sized parts" does not necessarily mean the same shape when using an area model. So if you teach second grade, make sure to include examples that illustrate this concept. Many children, in particular children with disabilities, will need to cut and move pieces around to check to make sure the parts are indeed equal in size.

In the "Fair and Unfair Shares" activity, the wholes are already partitioned either correctly or incorrectly; the children are not involved in the partitioning. So the most important part of this activity is the discussion. Use the discussion to reinforce the idea that all the pieces need to be shared and shared equally.

In the following activity, children create designated equal shares using physical models as opposed to drawing their own representations. You may want to start with an activity like this before you move to asking children to draw and partition their own representations.

Figure 14.6 Children learning about fractions through partitioning need to recognize when shares are not equal.

Activity 14.2 FINDING FAIR SHARES

Give children manipulatives identifying which piece represents one whole and have them find thirds or fourths or other fractional parts. Use a familiar context, such as friends sharing sandwiches or pizzas. (The physical models should never have fractions written on them.) Some ideas are suggested in Figure 14.7. Emphasize "ths" as you say the fractional parts, particularly for ELLs who may not hear the difference between fraction parts and wholes (e.g., *fourths* sounds like "fours"). Also write and discuss the meaning of the words *whole* and *hole*.

In Activity 14.2, children do not necessarily have to think of equal-sized pieces because the manipulatives automatically create them. Emphasize the need for equal-sized pieces whether manipulatives or student-generated representations are used. Activity 14.3 uses examples of line segments (length model) in which the partitioning is not completely illustrated. This can help children develop a stronger understanding of equal parts.

Teaching Tip

Activities such as Activity 14.2 are especially interesting when different wholes can be designated in the same physical model. That way, a given fractional part does not get identified with a special shape or color but instead with the relationship of the part to the designated whole.

Figure 14.7 Given a whole, find fractional parts.

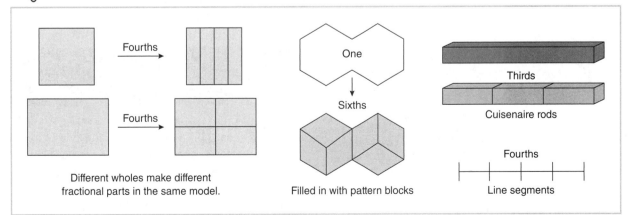

Different wholes make different fractional parts in the same model.

Filled in with pattern blocks

Cuisenaire rods

Line segments

Activity 14.3 HOW MUCH DID SHE SHARE?

Give children line segments partitioned such that only some of the partitions are showing. Use a context such as someone sharing licorice strings. For each line segment, ask "How much did Holly share? How do you know?"

Children can justify their reasoning by measuring the size of the sections that have been partitioned using paper strips or Cuisenaire rods.

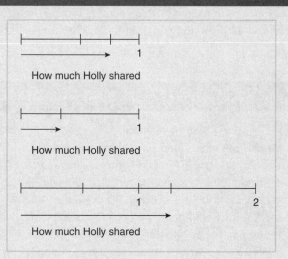

Teaching Tip

Make sure to use fractions greater than 1 ($\frac{10}{4}$) and mixed numbers ($2\frac{1}{2}$) along with fractions between 0 and 1. This helps children see that fractions can be any size and that they often fall between whole-number values.

Figure 14.8

Iterating fractional parts in an area model (see Blackline Masters 35–36).

BLM

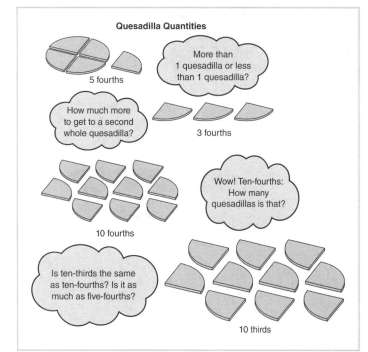

Children should engage in counting by fractional amounts to reinforce that fractions are numbers. Iterating or counting can be done with length models as well as area models. Display some circular fractional pieces in groups as shown in Figure 14.8. For each collection, tell children what type of piece is being shown and simply count them together: "*One*-fourth, *two*-fourths, *three*-fourths, *four*-fourths, *five*-fourths." Ask, "If we have five-fourths, is that more than one whole, less than one whole, or the same as one whole?"

As children count collections of parts, discuss the relationship to one whole. Make informal comparisons between different collections. "Why does it take more fourths to make a whole than thirds?" "Why did we get two wholes with four halves but just a little more than one whole with four thirds?" Take this opportunity to connect this language to mixed numbers. "What is another way we could say ten-fourths?" (Possible responses are two wholes and two-fourths, or two wholes and one-half, or one whole and six-fourths.)

With this introduction, children are ready for the following activity.

Activity 14.4 MORE, LESS, OR EQUAL TO ONE WHOLE

Give children a collection of fractional parts (all the same size pieces) and indicate the kind of fractional part they have. (Use either area or length models. Set models are too difficult for young children to use for iteration.) Parts can be drawn on a worksheet or physical models can be placed in plastic bags with an identifying card. For example, if done with Cuisenaire rods or fraction strips, the collection might have seven light green rods/strips with a caption or note indicating "each piece is an eighth." The task is to decide whether the collection is less than one whole, equal to one whole, or more than one whole. Ask children to draw pictures and/ or use fraction words to explain their answer. Adding a context, such as people sharing candy bars, pizzas, or sticks of clay, can help children understand and reason through the problem.

To develop a more comprehensive understanding of fractions, children need experiences partitioning regions or shapes (area models) as well as lengths and sets of objects. In the story problems you pose, make sure to include a variety of situations that can be represented with these different models. For example, the following story problems fit a length model, a set model, and an area model respectively:

- Marley, Zack, Rita, and Hannah want to share 5 pretzel sticks equally. How much will each of them get? (length)
- Marley and Zack want to share 11 grapes equally. How much will each of them get? (set)
- Marley, Zack, and Mia want to share 7 pieces of poster board equally. How much will each of them get? (area)

The objects to be shared can be drawn on paper as rectangles, circles, or line segments along with a statement of the problem. Some children may need to cut and physically distribute the pieces, so another possibility is to cut out construction paper circles or rectangles to represent the objects to be shared. You could use thin rectangles to represent objects of length. Children can use connecting cubes to make bars that they can separate into pieces. Or they can use more traditional fraction models such as circular "pie" pieces (area), Cuisenaire rods (length), or counters of different colors (sets).

As you create story problems and tasks for the children, remember the big ideas you are trying to help them construct: (1) Fractions are numbers and (2) fractional parts are equal shares or equal-sized portions of a whole or unit.

Fraction Ordering and Equivalence

Look for opportunities when children are solving equal sharing story problems in which they have what appear to be different answers but are actually equivalent amounts. For example, for the problem *4 children equally share 6 pancakes*, one child may distribute one whole pancake to each person and then halve the remaining two and say that each person gets *one and one-half* pancakes. A second child may also distribute one whole pancake to each person but partition the remaining two pancakes into fourths and say that each person gets *one and two-fourths*. A third child may partition each of the 6 pancakes into 4 equal parts (fourths) and say that each person gets *six fourths*. (See Figure 14.9.) Use the children's solutions to help them see that the same quantity is shared in each case. You can have children count the pieces together: "*one*-fourth, *two*-fourths, *three*-fourths, *four*-fourths, *five*-fourths, *six*-fourths." Ask, "If we have six-fourths, is that more than one whole, less than one whole, or the same as one whole?"

Once children are successful with equal sharing problems over an extended period of time (months, not days), you can extend sharing problems to situations in which children compare fractional amounts. For example, children can compare the amounts people would get if 2, 3, 4, and 6 people shared a brownie. *The Doorbell Rang* (Hutchins, 1986) is a great children's book that builds on the idea that as the number of sharers involved

Standards for
Mathematical Practice

◀ **7 Look for and make use of structure**

Figure 14.9

Solutions for an equal sharing story problem.

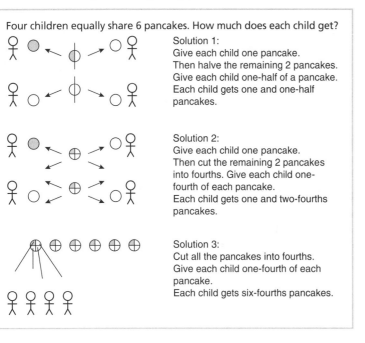

Four children equally share 6 pancakes. How much does each child get?

Solution 1:
Give each child one pancake.
Then halve the remaining 2 pancakes.
Give each child one-half of a pancake.
Each child gets one and one-half pancakes.

Solution 2:
Give each child one pancake.
Then cut the remaining 2 pancakes into fourths. Give each child one-fourth of each pancake.
Each child gets one and two-fourths pancakes.

Solution 3:
Cut all the pancakes into fourths.
Give each child one-fourth of each pancake.
Each child gets six-fourths pancakes.

increases, the smaller the shares become. Encourage children to use the formal fraction names in their comparisons; for example, one-third of a brownie is less than one-half of a brownie.

As already mentioned, when children use different partitioning strategies, you should look for opportunities to have them consider if the amounts in different solutions are equivalent (e.g., when one child gets $\frac{1}{2}$ and another child gets $\frac{2}{4}$). The following activity has children purposefully looking for different ways to partition the same quantity.

Activity 14.5 CUT THEM UP AGAIN!

Pose a sharing story problem for which children could partition the objects in multiple ways. For example, "4 children share 10 brownies so that each one will get the same amount. How much will each child get?" Tell children that their task is to find at least two different ways to share the objects. Some children will use trial and error while others will be more systematic in finding different ways to partition the objects. Have children share the different ways they have found to partition the objects. Then challenge them to determine if the different ways result in each child getting a different or equal amount of brownie. Have children explain their reasoning.

The next activity uses the idea of a missing value to help children find equivalent fractional amounts.

Activity 14.6 KEEPING IT FAIR

Pose a problem such as the following: "Suppose 6 children shared 8 cookies equally. If 3 more children arrive, how many cookies would you need if you want to give them the same amount as the first 6 children?" Some children will share 8 cookies equally among the 6 children to determine how much each person will get in that situation and then use that information to determine how much is needed for the additional 3 children. Others may reason that because 3 is half of 6, they can halve the 8 cookies to see that 4 cookies are needed for the additional 3 children. Make sure to have children share their reasoning for keeping it fair!

Using a length model helps to emphasize that a fraction is a quantity and it also allows children to compare fractions in terms of relative size. The following activity (adapted from Bay-Williams & Martinie, 2003) is a fun way to use a real-world context to engage children in thinking about fractions through a linear model.

Activity 14.7 WHO IS WINNING?

Friends are playing the game "Red Light–Green Light." The fractions tell how much of the distance each child has already moved. Who is winning? Challenge children to place the friends on a line to show where they are between the start and finish.

Mary: three-fourths   Harry: one-half   Larry: two-fourths

Hans: two-thirds   Angela: five-eighths   Greta: four-sixths

The game "Red Light–Green Light" may not be familiar to all children, especially ELLs. Modeling the game with children in the class is a good way to build background and also support children with disabilities.

From Fraction Words to Symbols

Notice that throughout this chapter we have used words to name fractional amounts. The earliest we recommend introducing fraction symbolism is toward the end of second grade. If you choose to do so, you will need to spend time helping children develop a strong understanding of what the top number (numerator) and bottom number (denominator) of a fraction tell us. Build on the ideas that children have already been using as they counted *one-fourth, two-fourths, three-fourths, four-fourths, five-fourths,* and so on.

The way that we write fractions with a top and a bottom number and a bar between is a convention—an arbitrary agreement for how to represent fractions. (By the way, always write fractions with a horizontal bar, not a slanted one. Write $\frac{3}{4}$, not ¾. It is easier for children to tell which number is on the top and which one is on the bottom.) As a convention, it falls in the category of things that you simply tell children. However, a good idea is to make the convention so clear by way of demonstration that children will tell you what the numerator and denominator stand for.

Display several collections of fractional parts in a manner similar to those in Figure 14.10. Have children count the parts together. After each count, write the correct fraction, indicating that this is how it is written as a symbol. Include sets that are more than 1, but write them as fractions greater than 1 (sometimes referred to as "improper" fractions) and not as mixed numbers. Include at least two pairs of sets with the same numerators such as $\frac{4}{8}$ and $\frac{4}{3}$. Likewise, include sets with the same denominators. After the class has counted and you have written the fraction for at least six sets of fractional parts, pose the following questions:

What does the denominator in a fraction tell us?

What does the numerator in a fraction tell us?

Teaching Tip

The phrase "improper fraction" is a misleading phrase that implies something is wrong with the fraction, when it is simply an equivalent representation. Instead use "fraction" or "fraction greater than 1."

Standards for Mathematical Practice

◀ **4 Model with mathematics**

Stop and Reflect

Before reading further, answer these two questions in your own words. Don't rely on formulations you've heard before. Think in terms of what we have been talking about—namely, fractional parts and counting fractional parts. Imagine counting a set of 5 eighths and a set of 5 fourths and writing the fractions for these sets. Use children's language in your formulations and try to come up with a way to explain these meanings that has nothing to do with the type of model involved. ■

Figure **14.10** Counting fractional parts.

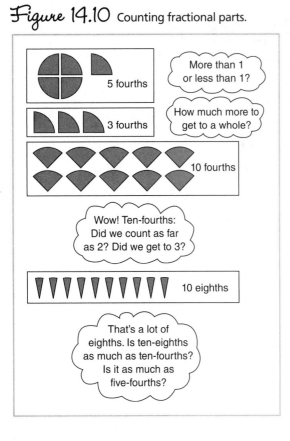

Here are some reasonable explanations for the numerator and denominator.

- *Numerator.* This is the counting number. It tells how many shares or parts we have. It tells how many have been counted. It tells how many parts we are talking about. It counts the parts or shares.

- *Denominator.* This tells what is being counted. It tells what fractional part is being counted. If the denominator is a 4, it means we are counting *fourths;* if it is a 6, we are counting *sixths;* and so on.

This formulation of the meanings of the numerator and denominator may seem unusual to you. It is often said that the numerator tells "how many" and the denominator tells "how many parts it takes to make a whole." This may be correct but can also be misleading. For example, a $\frac{1}{6}$ piece is often cut from a cake without making any slices in the remaining $\frac{5}{6}$ of the cake. That the cake is only in two pieces does not change the fact that the piece taken is $\frac{1}{6}$. Or if a pizza is cut in 12 pieces, two pieces still make $\frac{1}{6}$ of the pizza. In neither of these instances does the denominator tell how many pieces make a whole.

The iterative concept described earlier is most clear when focusing on these two ideas about fraction symbols:

- The top number counts (numerator).

- The bottom number tells *what is being counted* (denominator).

The *what* of fractions are the fractional parts. They can be counted. Fraction symbols are just a shorthand way of saying *how many* and *what.*

Equal Sharing Stories for Early Fractions

Content and Task Decisions

Grade Level: 1–2

Mathematics Goals

- To develop the equal sharing (division) meaning of fractions by investigating various contexts through story problems
- To introduce or reinforce the terms for fractional parts (e.g., *halves, fourths, quarters, eighths*)

Grade Level Guide

NCTM *Curriculum Focal Points*	*Common Core State Standards*
Composing and decomposing geometric shapes is one of the focal points for grade 1. Through this activity, children build "an understanding of part–whole relationships" (National Council of Teachers of Mathematics, 2006, p. 14). Developing an understanding of partitioning in the context of measurement is included in one of the focal points in grade 2. Composing and decomposing two-dimensional shapes are identified in grade 2 as a way to "develop foundations for understanding area, fractions, and proportions" (p. 14).	In first and second grades, children begin developing their understanding of fractions, particularly with thinking about partitioning quantities. In grade 1, children will "partition circles and rectangles into two and four equal shares, describe the shares using the words halves, fourths, and quarters, and use the phrases half of, fourth of, and quarter of. Describe the whole as two of, or four of the shares. Understand for these examples that decomposing into more equal shares creates smaller shares" (CCSSO, 2010, p. 16). In grade 2, children will "partition circles and rectangles into two, three, or four equal shares, describe the shares using the words halves, thirds, half of, a third of, etc., and describe the whole as two halves, three thirds, four fourths. Recognize that equal shares of identical wholes need not have the same shape" (CCSSO, 2010, p. 20).

Consider Your Children's Needs

Children have solved partition and measurement story problems with whole-number solutions. They understand that in a sharing situation all the objects should be shared and shared fairly.

For English Language Learners

- Use visuals for the opening story problem (real grapes or manipulatives to represent grapes) and model it with children in the class.
- Provide an opportunity for children to work with a partner who will be able to help with vocabulary.
- Encourage children to use both their native language and English as they work in groups.
- Using the same context (sharing quesadillas) across the problems in the lesson helps ELLs focus on the mathematics involved rather than having to make sense of a new and possibly unfamiliar context for each problem.

For Children with Special Needs

- After debriefing the problem with the grapes, use a think-aloud to highlight some of the thinking strategies that come into the decision making as you solve the problem. Jot down some of these ideas so that children can use them as a reference.
- Suggest to children who struggle with making equal partitions to use wooden coffee stirrers or thick uncooked spaghetti noodles to help them decide where to make their cuts.

Materials

Each child will need:

- Manipulatives, such as counters or cubes (at least 20)
- 15–20 circles cut from construction paper

Teacher will need:

- A way to project the stories and the solutions

Lesson

Before

Begin with a simpler version of the task:

- Ask children how they would solve the following story problem:

- "Four children want to fairly share 12 grapes. How many grapes will each child get?"
- Have them draw a picture or act out the story with manipulatives to determine the answer. Listen to children's ideas. Capitalize on ideas that emphasize the sharing action in the problem, in particular that all the grapes are shared and they are shared equally among the four children.

Present the focus task to the class:

- Children are to solve the following problems:
  - Two children want to share 5 quesadillas so that everyone gets the same amount. How much will each child get?
  - Four children want to share 9 quesadillas so that everyone gets the same amount. How much will each child get?
- Children should either use the construction paper circles or draw pictures and have a written explanation for their solutions that shows how much each child will get. Their explanation should include writing the fractional parts in words (e.g., *halves, fourths, eighths*) if they have been introduced to these terms. (See the fourth bullet under the *After* portion of lesson if you are using this lesson to introduce these terms.) Children should also be prepared to explain their thinking. Before you come together as a class, have children explain their ideas to a partner.

Provide clear expectations:

- Have children work independently and then share their work with a partner.

During

Initially:

- Be sure that children are using the construction paper circles or drawing pictures to help them think about how to do the problems and explain their thinking.

Ongoing:

- Look for children who partitioned their representations in different ways. Highlight those different ways in the *After* phase of the lesson.
- To differentiate for advanced learners, pose another problem to them in which the quantities must be split into smaller parts (say, 8 children and 11 quesadillas).
- Monitor partner discussions as children explain their thinking in order to address any misconceptions or difficulties during the whole-class discussion.

After

Bring the class together to share and discuss the tasks:

- For each problem, first get answers from different children in the class. If more than one answer is offered, simply record them and offer no evaluation.
- Have children come to the board to explain their strategies for thinking about the problem. You may need to ask questions about drawings or explanations to make sure everyone in the class follows the rationale. Encourage the class to comment or ask questions about the child's representation or thinking. Ask if others partitioned in a different way. If so, have the children come forward to share their solutions. If there are different answers, the class should evaluate the solution strategies and decide which answer is correct and why.
- Discuss the different partitions children use and how the action in the story is one of sharing fairly in which all the quesadillas are shared and everyone gets an equal share.
- If you are using this lesson to introduce the terms for fractional parts (e.g., *halves, fourths, quarters, eighths*), wait until a child has shared a solution that illustrates the fractional part you want to name. If possible, use the child's representation to point out that the whole is partitioned into, say, four equal parts and that we call those parts *fourths* or *quarters*.
- Children will likely use different ways to partition the circles (e.g., some children will distribute whole quesadillas first and then halves; others will halve all the quesadillas before distributing). It is important to have children compare and contrast the different approaches. Through questioning, help children understand that, while some solutions at first appear to be different, they are actually equivalent.

Assessment
Observe

- Are children using their understanding of sharing fairly to help them partition the amounts equally?
- Look for children who are not partitioning the circles into smaller parts and either want to ignore the extras or are okay with someone getting more than someone else. These children need more experience working with sharing tasks whose solutions are whole numbers.

Ask

- What is the problem asking you to partition?
- What is the whole?
- How much does each child get?

Building Measurement Concepts

BigIDEAS

1 Measurement involves a comparison of an attribute of an item or situation with a unit that has the same attribute. Lengths are compared to units of length, areas to units of area, time to units of time, and so on.

2 Before anything can be measured meaningfully, it is necessary to understand the attribute to be measured.

3 Estimation of measures and the development of benchmarks for frequently used units of measure help children increase their familiarity with units, preventing errors in measurements and aiding in the meaningful use of measurement.

4 Measurement instruments (e.g., rulers) are tools that replace the need for actual measurement units.

Measurement is one of the most useful mathematics content strands because it is so pervasive in our daily lives—buying apples, preparing recipes for a meal, determining how long it will take to get ready for school or work, deciding whether you need the 6-foot or 12-foot power cord, checking the loudness of your music or TV, hearing about the intensity of a tornado or hurricane, and more. Measurement is also embedded in the other strands of mathematics—number, geometry, and data in particular—and is used in science, social studies, art, and music.

Measurement can be thought of as the "assignment of a numerical value to an attribute or characteristic of an object" (National Council of Teachers of Mathematics, 2003, p. 1) and is not an easy topic for children to understand. Data from international studies consistently indicate that children in the United States are weaker in the area of measurement than any other topic in the mathematics curriculum (Thompson & Preston, 2004).

For grades pre-K–2, the primary emphasis is on helping children develop a conceptual understanding of the measurement process and the units and tools for measuring length and time. According to the *Common Core State Standards* (CCSSO, 2010), kindergartners should learn to describe measureable attributes of objects (e.g., length and weight), directly comparing two objects using words such as *taller, shorter, heavier, lighter, more,* and *less.* By first grade, children should compare objects indirectly using a third object and understand how to use multiple copies of

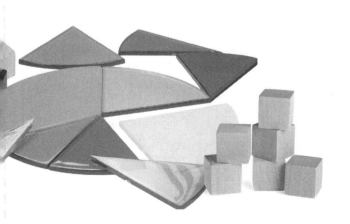

a unit to measure the length of an object. Second graders move to using standard measuring tools, such as rulers, yardsticks, and meter sticks, and to using number lines to represent whole numbers as lengths from zero. They also begin to explore the inverse relationship between the size of the measuring unit and the measure (i.e., number of units used). First graders begin to tell and write time in hours and half-hours and second graders extend that to 5-minute intervals and the use of a.m. and p.m. Money is also included under the study of measurement but does not occur until second grade.

The Meaning and Process of Measuring

Suppose that you asked your children to measure an empty bucket (see Figure 15.1). The first thing they would need to know is *what* about the bucket is to be measured. They might measure the height, depth, diameter (distance across), or circumference (distance around). All of these are length measures. The surface area of the side could be determined. A bucket also has capacity and weight. Each aspect that can be measured is an *attribute* of the bucket.

Once children determine the attribute to be measured, they need to choose a unit that has the attribute being measured. Length is measured with units that have length, area with units that have area, volume with units that have volume, weight with units that have weight, and so on.

Technically, a measurement is a number that indicates a comparison between the attribute of the object (or situation, or event) being measured and the same attribute of a given unit of measure. We commonly use small units of measure to determine a numeric relationship (the measurement) between what is measured and the unit. For example, to measure a length, the comparison can be done by lining up copies of the unit directly against the length being measured. For most attributes measured in schools, we can say that to measure

𝓕𝓲𝓰𝓾𝓻𝓮 15.1 Measuring different attributes of a bucket.

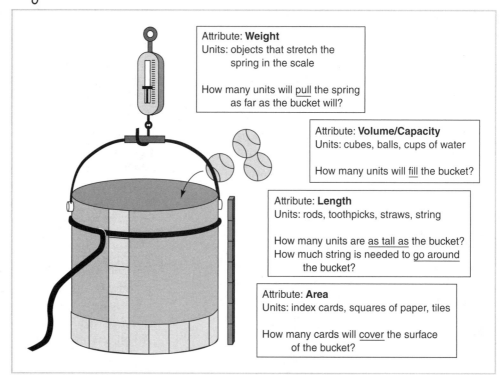

means that the attribute being measured is "filled" or "covered" or "matched" with a unit of measure with the same attribute (as illustrated in Figure 15.1).

In summary, to measure something, one must perform three steps:

1. Decide on the attribute to be measured.
2. Select a unit that has that attribute.
3. Compare the units—by filling, covering, matching, or using some other method—with the attribute of the object being measured. The number of units required to match the object is the measure.

Measuring instruments such as rulers, meter sticks, scales, and clocks are devices that make the filling, covering, or matching process easier. A ruler lines up the units of length and numbers them. A clock lines up units of time and marks them off.

◆ Measurement Concepts and Skills

If a typical group of first graders attempts to measure the length of their classroom by laying strips 1 meter long end to end, the strips sometimes overlap, and the line can weave in a snakelike fashion. Do they understand the concept of length as an attribute of the classroom? Do they understand that each 1-meter strip has this attribute of length? They most likely understand that they are counting a line of strips stretching from wall to wall. But they may not be aware that, when measuring, they are comparing the same attribute of the measuring unit (the 1-meter strip) and the object being measured (the classroom). The skill of measuring with a unit must be explicitly linked to the concept of measuring as a process of comparing attributes. Table 15.1 describes a recommended sequence of experiences that help children explicitly link measurement concepts and skills. We also briefly discuss the sequence here.

Table 15.1   Recommended Sequence of Experiences for Measurement Instruction

Step	Goal	Type of Activity	Notes
1—Making Comparisons	Children will understand the attribute to be measured.	Make comparisons based on the attribute, for example, longer/shorter, heavier/lighter. Use direct comparisons whenever possible.	When it is clear that the attribute is understood, there is no further need for comparison activities.
2—Using Models of Measuring Units	Children will understand how filling, covering, matching, or making other comparisons of an attribute with measuring units produces a number called a *measure.*	Use physical models of measuring units to fill, cover, match, or make the desired comparison of the attribute with the unit.	Begin with nonstandard units. Progress to the direct use of standard units when appropriate and certainly before using measuring tools.
3—Using Measuring Instruments	Children will use common measuring tools with understanding and flexibility.	Make measuring instruments and use them in comparison with the actual unit models to see how the measurement tool performs the same function as the individual units. Be certain to make direct comparisons between the student-made tools and the standard tools. Standard measuring instruments, such as rulers, make the filling, covering, or matching process easier.	Without a careful comparison with the standard tools, much of the value in student-made tools can be lost.

Making Comparisons

The first critical goal is for children to understand the attribute they are going to measure. When children compare objects on the basis of some measurable attribute, that attribute becomes the focus of the activity. For example, is the weight of one box more than, less than, or about the same as the weight of another? No measurement is required, but some manner of comparing one weight to the other must be devised. The attribute of "weight" (heaviness) is inescapable.

With a measure, such as length, you can sometimes make a direct comparison by lining up one object against another. But often an indirect method using a third object is necessary. For example, if children wanted to compare the height of a wastebasket to the distance around, they would need to use something like a string to make that comparison. The string is the intermediary, as it is impossible to directly compare these two lengths.

Teaching Tip

Use and encourage precise language when helping children make comparisons. Avoid using the phrase "bigger than" and instead use more specific language such as "longer than" or "is heavier."

◆ Standards for
Mathematical Practice

6 Attend to
precision ▶

Using Physical Models of Measuring Units

The second goal is for children to understand how matching, filling, covering, or making other comparisons of an attribute with measuring units produces a number called a measure. For most attributes that are measured in elementary schools, it is possible to have physical models of units of measure. Time and temperature are exceptions. Units can be both nonstandard (sometimes referred to as informal) units and standard units. For length, for example, a drinking straw cut into an arbitrary length (nonstandard) and a 1-foot-long strip of card stock (standard) might be used as units.

To help make the notion of units explicit and to aid children in understanding units, use as many copies of the unit as are needed to fill or match the attribute measured (this can be thought of as equal partitioning). The length of the room could be measured with giant footprints by placing card stock copies of the footprint end to end, completely "covering" the length of the room. Laying out copies of the same size unit and counting the units is called *iteration* (you may recall that counting same-size fractional parts is also called *iteration*). It is somewhat more difficult to use a single copy of a unit to complete this iteration. That means measuring a given length (say, with a single footprint) by repeatedly moving it from position to position and keeping track of where the last unit ended. Not only is this more difficult for younger children, but it also obscures the meaning of the measurement—to see how many units will fill the length.

It is useful to measure the same object with units of different sizes to help children understand that the size of the unit used is important. (This is an expectation for second graders in the *Common Core State Standards*.) For each differently sized unit, estimate the measure in advance and discuss the estimate afterward. Children should start to observe that smaller units produce larger numeric measures, and vice versa. This is a difficult concept for young children to understand but, with instruction, they can learn it (e.g., National Research Council, 2009). Children construct this inverse relationship by estimating, then experimenting, and finally reflecting on the measurements.

Figure 15.2

"How long is this crayon?"

Building and Using Measuring Instruments

Only after children understand and can use single units of measurement should they move to working with common measuring tools. On the 2003 NAEP exam (Blume, Galindo, & Walcott, 2007), only 20 percent of fourth graders could give the correct measure of an object not aligned with the end of a ruler, as in Figure 15.2. Even at the middle school level, only 56 percent of eighth graders answered the same situation accurately (Kloosterman, Rutledge, & Kenney,

2009). Students on the same exam also experienced difficulty when the increments on a measuring tool were not one unit. These results point to the difference between using a measuring tool and understanding how it works.

If children build simple measuring instruments using unit models with which they are familiar, it is more likely that they will understand how an instrument measures. A ruler is a good example. If children line up individual physical units, such as paper clips or 1-inch-long tiles, along a strip of card stock and mark them off, they can see that it is the spaces on rulers and not the hash marks or numbers that are important. It is essential that children discuss how measurement with iterating individual units compares with measurement using an instrument. Without this comparison and discussion, children may not understand that these two methods are essentially the same.

> *Teaching Tip*
>
> If your children have been using individual paper clips as units of measurement, ask them to create a chain of paper clips to be used as a ruler to make the transition from single units to instruments more apparent.

◆ Using Nonstandard Units

At the pre-K–2 level, a conceptual foundation for measuring various attributes (e.g., area, volume, capacity, and weight) is developed with a primary emphasis on the development of linear measurements. A common approach in primary grades is to begin measurement of any attribute with nonstandard units. The move to standard units should be guided by how well you believe your children are developing an understanding of measurement of that attribute.

The use of nonstandard units for beginning measurement activities is beneficial for the following reasons:

- Nonstandard units make it easier to focus directly on the attribute being measured. For example, when discussing how to measure the length of a bulletin board, units such as toothpicks, straws, or paper clips may be suggested. Each unit covers length—and actually accentuates length because each unit is thin and long—and each will give a different result. The discussion focuses on what it means to measure length.

- The use of nonstandard units avoids conflicting objectives in introductory lessons. Is your lesson about what it means to measure length or about understanding inches?

- By carefully selecting units, the size of the numbers in early measurements can be kept reasonable. The measures of length for first graders can be kept less than 20 units even when measuring long distances simply by using longer units.

- Nonstandard units provide a good rationale for standard units. The need for a standard unit can have more meaning when your children measure the same objects with their own units and arrive at different answers.

Although nonstandard units have these benefits, based on several research studies, Clements and Sarama (2009) caution that early measuring experiences with several different units can confuse children. While children are grappling with the concept of measurement, it is important to use a few nonstandard units that clearly demonstrate the attribute being measured (e.g., for length, toothpicks as opposed to square tiles or linking cubes). Early on, children need to understand the attribute being measured, the notion of matching, and the use of units of equal size. Once they demonstrate understanding of these concepts, you can introduce units of different sizes to provide the rationale for standard units.

◆ Developing Standard Units

Children who exhibit measurement sense are familiar with the standard measurement units, are able to make estimates in terms of these units, and meaningfully interpret measures depicted with standard units. Perhaps the biggest error in measurement instruction is the

failure to recognize and separate two types of objectives: (1) understanding the meaning and technique of measuring a particular attribute and (2) learning about the standard units commonly used to measure that attribute.

Teaching standard units of measure can be organized around three broad goals:

1. *Familiarity with the unit.* Children should have a basic idea of the size of commonly used units and what they measure. Being able to estimate a shelf as 5 feet long is as important as being able to measure the length of a shelf accurately.

2. *Ability to select an appropriate unit.* Children should know both what is a reasonable unit of measure in a given situation and the precision that is required. (Would you measure your lawn to purchase grass seed with the same precision you would use to measure a window to buy a pane of glass?) Children need practice in selecting appropriate standard units and judging the level of precision.

3. *Knowledge of relationships between units.* Children should know the relationships that are commonly used, such as those between inches, feet, and yards or minutes and hours.

Developing Unit Familiarity

One way to develop familiarity with standard units is through comparisons that focus on a single unit. The following activity provides this kind of experience and can be adapted for use with any standard unit.

Activity 15.1 **ABOUT ONE UNIT**

Give children a physical model of a standard unit and have them search for objects that have about the same measure as that one unit. For example, to develop familiarity with the meter, give children a piece of rope 1 meter long and have them look for objects in the classroom, outside on the playground, around the school building, or at home that are about 1 meter in length. Have them make lists of things that are about 1 meter long and separate lists for things that are a little shorter (or longer) or twice as long (or half as long). In the case of lengths, be sure to include circular lengths. Later, children can try to predict whether a given object is longer, shorter, or close to 1 meter. (Notice the use of terms such as *longer* rather than *more than*. Remember to use precise language!)

For larger standard units, such as 1 mile or 1 kilometer, enlist parents to help children find distances of that length. Suggest in a letter sent home that they check the distances around the neighborhood, to the school or shopping center, or along other frequently traveled paths. If possible, send home (or use in class) a 1-meter or 1-yard trundle wheel to measure distances.

For the standard weights of gram, kilogram, ounce, and pound, children can compare objects on a two-pan balance with single copies of these units. It may be more effective to work with 10 grams or 5 ounces so you don't have to use so many units to balance the pan. (Note that one slice of store-bought sandwich bread usually weighs about 1 ounce, so many objects will weigh much more than 1 ounce.) Children can be encouraged to bring in familiar objects from home to compare on the classroom scale.

A second approach to develop unit familiarity is to begin with familiar items and use their measures as references or benchmarks. A doorway is a bit more than 2 meters high. A bag of flour is a good reference for 5 pounds. A paper clip weighs about a gram and is about 1 centimeter wide. A gallon of milk weighs a little less than 4 kilograms. The following activity engages children in measuring familiar items in a variety of ways.

Activity 15.2 FAMILIAR REFERENCES

Use the book *Measuring Penny* (Leedy, 2000) to introduce children to the variety of ways familiar items can be measured. In this book, the author bridges between nonstandard units (e.g., dog biscuits, swabs, etc.) and standard units (inches, centimeters, etc.) to measure her pet dog Penny. Have children use the idea of measuring Penny to find something at home (or in class) to measure in as many ways as they can think of using standard units. The measures should be rounded to whole numbers. Discuss in class the familiar items chosen and their measures so that different ideas and benchmarks are shared. Many of the units used in *Measuring Penny* are common in the United States but not in other countries. Still, the book can be used to relate to how children from other countries measure length and volume.

Children's literature can also provide a way to engage children in developing familiarity with various lengths. For example, the children's book *Actual Size* (Jenkins, 2011a) portrays several different animals and insects (or a part of their body) in their actual size. From the head of a 23-foot-long crocodile to the hand of a gorilla to the $2\frac{1}{2}$-inch-tall mouse lemur, children can compare themselves and their classmates to these fascinating creatures while learning about linear measurement.

It can be interesting to have children find length benchmarks on their bodies. Couple the discussion of personal benchmarks with a discussion of growth because these benchmarks will change as they grow! Have children compare their references with their parents or an older sibling's benchmarks to see how they differ in size. Point out that children will likely need to adjust their benchmarks over time.

Activity 15.3 PERSONAL BENCHMARKS

Measure various parts of your body. About how long is your foot, your stride, your hand span (stretched and with fingers together), the width of your index finger or pinky finger, your arm span (finger to finger and finger to nose), and the distance around your wrist and around your waist? What is the height to your waist, shoulder, and head? Some of these measures may prove to be useful benchmarks for single or multiples of standard units. (The average child's fingernail is about 1 cm in width and most people find a 10-cm length somewhere on their hands.)

Choosing Appropriate Units

Should rooms be measured in feet or inches? Should concrete blocks be weighed in grams or kilograms? The answers to questions such as these involve more than simply knowing how big the units are, although that is certainly required. Another consideration involves the need for precision. If you were measuring your wall in order to cut a piece of molding or woodwork to fit, you would need to measure it very precisely. The smallest unit would be an inch or a centimeter, and you would also use small fractional parts. But

Standards for Mathematical Practice

5 Use appropriate tools strategically

if you were determining how many 8-foot molding strips to buy, the nearest foot would probably be sufficient.

Activity 15.4 GUESS THE UNIT

Find examples of measurements of all types in newspapers, on signs, or in other everyday situations. Present the context and measures but without units. The task is to predict what units of measure were used. Have children discuss their choices. For children with disabilities you may want to provide the headings for the possible units (e.g., inches, feet, yards, miles) so they can sort the real-world measures into these groups.

Important Standard Units and Relationships

Although a conceptual foundation for measuring many attributes is developed during grades pre-K–2, the primary emphasis is on the development of linear measurements, including work with standard linear units. Your state or local curriculum is the best guide to help you decide which linear units your children should learn. However, the position statement of the National Council of Teachers of Mathematics on the metric system is clear: "Because the metric system is an effective, efficient, base-ten measurement system used throughout the world, students need to develop an understanding of its units, and their relationship as well as fluency in its application to real world situations" (National Council of Teachers of Mathematics, 2011b). The statement goes on to say that because we are still using customary measures in day-to-day life children must work in that system as well. Countries worldwide have passed laws stating that international commerce must use metric units, so if U.S. students are going to be prepared for the global workplace, they must be knowledgeable and comfortable with metric units. The *Common Core State Standards* specifically state that, by the end of second grade, children should be familiar with centimeters and meters as well as inches and feet.

The relationships between units within either the metric or customary systems are conventions. As such, children must simply be told what the relationships are and instructional experiences must be devised to reinforce them. Typically, knowing basic relationships between units in a given measurement system becomes important in the intermediate grades. At the primary level, being able to pace off 3 meters—unit familiarity—is more important than knowing how many cups in a quart or inches in a yard. The *Common Core State Standards* support this stance by identifying measurement equivalents within the same system as being an expectation for fourth graders.

◆ Estimation and Approximation

Measurement estimation is the process of using mental and visual information to measure or make comparisons without using measuring instruments. It is a practical skill used by people almost every day. Do I have enough sugar to make cookies? Is this suitcase over the weight limit? Will my car fit into that parking space? Here are several reasons for including estimation in measurement activities:

- Estimation helps children focus on the attribute being measured and the measuring process. Think how you would estimate the area of the cover of this book using playing cards as the unit. To do so, you have to think about what area is and how the units might be placed on the book cover.

- Estimation provides an intrinsic motivation for measurement activities. It is interesting to see how close you can come in your estimate.
- When standard units are used, estimation helps develop familiarity with the unit. If you estimate the height of the door in meters before measuring, you must think about the size of a meter.
- The use of a benchmark to make an estimate lays the foundation for multiplicative reasoning. For example, someone might reason that the width of a picture is about twice the length of a ruler, or about 24 inches or 2 feet.

In all measuring activities, emphasize the use of approximate language. The desk is about 15 orange rods long. The chair is a little less than 4 straws high. Approximate language is very useful for young children because many measurements do not result in whole numbers. This is an opportunity to develop the idea that all measurements include some error. As children get older, they will begin to use fractional units or smaller units to measure with more precision. When this happens, acknowledge that the smaller unit or subdivision produces a greater degree of precision. Consider that a length measure can never be more than one-half unit in error. And because there is mathematically no "smallest unit," there is always some error involved. In other words, all measurements are approximations.

Standards for Mathematical Practice

◄ **6 Attend to precision**

Stop and Reflect

Why is it the case that a length measure can never be more than one-half unit in error? ■

Suppose you are measuring a length of ribbon with a ruler that only shows quarter inches; our unit is a quarter of an inch. If the length of ribbon falls between $3\frac{3}{4}$ and 4 inches, we would usually round to whichever number is closest to the length of ribbon. If the length of ribbon is more than halfway towards the 4-inch mark, we say it's 4 inches long. However, if the length of ribbon is less than halfway from $3\frac{3}{4}$, we say it is closer to $3\frac{3}{4}$ inches. In either case, we are within $\frac{1}{8}$ of an inch or one-half of the unit and are essentially ignoring the excess or deficiency—and this constitutes our "error." If we need more precision in our measurement, we use smaller units to ensure that our measurement rounding or error is within a range that we can accept.

Strategies for Estimating Measurements

Always begin a measurement activity with children making an estimate—whether they are using nonstandard or standard units. Here are four specific strategies that can be taught for estimating measures:

1. *Develop and use benchmarks or referents for important units.* Research shows that children who have acquired mental benchmarks or reference points for measurements and have practiced using them in class activities are much better estimators than children who have not learned to use benchmarks (Joram, 2003). Children must pay attention to the size of the unit to estimate well (Towers & Hunter, 2010). Referents should be things that are easily envisioned by the child. One example is the height of an average child (see Figure 15.3). Children should have a good referent for single units and also useful multiples of standard units.

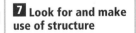

Standards for Mathematical Practice

◄ **7 Look for and make use of structure**

2. *Use "chunking" when appropriate.* Figure 15.3 shows an example indicated by the arrows. It may be easier to estimate the shorter chunks along the wall than to estimate the whole length. The weight of a stack of books is easier if some estimate is given to the weight of an "average" book.

Figure 15.3 Estimating measures using benchmarks and chunking.

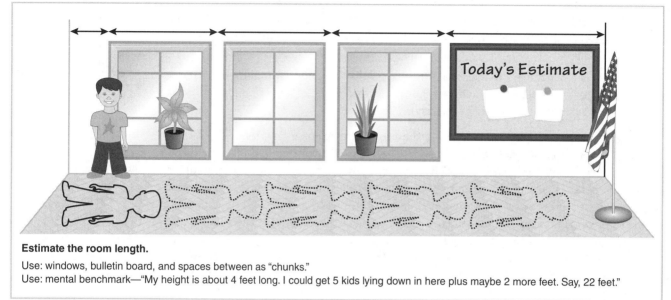

Estimate the room length.

Use: windows, bulletin board, and spaces between as "chunks."
Use: mental benchmark—"My height is about 4 feet long. I could get 5 kids lying down in here plus maybe 2 more feet. Say, 22 feet."

3. *Use subdivisions.* This is a strategy similar to chunking, with the chunks imposed on the object by the estimator. For example, if the wall length to be estimated has no useful chunks, it can be mentally divided in half and then in fourths or even eighths by repeated halving until a more manageable length is found. Length, volume, and area measurements all lend themselves to this technique.

4. *Iterate a unit mentally or physically.* For length, area, and volume, it is sometimes easy to mark off single units visually. You might use your hands or make marks or folds to keep track as you go. If a child knows, for example, that her stride is about $\frac{1}{2}$ meter long, she can walk off a length and then add to get an estimate. Hand and finger widths are useful for shorter measures.

Tips for Teaching Estimation

Each strategy just listed should be explicitly taught and discussed with children. Suggested benchmarks for useful measures can be developed and recorded on a class chart. Include items found at home. But the best approach to improving estimation skills is to have children do a lot of estimating. Keep the following tips in mind:

1. Help children learn strategies by having them first try a specified approach. Later activities should permit them to choose whatever techniques they wish.

2. Discuss how different children made their estimates. This will confirm that there is no single right way to estimate while reminding children of other useful approaches.

3. Accept a range of estimates. Think in relative terms about what is a good estimate. Within 10 percent for length is quite good. Even 30 percent "off" may be reasonable for weights or volumes.

4. Encourage children to give a range of estimates (e.g., the door is between 7 and 8 feet tall) that they believe includes the actual measure. This not only is a practical approach in real life but also helps focus on the approximate nature of estimation.

Teaching Tip

Do not promote a "winning" estimate. It discourages estimation and promotes only seeking the exact answer.

5. Make measurement estimation an ongoing activity. Post a daily measurement to be estimated. Children can record their estimates and discuss them in a 5-minute period. Teams of second graders can take turns determining the daily measurements to estimate each week.

6. Be precise with your language and do not use the word *measure* interchangeably with the word *estimate* (Towers & Hunter, 2010). Randomly substituting one word for the other will cause uncertainty and possibly confusion in children.

Measurement Estimation Activities

Estimation activities need not be elaborate. Any measurement activity can have an "estimate first" component. For more emphasis on the process of estimation itself, simply think of measures that can be estimated and have children estimate (without later measuring). The following activities provide two suggestions.

Activity 15.5 ESTIMATION QUICKIE

Select a single object such as a box, a pumpkin, a painting on the wall of the school, a jar, or even the principal! Each day, select a different attribute or dimension to estimate. For the pumpkin, for example, children can estimate its height, circumference, weight, volume, and surface area.

Activity 15.6 ESTIMATION SCAVENGER HUNT

Conduct estimation scavenger hunts. Give teams a list of either nonstandard or standard measurements and have them find things that are close to having those measurements. Do not allow children to use measuring instruments. A list might include the following items:

- A length of 3 meters
- Something that is as long as your mathematics book
- Something that weighs more than a paper clip but less than your mathematics book
- Something that has the same area as the palm of your hand

Let children suggest how to judge results in terms of accuracy.

Formative Assessment Note

Estimation tasks are a good way to assess children's understanding of both measurement and units. Use a checklist while children estimate measures of real objects inside and outside the classroom. Prompt them to explain how they arrived at their estimates to get a more complete picture of their measurement knowledge. Asking only for a numeric estimate and no explanation can mask a lack of understanding and will not give you the information you need to provide appropriate remediation.

In this chapter, we emphasize length, time, and money as these are the measurements highlighted in the pre-K–2 curriculum. We infuse ideas of teaching measurement and estimation using activities as examples.

 **Length**

Length is usually the first attribute children learn to measure. Be aware, however, that length measurement is not immediately understood by young children. Researchers (e.g., Clements & Sarama, 2009; Curry, Mitchelmore, & Outhred, 2006) have identified some of the more common misconceptions and difficulties children have when measuring length:

- Leaving gaps between units or overlapping units
- Using units that are not of equal size (e.g., measuring with paper clips of different sizes)
- Combining units of different sizes as if they were the same unit (e.g., combining 2 feet and 4 inches as "6 long")
- When using a ruler, beginning at "1" rather than "0" or measuring from the wrong end of the ruler
- Counting the marks on a ruler or the "points" between heel-to-toe steps rather than the spaces in between
- When comparing the length of two objects, comparing the objects at one end only

It is important to keep these misconceptions and difficulties in mind as you plan lessons and observe your children during measurement activities.

◆ Comparison Activities

At the pre-K–K level, children should begin with direct comparisons of two or more lengths and then move to indirect comparisons by the first grade (CCSSO, 2010; National Council of Teachers of Mathematics, 2006).

Activity 15.7 LONGER, SHORTER, SAME

Set up learning stations where children can explore which objects in a group are longer, shorter, or about the same in length as a specified "target" object. Change the target object and children may find that the shorter object is now longer than the target. A similar task can involve putting a set of objects in order from shortest to longest.

Activity 15.8 LENGTH (OR UNIT) HUNT

Give pairs of children a strip of card stock, a stick, a length of rope, or some other object with an obvious length dimension that will serve as a "target" unit. The task is for children to find five things in the room that are shorter than, longer than, or about the same length as their target unit. They can record what they find using pictures or words.

By making the target length a standard unit (e.g., a meter stick or a 1-meter length of rope), the activity can be repeated to provide familiarity with important standard units.

Throughout the school day, look for opportunities for children to compare lengths directly. For example, which block tower is taller, which clay snake is shorter, which chair is wider, and so on.

Indirect comparison, which means using another object to help make the measure, is the focus in the next activity. Children who can use a third object to compare the lengths of two other objects must have a transitive understanding of measurement. For example, if the length of a green pencil is shorter than the length of a blue pencil, and the length of the blue pencil is shorter than the length of a red pencil, then the length of the green pencil must be shorter than the length of the red pencil. Although transitivity is crucial to understanding measurement, not all children in grades K–1 will be able to follow this argument (Curry, Mitchelmore, & Outhred, 2006).

Activity 15.9 WILL IT FIT?

Challenge children to determine whether an object in the classroom or outside the classroom (maybe in the library or cafeteria or on the playground) would fit through the doorway of the classroom. For example, is the doorway wide enough for one of the tables in the cafeteria to go through? Will one of the shelves in the library fit through the doorway? What about the monkey bars on the playground? In pairs have children brainstorm ways they can check and then discuss and try some of their suggestions.

Children should also compare lengths that are not in straight lines. One way to do this is by using indirect comparisons. For example, children can wrap string around objects in a search for things that are, say, as long around as the distance from the floor to their belly button or as long as the distance around their head or waist.

Activity 15.10 CROOKED PATHS

Make some crooked or curvy paths on the floor (or outside) with masking tape or chalk. The task is to determine which path is longest, next longest, and so on. Children should suggest ways to measure the crooked paths so that they can be compared easily. If you wish to offer a hint, provide pairs of children with a long piece of string (at first make it longer than the path). Have children explain how they solved the problem. For children with disabilities, you may need to tape the end of the string to the beginning of the path and help them mark the final measurement on the string with a marker. Use another string for the other path in the same way. Then compare the string lengths.

In "Crooked Paths" some children may argue that the path that "looks longer" is the longer path, although a crooked and more compact path may actually be longer. You might want to show an example of two paths on the floor (one crooked path and one straight path that "looks longer" than the crooked path) and have children walk each path to see which takes longer to walk.

● Using Physical Models of Length Units

There are four important principles of iterating units of length, whether they are nonstandard or standard (Dietiker, Gonulates, Figueras, & Smith, 2010, p. 2). You will notice that these principles are related to some of the common difficulties children have with linear measurement that were identified earlier.

- All units must have equal length—if not, you cannot accumulate units by counting.
- All units must be placed on the path being measured—otherwise, a different quantity is being measured.

- The units must be without gaps—if not, part of the quantity is not being measured.
- The units must not overlap—otherwise, part of the quantity is measured more than once.

Children can begin to measure length using a variety of nonstandard units, including the following:

- *Giant footprints.* Cut out about 20 copies of a large footprint about $1\frac{1}{2}$ to 2 feet long on poster board.
- *Measuring ropes.* Cut rope into lengths of 1 meter. These ropes can measure the perimeter and the circumference of objects such as the teacher's desk, a tree trunk, or the class pumpkin.
- *Drinking straws.* Straws provide large quantities of a useful unit as they are easily cut into smaller units. They can also be linked together with a long string or slid onto a length of pipe cleaner, creating an excellent bridge to a ruler or measuring tape.
- *Short units.* Flat toothpicks, linking cubes, and paper clips are all useful nonstandard units for measuring shorter lengths. Cuisenaire rods are also useful because they are easily placed end to end and are also metric (centimeters) and so make an excellent bridge to a ruler. Paper clips can also be made into chains. Note that individual linking cubes do not explicitly exhibit the attribute of length as well as Cuisenaire rods, toothpicks, paper clips, and straws.

Keep in mind the word of caution mentioned earlier about using a few well-chosen nonstandard units to avoid confusing children with a variety of units. Once children demonstrate, in particular, that all the units used to measure a given length must be the same length, then you may want to increase the variety of nonstandard units available.

Formative Assessment Note

For a quick diagnostic interview, give a child the two diagrams as shown and ask him to tell you the length of each object. Does the child simply count the units for both objects or does he indicate the issue with the different length units in the second diagram? If the child simply counts the units, this is an indication that he does not understand that the units must be of equal size. Having the child use a wide variety of different kinds of units may actually be more confusing. Instead, having the child consistently use the same kind of unit in measurement activities may help him realize that the units need to be equal in length.

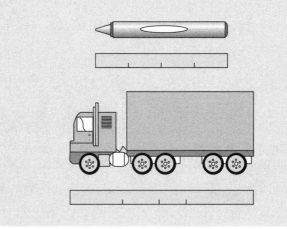

The following activity encourages children to develop their own approach to measuring lengths.

Activity 15.11 HOW LONG IS THE TEACHER?

Explain that you have just received an important request from the principal. She needs to know exactly how tall each teacher in the building is. The children are to decide how to measure the teachers and write a note to the principal explaining how tall their teacher is and detailing the process that they used. If you wish to give a hint, ask if it might be easier if they were to measure how long you are instead of how tall. You can ask, "Would it help if I lie down?" Have children make marks at your feet and head and draw a straight line between these marks.

Explain that the principal says they can use any nonstandard unit to measure with (provide a few choices until you are confident children understand the necessity to use equal-length units). For each choice of unit, supply enough units to more than cover your length. Put children in pairs and allow them to select one unit with which to measure. Ask children to make an estimate and then have them use their unit to measure.

After children complete their measuring, follow up with questions such as "How did you get your measurement?" "Did children who measured with the same unit get the same answers? If not, why not?" "How could the principal make a line that was as long as the teacher?" Focus on the value of carefully lining up units end to end. Discuss what happens if you overlap units, have gaps in the units, or don't follow a straight line.

Repeat the basic task of "How Long Is the Teacher?" with other measuring tasks, each time providing a choice of units and the requirement that children explain their measures. It is always helpful if the same lengths (e.g., heights, distances around) are measured by several pairs of children using the same unit so that possible errors can be discussed and the measuring process refined. The following activity adds an estimation component.

Activity 15.12 ESTIMATE AND MEASURE

Make lists of things in the room to measure (see Figure 15.4). Run a piece of masking tape along the dimension of objects to be measured. Include curves or other distances that are not straight lines. Have children make estimates before they measure. Young children will not be very good at estimating distances at first so it is important to provide them with some strategies for doing so (see section on "Tips for Teaching Estimation"). For example, have children make a row or chain of exactly 10 units to help them with their estimates. They can first lay 10 units against the object and then make their estimate. You can also do this activity using standard units.

Figure 15.4

Record sheet for measuring with informal length units.

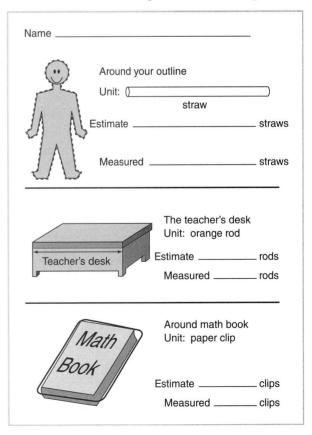

The *Common Core State Standards* recommend that second graders consider the relationship between the size of a unit and the resulting measure. Children can find it a challenge to understand that larger units will create a smaller measure and vice versa. Engage children in activities in which this issue is emphasized.

Activity 15.13 CHANGING UNITS

Have children measure a length with a specified unit. Then provide them with a different unit that is either twice as long or half as long as the original unit.

Their task is to predict the measure of the same length using the new unit. Children should write down their predictions and discuss how they made their estimations. Then have them make the actual measurement. Cuisenaire rods are excellent for this activity, but other nonstandard units are useful as well.

Standards for Mathematical Practice

2 Reason abstractly and quantitatively ▶

Teaching Tip

Some children will be challenged using units that are more difficult multiples of the original task. Starting with simpler multiples will help children more readily see the inverse relationship of size of unit to the numeric measure.

When first doing the "Changing Units" activity, show the second unit and discuss only if the measure will be smaller or larger using this unit. You will find that many children will think that the larger units will give the larger measure. Allow children to struggle with their reasoning and test their conjectures by actually measuring.

Formative Assessment Note

Observation and discussion during activities such as those just described provide evidence of how well your children understand length measurement. Additional tasks that can be used in diagnostic interviews include the following:

- Provide a box with assorted units of different sizes. Cuisenaire rods would be suitable. Have children use the materials in the box to measure a given length. Observe whether the child understands that all units must be of similar size. If different lengths of units are used, ask the child to describe his or her measurement.
- Ask children to draw a line or mark off a distance of a prescribed number of units. Observe whether children know to align the units in a straight line without overlaps or gaps.
- Provide a length of string. Tell children that the string is 6 units long. How could they use the string to make a length of 3 units? How could they make a length of 9 units? In this task, you are looking to see if children can mentally subdivide the given length (string) based on an understanding of its measure. That is, can children visualize that 6 units are matched to the string length and half of these would be 3 units?
- Have children measure two different objects. Then ask how much longer the longer object is. Observe whether children can use the measurements to answer or whether they need to make a third measurement to find the difference.

◆ Making and Using Rulers

The jump from measuring with individual units to using standard rulers can be challenging. One method to help children understand rulers is to have them make their own rulers.

Activity 15.14 MAKE YOUR OWN RULER

Use two colors of precut narrow strips of construction paper. For each unit, use a length that is at least twice as long as the width so that the notion of length is emphasized. For example, if you use inches as the unit, your narrow strips could be 1 inch long and $\frac{1}{2}$ inch wide (or tall). For centimeters, the strip could be 1 cm long and $\frac{1}{2}$ cm wide. Or you could use a nonstandard unit of 5 cm long and about $2\frac{1}{2}$ cm wide. Discuss how the strips could be used to measure by laying them end to end. Provide long strips of card stock at least twice the width of your unit. Have children make their own ruler (e.g., foot-long, 10-cm-long, 10-unit-long rulers) by gluing the units in alternating colors onto the card stock, as shown at the top of Figure 15.5.

Have children use their new rulers to measure items on a list you provide. Include lengths that are longer than their rulers. Discuss the results, including how they measured the longer items. It is possible that there will be discrepancies due to rulers that were not made properly or because a child does not understand how a ruler works. Use these discrepancies as opportunities to reinforce the four important principles mentioned earlier (i.e., units must align with no gaps or overlaps, units must have equal length, units must be placed along the path being measured).

Also, consider using larger nonstandard units such as multiple tracings of a child's footprint glued onto strips of cash register tape. These rulers can be used to measure longer lengths or distances.

Teaching Tip

Alternatively, children can color a strip of centimeter grid paper and number each section to create a metric ruler.

Challenge children to find more than one way to measure a length with a ruler. Do you have to start at the end? What if you start at another unit in the center? Does that matter? Children can eventually put numbers on their homemade rulers, as shown in Figure 15.5. To begin with, numbers can be written in the center of each unit as a way to precount the units. When numbers are written in the standard way, at the ends of the units, the ruler becomes a number line. This format is more sophisticated and should be carefully discussed with children—in particular, why the numbers are at the end of the unit. (See the discussion in Chapter 9 about meaningfully developing a number line representation with children. Look for opportunities to help children relate the number-line representation to length measurement.)

Help children make the connection between their handmade rulers and standard rulers by giving them a standard ruler and having them identify and discuss how the handmade and standard rulers are alike and how they are different. Ask questions such as "What are the units?" "What do the numbers mean?" "What are the marks for?" "Where do the units begin?" "Could you make a ruler with the same units as the standard ruler?"

Figure 15.5

Give meaning to numbers on rulers.

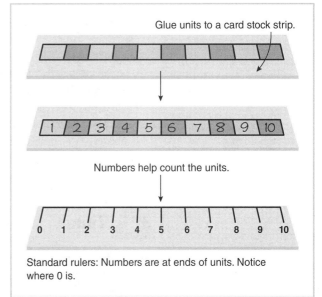

Standard rulers: Numbers are at ends of units. Notice where 0 is.

Figure 15.6

Use an unmarked ruler and ask children to measure an object. In the example shown, the correct length is 8 units. A child counting hash marks would respond with 9 units.

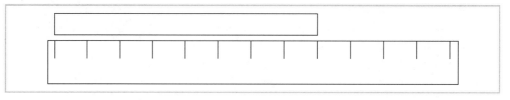

Formative Assessment Note

Research indicates that when children see standard rulers with the numbers on the hash marks, they often incorrectly believe that the numbers are counting the marks rather than indicating the units or spaces between the marks. As a performance assessment, provide children with a ruler, as shown in Figure 15.6, with hash marks but no numbers. Have children use the ruler to measure an item that is shorter than the ruler. Use a checklist to record whether the child counts spaces between the hash marks or counts the hash marks.

Another good performance assessment of ruler understanding is to have children measure with a "broken" ruler, one with the first two units broken off. Use your checklist to note whether children say that it is impossible to measure with such a ruler because there is no starting point. Those who understand rulers will be able to match and count the units meaningfully in their measures.

Observing how children use a ruler to measure an object that is longer than the ruler is also informative. If a child simply reads the last mark on the ruler, this is an indication that he or she does not understand how a ruler is a representation of a row of units.

technology note

GeoGebra offers a couple of interactive worksheets in which children are asked to measure given objects using a broken ruler. The worksheet at http://maine.edc.org/file.php/1/AssessmentResources/BrokenRulers132_L.html allows you to change the ruler from a standard ruler to a standard ruler that is broken along different intervals. There are nine objects children can measure, all of which are close enough in length to approximate to whole units. The rulers on this worksheet are all divided into fourths. Another worksheet uses a ruler that is divided into sixteenths and has children measuring various parts of pets (http://maine.edc.org/file.php/1/AssessmentResources/BrokenRulers_MeasureMe32_L.html). If children click on the hint button, a line is drawn along the path that should be measured.

 **Time**

Time is different from most other attributes that are commonly measured in school because it cannot be seen or felt and because it is more difficult for children to comprehend units of time or how those units are matched against a given time period or duration.

Comparison Activities

Time can be thought of as the duration of an event from its beginning to its end. As with other attributes, for children to adequately understand the attribute of time, they should make comparisons of events that have different durations. If two events begin at the same time, the shorter duration will end first and the other last longer. For example, which wind-up toy lasts longer? However, this form of comparison focuses on the ending of the duration rather than the duration itself. In order to think of time as something that can be measured, we need to focus on the duration itself.

Engaging tasks that address duration include the following:

- Stacking 10 blocks one at a time and then removing them one at a time
- Saying your full name
- Walking along a designated path
- Watering a plant
- Reading a page of a book

Children need to learn about seconds, minutes, and hours to develop some concept of how long these units are. Point out to children the duration of short and long events during the school day. Have children time familiar events in their daily lives: brushing teeth, eating dinner, riding to school, doing homework. Timing short events of $\frac{1}{2}$ minute to 2 minutes at school and at home can be fun and useful. Children can work in pairs and use a timer, such as a stopwatch, to time some of the tasks listed previously. For other examples, in *Just a Second* author Steve Jenkins (2011b) shares some interesting events that occur in just 1 second, 1 minute, and 1 hour.

Reading Clocks

The common instrument for measuring time is the clock. However, learning to tell time has little to do with time measurement and more to do with the skills of learning to read an instrument. Clock reading can be a difficult skill to teach. Starting in first grade children are usually taught to read clocks to the hour and then to the half hour. In second grade, they learn to read to 5-minute intervals (CCSSO, 2010). In the early stages of this sequence, children are shown clocks set exactly to the hour or half hour. Thus, many children who can read a clock at 7:00 or 2:30 are initially challenged by 6:58 or 2:33.

Digital clocks permit children to read times easily but do not relate times very well to benchmark times. To know that a digital reading of 7:58 is nearly 8 o'clock, the child must know that there are 60 minutes in an hour, that 58 is close to 60, and that 2 minutes is not a very long time. These concepts are challenging for many first-grade and second-grade children. The analog clock (with hands) shows "close to" times visually without the need for understanding big numbers or even how many minutes are in an hour.

The following suggestions can help children understand and read analog clocks by focusing on the actions and functions of the minute and hour hands on a clock.

1. Begin with a one-handed clock by breaking off the minute hand from a regular clock. Use lots of approximate language: "It's about 7 o'clock." "It's a little past 9 o'clock." "It's halfway between 2 o'clock and 3 o'clock" (see Figure 15.7).

2. Discuss what happens to the big hand as the little hand goes from one hour to the next. When the big hand is at 12, the hour hand is pointing exactly to a number. If the hour hand is about halfway between numbers, about where would the minute hand be? If the hour hand is a little past or before an hour (10 to 15 minutes), about where would the minute hand be?

Figure 15.7

Approximate time with one-handed clocks.

"About 7 o'clock"

"A little bit past 9 o'clock"

"Halfway between 2 o'clock and 3 o'clock"

3. Use two real clocks, one with only an hour hand and one with two hands. Cover the two-handed clock. Periodically during the day, direct attention to the one-handed clock. Discuss the time in approximate language. Have children predict where the minute hand should be. Uncover the other clock and check.

4. Teach time after the hour in 5-minute intervals. After step 3 has begun, count by fives going around the clock. Instead of predicting that the minute hand is "pointing at the 4," transition to the language "it is about 20 minutes after the hour." As skills develop, suggest that children always look first at the little or hour hand to learn approximately what time it is and then focus on the big or minute hand for precision.

5. Predict the reading on a digital clock when shown an analog clock, and vice versa; set an analog clock when shown a digital clock.

6. Relate the time after the hour to the time before the next hour. This is helpful not only for telling time but also for number sense.

The following activity assesses children's ability to read a clock.

Activity 15.15 ONE-HANDED CLOCKS

Prepare a page of clock faces (see Blackline Master 47). On each clock draw an hour hand with a variety of placements that are appropriate for your grade (e.g., on the hour, half past the hour, a quarter past the hour, a quarter until the hour, and close to but not on the hour). For each clock face, the children's task is to write the digital time and draw the corresponding minute hand on the clock. If you have ELLs, it is important to note that telling time is done differently in different cultures. For example, in Spanish any time past 30 minutes is stated as the next hour minus the time until that hour. For example, 10:45 is thought of as 15 minutes before 11, or 11 minus a quarter. Be explicit that in English it can be said either way—"10:45" or "a quarter till 11."

The "Time—Analog and Digital Clocks" applet at the National Library of Virtual Manipulatives allows children to change the time on an analog clock and see how it changes on the digital clock and vice versa (http://nlvm.usu.edu/en/nav/grade_g_1.html). The "Time—Match Clocks" applet at the same website displays a time on the analog clock and children have to match that time on the digital clock. Times are also shown on the digital clock that children match using the analog clock.

After children learn how to read a clock, the following activity not only motivates them to think about telling time, but it also helps them to consider the relationship between analog clock reading and digital recording.

Activity 15.16 READY FOR THE BELL

Give children a recording sheet with a set of clock faces (see Blackline Master 47). Secretly set a timer to go off at the hour, half hour, or minute. When the bell rings, children should look up and record the time on the clock face and in numerals on the recording sheet.

Although intervals of time (elapsed time) are a third-grade topic in the *Common Core State Standards*, time provides a good context for adding and subtracting numbers. "Ready for the Bell" provides opportunities for children to determine the time between timer rings.

You can also pose story problems about time, keeping in mind the problem structures for addition and subtraction that were discussed in Chapter 9. Consider the following examples:

- Sara started reading at 4:15 p.m. and stopped at 4:40 p.m. How long did Sara read? (Change Unknown)
- Sara read today for 50 minutes. She stopped reading at 6:30 p.m. What time did Sara start reading? (Start Unknown)
- Danny gets on the bus at 7:15 a.m. and arrives at school at 7:50 a.m. Callie gets on her bus at 7:25 a.m. and arrives at school at 8:05 a.m. Who has a longer bus ride? (Comparison: Difference Unknown)
- It takes Frank 15 minutes to get to school on his bus. If Kiera gets on her bus at 7:20 a.m. and rides the bus for 10 more minutes than Frank, what time does she arrive at school? (Comparison: Larger Unknown)

As discussed in Chapter 9, you can modify the difficulty of these problems by changing the numbers (e.g., use time on the hour or half hour to create easier problems, or use time in 5-minute intervals to increase the difficulty level). Start unknown and change unknown problems are also more difficult than result unknown problems. Make sure to provide a variety of problems in which the location of the unknown changes.

Money

Here is a list of the money ideas and skills typically required in the primary grades:

- Recognizing coins
- Identifying and using the value of coins
- Counting and comparing sets of coins
- Creating equivalent coin collections (same amounts, different coins)
- Selecting coins for a given amount
- Making change
- Solving word problems involving money starting in second grade (CCSSO, 2010)

Recognizing Coins and Identifying Their Values

The names of our coins are conventions of our social system. Children learn these names the same way that they learn the names of any physical objects in their daily environment—through exposure and repetition.

The value of each coin is also a convention that children must simply be told. For these values to make sense, children must have an understanding of 5, 10, and 25 and think of these quantities without seeing countable objects. Nowhere else do we say, "This is five," while pointing to a single item. A child who remains tied to counting objects to determine "how much" will be challenged to understand the values of coins. Lessons about coin values should focus on purchase power—a dime can buy the same thing that 10 pennies can buy.

◆ Counting Sets of Coins

Naming the total value of a group of coins is the same as mentally adding their values. Second graders can be asked to do the mental mathematics required in counting a collection of different coins. Children may sort their coins by value and start counting from the highest values, just as they often add or subtract the larger place values first. Or they may put coins together to make decade numbers, for example, adding a quarter and a nickel to make 30¢. With pennies aside, coins have the advantage of being in multiples of 5 and 10 and thereby lead to skip counting. The next activity helps prepare children for counting money.

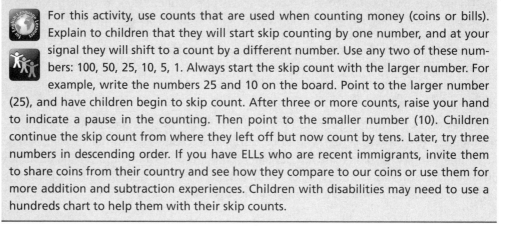

Activity 15.17 **MONEY SKIP COUNTING**

For this activity, use counts that are used when counting money (coins or bills). Explain to children that they will start skip counting by one number, and at your signal they will shift to a count by a different number. Use any two of these numbers: 100, 50, 25, 10, 5, 1. Always start the skip count with the larger number. For example, write the numbers 25 and 10 on the board. Point to the larger number (25), and have children begin to skip count. After three or more counts, raise your hand to indicate a pause in the counting. Then point to the smaller number (10). Children continue the skip count from where they left off but now count by tens. Later, try three numbers in descending order. If you have ELLs who are recent immigrants, invite them to share coins from their country and see how they compare to our coins or use them for more addition and subtraction experiences. Children with disabilities may need to use a hundreds chart to help them with their skip counts.

Formative Assessment Note

When a collection of coins is not arranged in descending order of values, children must first impose this order on the collection. This is a skill based only on the ability to compare numbers and recognize the value of the coins. Check to see if children can put a string of numbers such as this in order from greatest to least: 5, 1, 5, 25, 10, 1, 25, 10. For a child experiencing difficulty with this task, try a collection with no duplicates. If there is still difficulty, the child may need more experiences with counting, with the hundreds chart, and with other concept-development activities for place value.

If the child can put the numeral string in order but cannot order a set of coins, the problem is most likely a failure to have learned the values of the coins.

Working with coins requires not only adding up the values but also first mentally giving each coin a value. Engage children in using coins and developing addition concepts by having them add a mixed collection of coins.

Activity 15.18 **COIN-NUMBER ADDITION**

Using a projector, show a small collection of coins not arranged in any order. How many coins to use will vary with the experiences of your children. Begin with only dimes and pennies. Then add some nickels and eventually quarters. Give children time to identify the coins and write down the corresponding numeric values of the coins (e.g., 5 for a nickel, 25 for a quarter). Have children share what they have written down to make sure everyone has identified the correct amounts.

Now the children's task is to add the numbers mentally. Do not suggest how they add the numbers or in what order because there is almost always more than one good way to do this. For example, rather than add from the largest values to the smallest—the typical way coins are taught in books—it is also reasonable to use the 5s to make tens or other methods. For this collection, note that it is easy to add 5 and 25, then 10, then 7 (the last 5 and two 1s). Discuss with children how they added the collection.

```
   10      1      25
        5      5      1
```

When discussing solutions to this last activity, be sure to value any approach that works. However, pay special attention to those children who begin with the larger values and those who put combinations together utilizing thinking with tens. There is no reason to require children to add in any particular order, not with this activity or with coins.

As with time, you can also pose story problems about money using the problem structures for addition and subtraction discussed in Chapter 9. Consider the following examples:

- Alexis has some coins. Zig gives her 1 dime and 2 pennies. Now Alexis has 36¢. What coins did Alexis have to begin with? (Joining: Start Unknown)
- Jay has 2 quarters and a dime. He needs 95¢ to buy a notebook. How much more money does Jay need? (Part–Part–Whole: Part Unknown)
- Andy has $11.65. He gave Becky some money. Now Andy has $8.15. How much money did Andy give Becky? (Separate: Change Unknown)
- Wendy has $2.67. That is $1.25 more than what Keith has. How much money does Keith have? (Comparison: Smaller Unknown)

Again, changing the numbers and the location of the unknown will modify the level of difficulty.

◆ Making Change

When you pay for something at a store using cash, you may often give the clerk more money than the purchase price and you expect to receive the correct change back. Knowing how to make change is important for the clerk but also for the customers—so they can check to make sure they received the correct change!

Stop and Reflect

Before reading further, think about how you would make change from a hundred dollar bill for a purchase that cost $82. ∎

You may have thought, I can start at 100, go back 10 to 90, then back 8 more to 82—so the change would be $10 + 8$ or 18 dollars. You could also start at 100, go back 20 to 80, up 2 to 82, so that's $20 - 2$ or 18. You may have thought to start at 82, go 8 more to 90 and then 10 more to 100—that's $8 + 10$ or 18 dollars.

Making change is the same as finding a difference—specifically, a difference between the amount given to the clerk and the purchase price. We discussed a variety of ways to find a difference in Chapters 9 and 12. The third approach described earlier uses adding on to find a difference. This strategy is sometimes used to teach how to "make change" in school because it is useful for counting back change to the customer. Any of the ways previously described are appropriate to make change because they all use strategies based on number sense. Counting back change should be considered a separate skill. Because making change is related to strategies based on number sense, children should have experiences with these strategies before they are asked to make change with money.

The following activity builds from children's experiences using various strategies to find a difference.

Activity 15.19 HOW MUCH IS THE CHANGE?

Write a target number on the board. This number should be the same as an amount of money that might be given to a store clerk in a purchase, most likely 25, 50, 75, or 100. To the left of this target, write a smaller starting number and an arrow. Here are some examples:

$$13 \rightarrow 25 \qquad 56 \rightarrow 75 \qquad 29 \rightarrow 50$$

In creating the amounts for this activity, think in terms of purchases. If the target is 75, that means you gave the clerk 75¢. You would only do this for items costing more than 50¢. Similarly, for a target of 50, use numbers greater than 25. For a target of 100, any smaller number would be appropriate because you may have given the clerk a dollar bill.

Embed the numbers in story problems that describe making a purchase. Explain to the children that the first number written represents the amount of the purchase and the second number represents the amount of money given to the store clerk. The children's task is to find the difference (i.e., the change) using a strategy that they can explain. They may need to write down intermediate results. Discuss the solution methods used by different children.

The next activity extends "How Much Is the Change?" and attempts to draw children's attention to the notion of using the fewest possible coins.

Activity 15.20 HOW MUCH IS THE CHANGE WITH COINS?

On the board, write start and target numbers as in "How Much Is the Change?" Then write on the board the values of the coins: 25, 10, 5, 1. In this task, children must use only the numbers (i.e., coins) in the list to create the difference. As they use a number, they should write it down. Challenge children to try to use as few "coins" as possible or, in other words, as many of the larger numbers as possible. For example, if the target is 75 with a start of 58, they could write 1, 1, 10, 5. Have children discuss their solutions.

When your children are ready, "How Much Is the Change with Coins?" can be extended to values greater than a dollar (greater than targets of 100¢).

This sequence of suggested activities is not a surefire solution to the difficulties children experience with money. It is designed to build on number and place-value skills and concepts that were developed without or before using coins.

The Coin Box applet found at Illuminations on NCTM's website (http://illuminations.nctm.org/ActivityDetail .aspx?ID=217) poses tasks that allow children to count coins, collect a given amount of money, exchange a given collection of coins for the fewest coins, and make change. There are two options to display coins— one that uses only the pictures of coins and another that places the coin onto a grid that indicates its value (e.g., a nickel is displayed on a 1 by 5 grid; a dime is displayed on a 2 by 5 grid). You can find another applet under "Money" at http://nlvm.usu.edu/en/nav/grade_g_1.html that uses coins and bills. In this applet children can count the money displayed, pay an exact amount, and make a dollar by dragging coins into a box. They can also check their work, receiving feedback that indicates if they are correct or if they have placed too much or too little in the box.

Other Measurable Attributes

Although children in grades pre-K–2 focus on measuring length, time, and money, they also need experience with other measureable attributes, such as area, weight, and volume. Here we offer some ideas and activities for initial experiences with these attributes.

♦ Area

Area is the two-dimensional space inside a region. As with other attributes, children must first understand the attribute of area before measuring.

Comparison Activities

One purpose of early comparison activities with areas is to help children distinguish between size (or area) and shape, length, and other dimensions. A long, skinny rectangle may have less area than a triangle with shorter sides. Also important to understand is the idea that rearranging areas into different shapes does not affect the amount of area. These ideas are especially difficult for young children to understand.

Direct comparison of two areas is frequently impossible except when the shapes involved have some common dimension or property. For example, two rectangles with the same width can be compared directly. Comparison of these special shapes, however, fails to deal with the attribute of area. Instead, activities in which one area is rearranged (conservation of area) are suggested. Cutting a shape into two parts and reassembling it in a different shape can show that the before and after shapes have the same area, even though they are different shapes. This idea is not at all obvious to children in grades pre-K–2.

Figure **15.8** Different shapes, same area.

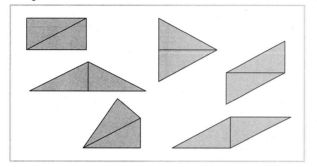

Activity 15.21 **TWO-PIECE SHAPES**

Cut out a large number of rectangles of the same area, about 3 inches by 5 inches, or use unruled index cards with these dimensions. Each pair of children will need six rectangles. Have them fold and cut the rectangles on the diagonal, making two identical triangles. Next, have them rearrange the triangles into different shapes, including back into the original rectangle. The rule is that only sides of the same length can be matched up and must be matched exactly. Have pairs of children find all the shapes that can be made this way, gluing the triangles on paper as a record (see Figure 15.8). Discuss the area and shape of the different responses. Does one shape have a greater area than the rest? How do you know? Did one take more paper to make? Help children conclude that although each figure is a different shape, all the figures have the same *area*.

Using Physical Models of Area Units

Although squares are the most common area units, any tile that conveniently fills up a plane region can be used. Nonstandard units, such as index cards or playing cards, can be used initially to explore the concept of area. Here are some suggestions for nonstandard area units:

- *Round counters, chips, or pennies.* It is not necessary that the area units fit with no gaps for early explorations.
- *Cardboard squares.* Squares that are about 20 cm per side work well for large areas. Smaller units should be about 5 cm to 10 cm on a side.
- *Sheets of newspaper.* These make excellent units for very large areas.
- *Pattern blocks.* The hexagon, trapezoid, blue rhombus, and triangle are easily compared to each other by laying one on top of the other.

In addition, standard units can be used:

- Color tiles (1-inch sides).
- White Cuisenaire rods or the unit cube from base-ten blocks (1-cm sides).

Children can use units to measure surfaces in the room such as desktops, bulletin boards, and books. Large regions can be outlined with masking tape on the floor. Small regions can be duplicated on paper so that children can work at stations.

In area measurements, there may be lots of units that only partially fit. To avoid this issue as children begin their initial explorations with area, create tasks by building a shape with units and drawing the outline. Give this outline to children for them to determine how many units are needed to cover the outlined region.

The following activity is a good way to see what ideas your children have about units of area.

Activity 15.22 **FILL AND COMPARE**

Draw two rectangles and a blob shape on a sheet of paper. Make it so that the three areas are not the same but with no area that is clearly largest or smallest. The children's first task is to estimate which is the smallest and the largest of the three shapes. After recording their estimate, they should use multiples of the same unit to fill in the shapes (e.g., color tiles, round counters). Alternatively, they can trace or glue the same two-dimensional unit on the shapes. Children should explain what they discovered.

Your objective in the beginning is to develop the idea that area is measured by covering or tiling. Groups are likely to come up with different measures for the same region. Discuss these differences with the children and point to the difficulties involved in making estimates around the edges. Avoid the idea that there is one "right" approach.

◆ Volume and Capacity

Volume and *capacity* are both terms for measures of the "size" of three-dimensional regions. The term *capacity* is generally used to refer to the amount that a container will hold. Standard units of capacity include quarts and gallons, liters and milliliters—units used for liquids as well as the containers that hold them. The term *volume* can be used to refer to the capacity of a container but is also used for the size of solid objects. Standard units of volume are expressed in terms of length units, such as cubic inches or cubic centimeters.

Comparison Activities

Comparing the volumes of solid objects is very difficult. For primary grade children, it is appropriate to focus on capacity. A simple method of comparing capacity is to fill one container with something and then pour this amount into the comparison container.

Young children should have lots of experiences directly comparing the capacities of different containers such as cans, small boxes, and plastic containers. The following activity is appropriate for pre-K–2 children.

▶ *Activity* 15.23 **CAPACITY SORT**

Provide a variety of containers with one marked as the "target." The children's task is to sort the collection into those that hold more than, less than, or about the same amount as the target container. Provide a recording sheet on which each container is listed and a place to circle "holds more," "holds less," and "holds about the same." List the choices twice for each container—one to record an estimate and one for the actual measure. Provide a filler (such as beans, rice, or Styrofoam peanuts), scoops, and funnels. Working in pairs, have children measure and record results. Discuss what children noticed in their estimating and measuring (e.g., rounder/fatter shapes seem to hold more).

Using Physical Models of Volume and Capacity Units

Two types of units can be used to measure volume and capacity: solid units and containers. Solid units are things like wooden cubes or old tennis balls that can be used to fill the container being measured. The other type of unit model is a small container that is filled and poured repeatedly into the container being measured. The following are a few examples of units that you might want to collect.

- Plastic liquid medicine cups
- Plastic jars and containers of almost any size
- Wooden cubic blocks or blocks of any shape (a lot and all the same size)
- Styrofoam packing peanuts (which still produce conceptual measures of volume even though they do not pack perfectly)

Remember your goal is to help children develop an understanding of the concept of capacity or volume. Children often think that a tall, narrow container holds more than a short, wide one because it is difficult for them to attend to two dimensions, the height and width. By having them explore capacity using a variety of containers, you can challenge this misconception.

You can also have children begin to use cups, pints, quarts, and gallon containers to help them begin to get a sense of their sizes. Having them use, for example, a measuring cup to fill a pint container or a pint container to fill a gallon container can help them begin to develop a sense of the relative sizes of customary units of capacity.

◆ Weight and Mass

Weight is a measure of the pull or force of gravity on an object. Mass is the amount of matter in an object and a measure of the force needed to accelerate it. On the moon, where gravity is much less than on Earth, an object has a smaller weight but the identical mass as on Earth. For practical purposes, on Earth, the measures of mass and weight will be about the same. In this discussion, the terms *weight* and *mass* will be used interchangeably.

Comparison Activities

Starting in kindergarten, children can begin exploring the concept of heavier and lighter. The most conceptual way for children to compare the weights of two objects is to hold one in each hand, extend their arms, and experience the relative downward pull on each—effectively communicating to a pre-K–1 child what "heavier" or "weighs more" means. This personal experience can then be transferred to one of two basic types of scales—balances and spring scales.

When introducing children to a balance, have them hold two different objects, one in each hand, and estimate which of two objects is heavier. When they then place the objects in the two pans of a balance, the pan that goes down can be understood to hold the heavier object. Even a relatively simple balance will detect small differences. If two objects are placed one at a time in a spring scale, the heavier object pulls the pan down farther. Both balances and spring scales have real value in the classroom. (Technically, spring scales measure weight and balance scales measure mass. Why?) With either scale, sorting and ordering tasks are possible with very young children.

Using Physical Models of Weight or Mass Units

Any collection of uniform objects with the same mass can serve as weight units. For very light objects, large paper clips, wooden blocks, or plastic cubes work well. You can also use U.S. coins for weight units. For example, all U.S. nickels weigh 5 grams and pennies weigh 2.5 grams. Large metal washers found in hardware stores are effective for weighing slightly heavier objects. You will need to rely on standard weights to weigh things as heavy as a kilogram or more.

Weight cannot be measured directly (i.e., you can't see weight), so either a two-pan balance or a spring scale must be used. In a balance scale, place an object in one pan and weights in the other until the two pans balance. In a spring scale, first place the object in and mark the position of the pan on a piece of paper taped behind the pan. Remove the object and place just enough weights in the pan to pull it down to the same level. Discuss how equal weights will pull the spring or rubber band with the same force.

Although the notion of units of weight or mass appears in the expectations of the *Common Core State Standards* for third graders, it is good preparation for younger children to explore the attribute of weight using informal units. Plus, you can make the connection to the equal sign as discussed in Chapter 13, in which pan balances are used to think about creating equivalent quantities on each side.

Expanded Lesson

Crooked Paths

Content and Task Decisions

Grade Level: K–1

Mathematics Goals

- To help children understand that length is an attribute that need not be in a straight line (e.g., the distance around an object or a nonstraight path has length, just as does a straight object)
- To use a nonstandard measurement tool (e.g., string, blocks) to measure lengths

Grade Level Guide

NCTM *Curriculum Focal Points*	*Common Core State Standards*
Children in prekindergarten think about which objects have the attribute of length and can compare objects' lengths. In kindergarten, children use length to compare objects. First graders measure using multiple copies of units end to end.	Kindergarten students begin to describe attributes of objects that can be measured with length. In grade 1, one of four focal areas is children measuring lengths indirectly and by iterating (or using groups of the same unit).

Consider Children's Needs

Children have made comparisons of straight objects or paths and have learned the meaning of *longer* and *shorter* in that context. Children have not used units or rulers to measure lengths.

For English Language Learners

- Children may need language support for the terms *longer, shorter, straight,* and *crooked.* You can have the children model what these terms mean and/or use objects to illustrate their meaning. Also, reinforce the meaning of *estimate.*
- Use pair-share and/or encourage use of native language in the *After* phase when the children are explaining their thinking about the longer paths.

For Children with Disabilities

- Tape the end of the string to the beginning of the path, then mark the end of the measurement on the string with a marker. Use another string for the other path in the same way. Then compare the lengths.
- Children may have trouble with thinking about the estimates of length when one path is "crooked." You might want to show an example of two paths on the floor (one crooked and one straight) and have the children walk each to see which takes longer to walk. Then they can think about estimating the paths made in the learning stations.

Materials

- Masking tape
- Rope, string, or yarn that is at least 10 feet long for each station
- One "Crooked Paths" recording sheet for every pair of children (Blackline Master 48)

Lesson

Before

This will be a station activity. Set up three identical stations around the room. Each station consists of two crooked paths made of masking tape. Try to make them about the same in each station. Path A is a zigzag of four straight-line segments that total about 9 feet. Path B is more S-shaped and is about 7 feet long. Make path B "look" longer by spreading it out more.

Begin with a simpler version of the task:

- Show the class pairs of straight objects, such as a pencil and a crayon, or two lines drawn on the board. For each pair, ask, "Which is longer? Which is shorter? How can we tell?"
- On the board, draw a half-circle and beneath it a line segment about as long as the diameter. Ask, "How can

we tell which of these is longer?" Solicit ideas. Be sure the children hear the idea that the curve is longer than the line segment and that some children provide good reasons. For example, say, "If you had to walk on these, it would take longer to walk the curved path."

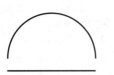

Present the focus task to the class:

- Gather the children around one station. Say, "One path might be longer or they might be the same. Your task is to decide."

- Show the children the worksheets and explain how to use them. Explain that they are to circle the path that is longer or circle both paths if they think they are the same. Then they are to draw a picture to show how they decided. Have the children work in pairs.

- Ask the children which path they think is longer or whether they think they are the same. Say, "Before you begin work, put an X on the picture of the path that you think is longer. This is your estimate." Have a few children share their estimates and their reasoning.

- Show the children that there is string for comparing lengths, but they can use linked paper clips, blocks, or whatever materials they want to help them decide.

Provide clear expectations:

- Children will work with partners at the stations.

During

- Monitor station activity but do not interfere. Be sure the children are completing worksheets to the best of their abilities.

- If a pair seems unable to make a decision, ask, "If a toy car was going to go along these paths, which path would it travel longer on?" or, "Could you use some blocks from over in the block corner to help?"

- For children who need a greater challenge, ask them to make a row of blocks in a straight line that is just as long as the curvy path.

After

Bring the class together to share and discuss the task:

- Remind the children of the task of comparing the two paths. Have the children refer to their worksheets as they talk about what they did.

- Ask, "How many thought the zigzag path was longer?" Count and record on the board next to a zigzag. "How many thought the curvy path was longer?" Count and record. "How many thought they were about the same?" Count and record. Ask the children if the estimates they made were the same as the result that they figured out. Were they surprised? Why?

- Select pairs to explain what they did. Get as many different ideas and methods as possible.

- If the children disagree about which path is longer, have them explain their reasoning in a way that might convince those who disagree. Give the children the opportunity to change their minds, but ask, "What made you change your minds?"

Assessment

Observe

- Look for children who understand how length can exist on a curved path (correctly compare or make appropriate attempt). This can be a checklist item based on the discussion or observations.

- For children who used units, did they use like-sized units or make appropriate use of materials?

Ask

- Which path is longer? How do you know?

- How can path A be longer if it takes less room to make on the floor than path B?

16

Developing Geometric Reasoning and Concepts

Big IDEAS

1 What makes shapes alike and different can be determined by an array of geometric properties and defining characteristics. For example, a square is like a rectangle because it has two pairs of parallel sides and four right angles; some rectangles are different from squares because they do not have four equal sides.

2 Shapes can be described in terms of their location in a plane or in space. Initially children use the words of everyday language such as *above, below, next to, in front of,* and *beside* to describe location and then later transition to simple coordinate systems to describe locations more precisely.

3 Shapes can be moved in a plane or in space without changing the shape's properties. These movements can be described in terms of translations (slides), reflections (flips), and rotations (turns).

4 Visualization is "geometry done with the mind's eye." It involves being able to create and move mental images of shapes, thinking about how they look from different viewpoints, and predicting the results of various transformations.

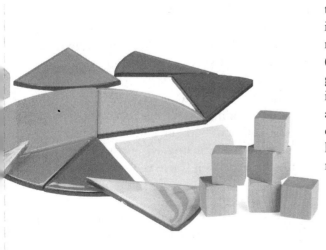

According to the NCTM *Principles and Standards for School Mathematics* (National Council of Teachers of Mathematics, 2000), "At the core of mathematics in the early years are the Number and Geometry strands" (p. 77). This sentiment is also seen in the *Curriculum Focal Points* (National Council of Teachers of Mathematics, 2006) in which geometry is included as one of three focal points in grades pre-K–1 and as a connection to the focal points in grade 2. The *Common Core State Standards* (CCSSO, 2010) highlight geometry as one of the critical areas across grades K–2 (see Appendix B). The National Research Council (2009) in its publication *Mathematics Learning in Early Childhood* also supports an emphasis on geometry in the early grades. All of these directives are clear that geometry instruction in grades pre-K–2 should help children learn more about the world they live in while also playing a significant role in supporting the development of number concepts.

Geometry Goals for Young Children

It is useful to think about your geometry objectives in terms of two related frameworks: (1) spatial sense and geometric reasoning and (2) the specific geometry content found in your state or district objectives. The first framework has to do with the way children think and reason about shape and space. A well-researched theoretical basis that describes the development of geometric thought informs this framework. The second framework is content in the more traditional sense—knowing about shapes, such as squares, triangles, circles, prisms, cubes, and cylinders, parallel lines, symmetry, and so forth. The *Common Core State Standards* (CCSSO, 2010) and *Curriculum Focal Points* (National Council of Teachers of Mathematics, 2006) help describe content goals across the grades:

- In kindergarten, children are expected to identify and describe various two- and three-dimensional shapes and describe their relative position using everyday language (e.g., *above*, *below*, *beside*). They should also draw and build shapes as well as compose larger shapes from smaller ones.

- In first grade, children should be able to distinguish between a shape's defining attributes (e.g., number of sides, closed) and irrelevant attributes (e.g., color, size, orientation). They also work on composing shapes to create new shapes and begin to decompose shapes into smaller shapes.

- Second graders are expected to be able to recognize and draw shapes given specific attributes (e.g., number of angles, equal length sides, and "square" angles). They continue to work on decomposing shapes into smaller shapes.

In order to best help children grow in their understanding of geometry, we need to understand both aspects of geometry—reasoning and content.

◆ Spatial Sense and Geometric Reasoning

Spatial sense can be defined as an intuition about shapes and the relationships between shapes and is considered a core area of mathematical study in the early grades (Sarama & Clements, 2009). Spatial sense includes the ability to mentally visualize objects and spatial relationships, including being able to mentally move objects around. It also includes familiarity with geometric descriptions of objects and position. People with well-developed spatial sense appreciate geometric form in art, nature, and architecture and they use geometric ideas to describe and analyze their world.

Some people say that you either are or are not born with spatial sense. This simply is not true! Meaningful experiences with shape and spatial relationships, when provided consistently over time, can and do develop spatial sense. Between 1990 and 2000, National Assessment of Educational Progress (NAEP) data indicated a steadily continuing improvement in children's geometric reasoning at grade 8 (Sowder & Wearne, 2006). However, students did not just get smarter. Instead, there has been an increasing emphasis on geometry at all grades, but particularly so in the elementary grades. The *Principles and Standards for School Mathematics* support this notion that all students can grow in their geometric skills and understandings: "The notion of building understanding in geometry across the grades, from informal to more formal thinking, is consistent with the thinking of theorists and researchers" (National Council of Teachers of Mathematics, 2000, p. 41).

◆ Geometric Content

For too long, geometry curricula in the United States emphasized the learning of terminology. Geometry, in fact, involves a number of aspects that apply to all grade levels:

- *Shapes and Properties* includes a study of the properties of shapes in two and three dimensions, as well as a study of the relationships built on properties.

- *Transformation* includes a study of translations, reflections, and rotations (slides, flips, and turns), the study of symmetries, and the concept of similarity.

- *Location* refers to ways of specifying how objects are located in the plane or in space, such as coordinate geometry.

- *Visualization* includes the recognition of shapes in the environment, developing relationships between two- and three-dimensional objects, and the ability to recognize, draw, and think about objects from different viewpoints.

The chapter is organized around these four categories with experiences suggested for each category. You will note that more attention is devoted to the topic shapes and properties as that category aligns with the emphasis of the *Common Core State Standards* for grades pre-K–2. However, you should also note that experiences targeted toward each of the categories have potential to enhance children's understanding in the other categories.

Developing Geometric Reasoning

Although not all people think about geometric ideas in the same manner, we are all capable of developing the ability to think and reason in geometric contexts. The research of two Dutch educators, Pierre van Hiele and Dina van Hiele-Geldof, provides insight into the differences in individuals' geometric thinking and how those differences come to be. The van Hiele theory significantly influences geometry curricula worldwide.

◆ The van Hiele Levels of Geometric Thought

The van Hiele model is typically described as a five-level hierarchy of ways of understanding spatial ideas. Each level describes the thinking processes used in geometric contexts. Specifically, the levels describe what types of geometric ideas we think about (called *objects of thought*) and how we think about those ideas. Clements and Battista (1992) proposed the existence of a level prior to the first level in the van Hiele model. We include this level because of its power to help you make sense of some of your young children's geometric reasoning (see Figure 16.1); however, we have left this initial level unnumbered and maintained the original numbering of the van Hiele levels to be consistent with other resources and the other volumes in this series.

Pre-Recognition

The objects of thought at this level are specific visible or tactile objects.

Children at this level are unable to identify and distinguish between many common shapes. They may notice only a subset of the visual characteristics of a shape, which results in an inability to distinguish between some shapes. For example, they may be able to distinguish between a circle and a square but not between a square and a triangle. Most children at this level will know something about circles and squares. They tend to be less accurate identifying triangles and rectangles. At this level children may identify any shape that has a prominent

Figure 16.1 The van Hiele theory of geometric thought, modified to include the pre-recognition level.

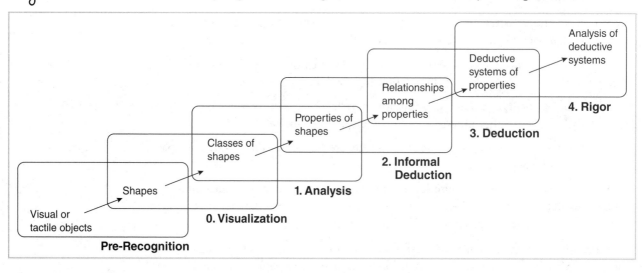

"point" as a triangle and any four-sided shape with long parallel sides as a rectangle (Clements & Sarama, 2000a).

The products of thought at the pre-recognition level are shapes and what they "look like."

Level 0: Visualization

The objects of thought at level 0 are shapes and what they "look like."

Children at level 0 recognize and name figures based on the global, visual characteristics of the figure—a gestalt-like approach to shape. For example, a square is defined by a child at this level as a square "because it looks like a square." Because appearance is dominant at this level, appearances can overpower properties of a shape. For example, a rotated square whose sides are all at a 45-degree angle to the vertical may now be called a diamond and no longer a square according to children at this level. Children at level 0 will sort and classify shapes based on their appearances—"I put these together because they are all pointy" (or "fat," or "look like a house," or "are dented in," and so on). With a focus on the appearances of shapes, children are able to see how shapes are alike and different. As a result, children at this level can create and begin to understand classifications of shapes.

The products of thought at level 0 are classes or groupings of shapes that seem to be "alike."

Level 1: Analysis (also known as Description)

The objects of thought at level 1 are classes of shapes rather than individual shapes.

Children at the analysis or description level see shapes as a collection of properties. Consequently, in describing a shape, level 1 thinkers are likely to list as many properties of a shape as they know. They do not see relationships between these properties and so cannot determine which properties are sufficient in describing a shape. They are able to consider all shapes within a class rather than just the single shape on their desk. Instead of talking about this rectangle, they can talk about all rectangles. By focusing on a class of shapes, children are able to think about what makes a rectangle a rectangle (four sides, opposite sides parallel, opposite sides of the same length, four right angles, congruent diagonals, etc.). The irrelevant features (e.g., size or orientation) fade into the background and children begin to appreciate that a collection of shapes goes together because of properties. If a shape belongs to a particular class such as cubes, it has the corresponding properties of that class. "All cubes have six congruent faces, and each of those faces is a square." These properties are only implicit at level 0. Children operating at level 1 may be able to list all the properties of squares, rectangles, and parallelograms but not see that these are subclasses of one another, that is, that all squares are rectangles and all rectangles are parallelograms.

The products of thought at level 1 are the properties of shapes.

Level 2: Informal Deduction

The objects of thought at level 2 are the properties of shapes.

Children at the informal deduction level are able to develop relationships between properties and between shapes. "If all four angles are right angles, the shape must be a rectangle. If it is a square, all angles are right angles. If it is a square, it must be a rectangle." With greater ability to engage in "if–then" reasoning, children can classify shapes using only a minimum set of defining characteristics. For example, four congruent sides and at least one right angle are sufficient to define a square. Rectangles are parallelograms with a right angle. Observations go beyond properties themselves and begin to focus on logical arguments about the properties. Children at level 2 will be able to follow and appreciate informal deductive arguments about shapes and their properties. "Proofs" may be more intuitive than rigorously deductive; however, there is an appreciation that a logical argument is compelling. An appreciation of the axiomatic structure (an agreed-on set of rules) of a formal deductive system, however, remains under the surface.

The products of thought at level 2 are relationships among properties of geometric objects.

Level 3: Deduction

The objects of thought at level 3 are relationships among properties of geometric objects.

At level 3, students move from thinking about properties to reasoning and generating proofs that are based on the properties. As this analysis of the informal arguments takes place, the structure of the system, complete with axioms, definitions, theorems, corollaries, and postulates, begins to develop and can be appreciated as the necessary means of establishing geometric truth. The student at this level is able to work with abstract statements about geometric properties and make conclusions based more on logic than intuition. A student operating at level 3 is not only aware that the diagonals of a rectangle bisect each other (level 2) but also has an appreciation of the need to prove this from a series of deductive arguments.

The type of reasoning that characterizes a level 3 thinker is the same reasoning required in high school geometry, where students build on a list of axioms and definitions to create theorems. In a very global sense, high school geometry students are working to create a complete geometric deductive system.

The products of thought at level 3 are deductive axiomatic systems for geometry.

Level 4: Rigor

The objects of thought at level 4 are deductive axiomatic systems for geometry.

At the highest level of the van Hiele hierarchy, the objects of thought are axiomatic systems themselves, not just the deductions within a system. There is an appreciation of the distinctions and relationships between different axiomatic systems. For example, spherical geometry is based on lines drawn on a sphere rather than in a plane. This geometry has its own set of axioms and theorems and is generally found at the level of college geometry courses.

We have given brief descriptions of all six levels to illustrate the scope of the van Hiele theory. Most children at the pre-K–2 grades will be at the pre-recognition level or level 0 (visualization) with some children moving to level 1 (analysis). Consequently, a significant number of the activities in this chapter address the first two levels.

Characteristics of the van Hiele Levels

Five related characteristics of the van Hiele levels merit special attention.

- The products of thought at each level are the same as the objects of thought at the next level, as illustrated in Figure 16.1. The objects (ideas) must be created at one level so that relationships between these objects of thought can become the focus of the next level.

- The levels are not age dependent. A third grader or a high school student could be at level 1.

- The levels are sequential. To arrive at any level above the pre-recognition level, children must move through all prior levels. To move through a level means that children have experienced geometric thinking appropriate for that level and have created in their own minds the types of objects or relationships that are the focus of thought at the next level.

- Advancement through the levels requires geometric *experiences*. Children should explore, talk about, and interact with content at the next level while increasing their experiences at their current level.

- When instruction or language is at a level higher than that of the children, children will be unable to understand the concept being developed. They may memorize a fact (e.g., all squares are rectangles) but not construct the actual relationship between the properties involved.

⬡ Implications for Instruction

If students are to be prepared for the deductive geometry of high school and beyond, reaching van Hiele level 2 by the end of the eighth grade is critical. All teachers should be aware that the experiences they provide are the single most important factor in moving children up this developmental ladder.

The van Hiele theory and the developmental perspective of this book highlight the necessity of teaching at the child's level of thought. However, almost any activity can be modified to span two levels of thinking. For many activities, you will need to adapt the activity to the level of individual children so you can challenge them to operate at the next higher level.

As you choose activities for your children, keep in mind four features of effective geometry instruction for young children (Clements & Sarama, 2009):

- *Show and compare diverse examples and nonexamples.* Show examples and nonexamples that look alike to help children attend to a shape's relevant attributes.

- *Facilitate discussions about shapes and their attributes.* When you encourage children to describe shapes, expect them to initially use visual descriptions (e.g., long, pointy, etc.) but try to focus their attention on the relevant attributes (e.g., number of sides, sides of equal length).

- *Examine a wider variety of shape classes.* Children in early childhood classrooms should experiment with and describe shapes beyond the typical circle, square, triangle, and rectangle. Their experiences should extend to semicircles, trapezoids, pentagons, hexagons, cubes, prisms, cones, and cylinders as well as different kinds of triangles and quadrilaterals.

- *Challenge children with a wide range of geometric tasks.* The use of physical materials, drawings, and computer models at every level of geometric thought is a must. Activities should also require and support children's reflection about the ideas they are learning.

From Pre-Recognition to Level 0 (Visualization)

Children transitioning from the pre-recognition level to level 0 can be supported as follows:

- Provide opportunities for children to identify shapes in their classroom, school, and community.

- Involve children in lots of experiences sorting shapes and describing why they believe a particular shape belongs to a group as well as why a particular shape does not belong. Include a sufficient variety of examples of shapes so that irrelevant features (e.g., orientation, size, color) do not become important.

- Provide lots of experiences for children to copy and build shapes using a wide variety of materials. These activities should help children focus on the relevant and irrelevant attributes of shapes.

From Level 0 (Visualization) to Level 1 (Analysis)

Children moving from level 0 to level 1 can be supported as follows:

- Challenge children to test ideas about shapes using a variety of examples from a particular category. Say to them, "Let's see if that is true for other rectangles," or "Can you draw a triangle that does not have a right angle?" In general, encourage children to see whether observations made about a particular shape apply to other shapes of a similar kind.

- Provide ample opportunities for children to draw, build, make, put together (compose), and take apart (decompose) shapes in both two and three dimensions. These activities should be built around understanding and using specific characteristics or properties.

- Emphasize the properties of figures rather than simple identification. As new geometric concepts are learned, the number of properties that figures have can be expanded.

- Apply ideas to entire classes of figures (e.g., *all* rectangles, *all* prisms) rather than to individual models. For example, find ways to sort all possible triangles into groups. From these groups, define types of triangles.

Task Selection and Levels of Thought

No simple assessment exists to identify the exact level at which a child is functioning. However, using the descriptors at the levels of thinking can be helpful. As children are engaged in an activity or a diagnostic interview, listen to children discuss their thinking. Can they identify common shapes? Do they understand that shapes do not change when the orientation or size changes? Do they use properties in their descriptions and discussions of shapes? Can they talk about shapes as classes? Do they, for example, refer to "rectangles" or do they base their discussion around a particular rectangle? With careful observations such as these, you will soon be able to distinguish among children at the first three levels.

The remainder of this chapter offers a sample of activities organized around the four content goals of the NCTM *Principles and Standards for School Mathematics*: Shapes and Properties, Transformations, Location, and Visualization. Within each of these sections, activities are further sorted according to the most appropriate van Hiele levels for grades pre-K–2. Understand that all of these subdivisions are quite fluid. An activity found at one level of thinking can easily be adapted to an adjacent level simply by the way it is presented to children.

Learning about Shapes and Properties

Although the van Hiele theory applies to all students of all ages learning any geometric content, it may be easier to apply the theory to the shapes and properties category. In this content area, children are finding out what makes shapes alike and different, and in the process they will begin to discover properties of the shapes, including the conventional names for these properties. With sufficient experiences, children can begin to develop classifications of special shapes (e.g., triangles, quadrilaterals) and learn that some properties apply to entire classes of shapes. As children explore their geometric world, they should have experiences with a rich variety of both two- and three-dimensional shapes.

Shapes and Properties Activities for Pre-Recognition Thinkers

The following activity can be modified to accommodate children at the pre-recognition level, level 0, and level 1 by altering the object of the search. Here we focus on children at the pre-recognition level.

Activity 16.1 SHAPE SHOW AND HUNT

Show a couple of examples of the target shape and name the shape. Explicitly point out the relevant attributes on the target shape (e.g., straight or curved sides, number of sides, right angles, and so on). Make sure children, especially ELLs, understand the terms you use such as *square corners* and *right turns*. You can compare a square corner or right angle to a capital "L" or the corner of a sheet of paper or an index card. Use masking tape to create a large target shape on the community rug so that children can walk around the shape. You can also have the children draw the shape in the air. Now the task is for children to find one or two items in the classroom, on the playground, in the library, or somewhere else at school that have this same shape or attribute. If searching outside the classroom, you may want to take pictures of the examples children find so that you can show the examples later. As children find their examples, ask them how they know it is the target shape. Listen for how they describe their example. What are they focusing on? What words are they using? For children with disabilities, provide a cutout of the target shape that children can take with them as they search for an example.

Have children search not just for triangles, circles, squares, and rectangles but also for properties of shapes. A shape hunt will be much more successful if you let children look for either one thing or for a specific list. Some examples children can search for are the following:

- Right angles ("square corners")
- Curved surfaces or curved lines
- Two or more shapes that can be put together to make another shape
- Circles inside each other (concentric)
- Shapes with "dents" (concave) or without "dents" (convex)
- Solids that are like a box (prism), a cylinder, a pyramid, a cone
- Five shapes that are alike in some way

Activity 16.2 MATCH IT–NAME IT

Create a variety of familiar shapes from the assorted two-dimensional shapes in the Blackline Masters (20–26) using card stock in two colors. Create multiples of the same shapes. Give each child a shape from the set. Select a shape that matches one of the children's shapes but in a different color. Ask the children to stand up if they think they have a shape that matches your shape. Have children (either those standing or others) explain how they know the shapes match and to name the shape. Then have children try to find matches for their shapes with children sitting near them. Have children share their matches and encourage them to try to name the shapes.

BLM

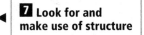

Standards for
Mathematical Practice

◀ **7** **Look for and make use of structure**

The next activity introduces children to three-dimensional shapes and is adapted from Clements and Sarama (2000b).

Activity 16.3 GETTING INTO SHAPE

After identifying and talking about the relevant attributes of a three-dimensional shape, have the children pretend they are inside of it. For example, after showing the children an oatmeal box (cylinder), tell them to pretend they are inside of it. Tell them to close their eyes and touch the walls of the cylinder. Ask them to describe the walls. Then have them pretend to trace the top of the cylinder and then the bottom of the cylinder with their finger. Ask, "What is the shape you traced?" The activity can be repeated with other shapes, such as a prism, where they are feeling and trying to identify each face. Try to find large boxes or tubes for your children to get in so they can actually feel the inside and outside of the shapes.

Source: D. H. Clements and J. Samara, *Young Mathematicians at Work: Constructing Algebra.* Reprinted with permission. Copyright 2010 by the National Council of Teachers of Mathematics. All rights reserved.

Children at the pre-recognition level tend to ignore some of the attributes of shapes. The next two activities help to draw their attention to shapes' attributes as children consider examples and nonexamples of shapes.

Activity 16.4 IS IT OR ISN'T IT?

Show children an example of a two-dimensional shape that you've drawn on the board. Ask them for the name of the shape and ask them to tell why it is that shape. Draw another shape that is somehow different from the first shape—it could be another example of the shape or a nonexample that looks like the target shape and that children could mistake for the shape. For example, if the target shape is a triangle, display triangles that are "skinny" or oriented with the vertex pointing down. Or display a three-sided shape whose sides are not straight. You can also provide counterexamples such as a "triangle" musical instrument that has an open side. Have children identify and discuss the differences. Summarize by highlighting the relevant features of the target shape.

Clements and Sarama (2009) recommend pairing examples and nonexamples that look alike so as to focus attention on a shape's critical attributes. The next activity provides this kind of experience.

🔳 Standards for
Mathematical Practice

| **6** Attend to
precision |

Figure 16.2

"Tricky Shapes"
uses examples and
nonexamples that look
alike to help children
attend to critical
attributes.

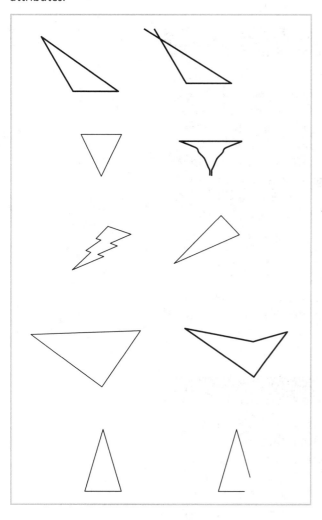

Teaching Tip

Along the way, the names of any new shapes and their properties can be introduced and placed on the math word wall.

Activity 16.5 **TRICKY SHAPES**

Provide pairs of children with a worksheet that has several examples and nonexamples
of a target shape (see Figure 16.2). They are to identify the examples and explain why
they are that shape. They are also to describe why the nonexamples are not the shape.
Facilitate a discussion with the whole class. Summarize by reviewing the relevant features
of the target shape.

The following activity requires children to think about the attributes of target shapes so
that they can then build them.

Activity 16.6 **BUILD IT**

Provide children with drawings of four or five varied examples of a target shape and plastic (flat) coffee stirrers
cut to various lengths or a manipulative such as D-Stix.
(D-Stix kits contain six to nine sticks of different lengths
that can be used to make two- and three-dimensional
shapes.) Children make the shapes by placing the stirrers
on the drawings with the stirrers "connected" or touching at their endpoints. Have children name the shape and
talk about the attributes. Challenge children to create
examples of a target shape without having access to a
drawing as a model.

Clements and Sarama (2000a) describe how a kindergarten teacher challenged her children to create shapes with
their bodies. Two children in the class created a rhombus by
sitting on the floor facing each other with their legs spread
and feet together. One child in the classroom suggested that
if another child lay across their feet, they would have two
triangles. See how creative your children can be!

Shapes and Properties Activities 🔷 for Level 0 (Visualization) Thinkers

The emphasis at level 0 is on the shapes that children can
observe, feel, build, take apart, and perceive in many ways.
The general goal is to explore how shapes are alike and different and use these ideas to create classes of shapes (both
physically and mentally). Some of these classes of shapes
have names—rectangles, triangles, prisms, cylinders, and so
on. Properties of shapes, such as parallel sides, symmetry,
right angles, and so on, are included at this level but only
in an informal, observational manner. Children need experience with a wide variety of two- and three-dimensional
shapes. The triangles you use should be more than just

equilateral and not always shown with the vertex at the top. Shapes should have curved sides, straight sides, and combinations of these.

Sorting and Classifying

As young children work at classification of shapes, be prepared for them to notice features that you do not consider to be "real" geometric attributes, such as "skinny" or "looks like a rocket." Children at this level will also attach to shapes ideas that are not part of the shape, such as "points up" or "has a side that is the same as the edge of the board."

For variety in two-dimensional shapes, create your own materials using something like the 2-D Shapes in the Blackline Masters (20–26). Make multiple copies so that groups of children can all work with the same shapes. Once you have your sets constructed, the following activity provides several ideas.

Activity 16.7 SHAPE SORTS

Have children work in groups of four on the following related activities using a set of two-dimensional shapes like those in Figure 16.3. Do the activities in the order shown.

- Each child randomly selects a shape. In turn, the children tell one or two things they find interesting about their shape.
- Children each randomly select two shapes and try to find something that is alike about their two shapes and something that is different.
- The group selects one target shape at random and places it in the center of the workspace. Their task is to find all other shapes that are like the target shape according to the same rule. For example, if they say, "This shape is like the target shape because it has a curved side and a straight side," then all other shapes that they put in the collection must have these properties. Do a second sort with the same target shape but use a different property.
- Do a "secret sort." You (or one of the children) create a small collection of about five shapes that fit a secret rule. Leave other shapes that belong in your set in the pile. Children try to find additional pieces that belong to the set and/or guess the secret rule.

Figure 16.3

A collection of shapes for sorting. See Blackline Masters 20–26 for these shapes and others.

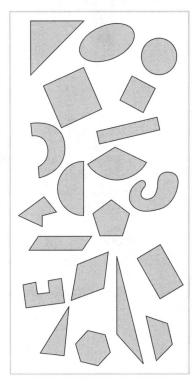

Figure 16.4 illustrates a few of the many possible ways a set might be sorted. Most of these activities can and should be done with three-dimensional shapes as well.

These activities can elicit a wide variety of ideas as children examine the shapes. They may start describing the shapes with ideas such as "curvy" or "looks like a tree" rather than typical geometric properties. But as children notice more sophisticated properties you can attach appropriate names to them. For example, some children may notice that some shapes have corners "like a square" (explain that those are also called right angles) or that "these shapes are the same on both sides" (symmetrical).

What makes Activity 16.7 a level 0 activity is that children are operating on the shapes that they see in front of them and are beginning to see similarities and differences in shapes. By forming groups of shapes, they begin to imagine shapes that are not in the collection that belong to the classes or groups they identify.

Teaching Tip

In any sorting activity, the children—not the teacher—should decide how to sort. This allows the children to do the activity using ideas they own and understand. By listening to the kinds of attributes that they use in their sorting, you will be able to tell which properties they know and use and how they think about shapes.

Figure 16.4

By sorting shapes, children begin to recognize properties.

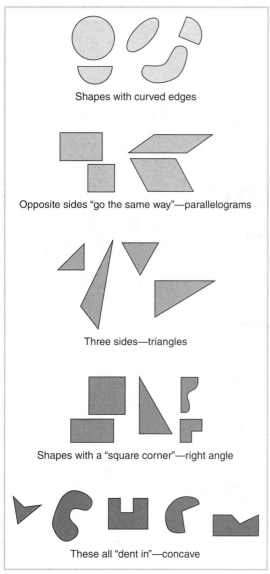

Shapes with curved edges

Opposite sides "go the same way"—parallelograms

Three sides—triangles

Shapes with a "square corner"—right angle

These all "dent in"—concave

The secret sorting in Activity 16.7 is one option for introducing a new property. For example, sort the shapes so that all have at least one right angle or "square corner." When children discover your rule, you have an opportunity to talk more about that property and name the property "right angle."

The following activity is also done with the two-dimensional shapes.

Activity 16.8 WHAT'S MY SHAPE?

BLM

From the Blackline Masters 20–26, make a double set of two-dimensional assorted shapes on card stock. Cut out one set of shapes and glue each shape inside a folded half-sheet of construction paper to make "secret-shape" folders. You can also cut file folders to create mini folders for the secret shapes.

In a group, one child is designated the leader and given a secret-shape folder. The other children are to find the shape that matches the shape in the folder by asking only "yes" or "no" questions. The group can eliminate shapes as they get answers that help narrow down the possibilities. They are not allowed to point to a piece and ask, "Is it this one?" Rather, they must continue to ask questions about properties or characteristics that reduce the choices to one shape. The final piece is checked against the one in the leader's folder. You may need to provide a list of properties and characteristics (e.g., number of sides) to support children with disabilities in their question asking.

The difficulty of Activity 16.8 largely depends on the shape in the folder. The more shapes in the collection that share properties with the secret shape, the more difficult the task.

This activity can be adapted for three-dimensional shapes by using two sets of three-dimensional models. The leader can place the secret shape under a cloth or in a shoe box. Power Solids, Polydrons, and other collections of three-dimensional shapes are available through various catalogs. Another option is to collect real objects such as cans, boxes, balls, and Styrofoam shapes. Figure 16.5 illustrates some classifications of solids.

Formative Assessment Note

Using three-dimensional shapes, adapt Activity 16.7 "Shape Sorts" for a diagnostic interview. Make sure you have a collection of solids that offers sufficient variability (curved surfaces, etc.).

The ways children describe these three-dimensional shapes provides good evidence of their level of thinking. The classifications made by level 0 thinkers are generally restricted to the shapes they have in front of them. Level 1 thinkers will begin to create categories based on properties, and their language will indicate that they know there are many more shapes in the group than those that are physically present. Children may say things such as, "These shapes have square corners sort of like rectangles," or "These look like boxes. All the boxes have square (rectangular) sides."

Figure 16.5 Early classifications of three-dimensional shapes.

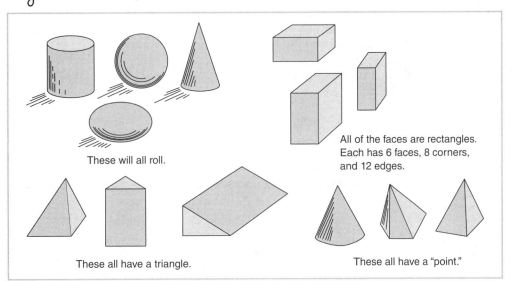

These will all roll.

All of the faces are rectangles. Each has 6 faces, 8 corners, and 12 edges.

These all have a triangle.

These all have a "point."

The next activity helps draw children's attention away from appearance to relevant attributes.

◣ *Activity* 16.9 **FEELING IT**

You will need two sets of shapes, one that you will display and one that you will use to select a secret shape from. On one day, focus on two-dimensional shapes. On another day, use three-dimensional shapes. Give children time to explore the displayed shapes, asking them to run their fingers along the sides and around the corners (for two-dimensional shapes). Secretly select one of the shapes from your set and place it in a box or a bag. Use a box with holes cut into the sides or a bag that has elastic around the top—or you could use a long sock. The idea is for children to be able to get their hands into the box, bag, or sock without being able to peek! Have the children feel the secret shape and try to guess what shape it is. You can have one child feel the shape and describe it to others so that they can decide which of the displayed shapes it matches.

Composing and Decomposing Shapes

Children need to freely explore how shapes fit together to form larger shapes (compose) and how larger shapes can be made of smaller shapes (decompose). Among two-dimensional shapes for these activities, pattern blocks and tangrams are the best known. Use pattern blocks or shapes cut from card stock to create designs for children to copy (see Figure 16.6). To increase the level of difficulty, only provide the outside outline of the design. Children can then create their own designs using these materials.

Many pattern block designs and artwork created by children will have an element of symmetry in them. Although symmetry is not a core idea in the *Common Core State Standards* for grades K–2, you can use children's creations to introduce this idea informally.

Figure 16.7 shows tangram puzzles in increasing order of difficulty. A pattern for tangrams can be found in Blackline Master 27.

BLM

Figure **16.6** Assorted materials for composing and decomposing activities.

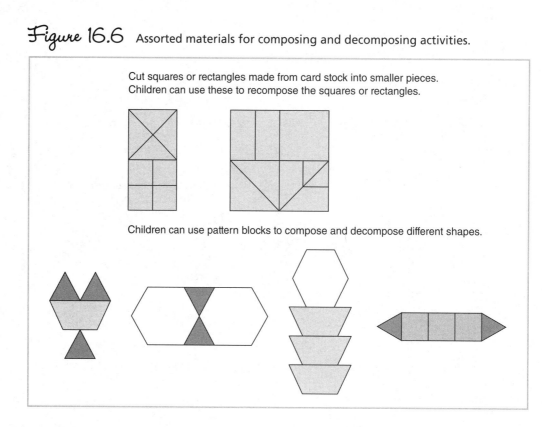

Cut squares or rectangles made from card stock into smaller pieces. Children can use these to recompose the squares or rectangles.

Children can use pattern blocks to compose and decompose different shapes.

Figure **16.7** Four types of tangram puzzles illustrate a range of difficulty levels.

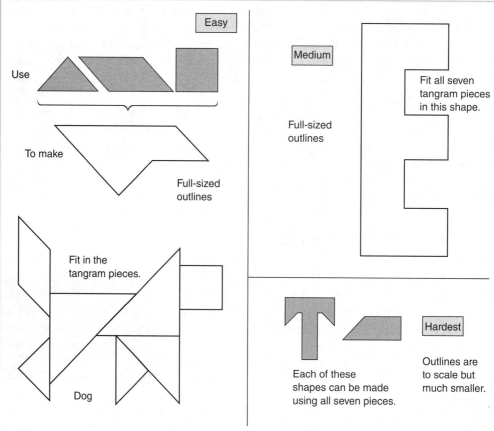

technology note

"Patch Tool" at NCTM's Illuminations site provides a computerized environment where children can compose shapes using different pattern blocks (http://illuminations.nctm.org/ActivityDetail.aspx?ID=27). It also provides five outlines of different designs where children have to decide which shapes are used to complete the designs. The National Library of Virtual Manipulatives has a tangram applet with a set of fourteen puzzle figures that can be made using all seven of the pieces (http://nlvm.usu.edu/en/nav /category_g_1_t_3.html). The e-version of tangrams has the advantage of motivation and the fact that you must be much more deliberate in arranging the shapes.

The geoboard is one of the best devices for creating two-dimensional shapes. Here are just two of many possible activities appropriate for level 0.

Figure 16.8 Shapes on geoboards (see Blackline Masters 28–29).

Have children copy shapes from pattern cards onto a geoboard.

◆ *Activity* 16.10 GEOBOARD COPY

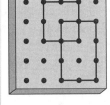

Using their own geoboards, children copy shapes, designs, and patterns from prepared cards (use Blackline Masters 28–29 to create cards) or from a geoboard projected by the teacher. Begin with designs using one band; then create more complex designs (see Figure 16.8).

◆ *Activity* 16.11 CUT IT UP/BUILD IT UP

Children copy a shape from a card onto their geoboards and then subdivide or cut the shape into smaller shapes. Specify the number of smaller shapes. Also specify whether the shapes should all be the same size or simply of the same type as shown in Figure 16.9. Alternatively, children can start with a smaller shape and duplicate the shape to create a larger shape.

Teaching Tip

Have lots of geoboards available in the classroom. It is better for two or three children to have 10 or 12 boards at a station than for each to have only one. That way, a variety of shapes can be made and compared before they are changed.

Teach children from the very beginning to copy their geoboard designs on geoboard paper (use Blackline Masters 28–29). To help children transfer their designs to paper, suggest that they first mark the dots on the paper for the corners of their shape by identifying the location of the pegs (e.g., "second row, first peg"). With the corners identified, it is much

Figure 16.9

Decomposing and composing shapes (see Blackline Masters 28–29).

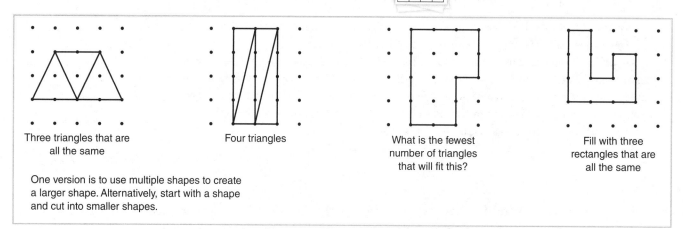

One version is to use multiple shapes to create a larger shape. Alternatively, start with a shape and cut into smaller shapes.

easier for them to draw lines between corners to make the shapes. These drawings can be placed in groups for classification and discussion, made into booklets illustrating a new idea that is being discussed, or sent home to families.

The NCTM e-Standards provides electronic geoboard activities entitled "Investigating the Concept of a Triangle and Properties of Polygons" (www.nctm.org/standards/content.aspx?menu_id=1155&id=26867). Children can select and delete bands and select and delete vertices as they create triangles and other polygons. The geoboard applet from the National Library of Virtual Manipulatives (http://nlvm.usu.edu /en/nav/category_g_1_t_3.html) is essentially the same kind of set up with some additional features.

The following activity provides children more opportunities to decompose two-dimensional shapes.

Activity 16.12 TWO SHAPES FROM ONE

Provide children with a variety of cut-out shapes or outlines of shapes on a recording sheet. Their task is to connect any two sides of the shape with a straight line, forming two new shapes (see Figure 16.10). Challenge them to classify each new shape using properties.

"Shape Tools" at NCTM's Illuminations site allows children to decompose pattern blocks and then compose them into different shapes (http://illuminations.nctm.org/ActivityDetail.aspx?ID=35). Children can use "Shape Cutter" at the same site to create and decompose a wide variety of shapes and then compose them into new shapes (http://illuminations.nctm.org/ActivityDetail.aspx?ID=72).

Building Shapes

Building activities at level 0 help children pay attention to the properties of shapes. For building two-dimensional models, use an activity like Activity 16.6, "Build It," but do not provide drawings as models for children. Challenge them to create two or more examples of a target shape and explain why they are that shape. See whether others in the class agree with their explanations.

Building three-dimensional shapes is a little more difficult than building two-dimensional shapes. A variety of commercial materials permit fairly creative construction of geometric solids (e.g., Polydron and the Zome System). The following are three approaches to making handmade models.

- *Plastic coffee stirrers with modeling clay or pipe cleaners.* Plastic stirrers can be cut into different lengths and used to build the edges of the three-dimensional shape. To connect corners, use small balls of clay or insert pipe cleaners cut into 2-inch lengths into the ends of the stirrers.

- *Plastic drinking straws with flexible joints.* Cut the straws lengthwise from the top down to the flexible joint. These slit ends can then be inserted into the uncut bottom ends of other straws, making a strong but flexible joint. Three or more straws are joined in this fashion to form two-dimensional polygons. To make skeletal solids, use tape or twist ties to join polygons side to side.

- *Rolled newspaper rods.* Fantastic superlarge skeletons can be built using newspaper and masking tape or duct tape (see Figure 16.11).

With these homemade models, children should compare the rigidity of a triangle with the lack of rigidity of polygons with more than three sides. Point out that triangles are used in

> **◆ Standards for Mathematical Practice**
>
> **3 Construct viable arguments and critique the reasoning of others**

Figure 16.10 Start with a shape and then draw a segment to divide the shape into two new shapes.

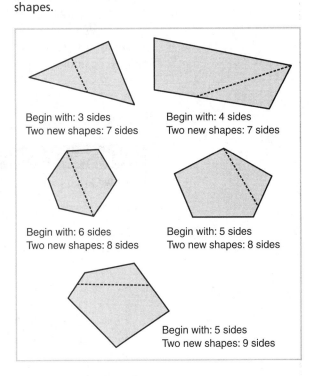

Begin with: 3 sides
Two new shapes: 7 sides

Begin with: 4 sides
Two new shapes: 7 sides

Begin with: 6 sides
Two new shapes: 8 sides

Begin with: 5 sides
Two new shapes: 8 sides

Begin with: 5 sides
Two new shapes: 9 sides

Figure 16.11

Large skeletal structures and special shapes can be built with tightly rolled newspaper.

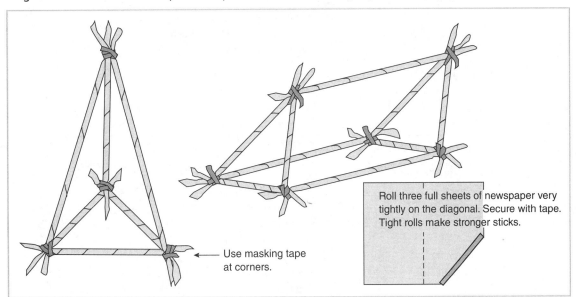

← Use masking tape at corners.

Roll three full sheets of newspaper very tightly on the diagonal. Secure with tape. Tight rolls make stronger sticks.

many bridges, in the long booms of construction cranes, in gates, and in the structural parts of buildings. Discuss why this may be so.

◈ Shapes and Properties Activities for Level 1 (Analysis/Description) Thinkers

As children move to level 1 thinking, their attention turns more to properties of shapes. They do not see relationships between shapes and between properties, so that is an emphasis for instruction at this level. Level 1 thinkers will continue to use models and drawings of shapes. Their understanding of the properties of shapes—such as relationships of side lengths, size of angles, symmetry, parallel sides, and so on—continues to be refined.

The definitions of two- and three-dimensional shapes support the exploration of the relationships between shapes. Table 16.1 lists some important categories of two-dimensional shapes. Examples of these shapes can be found in Figure 16.12.

Table 16.1 Categories of Two-Dimensional Shapes

Shape	Description
Simple Closed Curves	
Concave, convex	An intuitive definition of *concave* might be "having a dent in it." If a simple closed curve is not concave, it is convex.
Symmetrical, nonsymmetrical	Shapes may have one or more lines of symmetry and may or may not have rotational symmetry. These concepts will require more detailed investigation.
Polygons Concave, convex Symmetrical, nonsymmetrical	Simple closed curves with all straight sides.
Regular	All sides and all angles are congruent.
Triangles	
Triangles	Polygons with exactly three sides.
Classified by sides Equilateral Isosceles Scalene	All sides are congruent. At least two sides are congruent. No two sides are congruent.
Classified by angles Right Acute Obtuse	Has a right angle. All angles are smaller than a right angle. One angle is larger than a right angle.
Convex Quadrilaterals	
Convex quadrilaterals Kite Trapezoid Isosceles trapezoid Parallelogram Rectangle Rhombus Square	Convex polygons with exactly four sides. Two opposing pairs of congruent adjacent sides. At least one pair of parallel sides. A pair of opposite sides is congruent. Two pairs of parallel sides. Parallelogram with a right angle. Parallelogram with all sides congruent. Parallelogram with a right angle and all sides congruent.

Figure 16.12   Classification of two-dimensional shapes.

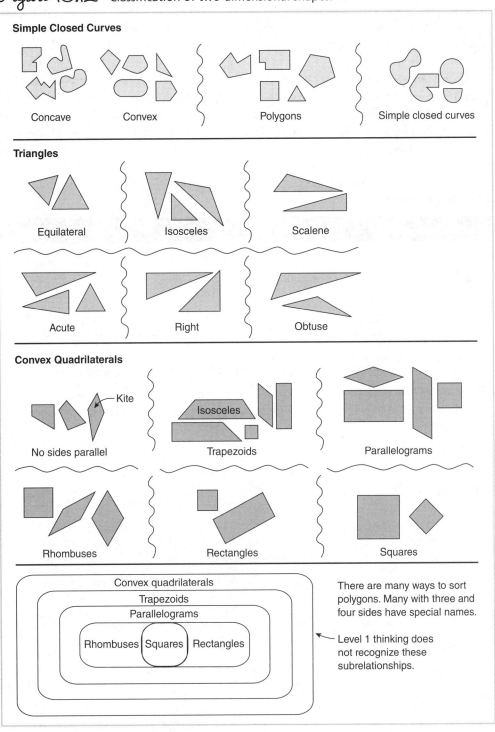

In the classification of quadrilaterals and parallelograms, some subsets overlap. For example, a square is a rectangle and a rhombus. All parallelograms are trapezoids, but not all trapezoids are parallelograms.* Children at level 1 commonly have difficulty seeing

*Some definitions of trapezoid specify *only one* pair of parallel sides, in which case parallelograms would not be trapezoids. The University of Chicago School Mathematics Project (UCSMP) uses the "at least one pair" definition, meaning that parallelograms and rectangles are trapezoids.

this type of subrelationship. They may quite correctly list all the properties of a square, a rhombus, and a rectangle and still might identify a square as a "nonrhombus" or a "non-rectangle." You can suggest to children to consider how one of their classmates can belong to more than one club or team. A square is an example of a quadrilateral that belongs to two other clubs.

Important and interesting shapes and relationships also exist in three dimensions. Table 16.2 describes classifications of solids. Figure 16.13 shows examples of cylinders and prisms. Note that prisms are defined here as a special category of cylinder—a cylinder with a polygon for a base (Zwillinger, 2011). Figure 16.14 shows a comparable grouping of cones and pyramids.

Table 16.2 Categories of Three-Dimensional Shapes

Shape	Description
Sorted by Edges and Vertices	
Sphere and "egglike" shapes	Shapes with no edges and no vertices (corners).
	Shapes with edges but no vertices (e.g., a flying saucer).
	Shapes with vertices but no edges (e.g., a football).
Sorted by Faces and Surfaces	
Polyhedron	Shapes made of all faces (a face is a flat surface of a solid). If all surfaces are faces, all the edges will be straight lines.
	Some combination of faces and rounded surfaces (cylinders are examples, but this is not a definition of a cylinder).
	Shapes with curved surfaces.
	Shapes with and without edges and with and without vertices.
	Faces can be parallel. Parallel faces lie in places that never intersect.
Cylinders	
Cylinder	Two congruent, parallel faces called bases. Lines joining corresponding points on the two bases are always parallel. These parallel lines are called elements of the cylinder.
Right cylinder	A cylinder with elements perpendicular to the bases. A cylinder that is not a right cylinder is an oblique cylinder.
Prism	A cylinder with polygons for bases. All prisms are special cases of cylinders (Zwillinger, 2011).
Rectangular prism	A cylinder with rectangles for bases.
Cube	A square prism with square sides.
Cones	
Cone	A solid with exactly one face and a vertex that is not on the face. Straight lines (elements) can be drawn from any point on the edge of the base to the vertex. The base may be any shape at all. The vertex need not be directly over the base.
Circular cone	Cone with a circular base.
Pyramid	Cone with a polygon for a base. All faces joining the vertex are triangles. Pyramids are named by the shape of the base: triangular pyramid, square pyramid, octagonal pyramid, and so on. All pyramids are special cases of cones (Zwillinger, 2011).

Figure 16.13 Cylinders and prisms.

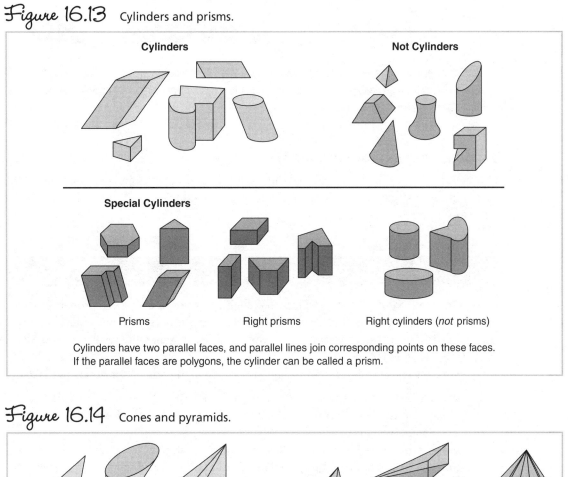

Cylinders have two parallel faces, and parallel lines join corresponding points on these faces. If the parallel faces are polygons, the cylinder can be called a prism.

Figure 16.14 Cones and pyramids.

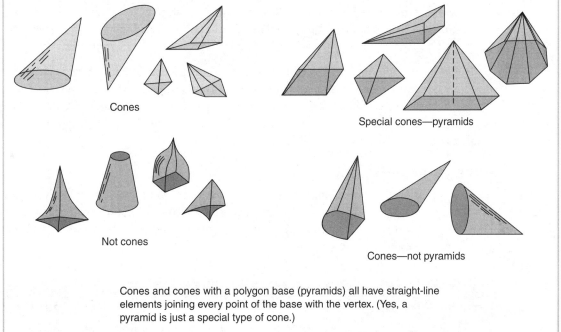

Cones and cones with a polygon base (pyramids) all have straight-line elements joining every point of the base with the vertex. (Yes, a pyramid is just a special type of cone.)

Many textbooks limit the definition of cylinders to circular cylinders. These books do not have special names for other cylinders. Under that definition, the prism is not a special case of a cylinder. This points to the fact that definitions are conventions, and not all conventions are universally agreed upon.

t·e·c·h·n·o·l·o·g·y ⏻
note

At NCTM's Illuminations Activity called "Geometric Solids" (http://illuminations.nctm.org/ActivityDetail
.aspx?ID=70) children can explore a variety of geometric solids by rotating the solids and coloring and
counting faces, edges, and vertices.

◆ Standards for
Mathematical Practice

**1 Make sense
of problems and
persevere in
solving them**

Building Shapes from Properties

Through building or drawing, children can focus on the properties and defining features of
shapes. In the next activity, children are challenged to build two-dimensional shapes accord-
▶ ing to given properties.

◆ *Activity* 16.13 **CAN YOU MAKE IT?**

Create a collection of challenges. Each challenge describes one or more properties of a
shape, and the challenge is to create a shape with these properties on a geoboard or
using plastic (flat) coffee stirrers cut to various lengths or a manipulative such as D-Stix.
The list that follows is only a sample. Try combining two or more properties to create new
challenges. Also have children create challenges that can be posted for others to make.

- A shape with only one square corner and four sides
- A shape with two square corners (or three, four, five, or six square corners)
- A shape with two pairs of parallel lines
- A shape with two pairs of parallel lines and no right angles
- A shape with one or two lines of symmetry (if your class has discussed symmetry)

If you keep track of solutions to the challenges in the last activity, there is an added
possibility of creating classes of shapes possessing certain properties that may result in definitions of new classes of shapes. The activity can also include impossible tasks, such as a
four-sided shape with exactly three right angles. Also, a triangle with three congruent sides
(equilateral) is not possible on a geoboard.

Sorting and Classifying

For children at level 1, classifying and sorting activities should focus more closely on the
properties that make the shape what it is (not just that it looks like the others in the group).
The next activity focuses children's attention on properties and provides a good way to introduce a category of shapes.

◆ *Activity* 16.14 **MYSTERY DEFINITION**

Use a projector to show a collection of shapes that have one or more properties in
common and another collection of shapes that do not have this commonality, such
as in Figure 16.15. For your first collection be certain that you have allowed for all possible
variables. In Figure 16.15, for example, a square is included in the set of rhombi. Similarly,
choose nonexamples to be as close to the positive examples as is necessary to help with
an accurate definition. The third or mixed set should also include those nonexamples with
which children are most likely to be confused. Children should justify their choices. Note that
the use of examples and nonexamples is particularly helpful for children with disabilities.

◆ Standards for
Mathematical Practice

**1 Make sense
of problems and
persevere in
solving them**

The value of the "Mystery Definition" approach of Activity 16.14 is that children develop ideas and definitions based on their own concept development. After their definitions have been discussed, compared, and refined as needed, you can offer the conventional definition for the sake of clarity.

The next activity introduces children to the idea that there are different categories of triangles. It is not necessary that children in grades pre-K–2 know the different names (e.g., equilateral, isosceles, scalene), only that some shapes can be further categorized based on their properties.

Activity 16.15 TRIANGLE SORT

Children work in groups of three to four. Each group will need a set of the Assorted Triangles (see Blackline Master 37). There are examples of right, acute, and obtuse triangles and equilateral, isosceles, and scalene triangles. Ask the children to sort the triangles in some way so that no triangle belongs to two groups. Have them describe and discuss their groupings. If no group used length of sides to form their groups, ask them to sort the entire collection by comparing the length of the sides in each triangle. Again, no triangle should belong to two groups. When they complete this sort, have them describe and discuss their groupings. Provide appropriate terminology as ideas arise. For example, you can say, "A triangle that has all equal sides is a special triangle called an equilateral triangle." Add this new terminology and corresponding illustrations to the math word wall.

In the following activity, children explore the idea that squares, rectangles, and rhombi have properties in common.

Activity 16.16 PROPERTY LISTS FOR QUADRILATERALS

Prepare handouts for parallelograms, rhombi, rectangles, and squares (see Blackline Masters 38–41 and Figure 16.16). Assign groups of three or four children to work with one type of quadrilateral. The task is for each group to use the examples on the handouts to describe the sides and angles (corners) of the shapes. For ELLs, make sure they understand the meaning of the terms *side* and *angle*. Anything that children list

Figure 16.15 A mystery definition.

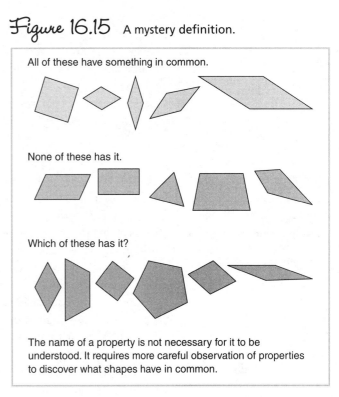

All of these have something in common.

None of these has it.

Which of these has it?

The name of a property is not necessary for it to be understood. It requires more careful observation of properties to discover what shapes have in common.

Figure 16.16

Shapes for "Property Lists for Quadrilaterals" activity (see Blackline Masters 38–41).

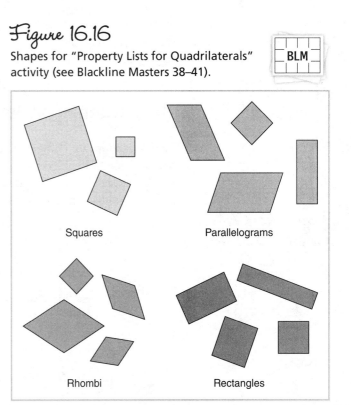

Squares   Parallelograms

Rhombi   Rectangles

has to apply to all of the shapes on their sheet. They will need tools such as index cards (to check right angles, to compare side lengths) and tracing paper (for identifying angle congruence). Encourage children to say the words "at least" when describing how many of something; for example, "rectangles have at least two sides that are equal" because squares—included in the rectangles—have four. Groups then share their lists with the class and eventually a class list for each category of shape will be developed.

Standards for Mathematical Practice

3 Construct viable arguments and critique the reasoning of others

▶ This last activity may take two or three days. Share lists beginning with parallelograms, then rhombi, then rectangles, and finally squares. Have one group present its list. Then others who worked on the same shape should add to or subtract from it. The class must agree with everything that is put on the list. As new relationships come up in this presentation-and-discussion period, you can introduce proper terminology. For example, if an angle is larger than a right angle, then it is called obtuse. Other terms such as *acute*, *parallel*, and so on can be clarified as you help children write their descriptions.

Compare the last activity, "Property Lists for Quadrilaterals," with Activity 16.7, "Shape Sorts." In "Shape Sorts," the objects of children's thought are the very shapes that are in front of them. The results of that activity are collections or classifications of shapes. For young children, these classifications will be nonstandard groupings that make sense to the children—fat, tall, pointy, looks like houses, and so on. Soon they will also construct standard groupings that have standard names—squares, triangles, rectangles, prisms, and so on—as you supply the appropriate names as the collections are developed.

In "Property Lists for Quadrilaterals," the children only see a small collection of shapes at the top of their paper. However, the object of their thinking is the entire class of shapes for which these few are representative. In "Property Lists for Quadrilaterals" the object of thinking is the very type of thing (a class of shapes) that was the product of thinking in "Shape Sorts" at level 0.

Learning about Transformations

Transformations are changes in position or size of a shape. Movements that do not change the size or shape of the object are called "rigid motions." Usually, three transformations are discussed: translations or slides, reflections or flips, and rotations or turns. Symmetry is included under the study of transformations due to its link to reflections.

Figure 16.17
Translation (slide), reflection (flip), rotation (turn).

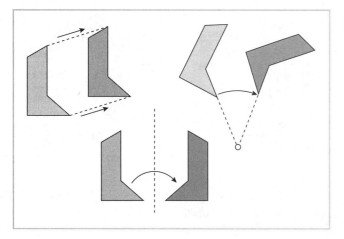

Transformation Activities for Pre-Recognition and Level 0 Thinkers

Transformations at these levels involve an introduction to the basic concepts of slides, flips, and turns. At the primary level, the terms *slide*, *flip*, and *turn* are adequate. The goal is to help children recognize these transformations and to begin to explore their effects on simple shapes. Use a nonsymmetrical shape to introduce these ideas (see Figure 16.17).

When putting together puzzles, children use geometric motions intuitively as they turn, flip, and slide pieces into place. Have them discuss how they are moving the pieces to make them fit. Use these experiences to help young children learn that changing an object's position or orientation does not change the shape.

Clements and Sarama (2009) recommend having children use computer programs and applets to explore slides, flips, and turns of objects because children have to purposefully select the screen tools to perform the geometric motion, which makes the motions more explicit to children. Some applets for exploring transformations are listed in the next Technology Note.

The NCTM's Illuminations Activities called "Patch Tool" (http://illuminations.nctm.org/ActivityDetail .aspx?ID=27) and "Shape Tool" (http://illuminations.nctm.org/ActivityDetail.aspx?ID=35) allow children to flip and rotate shapes to create various patterns and fill in designs, which informally introduce them to geometric transformations.

◈ Transformation Activities for Level 1 Thinkers

More Complex Slides, Flips, and Turns

Flags can provide an interesting context for children to think about slides, turns, and flips because of how flags move in the wind. Read to children a book about different flags or share pictures of flags used by different countries (e.g., *Flags of the World* by Selvie Bednar, 2009). Then use the following activity to explore these motions.

Activity 16.17 MOTION FLAG

Using the Motion Flag Blackline Masters 42–43, make copies of the first Motion Flag and then copy the mirror image on the backs of these copies (see Figure 16.18). You want the back image to match the front image when held to the light. Cut off the excess paper to leave a square. Alternatively, you can make the same design on squares of card stock using a marker. Give all children a two-sided Motion Flag. It might be helpful, especially for children with disabilities, to give them two Motion Flags, one to leave at the original position and the other to manipulate.

Demonstrate each of the possible motions. A slide is simply a slide. The figure does not rotate or turn over. Demonstrate turns. (With young children, use only clockwise turns for this activity.) Similarly, demonstrate a horizontal flip (top goes to bottom) and a vertical flip (left goes to right). For all children, especially ELLs, it is important that these demonstrations include explicit practice with the terms and that visuals are posted for reference. Practice by having everyone start with their Motion Flag in the same orientation. As you announce one of the moves, children slide, flip, or turn their Motion Flag accordingly.

Then display two Motion Flags side by side in any orientation. The task is to decide what motion or combination of motions will get the flag on the left to match the flag on the right. Children use their own flag to work out a solution. Test the solutions that children offer. If both flags are in the same position, call that a slide.

Figure 16.18

Motion Flag is used to show slides, flips, and turns (see Blackline Masters 42–43).

Once children understand how to use the Motion Flag, they can work in pairs. They begin with their Motion Flags in the same position. One child then changes his or her Motion Flag and challenges the other child to say what motion is required to make the two Motion Flags match. The solution is then tested and the roles reversed.

Stop and Reflect

Begin with the Motion Flag in the left position shown in Figure 16.18. Now place a second Motion Flag next to the first. Will it take one move or more than one move (transformation) to get from the first to the second Motion Flag? Can you describe all of the positions that require more than one move? Are there any positions that require more than two moves? ■

At first, children will be confused when they can't get their Motion Flag into the new position with one move. This causes an excellent problem. Don't be too quick to suggest that it may take two moves. If flips across each of the two diagonals are added to the motions along with vertical and horizontal flips, the Motion Flag can assume any new position in exactly one move.

Line Symmetry

Transformations for level 1 thinkers should involve the initial development of line symmetry. If a shape can be folded on a line so that the two halves match exactly, then it is said to have line symmetry (or mirror symmetry). Notice that the fold line is actually a line of reflection—the portion of the shape on one side of the line is reflected onto the other side—demonstrating a connection between line symmetry and transformations (flips).

One way to introduce line symmetry to children is to show examples and nonexamples using an "all-of-these" or "none-of-these" approach as in Figure 16.15. As another possibility, consider the following example that creates a line of symmetry: Fold a sheet of paper in half. Start somewhere along the fold and cut out a shape of your choosing. Open the paper and describe what you notice.

A third way to introduce line symmetry is to have children create designs with mirror images, as in the following activity.

Activity 16.18 PATTERN BLOCK MIRROR SYMMETRY

Children need a plain sheet of paper with a straight line through the middle. Using no more than six to eight pattern blocks, they make a design completely on one side of the line that touches the line in some way. When the one side is finished, children try to make the mirror image of their design on the other side of the line. After it is built, they use a mirror (or a Mira, a red plastic image reflector) to check their work. With the mirror sitting perpendicular on the line, they should see exactly the same image as they see when they lift the mirror.

Children often refer to the ideas of line and rotational symmetry when working with pattern blocks and other designs. They may observe, "When I turn the (equilateral) triangle a little, it fits back on top of itself" or "I can fold my butterfly drawing and it matches!" Capitalize on these opportunities to discuss the idea of symmetry so your children have a strong foundation for more formal study that will come later.

Learning about Location

In pre-K and kindergarten, children learn about everyday positional descriptions—above, below, beside, in front of, behind, and next to (CCSSO, 2010). These informal indicators of location are useful for helping children begin to specify locations. However, helping children refine the way they reason and communicate about direction, distance, and location enhances spatial understandings. Geometry, measurement, and algebra are all supported by the use of a grid system with numbers or coordinates attached that can specify the location. Children at the primary level can begin to think in terms of a grid system to identify location to help prepare them for more sophisticated ways of reasoning about location.

◆ Location Activities for Pre-Recognition Thinkers

At the pre-recognition level, children are learning to use language to describe an object's relative position in space. In learning to describe location, children need opportunities in which they have to pay attention to the space around them and how it is organized. Using and building simple maps can help children become more aware of their environment and how they navigate through it (e.g., Clements & Sarama, 2009). Clements (1999) found that children develop the ability to navigate by first paying attention to landmarks in their environment. In Activity 16.19, children use a simple map that includes landmarks to locate hidden objects.

Activity 16.19 **PLAYGROUND SCAVENGERS**

Prepare some simple maps of your playground area that identify some big landmarks and different paths. Give different groups of children different maps. Children will use their map to move from one location to another to find a hidden treasure. On each map, highlight the starting point and the ending point and draw a path along the route you want children to take.

After children have some experience using simple maps, having them create their own maps will help them notice landmarks and how those landmarks are positioned as they are challenged to identify a path that connects these landmarks.

Activity 16.20 **MAKING MAPS**

Identify landmarks in your classroom that children can use to design a map showing a path from one landmark to another. For example, children can create a map between the block area and the sink. Mark the path first with masking tape and have children walk along the path, drawing their attention to objects they pass along the way. (These are other landmarks that they can and should include on their maps.) After they create their map, they can walk along the path again and add additional landmarks to their maps.

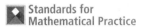 Standards for
Mathematical Practice

◄ **4** Model with mathematics

The maps young children create can vary greatly due to individual children's drawing skills. You do not want children to get bogged down in providing a lot of detail in representing landmarks. Encourage them to use simple drawings or provide cutout pictures of the landmarks that they can glue to their maps so they can attend more to the positions of the landmarks in relation to each other and the path.

Figure **16.19**

The "Hidden Positions" game. Players must communicate verbally the positions of their blocks on the grid.

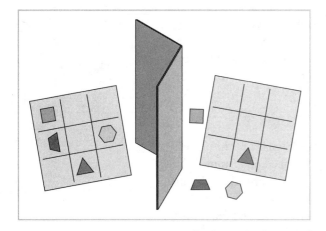

◆ Location Activities for Level 0 Thinkers

When children are able to attend to and describe landmarks in the space around them, it is time to help them see the value of a way to specify location without pointing. Activity 16.21 can help children refine their ways of describing location.

Activity 16.21 HIDDEN POSITIONS

For the game boards, draw an 8-inch square on card stock. Subdivide the squares into a 3 by 3 grid. Two children sit with a "screen" separating their desktop space so that neither child can see the other's grid (see Figure 16.19). Each child has four different pattern blocks. The first player places a block on four different sections of the grid. He then tells the other player where to put blocks on her grid to match his own. When all four pieces are positioned, the two grids are checked to see if they are alike. Then the players switch roles. Model the game once by taking the part of the first child. Use words such as *top row, middle row, last row, above, below, next to,* and *beside.* Children can play in pairs as a station activity. For children with disabilities, consider starting with just one shape. Then move on to two shapes and so on. For children ready for a greater challenge, increase the size of the grid.

Next, children can begin to use simple coordinates to describe positions. By extending the grid in "Hidden Positions" to a 6 by 6 grid, the need arises for a system to label positions. Use a simple coordinate grid like the one shown in Figure 16.20 (see Blackline Master 44). Explain how to use two numbers to designate an intersection point on the grid. The first number tells how far to move to the right. The second number tells how far to move up. Initially use the words along with the numbers: "right 3 and up 0." Be sure to include 0 in your introduction. Select a point on the grid and have children decide what two numbers name that point. If your point is at (2,4) and children incorrectly say "four, two," then simply indicate where the point is that they named.

The next activity explores the notion of different paths on a grid.

BLM

Figure **16.20**

A simple coordinate grid. The X is at (3,2) and the O is at (1,3). Use the grid to play "Three in a Row" (like "Tic-Tac-Toe"). Put marks on intersections, not spaces.

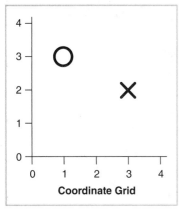

Activity 16.22 PATHS

BLM

On a sheet of 2-cm grid paper (see Blackline Master 30), mark two different points A and B as shown in Figure 16.21. Using a projector or floor tiles, demonstrate how to describe a path from A to B. For the points in the figure, one path is "up 5 and right 6." Another path might be "right 2, up 2, right 2, up 3, right 2." Count the length of each path. As long as you always move toward the target point (in this case either right or up), the path lengths will always be the same. Here they are 11 units long. Children draw three paths on their papers from A to B using different-colored crayons. For each path they write directions that describe their paths. They should check the lengths of each path. Ask the children, for example, "What is the greatest number of turns that you can make in your path? What is the smallest number? Where would A and B have to be in order to get there with no turns?"

technology ⏻
note

NCTM's e-Example 4.3 (found at www.nctm.org/standards/content.aspx?menu_id=1155&id=26868) is similar to "Paths" but offers some additional challenges. Children move a ladybug by listing directions that will hide the ladybug beneath a leaf. When the directions are complete, the ladybug is set in motion to follow them. The ladybug can also be directed to draw shapes such as a rectangle or to travel through mazes. Creating directions and predicting their outcome will help children develop ideas about navigation and location as they hone their visualization skills.

Figure 16.21

Coloring in different paths on a grid. What is the fewest number of turns needed to get from A to B? The most?

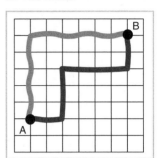

If you add a coordinate system to the grid in "Paths," children can describe their paths with coordinates: For example, one of the paths in Figure 16.21 can be described as follows:

$$(1,2) \rightarrow (3,2) \rightarrow (3,5) \rightarrow (7,5) \rightarrow (7,7)$$

Once a coordinate system has been introduced, children may want to use it in a simple game similar to the commercial game called "Battleship." Each player has a grid similar to the one in Figure 16.20. Players secretly put their initials on five intersections of their own grid. Then, with the grids kept separate as in "Hidden Positions," the players take turns trying to "hit" the other player's targets by naming a point on the grid using coordinates. The other player indicates if the "shot" was a hit or a miss. When a player scores a hit, he or she gets another turn. Each player keeps track of where he or she has taken shots, recording an "X" for a hit and a "0" for a miss. The game ends when one player has hit all of the other player's targets.

Learning about Visualization

Visualization could be called "geometry done with the mind's eye." It involves being able to create and move mental images of shapes, thinking about how they look from different viewpoints, and predicting the results of various transformations. It involves imagining the impact of certain actions on two- and three-dimensional shapes, such as what the parts would look like if you cut a shape in half. Many of the activities described in the previous sections can be used to develop children's visualization skills if they are asked to think about, manipulate, or transform a shape mentally—experimenting in their "mind's eye" to make predictions and then checking and reflecting on their predictions.

The following activity is a great example of how you can ask children to use their "mind's eye" to predict the outcome of manipulating a shape. It is based on an idea found in the NCTM's *Principles and Standards for School Mathematics* section on geometry in pre-K–2.

◀ *Activity* 16.23 **NOTCHES AND HOLES**

Use a half-sheet of paper that will easily fit on a projector. Fold it in half. Children make a sketch of the paper when it is opened, showing a line for the fold. With the paper folded, cut notches in one or two sides and/or cut off one or two corners. You can also use a paper punch to make a hole or two. While still folded, place the paper on the overhead showing the notches and holes. The folded edge should be to the left (see Figure 16.22). The task is for children to draw the notches and holes that they think will appear when you open the paper.

Figure 16.22 An example for the "Notches and Holes" activity.

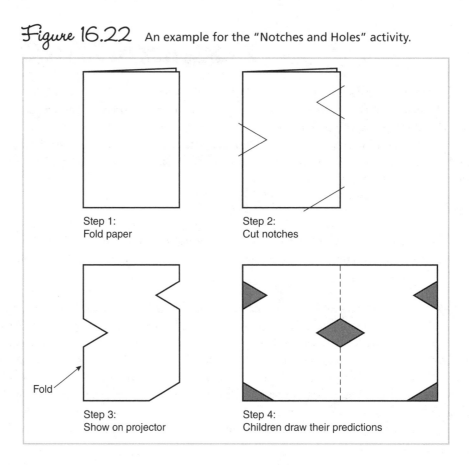

Step 1:
Fold paper

Step 2:
Cut notches

Fold

Step 3:
Show on projector

Step 4:
Children draw their predictions

Stop and Reflect

Stop now and try the "Notches and Holes" activity yourself. Try cuts in various places on the folded paper. Can you predict what the unfolded paper will look like? ■

The activity "Notches and Holes" can be modified for use with children who are at any level of geometric thought. To introduce this activity, begin with only one fold and only one cut. Adding additional cuts and additional folds increases the challenge. Having to predict the result helps build visualization skills and is also very motivating!

◆ Visualization Activities for Pre-Recognition Thinkers

Children at the pre-recognition level may notice only a subset of the visual characteristics of a shape, which results in an inability to distinguish between some shapes. Therefore, visualization activities for this level will have children trying to attend to the details of images. The following activity is based on an idea from NCTM's *Principles and Standards for Mathematics* (National Council of Teachers of Mathematics, 2000).

Activity 16.24 **CAN YOU REMEMBER?**

Draw some simple sketches of figures that will be easy for children to reproduce. Some examples are shown in Figure 16.23. Display one of the sketches for about 5 seconds. Then have children attempt to reproduce it on their own. Show the same figure again for a few seconds and allow children to modify their drawings. Repeat with additional figures.

Ask children to share how they thought about the figure or to describe in words what helped them remember what they saw. As children learn to verbally describe what they see, their visual memory will improve. Have children with disabilities identify the displayed figure from a set of figures that look alike.

Standards for Mathematical Practice

7 Look for and make use of structure

Visualization skills can also be developed through the map-building activities that are used to help children learn about location. Consider the following task that you can pose just after your class returns to the classroom from another location in the building:

Imagine that we are walking back to our classroom from the gym. What are some of the landmarks that we pass along the way?

After children have had time to visualize the path between the gym and their classroom, make a list of the landmarks that children thought of and take it with the class the next time you walk that path.

Figure 16.23
Examples of designs to use in the "Quick Images" activity.

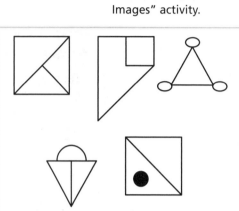

Visualization Activities for Level 0 Thinkers

Remember children at level 0 (visualization) are thinking about shapes in terms of the way they look. Visualization activities for this level will have children using a variety of physical shapes and drawings and will challenge them to think about these shapes in different orientations.

Finding out how many different shapes can be made with a given number of simple tiles requires that children mentally flip and turn shapes in their minds and find ways to decide whether they have found them all. That is the focus of the next activity.

Activity 16.25 PENTOMINOES

A pentomino is a shape formed by joining five squares as if cut from a square grid. Each square must have at least one side in common with another. Provide children with five square tiles and a sheet of square grid paper for recording. Challenge them to see how many different pentomino shapes they can find. Shapes that are flips or turns of other shapes are not considered different. Do not tell children how many pentomino shapes there are. Good discussions will come from deciding if some shapes are really different and if all shapes have been found.

Standards for Mathematical Practice

1 Make sense of problems and persevere in solving them

Once children have decided that there are just 12 pentominoes (see Figure 16.24), glue the grids with the children's pentominoes onto card stock and let them cut out the 12 shapes. Following is a variety of additional activities that can be done with pentominoes.

- Try to fit all 12 pieces into an 8 by 8 square.
- Use each of the 12 shapes as a tessellation tile and create a tessellation design.
- Examine each of the 12 pentominoes and decide which ones will fold up to make an open box. For those that are "box makers," which square is the bottom?

Figure 16.24

There are 12 different pentomino shapes.

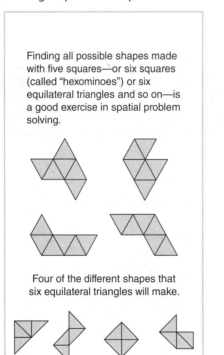

It is also fun to explore the number of shapes that can be made from six equilateral triangles or from four 45-degree right triangles (halves of squares) (see Figure 16.25). With the right triangles, sides that touch must be the same length. How many of each of these "ominoes" do you think there are?

Another aspect of visualization for young children is to be able to think about solid shapes in terms of their faces or sides. For these activities you will need to make "face cards" by tracing around the different faces of a three-dimensional shape, making either all faces on one card or a set of separate cards with one face per card (see Figure 16.26).

◆ Activity 16.26 FACE MATCHING

There are two versions of the task: Given a face card, find the corresponding solid, or given a solid, find the face card. With a collection of single-face cards, children can select the cards that go with a particular solid. For another variation, stack all of the single-face cards for one solid face down. Turn them up one at a time as clues to finding the solid.

Visualization involves creating and manipulating mental images. You can use activities in the other geometry categories (e.g., shapes and properties, transformation, location) to help children improve their visualization skills simply by asking them to recall and describe a hidden shape, describe how a shape would look from a different viewpoint, and predict what will happen before they manipulate (e.g., decompose, compose, flip, slide, turn) shapes. Look for those opportunities as you plan lessons and as you interact with your children.

Figure 16.25

Finding all possible shapes.

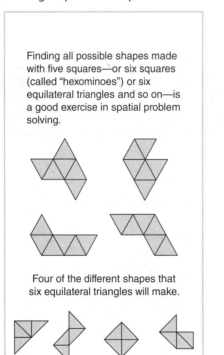

Finding all possible shapes made with five squares—or six squares (called "hexominoes") or six equilateral triangles and so on—is a good exercise in spatial problem solving.

Four of the different shapes that six equilateral triangles will make.

Four of the different shapes that four "half-square" triangles will make.

Figure 16.26

Matching face cards with solid shapes.

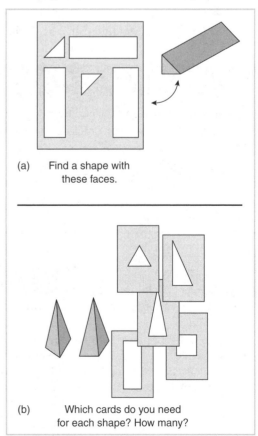

(a) Find a shape with these faces.

(b) Which cards do you need for each shape? How many?

Expanded Lesson

Shape Sorts

Content and Task Decisions

Grade Level: K–2

Mathematics Goals

- To develop an awareness of the wide variety of ways that two-dimensional shapes can be alike
- To establish classifications of shapes by various properties, including both traditional categorizations and informal, child-generated categories
- To introduce the names of common shapes or important properties (when and if the opportunity arises within the activity)

Grade Level Guide

NCTM *Curriculum Focal Points*	Common *Core State Standards*
Kindergartners use ideas about shapes to describe geometric ideas. In first and second grades children recognize that shapes have properties that help describe how they are alike and different from other shapes.	Kindergartners identify, describe, analyze, and compare shapes. They can use informal language to describe the shapes to point out their common attributes and differences. First and second graders use reasoning to distinguish between defining and non-defining attributes and they can draw shapes that have specific defining attributes.

Consider Your Children's Needs

Children need no prerequisite knowledge for this lesson. The activity will naturally adjust itself to the ideas held by the children. The level of vocabulary and the types of observations that children make will depend on their prior geometric experiences and their verbal skills.

For English Language Learners

- As children describe what they notice about a shape, or are identifying how their shape is like another, ask that they point at the aspect of the shape(s) they are describing so that everyone can understand.

- Record a list of the ideas children share to describe their shapes and draw a sketch next to it as a reminder.

For Children with Disabilities

- In the first part of the lesson, as children brainstorm different possible ideas that describe their shapes, record some of these on the board so that children can use these examples later as a guide for their own "target shape rule."
- Make sure the rule for a given target shape is written down near the target shape so that children with disabilities can refer to it during the session.

Materials

Each group of three to five children will need:

- Collection of two-dimensional shapes (Blackline Masters 20–26 provide a collection of 49 shapes. Duplicate each set on card stock and cut out the shapes. You may want to laminate the card stock before you cut out the shapes. Only use one color card stock so that the attribute of color does not become a focus for some children.)

Lesson

Before

Begin with a simpler version of the task:

- Gather children in a circle where all can see and have access to one set of shapes.
- Have each child select a shape. Ask children to think of things that they can say about their shape. Go around the group and ask children to hold up their shape and tell one or two of their ideas.
- Return all shapes to the pile and select one shape. Place this "target" shape for all to see. Each child is to find a shape that is like the target shape in some way. Again, have children share their ideas. You may want to repeat this with another shape.

Present the focus task to the class:

- Each group of children is to select one shape from the collection to be the target shape just as you did.

Then they announce their "rule" to the group. Then other children are to find as many other shapes that are like the target shape as they can. However, all the shapes they find must be like the target shape *in the same way.* For example, if the child uses "has straight sides" as a rule, each child in turn adds other shapes to the "has straight sides" group. They cannot also use another descriptor of the target shape such as "has a square corner" to add to the group. That would be two different ways or two rules.

- Explain that when you visit each group, you want to see a collection of shapes that go together according to the same rule. You will see if you can guess their rule by looking at the shapes they have put together.

- When you have checked their first rule, you will select a new target shape for them. They should make a new collection of shapes using a different rule. When they have finished, each child should draw a new shape on paper that would fit the rule. All of the drawings should then be alike in the same way. (For kindergarten and first-grade children, you will probably explain this part as you visit their group.)

Provide clear expectations:

- Children are to work in groups of three to five members.
- Children should take turns choosing descriptive properties (attributes) for the target shape.

During

- Listen carefully for the types of ideas that children are using. Are they using "nongeometric" language such as "pointy," "looks like a house," or "has a straight bottom," or are they beginning to talk about more geometric properties such as "square corners," "sides that go the same way" (parallel), or "dented in" (concave)? If they are using shape names, are they using them correctly?

- Introduce and reinforce correct terminology for shapes; however, do not make terminology and definitions a focus of the activity. Allow children to use their own ideas.

- To differentiate, you may want to challenge children by quickly creating a small group of shapes that go together according to a secret rule. See if they can figure out what the rule is and find other shapes that go with your collection.

After

Bring the class together to share and discuss the task:

- Collect children's drawings, keeping the groups intact. Gather children together so that all will be able to see the drawings. (This could be done the day after the *During* portion of the lesson.)

- Display the drawings from one group. Have children from other groups see if they can guess the rule for the drawings. If the drawings are not adequate to identify the rule, have those who made the drawings find a few shapes from the collection of shapes that also fit the rule.

- To expand children's ideas or interject new ideas, you may want to create a set of shapes using a secret rule, as described previously. Base your rule on a property of the shapes that the children have not yet thought of.

Assessment

Observe

- Do not think of this activity as something that children should master. This lesson can be repeated numerous times over the course of the year. As children have more and more experiences with shapes, they will be able to create different, more sophisticated sorting rules.

- Watch for children who talk about shapes in terms of relative attributes such as "bottom," "pointing up," or "has a side near the windows." These same children will not recognize a square as such if it has been turned to look like a diamond. When this happens, pick up the shape, turn it slowly, and ask the children if it is still pointing up (or whatever other attribute they are discussing). Point out that the shape doesn't change, only the way it is positioned.

- If you have introduced vocabulary that is important, you can informally assess children's knowledge of that vocabulary during this activity. Every type of shape that a primary-grade child needs to know is included in the set. There are also examples of right angles, parallel lines, concave and convex shapes, shapes with line symmetry, and shapes with rotational symmetry.

Ask

- How are these shapes alike?
- What other shapes are like the ones in this group?
- What is a shape that does NOT belong? Why?

17

Helping Children Use Data

BigIDEAS

1 Doing statistics involves a four-step process: formulating questions, collecting data, analyzing data, and interpreting results.

2 Data are gathered and organized in order to answer questions.

3 A collection of objects with various attributes can be classified or sorted in different ways. A single object can belong to more than one class. Classification is fundamental to data analysis.

4 Different types of graphs and other data representations provide different information about the data and, hence, the population from which the data are taken. The choice of graphical representation can affect how well the data are understood.

5 Graphs can provide a sense of the shape of the data, including how spread out or clustered the data are. Having a sense of the shape of data is having a big picture of the data rather than the data being simply a collection of numbers.

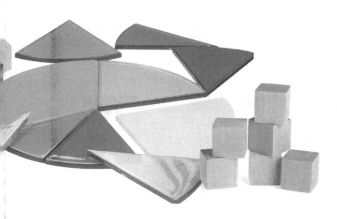

Graphs and statistics bombard the public in areas such as advertising, opinion polls, population trends, health risks, and progress of children in schools. We hear that the average amount of rainfall this summer is more than it was last summer or that the average American family consists of 3.19 people. We read on the U.S. Census website (www.census.gov) that the median home price in May 2000 was $164,700, and in May 2011 it was $222,000. The mean home price in May 2011 was $262,700. Knowing these statistics should raise an array of questions: How were these data gathered? What was the purpose? What does it mean to have an average of 3.19 people? Why are the median and the mean for home sales so different? Which statistic makes more sense for communicating about the prices of homes?

Statistical literacy is critical to understanding the world around us, essential for effective citizenship, and vital for developing the ability to question information presented in the media (Shaughnessy, 2007). Misuse of statistics occurs even in trustworthy sources such as newspapers, where graphs are often designed to exaggerate a finding. Therefore, it is crucial that students develop an understanding of the basic concepts of statistics. Children at the pre-K–2 level can begin developing this understanding. The *Common Core State Standards for Mathematics* (CCSSO, 2010) and the *Curriculum Focal Points* (National Council of Teachers of Mathematics, 2006) indicate that pre-K–K children should learn how data can be categorized while children in first and second grades should collect, organize, represent, and interpret data using picture and bar graphs. Second graders extend their work to generating and representing measurement data on line plots. The focus of the learning at these and every grade level should be on ways to use, present, and interpret data in the context of real questions.

The Process of Doing Statistics

Doing statistics is, in fact, a different process from doing mathematics. As Richard Scheaffer (2006), past president of the American Statistics Association, notes,

> Mathematics is about numbers and their operations, generalizations and abstractions; it is about spatial configurations and their measurement, transformations, and abstractions. . . . Statistics is also about numbers—but numbers in context: these are called data. Statistics is about variables and cases, distribution and variation, purposeful design or studies, and the role of randomness in the design of studies, and the interpretation of results. (pp. 310–311)

Statistics and mathematics are two different fields; however, statistical questions are often asked in assessments with questions that are mathematical in nature rather than statistical. The harm in this is that children are not focusing on statistical reasoning, as shown by the following exemplars from Scheaffer (2006).

1. The average weight of 50 prize-winning tomatoes is 2.36 pounds. What is the combined weight, in pounds, of these 50 tomatoes? (NAEP sample question)

    a. 0.0472   b. 11.8   c. 52.36   d. 59   e. 118

2. Table 17.1 gives the times each girl has recorded for seven trials of the 100-meter dash this year. Only one girl may compete in the upcoming track meet. Which girl would you select for the meet and why?

Stop and Reflect

Before reading further, label each of the preceding questions as "doing mathematics" or "doing statistics." ■

So, which of these problems involves statistical reasoning? Both? Neither? As explained by Schaeffer, only the second one is statistical in nature. The first requires computing with multiplication—mathematical thinking, not statistical thinking. The second question is statistical in nature because the situation requires analysis—graphs or averages might be used to determine a solution. The mathematics here is basic; the focus is on statistics. Also notice the context is central to responding to the second question, which is an indication that it is statistical reasoning.

Table 17.1   Race Time for Three Runners

Runner	Race						
	1	2	3	4	5	6	7
Suzie	15.2	14.8	15.0	14.7	14.3	14.5	14.5
Tanisha	15.8	15.7	15.4	15.0	14.8	14.6	14.5
Dara	15.6	15.5	14.8	15.1	14.5	14.7	14.5

Just as learning addition involves much more than the procedure for combining, doing statistics is much more than the process of creating a bar graph or line plot. To *meaningfully* engage children in learning and doing statistics, they should be involved in the full process, from asking and defining questions to collecting and analyzing data to interpreting data. This chapter is organized around this process, which is presented in Figure 17.1.

 **Formulating Questions**

The first goal in the Data Analysis and Probability standard of *Principles and Standards for School Mathematics* says that children should "formulate questions that can be addressed with data and collect, organize, and display relevant data to answer them" (National Council of Teachers of Mathematics, 2000, p. 48). Notice that data collection should be for a purpose—to answer a question—just as in the real world. Then the analysis of data should add information about some aspect of our world. This process of gathering data to answer questions and make informed decisions is what political pollsters, advertising agencies, market researchers, census takers, wildlife managers, and hosts of others do.

Whether the question is teacher initiated or student initiated, children should engage in conversations about how well-defined the question is. For example, if the teacher asks, "How many brothers and sisters do you have?" there may be a need to discuss half siblings. If children want to know how many shoes each classmate owns, questions may arise as to whether they should count bedroom slippers and flip-flops.

When children formulate the questions they want to ask, the data they gather become more and more meaningful. How they organize the data and the techniques for analyzing them have a purpose. For example, one class of children might gather data concerning which cafeteria foods are most often thrown in the garbage. As a result of these efforts, certain items could be removed from the regular menu. The experience can illustrate to children the power of organized data, and it can help them get food that they like better!

Often the need to gather data will come from the class naturally in the course of discussion or from questions arising in other content areas. Science, of course, is full of measurements and thus abounds in data analysis possibilities. Social studies is also full of opportunities to pose questions requiring data collection. The next few sections suggest some ideas related to these content areas as well as additional ideas.

Figure 17.1 Process of doing statistics.

Step 1: Formulate Questions
Clarify the problem at hand.
Formulate one (or more) questions that can be answered with data.

Step 2: Collect Data
Design a plan to collect appropriate data.
Employ the plan to collect the data.

Step 3: Analyze Data
Select appropriate graphical and numerical methods.
Use these methods to analyze the data.

Step 4: Interpret Results
Interpret the analysis.
Relate the interpretation to the original question.

Source: Franklin, C. A., Kader, G., Mewborn, D., Moreno, J., Peck, R., Perry, M., & Scheaffer, R. (2005). *Guidelines for Assessment and Instruction in Statistics Education: A Pre-K-12 Curriculum Framework.* Alexandria, VA: American Statistical Association. Reprinted with permission. Copyright 2005 by the American Statistical Association. All rights reserved.

Questions about "Me and My Classmates"

Young children want to learn about each other, their families and pets, measures such as arm span or time to get to school, their likes and dislikes, and so on. At the pre-K–2 level, the easiest questions to deal with are those that can be answered by each class member contributing one piece of data. Here are a few ideas:

- *Favorites:* TV show, game, movie, ice cream, video game, fruit, season of the year, color, sport, sports team (if many possibilities, start by restricting the number of choices)

- *Numbers:* Number of pets, siblings, or letters in name; hours watching TV, hours of sleep, or hours spent on the computer
- *Measures:* Height, arm span, length of foot, long-jump distance, time to run around the swing set on the playground, minutes spent traveling to school, daily temperature, shadow length

🔹 Questions beyond Self and Classmates

Eventually, you will sense that your children are ready to ask questions about things beyond themselves and their classmates.

Content Area Questions

Discussions about communities provide a good way to integrate social studies and mathematics. As you study the community in which children live, many questions arise:

- How many different kinds of restaurants or stores are in our community (fast-food restaurants versus "sit-down" restaurants; Italian, Mexican, or American; convenience stores, grocery stores, clothing stores, variety stores)?
- How many responses are made by local firefighters each month? How many different types of responses are made by local firefighters each month (fire, medical, hazardous, public service)? (Data can usually be found on websites of local institutions.)
- How many state and local government officials are elected by voters?

The newspaper itself suggests all sorts of data-related questions. For example, how many advertisements are included in the newspaper on different days of the week? How many sports stories are about different types of sports (e.g., basketball, football, swimming, etc.)? How many pages is the local paper each day of the week?

Science is another area in which questions can be asked and data gathered. In particular, experiments can be a great source for questions.

- How many plastic bottles or aluminum cans are placed in the school's recycling bins over a given week?
- How many times do different types of balls bounce when each is dropped from the same height?
- How many days does it take for different types of bean, squash, and pea seeds to germinate when kept in moist paper towels?
- Which brand of bubble gum will give you the largest bubble?
- Do some liquids expand more than others when frozen?
- Does a plant grow faster when watered with water, soda, or milk?

Children can also develop questions before going on a field trip (Mokros & Wright, 2009). While on the field trip, they can gather data to help answer those questions. For example, if visiting a zoo, children might look for the number of animals that are smaller than a small dog, like a Jack Russell terrier, or how many animals are larger than a large dog, like a golden retriever. (Make sure the animals or objects chosen are ones that all the children are familiar with!) Other questions might be "How many animals have wings and how many don't?" or "Are there more animals with fur than not?" or "How many animals have no legs, two legs, four legs, or more legs?" or "How many animals move around in various ways (e.g., fly, slither, crawl on four legs, walk on two legs, etc.)?" You can work with zoo personnel before going on the trip to identify possible topics to share with children to help them develop questions that they are curious about.

Comparisons

Another type of progression from the questions children ask about themselves and their class-mates is to consider if they as a class are alike or different from other groups. Do other second-grade children spend the same amount of time watching TV or like the same foods as they do? How much taller are children in the next grade or two grades ahead of them?

Comparisons can also be made between your own class and selected groups of adults to which the children have access, such as parents or faculty.

Teaching Tip

If your children have "buddies" in the upper grades, they can collect data from their buddies.

To further expand your children's perspective, you might explore ways that your class can compare themselves or their data with similar classes in other places in the state, other states, or perhaps even in a foreign country. This can open up not just a source of interesting data but also a way for your children to see beyond their own localities.

Data Collection

There are two main types of data—*categorical* and *numerical*. Categorical data refer to information about things that can be grouped by labels such as favorite after-school activity, colors of cars in the school parking lot, and the most popular name to give the class guinea pig. Categorical data are ordered arbitrarily—in other words, the bars in a bar graph could be put in any arrangement.

Numerical data, on the other hand, are ordered numerically, such as on a number line, and could include fractions or decimals. This kind of data includes how many miles to school, the temperature in your town over a one-week period, or the weight of the children's backpacks.

Teaching Tip

Note that the word *data* is plural—hence, we say "data are." The singular form of the word is *datum*.

◆ Collecting Data

Gathering data is not easy for children, especially young children. A teacher asked her first graders to gather data on "Are you 6?" After hearing the request, 18 eager children began asking others in the class if they were 6 and tallying yes or no responses. Eventually they realized that they had no idea whom they had asked more than once or whom they had not asked at all. This provided an excellent entry into a discussion about how statisticians gather data. Have your children brainstorm ways to gather the needed data in an organized manner. One kindergarten teacher asked her children to think of an organized way they could gather data from their classmates about their favorite flavors of ice cream. These kindergartners decided a class list would help them keep track of who had been asked and what their response had been (Cook, 2008).

Data can also be collected through observation. This creates a shared context for children in that they all will be a part of observing phenomena. For example, set up a bird feeder outside the classroom window and collect data at different times during the day to either count the number or type of birds. Children can also collect observational data on field trips (Mokros & Wright, 2009) and at evening or weekend activities with their families.

◆ Using Existing Data Sources

Data do not always have to be collected by children; existing data abound in various places, such as print resources and databases on the Internet.

Newspapers, almanacs, sports record books, maps, and various government publications are sources of data that may be used to answer children's questions. Children's literature is also an excellent and engaging resource. Children can tally words in a repeating verse like "Hickory, Dickory, Dock" (Niezgoda & Moyer-Packenham, 2005). Similarly, books like *Goodnight Moon* (Brown, 2005) and *Green Eggs and Ham* (Seuss, 1960) have many repeated words or phrases.

Children may be interested in facts about another country as a result of a social studies unit or a country in the news. Olympic records in various events over the years or data related to environmental issues are other examples of topics around which children's questions may be formulated. For these and hundreds of other questions, data can be found on the Web. Following are a few websites with a lot of interesting data.

- State Data Map (http://illuminations.nctm.org/ActivityDetail.aspx?ID=151) is a source that displays state data on population, land area, political representation, gasoline use, and more.

- Olympic Records (www.olympic.org/medallists-results) provides information about medalists in every Olympic event since 1896.

- Internet Movie Database (www.imdb.com) offers information about movies of all genres.

- Google Earth (http://earth.google.com) allows you to take a virtual trip to explore cities and regions in any place in the world.

 **Data Analysis**

Data analysis begins with organizing the data in a meaningful way, such as sorting or graphing, with the resulting visual providing a kind of summary for the data. The data are then analyzed with a focus on how the information answers the question that provided the purpose for collecting the data.

⬡ Classification

Initially young children tend to not use categories to represent data and instead simply put the data in one list (Clements & Sarama, 2009). For example, if children were asked to represent the class data about how children arrived at school, some children may simply list each child and their response. Classification involves making decisions about how to categorize things, a basic activity that is fundamental to data analysis. In order to formulate questions and decide how to represent data that have been gathered, decisions must be made about how things might be categorized. For example, children might group farm animals by number of legs; by type of product they provide; by those that work, provide food, or are pets; by size or color; by the type of food they eat; and so on. Each of these groupings is based on a different attribute of the animals. Those decisions about how things might be categorized need to become an emphasis in the early grades.

According to the *Curriculum Focal Points* (National Council of Teachers of Mathematics, 2006) and the *Common Core State Standards* (CCSSO, 2010), classification by attributes is a topic for pre-K–K children. Attribute activities are explicitly designed to develop flexible reasoning about the characteristics of data.

Classifications Using Attribute Materials

Attribute materials can be sets of objects that lend themselves to being sorted and classified in different ways—for example, seashells, leaves, children's shoes, or the children themselves. The attributes are the ways that the materials can be sorted. For example, hair color, height,

Figure 17.2

A teacher-made attribute set. Woozle cards can be duplicated on card stock, quickly colored in two colors, laminated, and cut into individual cards (see Blackline Master 49).

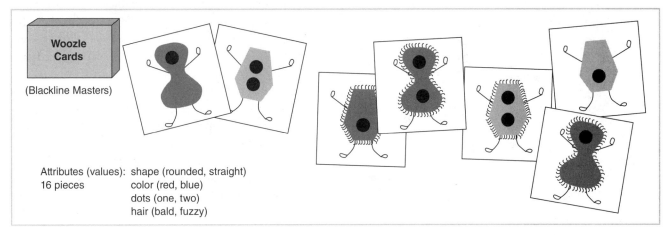

Attributes (values): shape (rounded, straight)
16 pieces   color (red, blue)
              dots (one, two)
              hair (bald, fuzzy)

and gender are attributes of children. Each attribute has a number of different values: for example, blond, brown, or red (for the attribute of hair color); tall or short (for height); male or female (for gender). A teacher-made attribute set is displayed in Figure 17.2 (see also Blackline Master 49).

Commercially available attribute blocks are sets of 60 plastic attribute pieces with each piece having four attributes: color (red, yellow, blue), shape (circle, triangle, rectangle, square, hexagon), size (big, little), and thickness (thick, thin). The specific values, number of values, or number of attributes that a set may have is not important.

Initially, do attribute activities by sitting in a large circle on the floor where all children can see and have access to the materials to be sorted. The following activity is a simple Venn diagram activity that pre-K–K children will enjoy.

BLM

Activity 17.1 WHAT ABOUT "BOTH"?

Give children two large loops of string and attribute blocks. Direct them to put all the red pieces inside one string and all triangles inside the other. Let the children try to resolve the difficulty of what to do with the red triangles. When the notion of overlapping the strings to create an area common to both loops is clear, more challenging activities can be explored. It will be helpful, especially for children with disabilities, to place labels on each loop of the string.

Standards for Mathematical Practice

1 Make sense of problems and persevere in solving them

The Attribute Blocks applet at http://nlvm.usu.edu/en/nav/grade_g_1.html provides several classification problems for children to do. They are shown a set of blocks inside a loop having the same shape, size, or color. Their task is to drag inside the loop other blocks that belong according to the target attribute.

Figure 17.3 A three-loop activity with attribute pieces.

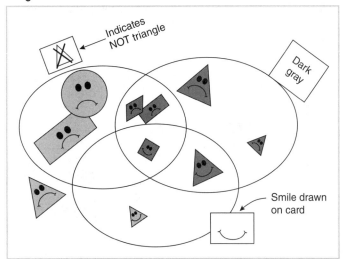

Indicates NOT triangle

Dark gray

Smile drawn on card

As shown in Figure 17.3, the labels need not be restricted to single attributes. If a piece does not fit in any region, it is placed outside of all of the loops.

As children progress, introduce labels for negative attributes such as "not red" or "not small." Also important is the eventual use of *and* and *or* connectives to form two-value rules such as "red and square" and "big or happy." This use of *and*, *or*, and *not* significantly widens children's classification schemes.

An engaging and challenging activity is to infer how things have been classified when the loops are not labeled. The following activities require children to make and test conjectures about how things are being classified.

Standards for Mathematical Practice

1 **Make sense of problems and persevere in solving them**

▶

Activity 17.2 GUESS MY RULE

For this activity, try using children instead of shapes as attribute "pieces." Decide on an attribute such as "blue jeans" or "stripes on clothing" but do not tell your rule to the class. Silently look at one child at a time and move the child to the left or right according to this secret rule. After a number of children have been sorted, have the next child come up and ask children to predict in which group he or she belongs.

Before the rule is articulated, continue the activity for a while so that others in the class will have an opportunity to determine the rule. The same activity can be done with virtually any materials that can be sorted, such as children's shoes, shells, or buttons. Encourage ELLs to use their native language and English to describe the rule.

Activity 17.3 HIDDEN LABELS

Create label cards for the loops of string used to make the Venn diagram. Place two of the cards face down, one on each loop. Ask children to select an attribute piece for you to place. For ELLs and children with disabilities, provide a list of the labels with pictures and/or translations for each as a reference. Begin to sort pieces according to the hidden rules. As you sort, have children try to determine what the labels are for each of the loops. Let children who think they have guessed the labels try to place a piece in the proper loop but avoid having them guess the labels aloud. Children who think they know the labels can also be asked to "play teacher" and respond to the guesses of the others. Point out that one way to test an idea about the labels is to select a piece that you think might go in a particular section. Wait to turn the label cards up until most children have figured out the rule.

Classifications Using Content Areas

"Guess My Rule" and "Hidden Labels" can and should be repeated with real-world materials connected to other content areas and to children's experiences. For example, if you are doing a unit on wildlife in the backyard, you can use pictures of creatures (see Figure 17.4)

Figure 17.4 Guess the rule that was used to sort these bugs.

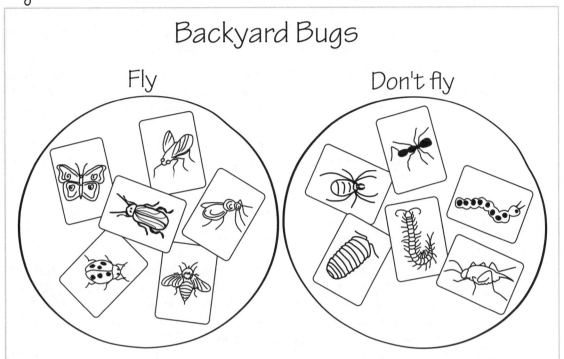

to sort by relevant attributes and have children guess the sorting rule. Following are additional ideas that can be used for classification activities related to social studies and science.

For social studies, children could sort and eventually graph data about:

- Places in the United States and outside the United States
- Country or state of origin of classmates
- Past, present, and future events
- Goods (e.g., bread, milk, apples, pants, socks, shoes) and services (e.g., waiting tables at a restaurant, mowing yards, repairing cars)
- Continents and oceans

For science, children might classify and graph data using the following attributes:

- Sensory descriptors for items such as sweet/sour/bitter/salty, rough/smooth, hard/soft, cold/warm, loud/soft, high/low, and bright/dull
- Relative size or weight of a collection of objects (big/little, large/small, heavy/light, wide/thin, long/short)
- Position of objects found in the classroom (over/under, in/out, above/below, left/right)
- Speed (fast/slow) of different animals (e.g., turtles, ants, snakes, cheetahs) or transportation (e.g., car, bicycle, airplane, walking)
- Materials or objects that float or sink in water
- Weather observations (e.g., sunny, cloudy, raining, snowing)
- Materials in the recycling bin (plastics, aluminum, glass, paper)
- Substances that will or will not dissolve in water

- Characteristics of plants (edible/nonedible, flowering/nonflowering, evergreen/deciduous)
- Physical characteristics of animals (body coverings or methods of movement)
- Other characteristics of animals (wild/tame, water homes/land homes, hibernate/do not hibernate, migrate/do not migrate, camouflage/no camouflage)

To connect reading and data, children can sort and analyze data within a book (e.g., kinds of animals, shapes, locations). Children can also keep track of the kinds of books they read as a class (by topic area) or the number of times different words are used in a story.

Hopefully, these lists communicate how children can use data across content areas. Using ideas related to content and the real world helps children understand that data analysis is useful as well as engaging!

Formative Assessment Note

The ability to classify is an important skill for early data analysis. You can assess your children's ability to classify by observing them in small groups or listening to children as they participate in full-class discussions. As you discuss a particular classification with children, ask them to justify their placement of items. Requiring children to explain their reasoning will provide you with much more information than if you simply accept answers. Here are some suggestions for what to listen and look for:

- After gathering data, do children use categories to sort the data or do they focus on the particulars (e.g., list each child in the class and their favorite ice cream)?
- Are children able to place items into categories once they have been identified? Do they use valid reasons for placing items in a category?
- Do children contribute to ideas for classification schemes?
- Do children understand that different classification schemes will result in a different organization of the items being sorted? For example, children's names may be sorted by number of letters, and they can also be sorted by which part of the alphabet they begin with—first half or second half. These two schemes would result in different classifications.
- Do children correctly use an overlapping category—items that belong to two different groups at the same time?
- Can children correctly use the logical connectors *and* and *or* and the adjective *not* when creating classifications?

◆ Graphical Representations

A graph provides a visual image of the data that cannot be captured in other forms. The loops used with the attribute materials provide a first form of graphical representation. The class can "graph" data about themselves by placing information in loops with labels. A graph of "Our Pets" might consist of a picture of each child's pet or favorite stuffed animal (in lieu of a pet) that can be affixed to a wall display showing how the pets were classified. Different classifications would produce different graphs. For example, the graphs could show pets by the number of legs; by fur, feathers, or scales; by how long they have been with the family; and so on.

How data are organized should be directly related to the question that caused you to collect the data in the first place. For example, suppose that children want to know how many pockets they have on their clothing (Russell, 2006). Data collection involves each child in the room counting his or her pockets.

Stop and Reflect

If your second-grade class had collected these data, what methods might you suggest they use for organizing and graphing them? Is one of your ideas better than others for answering the question about how many pockets? ■

A bar graph made with one bar for every child will certainly tell how many pockets each child has. However, is it the best way to answer the question? If the data were categorized by number of pockets, then a graph showing the number of children with no pockets, one pocket, two pockets, three pockets, and so on will easily show which number of pockets is most common and how the number of pockets varies across the class.

Children should be involved in deciding how they want to represent their data. However, for children with little experience with the various methods of picturing data, you will need to introduce options. Graph the data using these options and facilitate a discussion with the class to decide which method might be best and why.

Once children have made the display, they should discuss the meanings of various parts of the representation. Analyzing data that are numerical (number of pockets) versus categorical (color of socks) is an added challenge for children as they struggle to make sense of the graphs. If, for example, the graph has seven stickers above the five, children may think that five people have seven pockets or seven people have five pockets. Children should be challenged to determine how this issue can be remedied.

Often young children have difficulty distinguishing between the data and the larger event from which the data were collected. They can think of the data as triggers or "pointers" to the event, not as abstracting specific information about the event (Konold, Higgins, Russell, & Khalil, 2004). For example, instead of recognizing that more children in the class have two pockets than five pockets, they may describe how they can put their lunch money in their front pocket or that they counted their pockets by twos. Focusing on the meaning of the symbols used in a graphical representation of the data as well as having children make comparisons between different groups (e.g., How many pockets do fifth graders have?) can help make the intent of the graph more salient for children (Russell, 2006).

The goal is to help children see that graphs tell information and that different types of representations tell different things about the same data. The value of having children actually construct their own graphs is not so much that they learn the techniques as that they are personally invested in the data and that they learn how a graph conveys information. Once a graph is constructed, the most important activity is discussing what it tells the people who see it, especially those who were not involved in making the graph. Discussions about graphs of real data that the children have themselves been involved in gathering will help them analyze and interpret other graphs that they see in books and newspapers and on TV.

What we should *not* do is only concentrate on the details of graph construction. Your objectives should focus on the issues of analysis and communication, which are much more important than the technique! In the real world, technology will take care of details.

Children should construct graphs or charts by hand and with technology. First, encourage them to make graphs that make sense to them and that they feel communicate the information they wish to convey. The intent is to get the children involved in accurately communicating a message about their data.

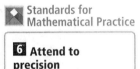

Standards for
Mathematical Practice

6 Attend to
precision

Standards for
Mathematical Practice

1 Make sense
of problems and
persevere in
solving them

Considering the complexities of graphs and the results of various research studies, Friel, Curcio, and Bright (2001) recommend the following progression for the introduction of different kinds of graphs in grades pre-K–2:

- Object graphs
- Picture graphs
- Line plots
- Bar graphs

These types of graphs help children focus on the count or frequency for each value along the vertical scale. They also progress from graphs where each piece of data is evident to graphs where the individual data values may seem to disappear—at least from the perspective of a child. At first glance, this progression does not follow the one recommended in the *Common Core State Standards* (CCSSO, 2010) and the *Curriculum Focal Points* (National Council of Teachers of Mathematics, 2006) because line plots appear after bar graphs in both of these documents. We address this issue in the sections on bar graphs and line plots.

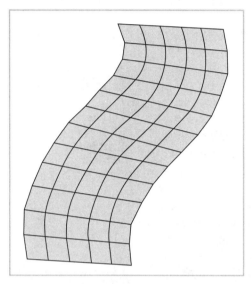

Figure 17.5
A graph mat for displaying real objects can be made from a sheet of plastic such as a shower curtain liner.

Object Graphs

An object graph uses the actual objects being graphed. Examples include types of shoes, favorite fruit, and shapes of buttons. Figure 17.5 shows a graph mat that can be used on the floor to display the objects in an organized manner. The mat can be made from a sheet of plastic about 8 to 10 feet long. Make 5 or 6 columns with 12 to 15 squares in each column. Children place each object in a square so that comparisons and counts are easily made. No numeric scale is necessary. Notice that an object graph is a small step from sorting. If real objects are sorted into groups, those groups can be lined up for comparison—an object graph!

Picture Graphs

Picture graphs (also called pictographs) move up a level of abstraction by using a drawing or picture of some sort that represents what is being graphed. The picture can represent one piece of data or it can represent a designated quantity. For example, a picture of a book can be assigned to mean five books in a graph of how many books were read each day of the week. When children view the graph and see four books for Monday, they skip count to determine that twenty books were read on Monday.

Teaching Tip

Pictographs are a great way to connect to skip counting and early experiences with multiplication.

Children can make their own drawings for pictographs, but this can often become time consuming and tedious. There are various ways to make pictographs easier to create and thereby keep the focus on the meaning of the graph rather than the creation of it. You can duplicate student-made drawings. You can use clip art and create a full page of images that can be colored (optional) and cut out to suit particular needs. If you have a die-cut machine, you can use available shapes to help you pick a topic for a graph. For example, if your die-cut has various vehicles (cars, trains, bus, bike, boat, etc.), children can use those shapes to indicate each of the vehicles they have ridden in this year. Stickers can also be a quick way to make a pictograph.

Bar Graphs

After object and picture graphs, bar graphs are among the first ways used to group and present data with children in grades pre-K–2. The following activity can be used to introduce children to the idea of using bar graphs to organize data.

Activity 17.4 ORGANIZING CARDS

Each pair of children needs a set of about 12 information cards that have two attributes written on them. (See Figure 17.6a for examples of cards.) Tell the children that these cards describe children from another class and their task is to sort and organize the cards so that they can find out some things about this class. Emphasize that they need to focus on the class and not on individual children. After pairs have organized their cards in some way, have the children walk around to look at the different arrangements. (See Figure 17.6b for possible arrangements.) You may want to draw the different arrangements on the board for children to see while the class discusses the different ways. First ask, "What can you tell about the class when the cards are arranged this way or that way?"

Ask "how many" type questions, such as "Which arrangement helps us see how many children like chocolate ice cream?" or "Can we tell how many more boys than girls are in the class with this arrangement?" or "Which arrangement helps you see which ice cream flavor is most liked?" You can also have pairs of children gather and organize their cards as you ask each question so that the answer to the question is more apparent. Have children justify how their arrangement helps to answer a given question.

Standards for
Mathematical Practice

2 **Reason abstractly and quantitatively**

Initially bar graphs should be made with each bar consisting of countable parts so that the individual pieces of data do not seem to disappear. The information cards in the previous activity, "Organizing Cards," served this purpose. Having children use something to represent the pieces of data or the things being counted helps transition from object and picture graphs to bar graphs. An easy idea is to use sticky notes to represent the individual pieces of data. These can be posted directly to the board or to a chart and rearranged if needed. To help children keep their notes in line you may wish to use a gridded chart similar to the graph mat described in the section on object graphs.

Figure 17.6 "Organizing Cards" activity.

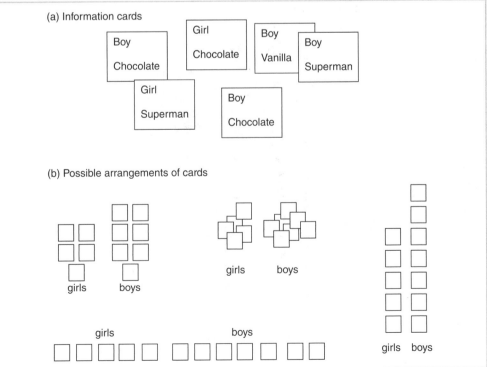

After identifying a question, make a quick graph of class data by following these steps:

1. Decide as a class which groups of data will make up the different bars. It is good to have two to six different bars in a graph.

2. Have children look at the choices and decide where they will place their sticky note. Have them write their name on the note.

3. In small groups, have children place their entry on the graph.

Figure 17.7 illustrates two additional quick ways to gather information (step 2 of the process of doing statistics) and analyze it (step 3). A class of 25 to 30 children can make a graph in less than 10 minutes, leaving ample time to use the graph for questions and observations (step 4).

The next transition is to begin using rectangular bars as seen in traditional bar graphs, but have children shade each bar with alternating colors to keep individual pieces of data visible. Friel, Curcio, and Bright (2001) also recommend using grid lines to help children read the counts or frequencies and label the bars with numerical values.

Figure **17.7** Some ideas for quick graphs that can be used again and again.

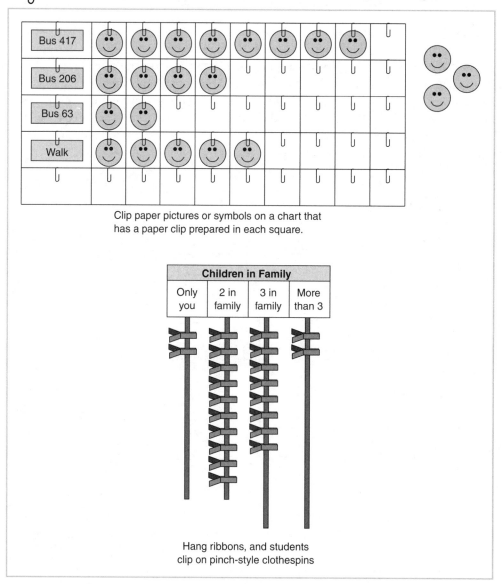

Clip paper pictures or symbols on a chart that has a paper clip prepared in each square.

Hang ribbons, and students clip on pinch-style clothespins

The following activity uses traditional bar graphs in which the individual pieces of data (inches or centimeters) disappear and children focus on each bar as a whole.

Activity 17.5 STORM CHASER

This activity involves children collecting data over time about the amount of rainfall (or snowfall) right outside their classroom. Install a rain (or snow) gauge outside the classroom in a location where it can be easily accessed. After a heavy rain (or snow) storm, send a pair of children outside with a piece of cash register tape. Their task is to cut the tape as long as the height of the rain on the scale. Then they should mark the tape with the date of the storm. Place the strips chronologically on a base line labeled with the month and day. These strips form a bar graph that can be added to and analyzed over the year. Have children to round to the nearest $\frac{1}{2}$ or $\frac{1}{4}$ inch. For example, if it rained about 1 inch on October 5, about $\frac{1}{4}$ inch on October 10, and about $\frac{1}{2}$ inch on October 23, there would be 3 bars with the indicated heights (1 inch, $\frac{1}{4}$ inch, $\frac{1}{2}$ inch), each labeled with the corresponding date. If the storm occurred over the weekend, the children can problem solve how they want to record that observation (one strip of paper for the whole weekend if it is one storm, cut the piece in half if there are two storms, or consult the news for approximate rainfalls). The important components are combining and comparing the data—how does the storm total in October compare to the total in April? Note that this paper strip to bar graph approach can also be used with monitoring plant growth as well as other similar activities.

Bar graphs can clearly show the category that is the largest and the one that is the smallest, as well as tell exactly how large each category is. They can also be a source for creating put-together, take-apart, and comparison word problems.

Figure 17.8

Using bar graphs to create story problems.

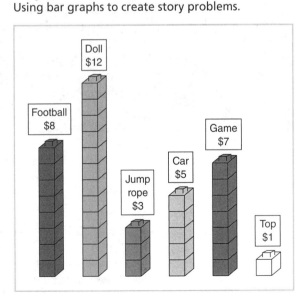

Activity 17.6 STORY BARS

Have children make a bar graph of some data using plastic connecting cubes such as Unifix. Choose a situation with 5 or 6 bars with no more than 10 or 12 cubes in each. For example, the graph in Figure 17.8 shows prices for six toys. The task for children is to use the graph itself to create at least two story problems about the toy prices. For example, one problem might be "How much more money does the doll cost than the football?" Another problem could be "If you had $20, which toys could you buy? How much change would you get back?" They can swap their story problems with a partner or you can pose some of the problems to the entire class.

Figure 17.9

A line plot that answers the question, "Do all the small boxes of raisins have the same number of raisins?"

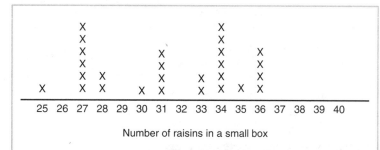

Number of raisins in a small box

Line Plots

Object, picture, and bar graphs are useful for illustrating categorical data, for example, favorite colors or TV shows. When data are numerical (i.e., grouped along a continuous scale), they should be ordered along a number line.

Line plots are counts of things along a numeric scale. To make a line plot, a number line is drawn and an X is made above the corresponding value on the line for every corresponding data element (in middle school and beyond the X is replaced by dots and the graph is then called a dot plot). One advantage of a line plot is that every piece of data is shown on the graph. It is also a very easy type of graph for children to make. It is essentially a bar graph arranged along a numerical scale with a potential bar for every indicated value on the horizontal scale. A simple example is shown in Figure 17.9 that answers the question, "Do all the small boxes of raisins have the same number of raisins?" (Friel et al., 2001).

The following activity helps develop this representation of numerical information.

 Teaching Tip

Having children be "in the graph" is an important experience that will enable them to better understand the more abstract representation.

Teaching Tip

A common error that children make, especially when using technology to create graphs, is to use a line graph instead of a line plot. In line graphs we assume that the points on the line between the identified values are feasible values (e.g., those temperatures were passed through on the way from one identified value to the next). Data used with line plots are not continuous in that sense.

Activity 17.7 STAND BY ME

Create a line plot on the floor of the classroom. Use masking tape to mark a line and label it with numbers ranging from 2 minutes to 20 minutes (or whatever is appropriate for your children). Have children write on a sticky note how many minutes it takes them to travel to school. Then they are to stand on the location above that number on the line. Use the sticky notes to recreate the line plot above a piece of cash register tape on the board. (Label the cash register tape with the same numbers as the masking tape line, e.g., 2 minutes to 20 minutes.) Then children can better interpret the data.

Ask children to draw some conclusions about the different travel times of children in the class. What are the differences in times? What is the total of the five longest trips? How long does Emma travel over the five days during the school week (back and forth)? You can also use the data to create word problems.

Formative Assessment Note

Your goal is for children to understand that a graph helps answer a question and that different graphs tell us different things about the data. Children should write about their graphs, explaining what the graph shows.

Interpreting Results

Once a graph has been constructed, it is time for the fourth step in the process of doing statistics: interpretation. You can start by engaging the class in a discussion of what information the graph shows or conveys. "What can you tell about our class by looking at this shoe graph?" Graphs convey factual information (e.g., more people wear sneakers than any other kind of shoe) and also provide opportunities to make inferences that are not directly observable in the graph (e.g., kids in this class do not like to wear leather shoes).

When asked about graphs, young children tend to initially focus on individual pieces of data in a data display and not on the data as a whole (Clements & Sarama, 2009). So when asked to describe something about a graph, they may state, "There I am! I ride the bus to school." However, much more can be said about a set of data than about the individual pieces of data.

Figure 17.10

Two bar graphs for 25 children. The shapes of the data in these two graphs are quite different. One is spread equally whereas the other has two high values and three low values.

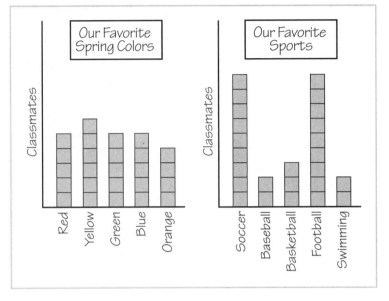

The idea is to help children consider the data set as a whole. One way to accomplish this is to try to focus their attention on the *shape of data:* a sense of how the data are spread or grouped. In grades pre-K–2 this can be discussed informally by looking at almost any graph.

Whenever there are two or more graphs of the same type, it is worth talking with children about the overall look of the graphs—how they are alike and how they are different. Consider, for example, the two graphs in Figure 17.10, showing data that have been gathered from a class of 25 children. In Our Favorite Spring Colors graph, the children are almost distributed equally though there is a most favored color. In Our Favorite Sports graph, two sports received most of the votes from the class and the remainder of the class is somewhat spread among the other three.

When data are depicted on a number line, such as on a line plot, the idea of data as being spread out or grouped together also takes on a numeric meaning. For example, in a measure of the heights of boys and girls in inches, we might notice that the girls' heights are spread over a wider range than the boys' heights. The boys' heights may cluster more around a particular height.

As discussed earlier in this chapter, sometimes questions focus on mathematical ideas rather than statistical ideas. Although it is helpful to ask mathematical questions, it is essential to ask questions that are statistical in nature. That means the questions focus on the context of the situation, seeing what can be learned or inferred from the data. During the interpretation phase, children might even want to create a different data display to get a different look at the data or gather data from a different class to see how their results compare.

Different researchers have recommended questions that focus on statistical thinking (Franklin et al., 2005; Friel, O'Conner, & Mamer, 2006; Russell, 2006; Shaughnessy, 2006). Here are some ideas from their lists to get you started on having meaningful discussions about interpreting data:

- What do the numbers tell us about our class (or another class)?
- If we asked another class the same questions, how would that data look? What if we asked a larger group, how would the data look?

Standards for Mathematical Practice

3 Reason abstractly and quantitatively

- How do the numbers in this graph *compare* to this graph?
- Where are the data "clustering"? Where are the data that are *not* in the cluster?
- What does the graph *not* tell us?
- What new questions arise from these data?
- What is the maker of the graph trying to tell us?

These prompts apply across many data displays. It certainly should be a major focus of your instruction. Consider it the *After* phase of your lesson, although some of these questions will be integrated in the *During* phase as well. The emphasis of the questions in this phase is on getting children to notice differences in the data and provide possible reasons for those differences (Franklin & Mewborn, 2008).

Our world is inundated with data. It is essential that we prepare our children to be literate about what can be interpreted from data and what cannot be interpreted from data. It is not too early to start this preparation in grades pre-K–2.

Expanded Lesson

Using Data to Answer a Question

Content and Task Decisions

Grade Level: K–2

Mathematics Goals

- To determine a question that can be answered through gathering data
- To determine how to gather the data
- To use data to create graphs
- To use graphs to answer questions concerning a population

Grade Level Guide

NCTM *Curriculum Focal Points*	*Common* *Core State Standards*
Children in kindergarten collect data and use counting to answer questions. By first grade, children are representing data in picture graphs and bar graphs.	First graders organize, represent, and interpret data. They are able to ask and answer questions by comparing data. By second grade, children are able to draw picture graphs and bar graphs (using a single unit scale) to represent data. They are also able to use the information in a bar graph to answer problems.

Consider Your Children's Needs

This lesson assumes that the children have had experiences with several different types of graphs, including Venn diagrams and some form of bar graph, and that they are able to use tallies or numbers for gathering data. You may also want to allow the children to do this phase of the lesson using appropriate graphing programs on the computer. Involve the children in selecting questions that are of interest to them and are culturally relevant.

For English Language Learners

- Include written prompts and pair-share for the discussions at the start of this lesson as a way to increase the participation of ELLs.

- Model the process of gathering data using children from the class. You can model "how to" and "how not to" as a way to help all the children (particularly ELLs) comprehend the process.

- In selecting how the data will be displayed, show illustrations of different options and have them labeled with the appropriate terminology.

For Children with Disabilities

- Provide a table with the possible answers for children with disabilities if they are collecting data from another class. This will support them in organizing the tallies.

- When the children are creating a bar graph, have them make an X in the grid prior to coloring. This will help them focus on the quantity to ensure accuracy.

- When analyzing the data, pose some questions that will help the children compare data points in a think-aloud mode. Some children with disabilities may need to hear the way you compare data to help them draw conclusions and answer the question.

Materials

- Large pieces of paper, such as chart paper
- Grid paper, such as a 1-cm grid (see Blackline Master 31)
- Chart grid paper (optional)
- Markers/crayons
- Connecting cubes or other manipulatives for graphing data
- Computers (visit http://nlvm.usu.edu for free graph-making programs)

Lesson

This lesson may require several days to complete. It employs the four-step process of doing statistics: (1) What question do we want to answer? (2) How will we collect the data? (3) What type of analysis (e.g., a graph) should we use to view our data? (4) What do the data tell us about our question? In this lesson, the process is split into two tasks with the fourth phase addressed in the *After* portion of the second task.

LESSON PART I

Before

Present the first task to the class:

- Engage the children in a discussion of what question they would like to answer. How you guide this discussion will vary with the age of the children and perhaps their recent experiences, such as a field trip, a unit of study in science, or a book that has been read to the class. Consider such ideas as favorites (books, food, etc.), nature or science (weather, what lives in our yards), comparisons (something about your class as compared with another class, children compared to adults), measures (heights, arm spans), how many (pets, hours watching TV, minutes spent brushing teeth), and so on.

- Once a question or questions are determined, talk about how information (data) can be collected. If a survey is required, you will probably need to help the children formulate one to three questions that have simple responses—not full sentences or explanations. What is important is that the children are personally invested in the decisions. Remember to limit options to a reasonable amount when deciding on choices for answers (such as in a question about favorites).

- Discuss *how* they can gather data to answer the question. This is not easy, as the children will need to think about ways to get data from all classmates without duplicating, for example. Set the children to gathering the data. If the collection involves getting data from home or from another class, you will need to help the children be very organized about doing this so that real data are available when you need them.

Provide clear expectations:

- The children may be working in groups to answer different questions, or this may be a whole-class project. During the second task, the children will work best in groups of two or three. This may mean that there will be multiple groups working on the same question and/or with the same data.

- Materials should be available for the children to select what they desire for their group when they are organizing and displaying their data.

- Children may use computer graphing to display their data.

During

- Monitor the data collection to be sure it is being gathered appropriately and recorded such that the children will know what the data mean.

After

Bring the class together to share and discuss the task:

- When the data have been collected, briefly discuss what data the class, groups, or individuals have gathered.

- Ask the children what they notice about their data. They might be able to say some comparison statements. Can they answer the question(s) they posed? What new questions might emerge?

- Suggest to the children that they might be able to learn more about their question if they display their data in some kind of graph. At this point, a new problem develops, as presented in the second task.

LESSON PART II

Before

- Decide on a type of graph to make with the data that will help answer your question. Make the graph.

- Engage the class in thinking about the various types of graphs that they know how to make and ask for ideas about matching a type of graph with the question to be answered and the data gathered. You may need to remind the children about techniques they have seen or that are available on the computer.

- Show the children the types of materials available to them, including the computer. They are to select a type of graph, then use the data they have collected to create a presentation of the data in a way that they believe answers the question.

During

Initially:

- Be sure the children are productively working. Move around to the groups to answer any questions.

Ongoing:

- Have the children use the grid paper to create bar graphs. Try to make sure the graphs represent the data and will not distort conclusions.

- Encourage the children to add titles (linked to the question answered) and labels to their posters or presentations to help explain the data shown in the graph.

After

- Have groups display their graphs. Take turns having children explain their graphs and what their graph tells us related to the original questions.

- Discuss which graphs best answered the question and why, or what advantages one graph (e.g., Venn diagram) has over another (e.g., bar).

- Ask the children whether they can answer other questions using the data.
- Finally, ask the children what new questions might be asked, having learned what they did from this question.

Assessment

Observe

- Are the children using a table, checklist, or tally to gather their data? Do they have a process in place to ensure they gather data from each person only once?
- Are the children considering appropriate types of graphs? Do they understand how the type of data limits what makes sense for a graph?

- Are the children able to actually create the graph?
- Do the children know how to interpret the data in the graph? Can they make conjectures?

Ask

- What do we need to consider when planning a survey or question?
- What do you need to do to gather data correctly?
- How did you decide on the type of graph to make?
- How did you create your graph?
- What does (indicate specific data point) mean on the graph?
- What do the data tell us about the question posed?

Common Core State Standards

Standards for Mathematical Practice

The Standards for Mathematical Practice describe varieties of expertise that mathematics educators at all levels should seek to develop in their students. These practices rest on important "processes and proficiencies" with longstanding importance in mathematics education. The first of these are the NCTM process standards of problem solving, reasoning and proof, communication, representation, and connections. The second are the strands of mathematical proficiency specified in the National Research Council's report *Adding It Up*: adaptive reasoning, strategic competence, conceptual understanding (comprehension of mathematical concepts, operations and relations), procedural fluency (skill in carrying out procedures flexibly, accurately, efficiently and appropriately), and productive disposition (habitual inclination to see mathematics as sensible, useful, and worthwhile, coupled with a belief in diligence and one's own efficacy).

1 Make sense of problems and persevere in solving them.

Mathematically proficient students start by explaining to themselves the meaning of a problem and looking for entry points to its solution. They analyze givens, constraints, relationships, and goals. They make conjectures about the form and meaning of the solution and plan a solution pathway rather than simply jumping into a solution attempt. They consider analogous problems, and try special cases and simpler forms of the original problem in order to gain insight into its solution. They monitor and evaluate their progress and change course if necessary. Older students might, depending on the context of the problem, transform algebraic expressions or change the viewing window on their graphing calculator to get the information they need. Mathematically proficient students can explain correspondences between equations, verbal descriptions, tables, and graphs or draw diagrams of important features and relationships, graph data, and search for regularity or trends. Younger students might rely on using concrete objects or pictures to help conceptualize and solve a problem. Mathematically proficient students check their answers to problems using a different method, and they continually ask themselves, "Does this make sense?" They can understand the approaches of others to solving complex problems and identify correspondences between different approaches.

2 Reason abstractly and quantitatively.

Mathematically proficient students make sense of quantities and their relationships in problem situations. They bring two complementary abilities to bear on problems involving quantitative relationships: the ability to *decontextualize*—to abstract a given situation and represent it symbolically and manipulate the representing symbols as if they have a life of their own, without necessarily attending to their referents—and the ability to *contextualize*, to pause as needed during the manipulation process in order to probe into the referents for the symbols involved. Quantitative reasoning entails habits of creating a coherent representation of the problem at hand; considering the units involved; attending to the meaning of quantities, not just how to compute them; and knowing and flexibly using different properties of operations and objects.

3 Construct viable arguments and critique the reasoning of others.

Mathematically proficient students understand and use stated assumptions, definitions, and previously established results in constructing arguments. They make conjectures and build a logical progression of statements to explore the truth of their conjectures. They are able to analyze situations by breaking them into cases, and can recognize and use counterexamples. They justify their conclusions, communicate them to others, and respond to the arguments of others. They reason inductively about data, making plausible arguments that take into account the context from which the data arose. Mathematically proficient students are also able to compare the effectiveness of two plausible arguments, distinguish correct logic or reasoning from that which is flawed, and—if there is a flaw in an argument—explain what it is. Elementary students can construct arguments using concrete referents such as objects, drawings, diagrams, and actions. Such arguments can make sense and be correct, even though they are not generalized or made formal until later grades. Later, students learn to determine domains to which an argument applies. Students at all grades can listen or read the arguments of others, decide whether they make sense, and ask useful questions to clarify or improve the arguments.

4 Model with mathematics.

Mathematically proficient students can apply the mathematics they know to solve problems arising in everyday life, society, and the workplace. In early grades, this might be as simple as writing an addition equation to describe a situation. In middle grades, a student might apply proportional reasoning to plan a school event or analyze a problem in the community. By high school, a student might use geometry to solve a design problem or use a function to describe how one quantity of interest depends on another. Mathematically proficient students who can apply what they know are comfortable making assumptions and approximations to simplify a complicated situation, realizing that these may need revision later. They are able to identify important quantities in a practical situation and map their relationships using such tools as diagrams, two-way tables, graphs, flowcharts and formulas. They can analyze those relationships mathematically to draw conclusions. They routinely interpret their mathematical results in the context of the situation and reflect on whether the results make sense, possibly improving the model if it has not served its purpose.

5 Use appropriate tools strategically.

Mathematically proficient students consider the available tools when solving a mathematical problem. These tools might include pencil and paper, concrete models, a ruler, a protractor, a calculator, a spreadsheet, a computer algebra system, a statistical package, or dynamic geometry software. Proficient students are sufficiently familiar with tools appropriate for their grade or course to make sound decisions about when each of these tools might be helpful, recognizing both the insight to be gained and their limitations. For example, mathematically proficient high school students analyze graphs of functions and solutions generated using a graphing calculator. They detect possible errors by strategically using estimation and other mathematical knowledge. When making mathematical models, they know that technology can enable them to visualize the results of varying assumptions, explore consequences, and compare predictions with data. Mathematically proficient students at various grade levels are able to identify relevant external mathematical resources, such as digital content located on a website, and use them to pose or solve problems. They are able to use technological tools to explore and deepen their understanding of concepts.

6 Attend to precision.

Mathematically proficient students try to communicate precisely to others. They try to use clear definitions in discussion with others and in their own reasoning. They state the meaning of the symbols they choose, including using the equal sign consistently and appropriately. They are careful about specifying units of measure, and labeling axes to clarify the correspondence with quantities in a problem. They calculate accurately and efficiently, express numerical answers with a degree of precision appropriate for the problem context. In the elementary grades, students give carefully formulated explanations to each other. By the time they reach high school they have learned to examine claims and make explicit use of definitions.

7 Look for and make use of structure.

Mathematically proficient students look closely to discern a pattern or structure. Young students, for example, might notice that three and seven more is the same amount as seven and three more, or they may sort a collection of shapes according to how many sides the shapes have. Later, students will see 7×8 equals the well remembered $7 \times 5 + 7 \times 3$, in preparation for learning about the distributive property. In the expression $x^2 + 9x + 14$, older students can see the 14 as 2×7 and the 9 as $2 + 7$. They recognize the significance of an existing line in a geometric figure and can use the strategy of drawing an auxiliary line for solving problems. They also can step back for an overview and shift perspective. They can see complicated things, such as some algebraic expressions, as single objects or as being composed of several objects. For example, they can see $5 - 3(x - y)^2$ as 5 minus a positive number times a square and use that to realize that its value cannot be more than 5 for any real numbers x and y.

8 Look for and express regularity in repeated reasoning.

Mathematically proficient students notice if calculations are repeated, and look both for general methods and for shortcuts. Upper elementary students might notice when dividing 25 by 11 that they are repeating the same calculations over and over again, and conclude they have a repeating decimal. By paying attention to the calculation of slope as they re-peatedly check whether points are on the line through $(1, 2)$ with slope 3, middle school students might abstract the equation $(y - 2)/(x - 1) = 3$. Noticing the regularity in the way terms cancel when expanding $(x - 1)(x + 1)$, $(x - 1)(x^2 + x + 1)$, and $(x - 1)(x^3 + x^2 + x + 1)$ might lead them to the general formula for the sum of a geometric series. As they work to solve a problem, mathematically proficient students maintain oversight of the process, while attending to the details. They continually evaluate the reasonableness of their intermediate results.

Connecting the Standards for Mathematical Practice to the Standards for Mathematical Content

The Standards for Mathematical Practice describe ways in which developing student practitioners of the discipline of mathematics increasingly ought to engage with the subject matter as they grow in mathematical maturity and expertise throughout the elementary, middle and high school years. Designers of curricula, assessments, and professional development should all attend to the need to connect the mathematical practices to mathematical content in mathematics instruction.

The Standards for Mathematical Content are a balanced combination of pro-cedure and understanding. Expectations that begin with the word "understand" are often especially good opportunities to connect the practices to the content. Students who lack understanding of a topic may rely on procedures too heavily. Without a flex-ible base from which to work, they may be less likely to consider analogous problems, represent problems coherently, justify conclusions, apply the mathematics to practi-cal situations, use technology mindfully to work with the mathematics, explain the mathematics accurately to other students, step back for an overview, or deviate from a known procedure to find a shortcut. In short, a lack of understanding effectively pre-vents a student from engaging in the mathematical practices.

In this respect, those content standards which set an expectation of understand-ing are potential "points of intersection" between the Standards for Mathematical Content and the Standards for Mathematical Practice. These points of intersection are intended to be weighted toward central and generative concepts in the school mathematics curriculum that most merit the time, resources, innovative energies, and focus necessary to qualitatively improve the curriculum, instruction, assessment, pro-fessional development, and student achievement in mathematics.

Common Core State Standards

Grades K–2 Critical Content Areas and Overviews

CCSS Mathematics | Grade Kindergarten Critical Areas

In Kindergarten, instructional time should focus on two critical areas:

1. representing and comparing whole numbers, initially with sets of objects;
2. describing shapes and space.

More learning time in Kindergarten should be devoted to number than to other topics.

1. *Students use numbers, including written numerals, to represent quantities and to solve quantitative problems, such as counting objects in a set; counting out a given number of objects; comparing sets or numerals; and modeling simple joining and separating situations with sets of objects, or eventually with equations such as $5 + 2 = 7$ and $7 - 2 = 5$.* (Kindergarten students should see addition and subtraction equations, and student writing of equations in kindergarten is encouraged, but it is not required.) Students choose, combine, and apply effective strategies for answering quantitative questions, including quickly recognizing the cardinalities of small sets of objects, counting and producing sets of given sizes, counting the number of objects in combined sets, or counting the number of objects that remain in a set after some are taken away.

2. *Students describe their physical world using geometric ideas (e.g., shape, orientation, spatial relations) and vocabulary.* They identify, name, and describe basic two-dimensional shapes, such as squares, triangles, circles, rectangles, and hexagons, presented in a variety of ways (e.g., with different sizes and orientations), as well as three-dimensional shapes such as cubes, cones, cylinders, and spheres. They use basic shapes and spatial reasoning to model objects in their environment and to construct more complex shapes.

Grade K Overview

Counting and Cardinality

- Know number names and the count sequence.
- Count to tell the number of objects.
- Compare numbers.

Source: © Copyright 2010. National Governors Association Center for Best Practices and Council of Chief State School Officers. All rights reserved.

Operations and Algebraic Thinking

- Understand addition as putting together and adding to, and understand subtraction as taking apart and taking from.

Number and Operations in Base Ten

- Work with numbers 11–19 to gain foundations for place value.

Measurement and Data

- Describe and compare measurable attributes.
- Classify objects and count the number of objects in each category.

Geometry

- Identify and describe shapes.
- Analyze, compare, create, and compose shapes.

CCSS Mathematics | Grade 1 Critical Areas

In Grade 1, instructional time should focus on four critical areas:

1. developing understanding of addition, subtraction, and strategies for addition and subtraction within 20;
2. developing understanding of whole number relationships and place value, including grouping in tens and ones;
3. developing understanding of linear measurement and measuring lengths as iterating length units; and
4. reasoning about attributes of, and composing and decomposing geometric shapes.

1. *Students develop strategies for adding and subtracting whole numbers based on their prior work with small numbers.* They use a variety of models, including discrete objects and length-based models (e.g., cubes connected to form lengths), to model add-to, take-from, put-together, take-apart, and compare situations to develop meaning for the operations of addition and subtraction, and to develop strategies to solve arithmetic problems with these operations. Students understand connections between counting and addition and subtraction (e.g., adding two is the same as counting on two). They use properties of addition to add whole numbers and to create and use increasingly sophisticated strategies based on these properties (e.g., "making tens") to solve addition and subtraction problems within 20. By comparing a variety of solution strategies, children build their understanding of the relationship between addition and subtraction.

2. *Students develop, discuss, and use efficient, accurate, and generalizable methods to add within 100 and subtract multiples of 10.* They compare whole numbers (at least to 100) to develop understanding of and solve problems involving their relative sizes. They think of whole numbers between 10 and 100 in terms of tens and ones (especially recognizing the numbers 11 to 19 as composed of a ten and some ones). Through activities that build number sense, they understand the order of the counting numbers and their relative magnitudes.

3. *Students develop an understanding of the meaning and processes of measurement, including underlying concepts such as iterating (the mental activity of building up the length of an object with equal-sized units) and the transitivity principle for indirect measurement.*[1]

4. *Students compose and decompose plane or solid figures (e.g., put two triangles together to make a quadrilateral) and build understanding of part-whole relationships as well as the properties of the original and composite shapes.* As they combine shapes, they recognize them from different perspectives and orientations, describe their geometric attributes, and determine how they are alike and different, to develop the background for measurement and for initial understandings of properties such as congruence and symmetry.

Grade 1 Overview

Operations and Algebraic Thinking

- Represent and solve problems involving addition and subtraction.
- Understand and apply properties of operations and the relationship between addition and subtraction.
- Add and subtract within 20.
- Work with addition and subtraction equations.

Number and Operations in Base Ten

- Extend the counting sequence.
- Understand place value.
- Use place value understanding and properties of operations to add and subtract.

Measurement and Data

- Measure lengths indirectly and by iterating length units.
- Tell and write time.
- Represent and interpret data.

Geometry

- Reason with shapes and their attributes.

CCSS Mathematics | Grade 2 Critical Areas

In Grade 2, instructional time should focus on four critical areas:

1. extending understanding of base-ten notation;
2. building fluency with addition and subtraction;
3. using standard units of measure; and
4. describing and analyzing shapes.

---

[1]Students should apply the principle of transitivity of measurement to make indirect comparisons, but they need not use this technical term.

1. *Students extend their understanding of the base-ten system.* This includes ideas of counting in fives, tens, and multiples of hundreds, tens, and ones, as well as number relationships involving these units, including comparing. Students understand multi-digit numbers (up to 1000) written in base-ten notation, recognizing that the digits in each place represent amounts of thousands, hundreds, tens, or ones (e.g., 853 is 8 hundreds + 5 tens + 3 ones).

2. *Students use their understanding of addition to develop fluency with addition and subtraction within 100.* They solve problems within 1000 by applying their understanding of models for addition and subtraction, and they develop, discuss, and use efficient, accurate, and generalizable methods to compute sums and differences of whole numbers in base-ten notation, using their understanding of place value and the properties of operations. They select and accurately apply methods that are appropriate for the context and the numbers involved to mentally calculate sums and differences for numbers with only tens or only hundreds.

3. *Students recognize the need for standard units of measure (centimeter and inch) and they use rulers and other measurement tools with the understanding that linear measure involves an iteration of units.* They recognize that the smaller the unit, the more iterations they need to cover a given length.

4. *Students describe and analyze shapes by examining their sides and angles. Students investigate, describe, and reason about decomposing and combining shapes to make other shapes.* Through building, drawing, and analyzing two- and three-dimensional shapes, students develop a foundation for understanding area, volume, congruence, similarity, and symmetry in later grades.

Grade 2 Overview

Operations and Algebraic Thinking

- Represent and solve problems involving addition and subtraction.
- Add and subtract within 20.
- Work with equal groups of objects to gain foundations for multiplication.

Number and Operations in Base Ten

- Understand place value.
- Use place value understanding and properties of operations to add and subtract.

Measurement and Data

- Measure and estimate lengths in standard units.
- Relate addition and subtraction to length.
- Work with time and money.
- Represent and interpret data.

Geometry

- Reason with shapes and their attributes.

A Guide to the Blackline Masters

This appendix contains thumbnails of all of the Blackline Masters that are referenced throughout the book. Each full-size master can easily be downloaded from the PD Toolkit at http://pdtoolkit.pearson.com. Once downloaded, you may print as many copies as you need. Keep the files on your computer.

Tips for the Use of the Blackline Masters

When a blackline is to be used either as a workmat for children or will be cut apart into smaller pieces, the best advice is to duplicate the master on card stock. Card stock (also known as index stock) is heavy paper that comes in a variety of colors and can be found at copy or office supply stores.

Workmats such as the ten-frame mat and the place-value mat are best if not laminated. Lamination makes the mats slippery so that counters slide around or off.

With materials that require cutting into smaller pieces, we suggest that you laminate the card stock before you cut out the pieces. This will preserve the materials for several years and save valuable time in the future. Here are some additional, specific instructions for certain masters.

- Dot Cards (BLMs 3–8): Make each set of six pages a different color. Otherwise, it is difficult to tell to which set a stray card belongs.

- Little Ten-Frames (BLMs 17 and 18): Make the full ten-frames on one color of card stock and the less-than-ten sheet on another. One set consists of the ten cards of each type, cut from a strip of ten on the master.

- Assorted Shapes (BLMs 20–26): Make each set of seven pages a different color. Otherwise, it is very difficult to tell to which set a stray shape belongs.

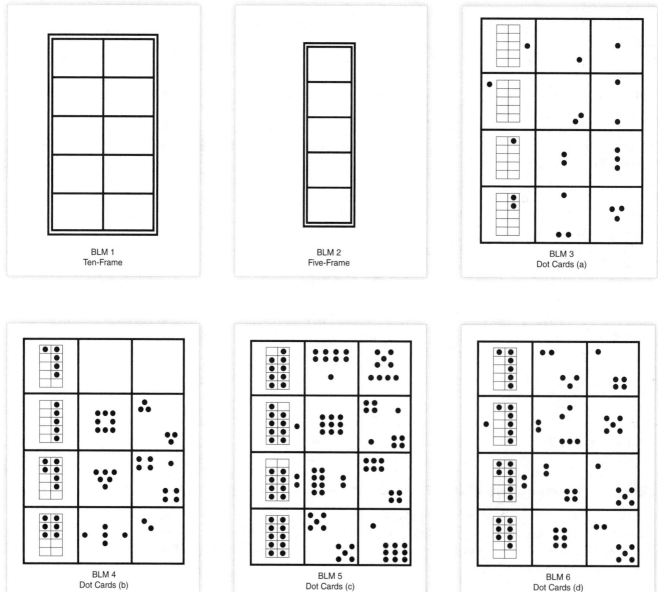

BLM 1
Ten-Frame

BLM 2
Five-Frame

BLM 3
Dot Cards (a)

BLM 4
Dot Cards (b)

BLM 5
Dot Cards (c)

BLM 6
Dot Cards (d)

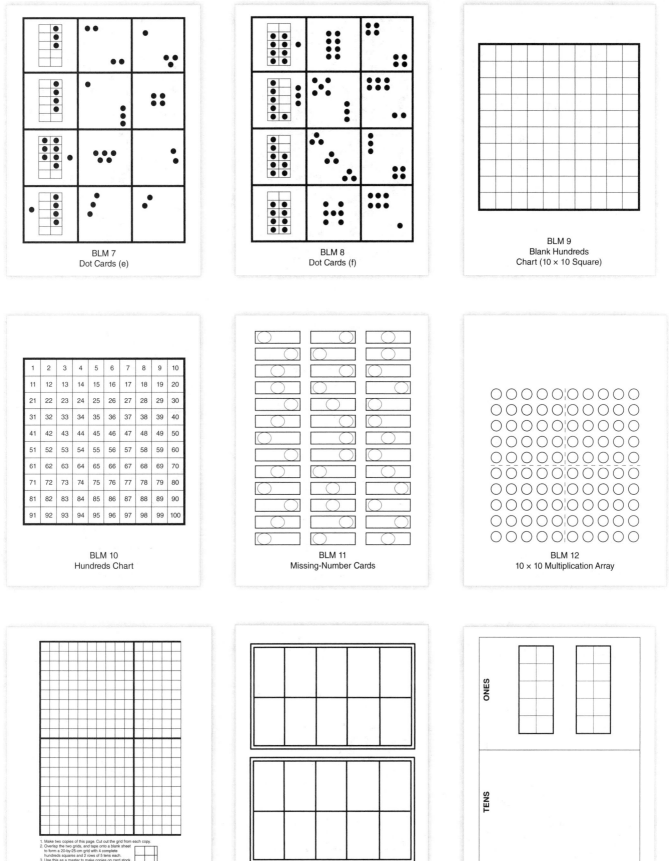

BLM 7
Dot Cards (e)

BLM 8
Dot Cards (f)

BLM 9
Blank Hundreds
Chart (10 × 10 Square)

BLM 10
Hundreds Chart

BLM 11
Missing-Number Cards

BLM 12
10 × 10 Multiplication Array

BLM 13
Base-Ten Materials Grid

BLM 14
Double Ten-Frame

BLM 15
Place-Value Mat (with Double Ten-Frames)

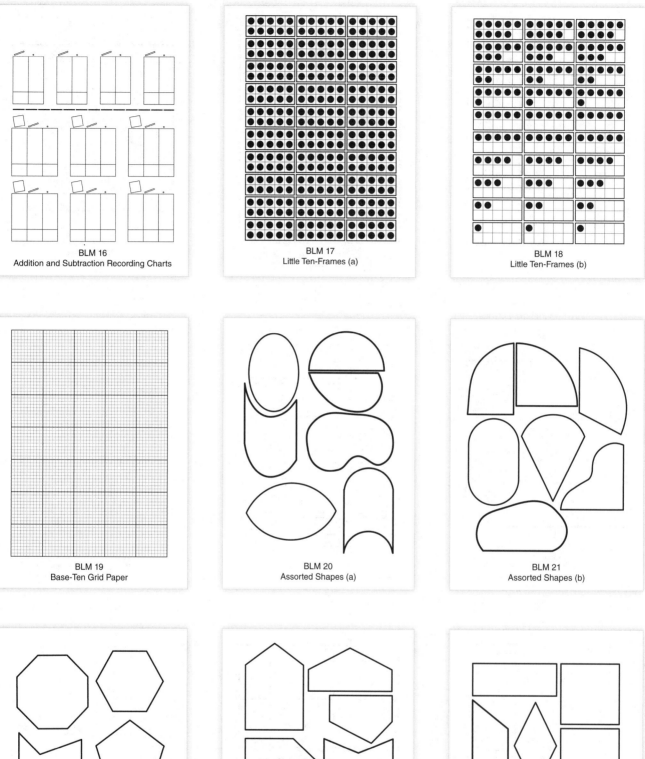

BLM 16
Addition and Subtraction Recording Charts

BLM 17
Little Ten-Frames (a)

BLM 18
Little Ten-Frames (b)

BLM 19
Base-Ten Grid Paper

BLM 20
Assorted Shapes (a)

BLM 21
Assorted Shapes (b)

BLM 22
Assorted Shapes (c)

BLM 23
Assorted Shapes (d)

BLM 24
Assorted Shapes (e)

BLM 25
Assorted Shapes (f)

BLM 26
Assorted Shapes (g)

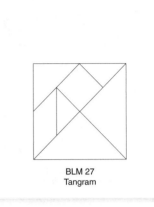

BLM 27
Tangram

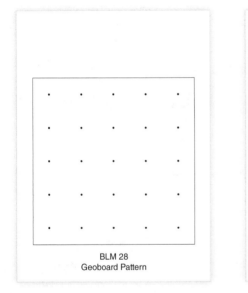

BLM 28
Geoboard Pattern

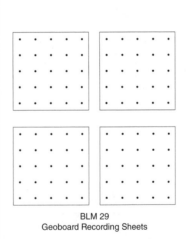

BLM 29
Geoboard Recording Sheets

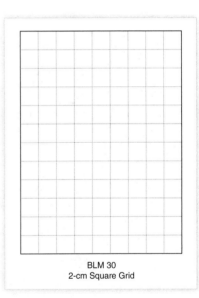

BLM 30
2-cm Square Grid

BLM 31
1-cm Square Grid

BLM 32
0.5-cm Square Grid

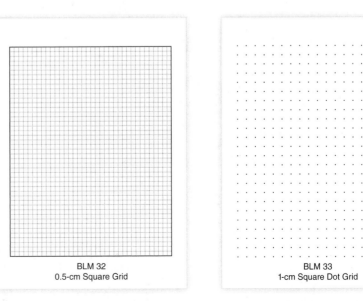

BLM 33
1-cm Square Dot Grid

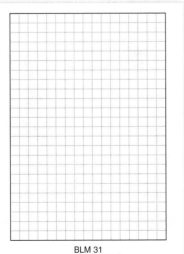

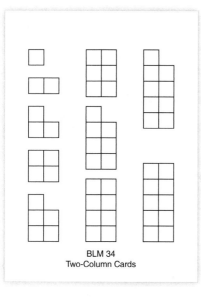

BLM 34
Two-Column Cards

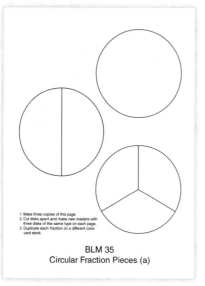

BLM 35
Circular Fraction Pieces (a)

1. Make three copies of this page.
2. Cut disks apart and make new masters with three disks of the same type on each page.
3. Duplicate each fraction on a different color card stock.

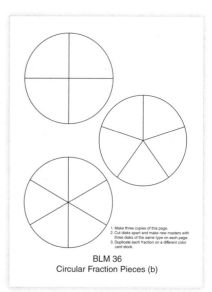

BLM 36
Circular Fraction Pieces (b)

1. Make three copies of this page.
2. Cut disks apart and make new masters with three disks of the same type on each page.
3. Duplicate each fraction on a different color card stock.

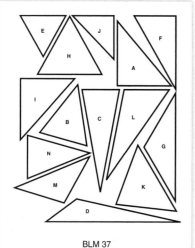

BLM 37
Assorted Triangles

Parallelograms

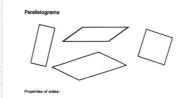

Properties of sides:

Properties of angles:

BLM 38
Property Lists for
Quadrilaterals (Parallelograms)

Rhombuses

Properties of sides:

Properties of angles:

BLM 39
Property Lists for
Quadrilaterals (Rhombuses)

Rectangles

Properties of sides:

Properties of angles:

BLM 40
Property Lists for
Quadrilaterals (Rectangles)

Squares

Properties of sides:

Properties of angles:

BLM 41
Property Lists for
Quadrilaterals (Squares)

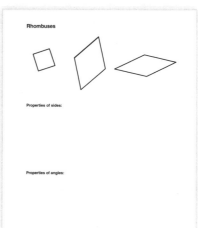

Directions: Make copies of side 1.
Then copy side 2 on the reverse of side 1.
Check the orientation and alignment with
one copy. When oriented and aligned correctly,
the two sides will line up when held to the light.

BLM 42
Motion Flag (Side 1)

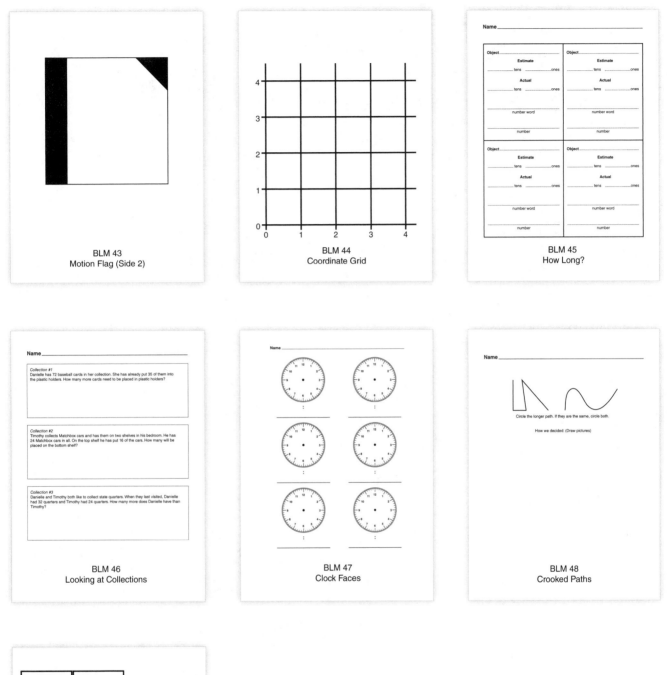

BLM 43
Motion Flag (Side 2)

BLM 44
Coordinate Grid

BLM 45
How Long?

BLM 46
Looking at Collections

BLM 47
Clock Faces

BLM 48
Crooked Paths

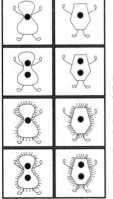

BLM 49
Woozle Cards

Make two copies for each set of Woozle Cards. Use white or off-white card stock. Before laminating, color the bodies in one set light blue and the other set red. Cut into individual cards.

Ambrose, R. (2002). Are we overemphasizing manipulatives in the primary grades to the detriment of girls? *Teaching Children Mathematics, 9*(1), 16–21.

Ashcraft, M. H., & Christy, K. S. (1995). The frequency of arithmetic facts in elementary texts: Addition and multiplication in grades 1–6. *Journal for Research in Mathematics Education, 26,* 396–421.

Aspiazu, G. G., Bauer, S. C., & Spillett, M. D. (1998). Improving the academic performance of Hispanic youth: A community education model. *Bilingual Research Journal, 22*(2), 1–20.

Assouline, S. G., & Lupkowski-Shoplik, A. (2011). Developing math talent: A comprehensive guide to math education for gifted students in elementary and middle school (2nd ed.). Waco, TX: Prufrock Press.

Averill, R., Anderson, D., Easton, H., Te Maro, P., Smith, D., & Hynds, A. (2009). Culturally responsive teaching of mathematics: Three models from linked studies. *Journal for Research in Mathematics Education, 40*(2), 157–186.

Ball, D. L., & Bass, H. (2003). Making mathematics reasonable in school. In J. Kilpatrick, W. G. Martin, & D. Schifter (Eds.), *A research companion to Principles and Standards for School Mathematics* (pp. 27–44). Reston, VA: National Council of Teachers of Mathematics.

Baroody, A. J. (1985). Mastery of the basic number combinations: Internalization of relationships or facts? *Journal for Research in Mathematics Education, 16*(2), 83–98.

Baroody, A. J. (2003). The development of adaptive expertise and flexibility: The integration of conceptual and procedural knowledge. In A. J. Baroody & A. Dowker (Eds.), *The development of arithmetic concepts and skills: Constructing adaptive expertise* (pp. 1–34). Mahwah, NJ: Erlbaum.

Baroody, A. J. (2006). Why children have difficulties mastering the basic number combinations and how to help them. *Teaching Children Mathematics, 13*(1), 22–31.

Baroody, A. J. (2011). Learning: A framework. In F. Fennell (Ed.), *Achieving fluency in special education and mathematics* (pp. 15–58). Reston, VA: National Council of Teachers of Mathematics.

Baroody, A. J., Bajwa, N. P., & Eiland, M. (2009). Why can't Johnny remember the basic facts? *Developmental Disabilities Research Reviews, 15,* 69–79.

Bay, J. M., Reys, B. J., & Reys, R. E. (1999). The top 10 elements that must be in place to implement standards-based mathematics curricula. *Phi Delta Kappan, 80*(7), 503–506.

Bay-Williams, J. (2010). Influences on student outcomes: Teachers' classroom practices. In D. Lambdin (Ed.), *Teaching and learning mathematics: Translating research to the classroom* (pp. 31–36). Reston, VA: National Council of Teachers of Mathematics.

Bay-Williams, J. M., & Martinie, S. L. (2003). Thinking rationally about number in the middle school. *Mathematics Teaching in the Middle School, 8*(6), 282–287.

Bay-Williams, J. M., & Meyer, M. R. (2003). What parents want to know about standards-based mathematics curricula. *Principal Leadership, 3*(7), 54–60.

Bednar, S. (2009). *Flags of the world.* New York, NY: Abrams Books.

Blanton, M. L. (2008). *Algebra in the elementary classroom: Transforming thinking, transforming practice.* Portsmouth, NH: Heinemann.

Bley, N. S., & Thornton, C. A. (1995). *Teaching mathematics to students with learning disabilities* (3rd ed.). Austin, TX: Pro-Ed.

Blume, G., Galindo, E., & Walcott, C. (2007). Performance in measurement and geometry from the viewpoint of *Principles and Standards for School Mathematics.* In P. Kloosterman & F. Lester, Jr. (Eds.), *Results and interpretations of the 2003 mathematics assessment of the National Assessment of Educational Progress* (pp. 95–138). Reston, VA: National Council of Teachers of Mathematics.

Boaler, J. (2006). Promoting respectful learning. *Educational Leadership, 63*(5), 74–78.

Booth, J., & Siegler, R. (2008). Numerical magnitude representations influence arithmetic learning. *Child Development, 79*(4), 1016–1031.

Bray, W. S. (2009). The power of choice. *Teaching Children Mathematics, 16*(3), 178–184.

Breyfogle, M., & Williams, L. (2008/2009). Designing and implementing worthwhile tasks. *Teaching Children Mathematics, 15*(5), 276–280.

Brown, M. (2005). *Goodnight moon.* New York, NY: Harper Collins.

Brownell, W., & Chazal, C. (1935). The effects of premature drill in third grade arithmetic. *Journal of Educational Research, 29*(1), 17–28.

Bruner, J. (1966). *Toward a theory of instruction.* Cambridge, MA: Harvard University Press.

Carpenter, T. P., Fennema, E., Franke, M. L., Levi, L., & Empson, S. B. (1999). *Children's mathematics: Cognitively guided instruction.* Portsmouth, NH: Heinemann.

Carpenter, T. P., Franke, M. L., Jacobs, V. R., Fennema, E., & Empson, S. B. (1998). A longitudinal study of invention and understanding in children's multidigit addition and subtraction. *Journal for Research in Mathematics Education, 29*(1), 3–20.

Carpenter, T. P., Franke, M. L., & Levi, L. (2003). *Thinking mathematically: Integrating arithmetic and algebra in elementary school.* Portsmouth, NH: Heinemann.

Carraher, D. W., & Schliemann, A. D. (2007). Early algebra and algebraic reasoning. In F. Lester (Ed.), *Second handbook of research on mathematics teaching and learning: A project of the National Council of Teachers of Mathematics* (Vol. II, pp. 609–705). Charlotte, NC: Information Age Publishing.

Carter, S. (2008). Disequilibrium and questioning in the primary classroom: Establishing routines that help students learn. *Teaching Children Mathematics, 15*(3), 134–137.

Cassone, J. D. (2009). Differentiating mathematics by using task difficulty. In D. Y. White & J. S. Spitzer (Eds.), *Mathematics for every student: Responding to diversity, grades Pre-K–5* (pp. 89–98). Reston, VA: National Council of Teachers of Mathematics.

CCSSO (Council of Chief State School Officers). (2010). *Common core state standards.* Retrieved from http://corestandards.org

CCSSO (Council of Chief State School Officers). (2011). *Application of Common Core State Standards for English language learners*. Retrieved from www.corestandards.org/assets/application-for-english-learners.pdf

Celedón-Pattichis, S. (2009). What does that mean? Drawing on Latino and Latina students' language and culture to make mathematical meaning. In M. W. Ellis (Ed.), *Responding to diversity: Grades 6–8* (pp. 59–74). Reston, VA: National Council of Teachers of Mathematics.

Celedón-Pattichis, S., & Ramirez, N. G. (2012). *Beyond good teaching: Advancing mathematics education for ELLs*. Reston, VA: National Council of Teachers of Mathematics.

Chapin, S., O'Connor, C., & Anderson, N. (2009). *Classroom discussions: Using math talk to help students learn* (2nd ed.). Sausalito, CA: Math Solutions.

Christelow, E. (2004). *Five little monkeys play hide-and-seek*. New York, NY: Clarion.

Civil, M., & Menendez, J. M. (2010). *NCTM research brief: Involving Latino and Latina parents in their children's mathematics education*. Retrieved from www.nctm.org/uploadedFiles/Research_News_and_Advocacy/Research/Clips_and_Briefs/Research_brief_17-civil.pdf

Civil, M., & Planas, N. (2010). Latino/a immigrant parents' voices in mathematics education. In E. L. Grigorenko & R. Takanishi (Eds.), *Immigration, diversity, and education* (pp. 130–150). New York, NY: Routledge.

Clement, L. (2004). A model for understanding, using, and connecting representations. *Teaching Children Mathematics, 11*(2), 97–102.

Clements, D. (1999). Geometric and spatial thinking in young children. In J. Copely (Ed.), *Mathematics in the early years* (pp. 66–79). Reston, VA: National Council of Teachers of Mathematics.

Clements, D. H., & Battista, M. T. (1992). Geometry and spatial reasoning. In D. A. Grouws (Ed.), *Handbook of research on mathematics teaching and learning* (pp. 420–464). Old Tappan, NJ: Macmillan.

Clements, D. H., & Sarama, J., (2000a). Young children's ideas about geometric shapes. *Teaching Children Mathematics, 6*(8), 482–488.

Clements, D. H., & Sarama, J. (2000b). The earliest geometry. *Teaching Children Mathematics, 7*(2), 82–86.

Clements, D. H., & Sarama, J. (2007). Early childhood mathematics learning. In F. K. Lester, Jr. (Ed.), *Second handbook on mathematics teaching and learning* (pp. 461–555). Charlotte, NC: Information Age Publishing.

Clements, D. H., & Sarama, J. (2009). *Learning and teaching early math: The learning trajectories approach*. New York, NY: Routledge.

Cook, C. D. (2008). I scream, you scream: Data analysis with kindergartners. *Teaching Children Mathematics, 14*(9), 538–540.

Cooper, H. (2007). *The battle over homework: Common ground for administrators, teachers, and parents* (3rd ed.). Thousand Oaks, CA: Corwin Press.

Cramer, K., & Henry, A. (2002). Using manipulative models to build number sense for addition of fractions. In B. Litwiller (Ed.), *Making sense of fractions, ratios, and proportions* (pp. 41–48). Reston, VA: National Council of Teachers of Mathematics.

Cramer, K., Wyberg, T., & Leavitt, S. (2008). The role of representations in fraction addition and subtraction. *Mathematics Teaching in the Middle School, 13*(8), 490–496.

Crespo, S., & Kyriakides, A. (2007). To draw or not to draw: Exploring children's drawings for solving mathematics problems. *Teaching Children Mathematics, 14*(2), 118–125.

Cummins, J. (1994). Primary language instruction and the education of language minority students. In C. F. Leyba (Ed.), *Schooling and language minority students: A theoretical framework* (pp. 3–46). Los Angeles: California State University, National Evaluation, Dissemination and Assessment Center.

Curry, M., Mitchelmore, M., & Outhred, L. (2006). Development of children's understanding of length, area, and volume measurement principles. In J. Novotná, H. Moraová, M. Krátká, & N. Stehlíková (Eds.). *Proceedings for 30th Conference of the International Group for the Psychology of Mathematics Education,* Vol. 2, pp. 377–384.

Daro, P., Mosher, F., & Corcoran, T. (2011). *Learning trajectories in mathematics: A foundation for standards, curriculum assessment and instruction*. Philadelphia, PA: Consortium for Policy Research in Education.

Dietiker, L., Gonulates, F., Figueras, J., & Smith, J. P. (2010, April). *Weak attention to unit iteration in U.S. elementary curriculum materials*. Presentation at the annual conference of the American Educational Research Association, Denver, CO.

Dougherty, B., Flores, A., Louis, E., & Sophian, C. (2010). *Developing essential understanding of number and numeration for teaching mathematics in prekindergarten–grade 2*. Reston, VA: National Council of Teachers of Mathematics.

Drescher, D. (2008). *What's hiding in there?* Edinburgh, Scotland: Floris.

Echevarria, J., Vogt, M. E., & Short, D. (2008). *Making content comprehensible for English learners: The SIOP model* (3rd ed.). Boston, MA: Allyn & Bacon.

Else-Quest, N. M., Hyde, J. S., & Hejmadi, A. (2008). Mother and child emotions during mathematics homework. *Mathematical Thinking and Learning, 10*, 5–35.

Empson, S. (2002). Organizing diversity in early fraction thinking. In B. Litwiller (Ed.), *Making sense of fractions, ratios, and proportions* (pp. 29–40). Reston, VA: National Council of Teachers of Mathematics.

Empson, S., & Levi, L. (2011). *Extending children's mathematics: Fractions and decimals*. Portsmouth, NH: Heinemann.

Falkner, K. P., Levi, L., & Carpenter, T. P. (1999). Children's understanding of equality: A foundation for algebra. *Teaching Children Mathematics, 6*(4), 232–236.

Fernandez, A., Anhalt, C., & Civil, M. (2009). Mathematical interviews to assess Latino students. *Teaching Children Mathematics, 16*(3), 162–169.

Fleischman, H. L., Hopstock, P. J., Pelczar, M. P., & Shelley, B. E. (2010). Highlights from PISA 2009: Performance of U.S. 15-year-old students in reading, mathematics, and science literacy in an international context (NCES 2011–004). Washington, DC: U.S. Government Printing Office.

Forbringer, L., & Fahsl, A. J. (2010). Differentiating practice to help students master basic facts. In D. Y. White & J. S. Spitzer (Eds.), *Responding to diversity: Grades pre-K–5* (pp. 7–22). Reston, VA: National Council of Teachers of Mathematics.

Fosnot, C. (2007). *The sleepover*. Portsmouth, NH: Heinemann.

Fosnot, C. T., & Dolk, M. (2001). *Young mathematicians at work: Constructing number sense, addition, and subtraction*. Portsmouth, NH: Heinemann.

Fosnot, C. T., & Jacob, B. (2007). *Young mathematicians at work: Constructing algebra*. Portsmouth, NH: Heinemann.

Fosnot, C. T., & Jacob, B. (2010). *Young mathematicians at work: Constructing algebra*. Reston, VA: National Council of Teachers of Mathematics.

Franklin, C. A., Kader, G., Mewborn, D., Moreno, J., Peck, R., Perry, M., & Scheaffer, R. (2005). *Guidelines for assessment and instruction in statistics education (GAISE) report*. Alexandria, VA: American Statistical Association.

Franklin, C. A., & Mewborn, D. S. (2008). Statistics in the elementary grades: Exploring distribution of data. *Teaching Children Mathematics, 15*(1), 10–16.

Frayer, D. A., Fredrick, W. C., & Klausmeier, H. J. (April, 1969). *A schema for testing the level of concept mastery (Working Paper No. 16)*. University of Wisconsin Center for Educational Research.

Friel, S. N., Curcio, F. R., & Bright, G. W. (2001). Making sense of graphs: Critical factors influencing comprehension and instructional implications. *Journal for Research in Mathematics Education, 32*, 124–158.

Friel, S. N., O'Conner, W., & Mamer, J. D. (2006). More than "meanmedianmode" and a bar graph: What's needed to have a statistical conversation? In G. F. Burrill & P. C. Elliott (Eds.), *Thinking and reasoning about data and chance: 68th NCTM yearbook* (pp. 117–138). Reston, VA: National Council of Teachers of Mathematics.

Fuchs, L. S., & Fuchs, D. (2001). Principles for the prevention and intervention of mathematics difficulties. *Learning Disabilities Research and Practice, 16*(2), 85–95.

Fuchs, L. S., Fuchs, D., Yazdian, L., & Powell, S. R. (2002). Enhancing first-grade children's mathematics development with peer-assisted learning strategies. *School Psychology Review, 31*(4), 569–583.

Fuson, K. C. (1984). More complexities in subtraction. *Journal for Research in Mathematics Education, 15*(3), 214–225.

Fuson, K. C. (1992). Research on whole number addition and subtraction. In D. A. Grouws (Ed.), *Handbook of research on mathematics teaching and learning* (pp. 243–275). New York, NY: Macmillan.

Fuson, K. C. (2003). Developing mathematical power in whole number operations. In J. Kilpatrick, W. G. Martin, & D. Schifter (Eds.), *A research companion to Principles and Standards in School Mathematics* (pp. 68–94). Reston, VA: National Council of Teachers of Mathematics.

Fuson, K. C. (2006). Research on whole number addition and subtraction. In D. Grouws (Ed.), *Handbook of research on mathematics teaching and learning* (pp. 243–275). Charlotte, NC: Information Age Publishing.

Gagnon, J., & Maccini, P. (2001). Preparing students with disabilities for algebra. *Teaching Exceptional Children, 34*(1), 8–15.

Gallagher, J., & Gallagher, S. (1994). *Teaching the gifted child*. Boston, MA: Allyn and Bacon.

Garrison, L. (1997). Making the NCTM's Standards work for emergent English speakers. *Teaching Children Mathematics, 4*(3), 132–138.

Gavin, M. K., & Sheffield, L. J. (2010). Using curriculum to develop mathematical promise in the middle grades. In M. Saul, S. Assouline, & L. J. Sheffield (Eds.), *The peak in the middle: Developing mathematically gifted students in the middle grades* (pp. 51–76). Reston, VA: National Council of Teachers of Mathematics, National Association of Gifted Children, and National Middle School Association.

Gersten, R., Beckmann, S., Clarke, B., Foegen, A., Marsh, L., Star, J. R., & Witzel, B. (2009). *Assisting students struggling with mathematics: Response to Intervention (RtI) for elementary and middle schools* (NCEE 2009-4060). Washington, DC: National Center for Education Evaluation and Regional Assistance, Institute of Education Sciences, U.S. Department of Education. Retrieved from http://ies.ed.gov /ncee/wwc/publications/practiceguides

Gilbert, M. C., & Musu, L. E. (2008). Using TARGETTS to create learning environments that support mathematical understanding and adaptive motivation. *Teaching Children Mathematics, 15*(3), 138–143.

Gómez, C. L. (2010). Teaching with cognates. *Teaching Children Mathematics, 16*(8), 470–474.

González, N., Moll, L. C., & Amanti, C. (Eds.). (2005). *Funds of knowledge: Theorizing practices in households and classrooms*. Mahwah, NJ: Lawrence Erlbaum.

Gravemeijer, K., & van Galen, F. (2003). Facts and algorithms as products of students' own mathematical activity. In J. Kilpatrick, W. G. Martin, & D. Schifter (Eds.), *A research companion to Principles and Standards for School Mathematics* (pp. 114–122). Reston, VA: National Council of Teachers of Mathematics.

Greenes, C., Teuscher, D., & Regis, T. (2010). Preparing teachers for mathematically talented middle school students. In M. Saul, S. Assouline, & L.J. Sheffield (Eds.), *The peak in the middle: Developing mathematically gifted students in the middle grades* (pp. 77–91). Reston, VA: National Council of Teachers of Mathematics, National Association of Gifted Children, and National Middle School Association.

Griffin, L., & Lavelle, L. (2010, April). *Assessing mathematical understanding: Using one-on-one mathematics interviews with K–2 students*. Presentation given at the Annual Conference of the National Council of Supervisors of Mathematics, San Diego, CA.

Gutiérrez, R. (2009). Embracing the inherent tensions in teaching mathematics from an equity stance. *Democracy and Education, 18*(3), 9–16.

Gutstein, E., & Romberg, T. A. (1995). Teaching children to add and subtract. *Journal of Mathematical Behavior, 14*, 283–324.

Haas, E., & Gort, M. (2009). Demanding more: Legal standards and best practices for English language learners. *Bilingual Research Journal, 32*, 115–135.

Hamm, D. (1994). *How many feet in the bed?* New York, NY: Simon and Schuster.

Hattie, J. (2009). *Visible learning: A synthesis of over 800 meta-analyses relating to achievement*. New York, NY: Routledge.

Heddens, J. (1964). *Today's mathematics: A guide to concepts and methods in elementary school mathematics*. Chicago, IL: Science Research Associates.

Henderson, A. T., Mapp, K. L., Jordan, C., Orozco, E., Averett, A., Donnelly, D., Buttram, J., Wood, L., Fowler, M., & Myers, M. (2002). *A new wave of evidence: The impact of school, family, and community connections on student achievement*. Austin, TX: Southwest Education Development Laboratory.

Henry, V. J., & Brown, R. S. (2008). First-grade basic facts: An investigation into teaching and learning of an accelerated, high-demand memorization standard. *Journal for Research in Mathematics Education, 39*(2), 153–183.

Hiebert, J., Carpenter, T. P., Fennema, E., Fuson, K., Wearne, D., Murray, H., Olivier, A., & Human, P. (1997). *Making sense: Teaching and learning mathematics with understanding.* Portsmouth, NH: Heinemann.

Hiebert, J., & Grouws, D. A. (2007). The effects of classroom mathematics teaching on students' learning. In F. K. Lester (Ed.), *Second handbook of research on mathematics teaching and learning* (pp. 371–404). Charlotte, NC: Information Age Publishing.

Hodges, T. E., Cady, J., & Collins, R. L. (2008). Fraction representation: The not-so-common denominator among textbooks. *Mathematics Teaching in the Middle School, 14*(2), 78–84.

Hoffman, B. L., Breyfogle, M. L., & Dressler, J. A. (2009). The power of incorrect answers. *Mathematics Teaching in the Middle School, 15*(4), 232–238.

Hong, L. (1993). *Two of everything.* Morton Grove, IL: Albert Whitman & Company.

Howden, H. (1989). Teaching number sense. *Arithmetic Teacher, 36*(6), 6–11.

Huff, K., & Goodman, D. P. (2007). The demand for cognitive diagnostic assessment. In J. P. Leighton & M. J. Gierl (Eds.), *Cognitive diagnostic assessment for education: Theory and applications* (pp. 19–60). New York, NY: Cambridge.

Hutchins, P. (1986). *The doorbell rang.* New York, NY: Greenwillow Books.

Jacobs, V. R., & Ambrose, R. C. (2008). Making the most of story problems. *Teaching Children Mathematics, 15*(5), 260–266.

Janzen, J. (2008). Teaching English language learners in the content areas. *Review of Educational Research, 78*(4), 1010–1038.

Jenkins, S. (2011a). *Actual size.* Boston, MA: Houghton Mifflin.

Jenkins, S. (2011b). *Just a second.* New York, NY: Houghton Mifflin.

Joram, E. (2003). Benchmarks as tools for developing measurement sense. In D. H. Clements (Ed.), *Learning and teaching measurement* (pp. 57–67). Reston, VA: National Council of Teachers of Mathematics.

Kamii, C. K. (1985). *Young children reinvent arithmetic.* New York, NY: Teachers College Press.

Kamii, C. K., & Anderson, C. (2003). Multiplication games: How we made and used them. *Teaching Children Mathematics, 10*(3), 135–141.

Kamii, C. K., & Dominick, A. (1998). The harmful effects of algorithms in grades 1–4. In L. J. Morrow (Ed.), *The teaching and learning of algorithms in school mathematics* (pp. 130–140). Reston, VA: National Council of Teachers of Mathematics.

Kaput, J. J. (2008). What is algebra? What is algebraic reasoning? In J. J. Kaput, D. W. Carraher, & M. L. Blanton (Eds.), *Algebra in the early grades.* Reston, VA: National Council of Teachers of Mathematics.

Karp, K., & Howell, P. (2004). Building responsibility for learning in students with special needs. *Teaching Children Mathematics, 11*(3), 118–126.

Keiser, J. M. (2010). Shifting our computational focus. *Mathematics Teaching in the Middle School, 16*(4), 216–223.

Kenney, P. A., & Kouba, V. L. (1997). What do students know about measurement? In P. A. Kenney & E. Silver (Eds.), *Results from the sixth mathematics assessment of the National Assessment of Educational Progress* (pp. 141–163). Reston, VA: National Council of Teachers of Mathematics.

Kersaint, G., Thompson, D. R., & Petkova, M. (2009). *Teaching mathematics to English language learners.* New York, NY: Routledge.

Khisty, L. L. (1997). Making mathematics accessible to Latino students: Rethinking instructional practice. In M. Kenney & J. Trentacosta (Eds.), *Multicultural and gender equity in the mathematics classroom: The gift of diversity* (pp. 92–101). Reston, VA: National Council of Teachers of Mathematics.

Kilic, H., Cross, D. I., Ersoz, F. A., Mewborn, D. S., Swanagan, D., & Kim, J. (2010). Techniques for small-group discourse. *Teaching Children Mathematics, 16*(6), 350–357.

Kingore, B. (2006, Winter). Tiered instruction: Beginning the process. *Teaching for High Potential,* 5–6.

Klein, A. S., Beishuizen, M., & Treffers, A. (2002). The empty number line in Dutch second grade. In J. Sowder & B. Schapelle (Eds.), *Lessons learned from research* (pp. 41–44). Reston, VA: National Council of Teachers of Mathematics.

Kliman, M. (1999). Beyond helping with homework: Parents and children doing mathematics at home. *Teaching Children Mathematics, 6*(3), 140–146.

Kloosterman, P., Rutledge, Z., & Kenney, P. (2009). Exploring the results of the NAEP: 1980s to the present. *Mathematics Teaching in the Middle School, 14*(6), 357–365.

Knuth, E. J., Stephens, A. C., McNeil, N. M., & Alibali, M. W. (2006). Does understanding the equal sign matter? Evidence from solving equations. *Journal for Research in Mathematics Education, 37*(4), 297–312.

Konold, C., Higgins, T., Russell, S., & Khalil, K. (2004). *Data seen through different lenses.* Amherst, MA: University of Massachusetts. Retrieved from www.srri.umass.edu/publications/konold-2004dst

Labinowicz, E. (1985). *Learning from children: New beginnings for teaching numerical thinking.* Menlo Park, CA: AWL Supplemental.

Lamon, S. J. (2012). *Teaching fractions and ratios for understanding: Essential content knowledge and instructional strategies for teachers* (3rd ed.). New York, NY: Routledge.

Leedy, L. (2000). *Measuring Penny.* New York, NY: Henry Holt and Company.

Lesh, R. A., Cramer, K., Doerr, H., Post, T., & Zawojewski, J. (2003). Model development sequences. In R. A. Lesh & H. Doerr (Eds.), *Beyond constructivism: A models and modeling perspective on mathematics teaching, learning, and problem solving* (pp. 35–58). Mahwah, NJ: Lawrence Erlbaum.

Lewis, T. (2005). Facts + fun = fluency. *Teaching Children Mathematics, 12*(1), 8–11.

Mack, N. K. (2001). Building on informal knowledge through instruction in a complex content domain: Partitioning, units, and understanding multiplication of fractions. *Journal for Research in Mathematics Education, 32,* 267–295.

Mack, N. K. (2011). Enriching number knowledge. *Teaching Children Mathematics, 18*(2), 101–109.

Maida, P. (2004). Using algebra without realizing it. *Mathematics Teaching in the Middle School, 9*(9), 484–488.

Maldonado, L. A., Turner, E. E., Dominguez, H., & Empson, S. B. (2009). English language learning from, and contributing to, mathematical discussions. In D. Y. White & J. S. Spitzer (Eds.), *Responding to diversity: Grades pre-K–5* (pp. 7–22). Reston, VA: National Council of Teachers of Mathematics.

Mann, R. L. (2004). Balancing act: The truth behind the equals sign. *Teaching Children Mathematics, 11*(2), 65–69.

Mathis, S. B. (1986). *The hundred penny box.* New York, NY: Puffin Books.

Mazzocco, M. M. M., Devlin, K. T., & McKenney, S. J. (2008). Is it a fact? Timed arithmetic performance of children with mathematical learning disabilities (MLD) varies as a function of how MLD is defined. *Developmental Neuropsychology, 33*(3), 318–344.

McNamara, J. C. (2010). Two of everything. *Teaching Children Mathematics, 17*(3), 132–136.

McNeil, N. M., & Alibali, M. W. (2005). Knowledge change as a function of mathematics experience: All contexts are not created equal. *Journal of Cognition and Development, 6*, 285–306.

McNeil, N. M., Grandau, L., Knuth, E. J., Alibali, M. W., Stephens, A. C., Hattikudur, S., & Krill, D. E. (2006). Middle school students' understanding of the equal sign: The books they read can't help. *Cognition & Instruction, 24*(3), 367–385.

Meyer, M., & Arbaugh, F. (2008). Professional development for administrators: What they need to know to support curriculum adoption and implementation. In M. Meyer, C. Langrall, F. Arbaugh, D. Webb, & M. Hoover (Eds.), *A decade of middle school mathematics curriculum implementation: Lessons learned from the Show-Me Project* (pp. 201–210). Charlotte, NC: Information Age Publishing.

Mokros, J., & Wright, T. (2009). Zoos, aquariums, and expanding students' data literacy. *Teaching Children Mathematics, 15*(9), 524–530.

Molina, M., & Ambrose, R. C. (2006). Fostering relational thinking while negotiating the meaning of the equals sign. *Teaching Children Mathematics, 13*(2), 111–117.

Moschkovich, J. (2009). *NCTM research brief: Using two languages when learning mathematics: How can research help us understand mathematics learners who use two languages?* Reston, VA: National Council of Teachers of Mathematics.

Murray, M., & Jorgensen, J. (2007). *The differentiated math classroom: A guide for teachers, K–8.* Portsmouth, NH: Heinemann.

National Center for Education Statistics (NCES). (2011). *The condition of education 2011 (NCES 2011-033).* Washington, DC: U.S. Department of Education.

National Council of Teachers of Mathematics. (2000). *Principles and standards for school mathematics.* Reston, VA: Author.

National Council of Teachers of Mathematics. (2003). *Navigating through measurement in prekindergarten–grade 2.* Reston, VA: Author.

National Council of Teachers of Mathematics. (2006). *Curriculum focal points for prekindergarten through grade 8 mathematics: A quest for coherence.* Reston, VA: Author.

National Council of Teachers of Mathematics. (2007). *Research brief: Effective strategies for teaching students with difficulties in mathematics.* Retrieved from www.nctm.org/news/content.aspx?id=8452

National Council of Teachers of Mathematics. (2011a, March). *Position statement on interventions.* Retrieved June 5, 2011, from www.nctm.org/about/content.aspx?id=30506

National Council of Teachers of Mathematics. (2011b, March). *Position statement on the metric system.* Retrieved from www.nctm.org/about/content.aspx?id=29000

National Research Council. (2001). *Adding it up: Helping children learn mathematics.* J. Kilpatrick, J. Swafford, & B. Findell (Eds.). Washington, DC: National Academies Press.

National Research Council Committee. (2009). *Mathematics learning in early childhood: Paths toward excellence and equity.* Washington, DC: National Academies Press.

Nebesniak, A. L., & Heaton, R. M. (2010). Student confidence and student involvement. *Mathematics Teaching in the Middle School, 16*(2), 97–103.

Neumann, M. D. (2005). Freedom quilts: Mathematics on the Underground Railroad. *Teaching Children Mathematics, 11*(6), 316–321.

Niezgoda, D. A., & Moyer-Packenham, P. S. (2005). Hickory, dickory, dock: Navigating through data analysis. *Teaching Children Mathematics, 11*(6), 292–300.

Norton, A., & D'Ambrosio, B. S. (2008). ZPC and ZPD: Zones of teaching and learning. *Journal for Research in Mathematics Education, 39*(3), 220–246.

Numeroff, L. (1985). *If you give a mouse a cookie.* New York, NY: Harper Collins.

Olive, J. (2002). Bridging the gap: Using interactive computer tools to build fraction schemes. *Teaching Children Mathematics, 8*(6), 356–61.

Parker, R., & Breyfogle, L. (2011). Learning to write about mathematics. *Teaching Children Mathematics, 18*(2), 90–99.

Patall, E. A., Cooper, H., & Robinson, J. C. (2008). Parent involvement in homework: A research synthesis. *Review of Educational Research, 78*(4), 1039–1101.

Perkins, I., & Flores, A. (2002). Mathematical notations and procedures of recent immigrant students. *Teaching Children Mathematics, 7*(6), 346–351.

Pesek, D., & Kirshner, D. (2002). Interference of instrumental instruction in subsequent relational learning. In J. Sowder & B. P. Schappelle (Eds.), *Lessons learned from research* (pp. 101–107). Reston, VA: National Council of Teachers of Mathematics.

Petit, M., & Zawojewski, J. (2010). Formative assessment in elementary school mathematics. In D. Lambdin & F. K. Lester, Jr. (Eds.), *Teaching and learning mathematics: Translating research for elementary school teachers* (pp. 73–79). Reston, VA: National Council of Teachers of Mathematics.

Philipp, R., Cabral, C., & Schappell, B. (2012). *IMAP integrating mathematics and pedagogy.* New York, NY: Pearson.

Philipp, R., & Vincent, C. (2003). Reflecting on learning fractions without understanding. *OnMath, 2*(7).

Piaget, J. (1976). *The child's conception of the world.* Totowa, NJ: Littlefield, Adams.

Pinczes, E. (1999). *One hundred hungry ants.* New York, NY: Houghton Mifflin.

Pinczes, E. (2002). *Remainder of one.* New York, NY: Houghton Mifflin.

Post, T. R., Wachsmuth, I., Lesh, R. A., & Behr, M. J. (1985). Order and equivalence of rational numbers: A cognitive analysis. *Journal for Research in Mathematics Education, 16*(1), 18–36.

Pothier, Y., & Sawada, D. (1990). Partitioning: An approach to fractions. *Arithmetic Teacher, 38*(4), 12–17.

RAND Mathematics Study Panel. (2003). *Mathematical proficiency for all students: Toward a strategic research and development program in mathematics education* (Issue 1643). Santa Monica, CA: Rand Corporation.

Rasmussen, C., Yackel, E., & King, K. (2003). Social and sociomathematical norms in the mathematics classroom. In H. L. Schoen & R. I. Charles (Eds.), *Teaching mathematics through problem solving: Grades 6–12* (pp. 143–154). Reston, VA: National Council of Teachers of Mathematics.

Rathmell, E. C., Leutzinger, L. P., & Gabriele, A. (2000). *Thinking with numbers.* Cedar Falls, IA: Thinking with Numbers.

Ravenna, G. (2008). *Factors influencing gifted students' preferences for models of teaching.* Dissertation, University of Southern California.

Reis, S., & Renzulli, J. S. (2005). *Curriculum compacting: An easy start to differentiating for high potential students.* Waco, TX: Prufrock Press.

Renzulli, J. S., Gubbins, E. J., McMillen, K. S., Eckert, R. D., & Little, C. A. (Eds.). (2009). *Systems & models for developing programs for the gifted & talented* (2nd ed.). Mansfield Center, CT: Creative Learning Press, Inc.

Rittle-Johnson, B., Star, J. R., & Durkin, K. (2010, April). Developing procedural flexibility: When should multiple solution methods be introduced? Paper presented at the Annual Conference of the American Educational Research Association, Denver, CO.

Roberts, S. (2003). Snack math: Young children explore division. *Teaching Children Mathematics, 9*(5), 258–261.

Robinson, J. P. (2010). The effects of test translation on young English learners' mathematics performance. *Educational Researcher, 39*(8), 582–590.

Rodríguez-Brown, F. V. (2010). Latino families: Culture and schooling. In E. G. Murillo, Jr., S. A. Villenas, R. T. Galván, J. S. Muñoz, C. Martínez, & M. Machado-Casas (Eds.), *Handbook of Latinos and education: Theory, research, and practice* (pp. 350–360). New York, NY: Routledge.

Ross, S. H. (1986). *The development of children's place-value numeration concepts in grades two through five.* Presented at the annual meeting of the American Educational Research Association, San Francisco. (ERIC Document Reproduction Service No. ED 2773 482)

Ross, S. H. (1989). Parts, wholes, and place value: A developmental perspective. *Arithmetic Teacher, 36*(6), 47–51.

Ross, S. R. (2002). Place value: Problem solving and written assessment. *Teaching Children Mathematics, 8*(7), 419–423.

Rotigel, J., & Fellow, S. (2005). Mathematically gifted students: How can we meet their needs? *Gifted Child Today, 27*(4), 46–65.

Ruschak, L., & Carter, D. (1990). *Snack attack: A tasty pop-up book.* New York, NY: Simon & Schuster.

Russell, S. J. (2006). What does it mean that "5 has a lot"? From the world to data and back. In G. F. Burrill & P. C. Elliott (Eds.), *Thinking and reasoning about data and chance: 68th NCTM yearbook* (pp. 17–30). Reston VA: National Council of Teachers of Mathematics.

Sadler, P., & Tai, R. (2007). The two pillars supporting college science. *Science, 317*(5837), 457–458.

Sarama, J., & Clements, D. H. (2009). *Early childhood mathematics education research: Learning trajectories for young children.* New York, NY: Routledge.

Saul, M., Assouline, S., & Sheffield, L. J. (Eds.) (2010). *The peak in the middle: Developing mathematically gifted students in the middle grades.* Reston, VA: National Council of Teachers of Mathematics, National Association of Gifted Children, and National Middle School Association.

Scheaffer, R. L. (2006). Statistics and mathematics: On making a happy marriage. In G. F. Burrill & P. C. Elliott (Eds.), *Thinking and reasoning about data and chance: 68th NCTM yearbook* (pp. 309–322). Reston, VA: National Council of Teachers of Mathematics.

Schifter, D. (1999). Reasoning about operations: Early algebraic thinking, grades K through 6. In L. Stiff & F. Curcio (Eds.), *Developing mathematical reasoning in grades K–12* (pp. 62–81). Reston, VA: National Council of Teachers of Mathematics.

Schifter, D., Bastable, V., & Russell, S. J. (1999). *Making meaning for operations: Facilitator's guide* (Developing mathematical ideas: Number and operations, part 2). Parsippany, NJ: Dale Seymour.

Schifter, D., Monk, G. S., Russell, S. J., & Bastable, V. (2007). Early algebra: What does understanding the laws of arithmetic mean in the elementary grades? In J. Kaput, D. Carraher, & M. Blanton (Eds.), *Algebra in the early grades.* Mahwah, NJ: Lawrence Erlbaum.

Scott, T., & Lane, H. (2001). Multi-tiered interventions in academic and social contexts. Unpublished manuscript, University of Florida, Gainesville.

Secada, W. G. (1983). *The educational background of limited-English-proficient students: Implications for the arithmetic classroom.* Arlington Heights, IL: Bilingual Education Service Center. (ERIC Document Reproduction Service No. ED 237318)

Seeley, C. L. (2009). *Faster isn't smarter: Messages about math, teaching, and learning in the 21st century.* Sausalito, CA: Math Solutions.

Setati, M. (2005). Teaching mathematics in a primary multilingual classroom. *Journal for Research in Mathematics Education, 36*(5), 447–466.

Seuss, Dr. (1960). *Green eggs and ham.* New York, NY: Random House.

Shaughnessy, J. M. (2006). Research on students' understanding of some big concepts in statistics. In G. F. Burrill & P. C. Elliott (Eds.), *Thinking and reasoning about data and chance: 68th NCTM yearbook* (pp. 77–98). Reston, VA: National Council of Teachers of Mathematics.

Shaughnessy, J. M. (2007). Research on statistics learning and reasoning. In F. Lester, Jr. (Ed.), *Second handbook of research on mathematics teaching and learning* (pp. 957–1010). Reston, VA: National Council of Teachers of Mathematics.

Sheffield, L. J. (Ed.). (1999). *Developing mathematically promising students.* Reston, VA: National Council of Teachers of Mathematics.

Siebert, D., & Gaskin, N. (2006). Creating, naming, and justifying fractions. *Teaching Children Mathematics, 12*(8), 394–400.

Siegler, R. S., Carpenter, T., Fennell, F., Geary, D., Lewis, J., Okamoto, Y., Thompson, L., & Wray, J. (2010). *Developing effective fractions instruction for kindergarten through 8th grade: A practice guide* (NCEE 2010-4039). Retrieved from http://ies.ed.gov/ncee/wwc/practiceguide.aspx?sid=15

Siegler, R. S., & Ramani, G. B. (2009). Playing linear number board games—but not circular ones—improves low-income preschoolers' numerical understanding. *Journal of Educational Psychology, 101*, 545–560.

Skemp, R. (1978). Relational understanding and instrumental understanding. *Arithmetic Teacher, 26*(3), 9–15.

Small, M. (2009). Good questions: Great ways to differentiate mathematics instruction. Reston, VA: National Council of Teachers of Mathematics.

Smith, M., Hughes, E., Engle, R., & Stein, M. (2009). Orchestrating discussions. *Mathematics Teaching in the Middle School, 14*(9), 548–556.

Smith, M. S., & Stein, M. K. (1998). Selecting and creating mathematical tasks: From research to practice. *Mathematics Teaching in the Middle School, 3*, 344–350.

Sousa, D., & Tomlinson, C. (2011). *Differentiation and the brain: How neuroscience supports the learner-friendly classroom.* Bloomington, IN: Solution Tree Press.

Sowder, J. T., & Wearne, D. (2006). What do we know about eighth-grade student achievement? *Mathematics Teaching in the Middle School, 11*(6), 285–293.

Steffe, L., & Cobb, P. (1988). *Construction of arithmetic meanings and strategies.* New York, NY: Springer-Verlag.

Stephan, M., & Whitenack, J. (2003). Establishing classroom social and sociomathematical norms for problem solving. In F. K. Lester, Jr., & R. I. Charles (Eds.), *Teaching mathematics through problem solving: Grades pre-K–6* (pp. 149–162). Reston, VA: National Council of Teachers of Mathematics.

Stiggins, R. (2009). Assessment for learning in upper elementary grades. *Phi Delta Kappan, 90*(6), 419–421.

Storeygard, J. (2010). *My kids can: Making math accessible to all learners, K–5.* Portsmouth, NH: Heinemann.

Sullivan, P., & Lilburn, P. (2002). *Good questions for math teaching: Why ask them and what to ask, K–6.* Sausalito, CA: Math Solutions.

Thompson, T. D., & Preston, R. V. (2004). Measurement in the middle grades: Insights from NAEP and TIMSS. *Mathematics Teaching in the Middle School, 9*(9), 514–519.

Tobias, S. (1995). *Overcoming math anxiety.* New York, NY: W. W. Norton & Company.

Tomlinson, C. (1999). Mapping a route towards differentiated instruction. *Educational Leadership, 57*(1), 12–16.

Tomlinson, C. (2003). *Fulfilling the promise of the differentiated classroom: Strategies and tools for responsive teaching.* Alexandria. VA: Association of Supervision and Curriculum Development.

Torbeyns, J., De Smedt, B., Ghesquiere, P., & Verschaffel, L. (2009). Acquisition and use of shortcut strategies by traditionally schooled children. *Educational Studies in Mathematics, 71*, 1–17.

Torgesen, J. K. (2002). The prevention of reading difficulties. *Journal of School Psychology, 40*(1), 7–26.

Towers, J., & Hunter, K. (2010). An ecological reading of mathematical language in a grade 3 classroom: A case of learning and teaching measurement estimation. *The Journal of Mathematical Behavior, 29*, 25–40.

Turner, E. E., Celedón-Pattichis, S., Marshall, M., & Tennison, A. (2009). "Fijense amorcitos, les voy a contra una historia": The power of story to support solving and discussing mathematical problems among Latino and Latina kindergarten students. In D. Y. White & J. S. Spitzer (Eds.), *Responding to diversity: Grades pre-K–5* (pp. 23–42). Reston, VA: National Council of Teachers of Mathematics.

Tzur, R. (1999). An integrated study of children's construction of improper fractions and the teacher's role in promoting learning. *Journal for Research in Mathematics Education, 30*, 390–416.

Van Tassel-Baska, J., & Brown, E. F. (2007). Toward best practice: An analysis of the efficacy of curriculum models in gifted education. *Gifted Child Quarterly, 51*(4), 342–358.

Verschaffel, L., Greer, B., & De Corte, E. (2007). Whole number concepts and operations. In F. Lester (Ed.), *Second handbook of research on mathematics teaching and learning* (pp. 557–628). Reston, VA: National Council of Teachers of Mathematics.

Vygotsky, L.S. (1978). *Mind and society.* Cambridge, MA: Harvard University Press.

Wallace, A. (2007). Anticipating student responses to improve problem solving. *Mathematics Teaching in the Middle School, 12*(9), 504–511.

Wallace, A. H., & Gurganus, S. P. (2005). Teaching for mastery of multiplication. *Teaching Children Mathematics, 12*(1), 26–33.

Warren, E., & Cooper, T. J. (2008). Patterns that support early algebraic thinking in elementary school. In C. E. Greenes & R. Rubenstein (Eds.), *Algebra and algebraic thinking in school mathematics: 70th NCTM yearbook* (pp. 113–126). Reston, VA: National Council of Teachers of Mathematics.

Wearne, D., & Kouba, V. L. (2000). Rational numbers. In E. A. Silver & P. A. Kenney (Eds.), *Results from the seventh mathematics assessment of the National Assessment of Educational Progress* (pp. 163–191). Reston, VA: National Council of Teachers of Mathematics.

Whiteford, T. (2009/2010). Is mathematics a universal language? *Teaching Children Mathematics, 16*(5), 276–283.

Wiggins, G., & McTighe, J. (2005). *Understanding by design* (2nd ed.). Alexandria, VA: Association for Supervision and Curriculum Development.

Wiliam, D. (2010). *Practical techniques for formative assessment.* Presentation given in Boras, Sweden, September 2010. Retrieved June 11, 2011, from www.slideshare.net/BLoPP/dylan-wiliam-bors-2010

Witzel, B. S. (2005). Using CRA to teach algebra to students with math difficulties in inclusive settings. *Learning Disabilities—A Contemporary Journal, 3*(2), 49–60.

Wood, T., & Turner-Vorbeck, T. (2001). Extending the conception of mathematics teaching. In T. Wood, B. S. Nelson, & J. Warfield (Eds.), *Beyond classical pedagogy: Teaching elementary school mathematics* (pp. 185–208). Mahwah, NJ: Lawrence Erlbaum.

Wood, T., Williams, G., & McNeal, B. (2006). Children's mathematical thinking in different classroom cultures. *Journal for Research in Mathematics Education, 37*(3), 222–255.

Woodward, J. (2006). Developing automaticity in multiplication facts: Integrating strategy instruction with timed practice drills. *Learning Disability Quarterly, 29*(4), 269–89.

Wright, R., Martland, J., Stafford, A., & Stanger, G. (2008). *Teaching number: Advancing children's skills and strategies.* London: Sage.

Wright, R., Stanger, G., Stafford, A., & Martland, J. (2006). *Teaching number in the classroom with 4–8-year-olds.* London: Sage.

Yackel, E., & Cobb, P. (1996). Sociomathematical norms, argumentation, and autonomy in mathematics. *Journal for Research in Mathematics Education, 27*(4), 458–477.

Ysseldyke, J. (2002). Response to "Learning disabilities: Historical perspectives." In R. Bradley, L. Danielson, & D. Hallahan (Eds.), *Identification of learning disabilities: Research to practice* (pp. 89–98). Mahwah, NJ: Erlbaum.

Zwillinger, D. (Ed.) (2011). *Standard mathematical tables and formulae* (32nd ed.). Boca Raton, FL: CRC Press.